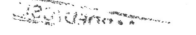

DATE DUE

PREFACE

Paul Hong, the owner of International Industrial Glue Inc., is anxious about the future of his business. Although his company has been very successful as an importer and distributor of industrial glue products, he is worried about new competition through the World Wide Web. He knows that the Web facilitates new competitors to enter his business, existing competitors to expand their businesses, and manufacturers to establish relationships directly with his customers. He also realizes that the Web provides tremendous opportunities for his business to grow and to enter new markets.

Paul Hong's main concern is the expansion of his company's website to enable his business to grow and fend off competition. The current website contains product descriptions, company information, and product support details. Although the site's attractive layout and graphics have attracted new customers, the business seems largely unchanged except for communication generated through the website. In addition, the site is cumbersome to maintain because individual Web pages must be changed as product details change.

He has contracted with Web Development Frontiers to make recommendations about a new website. After several weeks of careful study, Julia Sanchez, a principal at Web Development Frontiers, presents two alternative visions for his website:

- An interactive site that provides a dynamic catalog of products, online ordering, order and shipment tracking, and a knowledge base of product support cases
- A personalized site that provides a unique appearance for each customer as well as interactive capabilities

Both choices involve significant usage of database technology. In the first choice, database technology supports the catalog of products, online ordering capabilities, order and shipment tracking, and knowledge base. In the second choice, database technology supports the generation of pages that a user sees along with the interactive capabilities. In addition, new database and Web technology supports industry standard vocabulary for glue product data so that this data can be easily exchanged among industrial glue manufacturers, distributors, wholesalers, and retailers.

INTRODUCTION

This textbook provides a foundation to understand the database technology supporting new opportunities in electronic commerce such as those faced by Paul Hong. As a new student of database management, you need to first master traditional skills in database application development and database design. This textbook provides tools to help you acquire skills to solve basic and advanced problems in query formulation, application data requirements, data modeling, and normalization.

After establishing these skills, you are ready to study the role of database specialists and the processing environments in which databases are used. This textbook presents the fundamental database technologies in each processing environment and relates these technologies to new advances in electronic commerce. You will learn the vocabulary, architectures, and design issues that provide a background for advanced study of individual database management systems and electronic commerce applications.

COMPETITIVE ADVANTAGES

This textbook provides outstanding features unmatched in competing textbooks. The unique features include detailed SQL coverage for both Access and Oracle, problem-solving guidelines to aid acquisition of key skills, carefully designed sample databases and examples, a comprehensive case- study, advanced topic coverage, a free data modeling tool called ER Assistant, and optional integrated labs. These features provide a complete package for an introductory database course. Each of these features is described in more detail below.

- *SQL Coverage:* The breadth and depth of the SQL coverage in this text is unmatched by competing textbooks. Part 1 provides a thorough coverage of the CREATE TABLE, SELECT, UPDATE, INSERT, DELETE, and CREATE VIEW statements. Numerous examples of basic, intermediate, and advanced problems are presented. Chapter 12 on database administration covers other important statements in the SQL2 standard including the GRANT, CREATE DOMAIN, CREATE ASSERTION, and CREATE TRIGGER statements. Chapter 13 on transaction processing covers the BEGIN TRANSACTION, COMMIT, SET TRANSACTION, and SET CONSTRAINTS statements. Chapter 16 provides a significant introduction to SQL3, the emerging standard for object-relational databases. To make the SQL syntax precise, appendices in a number of chapters present the SQL2 syntax for each statement.

- *Access and Oracle Coverage:* The Part 1 chapters provide detailed coverage of both Access and Oracle SQL. Each example for the SELECT, INSERT, UPDATE, DELETE, and CREATE VIEW statements are shown for both database management systems. In addition, the Part 1 chapters cover SQL2 to support instruction with other prominent database management systems.

- *Problem-Solving Guidelines:* Students need more than explanations of concepts and examples to solve problems. Students need guidelines to help structure their thinking process to tackle problems in a systematic manner. The guidelines provide mental models to help students apply the concepts to solve basic and advanced problems. The textbook provides the following problem-solving guidelines that are missing in competing textbooks:
  - Conceptual evaluation process providing a simple execution model for SQL SELECT statements
  - Query formulation questions presenting checklists that students can use when mapping a narrative retrieval problem into a database representation
  - The "count" method depicting a simple approach to formulate queries that involve the difficult division operator of Relational Algebra
  - Analysis steps defining the data requirements for hierarchical forms

- Transformation operators supporting the generation of alternative Entity Relationship Diagrams
- Simple Synthesis Procedure providing a simple approach to achieving Boyce-Codd Normal Form
- Form analysis steps demonstrating how to derive an Entity Relationship Diagram that represents a data entry form
- Index selection heuristics demonstrating simple yet practical rules for making physical database design choices

- *Sample Databases and Examples:* Two sample databases are used throughout the Part 1 chapters to provide consistency and continuity. The University database is used in the chapter examples, while the Order Entry database is used in end of chapter problems. Numerous examples and problems with these databases depict the fundamental skills of query formulation and application data requirements. Revised versions of the databases provide separation between basic and advanced examples. The website contains CREATE TABLE statements, sample data, data manipulation statements, and Access database files for both databases. Icons for the University and Order Entry databases are placed in the margins of the text to call out to students when an example begins.

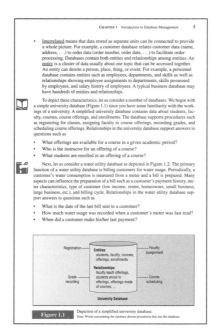

Chapters in Parts 2 and 3 use additional databases to broaden exposure to more diverse business situations. Students need exposure to a variety of business situations to acquire database design skills and understand concepts important to database specialists. Other databases covering water utility operations, patient visits, academic paper processing, personal financial tracking, airline reservations, placement office operations, consumer products reporting, and real estate sales supplement the University and Order Entry databases in the chapter examples and end of chapter problems.

- *Comprehensive Case Study:* The Student Loan Unlimited Case is found at the end of Part 2. The details of the case along with its solution helps tie together the concepts students learned in the preceding ten chapters on application development and database design. The follow-up problems at the end of the chapter provide additional opportunities for students to apply their knowledge on a realistic case.

- *Optional Integrated Labs:* Database management is best taught when concepts are closely linked to the practice of designing and implementing databases using a commercial DBMS. To help students apply the concepts described in the textbook, optional supplementary lab materials are available on CD-ROM and on the text's website. The CD-ROM contains labs for both Microsoft Access 97 and Access 2000 as well as sample databases and practice exercises. The Microsoft Access labs integrate a detailed coverage of Access with the application development concepts covered in the Part 1 chapters. In addition, the text's website will contain two more labs on Visio Professional 5 and 2000. The Visio labs explain how to use Visio Professional to build Entity Relationship Diagrams using the Crow's Foot notation covered in the Part 2 chapters.

- *Free Data Modeling Tool:* ER Assistant provides a simple interface for drawing and converting Entity Relationship Diagrams as presented in the Part 2 chapters on database development. This unique, DBMS independent program is packaged free with each student copy of the text. Students can quickly become productive with this program enabling them to focus on the concepts of data modeling rather than the details of a complex CASE tool.

- *Current and Cutting-Edge Topics:* This book covers some topics that are missing from competing textbooks: advanced query problems, updateable views, data requirements for data entry forms and reports, view integration, workflow management, data warehousing architectures, Web database connectivity architectures, object database architectures, SQL3, and transaction design principles. These topics can help motivated students obtain a deeper understanding of database management.

- *Complete Package for Course:* Depending on the course criteria, some students may need to purchase as many as five books for an introductory database course: a text book covering principles, laboratory books covering details of a DBMS and a CASE tool, a supplemental SQL book, and a casebook with realistic practice problems. This textbook and supplemental material provides one complete and less expensive source for the student. In addition to the expense of using many separate books and lab manuals oftentimes by different authors and publishers, the separate books lack an integrated approach.

TEXT AUDIENCE

This book is intended for a first undergraduate or graduate course in database management. At the undergraduate level, students should have a concentration (major or minor) or active interest in information systems. For two-year institutions, the instructor may want to skip the advanced topics and place more emphasis on the optional Access labs. Undergraduate students should have a first course covering general information systems concepts, spreadsheets, word processing, and possibly a brief introduction to databases. A previous course in computer programming can be a useful background but is not mandatory. This textbook makes reference to computer programming in some places but database programming is not covered.

At the graduate level, this book is suitable in either MBA or Master of Science (in information systems) programs. The advanced material in this book should be especially suitable for Master of Science students.

ORGANIZATION

As the title suggests, *Database Application Development and Design* emphasizes two sets of skills.

The chapters in Part 1 help students to acquire the skills for building database applications. Chapter 1 covers basic concepts of database management including database characteristics, features and architectures of database management systems, market for database management systems, and organizational impacts of database technology. Chapter 2 provides background on the relational data model including data definition concepts and relational algebra operators. Chapter 3 shows numerous examples of basic and intermediate SQL along with fundamental query formulation skills. Chapter 4 presents additional examples of intermediate and advanced SQL along with corresponding query formulation skills. Chapter 5 describes the motivation, definition, and usage of relational views along with specification of view definitions for data entry forms and reports.

The chapters in Part 2 emphasize practical skills and design processes for each step of the development process. Chapter 6 introduces the context, objectives, phases, and tools of the database development process. Chapter 7 presents the Crow's Foot notation of the Entity Relationship Model, the practice of data modeling on narrative problems, and conversion of Entity Relationship Diagrams into relational tables. Chapter 8 covers the motivation, functional dependencies, normal forms, and practical considerations of data normalization. Chapter 9 describes view design and view integration, data modeling concepts for large database development efforts. Chapter 10 contains broad coverage of physical database design including the objectives, inputs, file structure and query optimization background, and important design choices. Chapter 11 provides a comprehensive case study that enables students to gain insights about the difficulties of applying the skills to a realistic business database.

The chapters in Part 3 emphasize the role of database specialists and the details of managing databases in various operating environments. Chapter 12 provides a context for the other chapters through coverage of the responsibilities, tools, and processes used by database administrators and data administrators. The other chapters in Part 3 provide a foundation for managing databases in important environments: Chapter 13 on transaction processing, Chapter 14 on data warehouses, Chapter 15 on distributed processing and data, and Chapter 16 on object database management. These chapters emphasize concepts, architectures, and design choices important to database specialists.

TEXT APPROACH AND THEME

To support acquisition of the necessary skills for learning and understanding application development, database design, and managing databases, this book adheres to three guiding principles:

1. *Combine concepts and practice.* Database management is more easily learned when concepts are closely linked to the practice of designing and implementing databases using a commercial DBMS. The textbook and the

accompanying supplements have been designed to provide close integration between concepts and practice through the following features:

- SQL examples for both Access and Oracle as well as SQL2 coverage
- Emphasis of the relationship between application development and query formulation skills
- Usage of data modeling notation supported by professional CASE tools (Visio Professional) and an easy to use academic tool (ER Assistant)
- Supplemental labs that combine textbook concepts with details of commercial DBMSs

2. *Emphasize problem-solving skills.* This book features problem-solving guidelines to help students master the fundamental skills of data modeling, normalization, query formulation, and application development. The textbook and associated supplements provide a wealth of questions, problems, case studies, and laboratory practices in which students can apply their skills. With mastery of the fundamental skills, students will be poised for future learning about databases and change the way they think about computing, in general.

3. *Provide introductory and advanced material.* Business students who use this book may have a variety of backgrounds. This book provides enough depth to satisfy the most eager students. However, the advanced parts are placed so that they can be skipped by the less inclined.

PEDAGOGICAL FEATURES

This book contains the following pedagogical features to help students work their way through chapter content in a sensible and organized fashion:

- *Learning Objectives* focus on the knowledge and skills students will acquire from studying the chapter.
- *Overviews* provide a snapshot or preview of chapter contents.
- *Key Terms* are highlighted and defined in the margins as they appear in the chapter.

- *Examples* are clearly separated from the rest of the chapter material for easier review and studying purposes.

- *Running Database Examples*—University and Order Entry database examples with icons in margins as helpful hints to students.
- *Closing Thoughts* summarize what students have learned in the chapter.
- *Review Concepts* are the important conceptual highlights from the chapter, instead of just a list of terminology.
- *Questions* are provided to review the chapter concepts.
- *Problems* are included to help students practice and implement what they've learned.
- *References for Further Study* point students to additional sources on chapter content.
- *Chapter Appendixes* provide more in-depth treatment of certain principles or practices.

At the end of the text, students will find the following additional resources:
- *Glossary:* Provides complete list of terms and definitions used throughout the text.
- *Bibliography:* A list of helpful industry, academic, and other printed material for further research or study.
- *Web Resources:* A list of helpful industry, academic, and other Web material for further research or study.

ACCESS LABS ON CD-ROM

Labs for both Microsoft Access 97 and 2000 are available on CD-ROM as packaging options with this text. The labs provide complete coverage of the features important to beginning database students as well as many advanced features. The lab chapters provide a mixture of guided practice and reference material organized into the following seven chapters:

Young U. Ryu, *University of Texas–Dallas*
Hsueh-Chi Joshua Shih, *National Yunlin University of Science and Technology*
Santosh S. Venkatraman, *University of Arkansas–Little Rock*
Peter Wolcott, *University of Nebraska–Omaha*

Your comments, especially the critical ones, have helped me tremendously in refining the textbook.

Third, I thank my McGraw-Hill/Irwin editors, Rick Williamson and Christine Wright, for their guidance in this process as well as Amy Hill, Jim Labeots, Mary Christianson, and the other McGraw-Hill folks who helped in the production and publication of this text. Finally, I thank my wife, Monique, for her help with the textbook and supplements along with her moral support for my effort.

Michael V. Mannino

BRIEF CONTENTS

PART 1

APPLICATION DEVELOPMENT WITH
RELATIONAL DATABASES   1

1

INTRODUCTION TO DATABASE
MANAGEMENT   3

2

THE RELATIONAL DATA MODEL   25

3

QUERY FORMULATION WITH SQL   61

4

ADVANCED QUERY FORMULATION WITH
SQL   115

5

APPLICATION DEVELOPMENT WITH
VIEWS   153

PART 2

DATABASE DEVELOPMENT   189

6

INTRODUCTION TO DATABASE
DEVELOPMENT   191

7

DATA MODELING   211

8

NORMALIZATION OF RELATIONAL TABLES   263

9

VIEW DESIGN AND INTEGRATION   291

10

PHYSICAL DATABASE DESIGN   315

11

DATABASE DESIGN FOR STUDENT LOAN
LIMITED   355

PART 3

MANAGING DATABASE
ENVIRONMENTS   385

12

DATA AND DATABASE ADMINISTRATION   387

13

TRANSACTION MANAGEMENT   417

14

DATA WAREHOUSE TECHNOLOGY AND
MANAGEMENT   453

15
CLIENT–SERVER PROCESSING AND DISTRIBUTED DATABASES *485*

16
OBJECT DATABASE MANAGEMENT SYSTEMS *525*

Glossary   551

Bibliography   565

Web Resources   569

Index   573

CONTENTS

PART 1

APPLICATION DEVELOPMENT WITH RELATIONAL DATABASES   1

....

1

INTRODUCTION TO DATABASE MANAGEMENT   3

Learning Objectives 3
Overview 3
1.1 Database Characteristics 4
1.2 Features of Database Management Systems 7
    1.2.1 Database Definition 7
    1.2.2 Nonprocedural Access 8
    1.2.3 Application Development and Procedural Language Interface 10
    1.2.4 Other Features 11
1.3 Development of Database Technology and Market Structure 12
    1.3.1 Evolution of Database Technology 13
    1.3.2 Current Market for Database Software 14
1.4 Architectures of Database Management Systems 15
    1.4.1 Data Independence and the Three Schema Architecture 15
    1.4.2 Distributed Processing and the Client–Server Architecture 17
1.5 Organizational Impacts of Database Technology 18
    1.5.1 Interacting with Databases 18
    1.5.2 Information Resource Management 19
Closing Thoughts 21
Review Concepts 21
Questions 22
Problems 23
References for Further Study 23

2

THE RELATIONAL DATA MODEL   25

Learning Objectives 25
Overview 25
2.1 Basic Elements 26
    2.1.1 Tables 26
    2.1.2 Connections among Tables 28
    2.1.3 Alternative Terminology 29
2.2 Integrity Rules 30
    2.2.1 Definition of the Integrity Rules 30
    2.2.2 Applying the Integrity Rules 31
    2.2.3 Graphical Representation of Referential Integrity 34
2.3 Delete and Update Actions for Referenced Rows 35
2.4 Operators of Relational Algebra 37
    2.4.1 Restrict (Select) and Project Operators 38
    2.4.2 Extended Cross Product Operator 39
    2.4.3 Join Operator 41
    2.4.4 Outer Join Operator 43
    2.4.5 Union, Intersection, and Difference Operators 45
    2.4.6 Summarize Operator 48
    2.4.7 Divide Operator 49
    2.4.8 Summary of Operators 50
Closing Thoughts 52
Review Concepts 52
Questions 53
Problems 53
References for Further Study 56
Appendix 2.A: CREATE TABLE Statements for the University Database Tables 57
Appendix 2.B: SQL2 Syntax Summary 59

3

QUERY FORMULATION WITH SQL   61

Learning Objectives   61
Overview   61
3.1 Background   62
 3.1.1 Brief History of SQL   62
 3.1.2 Scope of SQL   63
3.2 Getting Started with SELECT   64
 3.2.1 Single Table Problems   66
 3.2.2 Joining Tables   72
 3.2.3 Summarizing Tables with GROUP BY and
  HAVING   74
 3.2.4 Improving the Appearance of Results   77
3.3 Conceptual Evaluation Process for SELECT
 Statements   79
3.4 Critical Questions for Query Formulation   84
3.5 Refining Query Formulation Skills with Examples   85
 3.5.1 Joining Multiple Tables with the Cross Product
  Style   85
 3.5.2 Joining Multiple Tables with the Join Operator
  Style   89
 3.5.3 Self-Joins and Multiple Joins between Two
  Tables   91
 3.5.4 Combining Joins and Grouping   93
 3.5.5 Traditional Set Operators in SQL   94
3.6 SQL Modification Statements   96
Closing Thoughts   97
Review Concepts   98
Questions   102
Problems   103
References for Further Study   110
Appendix 3.A: SQL2 Syntax Summary   111
Appendix 3.B: Syntax Differences among Major Database
 Products   114

4

ADVANCED QUERY FORMULATION WITH SQL   115

Learning Objectives   115
Overview   115
4.1 Outer Join Problems   116
 4.1.1 SQL Support for Outer Join Problems   116
 4.1.2 Mixing Inner and Outer Joins   121
4.2 Understanding Nested Queries   123
 4.2.1 Type I Nested Queries   123
 4.2.2 Type II Nested Queries   125
 4.2.3 Solving Difference Problems with Type II Nested
  Queries   127

4.3 Formulating Division Problems   133
 4.3.1 Review of the Divide Operator   133
 4.3.2 Simple Division Problems   134
 4.3.3 Advanced Division Problems   136
4.4 Null Value Considerations   138
 4.4.1 Effect on Simple Conditions   138
 4.4.2 Effect on Compound Conditions   139
 4.4.3 Effect on Aggregate Calculations and
  Grouping   141
Closing Thoughts   142
Review Concepts   143
Questions   145
Problems   146
References for Further Study   149
Appendix 4.A: Microsoft Access Formulation of Division
 Problems   150
Appendix 4.B: SQL2 Syntax Summary   151

5

APPLICATION DEVELOPMENT WITH VIEWS   153

Learning Objectives   153
Overview   153
5.1 Background   154
 5.1.1 Motivation   154
 5.1.2 View Definition   155
5.2 Using Views for Retrieval   156
 5.2.1 Using Views in SELECT Statements   156
 5.2.2 Processing Queries with View References   158
5.3 Updating Using Views   160
 5.3.1 Single-Table Updatable Views   160
 5.3.2 Multiple-Table Updatable Views   164
5.4 Using Views in Hierarchical Forms   167
 5.4.1 What Is a Hierarchical Form?   167
 5.4.2 Relationship between Hierarchical Forms and
  Tables   168
 5.4.3 Query Formulation Skills for Hierarchical
  Forms   169
5.5 Using Views in Reports   173
 5.5.1 What Is a Hierarchical Report?   173
 5.5.2 Query Formulation Skills for Hierarchical
  Reports   175
Closing Thoughts   176
Review Concepts   177
Questions   177
Problems   178
References for Further Study   185
Appendix 5.A: SQL2 Syntax Summary   186
Appendix 5.B: Rules for Updatable Join Views in
 Oracle 8   187

P A R T   2

Database Development 189

6

Introduction to Database Development *191*

Learning Objectives *191*
Overview *191*
6.1 Information Systems *192*
   6.1.1 Components of Information Systems *192*
   6.1.2 Information Systems Development Process *193*
6.2 Goals of Database Development *195*
   6.2.1 Develop a Common Vocabulary *195*
   6.2.2 Define the Meaning of Data *195*
   6.2.3 Ensure Data Quality *196*
   6.2.4 Find an Efficient Implementation *197*
6.3 Database Development Process *197*
   6.3.1 Phases of Database Development *197*
   6.3.2 Skills in Database Development *201*
6.4 Tools of Database Development *203*
   6.4.1 Diagramming *204*
   6.4.2 Documentation *204*
   6.4.3 Analysis *204*
   6.4.4 Prototyping Tools *205*
   6.4.5 Commercial CASE Tools *205*
Closing Thoughts *208*
Review Concepts *208*
Questions *209*
Problems *210*
References for Further Study *210*

7

Data Modeling *211*

Learning Objectives *211*
Overview *211*
7.1 Introduction to Entity Relationship Diagrams *212*
   7.1.1 Basic Symbols *212*
   7.1.2 Relationship Cardinality *213*
   7.1.3 Comparison to Relational Database Diagrams *216*
7.2 Understanding Relationships *217*
   7.2.1 Identification Dependency (Weak Entities and
      Identifying Relationships) *217*
   7.2.2 Relationship Patterns *219*
   7.2.3 Equivalence between 1-M and M-N
      Relationships *223*
7.3 Classification in the Entity Relationship Model *224*
   7.3.1 Generalization Hierarchies *225*

7.3.2 Disjointness and Completeness Constraints *225*
7.3.3 Multiple Levels of Generalization *226*
7.4 Review of Notation and Comparison to Other
   Notations *227*
   7.4.1 Comprehensive ERD Example *227*
   7.4.2 Diagram Variations *227*
7.5 Developing an ERD for the Water Utility Database *230*
   7.5.1 Database Description *230*
   7.5.2 Initial ERD *231*
   7.5.3 Refinements to the Initial ERD *232*
   7.5.4 Finalizing the ERD *235*
7.6 Converting an ERD to Relational Tables *235*
   7.6.1 Basic Conversion Rules *236*
   7.6.2 Converting Optional 1-M Relationships *240*
   7.6.3 Converting Generalization Hierarchies *242*
   7.6.4 Converting 1-1 Relationships *245*
   7.6.5 Comprehensive Conversion Example *245*
Closing Thoughts *249*
Review Concepts *249*
Questions *250*
Problems *250*
References for Further Study *259*
Appendix 7.A: Class Diagram Notation of the Unified
   Modeling Language *260*

8

Normalization of Relational Tables *263*

Learning Objectives *263*
Overview *263*
8.1 Overview of Relational Database Design *264*
   8.1.1 Avoidance of Modification Anomalies *264*
   8.1.2 Functional Dependencies *265*
8.2 Normal Forms *267*
   8.2.1 First Normal Form *268*
   8.2.2 Second and Third Normal Form *269*
   8.2.3 Boyce-Codd Normal Form *271*
   8.2.4 Simple Synthesis Procedure *273*
8.3 Refining M-Way Relationships *276*
   8.3.1 Relationship Independence *276*
   8.3.2 Multivalued Dependencies and Fourth Normal Form
      (4NF) *279*
8.4 Higher-Level Normal Forms *280*
   8.4.1 Fifth Normal Form (5NF) *280*
   8.4.2 Domain Key Normal Form (DKNF) *281*
8.5 Practical Concerns about Normalization *281*
   8.5.1 Role of Normalization in the Database Development
      Process *282*
   8.5.2 Analyzing the Normalization Objective *282*
Closing Thoughts *283*

Review Concepts *283*
Questions *284*
Problems *285*
References for Further Study *290*

9

VIEW DESIGN AND INTEGRATION *291*

Learning Objectives *291*
Overview *291*
9.1 Motivation for View Design and Integration *292*
9.2 View Design with Forms *293*
    9.2.1 Form Analysis *293*
    9.2.2 Analysis of M-Way Relationships Using
        Forms *299*
9.3 View Integration *303*
    9.3.1 Incremental and Parallel Integration
        Approaches *304*
    9.3.2 View Integration Examples *307*
Closing Thoughts *309*
Review Concepts *310*
Questions *310*
Problems *311*
References for Further Study *313*

10

PHYSICAL DATABASE DESIGN *315*

Learning Objectives *315*
Overview *315*
10.1 Overview of Physical Database Design *316*
    10.1.1 Storage Level of Databases *316*
    10.1.2 Objectives and Constraints *318*
    10.1.3 Inputs, Outputs, and Environment *318*
    10.1.4 Difficulties *320*
10.2 Inputs of Physical Database Design *320*
    10.2.1 Table Profiles *320*
    10.2.2 Application Profiles *321*
10.3 File Structures *322*
    10.3.1 Sequential Files *322*
    10.3.2 Hash Files *323*
    10.3.3 Multiway Tree (Btree) Files *326*
    10.3.4 Summary of File Structures *331*
10.4 Query Optimization *332*
    10.4.1 Translation Tasks *332*
    10.4.2 Optimization Tips *335*
10.5 Index Selection *336*
    10.5.1 Problem Definition *336*
    10.5.2 Trade-offs and Difficulties *337*
    10.5.3 Selection Rules *340*
10.6 Additional Choices in Physical Database Design *342*
    10.6.1 Denormalization *342*
    10.6.2 Record Formatting *344*

10.6.3 Parallel Processing *345*
    10.6.4 Other Ways to Improve Performance *347*
Closing Thoughts *347*
Review Concepts *348*
Questions *348*
Problems *350*
References for Further Study *353*
Appendix 10.A: SQL2 Syntax Summary *354*

11

DATABASE DESIGN FOR STUDENT LOAN LIMITED *355*

Learning Objectives *355*
Overview *355*
11.1 Case Description *356*
    11.1.1 Overview *356*
    11.1.2 Flow of Work *356*
11.2 Conceptual Data Modeling *361*
    11.2.1 ERD for the Loan Origination Form *361*
    11.2.2 Incremental Integration after Adding the
        Disclosure Letter *363*
    11.2.3 Incremental Integration after Adding the Statement
        of Account *364*
    11.2.4 Incremental Integration after Adding the Loan
        Activity Report *366*
11.3 Refining the Conceptual Schema *367*
    11.3.1 Schema Conversion *367*
    11.3.2 Normalization *369*
11.4 Physical Database Design *370*
    11.4.1 Application and Table Profiles *370*
    11.4.2 Index Selection *372*
    11.4.3 Derived Data and Denormalization Decisions *373*
    11.4.4 Other Implementation Decisions *374*
Closing Thoughts *374*
Questions *374*
Problems *375*
Appendix 11.A: Glossary of Form and Report Fields *377*
Appendix 11.B: CREATE TABLE Statements *380*

PART 3

MANAGING DATABASE ENVIRONMENTS *385*

12

DATA AND DATABASE ADMINISTRATION *387*

Learning Objectives *387*
Overview *387*
12.1 Organizational Context for Managing Databases *388*

12.1.1 Database Support for Management Decision Making *388*

12.1.2 Information Resource Management to Knowledge Management *389*

12.1.3 Responsibilities of Data Administrators and Database Administrators *390*

12.2 Tools of Database Administration *392*

12.2.1 Security *392*

12.2.2 Integrity Constraints *395*

12.2.3 Triggers and Stored Procedures *398*

12.2.4 Data Dictionary Manipulation *400*

12.3 Processes for Database Specialists *401*

12.3.1 Data Planning *402*

12.3.2 Selection and Evaluation of Database Management Systems *403*

12.4 Managing Database Environments *407*

12.4.1 Transaction Processing *407*

12.4.2 Data Warehouse Processing *407*

12.4.3 Distributed Environments *408*

12.4.4 Object Database Management *408*

Closing Thoughts *409*

Review Concepts *410*

Questions *411*

Problems *413*

References for Further Study *413*

Appendix 12.A: SQL2 Syntax Summary *415*

13

TRANSACTION MANAGEMENT *417*

Learning Objectives *417*

Overview *417*

13.1 Basics of Database Transactions *418*

13.1.1 Transaction Examples *418*

13.1.2 Transaction Properties *420*

13.2 Concurrency Control *422*

13.2.1 Objective of Concurrency Control *422*

13.2.2 Interference Problems *422*

13.2.3 Concurrency Control Tools *424*

13.3 Recovery Management *429*

13.3.1 Data Storage Devices and Failure Types *429*

13.3.2 Recovery Tools *430*

13.3.3 Recovery Processes *431*

13.4 Transaction Design Issues *434*

13.4.1 Transaction Boundary and Hot Spots *434*

13.4.2 Example Transaction Boundary Design *435*

13.4.3 Isolation Levels *436*

13.4.4 Timing of Integrity Constraint Enforcement *438*

13.5 Workflow Management *439*

13.5.1 Characterizing Workflows *439*

13.5.2 Enabling Technologies *440*

Closing Thoughts *442*

Review Concepts *443*

Questions *444*

Problems *445*

References for Further Study *450*

Appendix 13.A: SQL2 Syntax Summary *451*

14

DATA WAREHOUSE TECHNOLOGY AND MANAGEMENT *453*

Learning Objectives *453*

Overview *453*

14.1 Basic Concepts *454*

14.1.1 Transaction Processing versus Decision Support *454*

14.1.2 Characteristics of Data Warehouses *455*

14.1.3 Architectures for Data Warehouses *456*

14.1.4 Data Mining *457*

14.1.5 Applications of Data Warehouses *459*

14.2 Multidimensional Representation of Data *460*

14.2.1 Example of a Multidimensional Data Cube *460*

14.2.2 Key Terminology *462*

14.2.3 Time-Series Data *464*

14.2.4 Data Cube Operations *465*

14.2.5 Relational Data Modeling for Multidimensional Data *468*

14.2.6 Multidimensional Database Technologies *469*

14.3 Building a Data Warehouse *472*

14.3.1 Requirements Specification *472*

14.3.2 Logical and Physical Design *473*

14.3.3 Data Extraction *475*

14.3.4 Practical Considerations *477*

14.4 Maintaining a Data Warehouse *478*

14.4.1 Query Phase *478*

14.4.2 Refresh Phase *479*

Closing Thoughts *479*

Review Concepts *480*

Questions *480*

Problems *481*

References for Further Study *483*

15

CLIENT–SERVER PROCESSING AND DISTRIBUTED DATABASES *485*

Learning Objectives *485*

Overview *485*

15.1 Overview of Distributed Processing and Distributed Data *486*

15.1.1 Evolution of Distributed Processing and Distributed Data *486*

15.1.2 Motivation for Distributed Processing *488*

15.1.3 Motivation for Distributed Data *489*
15.1.4 Summary of Advantages and Disadvantages *490*
15.2 Client–Server Database Architectures *490*
15.2.1 Design Issues *490*
15.2.2 Description of Architectures *492*
15.3 Web Database Connectivity *496*
15.3.1 Internet Basics *496*
15.3.2 Common Gateway Interface *499*
15.3.3 Server-Side Connectivity *500*
15.3.4 Client-Side Connectivity *501*
15.3.5 Summary of Web Database Connectivity
Approaches *502*
15.4 Architectures for Distributed Database Management
Systems *502*
15.4.1 Component Architecture *502*
15.4.2 Schema Architectures *505*
15.5 Transparency for Distributed Database Processing *507*
15.5.1 Motivating Example *507*
15.5.2 Fragmentation Transparency *509*
15.5.3 Location Transparency *510*
15.5.4 Local Mapping Transparency *511*
15.6 Distributed Database Processing *513*
15.6.1 Distributed Query Processing *513*
15.6.2 Distributed Transaction Processing *515*
Closing Thoughts *517*
Review Concepts *518*
Questions *519*
Problems *521*
References for Further Study *523*

16

OBJECT DATABASE MANAGEMENT SYSTEMS *525*

Learning Objectives *525*
Overview *525*

16.1 Motivation for Object Database Management *526*
16.1.1 Complex Data *526*
16.1.2 Type System Mismatch *527*
16.1.3 Application Examples *527*
16.2 Object-Oriented Principles *528*
16.2.1 Encapsulation *528*
16.2.2 Inheritance *530*
16.2.3 Polymorphism *531*
16.2.4 Programming Languages versus DBMSs *533*
16.3 Architectures for Object Database Management *534*
16.3.1 Large Objects and External Software *534*
16.3.2 Specialized Media Servers *535*
16.3.3 Object Database Middleware *536*
16.3.4 Object Relational Database Management Systems
for User-Defined Types *536*
16.3.5 Object-Oriented Database Management
Systems *538*
16.3.6 Summary of Object Database Architectures *539*
16.4 Database Definition and Manipulation Using
SQL3 *540*
16.4.1 User-Defined Types *540*
16.4.2 Table Definitions and Subtable Families *542*
16.4.3 Manipulating Complex Objects and Subtable
Families *545*
Closing Thoughts *546*
Review Concepts *547*
Questions *548*
Problems *549*
References for Further Study *550*

Glossary *551*
Bibliography *565*
Web Resources *569*
Index *573*

APPLICATION DEVELOPMENT WITH RELATIONAL DATABASES

CHAPTER 1 | *Introduction to Database Management*

CHAPTER 2 | *The Relational Data Model*

CHAPTER 3 | *Query Formulation with SQL*

CHAPTER 4 | *Advanced Query Formulation with SQL*

CHAPTER 5 | *Application Development with Views*

Part 1 provides a foundation for building database applications by helping students acquire skills in relational database concepts, query formulation, external view usage, and specification of data requirements for data entry forms and reports. Chapter 1 covers basic concepts of database management including database characteristics, features and architectures of database management systems, market for database management systems, and organizational impacts of database technology. Chapter 2 provides background on the relational data model including data definition concepts and relational algebra operators. Chapter 3 shows numerous examples of basic and intermediate SQL along with fundamental query formulation skills. Chapter 4 presents additional examples of intermediate and advanced SQL along with corresponding query formulation skills. Chapter 5 describes the motivation, definition, and usage of relational views along with specification of view definitions for data entry forms and reports.

Chapter 1

Introduction to Database Management

Learning Objectives

This chapter provides an introduction to database technology and the impact of this technology on organizations. After this chapter the student should have acquired the following knowledge and skills:

- Describe the characteristics of business databases and the features of database management systems.

- Appreciate the advances in database technology and the contribution of database technology to modern society.

- Understand the impact of database management system architectures on distributed processing and software maintenance.

- Perceive career opportunities related to database application development and database administration.

OVERVIEW

You may not be aware of it, but your life is dramatically affected by database technology. Computerized databases are vital to the functioning of modern organizations. You come into contact with databases on a daily basis through activities such as shopping at a supermarket, going to an automated teller machine, and registering for classes. The convenience of your daily life is partly due to proliferation of computerized databases and supporting database technology.

Database technology is not only improving the daily operations of organizations but also the quality of decisions that affect our lives. Databases contain a flood of data about many aspects of our lives: consumer preferences, telecommunications usage, credit history, television viewing habits, and so on. Database technology helps to summarize this mass of data into useful information for decision making. Management uses information gleaned from databases to make long-range decisions such as investing in plants and equipment, locating stores, adding new items to inventory, and entering new businesses.

This first chapter provides a starting point for your exploration of database technology. It surveys database characteristics, database management system features, system architectures, and human roles in managing and using databases. Other chapters in this part of the book explore the details of using database technology. This chapter provides a broad picture of database technology and shares the excitement about the journey ahead.

1.1 DATABASE CHARACTERISTICS

Every day, businesses collect mountains of facts about persons, things, and events such as credit card numbers, bank balances, and purchase amounts. Databases contain these sorts of simple facts as well as nonconventional information like photographs, fingerprints, product videos, and book abstracts. With the proliferation of the Internet and the means to capture data in computerized form, a vast amount of data is available at the click of a mouse button. With so much data available, organizing these data for ease of retrieval and maintenance is paramount. Thus, managing databases has become a vital task in most organizations.

Before learning about managing databases, you must first understand some important properties of databases:

Database a collection of <u>persistent</u> data that can be <u>shared</u> and <u>interrelated</u>.

- <u>Persistent</u> means that data reside on stable storage such as a magnetic disk. For example, organizations need to retain data about customers, suppliers, and inventory on stable storage because these data are repetitively used. A variable in a computer program is not persistent because it resides in main memory and disappears after the program terminates. Persistency does not mean that data last forever. When data are no longer relevant (such as a supplier going out of business), they are removed or archived.

  Persistency depends on relevance of intended usage. For example, the mileage you drive for work is important to maintain if you are self-employed. Likewise, the amount of your medical expenses is important if you can itemize your deductions. Because storing and maintaining data is costly, only data likely to be relevant to decisions should be stored.

- <u>Shared</u> means that a database can have multiple uses and users. A database provides a common memory for multiple functions in an organization. For example, a personnel database can support payroll calculations, performance evaluations, government reporting requirements, and so on. Many users can use a database at the same time. For example, many customers can simultaneously make airline reservations. Unless two users are trying to change the same part of the database at the same time, they can proceed without waiting on each other.

- <u>Interrelated</u> means that data stored as separate units can be connected to provide a whole picture. For example, a customer database relates customer data (name, address, . . .) to order data (order number, order date, . . .) to facilitate order processing. Databases contain both entities and relationships among entities. An <u>entity</u> is a cluster of data usually about one topic that can be accessed together. An entity can denote a person, place, thing, or event. For example, a personnel database contains entities such as employees, departments, and skills as well as relationships showing employee assignments to departments, skills possessed by employees, and salary history of employees. A typical business database may have hundreds of entities and relationships.

To depict these characteristics, let us consider a number of databases. We begin with a simple university database (Figure 1.1) since you have some familiarity with the workings of a university. A simplified university database contains data about students, faculty, courses, course offerings, and enrollments. The database supports procedures such as registering for classes, assigning faculty to course offerings, recording grades, and scheduling course offerings. Relationships in the university database support answers to questions such as

- What offerings are available for a course in a given academic period?
- Who is the instructor for an offering of a course?
- What students are enrolled in an offering of a course?

Next, let us consider a water utility database as depicted in Figure 1.2. The primary function of a water utility database is billing customers for water usage. Periodically, a customer's water consumption is measured from a meter and a bill is prepared. Many aspects can influence the preparation of a bill such as a customer's payment history, meter characteristics, type of customer (low income, renter, homeowner, small business, large business, etc.), and billing cycle. Relationships in the water utility database support answers to questions such as

- What is the date of the last bill sent to a customer?
- How much water usage was recorded when a customer's meter was last read?
- When did a customer make his/her last payment?

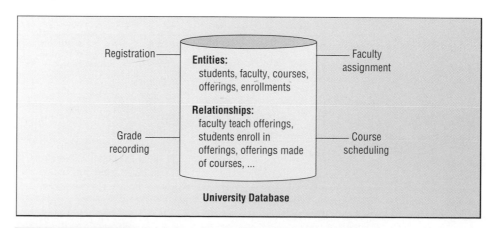

Figure 1.1   **Depiction of a simplified university database.**
Note: Words surrounding the database denote procedures that use the database.

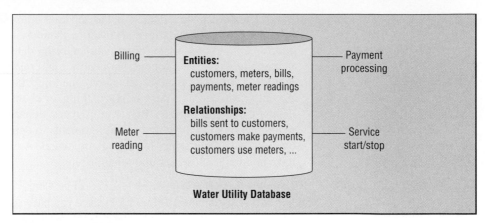

Figure 1.2 Depiction of a simplified water utility database.

Finally, let us consider a hospital database as depicted in Figure 1.3. The hospital database supports treatment of patients by physicians. Physicians make diagnoses and prescribe treatments based on symptoms. Many different health providers read and contribute to a patient's record. Nurses are responsible for monitoring symptoms and providing medication. Food staff prepare meals according to a treatment plan. Physicians prescribe new treatments based on the results of previous treatments and patient symptoms. Relationships in the database support answers to questions such as

- What are the most recent symptoms of a patient?
- Who prescribed a given treatment of a patient?
- What diagnosis did a doctor make for a patient?

These simplified databases lack many kinds of data found in real databases. For example, the simplified university database does not contain data about course prerequisites and classroom capacities and locations. Real versions of these databases would have many more entities and additional uses. Nevertheless, these simple databases have the essential characteristics of business databases: persistent data, multiple users and uses, and multiple entities connected by relationships.

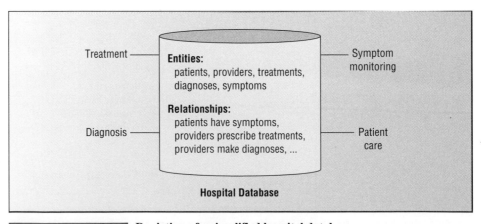

Figure 1.3 Depiction of a simplified hospital database.

1.2 FEATURES OF DATABASE MANAGEMENT SYSTEMS

Database Management System (DBMS) a collection of components that support data acquisition, dissemination, maintenance, retrieval, and formatting.

A database management system (DBMS) is a collection of software that supports the creation, use, and maintenance of databases. Initially, DBMSs provided efficient storage and retrieval of data. Due to marketplace demands and product innovation, DBMSs have evolved to provide a broad range of features for data acquisition, storage, dissemination, maintenance, retrieval, and formatting. The evolution of these features has made DBMSs rather complex. It can take years of study and use to master a particular DBMS. Because DBMSs continue to evolve, you must continually update your knowledge.

To provide insight about features that you will encounter in commercial DBMSs, Table 1–1 summarizes a common set of features. The remainder of this section presents examples of these features. Some examples are drawn from Microsoft Access, a popular desktop DBMS. Later chapters expand upon the introduction provided here.

Table a named, two-dimensional arrangement of data. A table consists of a heading part and a body part.

1.2.1 Database Definition

To define a database, the entities and relationships must be specified. In most commercial DBMSs, tables store collections of entities. A table (Figure 1.4) has a heading row (first row) showing the column names and a body (other rows) showing the contents of the table. Relationships indicate connections among tables. For example, the relationship

TABLE 1–1	Summary of Common Features of DBMSs
Feature	*Description*
Database definition	Language and graphical tools to define entities, relationships, integrity constraints, and authorization rights
Nonprocedural access	Language and graphical tools to access data without complicated coding
Application development	Graphical tools to develop menus, data entry forms, and reports
Procedural language interface	Language that combines nonprocedural access with full capabilities of a programming language
Transaction processing	Control mechanisms to prevent interference from simultaneous users and recover lost data after a failure
Database tuning	Tools to monitor and improve database performance

StdFirstName	StdLastName	StdCity	StdState	StdZip	StdMajor	StdClass	StdGPA
HOMER	WELLS	SEATTLE	WA	98121-1111	IS	FR	3.00
BOB	NORBERT	BOTHELL	WA	98011-2121	FIN	JR	2.70
CANDY	KENDALL	TACOMA	WA	99042-3321	ACCT	JR	3.50
WALLY	KENDALL	SEATTLE	WA	98123-1141	IS	SR	2.80
JOE	ESTRADA	SEATTLE	WA	98121-2333	FIN	SR	3.20
MARIAH	DODGE	SEATTLE	WA	98114-0021	IS	JR	3.60
TESS	DODGE	REDMOND	WA	98116-2344	ACCT	SO	3.30

Figure 1.4   **Display of student table in Microsoft Access.**

connecting the student table to the enrollment table shows the course offerings taken by each student.

Most DBMSs provide several tools to define databases. The Structured Query Language (SQL) is an industry standard language supported by most DBMSs. SQL can be used to define tables, relationships among tables, integrity constraints (rules that define allowable data), and authorization rights (rules that restrict access to data). Chapter 2 describes SQL statements to define tables and relationships.

In addition to SQL, many DBMSs provide graphical, window-oriented tools. Figures 1.5 and 1.6 depict graphical tools for defining tables and relationships. Using the Table Definition window in Figure 1.5, the user can define properties of columns such as the data type and field size. Using the Relationship Definition window in Figure 1.6, relationships among tables can be defined. After defining the structure, a database can be populated. The data in Figure 1.4 should be added after the Table Definition window and Relationship Definition window are complete.

> **SQL** an industry standard database language that includes statements for database definition, database manipulation, and database control.

1.2.2 Nonprocedural Access

The most important feature of DBMSs is the ability to answer queries. A query is a request for data to answer a question. For example, the user may want to know customers having large balances or products with strong sales in a particular region. Nonprocedural access allows users with limited computing skills to submit queries. The user specifies what parts of a database to retrieve, not the details of how retrieval occurs. The "how" part involves coding complex procedures with loops. Nonprocedural languages do not have looping statements (for, while, and so on) because only the "what" part is specified.

Nonprocedural access can reduce the number of lines of code by a factor of 100 as compared to procedural access. Because a large part of business software involves data access, nonprocedural access can provide a dramatic improvement in software productivity.

To appreciate the significance of nonprocedural access, consider an analogy to planning a vacation. You specify your destination, travel budget, length of stay, and departure date. These facts indicate the "what" of your trip. To specify the "how" of your

> **Nonprocedural Database Language** a language such as SQL that allows you to specify what part of a database to access rather than to code a complex procedure. Nonprocedural languages do not include looping statements.

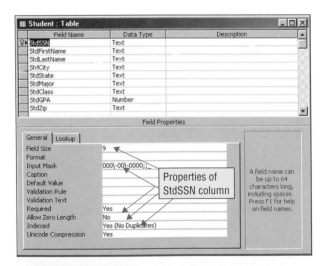

Figure 1.5   **Table Definition window in Microsoft Access.**

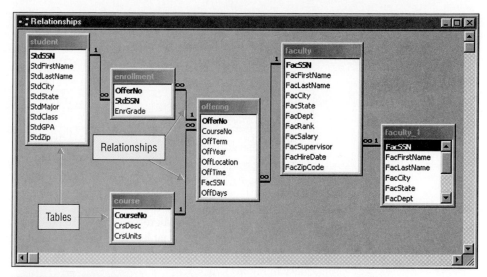

Figure 1.6   **Relationship Definition window in Microsoft Access.**

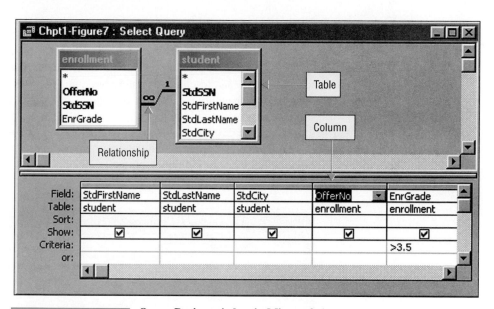

Figure 1.7   **Query Design window in Microsoft Access.**

trip, you need to indicate many more details such as the best route to your destination, the most desirable hotel, ground transportation, and so on. Your planning process is much easier if you have a professional to help with these additional details. Like a planning professional, a DBMS performs the detailed planning process to answer queries expressed in a nonprocedural language.

Most DBMSs provide more than one tool for nonprocedural access. The SELECT statement of SQL, described in Chapter 3, provides a nonprocedural way to access a database. Most DBMSs also provide graphical tools to access databases. Figure 1.7 depicts a

StdFirstName	StdLastName	StdCity	OfferNo	EnrGrade
MARIAH	DODGE	SEATTLE	1234	3.8
BOB	NORBERT	BOTHELL	5679	3.7
ROBERTO	MORALES	SEATTLE	5679	3.8
MARIAH	DODGE	SEATTLE	6666	3.6
LUKE	BRAZZI	SEATTLE	7777	3.7
WILLIAM	PILGRIM	BOTHELL	9876	4

Figure 1.8   **Result of executing query in Figure 1.7.**

graphical tool available in Microsoft Access. To pose a query to the database, a user only has to indicate the required tables, relationships, and columns. Access is responsible for knowing how to retrieve the requested data. Figure 1.8 shows the result of executing the query in Figure 1.7.

1.2.3 Application Development and Procedural Language Interface

Most DBMSs go well beyond simply accessing data. Graphical tools are provided for building complete applications using forms and reports. Data entry <u>forms</u> provide a convenient way to enter and edit data, while <u>reports</u> enhance the appearance of data that are displayed or printed. The form in Figure 1.9 can be used to add new course assignments for a professor and to change existing assignments. The report in Figure 1.10 uses indentation to show courses taught by faculty in various departments. The indentation style can be easier to view than the tabular style shown in Figure 1.8. Many forms and reports can be developed with a graphical tool without detailed coding. For example, Figures 1.9 and 1.10 were developed without coding. Chapter 5 describes concepts underlying form and report development.

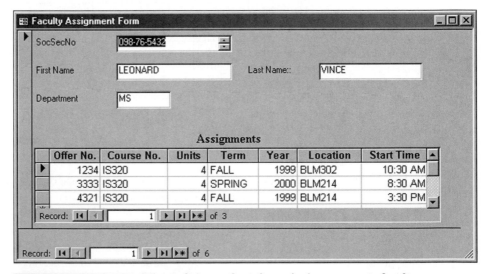

Figure 1.9   **Microsoft Access form for assigning courses to faculty.**

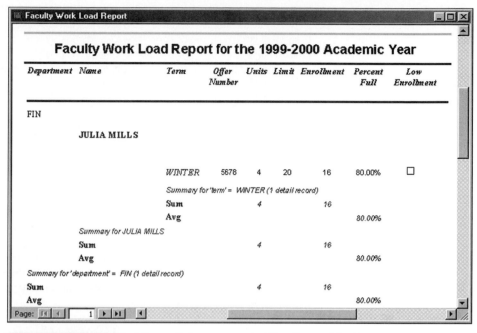

Figure 1.10   **Microsoft Access report of faculty workload.**

Nonprocedural access makes form and report creation possible without extensive coding. As part of creating a form or report, the user indicates the data requirements using a nonprocedural language (SQL) or graphical tool. To complete a form or report definition, the user indicates formatting of data, user interaction, and other details.

Procedural Language Interface a method to combine a nonprocedural language such as SQL with a programming language such as COBOL or Visual Basic.

In addition to application development tools, a procedural language interface adds the full capabilities of a computer programming language. Nonprocedural access and application development tools, though convenient and powerful, are sometimes not efficient enough or do not provide the level of control necessary for application development. When these tools are not adequate, DBMSs provide the full capabilities of a programming language. For example, Visual Basic for Applications (VBA) is a programming language that is integrated with Microsoft Access. VBA allows full customization of database access, form processing, and report generation. Most commercial DBMSs have a procedural language interface comparable to VBA. For example, Oracle has the language PL/SQL and Microsoft SQL Server has the language Transact-SQL.

1.2.4 Other Features

Transaction Processing reliable and efficient processing of large volumes of repetitive work. DBMSs ensure that simultaneous users do not interfere with each other and that failures do not cause lost work.

Transaction processing enables a DBMS to process large volumes of repetitive work. A transaction is a unit of work that should be processed reliably without interference from other users and without loss of data due to failures. Examples of transactions are withdrawing cash at an ATM, making an airline reservation, and registering for a course. A DBMS ensures that transactions are free of interference from other users, parts of a transaction are not lost due to a failure, and transactions do not make the database inconsistent. Transaction processing is largely a "behind the scenes" affair. The user does not know the details about transaction processing other than the assurances about reliability.

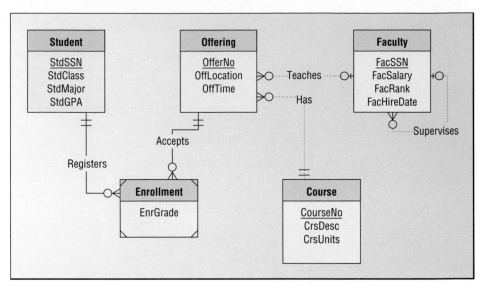

Figure 1.11 Entity relationship diagram (ERD) created with Visio Professional.

Database tuning includes a number of monitors and utility programs to improve performance. Some DBMSs can monitor how a database is used, the distribution of various parts of a database, and the growth of the database. Utility programs can be provided to reorganize a database, select physical structures for better performance, and repair damaged parts of a database.

Transaction processing and database tuning are most prominent on DBMSs that support large databases with many simultaneous users. These DBMSs are known as enterprise DBMSs because the databases they support are often critical to the functioning of an organization. Enterprise DBMSs usually run on powerful servers and have a high cost. In contrast, desktop DBMSs running on personal computers and small servers support limited transaction processing features but have a much lower cost. Desktop DBMSs support databases used by work teams and small businesses.

In addition to features provided directly by vendors of DBMSs, third-party software is also available for many DBMSs. In most cases, third-party software extends the features available with the database software. For example, many third-party vendors provide advanced database design tools that extend the database definition and tuning capabilities provided by DBMSs. Figure 1.11 shows a database diagram (an entity relationship diagram) created with Visio Professional, a tool for database design. The ERD in Figure 1.11 can be converted into the tables supported by most commercial DBMSs. In some cases, third-party software competes directly with the database product. For example, third-party vendors provide application development tools that can be used in place of the ones provided with the database product.

1.3 DEVELOPMENT OF DATABASE TECHNOLOGY AND MARKET STRUCTURE

The previous section provided a quick tour of the features found in typical DBMSs. The features in today's products are a significant improvement over just a few years ago. Database management, like many other areas of computing, has undergone tremendous technological growth. To provide you a context to appreciate today's DBMSs, this section reviews past changes in technology and suggests future trends. After this review, the current market for database software is presented.

1.3.1 Evolution of Database Technology

Table 1–2 depicts a brief history of database technology through four generations[1] of systems. The <u>first generation</u> supported sequential and random searching, but the user was required to write a computer program to obtain access. For example, a program could be written to retrieve all customer records or to just find the customer record with a specified customer number. Because first-generation systems did not offer much support for relating data, they are usually regarded as file processing systems rather than DBMSs. File processing systems can manage only one entity rather than many entities and relationships managed by a DBMS.

The <u>second-generation</u> products were the first true DBMSs as they could manage multiple entity types and relationships. However, to obtain access to data, a computer program still had to be written. Second-generation systems are referred to as "navigational" because the programmer had to write code to navigate among a network of linked records. Some of the second-generation products adhered to a standard database definition and manipulation language developed by the Committee on Data Systems Languages (CODASYL), a standards organization. The CODASYL standard had only limited market acceptance partly because IBM, the dominant computer company during this time, ignored the standard. IBM supported a different approach known as the hierarchical data model.

Rather than focusing on the second-generation standard, research labs at IBM and academic institutions developed the foundations for a new generation of DBMSs. The most important development involved nonprocedural languages for database access. <u>Third-generation</u> systems are known as relational DBMSs because of the foundation based on mathematical relations and associated operators. Optimization technology was developed so that access using nonprocedural languages would be efficient. Because nonprocedural access provided such an improvement over navigational access, third-generation systems supplanted the second generation. Since the technology was so different, most of the new systems were founded by start-up companies rather than

---

[1]The generations of DBMSs should not be confused with the generations of programming languages. In particular, fourth-generation language refers to programming language features, not DBMS features.

	TABLE 1–2	Brief Evolution of Database Technology	
Era	Generation	Orientation	Major Features
1960s	1st generation	File	File structures and proprietary program interfaces
1970s	2nd generation	Network navigation	Networks and hierarchies of related records, standard program interfaces
1980s	3rd generation	Relational	Nonprocedural languages, optimization, transaction processing
1990s	4th generation	Object	Multimedia, active, distributed processing, more powerful operators

by vendors of previous generation products. IBM was the major exception. It was IBM's weight that led to adoption of SQL as a widely accepted standard.

Fourth-generation DBMSs are extending the boundaries of database technology to unconventional data and the Internet. Fourth-generation systems can store and manipulate unconventional data types such as images, videos, maps, sounds, and animations. Because these systems view any kind of data as an object to manage, fourth-generation systems are sometimes called "object-oriented" or "object-relational." In addition to the emphasis on objects, the Internet is pushing DBMSs to develop new forms of distributed processing. Most DBMSs now feature convenient ways to publish static and dynamic data on the Internet. The market for fourth-generation systems is a battle between vendors of third-generation systems who are upgrading their products against a new group of systems developed by start-up companies. So far, the existing companies seem to have the upper hand.

1.3.2 Current Market for Database Software

According to Dataquest, a division of the Gartner Group, the sales of enterprise database software reached $7.1 billion in 1998, a 15 percent gain over 1997. Enterprise DBMSs use mainframe servers running IBM's MVS operating system and midrange servers running the Unix and Microsoft NT operating systems. Electronic commerce on the Internet has rejuvenated the market for enterprise database software. Before the advent of electronic commerce, enterprise DBMSs were becoming commodities and sales growth was stagnant. Dataquest projects sales of enterprise DBMSs to reach $10 billion by 2003.

According to Dataquest, five products dominate the market for enterprise database software as shown in Table 1–3. Although IBM holds the largest market share, Oracle dominates in the faster-growing Unix and NT markets. The overall market is very competitive with the major companies and smaller companies introducing many new features with each release.

In the market for desktop database software, Microsoft Access dominates at least in part because of the dominance of Microsoft Office. Desktop database software is pri-

TABLE 1–3	1998 Market Shares[2] by Revenue of Enterprise Database Software

Product	Market Share	Comments
IBM DB2	33%	Dominates the MVS and AS/400 environments; single-digit market share of Unix and NT environments
Oracle	29%	Dominates the Unix environment (61%); leader in the NT environment (46%)
Microsoft SQL Server	10%	30% market share from NT environment; no presence in other environments
Informix	4%	13% share of Unix environment (second behind Oracle)
Sybase SQL Server	4%	
Other	20%	Includes Computer Associates, NCR, Progress Software, NEC, and others

[2]Market shares according to a 1999 study by Dataquest, a division of the Gartner Group.

marily sold as part of office productivity software. With Microsoft Office holding about 90 percent of the office productivity market, Access holds a comparable share of the desktop database software market. Other significant products in the desktop database software market are Paradox, Approach, FoxPro, and FileMaker Pro.

To provide coverage of both enterprise and desktop database software, this book features significant coverage of Oracle and Microsoft Access. In addition, the emphasis on the SQL2 standard in Parts 1 and 3 provides database language coverage for the other major products.

1.4 ARCHITECTURES OF DATABASE MANAGEMENT SYSTEMS

To provide insight about the internal organization of DBMSs, this section describes two architectures or organizing frameworks. The first architecture describes an organization of database definitions to reduce the cost of software maintenance. The second architecture describes an organization of data and software to support remote access. These architectures promote a conceptual understanding rather than indicate how an actual DBMS is organized.

1.4.1 Data Independence and the Three Schema Architecture

In early DBMSs, there was a close connection between a database and computer programs that accessed the database. Essentially, the DBMS was considered part of a programming language. As a result, the database definition was part of the computer programs that accessed the database. In addition, the conceptual meaning of a database was not separate from its physical implementation on magnetic disk. The definitions about the structure of a database and its physical implementation were mixed inside computer programs.

The close association between a database and related programs led to problems in software maintenance. Software maintenance encompassing requirement changes, corrections, and enhancements can consume a large fraction of computer budgets. In early DBMSs, most changes to the database definition caused changes to computer programs. In many cases, changes to computer programs involved detailed inspection of the code, a labor-intensive process. This code inspection work is similar to "year 2000 compliance" where date formats must be changed to four digits. Performance tuning of a database was difficult because sometimes hundreds of computer programs had to be recompiled for every change. Because database definition changes are common, a large fraction of software maintenance resources was devoted to database changes. Some studies have estimated the percentage as high as 50 percent of software maintenance resources.

Data Independence a database should have an identity separate from the applications (computer programs, forms, and reports) that use it. The separate identity allows the database definition to be changed without affecting related applications.

The concept of data independence emerged to alleviate problems with program maintenance. Data independence means that a database should have an identity separate from the applications (computer programs, forms, and reports) that use it. The separate identity allows the database definition to be changed without affecting related applications. For example, if a new column is added to a table, applications not using the new column should not be affected. Likewise if a new table is added, only applications that need the new table should be affected. This separation should be even more pronounced if a change only affects physical implementation of a database. Database specialists should be free to experiment with performance tuning without worrying about making computer program changes.

In the mid 1970s, the concept of data independence led to the proposal of the Three Schema Architecture depicted in Figure 1.12. The word schema as applied to databases

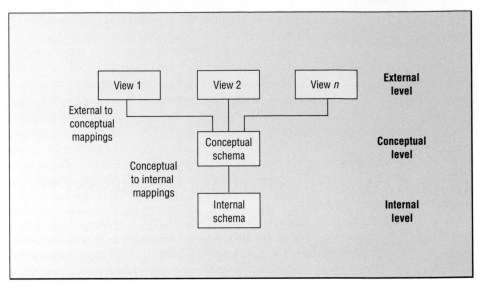

Figure 1.12   **Three Schema Architecture.**

means database description. The Three Schema Architecture includes three levels of database description. The <u>external</u> level is the user level. Each group of users can have a separate external view (or view for short) of a database tailored to the group's specific needs.

In contrast, the conceptual and internal schemas represent the entire database. The <u>conceptual schema</u> defines the entities and relationships. For a business database, the conceptual schema can be quite large, perhaps hundreds of entity types and relationships. Like the conceptual schema, the internal schema represents the entire database. However, the <u>internal schema</u> represents the storage view of the database whereas the conceptual schema represents the logical meaning of the database. The internal schema defines files, collections of data on a storage device such as a hard disk. A file can store one or more entities described in the conceptual schema.

To make the three schema levels clearer, Table 1–4 shows differences among database definition at the three schema levels using examples from the features described in Section 1.2. Even in a simplified university database, the differences among the schema levels are clear. With a more complex database, the differences would be even more pronounced with many more views, a much larger conceptual schema, and a more complex internal schema.

Three Schema Architecture an architecture for compartmentalizing database descriptions. The Three Schema Architecture was proposed as a way to achieve data independence.

TABLE 1–4	University Database Example Depicting Differences among Schema Levels

Schema Level	Description
External	HighGPAView: data required for the query in Figure 1.7
	FacultyAssignmentFormView: data required for the form in Figure 1.9
	FacultyWorkLoadReportView: data required for the report in Figure 1.10
Conceptual	Student, Enrollment, Course, Faculty, and Enrollment tables and relationships (Figure 1.6)
Internal	Files needed to store the tables; extra files (indexed property in Figure 1.5) to improve performance

The schema mappings describe how a schema at a higher level is derived from a schema at a lower level. For example, the external views in Table 1–4 are derived from the tables in the conceptual schema. The mapping provides the knowledge to convert a request using an external view (for example, HighGPAView) into a request using the tables in the conceptual schema. The mapping between conceptual and internal levels shows how entities are stored in files.

DBMSs, using schemas and mappings, ensure data independence. Typically, applications access a database using a view. The DBMS converts an application's request into a request using the conceptual schema rather than the view. The DBMS then transforms the conceptual schema request into a request using the internal schema. Most changes to the conceptual or internal schema do not affect applications because applications do not use the lower schema levels. The DBMS, not the user, is responsible for using the mappings to make the transformations. For more details about mappings and transformations, Chapter 5 describes views and transformations between the external and conceptual levels.

The Three Schema Architecture is an official standard of the American National Standards Institute (ANSI). However, the specific details of the standard were never widely adopted. Rather, the standard serves as a guideline about how data independence can be achieved. The spirit of the Three Schema Architecture is widely implemented in third- and fourth-generation DBMSs.

1.4.2 Distributed Processing and the Client–Server Architecture

With the growing importance of network computing and the Internet, distributed processing is becoming a crucial function of DBMSs. Distributed processing allows geographically dispersed computers to cooperate when providing data access. A large part of electronic commerce on the Internet involves accessing and updating remote databases. Many databases in retail, banking, and security trading are now available through the Internet. DBMSs use available network capacity and local processing capabilities to provide efficient remote database access.

Many DBMSs support distributed processing using a client–server architecture. A client is a program that submits requests to a server. A server processes requests on behalf of a client. For example, a client may request a server to retrieve product data. The server locates the data and sends them back to the client. The client may perform additional processing on the data before displaying the results to the user. As another example, a client submits a completed order to a server. The server validates the order, updates a database, and sends an acknowledgement to the client. The client informs the user that the order has been processed.

Client–Server Architecture an arrangement of components (clients and servers) and data among computers connected by a network. The client–server architecture supports efficient processing of messages (requests for service) between clients and servers.

To improve performance and availability of data, the client–server architecture supports many ways to distribute software and data in a computer network. The simplest scheme is just to place both software and data on the same computer (Figure 1.13(a)). To take advantage of a network, both software and data can be distributed. In Figure 1.13(b), the server software and the database are located on a remote computer. In Figure 1.13(c), the server software and the database are located on multiple remote computers.

The DBMS has a number of responsibilities in a client–server architecture. The DBMS provides software that can execute on both the client and the server. The client software is typically responsible for accepting user input, displaying results, and performing some processing of data. The server software validates client requests, locates remote databases, updates remote databases (if needed), and sends the data in a format that the client understands.

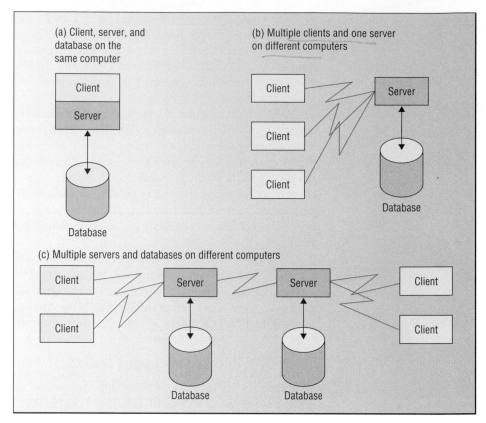

Figure 1.13 Typical client–server arrangements of database and software.

Client–server architectures provide a flexible way for DBMSs to interact with computer networks. The distribution of work among clients and servers and the possible choices to locate data and software are much more complex than described here. You will learn more details about client–server architectures in Chapter 15.

1.5 ORGANIZATIONAL IMPACTS OF DATABASE TECHNOLOGY

This section completes your introduction to database technology by discussing how databases affect organizations. The first section describes how you might interact with a database in an organization. The second section describes information resource management, an effort to control the data produced and used by an organization. Special attention is given to management roles that you may play as part of an effort to control information resources.

1.5.1 Interacting with Databases

Because databases are pervasive, there are a variety of ways in which you may interact with databases. The classification in Figure 1.14 distinguishes between functional users who interact with databases as part of their work and information systems professionals who participate in designing and implementing databases. Each box in the hierarchy rep-

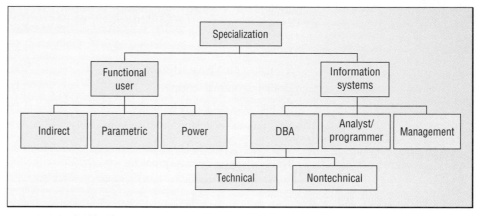

Figure 1.14   **Classification of roles.**

resents a role that you may play. You may simultaneously play more than one role. For example, a functional user in a job such as financial analysis may play all three roles in different databases. In some organizations, the distinction between functional users and information systems professionals is blurred. In these organizations, functional users may participate in designing and using databases.

Functional users can play a passive or an active role when interacting with databases. Indirect usage of a database is a passive role. An <u>indirect</u> user is given a report or some data extracted from a database. A parametric user is more active than an indirect user. A <u>parametric</u> user requests existing forms or reports using parameters, input values that change from usage to usage. For example, a parameter may indicate a date range, sales territory, or department name. The <u>power</u> user is the most active. Because decision-making needs can be difficult to predict, ad hoc or unplanned usage of a database is important. A power user is skilled enough to build a form or report when needed. Power users should have a good understanding of nonprocedural access, a skill described in the first part of this book.

Information systems professionals interact with databases as part of developing an information system. <u>Analyst/programmers</u> are responsible for collecting requirements, designing applications, and implementing information systems. They create and use external views to develop forms, reports, and other parts of an information system. Management has an oversight role in development of databases and information systems.

<u>Database administrators</u> assist both information systems professionals and functional users. Database administrators have a variety of both technical and nontechnical responsibilities (Table 1–5). Technical skills are more detail-oriented; nontechnical responsibilities are more people-oriented. The primary technical responsibility is database design. On the nontechnical side, the database administrator's time is split among a number of activities. Database administrators also can have responsibilities in planning databases and evaluating DBMSs.

Database Administrator
a support position that specializes in managing individual databases and DBMSs.

1.5.2 Information Resource Management

Information resource management is a response to the challenge of effectively utilizing information technology. The goal of <u>information resource management</u> is to use information technology as a tool for processing, distributing, and integrating information

TABLE 1–5	Responsibilities of the Database Administrator

Technical	*Nontechnical*
Designing conceptual schemas	Setting database standards
Designing internal schemas	Devising training materials
Monitoring database performance	Promoting benefits of databases
Selecting and evaluating database software	Consulting with users
Designing client–server databases	
Troubleshooting database problems	

throughout an organization. Management of information resources has many similarities with managing physical resources such as inventory. Inventory management involves activities such as safeguarding inventory from theft and deterioration, storing it for efficient usage, choosing suppliers, handling waste, coordinating movement, and reducing holding costs. Information resource management involves similar activities: planning databases, acquiring data, protecting data from unauthorized access, ensuring reliability, coordinating flow among information systems, and eliminating duplication.

As part of controlling information resources, new management responsibilities have arisen. The data administrator is a management role with many of these responsibilities, the major responsibility being planning the development of new databases. The data ad-

Data Administrator a management position that performs planning and policy setting for the information resources of an entire organization.

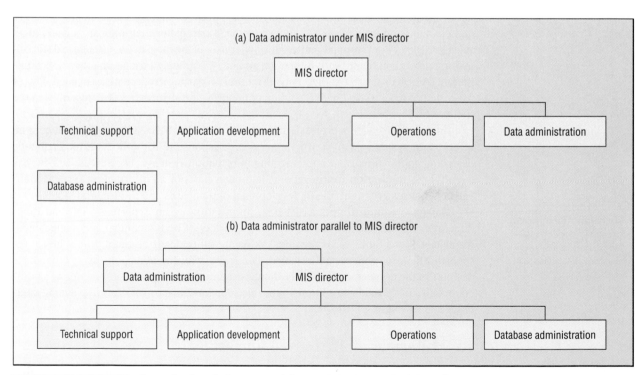

Figure 1.15   **Organizational placement of data and database administration.**

ministrator maintains an enterprise data architecture that describes existing databases and new databases and also evaluates new information technologies and determines standards for managing databases.

The data administrator typically has broader responsibilities than the database administrator. The data administrator is primarily a planning role, while the database administrator is a more technical role focused on individual databases and DBMSs. The data administrator also views the information resource in a broader context and considers all kinds of data, both computerized and noncomputerized. A major effort in many organizations is to computerize nontraditional data such as video, training materials, images, and correspondence. The data administrator develops long-range plans for nontraditional data, while the database administrator implements the plans using appropriate database technology.

Because of broader responsibilities, the data administrator typically is higher in an organization chart. Figure 1.15 depicts two possible placements of data administrators and database administrators. In a small organization, both roles may be combined in systems administration.

CLOSING THOUGHTS

Chapter 1 has provided a broad introduction to DBMSs. You should use this background to provide a context for the skills you will acquire in subsequent chapters. You learned that databases contain interrelated data that can be shared across multiple parts of an organization. DBMSs support transformation of data for decision making. To support this transformation, database technology has evolved from simple file access to powerful systems that support database definition, application development, transaction processing, and performance tuning. Nonprocedural access is the most vital element because it allows access without detailed coding. You learned about two architectures that provide organizing principles for DBMSs. The Three Schema Architecture supports data independence, an important concept for reducing the cost of software maintenance. Client–server architectures allow databases to be accessed over computer networks, a feature vital in today's networked world.

The skills emphasized in later chapters should enable you to work as an active functional user or analyst. Both kinds of users need to understand the skills taught in the first part of this book. This book also provides the foundation of skills to obtain a specialist position as a database or data administrator. The skills in the second and third parts of this book are most useful for a position as a database administrator. However, you probably will need to take additional courses, learn details of popular DBMSs, and acquire management experience before obtaining a specialist role. A position as a database or data administrator can be an exciting and lucrative career opportunity that you should consider.

REVIEW CONCEPTS

- Database characteristics: persistent, interrelated, and shared.
- Features of database management systems (DBMS).
- Nonprocedural access: a key to software productivity.
- Transaction: a unit of work that should be processed reliably.
- Application development using forms and reports.

- Procedural language interface for combining nonprocedural access with a programming language such as COBOL or Visual Basic.
- Data independence.
- Three Schema Architecture for reducing the impact of database definition changes.
- Client–server architecture for using databases over computer networks.
- Database specialist roles: database administrator and data administrator.
- Information resource management for utilizing information technology.

QUESTIONS

1. Describe a database that you have used on a job or as a consumer. List the entities and relationships that the database contains. If you are not sure, imagine the entities and relationships that are contained in the database.

2. For the database in question 1, list different user groups that can use the database.

3. For one of the groups in question 2, describe an application (form or report) that the group uses.

4. Describe the difference between a procedural and a nonprocedural language. What statements belong in a procedural language but not in a nonprocedural language?

5. Why is nonprocedural access an important feature of DBMSs?

6. What is the connection between nonprocedural access and application (form or report) development? Can nonprocedural access be used in application development?

7. For the database in question 1, describe a transaction that uses the database. How often do you think the transaction is submitted to the database? How many users submit transactions at the same time? Make guesses for the last two parts if you are unsure.

8. For the database you described in question 1, make a table to depict differences among schema levels. Use Table 1–4 as a guide.

9. What is the purpose of the mappings in the Three Schema Architecture? Is the user or the DBMS responsible for using the mappings?

10. Explain how the Three Schema Architecture supports data independence?

11. In a client–server architecture, why are processing capabilities divided between a client and a server? In other words, why not have the server do all the processing?

12. In a client–server architecture, why are data sometimes stored on several computers rather than on a single computer?

13. For the database in question 1, describe how functional users may interact with the database. Try to identify indirect, parametric, and power uses of the database.

14. Explain the differences in responsibilities between an active functional user of a database and an analyst. What schema level is used by both kinds of users?

15. Which role, database administrator or data administrator, is more appealing to you as a long-term career goal? Briefly explain your preference.

PROBLEMS

Because of the introductory nature of this chapter, there are no problems in this chapter. Problems appear at the end of most other chapters.

REFERENCES FOR FURTHER STUDY

The *Intelligent Enterprise Magazine* (http://www.iemagazine.com/) provides current information about business database issues, commercial DBMSs, and database development. *Advisor.com* (http://www.advisor.com/) provides detailed technical information about commercial DBMSs and database development. To learn more about the role of database specialists and information resource management, consult Davydov 1993; Guimaraes 1988; and Weldon 1981.

Chapter 2

The Relational Data Model

Learning Objectives

This chapter provides the foundation for using relational databases. After this chapter the student should have acquired the following knowledge and skills:

- Recognize relational database terminology.

- Understand the meaning of the integrity rules for relational databases.

- Understand the impact of referenced rows on maintaining relational databases.

- Understand the meaning of each relational algebra operator.

- List tables that must be combined to obtain desired results for simple retrieval requests.

OVERVIEW

Chapter 1 provided a starting point for your exploration of database technology. You broadly learned about database characteristics, DBMS features, system architectures, and human roles. This chapter narrows your focus to the relational data model. Relational DBMSs dominate the market for business DBMSs. You will undoubtedly use relational DBMSs throughout your career as an information systems professional. This chapter provides the background so that you may become proficient in developing applications for relational databases in later chapters.

To effectively use a relational database, you need two kinds of knowledge. First, you need to understand the structure and contents of the database tables. Understanding the connections among tables is especially critical because many database retrievals involve multiple tables. To help you understand relational databases, this chapter presents the basic terminology, the integrity rules, and a notation to visualize connections among tables. Second, you need to understand the operators of relational algebra as they are the building blocks of most commercial query languages. Understanding the operators will improve your knowledge of query languages such as SQL. To help you understand the meaning of each operator, this chapter provides a visual representation of each operator and several convenient summaries.

2.1 BASIC ELEMENTS

Relational database systems were originally developed because of familiarity and simplicity. Because tables are used to communicate ideas in many fields, the terminology of tables, rows, and columns is not intimidating to most users. During the early years of relational databases (1970s), the simplicity and familiarity of relational databases had strong appeal, especially as compared to the procedural orientation of other data models that existed at the time. Despite the familiarity and simplicity of relational databases, there is a strong mathematical basis also. The mathematics of relational databases involves thinking about tables as sets. The combination of familiarity and simplicity with a mathematical foundation is so powerful that relational DBMSs are commercially dominant.

This section presents the basic terminology of relational databases and introduces the CREATE TABLE statement of the Structured Query Language (SQL). Sections 2.2 through 2.4 provide more detail on the elements defined in this section.

2.1.1 Tables

A relational database consists of a collection of tables. Each table has a heading or definition part and a body or content part. The heading part consists of the table name and the column names. For example, a student table may have columns for social security number, name, street address, city, state, zip, class (freshman, sophomore, etc.), major, and cumulative grade point average (GPA). The body shows the rows of the table. Each row in a student table represents a student enrolled at a university. A student table for a major university may have more than 30,000 rows, too many to view at one time.

Table a two-dimensional arrangement of data. A table consists of a heading defining the table name and column names and a body containing rows of data.

To understand a table, it is also useful to view some of its rows. A table listing or datasheet shows the column names in the first row and the body in the other rows. Table 2–1 shows a table listing for the *Student* table. Three sample rows representing university students are displayed. In this book, the naming convention for column names includes a table abbreviation ("Std") followed by a descriptive name. Because column names often are used without identifying the associated tables, the abbreviation supports easy table association. Mixed case highlights the different parts of a column name.

TABLE 2–1	Sample Table Listing of the Student Table

StdSSN	StdFirstName	StdLastName	StdCity	StdState	StdZip	StdMajor	StdClass	StdGPA
123-45-6789	HOMER	WELLS	SEATTLE	WA	98121-1111	IS	FR	3.00
124-56-7890	BOB	NORBERT	BOTHELL	WA	98011-2121	FIN	JR	2.70
234-56-7890	CANDY	KENDALL	TACOMA	WA	99042-3321	ACCT	JR	3.50

Data Type defines a set of values and permissible operations on the values. Each column of a table is associated with a data type.

A CREATE TABLE statement can be used to define the heading part of a table. CREATE TABLE is a statement in the Structured Query Language (SQL). Because SQL is an industry standard language, the CREATE TABLE statement can be used to create tables in most DBMSs. The CREATE TABLE statement on the next page creates the *Student* table. For each column, the column name and the data type are specified. Data types indicate the kind of data (character, numeric, Yes/No, etc.) and permissible operations (numeric operations, string operations, etc.) for the column. Each data type has a name (for example, CHAR for character) and usually a length specification. Table 2–2 lists common data types[1] used in relational DBMSs.

[1]Data types are not standard across relational DBMSs. These data types are supported by most systems, although the name of the data type may differ.

TABLE 2–2	Brief Description of Common SQL Data Types

Data Type	Description
CHAR(L)	For fixed-length text entries such as state abbreviations and social security numbers. Each column value using CHAR contains the maximum number of characters (L) even if the actual length is shorter. Most DBMSs have an upper limit on the length (L) such as 255.
VARCHAR(L)	For variable-length text such as names and street addresses. Column values using VARCHAR contain only the actual number of characters, not the maximum length as for CHAR columns. Most DBMSs have an upper limit on the length such as 255.
FLOAT(P)	For columns containing numeric data with floating precision such as interest rate calculations and scientific calculations. The precision parameter P indicates the number of significant digits. Most DBMSs have an upper limit on P such as 38. Some DBMSs have two data types, REAL and DOUBLE PRECISION, for low- and high-precision floating-point numbers instead of the variable precision with the FLOAT data type.
DATE/TIME	For columns containing dates and times such as an order date. These data types are not standard across DBMSs. Some systems support three data types (DATE, TIME, and TIMESTAMP) while other systems support a combined data type (DATE) storing both the date and time.
DECIMAL(W,R)	For columns containing numeric data with a fixed precision such as monetary amounts. The W value indicates the total number of digits and the R value indicates the number of digits to the right of the decimal point. This data type is also called NUMERIC in some systems.
INTEGER	For columns containing whole numbers (i.e., numbers without a decimal point). Some DBMSs have the SMALLINT data type for very small whole numbers and the LONG data type for very large integers.
BOOLEAN	For columns containing data with two values such as true/false or yes/no.

```
CREATE TABLE Student
      (       StdSSN            CHAR(11),
              StdFirstName      VARCHAR(50),
              StdLastName       VARCHAR(50),
              StdCity           VARCHAR(50),
              StdState          CHAR(2),
              StdZip            CHAR(10),
              StdMajor          CHAR(6),
              StdClass          CHAR(6),
              StdGPA            DECIMAL(3,2) )
```

2.1.2 Connections among Tables

Relationship

connection between rows in two tables. Relationships are shown by column values in one table that match column values in another table.

It is not enough to understand each table individually. To understand a relational database, connections or relationships among tables also must be understood. The rows in a table are usually related to rows in other tables. Matching (identical) values show relationships between tables. Consider the sample *Enrollment* table (Table 2–3) in which each row represents a student enrolled in an offering of a course. The values in the *StdSSN* column of the *Enrollment* table match the *StdSSN* values in the sample *Student* table (Table 2–1). For example, the first and third rows of the *Enrollment* table have the same *StdSSN* value (123-45-6789) as the first row of the *Student* table. Likewise, the values in the *OfferNo* column of the *Enrollment* table match the *OfferNo* column in the *Offering* table (Table 2–4). Figure 2.1 shows a graphical depiction of the matching values.

The concept of matching values is crucial in relational databases. As you will see, relational databases typically contain many tables. Even a modest-size database can have 10 to 15 tables. Large databases can have hundreds of tables. To extract meaningful information, it is often necessary to combine multiple tables using matching values. By matching on *Student.StdSSN* and *Enrollment.StdSSN,* you could combine the *Student* and *Enrollment* tables.[2] Similarly, by matching on *Enrollment.OfferNo* and *Offering.OfferNo* you could combine the *Enrollment* and *Offering* tables. As you will see later in this chapter, the operation of combining tables on matching values is known as a join. Understanding the connections between tables (or ways that tables can be combined) is crucial for extracting useful data.

[2]When columns have identical names in two tables, it is customary to precede the column name with the table name and a period as *Student.StdSSN* and *Enrollment.StdSSN.*

TABLE 2–3	Sample Enrollment Table	
OfferNo	StdSSN	EnrGrade
1234	123-45-6789	3.3
1234	234-56-7890	3.5
4321	123-45-6789	3.5
4321	124-56-7890	3.2

TABLE 2–4	Sample Offering Table

OfferNo	CourseNo	OffTerm	OffYear	OffLocation	OffTime	FacSSN	OffDays
1111	IS320	SUMMER	2000	BLM302	10:30 AM		MW
1234	IS320	FALL	1999	BLM302	10:30 AM	098-76-5432	MW
2222	IS460	SUMMER	1999	BLM412	1:30 PM		TTH
3333	IS320	SPRING	2000	BLM214	8:30 AM	098-76-5432	MW
4321	IS320	FALL	1999	BLM214	3:30 PM	098-76-5432	TTH
4444	IS320	SPRING	2000	BLM302	3:30 PM	543-21-0987	TTH
5678	IS480	SPRING	2000	BLM302	10:30 AM	987-65-4321	MW
5679	IS480	SPRING	2000	BLM412	3:30 PM	876-54-3210	TTH
9876	IS460	SPRING	2000	BLM307	1:30 PM	654-32-1098	TTH

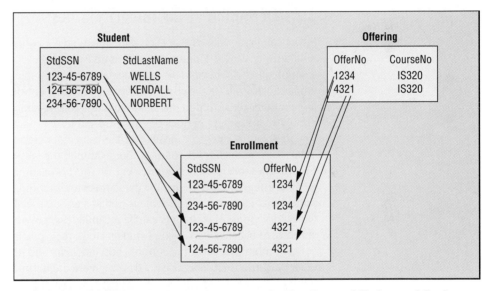

Figure 2.1	Matching values among the Enrollment, Offering, and Student tables.

2.1.3 Alternative Terminology

You should be aware that other terminology is used besides table, row, and column. Table 2–5 shows three roughly equivalent terminologies. The divergence in terminology is due to the different groups that use databases. The table-oriented terminology appeals to end users; the set-oriented terminology appeals to academic researchers; and the record-oriented terminology appeals to information systems professionals. In practice, these terms may be mixed. For example, in the same sentence you may hear both "tables" and "fields." You should expect to see a mix of terminology in your career.

TABLE 2–5	Alternative Terminology for Relational Databases		
Table-Oriented	*Set-Oriented*	*Record-Oriented*	
Table	Relation	Record type, file	
Row	Tuple	Record	
Column	Attribute	Field	

2.2 INTEGRITY RULES

In the previous section, you learned that a relational database consists of a collection of interrelated tables. To ensure that a database provides meaningful information, integrity rules are necessary. This section describes two important integrity rules (entity integrity and referential integrity), examples of their usage, and a notation to visualize referential integrity.

2.2.1 Definition of the Integrity Rules

Entity integrity[3] means that each table must have a column or combination of columns with unique values. Unique means that no two rows of a table have the same value. For example, *StdSSN* in *Student* is unique and the combination of *StdSSN* and *OfferNo* is unique in *Enrollment*. Entity integrity ensures that entities (people, things, and events) are uniquely identified in the database. For auditing and security reasons, it is often important that business entities be easily traceable.

Referential integrity means that the values of columns in one table must match the values of columns in other tables. For example, the value of *StdSSN* in each row of the *Enrollment* table must match the value of *StdSSN* in some row of the *Student* table. Referential integrity ensures that the database contains valid connections. For example, it is critical that each row of *Enrollment* contains a social security number of a valid student. Otherwise, some enrollments can be meaningless, possibly resulting in students denied enrollment because nonexisting students took their places.

For more precise definitions of entity integrity and referential integrity, a number of other definitions are necessary. These prerequisite definitions and the more precise definitions are presented below.

Definitions

- **Superkey:** a column or combination of columns containing unique values for each row. The combination of every column in a table is always a superkey because rows in a table must be unique.[4]
- **Candidate key:** a minimal superkey. A superkey is minimal if removing any columns makes it no longer unique.
- **Null value:** a special value that represents the absence of an actual value. A null value can mean that the actual value is unknown or does not apply to the given row.

---

[3]Entity integrity is also known as uniqueness integrity.
[4]The uniqueness of rows is a feature of the relational model that SQL2 does not require.

- **Primary key:** a specially designated candidate key. The primary key for a table cannot contain null values.
- **Foreign key:** a column or combination of columns in which the values must match those of a candidate key. A foreign key must have the same data type as its associated candidate key. In the CREATE TABLE statement of SQL2, a foreign key must be associated with a primary key rather than merely a candidate key.

Integrity Rules

- **Entity integrity rule:** No two rows of a table can contain the same value for the primary key. In addition, no row can contain a null value for any columns of a primary key.
- **Referential integrity rule:** Only two kinds of values can be stored in a foreign key:
    > a value matching a candidate key value in some row of the table containing the associated candidate key or
    > a null value.

2.2.2 Applying the Integrity Rules

To extend your understanding, let us apply the integrity rules to several tables in the university database. The primary key of *Student* is *StdSSN*. A primary key can be designated as part of the CREATE TABLE statement. To designate *StdSSN* as the primary key of *Student*, use a CONSTRAINT clause for the primary key at the end of the CREATE TABLE statement as shown below. The word PKStudent following the CONSTRAINT keyword is the name of the constraint.

```
CREATE TABLE Student
    (       StdSSN            CHAR(11),
            StdFirstName      VARCHAR(50),
            StdLastName       VARCHAR(50),
            StdCity           VARCHAR(50),
            StdState          CHAR(2),
            StdZip            CHAR(10),
            StdMajor          CHAR(6),
            StdClass          CHAR(2),
            StdGPA            DECIMAL(3,2),
    CONSTRAINT PKStudent PRIMARY KEY (StdSSN) )
```

Candidate keys that are not primary keys are declared with the UNIQUE keyword. The *Course* table (see Table 2–6) contains two candidate keys: *CourseNo* and *CrsDesc* (course description). The *CourseNo* column is the primary key because it is more stable than the *CrsDesc* column. Course descriptions may change over time, but the course numbers remain the same. In the CREATE TABLE statement, a constraint with the keyword UNIQUE follows the primary key constraint.

TABLE 2–6	Sample Course Table	
CourseNo	CrsDesc	CrsUnits
IS320	FUNDAMENTALS OF BUSINESS	4
IS460	SYSTEMS ANALYSIS	4
IS470	BUSINESS DATA COMMUNICATIONS	4
IS480	FUNDAMENTALS OF DATABASE	4

```
CREATE TABLE Course
    (        CourseNo    CHAR(6),
             CrsDesc     VARCHAR(250),
             CrsUnits    SMALLINT,
CONSTRAINT PKCourse PRIMARY KEY(CourseNo),
CONSTRAINT UniqueCrsDesc UNIQUE (CrsDesc) )
```

Some tables need more than one column in the primary key. In the *Enrollment* table, the combination of *StdSSN* and *OfferNo* is the only candidate key. Both columns are needed to identify a row. A primary key consisting of more than one column is known as a composite or a combined primary key.

Superkeys are usually not important to identify because they are common and contain columns that do not contribute to the uniqueness property. For example, the combination of *StdSSN* and *StdLastName* is unique. However, if *StdLastName* is removed, *StdSSN* is still unique.

For referential integrity, the columns *StdSSN* and *OfferNo* are foreign keys in the *Enrollment* table. The *StdSSN* column refers to *Student* and the *OfferNo* column refers to the *Offering* table (Table 2–4). An *Offering* row represents a course given in an academic period (summer, winter, etc.), year, time, location, and days of the week. The primary key of *Offering* is *OfferNo*. A course such as IS480 will have different offer numbers each time it is offered.

Referential integrity constraints can be defined similarly to the way of defining primary keys. For example, to define the foreign keys in *Enrollment,* use CONSTRAINT clauses for foreign keys at the end of the CREATE TABLE statement:

```
CREATE TABLE Enrollment
    (        OfferNo     INTEGER,
             StdSSN      CHAR(11),
             EnrGrade    DECIMAL(3,2),
CONSTRAINT PKEnrollment PRIMARY KEY(OfferNo, StdSSN),
CONSTRAINT FKOfferNo FOREIGN KEY (OfferNo) REFERENCES Offering,
CONSTRAINT FKStdSSN FOREIGN KEY (StdSSN) REFERENCES Student )
```

Allowing Null Values in Foreign Keys

Although referential integrity permits foreign keys to have null values, it is not common for foreign keys to have null values. When a foreign key is part of a primary key, null values are not permitted because of the entity integrity rule. For example, null values are not permitted for either *Enrollment.StdSSN* or *Enrollment.OfferNo* because each is part of the primary key.

When a foreign key is not part of a primary key, usage dictates whether null values should be permitted. For example, *Offering.CourseNo,* a foreign key referring to *Course* (Table 2–4), is not part of a primary key yet null values are not permitted. In most universities, a course cannot be offered before it is approved. Thus, an offering should not be inserted without having a related course.

In contrast, the *Offering.FacSSN* column referring to the faculty member teaching the offering may be null. The *Faculty* table (Table 2–7) stores data about instructors of courses. A null value for *Offering.FacSSN* means that a faculty member is not yet assigned to teach the offering. For example, an instructor is not assigned in the first and third rows of Table 2–4. Because offerings must be scheduled perhaps a year in advance, it is likely that instructors for some offerings will not be known until after the offering row is initially stored. Therefore, permitting null values in the *Offering* table is prudent.

In the CREATE TABLE statement, the NOT NULL clause indicates that a column cannot have null values. You indicate that nulls are not permitted by appending the NOT NULL clause after the data type specification. You also can specify the NOT NULL clause in a CONSTRAINT clause.

```
CREATE TABLE Student
      (        StdSSN          CHAR(11) NOT NULL,
               StdFirstName    VARCHAR(50) NOT NULL,
               StdLastName     VARCHAR(50) NOT NULL,
               StdCity         VARCHAR(50) NOT NULL,
               StdState        CHAR(2) NOT NULL,
               StdZip          CHAR(10) NOT NULL,
               StdMajor        CHAR(6),
               StdClass        CHAR(2) ,
               StdGPA          DECIMAL(3,2),
CONSTRAINT PKStudent PRIMARY KEY (StdSSN) )
```

TABLE 2–7 | **Sample *Faculty* Table**

FacSSN	FacFirstName	FacLastName	FacCity	FacState	FacDept	FacRank	FacSalary	FacSupervisor	FacHireDate	FacZipCode
098-76-5432	LEONARD	VINCE	SEATTLE	WA	MS	ASST	$35,000	654-32-1098	01-Apr-90	98111-9921
543-21-0987	VICTORIA	EMMANUEL	BOTHELL	WA	MS	PROF	$120,000		01-Apr-91	98011-2242
654-32-1098	LEONARD	FIBON	SEATTLE	WA	MS	ASSC	$70,000	543-21-0987	01-Apr-89	98121-0094
765-43-2109	NICKI	MACON	BELLEVUE	WA	FIN	PROF	$65,000		01-Apr-92	98015-9945
876-54-3210	CHRISTOPHER	COLAN	SEATTLE	WA	MS	ASST	$40,000	654-32-1098	01-Apr-94	98114-1332
987-65-4321	JULIA	MILLS	SEATTLE	WA	FIN	ASSC	$75,000	765-43-2109	01-Apr-95	98114-9954

Self-Referencing Relationship a relationship in which a foreign key refers to the same table. Self-referencing relationships represent associations among members of the same set.

Referential Integrity for Self-Referencing (Unary) Relationships

This section finishes with a discussion of <u>self-referencing relationships</u>, a special kind of referential integrity constraint. Self-referencing or unary relationships involve a single table. Self-referencing relationships are not common, but they are important when they occur. In the university database, a faculty member can supervise other faculty members and be supervised by a faculty member. For example, Victoria Emmanuel (second row) supervises Leonard Fibon (third row). The *FacSupervisor* column shows this relationship: the *FacSupervisor* value in the third row (543-21-0987) matches the *FacSSN* value in the second row. A referential integrity constraint involving the *FacSupervisor* column represents the self-referencing relationship. In the CREATE TABLE statement, the referential integrity constraint for a self-referencing relationship can be written the same way as other referential integrity constraints:

```
CREATE TABLE Faculty
      (       FacSSN          CHAR(11) NOT NULL,
              FacFirstName    VARCHAR(50) NOT NULL,
              FacLastName     VARCHAR(50) NOT NULL,
              FacCity         VARCHAR(50) NOT NULL,
              FacState        CHAR(2) NOT NULL,
              FacZipCode      CHAR(10) NOT NULL,
              FacHireDate     DATE,
              FacDept         CHAR(6) ,
              FacRank         CHAR(4),
              FacSalary       DECIMAL(10,2),
              FacSupervisor   CHAR(11),
CONSTRAINT PKFaculty PRIMARY KEY (FacSSN),
CONSTRAINT FKFacSupervisor FOREIGN KEY (FacSupervisor) REFERENCES Faculty )
```

2.2.3 Graphical Representation of Referential Integrity

In recent years, commercial DBMSs have provided graphical representations for referential integrity constraints. The graphical representation makes referential integrity easier to define and understand than the text representation in the CREATE TABLE statement. In addition, a graphical representation supports nonprocedural data access.

To depict a graphical representation, let us study the Relationship window in Microsoft Access. Access provides the Relationship window to visually define and display referential integrity constraints. Figure 2.2 shows the Relationship window for the tables of the university database. Each line represents a referential integrity constraint or relationship. In a relationship, the primary key table is known as the "1" table (for example, *Student*) and the foreign key table (for example, *Enrollment*) is known as the "M" (many) table.

The relationship from *Student* to *Enrollment* is called "1-M" (one to many) because a student can be related to many enrollments but an enrollment can be related to only one student. Similarly, the relationship from the *Offering* table to the *Enrollment* table means that an offering can be related to many enrollments but an enrollment can be re-

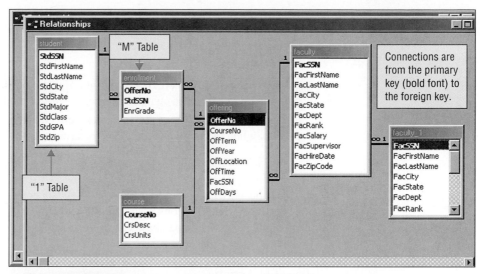

| **Figure 2.2** | **Relationship window for the university database.** |

lated to only one offering. You should practice by writing similar sentences for the other relationships in Figure 2.2.

M-N (many to many) relationships are not directly represented in the Relational Model. An M-N relationship means that rows from each table can be related to many rows of the other table. For example, a student enrolls in many course offerings and a course offering contains many students. In the Relational Model, a pair of 1-M relationships and a linking or associative table represents an M-N relationship. In Figure 2.2, the linking table *Enrollment* and its relationships with *Offering* and *Student* represent an M-N relationship between the *Student* and *Offering* tables.

Self-referencing relationships are represented indirectly in the Relationship window. The self-referencing relationship involving *Faculty* is represented as a relationship between the *Faculty* and *Faculty_1* tables. *Faculty_1* is not a real table as it is created only inside the Relationship window. Access can only indirectly show self-referencing relationships.

A graphical representation such as the Relationship window makes it easy to identify tables that should be combined to fulfill a retrieval request. For example, assume that you want to find instructors who teach courses with "database" in the course description. Clearly, you need the *Course* table to find "database" courses. You also need the *Faculty* table to display instructor data. Figure 2.2 shows that you also need the *Offering* table because *Course* and *Faculty* are not directly connected. Rather, *Course* and *Faculty* are connected through *Offering*. Thus, visualizing relationships helps to identify tables needed to fulfill retrieval requests. Before attempting the retrieval problems in later chapters, you should carefully study a graphical representation of the relationships. You should construct your own diagram if one is not available.

1-M Relationship a connection between two tables in which one row of a table can be referenced by many rows of a second table. 1-M relationships are the most common kind of relationship.

M-N Relationship a connection between two tables in which rows of each table can be related to many rows of the other table. M-N relationships cannot be directly represented in the Relational Model. Two 1-M relationships and a linking or associative table represent an M-N relationship.

2.3 DELETE AND UPDATE ACTIONS FOR REFERENCED ROWS

For each referential integrity constraint, you should carefully consider actions on <u>referenced</u> rows. A row is referenced if there is a matching row in a foreign key table. For example, the first row of the *Course* table

(Table 2–6) with *CourseNo* "IS320" is referenced by the first row of the *Offering* table (Table 2–4). It is natural to consider what happens to related *Offering* rows when the referenced *Course* row is deleted or the *CourseNo* is updated. More generally, these concerns can be stated as

> **Deleting a referenced row:**   What happens to related rows (that is, rows in the foreign key table) when the referenced row is deleted?
>
> **Updating the primary key of a referenced row:**   What happens to related rows when the primary key of the referenced row is updated?

Actions on referenced rows are important when changing the rows of a database. When developing data entry forms (discussed in Chapter 5), actions on referenced rows can be especially important. For example, if a data entry form permits deletion of rows in the *Course* table, actions on related rows in the *Offering* table must be carefully planned. Otherwise, the database can become inconsistent.

Possible Actions

There are several possible actions in response to the deletion of a referenced row or the update of the primary key of a referenced row. The appropriate action depends on the tables involved. The following list describes the actions and provides examples of usage.

- **Restrict:** Do not allow the action on the referenced row. For example, do not permit a *Student* row to be deleted if there are any related *Enrollment* rows. Similarly, do not allow *Student.StdSSN* to be changed if there are related *Enrollment* rows.

- **Cascade:** Perform the same action (cascade the action) to related rows. For example, if a *Student* is deleted, then delete the related *Enrollment* rows. Likewise, if *Student.StdSSN* is changed in some row, update *StdSSN* in the related *Enrollment* rows.

- **Nullify:** Set the foreign key of related rows to null. For example, if a *Faculty* row is deleted, then set *FacSSN* to NULL in related *Offering* rows. Likewise, if *Faculty.FacSSN* is updated, then set *FacSSN* to NULL in related *Offering* rows. The nullify action is not permitted if the foreign key does not allow null values. For example, the nullify option is not valid when deleting rows of the *Student* table because *Enrollment.StdSSN* is part of the primary key.

- **Default:** Set the foreign key of related rows to its default value. For example, if a *Faculty* row is deleted, then set *FacSSN* to a default faculty in related *Offering* rows. The default faculty might have an interpretation such as "to be announced." Likewise, if *Faculty.FacSSN* is updated, then set *FacSSN* to its default value in related *Offering* rows. The default action is an alternative to the null action as the default action avoids null values.

The delete and update actions can be specified in SQL using the ON DELETE and ON UPDATE clauses. These clauses are added as part of foreign key constraints. For example, the revised CREATE TABLE statement for the *Enrollment* table shows ON DELETE and ON UPDATE actions for the *Enrollment* table. NO ACTION means restrict (the first possible action). The keywords CASCADE, SET NULL, and SET DEFAULT can be used to specify the second through fourth options, respectively.

```
CREATE TABLE Enrollment
    (       OfferNo         INTEGER NOT NULL,
            StdSSN          CHAR(11) NOT NULL,
            EnrGrade        DECIMAL(3,2),
CONSTRAINT PKEnrollment PRIMARY KEY(OfferNo, StdSSN),
CONSTRAINT FKOfferNo FOREIGN KEY (OfferNo) REFERENCES Offering
            ON DELETE NO ACTION
            ON UPDATE CASCADE,
CONSTRAINT FKStdSSN FOREIGN KEY (StdSSN) REFERENCES Student
            ON DELETE NO ACTION
            ON UPDATE CASCADE )
```

Before finishing this section, you should understand the impact of referenced rows on insert operations. A referenced row must be inserted before its related rows. For example, before inserting a row in the *Enrollment* table, the referenced rows in the *Student* and *Offering* tables must exist. Referential integrity places an ordering on adding rows from different tables. When designing data entry forms, you should carefully consider the impact of referential integrity on the order that users complete forms.

2.4 OPERATORS OF RELATIONAL ALGEBRA

In previous sections of this chapter, you have studied the terminology and integrity rules of relational databases with the goal of understanding existing relational databases. In particular, understanding connections among tables was emphasized as a prerequisite to retrieving useful information. This section describes some fundamental operators that can be used to retrieve useful information from a relational database.

You can think of relational algebra similarly to the algebra of numbers except that the objects are different: algebra applies to numbers and relational algebra applies to tables. In algebra, each operator transforms one or more numbers into another number. Similarly, each operator of relational algebra *transforms a table (or two tables) into a new table.*

This section emphasizes the study of each relational algebra operator in isolation. For each operator, you should understand its purpose and inputs. While it is possible to combine operators to make complicated formulas, this level of understanding is not important for developing query formulation skills. Using relational algebra by itself to write queries can be awkward because of details such as ordering of operations and parentheses. Therefore, you should seek only to understand the meaning of each operator, not how to combine operators to write expressions.

The coverage of relational algebra groups the operators into three categories. The most widely used operators (restrict, project, and join) are presented first. The extended cross product operator is also presented to provide background for the join operator. Knowledge of these operators will help you to formulate a large percentage of queries. More specialized operators are covered in latter parts of the section. The more specialized operators include the traditional set operators (union, intersection, and difference) and advanced operators (summarize and divide). Knowledge of these operators will help you formulate more difficult queries.

2.4.1 Restrict (Select) and Project Operators

The restrict[5] (also known as select) and project operators produce subsets of a table. Because users often want to see a subset rather than an entire table, these operators are widely used. These operators are also popular because they are easy to understand.

The restrict and project operators produce an output table that is a subset of an input table (Figure 2.3). Restrict produces a subset of the rows, while project produces a subset of the columns. Restrict uses a condition or logical expression to indicate what rows should be retained in the output. Project uses a list of column names to indicate what columns to retain in the output. Restrict and project are often used together because tables can have many rows and columns. It is rare that a user wants to see all rows and columns.

The logical expression used in the restrict operator can include comparisons involving columns and constants. Complex logical expressions can be formed using the logical operators AND, OR, and NOT. For example, Table 2–8 shows the result of a restrict operation on Table 2–4 where the logical expression is: OffDays = 'MW' AND OffTerm = 'SPRING' AND OffYear = 2000.

A project operation can have a side effect. Sometimes after a subset of columns is retrieved, there are duplicate rows. When this occurs, the project operator removes the duplicate rows. For example, if *Offering.CourseNo* is the only column used in a project operation, only three rows are in the result (Table 2–9) even though the *Offering* table (Table 2–4) has nine rows. The column *Offering.CourseNo* contains only three unique values in

---

[5]In this book, the operator name restrict is used to avoid confusion with the SQL SELECT statement. The operator is more widely known as select.

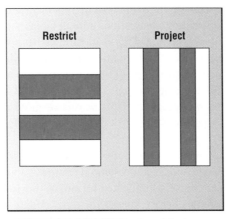

| **Figure 2.3** | **Graphical representation of restrict and project operators.** |

TABLE 2–8	Result of Restrict Operation on the Sample Offering Table (Table 2–4)						
OfferNo	CourseNo	OffTerm	OffYear	OffLocation	OffTime	FacSSN	OffDays
3333	IS320	SPRING	2000	BLM214	8:30 AM	098-76-5432	MW
5678	IS480	SPRING	2000	BLM302	10:30 AM	987-65-4321	MW

TABLE 2–9	Result of a Project Operation on *Offering.CourseNo*

CourseNo
IS320
IS460
IS480

Table 2–4. Note that if the primary key or a candidate key is included in the list of columns, the resulting table has no duplicates. For example, if *OfferNo* was included in the list of columns, the result table would have nine rows with no duplicate removal necessary.

This side effect is due to the "pure" nature of relational algebra. In relational algebra, tables are considered sets. Because sets do not have duplicates, duplicate removal is a possible side effect of the project operator. Commercial languages such as SQL usually take a more pragmatic view. Because duplicate removal can be computationally expensive, duplicates are not removed unless the user specifically requests it.

2.4.2 Extended Cross Product Operator

The extended cross product operator can combine any two tables. Other table combining operators have conditions about the tables to combine. Because of its unrestricted nature, the extended cross product operator can produce tables with excessive data. The extended cross product operator is important because it is a building block for the join operator. When you initially learn the join operator, knowledge of the extended cross product operator can be useful. After you gain experience with the join operator, you will not need to rely on the extended cross product operator.

Extended Cross Product
an operator that builds a table consisting of all possible combinations of rows, from each of the two input tables.

The extended cross product[6] (product for short) operator shows everything possible from two tables. The product of two tables is a new table consisting of all possible combinations of rows from the two input tables. Figure 2.4 depicts a product of two single column tables. Each result row consists of the columns of the *Faculty* table (only *FacSSN*) and the columns of the *Student* table (only *StdSSN*). The name of the operator (product) derives from the number of rows in the result. The number of rows in the resulting table is the product of the number of rows of the two input tables. In contrast, the number of result columns is the sum of the columns of the two input tables. In Figure 2.4, the result table has nine rows and two columns.

As another example, consider the product of the sample *Student* (Table 2–10) and *Enrollment* (Table 2–11) tables. The resulting table (Table 2–12) has nine rows (3×3) and seven columns ($4 + 3$). Note that most rows in the result are not meaningful as only three rows have the same value for *StdSSN*.

As these examples show, the extended cross product operator often generates excessive data. Excessive data are as bad as lack of data. For example, the product of a student table of 30,000 rows and an enrollment table of 300,000 rows is a table of nine billion rows! Most of these rows would be meaningless combinations. So it is rare that a cross product operation by itself is needed. Rather, the importance of the cross product operator is as a building block for other operators such as the join.

---

[6]The extended cross product operator is also known as the Cartesian product after French mathematician René Descartes.

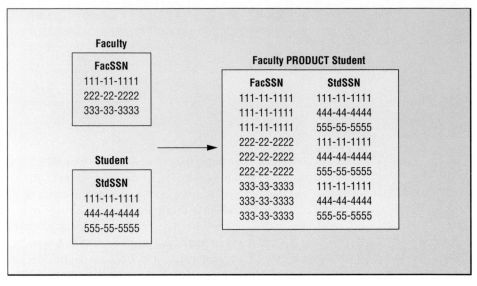

Faculty PRODUCT Student	
FacSSN	**StdSSN**
111-11-1111	111-11-1111
111-11-1111	444-44-4444
111-11-1111	555-55-5555
222-22-2222	111-11-1111
222-22-2222	444-44-4444
222-22-2222	555-55-5555
333-33-3333	111-11-1111
333-33-3333	444-44-4444
333-33-3333	555-55-5555

Figure 2.4 Cross product example.

TABLE 2–10	Sample *Student* Table		
StdSSN	StdLastName	StdMajor	StdClass
123-45-6789	WELLS	IS	FR
124-56-7890	NORBERT	FIN	JR
234-56-7890	KENDALL	ACCT	JR

TABLE 2–11	Sample *Enrollment* Table	
OfferNo	StdSSN	EnrGrade
1234	123-45-6789	3.3
1234	234-56-7890	3.5
4321	124-56-7890	3.2

TABLE 2–12	*Student* PRODUCT *Enrollment*					
Student.StdSSN	StdLastName	StdMajor	StdClass	OfferNo	Enrollment.StdSSN	EnrGrade
123-45-6789	WELLS	IS	FR	1234	123-45-6789	3.3
123-45-6789	WELLS	IS	FR	1234	234-56-7890	3.5
123-45-6789	WELLS	IS	FR	4321	124-56-7890	3.2
124-56-7890	NORBERT	FIN	JR	1234	123-45-6789	3.3
124-56-7890	NORBERT	FIN	JR	1234	234-56-7890	3.5
124-56-7890	NORBERT	FIN	JR	4321	124-56-7890	3.2
234-56-7890	KENDALL	ACCT	JR	1234	123-45-6789	3.3
234-56-7890	KENDALL	ACCT	JR	1234	234-56-7890	3.5
234-56-7890	KENDALL	ACCT	JR	4321	124-56-7890	3.2

2.4.3 Join Operator

Join is the most widely used operator for combining tables. Because most databases have many tables, combining tables is important. Join differs from cross product because join requires a matching condition on rows of two tables. Most tables are combined in this way. To a large extent, your skill in retrieving useful data will depend on your ability to use the join operator.

Join an operator that produces a table containing rows that match on a condition involving a column from each input table.

The join operator builds a new table by combining rows from two tables that match on a join condition. Typically, the join condition specifies that two rows have an identical value in one or more columns. When the join condition involves equality, the join is known as an equi-join, for equality join. Figure 2.5 shows a join of sample *Faculty* and *Offering* tables where the join condition is that the *FacSSN* columns are equal. Note that only a few columns are shown to simplify the illustration. The arrows indicate how rows from the input tables combine to form rows in the result table. For example, the first row of the *Faculty* table combines with the first and third rows of the *Offering* table to yield two rows in the result table.

Natural Join a commonly used join operator where the matching condition is equality (equi-join), one of the matching columns is discarded in the result table, and the join columns have the same unqualified names.

The natural join operator, a specialized kind of join, is the most common join operation. In a natural join operation, the join condition is equality (equi-join), one of the join columns is removed, and the join columns have the same unqualified[7] name. In Figure 2.5, the result table contains only three columns because the natural join removes one of the *FacSSN* columns. The particular column (*Faculty.FacSSN* or *Offering.FacSSN*) removed does not matter.

As another example, consider the natural join of *Student* (Table 2–13) and *Enrollment* (Table 2–14) shown in Table 2–15. In each row of the result, *Student.StdSSN*

---

[7]An "unqualified" name is the column name without the table name. The full name of a column includes the table name. Thus, the full names of the join columns in Figure 2.5 are *Faculty.FacSSN* and *Offering.FacSSN*.

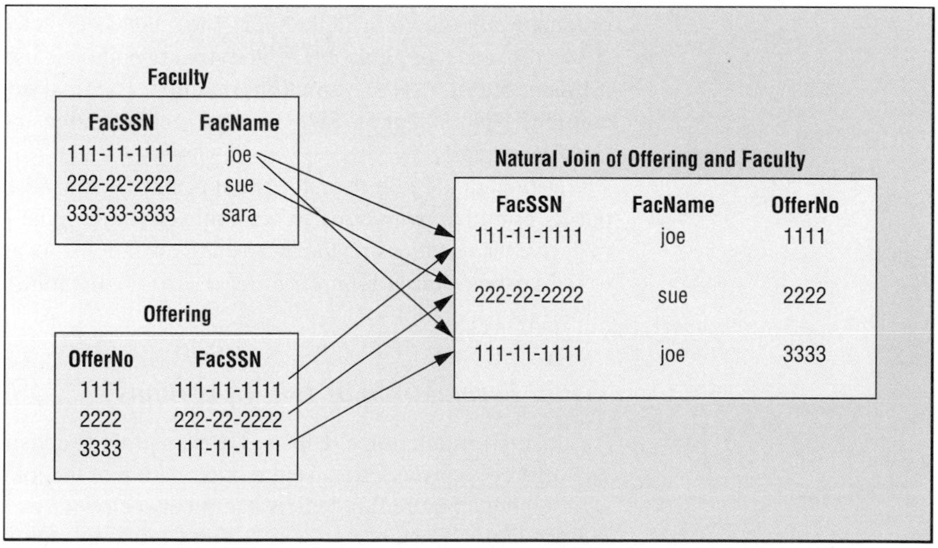

Figure 2.5   **Sample natural join operation.**

TABLE 2–13	Sample Student Table		
StdSSN	StdLastName	StdMajor	StdClass
123-45-6789	WELLS	IS	FR
124-56-7890	NORBERT	FIN	JR
234-56-7890	KENDALL	ACCT	JR

TABLE 2–14	Sample Enrollment Table	
OfferNo	StdSSN	EnrGrade
1234	123-45-6789	3.3
1234	234-56-7890	3.5
4321	124-56-7890	3.2

TABLE 2–15	Natural Join of *Student* and *Enrollment*				
Student.StdSSN	StdLastName	StdMajor	StdClass	OfferNo	EnrGrade
123-45-6789	WELLS	IS	FR	1234	3.3
124-56-7890	NORBERT	FIN	JR	4321	3.2
234-56-7890	KENDALL	ACCT	JR	1234	3.5

matches *Enrollment.StdSSN*. Only one of the join columns is included in the result. Arbitrarily, *Student.StdSSN* is shown although *Enrollment.StdSSN* could be included without changing the result.

Derivation of the Natural Join

The natural join operator is not primitive because it can be derived from other operators. The natural join operator consists of three steps:

1. A product operation to combine the rows.
2. A restrict operation to remove rows not satisfying the join condition.
3. A project operation to remove one of the join columns.

To depict these steps, the first step to produce the natural join in Table 2–15 is the product result shown in Table 2–12. The second step is to retain only the matching rows (rows 1, 6, and 8 of Table 2–12). A restrict operation is used with Student.StdSSN = Enrollment.StdSSN as the restriction condition. The final step is to eliminate one of the join columns (*Enrollment.StdSSN*). The project operation includes all columns except for *Enrollment.StdSSN*.

Although the join operator is not primitive, it can be conceptualized directly without its primitive operations. When initially learning the join operator, it can be helpful to derive the results using the underlying operations. As an exercise, you are encouraged to derive the result in Figure 2.5. After learning the join, you should not need to use the underlying operations.

Visual Formulation of Join Operations

As a query formulation aid, many DBMSs provide a visual way to formulate joins. Microsoft Access provides a visual representation of the join operator using the Query Design window. Figure 2.6 depicts a join between *Student* and *Enrollment* on *StdSSN* using the Query Design window. To form this join, you need only to select the tables. Access determines that you should join over the *StdSSN* column. Access assumes that most joins involve a primary key and foreign key combination. If Access chooses the join condition incorrectly, you can choose other join columns.

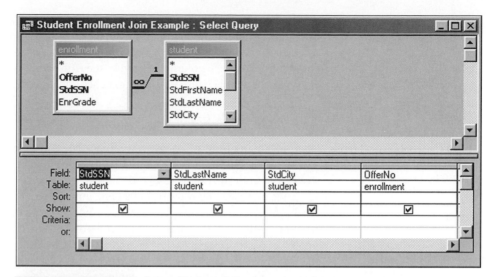

Figure 2.6   Query Design window showing a join between Student and Enrollment.

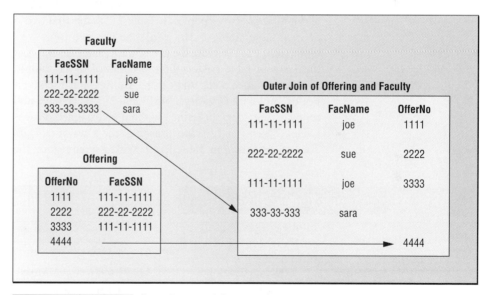

Figure 2.7   Sample outer join operation.

2.4.4 Outer Join Operator

The result of a join operation includes the rows matching on the join condition. Sometimes it is useful to include both matching and nonmatching rows. For example, sometimes you want to know offerings that have an assigned instructor as well as offerings without an assigned instructor. In these situations, the outer join operator is useful.

The <u>outer join</u> operator provides the ability to preserve <u>nonmatching rows</u> in the result as well as to include the matching rows. Figure 2.7 depicts an outer join between sample *Faculty* and *Offering* tables. Note that each table has one row that does not match any row in the other table. The third row of *Faculty* and the fourth row of *Offering* do not have matching rows in the other table. For nonmatching rows, null values are used to complete the column values in the other table. In Figure 2.7, blanks (no values) represent null values. The fourth result row is the nonmatched row of *Faculty* with a null value for the *OfferNo* column. Likewise, the fifth result row contains a null value for the first two columns because it is a nonmatched row of *Offering*.

Full versus One-Sided Outer Join Operators

Full Outer Join an operator that produces the matching rows (the join part) as well as the nonmatching rows from both tables.

One-Sided Outer Join an operator that produces the matching rows (the join part) as well as the nonmatching rows from the designated input table.

The outer join operator has two variations. The <u>full outer join</u> preserves nonmatching rows from both input tables. Figure 2.7 shows a full outer join because the nonmatching rows from both tables are preserved in the result. Because it is sometimes useful to preserve the nonmatching rows from just one input table, the <u>one-sided outer join</u> operator has been devised. In Figure 2.7, only the first four rows of the result would appear for a one-sided outer join that preserves the rows of the *Faculty* table. The last row would not appear in the result because it is an unmatched row of the *Offering* table. Similarly, only the first three rows and last row would appear in the result for a one-sided outer join that preserves the rows of the *Offering* table.

The outer join is useful in two situations. A full outer join can be used to combine two tables with some common columns and some unique columns. For example, to combine the *Student* and *Faculty* tables, a full outer join can be used to show all columns about all university people. In Table 2–18, the first two rows are only from the sample *Student* table (Table 2–16), while the last two rows are only from the sample *Faculty* table (Table 2–17). Note the use of null values for the columns from the other table. The third row in Table 2–18 is the row common to the sample *Faculty* and *Student* tables.

A one-sided outer join can be useful when a table has null values in a foreign key. For example, the *Offering* table (Table 2–19) can have null values in the *FacSSN* column representing course offerings without an assigned professor. A one-sided outer join between *Offering* and *Faculty* preserves the rows of *Offering* that do not have an assigned *Faculty,* as shown in Table 2–20. With a natural join, the first and third rows of Table

TABLE 2–16	Sample *Student* Table		
StdSSN	StdLastName	StdMajor	StdClass
123-45-6789	WELLS	IS	FR
124-56-7890	NORBERT	FIN	JR
876-54-3210	COLAN	MS	SR

TABLE 2–17	Sample *Faculty* Table		
FacSSN	FacLastName	FacDept	FacRank
098-76-5432	VINCE	MS	ASST
543-21-0987	EMMANUEL	MS	PROF
876-54-3210	COLAN	MS	ASST

TABLE 2–18	Result of Full Outer Join of Sample *Student* and *Faculty* Tables						
StdSSN	StdLastName	StdMajor	StdClass	FacSSN	FacLastName	FacDept	FacRank
123-45-6789	WELLS	IS	FR				
124-56-7890	NORBERT	FIN	JR				
876-54-3210	COLAN	MS	SR	876-54-3210	COLAN	MS	ASST
				098-76-5432	VINCE	MS	ASST
				543-21-0987	EMMANUEL	MS	PROF

TABLE 2–19	Sample *Offering* Table

OfferNo	CourseNo	OffTerm	FacSSN
1111	IS320	SUMMER	
1234	IS320	FALL	098-76-5432
2222	IS460	SUMMER	
3333	IS320	SPRING	098-76-5432
4444	IS320	SPRING	543-21-0987

TABLE 2–20	Result of One-Sided Outer Join between *Offering* (Table 2–19) and *Faculty* (Table 2–17)

OfferNo	CourseNo	OffTerm	Offering.FacSSN	Faculty.FacSSN	FacLastName	FacDept	FacRank
1111	IS320	SUMMER					
1234	IS320	FALL	098-76-5432	098-76-5432	VINCE	MS	ASST
2222	IS460	SUMMER					
3333	IS320	SPRING	098-76-5432	098-76-5432	VINCE	MS	ASST
4444	IS320	SPRING	543-21-0987	543-21-0987	EMMANUEL	MS	PROF

2–20 would not appear. As you will see in Chapter 5, one-sided joins can be useful in data entry forms.

Visual Formulation of Outer Join Operations

As a query formulation aid, many DBMSs provide a visual way to formulate outer joins. Access provides a visual representation of the one-sided join operator in the Query Design window. Figure 2.8 depicts a one-sided outer join that preserves the rows of the *Offering* table. The arrow from *Offering* to *Faculty* means that the nonmatched rows of *Offering* are preserved in the result. When combining the *Faculty* and *Offering* tables, Microsoft Access provides three choices: (1) show only the matched rows (a join), (2) show matched rows and nonmatched rows of *Faculty,* and (3) show matched rows and nonmatched rows of *Offering*. Choice (3) is shown in Figure 2.8. Choice (1) would appear similar to Figure 2.6. Choice (2) would have the arrow from *Faculty* to *Offering*.

2.4.5 Union, Intersection, and Difference Operators

Traditional Set Operators the union operator produces a table containing rows from either input table. The intersection operator produces a table containing rows common to both input tables. The difference operator produces a table containing rows from the first input table but not in the second input table.

The union, intersection, and difference table operators are similar to the traditional set operators. The traditional set operators are used to determine all members of two sets (union), common members of two sets (intersection), and members unique to only one set (difference), as depicted in Figure 2.9.

The union, intersection, and difference operators for tables apply to rows of a table but otherwise operate in the same way as the traditional set operators. A union operation retrieves all the rows in either table. For example, a union operator applied to two student tables at different universities can find all student rows. An intersection operation retrieves just the common rows. For example, an intersection operation can determine the students attending both universities. A difference operation retrieves the rows in the

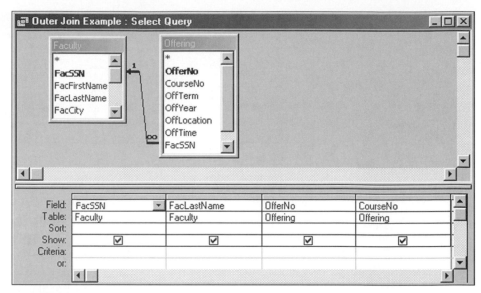

Figure 2.8 Query Design window showing a one-sided outer join.

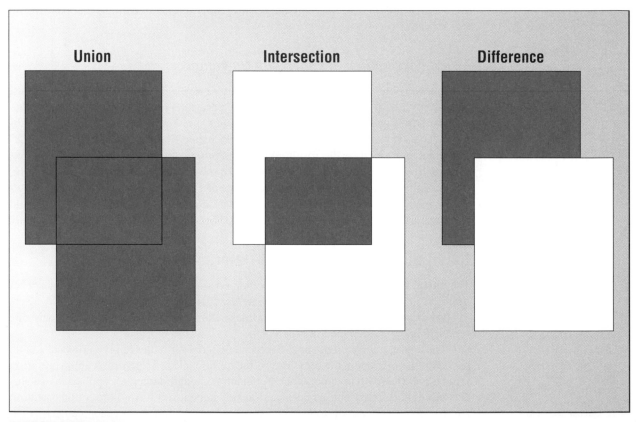

Figure 2.9 Venn diagrams for traditional set operators.

first table but not in the second table. For example, a difference operation can determine the students attending only one university.

Union Compatibility

Compatibility is a new concept for the table operators as compared to the traditional set operators. With the table operators, both tables must be union compatible because all columns are compared. Union compatible means that each table must have the same number of columns and each corresponding column must have the same data type. Union compatibility can be confusing because it requires positional correspondence of the columns. That is, the first columns of the two tables must have the same data type, the second columns must have the same data type, and so on.

To depict the union, intersection, and difference operators, let us apply them to the *Student1* and *Student2* tables (Tables 2–21 and 2–22). These tables are union compatible because they have identical columns listed in the same order. The results of union, intersection, and difference operators are shown in Tables 2–23 through 2–25, respectively. Even though we can determine that two rows are identical from looking only at *StdSSN*, all columns are compared due to the way that the operators are designed.

Note that the result of *Student1* DIFFERENCE *Student2* would not be the same as *Student2* DIFFERENCE *Student1*. The result of the latter (*Student2* DIFFERENCE *Student1*) is the second and third rows of *Student2* (rows in *Student2* but not in *Student1*).

Union Compatibility a requirement on the input tables for the traditional set operators. Both tables must have the same number of columns and each corresponding column must have the same data type.

TABLE 2–21	Student1 Table					
StdSSN	StdLastName	StdCity	StdState	StdMajor	StdClass	StdGPA
123-45-6789	WELLS	SEATTLE	WA	IS	FR	3.00
124-56-7890	NORBERT	BOTHELL	WA	FIN	JR	2.70
234-56-7890	KENDALL	TACOMA	WA	ACCT	JR	3.50

TABLE 2–22	Student2 Table					
StdSSN	StdLastName	StdCity	StdState	StdMajor	StdClass	StdGPA
123-45-6789	WELLS	SEATTLE	WA	IS	FR	3.00
995-56-3490	BAGGINS	AUSTIN	TX	FIN	JR	2.90
111-56-4490	WILLIAMS	SEATTLE	WA	ACCT	JR	3.40

TABLE 2–23	Student1 UNION Student2					
StdSSN	StdLastName	StdCity	StdState	StdMajor	StdClass	StdGPA
123-45-6789	WELLS	SEATTLE	WA	IS	FR	3.00
124-56-7890	NORBERT	BOTHELL	WA	FIN	JR	2.70
234-56-7890	KENDALL	TACOMA	WA	ACCT	JR	3.50
995-56-3490	BAGGINS	AUSTIN	TX	FIN	JR	2.90
111-56-4490	WILLIAMS	SEATTLE	WA	ACCT	JR	3.40

TABLE 2–24	Student1 INTERSECT Student2					
StdSSN	StdLastName	StdCity	StdState	StdMajor	StdClass	StdGPA
123-45-6789	WELLS	SEATTLE	WA	IS	FR	3.00

TABLE 2–25	Student1 DIFFERENCE Student2					
StdSSN	StdLastName	StdCity	StdState	StdMajor	StdClass	StdGPA
124-56-7890	NORBERT	BOTHELL	WA	FIN	FR	2.70
234-56-7890	KENDALL	TACOMA	WA	ACCT	JR	3.50

Because of the union compatibility requirement, the union, intersection, and difference operators are not as widely used as other operators. However, these operators do have some important, specialized uses. One use is to combine tables distributed over many locations. For example, suppose there is a student table at Big State University (*BSUStudent*) and a student table at University of Big State (*UBSStudent*). Because these tables have identical columns, the traditional set operators are applicable. To find students attending either university, use *UBSStudent* UNION *BSUStudent*. To find students only attending Big State, use *BSUStudent* DIFFERENCE *UBSStudent*. To find students attending both universities, use *UBSStudent* INTERSECT *BSUStudent*. Note that the resulting table in each operation has the same number of columns as the two input tables.

The traditional operators are also useful if there are tables that are similar but not union compatible. For example, the *Student* and *Faculty* tables have some identical columns (*StdSSN* with *FacSSN*, *StdLastName* with *FacLastName,* and *StdCity* with *FacCity*), but other columns are different. The union compatible operators can be used if the *Student* and *Faculty* tables are first made union compatible using the project operator discussed in Section 2.4.1.

2.4.6 Summarize Operator

Summarize is a powerful operator for decision making. Because tables can contain many rows, it is often useful to see statistics about groups of rows rather than individual rows. The summarize operator allows groups of rows to be compressed or summarized by a calculated value. Almost any kind of statistical function can be used to summarize groups of rows. Because this is not a statistics book, we will use only simple functions such as count, min, max, average, and sum.

The summarize operator compresses a table by replacing groups of rows with individual rows containing calculated values. A statistical or <u>aggregate function</u> is used for the calculated values. Figure 2.10 depicts a summarize operation for a sample enrollment table. The input table is grouped on the *StdSSN* column. Each group of rows is replaced by the average of the grade column.

As another example, Table 2–27 shows the result of a summarize operation on the sample *Faculty* table in Table 2–26. Note that the result contains one row per value of the grouping column, *FacDept*.

The summarize operator can include additional calculated values (also showing the minimum salary, for example) and additional grouping columns (also grouping on

Summarize an operator that produces a table with rows that summarize the rows of the input table. Aggregate functions are used to summarize the rows of the input table.

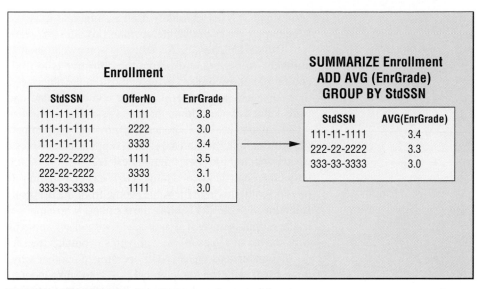

Figure 2.10	Sample summarize operation.

TABLE 2–26	Sample *Faculty* Table

FacSSN	FacLastName	FacDept	FacRank	FacSalary	FacSupervisor	FacHireDate
098-76-5432	VINCE	MS	ASST	$35,000	654-32-1098	01-Apr-90
543-21-0987	EMMANUEL	MS	PROF	$120,000		01-Apr-91
654-32-1098	FIBON	MS	ASSC	$70,000	543-21-0987	01-Apr-89
765-43-2109	MACON	FIN	PROF	$65,000		01-Apr-92
876-54-3210	COLAN	MS	ASST	$40,000	654-32-1098	01-Apr-94
987-65-4321	MILLS	FIN	ASSC	$75,000	765-43-2109	01-Apr-95

TABLE 2–27	Result Table for SUMMARIZE *Faculty* ADD AVG(*FacSalary*) GROUP BY *FacDept*

FacDept	FacSalary
MS	$66,250
FIN	$70,000

FacRank, for example). When grouping on multiple columns, each result row shows one combination of values for the grouping columns.

2.4.7 Divide Operator

Divide   an operator that produces a table in which the values of a column from one input table are associated with all the values from a column of the second table.

The divide operator is a more specialized and difficult operator than join because the matching requirement in divide is more stringent than join. For example, a join operator is used to retrieve offerings taken by *any* student. A divide operator is required to retrieve offerings taken by *all* (or every) students. Because divide has more stringent matching conditions, it is not as widely used as join, and it can be more difficult to understand. When appropriate, the divide operator provides a powerful way to combine tables.

The divide operator for tables is somewhat analogous to the divide operator for numbers. In numerical division, the objective is to find how many times one number contains another number. In table division, the objective is to find values of one column that contains *every* value in another column. Stated another way, the divide operator finds values of one column that are associated with *every* value in another column.

To understand more concretely how the divide operator works, consider an example with sample *Part* and *SuppPart* (supplier-part) tables as depicted in Figure 2.11. The divide operator uses two input tables. The first table (*SuppPart*) has two columns (a binary table) and the second table (*Part*) has one column[8] (a unary table). The result table has one column where the values come from the first column of the binary table. The result table in Figure 2.11 shows the suppliers who supply every part. The value s3 appears in the output because it is associated with *every* value in the *Part* table. Stated another way, the set of values associated with s3 contains the set of values in the *Part* table.

To understand the division operator in another way, rewrite the *SuppPart* table as three rows using the angle brackets $<>$ to surround a row: $<s3, \{p1, p2, p3\}>$, $<s0, \{p1\}>$, $<s1, \{p2\}>$. Rewrite the *Part* table as a set: $\{p1, p2\}$. The value s3 is in the result table because its set of second column values $\{p1, p2, p3\}$ contains the values in the second table $\{p1, p2\}$. The other *SuppNo* values (s0 and s1) are not in the result because they are not associated with all the values in the *Part* table.

As an example using the university database tables, Table 2–30 shows the result of a divide operation involving the sample *Enrollment* (Table 2–28) and *Student* tables (Table 2–29). The result shows offerings in which every student is enrolled. Only *OfferNo* 4235 has all three students enrolled.

2.4.8 Summary of Operators

To help you recall the relational algebra operators, Tables 2–31 and 2–32 provide a convenient summary of the meaning and usage of each operator. You might want to refer to these tables when studying query formulation in later chapters.

SuppPart			Part		SuppPart DIVIDEBY Part
SuppNo	**PartNo**		**PartNo**		**SuppNo**
s3	p1		p1		s3
s3	p2		p2		
s3	p3				
s0	p1				s3 {p1, p2, p3}
s1	p2				contains {p1, p2}

Figure 2.11   Sample divide operation.

[8]The divide by operator can be generalized to work with input tables containing more columns. However, the details are not important in this book.

TABLE 2–28	Sample *Enrollment* Table

OfferNo	StdSSN
1234	123-45-6789
1234	234-56-7890
4235	123-45-6789
4235	234-56-7890
4235	124-56-7890
6321	124-56-7890

TABLE 2–29	Sample *Student* Table

StdSSN
123-45-6789
124-56-7890
234-56-7890

TABLE 2–30	Result of *Enrollment* DIVIDEBY *Student*

OfferNo
4235

TABLE 2–31	Summary of Meanings of the Relational Algebra Operators

Operator	Meaning
Restrict (Select)	Extracts rows that satisfy a specified condition.
Project	Extracts specified columns.
Product	Builds a table from two tables consisting of all possible combinations of rows, one from each of the two tables.
Union	Builds a table consisting of all rows appearing in either of two tables.
Intersect	Builds a table consisting of all rows appearing in both of two specified tables.
Difference	Builds a table consisting of all rows appearing in the first table but not in the second table.
Join	Extracts rows from a product of two tables such that two input rows contributing to any output row satisfy some specified condition.
Outer Join	Extracts the matching rows (the join part) of two tables and the unmatched rows from both tables.
Divide	Builds a table consisting of all values of one column of a binary (2-column) table that match (in the other column) all values in a unary (1-column) table.
Summarize	Organizes a table on specified grouping columns. Specified aggregate computations are made on each value of the grouping columns.

TABLE 2–32	Summary of Usage of the Relational Algebra Operators

Operator	*Notes*
Union	Input tables must be union compatible.
Difference	Input tables must be union compatible.
Intersection	Input tables must be union compatible.
Product	Conceptually underlies join operator.
Restrict (Select)	Uses a logical expression.
Project	Eliminates duplicate rows if necessary.
Join	Only matched rows are in the result. Natural join eliminates one join column.
Outer join	Retains both matched and unmatched rows in the result. Uses null values for some columns of the unmatched rows.
Divide	Stronger operator than join, but less frequently used.
Summarize	Specify grouping column(s) if any and aggregate function(s).

CLOSING THOUGHTS

Chapter 2 has introduced the Relational Data Model as a prelude to developing queries, forms, and reports with relational databases. As a first step to work with relational databases, you should understand the basic terminology and integrity rules. You should be conversant reading table definitions in SQL and in other proprietary formats. To effectively query a relational database, you must understand the connections among tables. Most queries involve multiple tables using relationships defined by referential integrity constraints. A graphical representation such as the Relationship window in Microsoft Access provides a powerful tool to conceptualize referential integrity constraints. When developing forms that can change a database, it is important to respect the action rules for referenced rows.

The final part of this chapter described the operators of relational algebra. At this point, you should understand the purpose of each operator, the number of input tables, and other inputs used. You do not need to write complicated formulas that combine operators. Eventually, you should be comfortable understanding statements such as "write an SQL SELECT statement to join three tables." The SELECT statement will be discussed in Chapters 3 and 4, but the basic idea of a join is important to learn now. As you learn to extract data using the SQL SELECT statement in Chapter 3, you may want to review this chapter again. To help you remember the major points about the operators, the last section of this chapter presented several convenient summaries.

Understanding the operators will improve your knowledge of SQL and your query formulation skills. The meaning of SQL queries can be understood as relational algebra operations. Chapter 3 provides a flowchart demonstrating this correspondence. For this reason, relational algebra provides a yardstick to measure commercial languages: the commercial languages should provide at least the same retrieval ability as the operators of relational algebra.

REVIEW CONCEPTS

- Tables: heading and body.
- Primary keys and entity integrity rule.

- Foreign keys, referential integrity rule, and matching values.
- Visualizing referential integrity constraints.
- Relational Model representation of 1-M relationships, M-N relationships, and self-referencing relationships.
- Actions on referenced rows: cascade, nullify, restrict.
- Traditional set operators: union, intersection, difference, extended cross product.
- Union compatibility.
- Subset operators: restrict (select) and project.
- Matching value operators: join, full outer join, one-sided outer join, divide.
- Row compression operator: summarize.

QUESTIONS

1. How is creating a table similar to writing a chapter of a book?

2. With what terminology for relational databases are you most comfortable? Why?

3. What is the difference between a primary and a candidate key?

4. When is it not permissible for foreign keys to store null values?

5. What is the purpose of a database diagram such as the Access Relationship window?

6. How is a 1-M relationship represented in the Relational Model?

7. How is an M-N relationship represented in the Relational Model?

8. What is a self-referencing relationship?

9. How is a self-referencing relationship represented in the Relational Model?

10. Why is the restrict action for referenced rows more common than the cascade action?

11. Why study the operators of relational algebra?

12. Explain how the union, intersection, and difference operators for tables differ from the traditional operators for sets.

13. Why is the join operator so important for retrieving useful information?

14. What is the relationship between the join and the extended cross product operators?

15. What happens to unmatched rows with the join operator? Full outer join operator?

16. What is the difference between the full outer join and the one-sided outer join?

17. Define a decision-making situation that might require the summarize operator?

18. Why is the divide operator not as widely used as the join operator?

PROBLEMS

The problems use the *Customer, OrderTbl,* and *Employee* tables of the simplified Order Entry database. Other chapters of Part I extend the database to increase its usefulness. The *Customer* table records clients who have placed orders. The *OrderTbl* contains the

ORDER

basic facts about customer orders. The *Employee* table contains facts about employees who take orders. The primary keys of the tables are *CustNo* for *Customer,* *EmpNo* for *Employee,* and *OrdNo* for *OrderTbl.*

Customer						
CustNo	CustFirstName	CustLastName	CustCity	CustState	CustZip	CustBal
C0954327	Sheri	Gordon	Littleton	CO	80129-5543	$230.00
C1010398	Jim	Glussman	Denver	CO	80111-0033	$200.00
C2388597	Beth	Taylor	Seattle	WA	98103-1121	$500.00
C3340959	Betty	Wise	Seattle	WA	98178-3311	$200.00
C3499503	Bob	Mann	Monroe	WA	98013-1095	$0.00
C8543321	Ron	Thompson	Renton	WA	98666-1289	$85.00

Employee			
EmpNo	EmpFirstName	EmpLastName	EmpPhone
E1329594	Landi	Santos	(303) 789-1234
E8544399	Joe	Jenkins	(303) 221-9875
E8843211	Amy	Tang	(303) 556-4321
E9345771	Colin	White	(303) 221-4453
E9884325	Thomas	Johnson	(303) 556-9987
E9954302	Mary	Hill	(303) 556-9871

OrderTbl			
OrdNo	OrdDate	CustNo	EmpNo
O1116324	01/23/2000	C0954327	E8544399
O2334661	01/14/2000	C0954327	E1329594
O3331222	01/13/2000	C1010398	
O2233457	01/12/2000	C2388597	E9884325
O4714645	01/11/2000	C2388597	E1329594
O5511365	01/22/2000	C3340959	E9884325
O7989497	01/16/2000	C3499503	E9345771
O1656777	02/11/2000	C8543321	
O7959898	02/19/2000	C8543321	E8544399

1. Write a CREATE TABLE statement for the *Customer* table. Choose data types appropriate for the DBMS used in your course. Note that the CustBal column contains numeric data. The currency symbols are not stored in the database. The *CustFirstName* and *CustLastName* columns are required (not null).

2. Write a CREATE TABLE statement for the *Employee* table. Choose data types appropriate for the DBMS used in your course. The *OrdDate* column is required (not null).

3. Write a CREATE TABLE statement for the *OrderTbl* table. Choose data types appropriate for the DBMS used in your course.

4. Identify the foreign keys and draw a relationship diagram for the simplified Order Entry database. The *CustNo* column references the *Customer* table and the *EmpNo* column references the *Employee* table. For each relationship, identify the "1" table and the "Many" table.

5. Extend your CREATE TABLE statement from problem 3 with referential integrity constraints. Updates and deletes on related rows are restricted.

6. From examination of the sample data and your common understanding of order entry businesses, are null values allowed for the foreign keys in the *OrderTbl* table? Why or why not? Extend the CREATE TABLE statement in problem 5 to enforce the null value restrictions if any.

7. Show the result of a restrict operation that lists the orders in February 2000.

8. Show the result of a project operation that lists the *CustNo, CustFirstName,* and *CustLastName* columns of the *Customer* table.

9. Show the result of a project operation that lists the *CustCity and CustState* columns of the *Customer* table.

10. Show the result of a natural join that combines the *Customer* and *OrderTbl* tables.

11. Show the steps to derive the natural join for problem 10. How many rows and columns are in the extended cross product step?

12. Show the result of a natural join of the *Employee* and *OrderTbl* tables.

13. Show the result of a one-sided outer join between the *Employee* and *OrderTbl* tables. Preserve the rows of the *OrderTbl* table in the result.

14. Show the result of a full outer join between the *Employee* and *OrderTbl* tables.

15. Show the result of the restrict operation on *Customer* where the condition is *CustCity* equals "Denver" or "Seattle" followed by a project operation to retain the *CustNo, CustFirstName, CustLastName,* and *CustCity* columns.

16. Show the result of a summarize operation on *Customer.* The grouping column is *CustState* and the aggregate calculation is COUNT. COUNT shows the number of rows with the same value for the grouping column.

17. Show the result of a summarize operation on *Customer.* The grouping column is *CustState* and the aggregate calculations are the minimum and maximum *CustBal* values.

18. What tables are required to show the *CustLastName, EmpLastName,* and *OrdNo* columns in the result table?

19. Extend your relationship diagram from problem 4 by adding two tables (OrdLine and Product). Partial CREATE TABLE statements for the primary keys and referential integrity constraints are shown below:

```
CREATE TABLE Product ... PRIMARY KEY (ProdNo)
CREATE TABLE OrdLine ... PRIMARY KEY (OrdNo, ProdNo)
   FOREIGN KEY (OrdNo) REFERENCES Order
   FOREIGN KEY (ProdNo) REFERENCES Product
```

20. Extend your relationship diagram from problem 19 by adding another foreign key in the *Employee* table. The foreign key *SupEmpNo* is the employee number of the supervising employee. Thus, the *SupEmpNo* column references the *Employee* table.

21. What relational algebra operator do you use to find products contained in *every* order? What relational algebra operator do you use to find products contained in *any* order?

22. Are the *Customer* and *Employee* tables union compatible? Why or why not?

23. Using the database after problem 20, what tables must be combined to list the product names on order number 01116324?

24. Using the database after problem 20, what tables must be combined to list the product names ordered by customer number C0954327?

25. Using the database after problem 20, what tables must be combined to list the product names ordered by the customer named Sheri Gordon?

REFERENCES FOR FURTHER STUDY

Codd defined the Relational Model in a seminal paper in 1970. His paper inspired research projects at the IBM research laboratories and the University of California at Berkeley that led to commercial relational DBMSs. C. J. Date (1995) provides a syntax for relational algebra. Ullman (1988) and Elmasri and Navathe (1999) provide a more theoretical treatment of the Relational Model, especially the relational algebra.

Appendix 2.A CREATE TABLE Statements for the University Database Tables

The following are the CREATE TABLE statements for the university database tables (Tables 2–1, 2–3, 2–4, 2–6, and 2–7). The data types and names for standard data types can vary by DBMS. For example, Microsoft Access SQL supports the TEXT data type instead of CHAR and VARCHAR. In Oracle 8, you should use VARCHAR2 instead of VARCHAR.

```
CREATE TABLE Student
     (    StdSSN          CHAR(11)          NOT NULL,
          StdFirstName    VARCHAR(50)       NOT NULL,
          StdLastName     VARCHAR(50)       NOT NULL,
          StdCity         VARCHAR(50)       NOT NULL,
          StdState        CHAR(2)           NOT NULL,
          StdZip          CHAR(10)          NOT NULL,
          StdMajor        CHAR(6),
          StdClass        CHAR(2),
          StdGPA          DECIMAL(3,2),
CONSTRAINT PKStudent PRIMARY KEY (StdSSN) )
CREATE TABLE Course
     (    CourseNo        CHAR(6)           NOT NULL,
          CrsDesc         VARCHAR(250)      NOT NULL,
          CrsUnits        INTEGER,
     CONSTRAINT PKCourse PRIMARY KEY (CourseNo),
     CONSTRAINT UniqueCrsDesc UNIQUE (CrsDesc) )
CREATE TABLE Faculty
     (    FacSSN          CHAR(11)          NOT NULL,
          FacFirstName    VARCHAR(50)       NOT NULL,
          FacLastName     VARCHAR(50)       NOT NULL,
          FacCity         VARCHAR(50)       NOT NULL,
          FacState        CHAR(2)           NOT NULL,
          FacZipCode      CHAR(10)          NOT NULL,
          FacRank         CHAR(4),
          FacHireDate     DATE,
          FacSalary       DECIMAL(10,2),
          FacSupervisor   CHAR(11),
          FacDept         CHAR(6),
CONSTRAINT PKFaculty PRIMARY KEY (FacSSN),
CONSTRAINT FKFacSupervisor FOREIGN KEY (FacSupervisor)
     REFERENCES Faculty
          ON DELETE SET NULL
          ON UPDATE CASCADE)
```

```
CREATE TABLE Offering
    (        OfferNo         INTEGER              NOT NULL,
             CourseNo        CHAR(6)              NOT NULL,
             OffLocation     VARCHAR (50),
             OffDays         CHAR(6),
             OffTerm         CHAR(6)              NOT NULL,
             OffYear         INTEGER              NOT NULL,
             FacSSN          CHAR(11),
             OffTime         DATE,
CONSTRAINT PKOffering PRIMARY KEY (OfferNo),
CONSTRAINT FKCourseNo FOREIGN KEY (CourseNo) REFERENCES Course
             ON DELETE NO ACTION
             ON UPDATE NO ACTION,
CONSTRAINT FKFacSSN FOREIGN KEY (FacSSN) REFERENCES Faculty
             ON DELETE SET NULL
             ON UPDATE CASCADE     )
CREATE TABLE Enrollment
    (        OfferNo         INTEGER              NOT NULL,
             StdSSN          CHAR(11)             NOT NULL,
             EnrGrade        DECIMAL(3,2),
CONSTRAINT PKEnrollment PRIMARY KEY (OfferNo, StdSSN),
CONSTRAINT FKOfferNo FOREIGN KEY (OfferNo) REFERENCES Offering
             ON DELETE CASCADE
             ON UPDATE CASCADE,
CONSTRAINT FKStdSSN FOREIGN KEY (StdSSN) REFERENCES Student
             ON DELETE CASCADE
             ON UPDATE CASCADE     )
```

Appendix 2.B   **SQL2 Syntax Summary**

This appendix provides a convenient summary of the SQL2 syntax for the CREATE TABLE statement along with several related statements. For brevity, the syntax of the most common parts of the statements is described. For the complete syntax, refer to a SQL2 reference book such as Groff and Weinberg (1999). The conventions used in the syntax notation are listed before the statement syntax:

- Uppercase words denote reserved words.
- Mixed-case words without hyphens denote names that the user substitutes.
- The asterisk * after a syntax element indicates that a comma-separated list can be used.
- Names enclosed in angle brackets <> denote definitions defined later in the syntax. The definitions occur on a new line with the element and colon followed by the syntax.
- Square brackets [] enclose optional elements.
- Curly brackets {} enclose choice elements. One element must be chosen among the elements separated by the vertical bars | |.
- The parentheses () denote themselves.
- Double hyphens - - denote comments that are not part of the syntax.

CREATE TABLE[9] Syntax

```
CREATE TABLE TableName
   ( <Column-Definition>* [ , <Table-Constraint>* ] )
    <Column-Definition>: ColumnName DataType
     [ DEFAULT { DefaultValue | USER | NULL } ]
     [ [ CONSTRAINT ConstraintName ] NOT NULL ]
     [ [ CONSTRAINT ConstraintName ] UNIQUE ]
     [ [ CONSTRAINT ConstraintName ] PRIMARY KEY ]
     [ [ CONSTRAINT ConstraintName ] FOREIGN KEY REFERENCES TableName
         [ ( ColumnName ) ] [ ON DELETE <Action-Specification> ]
                            [ ON UPDATE <Action-Specification> ] ]
    <Table-Constraint>: [ CONSTRAINT ConstraintName ]
      { <Primary-Key-Constraint> |
        <Foreign-Key-Constraint> |
        <Uniqueness-Constraint> }
    <Primary-Key-Constraint>: PRIMARY KEY ( ColumnName* )
    <Foreign-Key-Constraint>: FOREIGN KEY ( ColumnName* )
      REFERENCES TableName ( ColumnName* )
      [ ON DELETE <Action-Specification> ]
      [ ON UPDATE <Action-Specification> ]
    <Action-Specification>: { CASCADE | SET NULL | SET DEFAULT | NO ACTION }
    <Uniqueness-Constraint>: UNIQUE ( ColumnName* )
```

---

[9]The CHECK constraint, an important kind of table constraint, is described in Chapter 12.

Other Related Statements

The ALTER TABLE and DROP TABLE statements support modification of a table definition and deletion of a table definition. The ALTER TABLE statement is particularly useful because table definitions often change over time. In both statements, the keyword RESTRICT means that the statement cannot be performed if related tables exist. The keyword CASCADE means that the same action will be performed on related tables.

```
ALTER TABLE TableName
  { ADD { <Column-Definition> | <Table-Constraint> } |
    ALTER ColumnName { SET DEFAULT DefaultValue | DROP DEFAULT } |
    DROP ColumnName { CASCADE | RESTRICT } |
    DROP CONSTRAINT ConstraintName {CASCADE | RESTRICT } }
DROP TABLE TableName { CASCADE | RESTRICT }
```

Notes on Oracle Syntax

The CREATE TABLE statement in Oracle 8 SQL conforms closely to the SQL2 standard. Here is a list of the most significant syntax differences:

- Oracle SQL does not support the ON UPDATE clause for referential integrity constraints.
- Oracle SQL only supports CASCADE as the action specification of the ON DELETE clauses. If an ON DELETE clause is not specified, the deletion is not allowed if related rows exist.
- Oracle SQL does not support dropping columns in the ALTER statement.
- Oracle SQL supports the MODIFY clause in place of the ALTER keyword in the ALTER statement (use MODIFY ColumnName instead of ALTER ColumnName).
- Oracle SQL supports data type changes using the MODIFY keyword in the ALTER statement.

Chapter 3

Query Formulation with SQL

Learning Objectives

This chapter provides the foundation for query formulation using the industry standard Structured Query Language (SQL). Query formulation is the process of converting a request for data into a statement of a database language such as SQL. After this chapter, the student should have acquired the following knowledge and skills:

■ Reason through the query formulation process using the three critical questions.

■ Write SQL SELECT statements for queries involving restriction, projection, join, and summarization operators.

■ Write SELECT statements for difficult joins involving three or more tables, self joins, and multiple joins between tables.

■ Understand the meaning of grouping queries using the conceptual process.

■ Write English descriptions to document SQL statements.

■ Write INSERT, UPDATE, and DELETE statements to change the contents of a database.

OVERVIEW

Chapter 2 provided a foundation for using relational databases. Most importantly, you learned about connections among tables and fundamental operators to extract useful data. This chapter shows you how to apply this knowledge in using the data manipulation statements of SQL.

Much of your skill with SQL or other computer languages is derived from imitating examples. This chapter provides many examples to facilitate your learning process. Initially you are presented with some easy examples so that you can plunge into SQL. To prime you for more difficult examples, two mental tools (conceptual evaluation process and critical questions) are presented. The conceptual evaluation process explains the meaning of the SELECT statement through the sequence of operations and intermediate tables that produce the result. The critical questions help you transform a problem statement into a relational database representation in a language such as SQL. These tools are used to help formulate and explain the advanced problems presented in the last part of this chapter.

3.1 BACKGROUND

Before using SQL, it is informative to understand its history and scope. The history reveals the origin of the name and the efforts to standardize the language. The scope puts the various parts of SQL into perspective. We have already seen the CREATE TABLE statement. The SELECT, UPDATE, DELETE, and INSERT statements are the subject of Chapters 3 and 4. To broaden your understanding, you should be aware of other parts of the language and different usage contexts.

3.1.1 Brief History of SQL

The Structured Query Language (SQL) has a short but colorful history. Table 3–1 depicts the highlights of SQL's development. SQL began life as the SQUARE language in IBM's System R project. The System R project was a response to the interest in relational databases sparked by Dr. Ted Codd, an IBM Fellow who wrote a famous paper in

TABLE 3–1	SQL Timeline
Year	Event
1972	System R project at IBM Research Labs
1974	SQUARE
1975	Language revision and name change to SEQUEL
1976	Language revision and name change to SEQUEL 2
1977	Name change to SQL
1978	First commercial implementation by Oracle Corporation
1981	IBM product SQL/DS featuring SQL
1986	SQL1 standard approved
1989	SQL1 standard enhanced
1992	SQL2 standard approved
1999	SQL3 standard approved

1970 about relational databases. The SQUARE language was somewhat mathematical in nature. After conducting human factors experiments, the IBM research team revised the language and renamed it SEQUEL (a follow-up to SQUARE). After another revision, the language was dubbed SEQUEL 2. Its current name, SQL, resulted from legal issues surrounding the name SEQUEL. Because of this naming history, a number of database professionals, particularly those working during the 1970s, pronounce the name as "sequel" rather than SQL.

SQL is now an international standard[1] although it was not always so. With the force of IBM behind SQL, many imitators used some variant of SQL. Such was the old order of the computer industry when IBM was dominant. It may seem surprising, but IBM was not the first company to commercialize SQL. Until a standards effort developed in the 1980s, SQL was in a state of confusion. Many vendors implemented different subsets of SQL with unique extensions. The standards efforts by the American National Standards Institute (ANSI), the International Organization for Standards (ISO), and the International Electrotechnical Commission (IEC) have restored some order. Although SQL was not initially the best database language developed, the standards efforts have improved the language as well as standardized its specification. The third standard (SQL3) was just approved in late 1999.

Because of the size of the current (SQL2) and the new (SQL3) standard, there are multiple levels that can be supported. The original standard contained about 150 pages, while the current standard contains more than 600 pages. In contrast, the new standard contains more than 2,100 pages. No vendor supports the entire SQL2 standard now. Most vendors support a super/subset of the standard. They support some levels of the standard and add their own extensions. With the new SQL3 standard, vendor implementations will likely be more fragmented because of the size and scope of the standard.

3.1.2 Scope of SQL

SQL was designed as a language for database definition, manipulation, and control. Table 3–2 shows a quick summary of the various statements in SQL. Only database administrators use most of the database definition and database control statements. You have already seen the CREATE TABLE statement in Chapter 2. Chapter 12 covers the GRANT, REVOKE, and CHECK statements. Chapter 5 covers the CREATE VIEW

TABLE 3–2	Selected SQL Statements	
Statement Type	*Statements*	*Purpose*
Database definition	CREATE SCHEMA, TABLE, INDEX, VIEW	Define a new database, table, index, or view
	ALTER TABLE	Modify table definition
Database manipulation	SELECT	Retrieve contents of tables
	UPDATE, DELETE, INSERT	Modify, remove, or add rows
Database control	COMMIT, ROLLBACK	Complete, undo transaction
	GRANT, REVOKE	Add or remove access rights
	CREATE ASSERTION	Define integrity constraint

[1] Dr. Michael Stonebraker, an early database pioneer, has even referred to SQL as "intergalactic data speak."

statement. The CREATE VIEW statement can be used by either database administrators or analysts. This chapter and Chapter 4 cover the database manipulation statements. Power users and analysts use the database manipulation statements. The transaction control statements (COMMIT and ROLLBACK) are used by analysts. Chapter 13 covers COMMIT and ROLLBACK along with other aspects of transaction processing.

SQL can be used in two contexts: stand-alone and embedded. In the <u>stand-alone</u> context, the user submits SQL statements with the use of a specialized editor. The editor alerts the user to syntax errors and sends the statements to the DBMS. In this chapter, we assume stand-alone usage. In the <u>embedded</u> context, an executing program submits SQL statements, and the DBMS sends results back to the program. The program includes SQL statements along with statements of the host programming language such as COBOL or Visual Basic. There are additional statements that allow other SQL statements (such as SELECT) to be used inside a computer program.

SQL Usage Contexts
SQL statements can be stand-alone, that is, used with a specialized editor, or embedded inside a computer program.

3.2 GETTING STARTED WITH SELECT

The SELECT statement supports data retrieval from one or more tables. This section describes a simplified format of the SELECT statement. More complex formats are presented in Chapter 4. The SELECT statement described here has the following format:

```
SELECT  <list of columns and expressions usually involving columns>
FROM  <list of tables and join operations>
WHERE  <list of row conditions connected by AND, OR, NOT>
GROUP BY  <list of grouping columns>
HAVING  <list of group conditions connected by AND, OR, NOT >
ORDER BY  <list of sorting specifications>
```

Expression a combination of constants, column names, functions, and operators that produces a value. In conditions and result columns, expressions can be used in any place that column names can appear.

In the above format, the uppercase words are keywords. You replace the angle brackets <> with information to make a meaningful statement. For example, after the keyword SELECT, type the list of columns that should appear in the result but do not type the angle brackets. The list can include a column such as StdFirstName or an expression involving constants, column names, and functions. Example expressions are price * qty and 1.1 * FacSalary. To make meaningful names for computed columns, you can rename a column in the result table using the AS keyword. For example, SELECT price * qty AS amount renames the expression price * qty to amount in the result table.

To depict this SELECT format and show the meaning of statements, this chapter shows numerous examples. Examples are provided for both Microsoft Access (1997 and 2000 versions), a popular desktop DBMS, and Oracle 8, a prominent enterprise DBMS. Most examples execute on both systems. Examples that only execute on one product are marked. In addition to the examples, Appendix B summarizes syntax differences among major DBMSs.

The examples use the university database tables introduced in Chapter 2. Tables 3–3 through 3–7 list the contents of the tables. CREATE TABLE statements are listed in Appendix 2.A of Chapter 2. For your reference, the relationship diagram showing the primary and foreign keys is repeated in Figure 3.1.

TABLE 3–3	Sample *Student* TABLE

StdSSN	StdFirstName	StdLastName	StdCity	StdState	StdZip	StdMajor	StdClass	StdGPA
123-45-6789	HOMER	WELLS	SEATTLE	WA	98121-1111	IS	FR	3.00
124-56-7890	BOB	NORBERT	BOTHELL	WA	98011-2121	FIN	JR	2.70
234-56-7890	CANDY	KENDALL	TACOMA	WA	99042-3321	ACCT	JR	3.50
345-67-8901	WALLY	KENDALL	SEATTLE	WA	98123-1141	IS	SR	2.80
456-78-9012	JOE	ESTRADA	SEATTLE	WA	98121-2333	FIN	SR	3.20
567-89-0123	MARIAH	DODGE	SEATTLE	WA	98114-0021	IS	JR	3.60
678-90-1234	TESS	DODGE	REDMOND	WA	98116-2344	ACCT	SO	3.30
789-01-2345	ROBERTO	MORALES	SEATTLE	WA	98121-2212	FIN	JR	2.50
876-54-3210	CRISTOPHER	COLAN	SEATTLE	WA	98114-1332	IS	SR	4.00
890-12-3456	LUKE	BRAZZI	SEATTLE	WA	98116-0021	IS	SR	2.20
901-23-4567	WILLIAM	PILGRIM	BOTHELL	WA	98113-1885	IS	SO	3.80

TABLE 3–4A	Sample *Faculty* TABLE (FIRST PART)

FacSSN	FacFirstName	FacLastName	FacCity	FacState	FacDept	FacRank	FacSalary
098-76-5432	LEONARD	VINCE	SEATTLE	WA	MS	ASST	$ 35,000
543-21-0987	VICTORIA	EMMANUEL	BOTHELL	WA	MS	PROF	$120,000
654-32-1098	LEONARD	FIBON	SEATTLE	WA	MS	ASSC	$ 70,000
765-43-2109	NICKI	MACON	BELLEVUE	WA	FIN	PROF	$ 65,000
876-54-3210	CRISTOPHER	COLAN	SEATTLE	WA	MS	ASST	$ 40,000
987-65-4321	JULIA	MILLS	SEATTLE	WA	FIN	ASSC	$ 75,000

TABLE 3–4B	Sample *Faculty* TABLE (SECOND PART)

FacSSN	FacSupervisor	FacHireDate	FacZipCode
098-76-5432	654-32-1098	01-Apr-1990	98111-9921
543-21-0987		01-Apr-1991	98011-2242
654-32-1098	543-21-0987	01-Apr-1989	98121-0094
765-43-2109		01-Apr-1992	98015-9945
876-54-3210	654-32-1098	01-Apr-1994	98114-1332
987-65-4321	765-43-2109	01-Apr-1995	98114-9954

TABLE 3–5	Sample *Offering* TABLE

OfferNo	CourseNo	OffTerm	OffYear	OffLocation	OffTime	FacSSN	OffDays
1111	IS320	SUMMER	2000	BLM302	10:30 AM		MW
1234	IS320	FALL	1999	BLM302	10:30 AM	098-76-5432	MW
2222	IS460	SUMMER	1999	BLM412	1:30 PM		TTH
3333	IS320	SPRING	2000	BLM214	8:30 AM	098-76-5432	MW
4321	IS320	FALL	1999	BLM214	3:30 PM	098-76-5432	TTH
4444	IS320	WINTER	2000	BLM302	3:30 PM	543-21-0987	TTH
5555	FIN300	WINTER	2000	BLM207	8:30 AM	765-43-2109	MW
5678	IS480	WINTER	2000	BLM302	10:30 AM	987-65-4321	MW
5679	IS480	SPRING	2000	BLM412	3:30 PM	876-54-3210	TTH
6666	FIN450	WINTER	2000	BLM212	10:30 AM	987-65-4321	TTH
7777	FIN480	SPRING	2000	BLM305	1:30 PM	765-43-2109	MW
8888	IS320	SUMMER	2000	BLM405	1:30 PM	654-32-1098	MW
9876	IS460	SPRING	2000	BLM307	1:30 PM	654-32-1098	TTH

TABLE 3–6	Sample *Course* TABLE

CourseNo	CrsDesc	CrsUnits
FIN300	FUNDAMENTALS OF FINANCE	4
FIN450	PRINCIPLES OF INVESTMENTS	4
FIN480	CORPORATE FINANCE	4
IS320	FUNDAMENTALS OF BUSINESS PROGRAMMING	4
IS460	SYSTEMS ANALYSIS	4
IS470	BUSINESS DATA COMMUNICATIONS	4
IS480	FUNDAMENTALS OF DATABASE MANAGEMENT	4

3.2.1 Single Table Problems

Let us begin with the simple SQL statement in Example 3.1. In all the examples, keywords appear in uppercase while information specific to the query appears in lower and mixed case. In Example 3.1, only the *Student* table is listed in the FROM clause because the conditions in the WHERE clause and columns after the SELECT keyword involve only the *Student* table. In some DBMSs, a semicolon is needed to terminate a statement.

EXAMPLE 3.1	Testing Rows Using the WHERE Clause

Retrieve the name, city, and grade point average (GPA) of students with a high GPA (greater than or equal to 3.7). The result follows the SELECT statement.

```
SELECT StdFirstName, StdLastName, StdCity, StdGPA
   FROM Student
   WHERE StdGPA >= 3.7
```

TABLE 3–7		Sample *Enrollment* TABLE			
OfferNo	StdSSN	EnrGrade	OfferNo	StdSSN	EnrGrade
1234	123-45-6789	3.3	5679	123-45-6789	2
1234	234-56-7890	3.5	5679	124-56-7890	3.7
1234	345-67-8901	3.2	5679	678-90-1234	3.3
1234	456-78-9012	3.1	5679	789-01-2345	3.8
1234	567-89-0123	3.8	5679	890-12-3456	2.9
1234	678-90-1234	3.4	5679	901-23-4567	3.1
4321	123-45-6789	3.5	6666	234-56-7890	3.1
4321	124-56-7890	3.2	6666	567-89-0123	3.6
4321	789-01-2345	3.5	7777	876-54-3210	3.4
4321	876-54-3210	3.1	7777	890-12-3456	3.7
4321	890-12-3456	3.4	7777	901-23-4567	3.4
4321	901-23-4567	3.1	9876	124-56-7890	3.5
5555	123-45-6789	3.2	9876	234-56-7890	3.2
5555	124-56-7890	2.7	9876	345-67-8901	3.2
5678	123-45-6789	3.2	9876	456-78-9012	3.4
5678	234-56-7890	2.8	9876	567-89-0123	2.6
5678	345-67-8901	3.3	9876	678-90-1234	3.3
5678	456-78-9012	3.4	9876	901-23-4567	4
5678	567-89-0123	2.6			

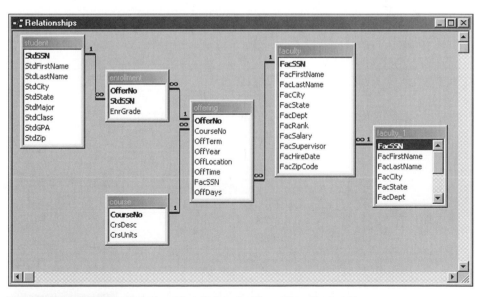

Figure 3.1   Relationship window for the university database.

StdFirstName	StdLastName	StdCity	StdGPA
CRISTOPHER	COLAN	SEATTLE	4.00
WILLIAM	PILGRIM	BOTHELL	3.80

TABLE 3–8	**Standard Comparison Operators**

Comparison Operator	Meaning
=	equal to
<	less than
>	greater than
<=	less than or equal to
>=	greater than or equal to
<> or !=	not equal (check your DBMS)

Table 3–8 depicts the standard comparison operators. Note that the symbol for some operators depends on the DBMS.

Example 3.2 is even simpler than Example 3.1. The result is identical to the original *Faculty* table in Table 3–4. Example 3.2 uses a shortcut to list all columns. The asterisk * in the column list means list all columns of the tables appearing in the FROM clause. The asterisk serves as a wildcard character matching all column names.

EXAMPLE 3.2	Show All Columns

List all columns and rows of the *Faculty* table. The resulting table is shown in two parts.

```
SELECT * FROM Faculty
```

FacSSN	FacFirstName	FacLastName	FacCity	FacState	FacDept	FacRank	FacSalary
098-76-5432	LEONARD	VINCE	SEATTLE	WA	MS	ASST	$35,000
543-21-0987	VICTORIA	EMMANUEL	BOTHELL	WA	MS	PROF	$120,000
654-32-1098	LEONARD	FIBON	SEATTLE	WA	MS	ASSC	$70,000
765-43-2109	NICKI	MACON	BELLEVUE	WA	FIN	PROF	$65,000
876-54-3210	CRISTOPHER	COLAN	SEATTLE	WA	MS	ASST	$40,000
987-65-4321	JULIA	MILLS	SEATTLE	WA	FIN	ASSC	$75,000

FacSSN	FacSupervisor	FacHireDate	FacZipCode
098-76-5432	654-32-1098	01-Apr-90	98111-9921
543-21-0987		01-Apr-91	98011-2242
654-32-1098	543-21-0987	01-Apr-89	98121-0094
765-43-2109		01-Apr-92	98015-9945
876-54-3210	654-32-1098	01-Apr-94	98114-1332
987-65-4321	765-43-2109	01-Apr-95	98114-9954

Example 3.3 depicts expressions in the SELECT and WHERE clauses. The expression in the SELECT clause increases the salary by 10 percent. The AS keyword is used to rename the computed column. Without renaming, most DBMSs will generate a meaningless name such as `Expr001`. The expression in the WHERE clause extracts the year from the hiring date. Because functions for the date data type are not standard, Access and Oracle formulations are provided. To become proficient with SQL on a particular DBMS, you will need to study the available functions especially with date columns.

EXAMPLE 3.3 (ACCESS)

Expressions in SELECT and WHERE Clauses

List the name, city, and increased salary of faculty hired after 1991. The **year** function extracts the year part of a column with a date data type.

```
SELECT FacFirstName, FacLastName, FacCity,
       FacSalary*1.1 AS IncreasedSalary, FacHireDate
FROM Faculty
WHERE year(FacHireDate) > 1991
```

FacFirstName	FacLastName	FacCity	IncreasedSalary	FacHireDate
NICKI	MACON	BELLEVUE	71500	01-Apr-1992
CRISTOPHER	COLAN	SEATTLE	44000	01-Apr-1994
JULIA	MILLS	SEATTLE	82500	01-Apr-1995

EXAMPLE 3.3 (ORACLE)

Expressions in SELECT and WHERE Clauses

The <u>to_char</u> function extracts the four-digit year from the *FacHireDate* column and the <u>to_number</u> function converts the character representation of the year into a number.

```
SELECT FacFirstName, FacLastName, FacCity,
       FacSalary*1.1 AS IncreasedSalary, FacHireDate
FROM Faculty
WHERE to_number(to_char(FacHireDate, 'YYYY'))> 1991
```

<u>Inexact matching</u> supports conditions that match some pattern rather than matching an identical string. One of the most common types of inexact matching is to find values having a common prefix such as 'IS4' (400 level IS courses). Example 3.4 uses the LIKE operator along with a pattern-matching character * to perform prefix matching. The string 'IS4*' means match strings beginning with 'IS4' and ending with anything. The wildcard character * matches any string. The Oracle formulation of Example 3.4 uses the percent symbol (%), the SQL2 standard for the wildcard character. Note that string constants must be enclosed in quotation marks.[2]

---

[2]Most DBMSs require the single quotes, the SQL2 standard. Microsoft Access allows either single or double quotes for string constants.

**EXAMPLE 3.4
(ACCESS)**

Inexact Matching with LIKE
List the senior level IS courses.

```
SELECT *
   FROM Course
   WHERE CourseNo LIKE 'IS4*'
```

CourseNo	CrsDesc	CrsUnits
IS460	SYSTEMS ANALYSIS	4
IS470	BUSINESS DATA COMMUNICATIONS	4
IS480	FUNDAMENTALS OF DATABASE MANAGEMENT	4

**EXAMPLE 3.4
(ORACLE)**

Inexact Matching with LIKE
List the senior level IS courses.

```
SELECT *
   FROM Course
   WHERE CourseNo LIKE 'IS4%'
```

Another common type of inexact matching is to match strings containing a substring. To perform this kind of matching, a wildcard character should be used before and after the substring. For example, to find courses containing the word "DATABASE" anywhere in the course description, write the condition `CrsDesc LIKE '*DATABASE*'` in Access or `CrsDesc LIKE '%DATABASE%'` in Oracle.

The wildcard character is not the only pattern-matching character. SQL2 specifies the underscore character _ to match any single character. Some DBMSs such as Access use the question mark ? to match any single character. In addition, most DBMSs have pattern-matching characters for matching a range of characters (for example, the digits 0 to 9) and any character from a list of characters. The symbols used for these other pattern-matching characters are not standard. To become proficient at writing inexact matching conditions, you should study the pattern-matching characters available with your DBMS.

In addition to performing pattern matching with strings, you can use <u>exact matching</u> with the equality = comparison operator. For example, the condition `CourseNo = 'IS480'` matches a single row in the *Course* table. For both exact and inexact matching, case sensitivity is an important issue. Some DBMSs such as Microsoft Access are not case sensitive. In Access SQL, the previous condition matches 'is480', 'Is480', and 'iS480' in addition to 'IS480'. Other DBMSs such as Oracle are case sensitive. In Oracle SQL, the previous condition matches only 'IS480', not 'is480', 'Is480', and 'iS480'. To alleviate confusion, you can use the Oracle <u>upper</u> or <u>lower</u> functions to convert strings to upper- or lowercase, respectively.

Example 3.5 depicts range matching on a column with a DATE data type. In Access SQL, pound symbols enclose date constants while in Oracle SQL, single quotation marks enclose date constants. Date columns can be compared just like numbers with the usual comparison operators (=, <, etc.). The BETWEEN-AND operator defines a closed interval (includes end points). In Access Example 3.5, the BETWEEN-AND condition is a shortcut for `FacHireDate>= #1/1/94# AND FacHireDate <= #12/31/95#`.

**BETWEEN-AND
Operator** a shortcut operator to test a numeric or date column against a range of values. The BETWEEN-AND operator returns true if the column is greater than or equal to the first value and less than or equal to the second value.

EXAMPLE 3.5
(ACCESS)

Conditions on Date Columns

List the name and hiring date of faculty hired in 1994 or 1995.

```
SELECT FacFirstName, FacLastName, FacHireDate
   FROM Faculty
   WHERE FacHireDate BETWEEN #1/1/1994# AND
         #12/31/1995#
```

FacFirstName	FacLastName	FacHireDate
CRISTOPHER	COLAN	01-Apr-94
JULIA	MILLS	01-Apr-95

EXAMPLE 3.5
(ORACLE)

Conditions on Date Columns

In Oracle SQL, the standard format for dates is DD-Mon-YYYY where DD is the day number, Mon is the month abbreviation, and YYYY is the four-digit year.

```
SELECT FacFirstName, FacLastName, FacHireDate
   FROM Faculty
   WHERE FacHireDate BETWEEN '1-Jan-1994' AND
         '31-Dec-1995'
```

Besides testing columns for specified values, you sometimes need to test for the lack of a value. Null values are used when there is no normal value for a column. A null can mean that the value is unknown or the value is not applicable to the row. For the *Offering* table, a null value for *FacSSN* means that the instructor is not yet assigned. Testing for null values is done with the IS NULL comparison operator. You also can test for a normal value using IS NOT NULL.

EXAMPLE 3.6

Testing for Nulls

List the offering number and course number of summer 2000 offerings without an assigned instructor.

```
SELECT OfferNo, CourseNo
   FROM Offering
   WHERE  FacSSN IS NULL AND OffTerm = 'SUMMER'
      AND  OffYear = 2000
```

OfferNo	CourseNo
1111	IS320

Mixing AND and OR
always use parentheses to make the grouping of conditions explicit.

Example 3.7 depicts a complex logical expression involving both logical operators AND and OR. When mixing AND and OR in a logical expression, it is a good idea to use parentheses. Otherwise, the reader of the SELECT statement may not understand how the AND and OR conditions are grouped. Without parentheses, you must depend on the default way that AND and OR conditions are grouped.

EXAMPLE 3.7

Complex Logical Expression

List the offer number, course number, and faculty social security number for course offerings scheduled in fall 1999 or winter 2000.

```
SELECT OfferNo, CourseNo, FacSSN
  FROM Offering
  WHERE (OffTerm = 'FALL' AND OffYear = 1999)
     OR (OffTerm = 'WINTER' AND OffYear = 2000)
```

OfferNo	CourseNo	FacSSN
1234	IS320	098-76-5432
4321	IS320	098-76-5432
4444	IS320	543-21-0987
5555	FIN300	765-43-2109
5678	IS480	987-65-4321
6666	FIN450	987-65-4321

3.2.2 Joining Tables

Example 3.8 demonstrates a join of the *Course* and *Offering* tables. The join condition `Course.CourseNo = Offering.CourseNo` is specified in the WHERE clause.

**EXAMPLE 3.8
(ACCESS)**

Join Tables but Show Columns from One Table Only

List the offering number, course number, days, and time of offerings containing the words "database" or "programming" in the course description and taught in spring 2000. The Oracle version of this example uses the % instead of the * as the wildcard character.

```
SELECT OfferNo, Offering.CourseNo, OffDays, OffTime
  FROM Offering, Course
  WHERE OffTerm = 'SPRING' AND OffYear = 2000
     AND (CrsDesc LIKE '*DATABASE*'
       OR CrsDesc LIKE '*PROGRAMMING*')
     AND Course.CourseNo = Offering.CourseNo
```

OfferNo	CourseNo	OffDays	OffTime
3333	IS320	MW	8:30 AM
5679	IS480	TTH	3:30 PM

There are two additional points of interest about Example 3.8. First, the *CourseNo* column names must be prefixed with a table name (*Course* or *Offering*). Otherwise, the SQL statement is ambiguous because *CourseNo* can refer to a column in either the *Course* or *Offering* table. Second, both tables must be listed in the FROM clause even though the result columns come from only the *Offering* table. The *Course* table is needed in the FROM clause because conditions in the WHERE clause reference *CrsDesc,* a column of the *Course* table.

Example 3.9 demonstrates another join, but this time the result columns come from both tables. There are conditions on each table in addition to the join conditions. The Oracle formulation uses the % instead of the * as the wildcard character.

EXAMPLE 3.9 (ACCESS)

Join Tables and Show Columns from Both Tables

List the offer number, course number, and name of the instructor of IS course offerings scheduled in fall 1999 taught by assistant professors.

```
SELECT OfferNo, CourseNo, FacFirstName, FacLastName
   FROM Offering, Faculty
   WHERE OffTerm = 'FALL' AND OffYear = 1999
      AND FacRank = 'ASST' AND CourseNo LIKE 'IS*'
      AND Faculty.FacSSN = Offering.FacSSN
```

OfferNo	CourseNo	FacFirstName	FacLastName
1234	IS320	LEONARD	VINCE
4321	IS320	LEONARD	VINCE

EXAMPLE 3.9 (ORACLE)

Join Tables and Show Columns from Both Tables

List the offer number, course number, and name of the instructor of IS course offerings scheduled in fall 1999 taught by assistant professors.

```
SELECT OfferNo, CourseNo, FacFirstName, FacLastName
   FROM Offering, Faculty
   WHERE OffTerm = 'FALL' AND OffYear = 1999
      AND FacRank = 'ASST' AND CourseNo LIKE 'IS%'
      AND Faculty.FacSSN = Offering.FacSSN
```

In the SQL2 standard, the join operation can be expressed directly in the FROM clause rather than being expressed in both the FROM and the WHERE clauses as shown in Examples 3.8 and 3.9. Because Oracle SQL does not support join operations in the FROM clause, there is no Oracle formulation for Example 3.10. To make a join operation in the FROM clause, use the keywords INNER JOIN as shown in Example 3.10. The join conditions are indicated by the ON keyword inside the FROM clause. Notice that the join condition no longer appears in the WHERE clause.

EXAMPLE 3.10 (ACCESS)

Join Tables Using a Join Operation in the FROM Clause

List the offer number, course number, and name of the instructor of IS course offerings scheduled in fall 1999 that are taught by assistant professors (result is identical to Example 3.9).

```
SELECT OfferNo, CourseNo, FacFirstName, FacLastName
   FROM Offering INNER JOIN Faculty
      ON Faculty.FacSSN = Offering.FacSSN
   WHERE OffTerm = 'FALL' AND OffYear = 1999
      AND FacRank = 'ASST' AND CourseNo LIKE 'IS*'
```

GROUP BY Reminder
the columns in the
SELECT clause must
either be in the GROUP
BY clause or be part of a
summary calculation with
an aggregate function.

3.2.3 Summarizing Tables with GROUP BY and HAVING

So far, the results of all examples in this section relate to individual rows. Even Example 3.9 relates to a combination of columns from individual *Offering* and *Faculty* rows. As mentioned in Chapter 2, it is sometimes important to show summaries of rows. The GROUP BY and HAVING clauses are used to show results about groups of rows rather than individual rows.

Example 3.11 depicts the GROUP BY clause to summarize groups of rows. Each result row contains a value of the grouping column (*StdMajor*) along with the aggregate calculation summarizing rows with the same value for the grouping column. The GROUP BY clause must contain every column in the SELECT clause except for aggregate expressions. For example, adding the *StdClass* column in the SELECT clause would make Example 3.11 invalid unless *StdClass* was also added to the GROUP BY clause.

EXAMPLE 3.11

Grouping on a Single Column

Summarize the average GPA of students by major.

```
SELECT StdMajor, AVG(StdGPA) AS AvgGPA
   FROM Student
   GROUP BY StdMajor
```

StdMajor	AvgGPA
ACCT	3.39999997615814
FIN	2.80000003178914
IS	3.23333330949148

COUNT Function Usage
COUNT(*) and
COUNT(column)
produce identical results
except when column
contains null values. See
Chapter 4 for more details
about the effect of null
values on aggregate
functions.

Table 3–9 shows the standard aggregate functions. If you have a statistical calculation that cannot be performed with these functions, check your DBMS. Most DBMSs feature many functions beyond these standard ones.

The COUNT, AVG, and SUM functions support the DISTINCT keyword to restrict the computation to unique column values. Example 3.12 demonstrates the DISTINCT

TABLE 3–9	**Standard Aggregate Functions**
Aggregate Function	*Meaning and Comments*
COUNT(*)	Computes the number of rows
COUNT(column)	Computes the number of non-null values in column; DISTINCT can be used to compute the number of unique column values.
AVG	Computes the average of a numeric column or expression excluding null values; DISTINCT can be used to compute the average of unique column values.
SUM	Computes the sum of a numeric column or expression excluding null values; DISTINCT can be used to compute the average of unique column values.
MIN	Computes the smallest value. For string columns, the collating sequence is used to compare strings.
MAX	Computes the largest value. For string columns, the collating sequence is used to compare strings.

keyword for the COUNT function. This example retrieves the number of offerings in a year as well as the number of distinct courses taught. Some DBMSs such as Microsoft Access do not support the DISTINCT keyword inside of aggregate functions.

EXAMPLE 3.12 (ORACLE)

Counting Rows and Unique Column Values
Summarize the number of offerings and unique courses by year.

```
SELECT OffYear, COUNT(*) AS NumOfferings,
        COUNT(DISTINCT CourseNo) AS NumCourses
FROM Offering
GROUP BY OffYear
```

OffYear	NumOfferings	NumCourses
1999	3	2
2000	10	6

WHERE vs. HAVING use the WHERE clause for conditions that can be tested on individual rows. Use the HAVING clause for conditions that can be tested only on groups. Conditions in the HAVING clause should involve aggregate functions whereas conditions in the WHERE clause cannot involve aggregate functions.

Examples 3.13 and 3.14 contrast the WHERE and HAVING clauses. In Example 3.13, the WHERE clause selects upper division (juniors or seniors) before grouping on major. Because the WHERE clause eliminates students before grouping occurs, only upper-division students are grouped. In Example 3.14, a HAVING condition retains groups with an average GPA greater than 3.1. The HAVING clause applies to groups of rows whereas the WHERE clause applies to individual rows. To use a HAVING clause, there must be a GROUP BY clause.

EXAMPLE 3.13

Grouping with Row Conditions
Summarize the average GPA of upper-division (junior or senior) students by major.

```
SELECT StdMajor, AVG(StdGPA) AS AvgGpa
FROM Student
WHERE StdClass = 'JR' OR StdClass = 'SR'
GROUP BY StdMajor
```

StdMajor	AvgGPA
ACCT	3.5
FIN	2.800000031789
IS	3.149999976158

EXAMPLE 3.14

Grouping with Row and Group Conditions
Summarize the average GPA of upper-division (junior or senior) students by major. Only list the majors with average GPA greater than 3.1.

```
SELECT StdMajor, AVG(StdGPA) AS AvgGpa
FROM Student
WHERE StdClass IN ('JR', 'SR')
GROUP BY StdMajor
HAVING AVG(StdGPA) > 3.1
```

HAVING Reminder the HAVING clause must be preceded by the GROUP BY clause.

StdMajor	AvgGPA
ACCT	3.5
IS	3.149999976158

One other point about Examples 3.13 and 3.14 is the use of the OR operator as compared to the IN operator (set element of operator). The WHERE condition in Examples 3.13 and 3.14 retains the same rows. The IN condition is true if *StdClass* matches any value in the parenthesized list. Chapter 4 provides additional explanation about the IN operator for nested queries.

To summarize all rows, aggregate functions can be used in SELECT without a GROUP BY clause as demonstrated in Example 3.15. The result is always a single row containing just the aggregate calculations.

EXAMPLE 3.15   Grouping All Rows

List the number of upper-division students and their average GPA.

```
SELECT COUNT(*) AS StdCnt, AVG(StdGPA) AS AvgGPA
   FROM Student
   WHERE StdClass = 'JR' OR StdClass = 'SR'
```

StdCnt	AvgGPA
8	3.0625

Sometimes it is useful to group on more than one column as demonstrated by Example 3.16. The result shows one row for each combination of *StdMajor* and *StdClass*. Some rows have the same value for both aggregate calculations because there is only one associated row in the Student table. For example, there is only one row for the combination ('ACCT', 'JR').

EXAMPLE 3.16   Grouping on Two Columns

Summarize the minimum and maximum GPA of students by major and class.

```
SELECT StdMajor, StdClass, MIN(StdGPA) AS MinGPA,
         MAX(StdGPA) AS MaxGPA
   FROM Student
   GROUP BY StdMajor, StdClass
```

StdMajor	StdClass	MinGPA	MaxGPA
ACCT	JR	3.5	3.5
ACCT	SO	3.3	3.3
FIN	JR	2.5	2.7
FIN	SR	3.2	3.2
IS	FR	3	3
IS	JR	3.6	3.6
IS	SO	3.8	3.8
IS	SR	2.2	4

A powerful combination is to use grouping with joins. There is no reason to restrict grouping to just one table. Often, more useful information is obtained by summarizing rows that result from a join. Example 3.17 demonstrates grouping applied to a join between *Course* and *Offering*. It is important to note that the join is performed before the grouping occurs. For example, after the join, there are six rows for BUSINESS PROGRAMMING. Because queries combining joins and grouping can be difficult to understand, Section 3.3 gives a more detailed explanation.

EXAMPLE 3.17 (ACCESS)	Combining Grouping and Joins

Summarize the number of IS course offerings by course description.

```
SELECT CrsDesc, COUNT(*) AS OfferCount
  FROM Course, Offering
  WHERE Course.CourseNo = Offering.CourseNo
     AND Course.CourseNo LIKE 'IS*'
  GROUP BY CrsDesc
```

CrsDesc	OfferCount
FUNDAMENTALS OF BUSINESS PROGRAMMING	6
FUNDAMENTALS OF DATABASE MANAGEMENT	2
SYSTEMS ANALYSIS	2

EXAMPLE 3.17 (ORACLE)	Combining Grouping and Joins

Summarize the number of IS course offerings by course description.

```
SELECT CrsDesc, COUNT(*) AS OfferCount
  FROM Course, Offering
  WHERE Course.CourseNo = Offering.CourseNo
     AND Course.CourseNo LIKE 'IS%'
  GROUP BY CrsDesc
```

3.2.4 Improving the Appearance of Results

We finish this section with two parts of the SELECT statement that can improve the appearance of results. Examples 3.18 and 3.19 demonstrate sorting using the ORDER BY clause. The sort sequence depends on the date type of the sorted field (numeric for numeric data types, ASCII collating sequence for string fields, and calendar sequence for data fields). By default, sorting occurs in ascending order. The keyword DESC can be used after a column name to sort in descending order as demonstrated in Example 3.19.

EXAMPLE 3.18	Sorting on a Single Column

List the GPA, name, city, and state of juniors. Order the result by GPA in ascending order.

```
SELECT StdGPA, StdFirstName, StdLastName, StdCity, StdState
  FROM Student
  WHERE StdClass = 'JR'
  ORDER BY StdGPA
```

StdGPA	StdFirstName	StdLastName	StdCity	StdState
2.50	ROBERTO	MORALES	SEATTLE	WA
2.70	BOB	NORBERT	BOTHELL	WA
3.50	CANDY	KENDALL	TACOMA	WA
3.60	MARIAH	DODGE	SEATTLE	WA

EXAMPLE 3.19

Sorting on Two Columns with Descending Order

List the rank, salary, name, and department of faculty. Order the result by ascending (alphabetic) rank and descending salary.

```
SELECT FacRank, FacSalary, FacFirstName, FacLastName,
       FacDept
FROM Faculty
ORDER BY FacRank, FacSalary DESC
```

FacRank	FacSalary	FacFirstName	FacLastName	FacDept
ASSC	75000.00	JULIA	MILLS	FIN
ASSC	70000.00	LEONARD	FIBON	MS
ASST	40000.00	CRISTOPHER	COLAN	MS
ASST	35000.00	LEONARD	VINCE	MS
PROF	120000.00	VICTORIA	EMMANUEL	MS
PROF	65000.00	NICKI	MACON	FIN

ORDER BY vs. DISTINCT use the ORDER BY clause to sort a result table on one or more columns. Use the DISTINCT keyword to remove duplicates in the result.

Some students confuse ORDER BY and GROUP BY. In most systems, GROUP BY has the side effect of sorting by the grouping columns. You should not depend on this side effect. If you just want to sort, use ORDER BY rather than GROUP BY. If you want to sort and group, use both ORDER BY and GROUP BY.

Another way to improve the appearance of the result is to remove duplicate rows. By default, SQL does not remove duplicate rows. Duplicate rows are not possible when the primary keys of the result tables are included. There are a number of situations in which the primary key does not appear in the result. Example 3.21 demonstrates the DISTINCT keyword to remove duplicates.

EXAMPLE 3.20

Result with Duplicates

List the city and state of faculty members.

```
SELECT FacCity, FacState
FROM Faculty
```

FacCity	FacState
SEATTLE	WA
BOTHELL	WA
SEATTLE	WA
BELLEVUE	WA
SEATTLE	WA
SEATTLE	WA

EXAMPLE 3.21

Eliminating Duplicates with DISTINCT

List the unique city and state combinations in the *Faculty* table.

```
SELECT DISTINCT FacCity, FacState
    FROM Faculty
```

FacCity	FacState
BELLEVUE	WA
BOTHELL	WA
SEATTLE	WA

3.3 CONCEPTUAL EVALUATION PROCESS FOR SELECT STATEMENTS

Conceptual Evaluation Process the sequence of operations and intermediate tables used to derive the result of a SELECT statement. The conceptual evaluation process may help you gain an initial understanding of the SELECT statement as well as help you to understand more difficult problems.

To develop a clearer understanding of the SELECT statement, it is useful to understand the evaluation process or sequence of steps to produce the desired result. The conceptual evaluation process describes operations (mostly relational algebra operations) that produce intermediate tables leading to the result table. You may find it useful to refer to the conceptual evaluation process when first learning to write SELECT statements. After you gain initial competence with SELECT, you should not need to refer to the conceptual evaluation process except to gain insight about difficult problems.

To demonstrate the conceptual evaluation process, consider Example 3.22 involving many parts of the SELECT statement. It involves multiple tables (*Enrollment* and *Offering* in the FROM clause), row conditions (following WHERE), aggregate functions (COUNT and AVG) over groups of rows (GROUP BY), a group condition (following HAVING), and sorting of the final result (ORDER BY).

EXAMPLE 3.22

Depict Many Parts of the SELECT Statement

List the course number, unique number, and average grade of students enrolled in fall 1999 IS course offerings in which more than one student is enrolled. Sort the result by course number in ascending order and average grade in descending order. The Oracle version of Example 3.22 is identical except for the % instead of the * as the wildcard character.

```
SELECT CourseNo, Enrollment.OfferNo,
        AVG(EnrGrade) AS AvgGrade
    FROM Enrollment, Offering
    WHERE CourseNo LIKE 'IS*' AND OffYear = 1999
        AND OffTerm = 'FALL'
        AND Enrollment.OfferNo = Offering.OfferNo
        AND Enrollment.OfferNo = Offering.CourseNo
    GROUP BY CourseNo, Enrollment.OfferNo
    HAVING COUNT(*) > 1
    ORDER BY CourseNo, 3 DESC
```

In the ORDER BY clause, note the number 3 as the second column to sort. The number 3 means sort by the third column (*AvgGrade*) in SELECT. Some DBMSs do not allow aggregate expressions or alias names (*AvgGrade*) in the ORDER BY clause.

Tables 3–10, 3–11, and 3–12 show the input tables and the result. Only small input and result tables have been used so that you can understand more clearly the process to derive the result. It does not take large tables to depict the conceptual evaluation process well.

TABLE 3–10	Sample *Offering* Table		
OfferNo	*CourseNo*	*OffYear*	*OffTerm*
1111	IS480	1999	FALL
2222	IS480	1999	FALL
3333	IS320	1999	FALL
5555	IS480	2000	WINTER
6666	IS320	2000	SPRING

TABLE 3–11	Sample *Enrollment* Table	
StdSSN	*OfferNo*	*EnrGrade*
111-11-1111	1111	3.1
111-11-1111	2222	3.5
111-11-1111	3333	3.3
111-11-1111	5555	3.8
222-22-2222	1111	3.2
222-22-2222	2222	3.3
333-33-3333	1111	3.6

TABLE 3–12	Example 3.22 Result	
CourseNo	*OfferNo*	*AvgGrade*
IS480	2222	3.4
IS480	1111	3.3

The conceptual evaluation process is a sequence of operations as indicated in Figure 3.2. This process is conceptual rather than actual because most SQL compilers can produce the same output using many shortcuts. Because the shortcuts are system specific rather than mathematical or performance oriented, we will not review them. The conceptual evaluation process provides a foundation for understanding the meaning of SQL statements that is independent of system and performance issues. The remainder of this section applies the conceptual evaluation process to Example 3.22.

1. The first step in the conceptual evaluation process combines the tables in the FROM clause with the cross product and join operators. In Example 3.22, a cross product operation is necessary because two tables are listed. A join operation is not necessary because the INNER JOIN keyword does not appear in the FROM statement. Recall that the cross product operator shows all possible rows by combining two tables. The resulting table contains the product of the number of rows and the sum of the columns. In this case, the cross product contains 35 rows (5 × 7) and 7 columns (3+4). Table 3–13 shows a partial result. As an exercise, you are encouraged to derive the entire result. As a notational shortcut here, the table name (abbreviated as *E* and *O*) is prefixed before the column name for *OfferNo*.

2. The second step uses a restriction operation to retrieve rows that satisfy the conditions in the WHERE clause from the result of step 1. We have four conditions: a join condition over *OfferNo*, a condition on *CourseNo*, a condition on *OffYear*, and a condition on *OffTerm*. Note that the condition on *CourseNo* includes the wildcard character *. Any course numbers beginning

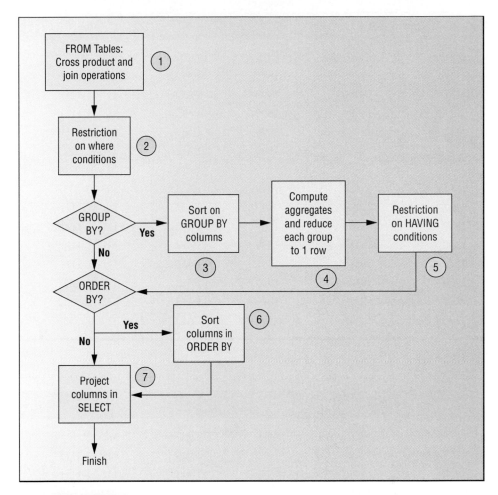

Figure 3.2   **Flowchart of the conceptual evaluation process.**

with IS match this condition. Table 3–14 shows that the result of the cross product (35 rows) is reduced to six rows.

3. The third step sorts the result of step 2 by the columns specified in the GROUP BY clause. The GROUP BY clause indicates that the output should relate to groups of rows rather than individual rows. If the output relates to individual rows rather than groups of rows, the GROUP BY clause is omitted. When using the GROUP BY clause, you must include <u>every</u> column from the SELECT clause except for expressions that involve an aggregate function.[3] Table 3–15 shows the result of step 2 sorted by *CourseNo* and *O.OfferNo*. Note that the columns have been rearranged to make the result easier to read.

4. The fourth step is only necessary if there is a GROUP BY clause. The fourth step computes aggregate function(s) for each group of rows and reduces each group to a single row. All rows in a group have the same values for the

---

[3]In other words, when using the GROUP BY clause, every column in the SELECT clause should either be in the GROUP BY clause or be an expression with an aggregate function.

TABLE 3–13	Partial Result of Step 1 for First Two *Offering* Rows (1111 and 2222)

O.OfferNo	CourseNo	OffYear	OffTerm	StdSSN	E.OfferNo	EnrGrade
1111	IS480	1999	FALL	111-11-1111	1111	3.1
1111	IS480	1999	FALL	111-11-1111	2222	3.5
1111	IS480	1999	FALL	111-11-1111	3333	3.3
1111	IS480	1999	FALL	111-11-1111	5555	3.8
1111	IS480	1999	FALL	222-22-2222	1111	3.2
1111	IS480	1999	FALL	222-22-2222	2222	3.3
1111	IS480	1999	FALL	333-33-3333	1111	3.6
2222	IS480	1999	FALL	111-11-1111	1111	3.1
2222	IS480	1999	FALL	111-11-1111	2222	3.5
2222	IS480	1999	FALL	111-11-1111	3333	3.3
2222	IS480	1999	FALL	111-11-1111	5555	3.8
2222	IS480	1999	FALL	222-22-2222	1111	3.2
2222	IS480	1999	FALL	222-22-2222	2222	3.3
2222	IS480	1999	FALL	333-33-3333	1111	3.6

TABLE 3–14	Result of Step 2

O.OfferNo	CourseNo	OffYear	OffTerm	StdSSN	E.OfferNo	EnrGrade
1111	IS480	1999	FALL	111-11-1111	1111	3.1
2222	IS480	1999	FALL	111-11-1111	2222	3.5
1111	IS480	1999	FALL	222-22-2222	1111	3.2
2222	IS480	1999	FALL	222-22-2222	2222	3.3
1111	IS480	1999	FALL	333-33-3333	1111	3.6
3333	IS320	1999	FALL	111-11-1111	3333	3.3

TABLE 3–15	Result of Step 3

CourseNo	O.OfferNo	OffYear	OffTerm	StdSSN	E.OfferNo	EnrGrade
IS320	3333	1999	FALL	111-11-1111	3333	3.3
IS480	1111	1999	FALL	111-11-1111	1111	3.1
IS480	1111	1999	FALL	222-22-2222	1111	3.2
IS480	1111	1999	FALL	333-33-3333	1111	3.6
IS480	2222	1999	FALL	111-11-1111	2222	3.5
IS480	2222	1999	FALL	222-22-2222	2222	3.3

GROUP BY columns. In Table 3–16, there are three groups {<IS320, 3333>, <IS480, 1111>, <IS480, 2222>}. Computed columns are added for aggregate functions in the SELECT and HAVING clauses. Table 3–16 shows two new columns for the AVG function in the SELECT clause and the COUNT function in the HAVING clause. Note that remaining columns are eliminated at this point because they are not needed in the remaining steps.

5. The fifth step eliminates step 4 rows that do not satisfy the HAVING condition. Table 3–17 shows that the first row in Table 3–16 is removed because it fails the HAVING condition. Note that the HAVING clause specifies a restriction operation for groups of rows. The HAVING clause cannot be present without a preceding GROUP BY clause. The conditions in the HAVING clause always relate to groups of rows, not to individual rows. Typically, conditions in the HAVING clause involve aggregate functions.

6. The sixth step sorts the results according to the ORDER BY clause. Note that the ORDER BY clause is optional. Table 3–18 shows the result table after sorting.

7. The seventh step performs a final projection. Columns appearing in the result of step 6 are eliminated if they do not appear in the SELECT clause. Table 3–19 (identical to Table 3–12) shows the result after the projection of step 6. The *Count(*)* column is eliminated because it does not appear in SELECT. The seventh step (projection) occurs after the sixth step (sorting) because the ORDER BY clause can contain columns that do not appear in the SELECT list.

This section finishes by discussing three major lessons about the conceptual evaluation process. These lessons are more important to remember than the specific details about the conceptual process.

- GROUP BY conceptually occurs after WHERE. If you have an error in a SELECT statement involving WHERE or GROUP BY, the problem is most likely in the WHERE clause. You can check the intermediate results after the WHERE clause by submitting a SELECT statement without the GROUP BY clause.

TABLE 3–16	Result of Step 4		
CourseNo	*O.OfferNo*	*AvgGrade*	*Count(*)*
IS320	3333	3.3	1
IS480	1111	3.3	3
IS480	2222	3.4	2

TABLE 3–17	Result of Step 5		
CourseNo	*O.OfferNo*	*AvgGrade*	*Count(*)*
IS480	1111	3.3	3
IS480	2222	3.4	2

TABLE 3–18	Result of Step 6		
CourseNo	*O.OfferNo*	*AvgGrade*	*Count(*)*
IS480	2222	3.4	3
IS480	1111	3.3	2

TABLE 3–19	Result of Step 7	
CourseNo	*O.OfferNo*	*AvgGrade*
IS480	2222	3.4
IS480	1111	3.3

- Grouping occurs only one time in the evaluation process. If your problem involves more than one independent aggregate calculation, you may need more than one SELECT statement.

- Using sample tables can help you analyze difficult problems. It is often not necessary to go through the entire evaluation process. Rather, use sample tables to understand only the difficult part. Section 3.5 and Chapter 4 depict the use of sample tables to help analyze some difficult problems.

3.4 CRITICAL QUESTIONS FOR QUERY FORMULATION

The conceptual evaluation process depicted in Figure 3.2 should help you understand the meaning of most SELECT statements, but it probably will not help you to formulate queries. Query formulation involves a mapping from a problem statement into a statement of a database language such as SQL as shown in Figure 3.3. In between the problem statement and the database language statement, you convert the problem statement into a database representation. Typically, the difficult part is to convert the problem statement into a database representation. This conversion involves a detailed knowledge of the tables and relationships and careful attention to possible ambiguities in the problem statement.

In converting from the problem statement into a database representation, you should answer three critical questions:

- What tables are needed?
- How are the tables combined?
- Does the output relate to individual rows or groups of rows?

For the first question, match the columns listed in the problem to be solved with columns from various tables. Include columns that are needed for output as well as for conditions. You also should include tables that are needed only to connect other tables. For example, if you want to join the *Student* and *Offering* tables, the *Enrollment* table should be included because it provides a connection to these tables. The *Student* and *Offering* tables cannot be combined directly. All tables needed in the query should be listed in the FROM clause.

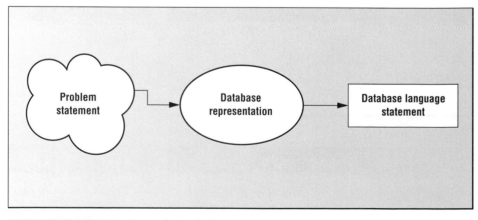

Figure 3.3 **Query formulation process.**

For the second question, most tables are combined by a join operation. In Chapter 4, you will use the outer join, difference, and division operators to combine tables. For now, just concentrate on combining tables with joins. You need to identify the matching columns for each join. In most joins, the primary key of one table is matched with a foreign key of another table. Occasionally, the primary key of both tables contains multiple columns. In this case, you need to match on both columns. In some situations, the matching columns do not involve a primary key/foreign key combination. You can perform a join as long as the matching columns have compatible data types. For example, when joining customer tables from different databases, there may not be a common primary key. Joining on other fields such as name, address, and so on may be necessary.

For the third question, look for computations involving aggregate functions. For example, the problem "list the name and average grade of students" contains an aggregate computation. Problems referencing an aggregate function indicate that the output relates to groups of rows. Hence the formulation requires a GROUP BY clause. If the problem contains conditions with aggregate functions, a HAVING clause should accompany the GROUP BY clause. For example, the problem "list the offer number of course offerings with more than 30 students" needs a HAVING clause with a condition involving the count function.

After answering these questions, you are ready to convert the database representation into a database language statement. To help in this process, you should develop a collection of statements for each kind of relational algebra operator using a database that you understand well. For example, you should have statements for problems that involve join operations, outer join operations, and other operators of relational algebra. As you increase your understanding of the database language, this conversion will become easy for most problems. For difficult problems such as those discussed in Section 3.5 and Chapter 4, relying on similar problems still may be useful because difficult problems are not common.

3.5 REFINING QUERY FORMULATION SKILLS WITH EXAMPLES

Let's apply your query formulation skills and knowledge of the SELECT statement to more difficult problems. All problems in this section involve the parts of SELECT discussed in Sections 3.2 and 3.3. The problems involve more difficult aspects such as joining more than two tables, grouping after joins of several tables, joining a table to itself, and traditional set operators.

3.5.1 Joining Multiple Tables with the Cross Product Style

Cross Product Style lists tables in the FROM clause and join conditions in the WHERE clause. The cross product style is easy to read but does not support outer join operations.

We begin with a number of join problems that are formulated using cross product operations in the FROM clause. This way to formulate joins is known as the cross product style because of the implied cross product operations. The next subsection uses join operations in the FROM clause to contrast the ways that joins can be expressed. In Example 3.23, some student rows appear more than once in the result. For example, Roberto Morales appears twice. Because of the 1-M relationship between the *Student* and *Enrollment* tables, a *Student* row can match multiple *Enrollment* rows.

EXAMPLE 3.23   Joining Two Tables

List the student name, offering number, and grade of students who have a grade ≥ 3.5 in a course offering.

```
SELECT StdFirstName, StdLastName, OfferNo, EnrGrade
  FROM Student, Enrollment
  WHERE EnrGrade >= 3.5
      AND Student.StdSSN = Enrollment.StdSSN
```

StdFirstName	StdLastName	OfferNo	EnrGrade
CANDY	KENDALL	1234	3.5
MARIAH	DODGE	1234	3.8
HOMER	WELLS	4321	3.5
ROBERTO	MORALES	4321	3.5
BOB	NORBERT	5679	3.7
ROBERTO	MORALES	5679	3.8
MARIAH	DODGE	6666	3.6
LUKE	BRAZZI	7777	3.7
BOB	NORBERT	9876	3.5
WILLIAM	PILGRIM	9876	4

Examples 3.24 and 3.25 depict duplicate elimination after a join. In Example 3.24, some students appear more than once as in Example 3.23. Because only student name appears in the output, duplicate rows appear. Example 3.25 uses the DISTINCT keyword to remove the duplicate rows.

EXAMPLE 3.24

Join with Duplicates

List the names of students who have a grade $\geq$ 3.5 in a course offering.

```
SELECT StdFirstName, StdLastName
  FROM Student, Enrollment
  WHERE EnrGrade >= 3.5
      AND Student.StdSSN = Enrollment.StdSSN
```

StdFirstName	StdLastName
CANDY	KENDALL
MARIAH	DODGE
HOMER	WELLS
ROBERTO	MORALES
BOB	NORBERT
ROBERTO	MORALES
MARIAH	DODGE
LUKE	BRAZZI
BOB	NORBERT
WILLIAM	PILGRIM

EXAMPLE 3.25

Join with Duplicates Removed

List the student names (without duplicates) who have a grade $\geq$ 3.5 in a course offering.

```
SELECT DISTINCT StdFirstName, StdLastName
  FROM Student, Enrollment
  WHERE EnrGrade >= 3.5
    AND Student.StdSSN = Enrollment.StdSSN
```

StdFirstName	StdLastName
BOB	NORBERT
CANDY	KENDALL
HOMER	WELLS
LUKE	BRAZZI
MARIAH	DODGE
ROBERTO	MORALES
WILLIAM	PILGRIM

Examples 3.26 through 3.29 depict problems involving more than two tables. In these problems, it is important to identify the tables in the FROM clause. Make sure that you examine conditions to test as well as columns in the result. In Example 3.28, the *Enrollment* table is needed even though it does not supply columns in the result or conditions to test. The *Enrollment* table is needed to connect the *Student* table with the *Offering* table. Example 3.29 extends Example 3.28 with details from the *Course* table. All five tables are needed to supply outputs, to test conditions, or to connect other tables.

EXAMPLE 3.26

Joining Three Tables with Columns from Only Two Tables
List the student name and the offering number in which the grade is greater than 3.7 and the offering is given in fall 1999.

```
SELECT StdFirstName, StdLastName, Enrollment.OfferNo
  FROM Student, Enrollment, Offering
  WHERE Student.StdSSN = Enrollment.StdSSN
    AND Offering.OfferNo = Enrollment.OfferNo
    AND OffYear = 1999 AND OffTerm = 'FALL'
    AND EnrGrade >= 3.7
```

StdFirstName	StdLastName	OfferNo
MARIAH	DODGE	1234

EXAMPLE 3.27

Joining Three Tables with Columns from Only Two Tables
List Leonard Vince's teaching schedule in fall 1999. For each course, list the offering number, course number, number of units, days, location, and time.

```
SELECT OfferNo, Offering.CourseNo, CrsUnits, OffDays,
          OffLocation, OffTime
  FROM Faculty, Course, Offering
  WHERE Faculty.FacSSN = Offering.FacSSN
    AND Offering.CourseNo = Course.CourseNo
    AND OffYear = 1999 AND OffTerm = 'FALL'
    AND FacFirstName = 'LEONARD'
    AND FacLastName = 'VINCE'
```

OfferNo	CourseNo	CrsUnits	OffDays	OffLocation	OffTime
1234	IS320	4	MW	BLM302	10:30 AM
4321	IS320	4	TTH	BLM214	3:30 PM

EXAMPLE 3.28

Joining Four Tables

List Bob Norbert's course schedule in spring 2000. For each course, list the offering number, course number, days, location, time, and faculty name.

```
SELECT Offering.OfferNo, Offering.CourseNo, OffDays,
       OffLocation, OffTime, FacFirstName, FacLastName
FROM Faculty, Offering, Enrollment, Student
WHERE Offering.OfferNo = Enrollment.OfferNo
    AND Student.StdSSN = Enrollment.StdSSN
    AND Faculty.FacSSN = Offering.FacSSN
    AND OffYear = 2000 AND OffTerm = 'SPRING'
    AND StdFirstName = 'BOB'
    AND StdLastName = 'NORBERT'
```

OfferNo	CourseNo	OffDays	OffLocation	OffTime	FacFirstName	FacLastName
5679	IS480	TTH	BLM412	3:30 PM	CRISTOPHER	COLAN
9876	IS460	TTH	BLM307	1:30 PM	LEONARD	FIBON

EXAMPLE 3.29

Joining Five Tables

List Bob Norbert's course schedule in spring 2000. For each course, list the offering number, course number, days, location, time, course units, and faculty name.

```
SELECT Offering.OfferNo, Offering.CourseNo, OffDays,
       OffLocation, OffTime, CrsUnits, FacFirstName,
       FacLastName
FROM Faculty, Offering, Enrollment, Student, Course
WHERE Faculty.FacSSN = Offering.FacSSN
    AND Offering.OfferNo = Enrollment.OfferNo
    AND Student.StdSSN = Enrollment.StdSSN
    AND Offering.CourseNo = Course.CourseNo
    AND OffYear = 2000 AND OffTerm = 'SPRING'
    AND StdFirstName = 'HOMER'
    AND StdLastName = 'WELLS'
```

OfferNo	CourseNo	OffDays	OffLocation	OffTime	CrsUnits	FacFirstName	FacLastName
5679	IS480	TTH	BLM412	3:30 PM	4	CRISTOPHER	COLAN
9876	IS460	TTH	BLM307	1:30 PM	4	LEONARD	FIBON

Example 3.30 demonstrates another way to combine the *Student* and *Faculty* tables. In Example 3.28, you saw it was necessary to combine the *Student, Enrollment, Offering,* and *Faculty* tables to find faculty teaching a specified student. To find students who are on the faculty (perhaps teaching assistants), the tables can be joined directly. Combining

the *Student* and *Faculty* tables in this way is similar to an intersection operation. However, intersection cannot actually be performed here because the *Student* and *Faculty* tables are not union compatible.

EXAMPLE 3.30

Joining Two Tables without Matching on a Primary and Foreign Key
List students who are on the faculty. Include all student columns in the result.

```
SELECT Student.*
  FROM Student, Faculty
  WHERE StdSSN = FacSSN
```

StdSSN	StdFirstName	StdLastName	StdCity	StdState	StdMajor	StdClass	StdGPA	StdZip
876-54-3210	CRISTOPHER	COLAN	SEATTLE	WA	IS	SR	4.00	98114-1332

Join Operator Style
lists join operations in the FROM clause using the INNER JOIN and ON keywords. The join operator style can be somewhat difficult to read for many join operations but supports outer join operations. The join operator style is a new element of SQL2.

A minor point about Example 3.30 is the use of the * after the SELECT keyword. Prefixing the * with a table name and period indicates all columns of the specified table are in the result. Using an * without a table prefix indicates that all columns from all FROM tables are in the result.

3.5.2 Joining Multiple Tables with the Join Operator Style

As demonstrated in Section 3.2, join operations can be expressed directly in the FROM clause using the INNER JOIN and ON keywords. This join operator style can be used to combine any number of tables. To ensure that you are comfortable using this style, this subsection presents examples of multiple table joins beginning with a two-table join in Example 3.31. Note that none of these examples executes in Oracle SQL.

EXAMPLE 3.31 (ACCESS)

Join Two Tables Using the Join Operator Style
Retrieve the name, city, and grade of students who have a high grade (greater than or equal to 3.5) in a course offering.

```
SELECT StdFirstName, StdLastName, StdCity, EnrGrade
  FROM Student INNER JOIN Enrollment
    ON Student.StdSSN = Enrollment.StdSSN
  WHERE EnrGrade >= 3.5
```

StdFirstName	StdLastName	StdCity	EnrGrade
CANDY	KENDALL	TACOMA	3.5
MARIAH	DODGE	SEATTLE	3.8
HOMER	WELLS	SEATTLE	3.5
ROBERTO	MORALES	SEATTLE	3.5
BOB	NORBERT	BOTHELL	3.7
ROBERTO	MORALES	SEATTLE	3.8
MARIAH	DODGE	SEATTLE	3.6
LUKE	BRAZZI	SEATTLE	3.7
BOB	NORBERT	BOTHELL	3.5
WILLIAM	PILGRIM	BOTHELL	4

The join operator style can be extended for any number of tables. Think of the join operator style as writing a complicated formula with lots of parentheses. To add another part to the formula, you need to add the arguments, operator, and another level of parentheses. For example, with the formula $(X + Y) * Z$, you can add another operation as $((X + Y) * Z) / W$. This same principle can be applied with the join operator style. Examples 3.32 and 3.33 extend Example 3.31 with additional conditions that need other tables. In both examples, another INNER JOIN is added to the end of the previous INNER JOIN operations. The INNER JOIN could also have been added at the beginning or middle if desired. The ordering of INNER JOIN operations is not important.

EXAMPLE 3.32 (ACCESS)

Join Three Tables Using the Join Operator Style

Retrieve the name, city, and grade of students who have a high grade (greater than or equal to 3.5) in a course offered in fall 1999.

```
SELECT StdFirstName, StdLastName, StdCity, EnrGrade
  FROM ( Student INNER JOIN Enrollment
    ON Student.StdSSN = Enrollment.StdSSN )
  INNER JOIN Offering
    ON Offering.OfferNo = Enrollment.OfferNo
  WHERE EnrGrade >= 3.5 AND OffTerm = 'FALL'
    AND OffYear = 1999
```

StdFirstName	StdLastName	StdCity	EnrGrade
CANDY	KENDALL	TACOMA	3.5
MARIAH	DODGE	SEATTLE	3.8
HOMER	WELLS	SEATTLE	3.5
ROBERTO	MORALES	SEATTLE	3.5

EXAMPLE 3.33 (ACCESS)

Join Four Tables Using the Join Operator Style

Retrieve the name, city, and grade of students who have a high grade (greater than or equal to 3.5) in a course offered in fall 1999 taught by Leonard Vince.

```
SELECT StdFirstName, StdLastName, StdCity, EnrGrade
  FROM ( (Student INNER JOIN Enrollment
    ON Student.StdSSN = Enrollment.StdSSN )
  INNER JOIN Offering
    ON Offering.OfferNo = Enrollment.OfferNo )
  INNER JOIN Faculty ON Faculty.FacSSN = Offering.FacSSN
  WHERE EnrGrade >= 3.5 AND OffTerm = 'FALL'
    AND OffYear = 1999 AND FacFirstName = 'LEONARD'
    AND FacLastName = 'VINCE'
```

StdFirstName	StdLastName	StdCity	EnrGrade
CANDY	KENDALL	TACOMA	3.5
MARIAH	DODGE	SEATTLE	3.8
HOMER	WELLS	SEATTLE	3.5
ROBERTO	MORALES	SEATTLE	3.5

The cross product and join operator styles can be mixed as demonstrated in Example 3.34. In most cases, it is preferable to use one style or the other, however.

**EXAMPLE 3.34
(ACCESS)**

Combine the Cross Product and Join Operator Styles

Retrieve the name, city, and grade of students who have a high grade (greater than or equal to 3.5) in a course offered in fall 1999 taught by Leonard Vince (same result as Example 3.33).

```
SELECT StdFirstName, StdLastName, StdCity, EnrGrade
   FROM ( (Student INNER JOIN Enrollment
      ON Student.StdSSN = Enrollment.StdSSN )
      INNER JOIN Offering
      ON Offering.OfferNo = Enrollment.OfferNo ),
      Faculty
   WHERE EnrGrade >= 3.5 AND OffTerm = 'FALL'
      AND OffYear = 1999 AND FacFirstName = 'LEONARD'
      AND FacLastName = 'VINCE'
      AND Faculty.FacSSN = Offering.FacSSN
```

The choice between the cross product and the join operator styles is largely a matter of preference. In the cross product style, it is easy to see the tables in the query. For multiple joins, the join operator style can be difficult to read because of nested parentheses. The primary advantage of the join operator style is that you can formulate queries involving outer joins as described in Chapter 4.

You should be conversant reading both join styles even if you only write queries using one style. You may need to maintain queries written with both styles. In addition, some visual query languages generate code in one of the styles. For example, Query Design, the visual query language of Microsoft Access, generates code in the join operator style.

3.5.3 Self-Joins and Multiple Joins between Two Tables

Self-Join a join between a table and itself (two copies of the same table). Self-joins are useful for finding relationships among rows of the same table.

Example 3.35 demonstrates a self-join, a join involving a table with itself. A self-join is necessary to find relationships among rows of the same table. The foreign key, *FacSupervisor,* shows relationships among *Faculty* rows. To find the supervisor name of a faculty member, match on the *FacSupervisor* column with the *FacSSN* column. The trick is to imagine that you are working with two copies of the *Faculty* table. One copy plays the role of the subordinate, while the other copy plays the role of the superior. In SQL, a self-join requires alias names (*Subr* and *Supr*) in the FROM clause to distinguish between the two roles or copies.

EXAMPLE 3.35

Self-Join

List faculty members who have a higher salary than their supervisor. List the social security number, the name, and the salary of the faculty member and the supervisor.

```
SELECT Subr.FacSSN, Subr.FacLastName, Subr.FacSalary,
         Supr.FacSSN, Supr.FacLastName, Supr.FacSalary
   FROM Faculty Subr, Faculty Supr
   WHERE Subr.FacSupervisor = Supr.FacSSN
      AND Subr.FacSalary > Supr.FacSalary
```

Subr.FacSSN	Subr.FacLastName	Subr.FacSalary	Supr.FacSSN	Supr.FacLastName	Supr.FacSalary
987-65-4321	MILLS	$75,000.00	765-43-2109	MACON	$65,000.00

Problems involving self-joins can be difficult to understand. If you are having trouble understanding Example 3.35, use the conceptual process to help. Start with a small *Faculty* table. Copy this table and use the names *Subr* and *Supr* to distinguish between the two copies. Join the two tables over *Subr.FacSupervisor* and *Supr.FacSSN*. If you need, derive the join using a cross product operation. You should be able to see that each result row in the join shows a subordinate and supervisor pair.

Problems involving self-referencing (unary) relationships are part of tree structured queries. In tree structured queries, a table can be visualized as a structure such as a tree or hierarchy. For example, the *Faculty* table has a structure showing an organization hierarchy. At the top, the college dean resides. At the bottom, faculty members without subordinates reside. Similar structures apply to the chart of accounts in accounting systems, part structures in manufacturing systems, and route networks in transportation systems.

A more difficult problem than a self-join is to find all subordinates (direct or indirect) in an organization hierarchy. This problem can be solved in SQL if the number of subordinate levels is known. One join for each subordinate level is needed. Without knowing the number of subordinate levels, this problem cannot be done in SQL2 although it can be solved in SQL3 and with proprietary extensions of SQL2. In SQL2, tree structured queries can be solved by using SQL inside a programming language.

Example 3.36 shows another difficult join problem. This problem involves two joins between the same two tables (*Offering* and *Faculty*). Alias table names (*O1* and *O2*) are needed to distinguish between the two copies of the *Offering* table used in the statement.

EXAMPLE 3.36   More Than One Join between Tables Using Alias Table Names
List the names of faculty members and the course number for which the faculty member teaches the same course as his or her supervisor in 2000.

```
SELECT FacFirstName, FacLastName, O1.CourseNo
    FROM Faculty, Offering O1, Offering O2
    WHERE Faculty.FacSSN = O1.FacSSN
        AND Faculty.FacSupervisor = O2.FacSSN
        AND O1.OffYear = 2000 AND O2.OffYear = 2000
        AND O1.CourseNo = O2.CourseNo
```

FacFirstName	FacLastName	CourseNo
LEONARD	VINCE	IS320
LEONARD	FIBON	IS320

If this problem is too difficult, use the conceptual evaluation process (Figure 3.2) with sample tables to gain insight. Perform a join between the sample *Faculty* and *Offering* tables, then join this result to another copy of *Offering* (*O2*) matching *FacSupervisor* with *O2.FacSSN*. In the resulting table, select the rows that have matching course numbers and year equal to 2000.

3.5.4 Combining Joins and Grouping

Example 3.37 demonstrates why it is sometimes necessary to group on multiple columns. After studying Example 3.37, you might be confused about the necessity to group on both *OfferNo* and *CourseNo*. One simple explanation is that any columns appearing in SELECT must be either a grouping column or an aggregrate expression. However, this explanation does not quite tell the entire story. Grouping on *OfferNo* alone produces the same values for the computed column *NumStudents* because *OfferNo* is the primary key. Including nonunique columns such as *CourseNo* adds information to each result row but does not change the aggregate calculations. If you do not understand this point, use sample tables to demonstrate it. When evaluating your sample tables, remember that joins occur before grouping.

EXAMPLE 3.37

Join with Grouping on Multiple Columns

List the course number, the offering number, and the number of students enrolled. Only include courses offered in spring 2000.

```
SELECT CourseNo, Enrollment.OfferNo, Count(*) AS
       NumStudents
  FROM Offering, Enrollment
  WHERE Offering.OfferNo = Enrollment.OfferNo
    AND OffYear = 2000 AND OffTerm = 'SPRING'
  GROUP BY Enrollment.OfferNo, CourseNo
```

CourseNo	OfferNo	NumStudents
FIN480	7777	3
IS460	9876	7
IS480	5679	6

Example 3.38 demonstrates another problem involving joins and grouping. An important part of this problem is to recognize the need for the *Student* table and the HAVING condition. They are needed because the problem statement refers to an aggregate function involving the *Student* table.

EXAMPLE 3.38

Joins, Grouping, and Group Conditions

List the course number, the offering number, and the average GPA of students enrolled. Only include courses offered in fall 1999 in which the average GPA of enrolled students is greater than 3.0.

```
SELECT CourseNo, Enrollment.OfferNo, Avg(GPA) AS AvgGPA
  FROM Student, Offering, Enrollment
  WHERE Offering.OfferNo = Enrollment.OfferNo
    AND Enrollment.StdSSN = Student.StdSSN
    AND OffYear = 1999 AND OffTerm = 'FALL'
  GROUP BY CourseNo, Enrollment.OfferNo
  HAVING Avg(GPA) > 3.0
```

CourseNo	OfferNo	AvgGPA
IS320	1234	3.23333330949148
IS320	4321	3.03333334128062

3.5.5 Traditional Set Operators in SQL

In SQL, you can directly use the traditional set operators with the UNION, INTER-SECT, and EXCEPT keywords. Some DBMSs including Microsoft Access do not support the INTERSECT and EXCEPT keywords. As with relational algebra, the problem is always to make sure that the tables are union compatible. In SQL, you can use a SELECT statement to make tables compatible. Examples 3.39 through 3.41 demonstrate set operations on column subsets of the *Faculty* and *Student* tables. The columns have been renamed to avoid confusion.

EXAMPLE 3.39	UNION Query

Show all faculty and students. Only show the common columns in the result.

```
SELECT FacSSN AS SSN, FacFirstName AS FirstName,
       FacLastName AS LastName, FacCity AS City, FacState
       AS State
   FROM Faculty
   UNION
SELECT StdSSN AS SSN, StdFirstName AS FirstName,
       StdLastName AS LastName, StdCity AS City, StdState
       AS State
   FROM Student
```

SSN	FirstName	LastName	City	State
098765432	LEONARD	VINCE	SEATTLE	WA
123456789	HOMER	WELLS	SEATTLE	WA
124567890	BOB	NORBERT	BOTHELL	WA
234567890	CANDY	KENDALL	TACOMA	WA
345678901	WALLY	KENDALL	SEATTLE	WA
456789012	JOE	ESTRADA	SEATTLE	WA
543210987	VICTORIA	EMMANUEL	BOTHELL	WA
567890123	MARIAH	DODGE	SEATTLE	WA
654321098	LEONARD	FIBON	SEATTLE	WA
678901234	TESS	DODGE	REDMOND	WA
765432109	NICKI	MACON	BELLEVUE	WA
789012345	ROBERTO	MORALES	SEATTLE	WA
876543210	CRISTOPHER	COLAN	SEATTLE	WA
890123456	LUKE	BRAZZI	SEATTLE	WA
901234567	WILLIAM	PILGRIM	BOTHELL	WA
987654321	JULIA	MILLS	SEATTLE	WA

**EXAMPLE 3.40
(ORACLE)**

INTERSECT Query

Show teaching assistants, faculty who are students. Only show the common columns in the result.

```
SELECT FacSSN AS SSN, FacFirstName AS FirstName,
        FacLastName AS LastName, FacCity AS City, FacState
        AS State
   FROM Faculty
      INTERSECT
SELECT StdSSN AS SSN, StdFirstName AS FirstName,
        StdLastName AS LastName, StdCity AS City, StdState
        AS State
   FROM Student
```

SSN	FirstName	LastName	City	State
876543210	CRISTOPHER	COLAN	SEATTLE	WA

**EXAMPLE 3.41
(ORACLE)**

Difference Query

Show faculty who are <u>not</u> students (pure faculty). Only show the common columns in the result. Oracle uses the MINUS keyword instead of the EXCEPT keyword used in SQL2.

```
SELECT FacSSN AS SSN, FacFirstName AS FirstName,
        FacLastName AS LastName, FacCity AS City, FacState
        AS State
   FROM Faculty
      MINUS
SELECT StdSSN AS SSN, StdFirstName AS FirstName,
        StdLastName AS LastName, StdCity AS City, StdState
        AS State
   FROM Student
```

SSN	FirstName	LastName	City	State
098765432	LEONARD	VINCE	SEATTLE	WA
543210987	VICTORIA	EMMANUEL	BOTHELL	WA
654321098	LEONARD	FIBON	SEATTLE	WA
765432109	NICKI	MACON	BELLEVUE	WA
987654321	JULIA	MILLS	SEATTLE	WA

By default, duplicate rows are removed in the results of SQL statements with the UNION, INTERSECT, and EXCEPT (MINUS) keywords. If you want to retain duplicate rows, use the ALL keyword after the operator. For example, the UNION ALL keyword performs a union operation but does not remove duplicate rows.

3.6 SQL Modification Statements

The modification statements support entering new rows (INSERT), changing columns in one or more rows (UPDATE), and deleting one or more rows (DELETE). Although well designed and powerful, they are not as widely used as SELECT because data entry forms are easier to use for end users.

The INSERT statement has two formats as demonstrated in Examples 3.42 and 3.43. In the first format, one row at a time can be added. You specify values for each column with the VALUES clause. You must format the constant values appropriate for each column. Refer to the documentation of your DBMS for details about specifying constants, especially string and date constants. Specifying a null value for a column is also not standard across DBMSs. In some systems, you simply omit the column name and the value. In other systems, you specify a particular symbol for a null value. Of course, you must be careful that the table definition permits null values for the column of interest. Otherwise, the INSERT statement will be rejected.

EXAMPLE 3.42   Single Row Insert

Insert a row into the *Student* table supplying values for all columns.

```
INSERT INTO Student (StdSSN, StdFirstName, StdLastName,
        StdCity, StdState, StdZip, StdClass, StdMajor, StdGPA)
    VALUES ('999999999', 'JOE', 'STUDENT", 'SEATAC',
        'WA', '98042-1121', 'FR', 'IS', 0.0)
```

The second format of the INSERT statement supports addition of a set of records as shown in Example 3.43. Using the SELECT statement inside the INSERT statement, you can specify any derived set of rows. You can use the second format when you want to create temporary tables for specialized processing.

EXAMPLE 3.43   Multiple Row Insert

Assume a new table *ISStudent* has been created previously. *ISStudent* has the same columns as *Student*. This INSERT statement adds rows from *Student* into *ISStudent*.

```
INSERT INTO ISStudent
    SELECT * FROM Student WHERE StdMajor = 'IS'
```

The UPDATE statement allows one or more rows to be changed. Any number of columns can be changed, although typically only one column at a time is changed. When changing the primary key, update rules on referenced rows may not allow the operation.

EXAMPLE 3.44   Single Column Update

Give faculty members in the MS department a 10 percent raise. Four rows are updated.

```
UPDATE Faculty
    SET FacSalary = FacSalary * 1.1
    WHERE FacDept = 'MS'
```

EXAMPLE 3.45	Update Multiple Columns

Change the major and class of Homer Wells. One row is updated.

```
UPDATE Student
   SET StdMajor = 'ACCT', StdClass = 'SO'
   WHERE StdFirstName = 'HOMER'
      AND StdLastName = 'WELLS'
```

The DELETE statement allows one or more rows to be removed. DELETE is subject to the rules on referenced rows. For example, a *Student* row cannot be deleted if related *Enrollment* rows exist and the deletion action is restrict.

EXAMPLE 3.46	Delete Selected Rows

Delete all IS majors who are seniors. Three rows are deleted.

```
DELETE FROM Student
   WHERE StdMajor = 'IS' AND StdClass = 'SR'
```

EXAMPLE 3.47	Delete All Rows in a Table.

Delete all rows in the *ISStudent* table

```
DELETE FROM ISStudent
```

Sometimes it is useful for the condition inside the WHERE clause of the DELETE statement to reference rows from other tables. Microsoft Access supports the join operator style to combine tables as shown in Example 3.48. You <u>cannot</u> use the cross product style inside a DELETE statement. Chapter 4 shows another way to reference other tables in a DELETE statement that most DBMSs (including Access and Oracle) support.

EXAMPLE 3.48 (ACCESS)	DELETE Statement Using the Join Operator Style

Delete offerings taught by Leonard Vince. Three Offering rows are deleted. In addition, this statement deletes related rows in the Enrollment table because the ON DELETE clause is set to CASCADE.

```
DELETE Offering.*
   FROM Offering INNER JOIN Faculty
      ON Offering.FacSSN = Faculty.FacSSN
   WHERE FacFirstName = 'LEONARD'
      AND FacLastName = 'VINCE'
```

CLOSING THOUGHTS

Chapter 3 has introduced you to the fundamental parts of the industry standard Structured Query Language (SQL). SQL has a wide scope covering database definition, manipulation, and control. As a result of careful analysis and compromise, standards groups have produced a well-designed language. SQL has become the common glue that binds the database industry. You will no doubt continually encounter SQL throughout your career.

This chapter has focused on the most widely used parts of the SELECT statement. Numerous examples were shown to demonstrate conditions on different data types, complex logical expressions, multiple table joins, summarization of tables with GROUP BY and HAVING, sorting of tables, and the traditional set operators. The subset of SELECT described in this chapter allows you to formulate problems involving the project, restrict, join, summarize, union, intersection, and difference operators of relational algebra. This chapter also briefly described the modification statements INSERT, UPDATE, and DELETE. These statements are not as complex and widely used as SELECT.

This chapter has emphasized several ways to help you formulate queries. A seven-step process using sample tables was introduced to help you see how a result is derived. You may find this evaluation process helps in your initial learning of SELECT as well as provides insight on more challenging problems. To help formulate queries, three questions were provided to guide you. You should explicitly or implicitly answer these questions before writing a SELECT statement to solve a problem. An understanding of both the critical questions and the conceptual evaluation process will provide you a solid foundation for using relational databases. Even with these formulation aids, you need to work many problems to learn query formulation and SELECT well.

This chapter covered an important subset of SELECT. Other parts of SELECT not covered in this chapter are outer joins, nested queries, and division problems. Chapter 4 covers advanced query formulation and additional parts of SELECT so that you can hone your skills.

REVIEW CONCEPTS

- SQL consists of statements for database definition (CREATE TABLE, ALTER TABLE, etc.), database manipulation (SELECT, INSERT, UPDATE, and DELETE), and database control (GRANT, REVOKE, etc.).
- SELECT is a complex statement. Chapter 3 covered SELECT statements with the format

  SELECT <list of column and column expressions>
  FROM <list of tables and join operations>
  WHERE <list of row conditions connected by AND, OR, and NOT>
  GROUP BY <list of columns>
  HAVING <list of group conditions connected by AND, OR, and NOT>
  ORDER BY <list of sorting specifications>

- Use the standard comparison operators to select rows:

  SELECT StdFirstName, StdLastName, StdCity, StdGPA
  FROM Student
  WHERE StdGPA >= 3.7

- Inexact matching is done with the LIKE operator and pattern-matching characters:

  Access:
  SELECT CourseNo, CrsDesc
  FROM Course
  WHERE CourseNo LIKE 'IS4*'

  Oracle:
  SELECT CourseNo, CrsDesc
  FROM Course
  WHERE CourseNo LIKE 'IS4%'

- Use BETWEEN . . . AND to compare dates:

  Access:

  ```
  SELECT FacFirstName, FacLastName, FacHireDate
    FROM Faculty
    WHERE FacHireDate BETWEEN #1/1/1994# AND
          #12/31/1995#
  ```

  Oracle:

  ```
  SELECT FacFirstName, FacLastName, FacHireDate
    FROM Faculty
    WHERE FacHireDate BETWEEN '1-Jan-1994' AND '31-Dec-
          1995'
  ```

- Use expressions in the SELECT and WHERE clauses:

  Access:

  ```
  SELECT FacFirstName, FacLastName, FacCity, FacSalary*1.1
          AS InflatedSalary, FacHireDate
    FROM Faculty
    WHERE year(FacHireDate) > 1991
  ```

  Oracle:

  ```
  SELECT FacFirstName, FacLastName, FacCity, FacSalary*1.1
          AS InflatedSalary, FacHireDate
    FROM Faculty
    WHERE to_number(to_char(FacHireDate, 'YYYY' ) ) >
          1991
  ```

- Test null values:

  ```
  SELECT OfferNo, CourseNo
    FROM Offering
    WHERE FacSSN IS NULL AND OffTerm = 'SUMMER'
    AND OffYear = 2000
  ```

- Create complex logical expressions with AND and OR:

  ```
  SELECT OfferNo, CourseNo, FacSSN
    FROM Offering
    WHERE (OffTerm = 'FALL' AND OffYear = 1999)
          OR (OffTerm = 'WINTER' AND OffYear = 2000)
  ```

- Sort results with the ORDER BY clause:

  ```
  SELECT StdGPA, StdFirstName, StdLastName, StdCity, StdState
    FROM Student
    WHERE StdClass = 'JR'
    ORDER BY StdGPA
  ```

- Eliminate duplicates with the DISTINCT keyword:

  ```
  SELECT DISTINCT FacCity, FacState
    FROM Faculty
  ```

- Qualify column names in join queries:

```
SELECT Course.CourseNo, CrsDesc
  FROM Offering, Course
  WHERE OffTerm = 'SPRING' AND OffYear = 2000
      AND Course.CourseNo = Offering.CourseNo
```

- Use the GROUP BY clause to summarize rows:

```
SELECT StdMajor, AVG(StdGPA) AS AvgGpa
  FROM Student
  GROUP BY StdMajor
```

- GROUP BY must precede HAVING:

```
SELECT StdMajor, AVG(StdGPA) AS AvgGpa
  FROM Student
  GROUP BY StdMajor
  HAVING AVG(StdGPA) > 3.1
```

- Use WHERE to test row conditions and HAVING to test group conditions:

```
SELECT StdMajor, AVG(StdGPA) AS AvgGpa
  FROM Student
  WHERE StdClass IN ('JR', 'SR')
  GROUP BY StdMajor
  HAVING AVG(StdGPA) > 3.1
```

- Difference between COUNT(*) and COUNT(DISTINCT column)—not supported by Access:

```
SELECT OffYear, COUNT(*) AS NumOfferings,
        COUNT(DISTINCT CourseNo) AS NumCourses
  FROM Offering
  GROUP BY OffYear
```

- Conceptual evaluation process lessons: use small sample tables, GROUP BY occurs after WHERE, only one grouping per SELECT statement.
- Query formulation questions: what tables?, how combined?, and row or group output?
- Join more than two tables with the cross product and join operator styles (not supported by Oracle):

```
SELECT OfferNo, Offering.CourseNo, CrsUnits, OffDays,
        OffLocation, OffTime
  FROM Faculty, Course, Offering
  WHERE Faculty.FacSSN = Offering.FacSSN
      AND Offering.CourseNo = Course.CourseNo
      AND OffYear = 1999 AND OffTerm = 'FALL'
      AND FacFirstName = 'LEONARD'
      AND FacLastName = 'VINCE'
SELECT OfferNo, Offering.CourseNo, CrsUnits, OffDays,
        OffLocation, OffTime
  FROM ( Faculty INNER JOIN Offering
        ON Faculty.FacSSN = Offering.FacSSN )
```

        INNER JOIN Course
            ON Offering.CourseNo = Course.CourseNo
       WHERE OffYear = 1999 AND OffTerm = 'FALL'
         AND FacFirstName = 'LEONARD'
         AND FacLastName = 'VINCE'

- Self-joins:

       SELECT Subr.FacSSN, Subr.FacLastName, Subr.FacSalary,
          Supr.FacSSN, Supr.FacLastName, Supr.FacSalary
       FROM Faculty Subr, Faculty Supr
       WHERE Subr.FacSupervisor = Supr.FacSSN AND
          Subr.FacSalary > Supr.FacSalary

- Combine joins and grouping:

       SELECT CourseNo, Enrollment.OfferNo, Count(*) AS
          NumStudents
       FROM Offering, Enrollment
       WHERE Offering.OfferNo = Enrollment.OfferNo
         AND OffYear = 2000 AND OffTerm = 'SPRING'
       GROUP BY Enrollment.OfferNo, CourseNo

- Traditional set operators and union compatibility:

       SELECT FacSSN AS SSN, FacLastName AS LastName FacCity
          AS City, FacState AS State
       FROM Faculty
        UNION
       SELECT StdSSN AS SSN, StdLastName AS LastName, StdCity
          AS City, StdState AS State
       FROM Student

- Use the INSERT statement to add one or more rows:

       INSERT INTO Student (StdSSN, StdFirstName, StdLastName,
          StdCity, StdState, StdClass, StdMajor, StdGPA)
       VALUES ('999999999', 'JOE', 'STUDENT', 'SEATAC', 'WA',
          'FR', 'IS', 0.0)

- Use the UPDATE statement to change columns in one or more rows:

       UPDATE Faculty
        SET FacSalary = FacSalary * 1.1
        WHERE FacDept = 'MS'

- Use the DELETE statement to remove one or more rows:

       DELETE FROM Student
        WHERE StdMajor = 'IS' AND StdClass = 'SR'

- Use a join operation inside a DELETE statement (Access only):

       DELETE Offering.*
        FROM Offering INNER JOIN Faculty
          ON Offering.FacSSN = Faculty.FacSSN
        WHERE FacFirstName = 'LEONARD'
         AND FacLastName = 'VINCE'

QUESTIONS

1. Why do some people pronounce SQL as "sequel"?

2. Why are the manipulation statements of SQL more widely used than the definition and control statements?

3. Is the SQL standard supported in whole or in part? Briefly explain.

4. From examples and discussion in Chapter 3, what parts of SELECT are not supported by all DBMSs?

5. Recite the rule about GROUP BY and HAVING.

6. Recite the rule about columns in SELECT when a GROUP BY clause is used.

7. How does a row condition differ from a group condition?

8. Why should row conditions be placed in the WHERE clause rather than the HAVING clause?

9. Why are most DBMSs not case sensitive when matching on string conditions?

10. Explain how working with sample tables can provide insight about difficult problems?

11. When working with date columns, why is it necessary to refer to documentation of your DBMS?

12. How do exact and inexact matching differ in SQL?

13. How do you know when the output of a query relates to groups of rows as opposed to individual rows?

14. What tables belong in the FROM statement?

15. Explain the cross product style for join operations.

16. Explain the join operator style for join operations.

17. Discuss the pros and cons of the cross product versus the join operator styles. Do you need to know both the cross product and the join operator styles?

18. What is a self-join? When is a self-join useful?

19. Provide a SELECT statement example in which a table is needed even though the table does not provide conditions to test or columns to show in the result.

20. What is the requirement to use the traditional set operators in SQL?

21. When combining joins and grouping, what conceptually occurs first, joins or grouping?

22. Why is the SELECT statement more widely used than the modification statements (INSERT, UPDATE, and DELETE)?

23. Provide an example of an INSERT statement that can insert multiple rows.

24. What is the relationship between the DELETE statement and the rules about deleting referenced rows?

25. What is the relationship between the UPDATE statement and the rules about updating the primary key of referenced rows?

PROBLEMS

The problems use the tables of the order entry database, an extension of the order entry tables used in the problems of Chapter 2. Table 3P–1 lists the meaning of each table and Figure 3P.1 shows the Access Relationship window. After the relationship diagram, row listings and Oracle CREATE TABLE statements are shown for each table. Note that the primary key of the *OrdLine* table is a combination of *OrdNo* and *ProdNo*. The *Employee* table has a self-referencing (unary) relationship to itself through the foreign key, *SupEmpNo*, the employee number of the supervising employee. In the relationship diagram, the table *Employee_1* is a representation of the self-referencing relationship, not a real table. The relationship from *OrderTbl* to *OrdLine* cascades deletions and primary key updates of referenced rows. All other relationships restrict deletions and primary key updates of referenced rows if related rows exist (NO ACTION).

TABLE 3P–1	Tables of the Order Entry Database
Table Name	*Description*
Customer	List of customers who have placed orders
OrderTbl	Contains the heading part of an order; Internet orders do not have an employee
Employee	List of employees who can take orders
OrdLine	Contains the detail part of an order
Product	List of products that may be ordered

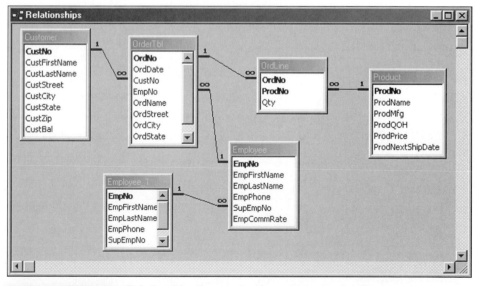

Figure 3P.1   **Relationship diagram for the order entry database.**

Customer							
CustNo	CustFirstName	CustLastName	CustStreet	CustCity	CustState	CustZip	CustBal
C0954327	Sheri	Gordon	336 Hill St.	Littleton	CO	80129-5543	$230.00
C1010398	Jim	Glussman	1432 E. Ravenna	Denver	CO	80111-0033	$200.00
C2388597	Beth	Taylor	2396 Rafter Rd.	Seattle	WA	98103-1121	$500.00
C3340959	Betty	Wise	4334 153rd NW	Seattle	WA	98178-3311	$200.00
C3499503	Bob	Mann	1190 Lorraine Cir.	Monroe	WA	98013-1095	$0.00
C8543321	Ron	Thompson	789 122nd St.	Renton	WA	98666-1289	$85.00
C8574932	Wally	Jones	411 Webber Ave.	Seattle	WA	98105-1093	$1,500.00
C8654390	Candy	Kendall	456 Pine St.	Seattle	WA	98105-3345	$50.00
C9128574	Jerry	Wyatt	16212 123rd Ct.	Denver	CO	80222-0022	$100.00
C9403348	Mike	Boren	642 Crest Ave.	Englewood	CO	80113-5431	$0.00
C9432910	Larry	Styles	9825 S. Crest Lane	Bellevue	WA	98104-2211	$250.00
C9543029	Sharon	Johnson	1223 Meyer Way	Fife	WA	98222-1123	$856.00
C9549302	Todd	Hayes	1400 NW 88th	Lynnwood	WA	98036-2244	$0.00
C9857432	Homer	Wells	123 Main St.	Seattle	WA	98105-4322	$500.00
C9865874	Mary	Hill	206 McCaffrey	Littleton	CO	80129-5543	$150.00
C9943201	Harry	Sanders	1280 S. Hill Rd.	Fife	WA	98222-2258	$1,000.00

OrderTbl								
OrdNo	OrdDate	CustNo	EmpNo	OrdName	OrdStreet	OrdCity	OrdState	OrdZip
O1116324	01/23/2000	C0954327	E8544399	Sheri Gordon	336 Hill St.	Littleton	CO	80129-5543
O1231231	01/23/2000	C9432910	E9954302	Larry Styles	9825 S. Crest Lane	Bellevue	WA	98104-2211
O1241518	02/10/2000	C9549302		Todd Hayes	1400 NW 88th	Lynnwood	WA	98036-2244
O1455122	01/09/2000	C8574932	E9345771	Wally Jones	411 Webber Ave.	Seattle	WA	98105-1093
O1579999	01/05/2000	C9543029	E8544399	Tom Johnson	1632 Ocean Dr.	Des Moines	WA	98222-1123
O1615141	01/23/2000	C8654390	E8544399	Candy Kendall	456 Pine St.	Seattle	WA	98105-3345
O1656777	02/11/2000	C8543321		Ron Thompson	789 122nd St.	Renton	WA	98666-1289
O2233457	01/12/2000	C2388597	E9884325	Beth Taylor	2396 Rafter Rd.	Seattle	WA	98103-1121
O2334661	01/14/2000	C0954327	E1329594	Mrs. Ruth Gordon	233 S. 166th	Seattle	WA	98011
O3252629	01/23/2000	C9403348	E9954302	Mike Boren	642 Crest Ave.	Englewood	CO	80113-5431
O3331222	01/13/2000	C1010398		Jim Glussman	1432 E. Ravenna	Denver	CO	80111-0033
O3377543	01/15/2000	C9128574	E8843211	Jerry Wyatt	16212 123rd Ct.	Denver	CO	80222-0022
O4714645	01/11/2000	C2388597	E1329594	Beth Taylor	2396 Rafter Rd.	Seattle	WA	98103-1121
O5511365	01/22/2000	C3340959	E9884325	Betty White	4334 153rd NW	Seattle	WA	98178-3311
O6565656	01/20/2000	C9865874	E8843211	Mr. Jack Sibley	166 E. 344th	Renton	WA	98006-5543
O7847172	01/23/2000	C9943201		Harry Sanders	1280 S. Hill Rd.	Fife	WA	98222-2258
O7959898	02/19/2000	C8543321	E8544399	Ron Thompson	789 122nd St.	Renton	WA	98666-1289
O7989497	01/16/2000	C3499503	E9345771	Bob Mann	1190 Lorraine Cir.	Monroe	WA	98013-1095
O8979495	01/23/2000	C9865874		Helen Sibley	206 McCaffrey	Renton	WA	98006-5543
O9919699	02/11/2000	C9857432	E9954302	Homer Wells	123 Main St.	Seattle	WA	98105-4322

Employee					
EmpNo	EmpFirstName	EmpLastName	EmpPhone	SupEmpNo	EmpCommRate
E1329594	Landi	Santos	(303) 789-1234	E8843211	0.02
E8544399	Joe	Jenkins	(303) 221-9875	E8843211	0.02
E8843211	Amy	Tang	(303) 556-4321	E9884325	0.04
E9345771	Colin	White	(303) 221-4453	E9884325	0.04
E9884325	Thomas	Johnson	(303) 556-9987		0.05
E9954302	Mary	Hill	(303) 556-9871	E8843211	0.02

Product					
ProdNo	ProdName	ProdMfg	ProdQOH	ProdPrice	ProdNextShipDate
P0036566	17 inch Color Monitor	ColorMeg, Inc.	12	$169.00	2/20/2000
P0036577	19 inch Color Monitor	ColorMeg, Inc.	10	$319.00	2/20/2000
P1114590	R3000 Color Laser Printer	Connex	5	$699.00	1/22/2000
P1412138	10 Foot Printer Cable	Ethlite	100	$12.00	
P1445671	8-Outlet Surge Protector	Intersafe	33	$14.99	
P1556678	CVP Ink Jet Color Printer	Connex	8	$99.00	1/22/2000
P3455443	Color Ink Jet Cartridge	Connex	24	$38.00	1/22/2000
P4200344	36-Bit Color Scanner	UV Components	16	$199.99	1/29/2000
P6677900	Black Ink Jet Cartridge	Connex	44	$25.69	
P9995676	Battery Back-up System	Cybercx	12	$89.00	2/1/2000

```
CREATE TABLE Customer
     (      CustNo          CHAR(8),
            CustFirstName   VARCHAR2(20) NOT NULL,
            CustLastName    VARCHAR2(30) NOT NULL,
            CustStreet      VARCHAR2(50),
            CustCity        VARCHAR2(30),
            CustState       CHAR(2),
            CustZip         CHAR(10),
            CustBal         DECIMAL(12,2) DEFAULT 0,
CONSTRAINT PKCustomer PRIMARY KEY (CustNo) )
```

OrdLine					
OrdNo	ProdNo	Qty	OrdNo	ProdNo	Qty
O1116324	P1445671	1	O3377543	P9995676	1
O1231231	P0036566	1	O4714645	P0036566	1
O1231231	P1445671	1	O4714645	P9995676	1
O1241518	P0036577	1	O5511365	P1412138	1
O1455122	P4200344	1	O5511365	P1445671	1
O1579999	P1556678	1	O5511365	P1556678	1
O1579999	P6677900	1	O5511365	P3455443	1
O1579999	P9995676	1	O5511365	P6677900	1
O1615141	P0036566	1	O6565656	P0036566	10
O1615141	P1445671	1	O7847172	P1556678	1
O1615141	P4200344	1	O7847172	P6677900	1
O1656777	P1445671	1	O7959898	P1412138	5
O1656777	P1556678	1	O7959898	P1556678	5
O2233457	P0036577	1	O7959898	P3455443	5
O2233457	P1445671	1	O7959898	P6677900	5
O2334661	P0036566	1	O7989497	P1114590	2
O2334661	P1412138	1	O7989497	P1412138	2
O2334661	P1556678	1	O7989497	P1445671	3
O3252629	P4200344	1	O8979495	P1114590	1
O3252629	P9995676	1	O8979495	P1412138	1
O3331222	P1412138	1	O8979495	P1445671	1
O3331222	P1556678	1	O9919699	P0036577	1
O3331222	P3455443	1	O9919699	P1114590	1
O3377543	P1445671	1	O9919699	P4200344	1

```
CREATE TABLE OrderTbl
    (       OrdNo           CHAR(8),
            OrdDate         DATE NOT NULL,
            CustNo          CHAR(8) NOT NULL,
            EmpNo           CHAR(8),
            OrdName         VARCHAR2(50),
            OrdStreet       VARCHAR2(50),
            OrdCity         VARCHAR2(30),
            OrdState        CHAR(2),
            OrdZip          CHAR(10),
CONSTRAINT PKOrderTbl PRIMARY KEY (OrdNo) ,
CONSTRAINT FKCustNo FOREIGN KEY (CustNo) REFERENCES Customer ,
CONSTRAINT FKEmpNo FOREIGN KEY (EmpNo) REFERENCES Employee )
```

```
CREATE TABLE OrdLine
     (      OrdNo          CHAR(8),
            ProdNo         CHAR(8),
            Qty            INTEGER DEFAULT 1,
CONSTRAINT PKOrdLine PRIMARY KEY (OrdNo, ProdNo),
CONSTRAINT FKOrdNo FOREIGN KEY (OrdNo) REFERENCES OrderTbl
  ON DELETE CASCADE,
CONSTRAINT FKProdNo FOREIGN KEY (ProdNo) REFERENCES Product )
```

```
CREATE TABLE Employee
     (      EmpNo           CHAR(8),
            EmpFirstName    VARCHAR2(20) NOT NULL,
            EmpLastName     VARCHAR2(30) NOT NULL,
            EmpPhone        CHAR(15),
            SupEmpNo        CHAR(8),
            EmpCommRate     DECIMAL(3,3) DEFAULT 0,
CONSTRAINT PKEmployee PRIMARY KEY (EmpNo),
CONSTRAINT FKSupEmpNo FOREIGN KEY (SupEmpNo) REFERENCES Employee )
```

```
CREATE TABLE Product
     (      ProdNo          CHAR(8),
            ProdName        VARCHAR2(50) NOT NULL,
            ProdMfg         VARCHAR2(20) NOT NULL,
            ProdQOH         INTEGER DEFAULT 0,
            ProdPrice       DECIMAL(12,2) DEFAULT 0,
            ProdNextShipDate DATE,
CONSTRAINT PKProduct PRIMARY KEY (ProdNo) )
```

Part 1: SELECT

1. List the customer number, name (first and last), and balance of customers.

2. List the customer number, name (first and last), and balance of customers who reside in Colorado (CustState is 'CO').

3. List all columns of the *Product* table for products costing more than $50. Order the result by product manufacturer (*ProdMfg*) and product name.

4. List the order number, order date, and shipping name (*OrdName*) of orders sent to addresses in Denver or Englewood.

5. List the customer number, name (first and last), city, and balance of customers who reside in Denver with a balance greater than $150 or who reside in Seattle with a balance greater than $300.

6. List the cities and states where orders have been placed. Remove duplicates from the result.

7. List all columns of the *OrderTbl* table for Internet orders placed in January 2000. An Internet order does not have an associated employee.

8. List all columns of the *OrderTbl* table for phone orders placed in February 2000. A phone order has an associated employee.

9. List all columns of the *Product* table that contain the words 'Ink Jet' in the product name.

10. List the order number, order date, and customer number of orders placed after January 23, 2000, that are shipped to Washington recipients.

11. List the order number, order date, customer number, and customer name (first and last) of orders placed in January 2000 sent to Colorado recipients.

12. List the order number, order date, customer number, and customer name (first and last) of orders placed in January 2000 placed by Colorado customers (*CustState*) but sent to Washington recipients (*OrdState*).

13. List the customer number, name (first and last), and balance of Washington customers who have placed one or more orders in February 2000. Remove duplicate rows from the result.

14. List the order number, order date, customer number, customer name (first and last), employee number, and employee name (first and last) of January 2000 orders placed by Colorado customers.

15. List the employee number, name (first and last), and phone of employees who have taken orders in January 2000 from customers with balances greater than $200. Remove duplicate rows in the result.

16. List the product number, name, and price of products ordered by customer number C0954327 in January 2000. Remove duplicate products in the result.

17. List the customer number, name (first and last), order number, order date, employee number, employee name (first and last), product number, product name, and order cost (`OrdLine.Qty * ProdPrice`) for products ordered on January 23, 2000, in which the order cost exceeds $150.

18. List the average balance of customers by city. Only include customers residing in Washington state ('WA').

19. List the average balance of customers by city and short zip code (the first five digits of the zip code). Only include customers residing in Washington state ('WA'). In Microsoft Access, the expression `left (CustZip, 5)` returns the first five digits of the zip code. In Oracle, the expression `substr (CustZip, 1, 5)` returns the first five digits.

20. List the average balance and number of customers by city. Only include customers residing in Washington state ('WA'). Eliminate cities in the result with less than two customers.

21. List the number of unique short zip codes and average customer balance by city. Only include customers residing in Washington state ('WA'). Eliminate cities in

the result in which the average balance is less than $100. (Note: this problem requires two SELECT statements in Access SQL.)

22. List the order number and the total amount of the order for orders on January 23, 2000. The total amount of an order is the sum of the quantity times the product price for each product on the order.

23. List the order number, order date, customer name (first and last), and total amount of the order for orders on January 23, 2000. The total amount of an order is the sum of the quantity times the product price for each product on the order.

24. List the customer number, customer name (first and last), the sum of the quantity of products ordered, and the total amount of products ordered in January 2000. Only include products in which the product name contains the string 'Ink Jet' or 'Laser'. Only include customers who have ordered more than three 'Ink Jet' or 'Laser' products in January 2000.

25. List the product number, product name, quantity of products ordered, and total amount of products ordered for products ordered in January 2000. Only include products that have more than five products ordered in January 2000. Sort the result by descending total amount.

26. List the order number, order date, customer number, customer name (first and last), customer state, and shipping state (*OrdState*) in which the customer state differs from the shipping state.

27. List the employee number, employee name (first and last), commission rate, supervising employee name (first and last), and commission rate of the supervisor.

28. List the employee number, employee name (first and last), and total amount of commissions on orders taken in January 2000. The amount of a commission is the sum of the dollar amount of products ordered times the commission rate of the employee.

29. List the union of the name, street, city, state, and zip of customers and order recipients. You need to use the concatenation function to combine the first and last names so that they can be compared to the order recipient name. In Access SQL, the & symbol is the concatenation function. In Oracle SQL, the ǁ symbol is the concatenation function.

30. List the first and last name of customers who have the same name (first and last) as an employee.

31. List the employee number and name (first and last) of second-level subordinates (subordinates of subordinates) of the employee named Thomas Johnson.

32. List the employee number and name (first and last) of the first- and second-level subordinates of the employee named Thomas Johnson. To distinguish the level of subordinates, include a computed column with subordinate level (1 or 2).

33. Using a mix of the join operator and the cross product styles, list the names (first and last) of customers who have placed orders taken by Amy Tang. Remove duplicate rows in the result. Note that Oracle does not support the join operator style.

34. Using the join operator style, list the product name and the price of all products ordered by Beth Taylor in January 2000. Remove duplicate rows from the result.

Part 2: INSERT, UPDATE, and DELETE statements

1. Insert yourself as a new row in the *Customer* table.

2. Insert your roommate, best friend, or significant other as a new row in the *Employee* table.

3. Insert a new *OrderTbl* row with you as the customer, the person from Problem 2 (Part 2) as the employee, and your choice of values for the other columns of the *OrderTbl* table.

4. Insert two rows in the *OrdLine* table corresponding to the *OrderTbl* row inserted in Problem 3 (Part 2).

5. Increase the price by 10 percent of products containing the words 'Ink Jet'.

6. Change the address (street, city, and zip) of the new row inserted in Problem 1 (Part 2).

7. Identify an order that respects the rules about deleting referenced rows to delete the rows inserted in Problems 1 to 4 (Part 2)?

8. Delete the new row(s) of the table listed first in the order for Problem 7 (Part 2).

9. Delete the new row(s) of the table listed second in the order for Problem 7 (Part 2).

10. Delete the new row(s) of the remaining tables listed in the order for Problem 7 (Part 2).

REFERENCES FOR FURTHER STUDY

Beyond the SQL coverage in this book, you will need specialized books on SQL2 such as Bowman, Emerson, and Darnovsky (1996); Cannan and Otten (1992); Celko (1997); Date and Darwen (1997); and Melton and Simon (1992). Groff and Weinberg (1999) provide a comprehensive review of the commercial dialects of SQL along with a CD-ROM with demonstration versions of Oracle, Microsoft SQL Server, Informix, Sybase, and DB2. The SQL Server Pro (http://www.inquiry.com/techtips/thesqlpro/) and the database information center of the *Intelligent Enterprise* magazine (http://www.iemagazine.com/) have plenty of practical advice about SQL. For product-specific SQL advice, the Advisor.com site (http://www.advisor.com/) features technical journals for Microsoft SQL Server and Microsoft Access and Visual Basic.

Appendix 3.A **SQL2 Syntax Summary**

This appendix summarizes the SQL2 syntax for the SELECT, INSERT, UPDATE, and DELETE statements presented in the chapter. The syntax is limited to the simplified structure presented in the chapter. More complex syntax is introduced in the following chapter. The conventions used in the syntax notation are identical to those used at the end of Chapter 2.

Simplified SELECT Syntax

```
<Select-Statement>: { <Simple-Select> | <Set-Select> }
  [ ORDER BY <Sort-Specification>* ]
<Simple-Select>:
  SELECT [ DISTINCT ] <Column-Specification>*
  FROM <Table-Specification>
  [ WHERE <Row-Condition> ]
  [ GROUP BY ColumnName* ]
  [ HAVING <Group-Condition> ]
<Column-Specification>: { <Column-List> | <Column-Item> }
<Column-List>: { * | TableName.* }—* is a literal here not a syntax symbol
<Column-Item>: <Column-Expression> [ AS ColumnName ]
<Column-Expression>:
  { <Scalar-Expression> | <Aggregate-Expression> }
<Scalar-Expression>:
  { (Scalar-Item) | <Scalar-Item> <Arith-Operator> <Scalar-Item> }
<Scalar-Item>: [ { + | - } ]
  { [ TableName.]ColumnName |
    Constant |
    FunctionName [ (Argument*) ] |
    <Scalar-Expression> |
    ( <Scalar-Expression> ) }
<Arith-Operator>: { + | − | * | / }
<Aggregate-Expression>:
  { SUM ( {<Scalar-Expression> | DISTINCT ColumnName } ) |
    AVG ( {<Scalar-Expression> | DISTINCT ColumnName } ) |
    MIN ( <Scalar-Expression> ) |
    MAX ( <Scalar-Expression> ) |
    COUNT ( [ DISTINCT ] ColumnName ) |
    COUNT ( * ) }—* is a literal symbol here, not a special syntax symbol
<Table-Specification>: { <Simple-Table>* | <Join-Operation> }
<Simple-Table>: TableName [ AliasName ]
<Join-Operation>:
  { TableName [ INNER ] JOIN TableName ON <Join-Condition> |
    { TableName | <Join-Operation> } [ INNER ] JOIN
```

```
    { TableName | <Join-Operation> } ON <Join-Condition> |
  ( <Join-Operation> ) }
<Join-Condition>: { <Simple-Join-Condition> | <Compound-Join-Condition> }
<Simple-Join-Condition>: <Scalar-Expression> <Comparison-Operator>
        <Scalar-Expression>
<Compound-Join-Condition>:
  { NOT <Join-Condition> |
    <Join-Condition> AND <Join-Condition> |
    <Join-Condition> OR <Join-Condition> |
    ( <Join-Condition> )
<Comparison-Operator>: { = | <|> | <= | >= | <> }
<Row-Condition>: { <Simple-Condition> | <Compound-Condition> }
<Simple-Condition>:
{ <Scalar-Expression> <Comparison-Operator> <Scalar-Expression> |
  <Scalar-Expression> [ NOT ] IN ( Constant* ) |
  <Scalar-Expression> BETWEEN <Scalar-Expression> AND <Scalar-Expression> |
  <Scalar-Expression> IS [NOT] NULL |
  ColumnName [ NOT ] LIKE StringPattern }
<Compound-Condition>:
  { NOT <Row-Condition> |
    <Row-Condition> AND <Row-Condition> |
    <Row-Condition> OR <Row-Condition> |
    ( <Row-Condition> ) }
<Group-Condition>: { <Simple-Group-Condition> | <Compound-Group-Condition> }
<Simple-Group-Condition>:—permits both scalar and aggregate expressions
  { <Column-Expression> ComparisonOperator < Column-Expression> |
    <Column-Expression> [ NOT ] IN ( Constant* ) |
    <Column-Expression> BETWEEN <Column-Expression> AND <Column-Expression> |
    <Column-Expression> IS [NOT] NULL |
    ColumnName [ NOT ] LIKE StringPattern }
<Compound-Group-Condition>:
  { NOT <Group-Condition> |
    <Group-Condition> AND <Group-Condition> |
    <Group-Condition> OR <Group-Condition> |
    ( <Group-Condition> ) }
<Sort-Specification>: { ColumnName | ColumnNumber } [ { ASC | DESC } ]
<Set-Select>: { <Simple-Select> | <Set-Select> } <Set-Operator>
        { <Simple-Select> | <Set-Select> }
<Set-Operator>: { UNION | INTERSECT | EXCEPT } [ ALL ]
```

INSERT Syntax

```
INSERT INTO TableName ( ColumnName* )
  VALUES ( Constant* )
INSERT INTO TableName [ ( ColumnName* ) ]
  <Simple-Select>
```

UPDATE Syntax

```
UPDATE TableName
  SET <Column-Assignment>*
  [ WHERE <Row-Condition> ]
  <Column-Assignment>: ColumnName = <Scalar-Expression>
```

DELETE Syntax

```
DELETE FROM TableName
  [ WHERE <Row-Condition> ]
DELETE TableName.*—* is a literal symbol here not a special syntax symbol
  FROM <Join-Operation>
  [ WHERE <Row-Condition> ]
```

Appendix 3.B   **Syntax Differences among Major Database Products**

Table 3B–1 summarizes syntax differences among Microsoft Access (1997 and 2000 versions), Oracle 8, Microsoft SQL Server, and IBM's DB2. The differences involve the parts of the SELECT statement presented in the chapter.

TABLE 3B–1	**SELECT Syntax Differences among Major Database Products**			
Element/Product	*Oracle 8*	*Access 97/2000*	*MS SQL Server 7*	*DB2*
Pattern-matching characters	%, __	*, ?	%, __	%, __
Case sensitivity in string matching	Yes	No	Yes	Yes
Date constants	Surround in single quotation marks	Surround in # symbols	Surround in single quotation marks	Surround in single quotation marks
Inequality symbol	<>	<>	!=	<>
Join operator style	No	Yes	Yes	Yes
Difference operations	MINUS keyword	Not supported	Not supported	EXCEPT keyword

Advanced Query Formulation with SQL

Learning Objectives

This chapter extends your query formulation skills by explaining advanced table-matching problems involving the outer join, difference, and division operators. Other parts of the SELECT statement are demonstrated to explain these advanced matching problems. In addition, the subtle effects of null values are explained to provide a deeper understanding of query formulation. After this chapter, you should have acquired the following knowledge and skills:

- Recognize Type I nested queries for joins and understand the conceptual evaluation process.

- Recognize Type II nested queries and understand the conceptual evaluation process.

- Recognize problems involving the outer join, difference, and division operators.

- Formulate problems involving the outer join, difference, and division operators.

- Understand the effect of null values on conditions, aggregate calculations, and grouping.

OVERVIEW

Chapter 3 provided a foundation for query formulation using SQL. Most importantly, you learned an important subset of SELECT and how to apply it to problems involving joins and grouping. This chapter extends your knowledge of query formulation to advanced matching problems. To solve these advanced matching problems, additional parts of the SELECT statement are introduced.

This chapter continues with the learning approaches of Chapter 3: provide many examples to imitate and conceptual models to help you reason through difficult problems. You first will learn how to formulate problems involving the outer join operator using new keywords in the FROM clause. You next will learn about nested queries and how they can be used in advanced matching problems. Then you will learn how to formulate problems involving the division operator using the GROUP BY clause and the COUNT function. Finally, you will learn the effect of null values on simple conditions, compound conditions with Boolean operators, aggregate calculations, and grouping. As in Chapter 3, all examples execute in both Microsoft Access (1997 and 2000 versions) and Oracle 8 except where noted.

4.1 OUTER JOIN PROBLEMS

One of the powerful but sometimes confusing aspects of SQL is the number of ways to express a join. In Chapter 3, you formulated joins using the cross product style and the join operator style. In the cross product style, you list the tables in the FROM clause and the join conditions in the WHERE clause. In the join operator style, you write join operations directly in the FROM clause using the INNER JOIN and ON keywords.

The major advantage of the join operator style is that problems involving the outer join operator can be formulated. Outer join problems cannot be formulated with the cross product style except with proprietary SQL extensions. This section demonstrates the join operator style for outer join problems and combinations of inner and outer joins. In addition, the proprietary outer join extension of Oracle is shown. For your reference, the relationship diagram of the university database is repeated from Chapter 3 (see Figure 4.1).

4.1.1 SQL Support for Outer Join Problems

A join between two tables generates a table with the rows that match on the join column(s). The outer join operator generates the join result (the matching rows) plus the nonmatching rows. A one-sided outer join generates a new table with the matching rows plus the nonmatching rows from one of the tables. For example, it can be useful to see all offerings listed in the output even if an offering does not have an assigned faculty.

SQL uses the LEFT JOIN and RIGHT JOIN keywords[1] to produce a one-sided outer join. The LEFT JOIN keyword means generate a table containing the matching rows and the nonmatching rows of the "left" table. The RIGHT JOIN keyword means generate a table containing the matching rows and the nonmatching rows of the "right" table. Thus, the result of a one-sided outer join depends on the direction (RIGHT or LEFT) and the position of the table names. Examples 4.1 and 4.2 demonstrate one-sided outer joins using both the LEFT and RIGHT keywords. The result rows with blank values for certain columns are nonmatched rows.

One-Sided Outer Join
an operator that generates the join result (the matching rows) plus the nonmatching rows from one of the input tables. SQL supports the one-sided outer join operator through the LEFT JOIN and RIGHT JOIN keywords.

---

[1]The full SQL keywords are LEFT OUTER JOIN and RIGHT OUTER JOIN. The SQL2 standard and most DBMSs allow omission of the OUTER keyword.

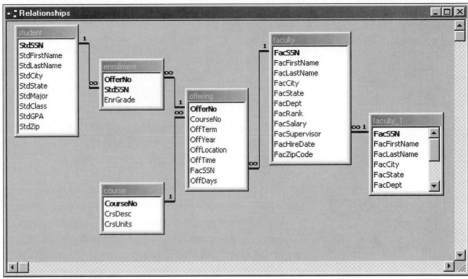

Figure 4.1   Relationship window for the university database.

**EXAMPLE 4.1
(ACCESS)**

One-Sided Outer Join Using LEFT JOIN

For IS course offerings, retrieve the offer number, the course number, the faculty number, and the faculty name. Include an offering in the result even if the faculty is not yet assigned.

```
SELECT OfferNo, CourseNo, Offering.FacSSN,
Faculty.FacSSN,
        FacFirstName, FacLastName
FROM Offering LEFT JOIN Faculty
        ON Offering.FacSSN = Faculty.FacSSN
WHERE CourseNo LIKE 'IS*'
```

OfferNo	CourseNo	Offering.FacSSN	Faculty.FacSSN	FacFirstName	FacLastName
1111	IS320				
2222	IS460				
1234	IS320	098-76-5432	098-76-5432	LEONARD	VINCE
3333	IS320	098-76-5432	098-76-5432	LEONARD	VINCE
4321	IS320	098-76-5432	098-76-5432	LEONARD	VINCE
4444	IS320	543-21-0987	543-21-0987	VICTORIA	EMMANUEL
8888	IS320	654-32-1098	654-32-1098	LEONARD	FIBON
9876	IS460	654-32-1098	654-32-1098	LEONARD	FIBON
5679	IS480	876-54-3210	876-54-3210	CHRISTOPHER	COLAN
5678	IS480	987-65-4321	987-65-4321	JULIA	MILLS

**EXAMPLE 4.2
(ACCESS)**

One-Sided Outer Join Using RIGHT JOIN
For IS course offerings, retrieve the offer number, course number, faculty number, and faculty name. Include an offering in the result even if the faculty is not yet assigned. The result is identical to Example 4.1.

```
SELECT OfferNo, CourseNo, Offering.FacSSN, Faculty.FacSSN,
         FacFirstName, FacLastName
  FROM Faculty RIGHT JOIN Offering
         ON Offering.FacSSN = Faculty.FacSSN
  WHERE CourseNo LIKE 'IS*'
```

Oracle developed a proprietary extension for one-sided outer joins before the join operator style was standardized in SQL2. To express a one-sided outer join in Oracle SQL, you use the notation (+) as part of a join condition in the WHERE clause. You place the (+) notation just after the join column of the "null" table, that is, the table with null values in the result. This placement reverses the usage of the SQL2 LEFT and RIGHT keywords by the table to preserve. The Oracle formulations of Examples 4.1 and 4.2 demonstrate the (+) notation.

**EXAMPLE 4.1
(ORACLE)**

One-Sided Outer Join Using LEFT JOIN
The (+) notation is placed after the *Faculty.FacSSN* column in the join condition because *Faculty* is the null table in the result.

```
SELECT OfferNo, CourseNo, Offering.FacSSN, Faculty.FacSSN,
         FacFirstName, FacLastName
  FROM Faculty, Offering
  WHERE  Offering.FacSSN = Faculty.FacSSN (+)
     AND CourseNo LIKE 'IS%'
```

**EXAMPLE 4.2
(ORACLE)**

One-Sided Outer Join Using RIGHT JOIN
The (+) notation is placed after the *Faculty.FacSSN* column in the join condition because *Faculty* is the null table in the result.

```
SELECT OfferNo, CourseNo, Offering.FacSSN, Faculty.FacSSN,
         FacFirstName, FacLastName
  FROM Faculty, Offering
  WHERE  Faculty.FacSSN (+) = Offering.FacSSN
     AND CourseNo LIKE 'IS%'
```

It should be noted that the proprietary extension of Oracle and other DBMSs is inferior to the SQL2 notation. The proprietary extension does not allow specification of the order of performing outer joins. This limitation can be problematic on difficult problems involving more than one outer join. In practice, this limitation is not too restrictive because problems with more than one outer join are not common.

Another use of the one-sided outer join operator is to generate a table with only nonmatching rows. The IS NULL comparison operator can remove rows that match, as demonstrated in Example 4.3.

**EXAMPLE 4.3
(ACCESS)**

One-Sided Outer Join with Only Nonmatching Rows
Retrieve the social security number, the name, the department, and the salary of faculty who are <u>not</u> students.

```
SELECT FacSSN, FacFirstName, FacLastName, FacSalary
FROM Faculty LEFT JOIN Student
        ON Faculty.FacSSN = Student.StdSSN
WHERE Student.StdSSN IS NULL
```

FacSSN	FacFirstName	FacLastName	FacSalary
098-76-5432	LEONARD	VINCE	$35,000.00
543-21-0987	VICTORIA	EMMANUEL	$120,000.00
654-32-1098	LEONARD	FIBON	$70,000.00
765-43-2109	NICKI	MACON	$65,000.00
987-65-4321	JULIA	MILLS	$75,000.00

**EXAMPLE 4.3
(ORACLE)**

One-Sided Outer Join with Only Nonmatching Rows
Retrieve the social security number, the name, the department, and the salary of faculty who are <u>not</u> students.

```
SELECT FacSSN, FacFirstName, FacLastName, FacSalary
 FROM Faculty, Student
 WHERE Faculty.FacSSN = Student.StdSSN (+)
        AND Student.StdSSN IS NULL
```

Full Outer Join   an operator that generates the join result (the matching rows) plus the nonmatching rows from both input tables. SQL supports the full outer join operator through the FULL JOIN keyword.

A <u>full outer join</u> generates a table with the matching rows plus the nonmatching rows from both tables. Typically, a full outer join is used to combine two similar but not union compatible tables. For example, the *Student* and *Faculty* tables are similar because they contain information about university people. However, they are not union compatible. They have common columns such as last name, city, and social security number but also unique columns such as GPA and salary. Occasionally, you will need to write a query that combines both tables. For example, find all university people within a certain city. A full outer join is used in such problems.

SQL2 provides the FULL OUTER JOIN keyword as demonstrated in Example 4.4. Note the null values in both halves (*Student* and *Faculty*) of the result.

**EXAMPLE 4.4
(SQL2)**

Full Outer Join
Combine the *Faculty* and *Student* tables using a full outer join. List the social security, the name (first and last), the salary (faculty only), and the GPA (students only) in the result. This SQL statement does not execute in Microsoft Access.

```
SELECT FacSSN, FacFirstName, FacLastName, FacSalary,
        StdSSN, StdFirstName, StdLastName, StdGPA
 FROM Faculty FULL JOIN Student
        ON Student.StdSSN = Faculty.FacSSN
```

FacSSN	FacFirstName	FacLastName	FacSalary	StdSSN	StdFirstName	StdLastName	StdGPA
				123456789	HOMER	WELLS	3
				124567890	BOB	NORBERT	2.7
				234567890	CANDY	KENDALL	3.5
				345678901	WALLY	KENDALL	2.8
				456789012	JOE	ESTRADA	3.2
				567890123	MARIAH	DODGE	3.6
				678901234	TESS	DODGE	3.3
				789012345	ROBERTO	MORALES	2.5
				890123456	LUKE	BRAZZI	2.2
				901234567	WILLIAM	PILGRIM	3.8
098765432	LEONARD	VINCE	35000				
543210987	VICTORIA	EMMANUEL	120000				
654321098	LEONARD	FIBON	70000				
765432109	NICKI	MACON	65000				
876543210	CRISTOPHER	COLAN	40000	876543210	CRISTOPHER	COLAN	4
987654321	JULIA	MILLS	75000				

Some DBMSs (such as Microsoft Access and Oracle 8) do not directly support the full outer join operator. In these systems, a full outer join can be formulated by taking the union of two one-sided outer joins using the steps shown below. The SELECT statement implementing these steps is shown in Example 4.5.

1. Construct a right join of *Faculty* and *Student* (nonmatched rows of *Student*).
2. Construct a left join of *Faculty* and *Student* (nonmatched rows of *Faculty*).
3. Construct a union of these two temporary tables. Remember when using the UNION operator, the two table arguments must be "union compatible": each corresponding column from both tables must have compatible data types. Otherwise, the UNION operator will not work as expected.

| EXAMPLE 4.5 (ACCESS) | Full Outer Join Using a Union of Two One-Sided Outer Joins |

Combine the *Faculty* and *Student* tables using a full outer join. List the social security number, the name (first and last), the salary (faculty only), and the GPA (students only) in the result. The result is identical to Example 4.4.

```
SELECT FacSSN, FacFirstName, FacLastName, FacSalary,
       StdSSN, StdFirstName, StdLastName, StdGPA
FROM Faculty RIGHT JOIN Student
     ON Student.StdSSN = Faculty.FacSSN
        UNION
SELECT FacSSN, FacFirstName, FacLastName, FacSalary,
       StdSSN, StdFirstName, StdLastName, StdGPA
FROM Faculty LEFT JOIN Student
     ON Student.StdSSN = Faculty.FacSSN
```

EXAMPLE 4.5 (ORACLE)

Full Outer Join Using a Union of Two One-Sided Outer Joins

Combine the *Faculty* and *Student* tables using a full outer join. List the social security number, the name (first and last), the salary (faculty only), and the GPA (students only) in the result. The result is identical to Example 4.4.

```
SELECT FacSSN, FacFirstName, FacLastName, FacSalary,
       StdSSN, StdFirstName, StdLastName, StdGPA
FROM Faculty, Student
WHERE Student.StdSSN = Faculty.FacSSN (+)
   UNION
SELECT FacSSN, FacFirstName, FacLastName, FacSalary,
       StdSSN, StdFirstName, StdLastName, StdGPA
FROM Faculty, Student
WHERE Student.StdSSN (+) = Faculty.FacSSN
```

4.1.2 Mixing Inner and Outer Joins

Inner and outer joins can be mixed as demonstrated in Examples 4.6 and 4.7. For readability, it is generally preferred to use the join operator style rather than to mix the join operator and cross product styles.

EXAMPLE 4.6 (ACCESS)

Mixing a One-Sided Outer Join and an Inner Join

Combine columns from the *Faculty, Offering,* and *Course* tables for IS courses offered in 2000. Include a row in the result even if there is not an assigned instructor.

```
SELECT OfferNo, Offering.CourseNo, OffTerm, CrsDesc,
       Faculty.FacSSN, FacFirstName, FacLastName
FROM ( Faculty RIGHT JOIN Offering
       ON Offering.FacSSN = Faculty.FacSSN )
     INNER JOIN Course
       ON Course.CourseNo = Offering.CourseNo
WHERE Course.CourseNo LIKE 'IS*' AND OffYear = 2000
```

OfferNo	CourseNo	OffTerm	CrsDesc	FacSSN	FacFirstName	FacLastName
1111	IS320	SUMMER	FUNDAMENTALS OF BUSINESS PROGRAMMING			
3333	IS320	SPRING	FUNDAMENTALS OF BUSINESS PROGRAMMING	098-76-5432	LEONARD	VINCE
4444	IS320	WINTER	FUNDAMENTALS OF BUSINESS PROGRAMMING	543-21-0987	VICTORIA	EMMANUEL
5678	IS480	WINTER	FUNDAMENTALS OF DATABASE MANAGEMENT	987-65-4321	JULIA	MILLS
5679	IS480	SPRING	FUNDAMENTALS OF DATABASE MANAGEMENT	876-54-3210	CHRISTOPHER	COLAN
8888	IS320	SUMMER	FUNDAMENTALS OF BUSINESS PROGRAMMING	654-32-1098	LEONARD	FIBON
9876	IS460	SPRING	SYSTEMS ANALYSIS	654-32-1098	LEONARD	FIBON

**EXAMPLE 4.6
(ORACLE)**

Mixing a One-Sided Outer Join and an Inner Join

Combine columns from the *Faculty, Offering,* and *Course* tables for IS courses offered in 2000. Include a row in the result even if there is not an assigned instructor.

```
SELECT OfferNo, Offering.CourseNo, OffTerm, CrsDesc,
        Faculty.FacSSN, FacFirstName, FacLastName
FROM Faculty, Offering, Course
WHERE Offering.FacSSN = Faculty.FacSSN (+)
    AND Course.CourseNo = Offering.CourseNo
    AND Course.CourseNo LIKE 'IS%' AND OffYear = 2000
```

**EXAMPLE 4.7
(ACCESS)**

Mixing a One-Sided Outer Join and Two Inner Joins

List the rows of the *Offering* table where there is at least one student enrolled, in addition to the requirements of Example 4.6. Remove duplicate rows when there is more than one student enrolled in an offering.

```
SELECT DISTINCT Offering.OfferNo, Offering.CourseNo,
        OffTerm, CrsDesc, Faculty.FacSSN, FacFirstName,
        FacLastName
FROM ( Faculty RIGHT JOIN Offering
        ON Offering.FacSSN = Faculty.FacSSN )
    INNER JOIN Course
        ON Course.CourseNo = Offering.CourseNo )
    INNER JOIN Enrollment
        ON Offering.OfferNo = Enrollment.OfferNo
WHERE Offering.CourseNo LIKE 'IS*' AND OffYear = 2000
```

OfferNo	CourseNo	OffTerm	CrsDesc	FacSSN	FacFirstName	FacLastName
5678	IS480	WINTER	FUNDAMENTALS OF DATABASE MANAGEMENT	987-65-4321	JULIA	MILLS
5679	IS480	SPRING	FUNDAMENTALS OF DATABASE MANAGEMENT	876-54-3210	CHRISTOPHER	COLAN
9876	IS460	SPRING	SYSTEMS ANALYSIS	654-32-1098	LEONARD	FIBON

**EXAMPLE 4.7
(ORACLE)**

Mixing a One-Sided Outer Join and Two Inner Joins

List the rows of the *Offering* table where there is at least one student enrolled, in addition to the requirements of Example 4.6. Remove duplicate rows when there is more than one student enrolled in an offering.

```
SELECT DISTINCT Offering.OfferNo, Offering.CourseNo,
        OffTerm, CrsDesc, Faculty.FacSSN,
        FacFirstName, FacLastName
FROM Faculty, Offering, Course, Enrollment
```

```
WHERE Offering.FacSSN = Faculty.FacSSN (+)
   AND Course.CourseNo = Offering.CourseNo
   AND Offering.OfferNo = Enrollment.OfferNo
   AND Course.CourseNo LIKE 'IS%' AND OffYear = 2000
```

4.2 UNDERSTANDING NESTED QUERIES

A nested query or subquery is a query (SELECT statement) inside a query. A nested query can appear as part of a condition in the WHERE or HAVING clauses. Nested queries can be used like a procedure (Type I nested query) in which the nested query is executed one time or like a loop (Type II nested query) in which the nested query is executed repeatedly. This section demonstrates examples of both kinds of nested queries and explains problems in which they can be applied.

Type I Nested Query a nested query in which the inner query does not reference any tables used in the outer query. Type I nested queries can be used for some join problems and some difference problems.

4.2.1 Type I Nested Queries

Type I nested queries are like procedures in a programming language. The nested query evaluates one time and produces a table. The nested (or inner) query does not reference the outer query. Using the IN comparison operator, a Type I nested query can be used to express a join. In Example 4.8, the nested query on the *Enrollment* table generates a list of qualifying social security number values. A row is selected in the outer query on *Student* if the social security number is an element of the nested query result.

EXAMPLE 4.8

Using a Type I Nested Query to Perform a Join

List the social security number, the name, and the major of students who have a high grade ($\geq$ 3.5) in a course offering.

```
SELECT StdSSN, StdFirstName, StdLastName, StdMajor
 FROM Student
 WHERE Student.StdSSN IN
    ( SELECT StdSSN FROM Enrollment
       WHERE EnrGrade >= 3.5 )
```

StdSSN	StdFirstName	StdLastName	StdMajor
123-45-6789	HOMER	WELLS	IS
124-56-7890	BOB	NORBERT	FIN
234-56-7890	CANDY	KENDALL	ACCT
567-89-0123	MARIAH	DODGE	IS
789-01-2345	ROBERTO	MORALES	FIN
890-12-3456	LUKE	BRAZZI	IS
901-23-4567	WILLIAM	PILGRIM	IS

Type I nested queries should be used only when the result does not contain any columns from the nested query. In Example 4.8, no columns from *Enrollment* are used in the result. In Example 4.9, the join between *Student* and *Enrollment* cannot be performed with a Type I nested query because *EnrGrade* appears in the result.

**EXAMPLE 4.9
(ACCESS)**

Combining a Type I Nested Query and the Join Operator Style

Retrieve the name, the city, and the grade of students who have a high grade (≥ 3.5) in a course offered in fall 1999.

```
SELECT StdFirstName, StdLastName, StdCity, EnrGrade
FROM Student INNER JOIN Enrollment
    ON Student.StdSSN = Enrollment.StdSSN
WHERE EnrGrade >= 3.5 AND Enrollment.OfferNo IN
    ( SELECT OfferNo FROM Offering
        WHERE OffTerm = 'FALL' AND OffYear = 1999 )
```

StdFirstName	StdLastName	StdCity	EnrGrade
CANDY	KENDALL	TACOMA	3.5
MARIAH	DODGE	SEATTLE	3.8
HOMER	WELLS	SEATTLE	3.5
ROBERTO	MORALES	SEATTLE	3.5

**EXAMPLE 4.9
(ORACLE)**

Combining a Type I Nested Query and the Cross Product Style

Retrieve the name, the city, and the grade of students who have a high grade (≥ 3.5) in a course offered in fall 1999.

```
SELECT StdFirstName, StdLastName, StdCity, EnrGrade
FROM Student, Enrollment
WHERE Student.StdSSN = Enrollment.StdSSN
    AND EnrGrade >= 3.5 AND Enrollment.OfferNo IN
    ( SELECT OfferNo FROM Offering
        WHERE OffTerm = 'FALL' AND OffYear = 1999 )
```

It is possible to have multiple levels of nested queries if desired. In a nested query, you can have another nested query using the IN comparison operator in the WHERE clause. In Example 4.10, the nested query on the *Offering* table has a nested query on the *Faculty* table. No *Faculty* columns are needed in the main query or in the nested query on *Offering*.

EXAMPLE 4.10

Using a Type I Nested Query Inside Another Type I Nested Query

Retrieve the name, the city, and the grade of students who have a high grade (≥ 3.5) in a course offered in fall 1999 taught by Leonard Vince.

```
SELECT StdFirstName, StdLastName, StdCity, EnrGrade
FROM Student, Enrollment
WHERE Student.StdSSN = Enrollment.StdSSN
    AND EnrGrade >= 3.5 AND Enrollment.OfferNo IN
    ( SELECT OfferNo FROM Offering
        WHERE OffTerm = 'FALL' AND OffYear = 1999
            AND FacSSN IN
            ( SELECT FacSSN FROM Faculty
                WHERE FacFirstName = 'LEONARD'
                    AND FacLastName = 'VINCE' ) )
```

StdFirstName	StdLastName	StdCity	EnrGrade
CANDY	KENDALL	TACOMA	3.5
MARIAH	DODGE	SEATTLE	3.8
HOMER	WELLS	SEATTLE	3.5
ROBERTO	MORALES	SEATTLE	3.5

The Type I style gives a visual feel to a query. You can visualize a Type I subquery as navigating between tables. Visit the table in the subquery to collect join values that can be used to select rows from the table in the outer query. The use of Type I nested queries is largely a matter of preference. Even if you do not prefer this join style, you should be prepared to interpret queries written by others with Type I nested queries.

The DELETE statement provides another use of a Type I nested query. A Type I nested query is useful when the deleted rows are related to other rows, as demonstrated in Example 4.11. Using a Type I nested query is the standard way to reference related tables in DELETE statements. Chapter 3 demonstrated the join operator style inside a DELETE statement, a proprietary extension of Microsoft Access. For your reference, Example 4.12 shows a DELETE statement using the join operator style that removes the same rows as Example 4.11.

EXAMPLE 4.11

DELETE Statement Using a Type I Nested Query

Delete offerings taught by Leonard Vince. Three Offering rows are deleted. In addition, this statement deletes related rows in the Enrollment table because the ON DELETE clause is set to CASCADE.

```
DELETE FROM Offering
  WHERE Offering.FacSSN IN
    ( SELECT FacSSN FROM Faculty
        WHERE FacFirstName = 'LEONARD'
        AND FacLastName = 'VINCE' )
```

EXAMPLE 4.12 (ACCESS)

DELETE Statement Using INNER JOIN Operation

Delete offerings taught by Leonard Vince. Three Offering rows are deleted. In addition, this statement deletes related rows in the Enrollment table because the ON DELETE clause is set to CASCADE.

```
DELETE Offering.*
  FROM Offering INNER JOIN Faculty
        ON Offering.FacSSN = Faculty.FacSSN
  WHERE FacFirstName = 'LEONARD'
        AND FacLastName = 'VINCE'
```

Type II Nested Query a nested query in which the inner query references a table used in the outer query. Type II nested queries are very useful for difference problems but should be avoided for join problems.

4.2.2 Type II Nested Queries

Type II nested queries have two distinguishing features. First, Type II nested queries reference one or more columns from an outer query. Type II nested queries are sometimes known as <u>correlated</u> subqueries because they reference columns used in outer queries. In contrast, Type I nested queries are not correlated with outer queries. In Example 4.13, note that *Student.StdSSN* in the inner query refers to the *Student* table used in the outer query. Whenever you see such a reference, the inner query is Type II.

| EXAMPLE 4.13 | Using a Type II Nested Query to Perform a Join |

List the social security number, the name (first and last), and the major of students who have a high grade (≥ 3.5) in a course offering. The result is identical to Example 4.8.

```
SELECT StdSSN, StdFirstName, StdLastName, StdMajor
FROM Student
WHERE EXISTS
    ( SELECT StdSSN FROM Enrollment
        WHERE Student.StdSSN = Enrollment.StdSSN
        AND EnrGrade >= 3.5 )
```

The second distinguishing feature of Type II nested queries involves execution. A Type II nested query executes one time for <u>each</u> row in the outer query. In this sense, a Type II nested query is similar to a nested loop that executes one time for each execution of the outer loop. In each execution of the inner loop, variables used in the outer loop are used in the inner loop. In other words, the inner query uses one or more values from the outer query in each execution.

In Example 4.13, each execution of the inner query uses the *Student.StdSSN* value from the current row of the outer query. To help you understand Example 4.13, Table 4–3 traces the execution of the nested query using Tables 4–1 and 4–2. The nested query

| TABLE 4–1 | Sample *Student* Table |

StdSSN	StdFirstName	StdLastName	StdMajor
123-45-6789	HOMER	WELLS	IS
124-56-7890	BOB	NORBERT	FIN
234-56-7890	CANDY	KENDALL	ACCT

| TABLE 4–2 | Sample *Enrollment* Table |

OfferNo	StdSSN	EnrGrade
1234	123-45-6789	3.6
4321	123-45-6789	3.5
4321	124-56-7890	3.2

| TABLE 4–3 | Execution Trace of Nested Query in Example 4.13 |

StdSSN	Result of subquery	EXISTS
123-45-6789	2 rows retrieved	true
124-56-7890	0 rows retrieved	false
234-56-7890	0 rows retrieved	false

executes three times, one time for each row in Table 4–1. For example, the first nested query execution uses the *StdSSN* value "123-45-6789" and retrieves the two matching rows in Table 4–2. The EXISTS comparison operator is true if the inner query evaluates to a nonempty table (one or more rows in the result). Thus, the result contains the first *Student* row because the EXISTS condition is true.

Type II nested queries can be combined with other join styles similar to Type I nested queries as demonstrated in Example 4.14. Note that Type II nested queries should not be used for a join when a column from the inner query is needed in the result.

EXAMPLE 4.14 (ACCESS)

Combining a Type II Nested Query and the Join Operator Style
Retrieve the name, the city, and the grade of students who have a high grade ($\geq$3.5) in a course offered in fall 1999. The result is identical to Example 4.9.

```
SELECT StdFirstName, StdLastName, StdCity, EnrGrade
FROM Student INNER JOIN Enrollment
      ON Student.StdSSN = Enrollment.StdSSN
WHERE EnrGrade >= 3.5 AND EXISTS
   ( SELECT * FROM Offering
       WHERE Enrollment.OfferNo = Offering.OfferNo
         AND OffTerm = 'FALL' AND OffYear = 1999 )
```

EXAMPLE 4.14 (ORACLE)

Combining a Type II Nested Query and the Cross Product Style
Retrieve the name, the city, and the grade of students who have a high grade ($\geq$3.5) in a course offered in fall 1999. The result is identical to Example 4.10.

```
SELECT StdFirstName, StdLastName, StdCity, EnrGrade
FROM Student, Enrollment
WHERE tudent.StdSSN = Enrollment.StdSSN
    AND EnrGrade >= 3.5 AND EXISTS
    ( SELECT * FROM Offering
        WHERE Enrollment.OfferNo = Offering.OfferNo
          AND OffTerm = 'FALL' AND OffYear = 1999 )
```

Because conceptually Type II nested queries are repeatedly executed, they are not typically used for join problems. Many SQL compilers will not recognize that some Type II nested queries are actually join operations. Thus, one of the other join styles is generally preferred for efficiency reasons. Type II nested queries are more typically used for difference problems, as demonstrated in the next subsection.

4.2.3 Solving Difference Problems with Type II Nested Queries

Type II nested queries are useful for problems involving the difference operator, as demonstrated in Example 4.15. The placement of the word "not" in the problem statement indicates that the result contains rows only in the *Faculty* table, not in the *Student* table. This requirement involves a difference operation. The Type II nested query provides a way to remove faculty members who are also students.

| EXAMPLE 4.15 | Using a Type II Nested Query for a Difference Problem |

Retrieve the social security number, the name (first and last), the department, and the salary of faculty who are <u>not</u> students.

```
SELECT FacSSN, FacFirstName, FacLastName, FacDept,
        FacSalary
FROM Faculty
WHERE NOT EXISTS
   ( SELECT * FROM Student
        WHERE Student.StdSSN = Faculty.FacSSN )
```

FacSSN	FacFirstName	FacLastName	FacDept	FacSalary
098-76-5432	LEONARD	VINCE	MS	$35,000.00
543-21-0987	VICTORIA	EMMANUEL	MS	$120,000.00
654-32-1098	LEONARD	FIBON	MS	$70,000.00
765-43-2109	NICKI	MACON	FIN	$65,000.00
987-65-4321	JULIA	MILLS	FIN	$75,000.00

To help you understand Example 4.15, Table 4–6 traces the execution of the nested query using Tables 4–4 and 4–5. The NOT EXISTS operator is true if the nested query returns 0 rows. Thus, a faculty row in the outer query is selected only if there are no matching student rows in the nested query. For example, the first two rows in Table 4–4 are se-

| TABLE 4–4 | Sample *Faculty* Table |

FacSSN	FacFirstName	FacLastName	FacRank
098-76-5432	LEONARD	VINCE	ASST
543-21-0987	VICTORIA	EMMANUEL	PROF
876-54-3210	CHRISTOPHER	COLAN	ASST

| TABLE 4–5 | Sample *Student* Table |

StdSSN	StdFirstName	StdLastName	StdMajor
123-45-6789	HOMER	WELLS	IS
124-56-7890	BOB	NORBERT	FIN
876-54-3210	CHRISTOPHER	COLAN	IS

| TABLE 4–6 | Execution Trace of Nested Query in Example 4.15 |

FacSSN	Result of subquery execution	NOT EXISTS
098-76-5432	0 rows retrieved	true
543-21-0987	0 rows retrieved	true
876-54-3210	1 row retrieved	false

lected because there are no matching rows in Table 4–5. The third row is <u>not</u> selected because the nested query returns one row (the third row of Table 4–5).

Example 4.16 shows another formulation that clarifies the meaning of the NOT EXISTS operator. Here, a faculty row is selected if the number of rows in the nested query is 0. Using the sample tables (Tables 4–4 and 4–5 above), the nested query result is 0 for the first two faculty rows.

EXAMPLE 4.16

Using a Type II Nested Query with the COUNT Function
Retrieve the social security number, the name, the department, and the salary of faculty who are <u>not</u> students. The result is the same as for Example 4.15.

```
SELECT FacSSN, FacFirstName, FacLastName, FacDept,
       FacSalary
 FROM Faculty
 WHERE 0 =
   ( SELECT COUNT(*) FROM Student
       WHERE Student.StdSSN = Faculty.FacSSN )
```

Other SQL Solutions for Difference Problems

Some difference problems can be solved using a Type I nested query in place of a Type II nested query, as demonstrated in Example 4.17. As long as the comparison among tables involves a single column (*FacSSN* in this problem), a Type I nested query can be used. On some DBMSs, the formulation with the Type I nested query will execute much faster than the formulation with the Type II nested query.

EXAMPLE 4.17

Using a Type I Nested Query for a Difference Problem
Retrieve the social security number, the name (first and last), the department, and the salary of faculty who are <u>not</u> students. The result is identical to Example 4.15.

```
SELECT FacSSN, FacFirstName, FacLastName, FacDept,
       FacSalary
 FROM Faculty
 WHERE FacSSN NOT IN
   ( SELECT StdSSN FROM Student )
```

Although SQL2 does have a difference operator (the EXCEPT keyword), it is sometimes not convenient because only the common columns can be shown in the result. Example 4.18 does not provide the same result as Example 4.15 because the columns unique to the *Faculty* table (*FacDept* and *FacSalary*) are not in the result. Another query that uses the first result must be formulated to retrieve the unique *Faculty* columns.

**EXAMPLE 4.18
(ORACLE)**

Difference Query
Show faculty who are <u>not</u> students (pure faculty). Only show the common columns in the result. Note that Microsoft Access does not support the EXCEPT keyword. Oracle uses the MINUS keyword instead of EXCEPT.

```
SELECT FacSSN AS SSN, FacFirstName AS FirstName,
         FacLastName AS LastName, FacCity AS City,
         FacState AS State
FROM Faculty
      MINUS
SELECT StdSSN AS SSN, StdFirstName AS FirstName,
         StdLastName AS LastName, StdCity AS City,
         StdState AS State
FROM Student
```

Difference Problems Cannot Be Solved with Inequality Joins

It is important to note that difference problems such as Example 4.15 cannot be solved with a join alone. Example 4.15 requires that every row of the *Student* table be searched to select a faculty row. In contrast, a join selects a faculty row when the first matching student row is found. To contrast difference and join problems, examine Example 4.19. Although it looks correct, it is not. Every faculty row will be in the result because there is at least one student row that does not match every faculty row.

EXAMPLE 4.19	Inequality Join

Erroneous formulation for the problem "Retrieve the social security number, the name (first and last), and the rank of faculty who are <u>not</u> students." The result contains all faculty rows.

```
SELECT DISTINCT FacSSN, FacFirstName, FacLastName,
                 FacRank
FROM Faculty, Student
WHERE Student.StdSSN <> Faculty.FacSSN
```

To understand Example 4.19, you can use the conceptual process discussed in Section 3.3. The result tables show the cross product (Table 4–7) of Tables 4–4 and 4–5 followed by the rows that satisfy the WHERE condition (Table 4–8). Notice that only one row of the cross product is deleted. The final result (Table 4–9) contains all rows of Table 4–4.

TABLE 4–7	Cross Product of Sample *Student* and *Faculty* Tables

FacSSN	FacFirstName	FacLastName	FacRank	StdSSN	StdFirstName	StdLastName	StdMajor
098-76-5432	LEONARD	VINCE	ASST	123-45-6789	HOMER	WELLS	IS
098-76-5432	LEONARD	VINCE	ASST	124-56-7890	BOB	NORBERT	FIN
098-76-5432	LEONARD	VINCE	ASST	876-54-3210	CHRISTOPHER	COLAN	IS
543-21-0987	VICTORIA	EMMANUEL	PROF	123-45-6789	HOMER	WELLS	IS
543-21-0987	VICTORIA	EMMANUEL	PROF	124-56-7890	BOB	NORBERT	FIN
543-21-0987	VICTORIA	EMMANUEL	PROF	876-54-3210	CHRISTOPHER	COLAN	IS
876-54-3210	CHRISTOPHER	COLAN	ASST	123-45-6789	HOMER	WELLS	IS
876-54-3210	CHRISTOPHER	COLAN	ASST	124-56-7890	BOB	NORBERT	FIN
876-54-3210	CHRISTOPHER	COLAN	ASST	876-54-3210	CHRISTOPHER	COLAN	IS

TABLE 4–8	Restriction of Table 4–7 to Eliminate Matching Rows						
FacSSN	**FacFirstName**	**FacLastName**	**FacRank**	**StdSSN**	**StdFirstName**	**StdLastName**	**StdMajor**
098-76-5432	LEONARD	VINCE	ASST	123-45-6789	HOMER	WELLS	IS
098-76-5432	LEONARD	VINCE	ASST	124-56-7890	BOB	NORBERT	FIN
098-76-5432	LEONARD	VINCE	ASST	876-54-3210	CHRISTOPHER	COLAN	IS
543-21-0987	VICTORIA	EMMANUEL	PROF	123-45-6789	HOMER	WELLS	IS
543-21-0987	VICTORIA	EMMANUEL	PROF	124-56-7890	BOB	NORBERT	FIN
543-21-0987	VICTORIA	EMMANUEL	PROF	876-54-3210	CHRISTOPHER	COLAN	IS
876-54-3210	CHRISTOPHER	COLAN	ASST	123-45-6789	HOMER	WELLS	IS
876-54-3210	CHRISTOPHER	COLAN	ASST	124-56-7890	BOB	NORBERT	FIN

TABLE 4–9	Projection of Table 4–8 to Eliminate *Student* Columns		
FacSSN	**FacFirstName**	**FacLastName**	**FacRank**
098-76-5432	LEONARD	VINCE	ASST
543-21-0987	VICTORIA	EMMANUEL	PROF
876-54-3210	CHRISTOPHER	COLAN	ASST

More Difficult Difference Problems

More difficult difference problems combine a difference operation with join operations. For example, consider the query to list students who took all of their IS offerings in winter 2000 from the same instructor. The query results should include students who took only one offering as well as students who took more than one offering.

- Construct a list of students who have taken IS courses in winter 2000 (a join operation).
- Construct another list of students who have taken IS courses in winter 2000 from more than one instructor (a join operation).
- Use a difference operation (first student list minus the second student list) to produce the result.

Conceptualizing a problem in this manner forces you to recognize that it involves a difference operation. If you recognize the difference operation, you can make a formulation in SQL involving a nested query (Type II with NOT EXISTS or Type I with NOT IN) or the EXCEPT keyword. Example 4.20 shows a NOT EXISTS solution in which the outer query retrieves a student row if the student does not have an offering from a <u>different</u> instructor in the inner query.

EXAMPLE 4.20 (ACCESS)	More Difficult Difference Problem Using a Type II Nested Query

List the social security number and the name of students who took all of their IS offerings in winter 2000 from the same instructor. Include students who took only one offering as well as students who took more than one offering. Note that in the nested query, the columns *Enrollment.StdSSN* and *Offering.FacSSN* refer to the outer query.

```
SELECT DISTINCT Enrollment.StdSSN, StdFirstName,
                StdLastName
FROM Student, Enrollment, Offering
WHERE Student.StdSSN = Enrollment.StdSSN
    AND Enrollment.OfferNo = Offering.OfferNo
    AND CourseNo LIKE 'IS*'AND OffTerm = 'WINTER'
    AND OffYear = 2000 AND NOT EXISTS
    ( SELECT * FROM Enrollment E1, Offering O1
        WHERE E1.OfferNo = O1.OfferNo
            AND Enrollment.StdSSN = E1.StdSSN
            AND O1.CourseNo LIKE 'IS*'
            AND O1.OffTerm = 'WINTER'
            AND O1.OffYear = 2000
            AND Offering.FacSSN <> O1.FacSSN )
```

StdSSN	StdFirstName	StdLastName
123-45-6789	HOMER	WELLS
234-56-7890	CANDY	KENDALL
345-67-8901	WALLY	KENDALL
456-78-9012	JOE	ESTRADA
567-89-0123	MARIAH	DODGE

EXAMPLE 4.20 (ORACLE)

More Difficult Difference Problem Using a Type II Nested Query
List the social security number and the name of students who took all of their IS offerings in winter 2000 from the same instructor. Include students who took only one offering as well as students who took more than one offering.

```
SELECT DISTINCT Enrollment.StdSSN, StdFirstName,
                StdLastName
FROM Student, Enrollment, Offering
WHERE Student.StdSSN = Enrollment.StdSSN
    AND Enrollment.OfferNo = Offering.OfferNo
    AND CourseNo LIKE 'IS%' AND OffTerm = 'WINTER'
    AND OffYear = 2000 AND NOT EXISTS
    ( SELECT * FROM Enrollment E1, Offering O1
        WHERE E1.OfferNo = O1.OfferNo
            AND Enrollment.StdSSN = E1.StdSSN
            AND O1.CourseNo LIKE 'IS%'
            AND O1.OffTerm = 'WINTER'
            AND O1.OffYear = 2000
            AND Offering.FacSSN <> O1.FacSSN )
```

Example 4.21 shows another example using the NOT EXISTS operator to solve a difference problem. Conceptually this problem involves a difference operation between two sets: the set of all faculty members and the set of faculty members teaching in the specified term. The difference operation can be implemented by selecting a faculty in the outer query list if the faculty does not teach an offering during the specified term in the inner query result.

EXAMPLE 4.21   Another Difference Problem Using a Type II Nested Query

List the name (first and last) and the department of faculty who are <u>not</u> teaching in winter term 2000.

```
SELECT FacFirstName, FacLastName, FacDept
  FROM Faculty
  WHERE NOT EXISTS
     ( SELECT * FROM Offering
         WHERE Offering.FacSSN = Faculty.FacSSN
           AND OffTerm = 'WINTER' AND OffYear = 2000 )
```

FacFirstName	FacLastName	FacDept
CHRISTOPHER	COLAN	MS
LEONARD	FIBON	MS
LEONARD	VINCE	MS

4.3 FORMULATING DIVISION PROBLEMS

Division problems can be some of the most difficult problems. Because of the difficulty, the divide operator of Chapter 2 is briefly reviewed. After this review, this section discusses some easier division problems before moving to more advanced problems.

4.3.1 Review of the Divide Operator

Divide an operator of relational algebra that combines rows from two tables. The divide operator produces a table in which the values of a column from one input table are associated with all the values from a column of the second table.

To review the divide operator, consider a simplified university database consisting of three tables: *Student1* (Table 4–10), *Club* (Table 4–11), and *StdClub* (Table 4–12), showing student membership in clubs. The divide operator is typically applied to linking tables showing M-N relationships. The *StdClub* table links the *Student1* and *Club* tables: a student may belong to many clubs and a club may have many students.

The divide operator builds a table consisting of the values of one column (*StdNo*) that match <u>all</u> of the values in a specified column (*ClubNo*) of a second table (*Club*). A typical division problem is to list the students who belong to <u>all</u> clubs. The resulting table contains only student S1 because S1 is associated with all four clubs.

TABLE 4–10	*Student1* Table Listing	
StdNo	SName	SCity
S1	JOE	SEATTLE
S2	SALLY	SEATTLE
S3	SUE	PORTLAND

TABLE 4–11	*Club* Table Listing			
ClubNo	CName	CPurpose	CBudget	CActual
C1	DELTA	SOCIAL	$1,000.00	$1,200.00
C2	BITS	ACADEMIC	$500.00	$350.00
C3	HELPS	SERVICE	$300.00	$330.00
C4	SIGMA	SOCIAL		$150.00

TABLE 4–12	*StdClub* Table Listing

StdNo	ClubNo
S1	C1
S1	C2
S1	C3
S1	C4
S2	C1
S2	C4
S3	C3

Division is more conceptually difficult than join because division matches on all of the values whereas join matches on a single value. If this problem involved a join, it would be stated as "list students who belong to <u>any</u> club." The key difference is the word "any" versus "all." Most division problems can be written with adjectives "every" or "all" between a verb phrase representing a table and a noun representing another table. In this example, the phrase "students who belong to all of the clubs" fits this pattern. Another example is "students who have taken every course."

4.3.2 Simple Division Problems

There are a number of ways to perform division in SQL. Some books describe an approach using Type II nested queries. Because this approach can be difficult to understand if you have not had a course in logic, a different approach is used here. The approach here uses the COUNT function with a nested query in the HAVING clause.

The basic idea is to compare the number of students associated with a club in the *StdClub* table with the number of clubs in the *Club* table. To perform this operation, group the *StdClub* table on *StdNo* and compare the number of rows in each *StdNo* group with the number of rows in the *Club* table. You can make this comparison using a nested query in the HAVING clause, as shown in Example 4.22.

EXAMPLE 4.22   Simplest Division Problem

List the student number of students who belong to all of the clubs.

```
SELECT StdNo
  FROM StdClub
  GROUP BY StdNo
  HAVING COUNT(*) = ( SELECT COUNT(*) FROM Club )
```

StdNo
S1

Note that the COUNT(*) on the left-hand side tallies the number of rows in the *StdNo* group. The right-hand side contains a nested query with only a COUNT(*) in the result. The nested query is Type I because there is no connection to the outer query. Therefore, the nested query only executes one time and returns a single row with a single value (the number of rows in the *Club* table).

Now let us examine some variations of the first problem. The most typical variation is to retrieve students who belong to a subset of the clubs rather than all of the clubs. For example, retrieve students who belong to all of the social clubs. To accomplish this change, you should modify Example 4.22 by including a WHERE condition in both the outer and the nested query. Instead of counting all *Student1* rows in a *StdNo* group, count only the rows where the club's purpose is social. Compare this count to the number of social clubs in the *Club* table. Example 4.23 shows these modifications.

EXAMPLE 4.23

Division Problem to Find a Subset Match
List the student number of students who belong to all of the social clubs.

```
SELECT StdNo
  FROM StdClub, Club
  WHERE StdClub.ClubNo = Club.ClubNo
    AND CPurpose = 'SOCIAL'
  GROUP BY StdNo
  HAVING COUNT(*) =
    ( SELECT COUNT(*) FROM Club
      WHERE CPurpose = 'SOCIAL' )
```

StdNo
S1
S2

Other variations are shown in Examples 4.24 and 4.25. In Example 4.24, a join between *StdClub* and *Student* is necessary to obtain the student name. Example 4.25 reverses the previous problems by looking for clubs rather than students.

EXAMPLE 4.24

Division Problem with Joins
List the student number and the name of students who belong to all of the social clubs.

```
SELECT Student1.StdNo, SName
  FROM StdClub, Club, Student1
  WHERE StdClub.ClubNo = Club.ClubNo
    AND Student1.StdNo = StdClub.StdNo
    AND CPurpose = 'SOCIAL'
  GROUP BY Student1.StdNo, SName
  HAVING COUNT(*) =
    ( SELECT COUNT(*) FROM Club
      WHERE CPurpose = 'SOCIAL' )
```

StdNo	SName
S1	JOE
S2	SALLY

EXAMPLE 4.25

Another Division Problem
List the club numbers of clubs that have all of the Seattle students as members.

```
SELECT ClubNo
  FROM StdClub, Student1
  WHERE Student1.StdNo = StdClub.StdNo
    AND SCity = 'SEATTLE'
  GROUP BY ClubNo
  HAVING COUNT(*) =
    ( SELECT COUNT(*) FROM Student1
        WHERE SCity = 'SEATTLE' )
```

ClubNo
C1
C4

4.3.3 Advanced Division Problems

Example 4.26 (using the original university database tables) depicts another complication of division problems in SQL. Before tackling this additional complication, let us examine a simpler problem. Example 4.26 can be formulated with the same technique as shown in Section 4.3.2. First, join the *Faculty* and *Offering* tables, select rows matching the WHERE conditions, and group the result by faculty name (first and last). Then compare the count of the rows in each faculty *name* group with the number of fall 1999, IS offerings from the *Offering* table.

**EXAMPLE 4.26
(ACCESS)**

Division Problem with a Join
List the social security number and the name (first and last) of faculty who teach all of the fall 1999 IS course offerings.

```
SELECT Faculty.FacSSN, FacFirstName, FacLastName
  FROM Faculty, Offering
  WHERE Faculty.FacSSN = Offering.FacSSN
    AND OffTerm = 'FALL'AND CourseNo LIKE 'IS*'
    AND OffYear = 1999
  GROUP BY Faculty.FacSSN, FacFirstName, FacLastName
  HAVING COUNT(*) =
    ( SELECT COUNT(*) FROM Offering
        WHERE OffTerm = 'FALL' AND OffYear = 1999
          AND CourseNo LIKE 'IS*' )
```

FacSSN	FacFirstName	FacLastName
098-76-5432	LEONARD	VINCE

**EXAMPLE 4.26
(ORACLE)**

Division Problem with a Join
List the social security number and the name (first and last) of faculty who teach all of the fall 1999 IS course offerings.

```
SELECT Faculty.FacSSN, FacFirstName, FacLastName
 FROM Faculty, Offering
 WHERE Faculty.FacSSN = Offering.FacSSN
     AND OffTerm = 'FALL' AND CourseNo LIKE 'IS%'
     AND OffYear = 1999
 GROUP BY Faculty.FacSSN, FacFirstName, FacLastName
 HAVING COUNT(*) =
     ( SELECT COUNT(*) FROM Offering
         WHERE OffTerm = 'FALL' AND OffYear = 1999
             AND CourseNo LIKE 'IS%' )
```

Example 4.26 is not particularly useful because it is unlikely that an instructor has taught every offering. Rather, it is more useful that an instructor has taught one offering of every course, as demonstrated in Example 4.27. Rather than counting the rows in each group, count the unique *CourseNo* values. This change is necessary because *CourseNo* is not unique in the *Offering* table. There can be multiple rows with the same *CourseNo,* corresponding to a situation where there are multiple offerings for the same course. The solution only executes in Oracle because Access does not support the DISTINCT keyword in aggregate functions. Appendix 4.A presents a solution for Example 4.27 without the DISTINCT keyword inside the COUNT function.

EXAMPLE 4.27
(ORACLE)

Division Problem with DISTINCT Inside COUNT
List the social security number and the name (first and last) of faculty who teach at least one section of all of the fall 1999 IS courses.

```
SELECT Faculty.FacSSN, FacFirstName, FacLastName
 FROM Faculty, Offering
 WHERE Faculty.FacSSN = Offering.FacSSN
     AND OffTerm = 'FALL' AND CourseNo LIKE 'IS%'
     AND OffYear = 1999
 GROUP BY Faculty.FacSSN, FacFirstName, FacLastName
 HAVING COUNT(DISTINCT CourseNo) =
     ( SELECT COUNT(DISTINCT CourseNo) FROM Offering
         WHERE OffTerm = 'FALL' AND OffYear = 1999
             AND CourseNo LIKE 'IS%' )
```

FacSSN	FacFirstName	FacLastName
098-76-5432	LEONARD	VINCE

Example 4.28 is another variation of the technique used in Example 4.27. The DISTINCT keyword is necessary so that students taking more than one offering from the same instructor are not counted twice. Note that the DISTINCT keyword is not necessary for the nested query because only rows of the *Student* table are counted.

EXAMPLE 4.28
(ORACLE)

Another Division Problem with DISTINCT Inside COUNT
List the faculty who have taught all of the seniors in their fall 1999 IS offerings.

```
SELECT Faculty.FacSSN, FacFirstName, FacLastName
FROM Faculty, Offering, Enrollment, Student
WHERE Faculty.FacSSN = Offering.FacSSN
   AND OffTerm = 'FALL' AND CourseNo LIKE 'IS%'
   AND OffYear = 1999 AND StdClass = 'SR'
   AND Offering.OfferNo = Enrollment.OfferNo
   AND Student.StdSSN = Enrollment.StdSSN
GROUP BY Faculty.FacSSN, FacFirstName, FacLastName
HAVING COUNT(DISTINCT Student.StdSSN) =
   ( SELECT COUNT(*) FROM Student
      WHERE StdClass = 'SR' )
```

FacSSN	FacFirstName	FacLastName
098-76-5432	LEONARD	VINCE

4.4 NULL VALUE CONSIDERATIONS

The last section of this chapter does not involve difficult matching problems or new parts of SQL. Rather, this section presents interpretation of query results when tables contain null values. These effects have largely been ignored until this section to simplify the presentation. Because most databases use null values, you need to understand the effects to attain a deeper understanding of query formulation.

Null values affect simple conditions involving comparison operators, compound conditions involving Boolean operators, aggregate calculations, and grouping. As you will see, some of the null value effects are rather subtle. Because of these subtle effects, a good table design minimizes, although it usually does not eliminate, the use of null values. The null effects described in this section are specified in the SQL2 standard. Because specific DBMSs may provide different results, you may need to experiment with your DBMS.

4.4.1 Effect on Simple Conditions

Simple conditions involve a comparison operator, a column or column expression, and a constant, column, or column expression. A simple condition results in a null value if either column (or column expression) in a comparison is null. A row qualifies in the result if the simple condition evaluates to true for the row. Rows evaluating to false and null are discarded. Example 4.29 depicts a simple condition evaluating to null for one of the rows.

EXAMPLE 4.29   Simple Condition Using a Column with Null Values

List the clubs (Table 4–11) with a budget greater than $200. The club with a null budget (C4) is omitted because the condition evaluates as a null value.

```
SELECT *
FROM Club
WHERE CBudget > 200
```

ClubNo	CName	CPurpose	CBudget	CActual
C1	DELTA	SOCIAL	$1,000.00	$1,200.00
C2	BITS	ACADEMIC	$500.00	$350.00
C3	HELPS	SERVICE	$300.00	$330.00

A more subtle result can occur when a simple condition involves two columns and at least one column contains null values. If neither column contains null values, every row will be in the result of either the simple condition or the opposite (negation) of the simple condition. For example, if $<$ is the operator of a simple condition, the opposite condition contains $\geq$ as its operator assuming the columns remain in the same positions. If at least one column contains null values, some rows will not appear in the result of either the simple condition or its negation. More precisely, rows containing null values will be excluded in both results, as demonstrated in Examples 4.30 and 4.31.

EXAMPLE 4.30

Simple Condition Involving Two Columns

List the clubs with the budget greater than the actual spending. The club with a null budget (C4) is omitted because the condition evaluates as a null value.

```
SELECT *
  FROM Club
  WHERE CBudget > CActual
```

ClubNo	CName	CPurpose	CBudget	CActual
C2	BITS	ACADEMIC	$500.00	$350.00

EXAMPLE 4.31

Opposite Condition of Example 4.30

List the clubs with the budget less than or equal to the actual spending. The club with a null budget (C4) is omitted because the condition evaluates as a null value.

```
SELECT *
  FROM Club
  WHERE CBudget <= CActual
```

ClubNo	CName	CPurpose	CBudget	CActual
C1	DELTA	SOCIAL	$1,000.00	$1,200.00
C3	HELPS	SERVICE	$300.00	$330.00

4.4.2 Effect on Compound Conditions

Compound conditions involve one or more simple conditions connected by the Boolean operators AND, OR, and NOT. Like simple conditions, compound conditions evaluate to true, false, or null. A row is selected if the entire compound condition in the WHERE clause evaluates to true.

To evaluate the result of a compound condition, the SQL2 standard uses truth tables with three values. A truth table shows how combinations of values (true, false, and null) combine with the Boolean operators. Truth tables with three values define a three-valued logic. Tables 4–13 through 4–15 depict truth tables for the AND, OR, and NOT operators. The internal cells in these tables are the result values. For example, the first internal cell (True) in Table 4–13 results from the AND operator applied to two conditions with true values. You can test your understanding of the truth tables using Examples 4.32 and 4.33.

TABLE 4–13	AND Truth Table		
AND	**True**	**False**	**Null**
True	True	False	Null
False	False	False	False
Null	Null	False	Null

TABLE 4–14	OR Truth Table		
OR	**True**	**False**	**Null**
True	True	True	True
False	True	False	Null
Null	True	Null	Null

TABLE 4–15	NOT Truth Table		
NOT	**True**	**False**	**Null**
	False	True	Null

EXAMPLE 4.32

Evaluation of a Compound OR Condition with a Null Value

List the clubs with the budget less than or equal to the actual spending or the actual spending less than $200. The club with a null budget (C4) is included because the second condition results in a true value.

```
SELECT *
FROM Club
WHERE CBudget <= CActual OR CActual <200
```

ClubNo	CName	CPurpose	CBudget	CActual
C1	DELTA	SOCIAL	$1,000.00	$1,200.00
C3	HELPS	SERVICE	$300.00	$330.00
C4	SIGMA	SOCIAL		$150.00

EXAMPLE 4.33

Evaluation of a Compound AND Condition with a Null Value

List the clubs (Table 4–11) with the budget less than or equal to the actual spending and the actual spending less than $500. The club with a null budget (C4) is not included because the first condition results in a null value.

```
SELECT *
FROM Club
WHERE CBudget <= CActual AND CActual < 500
```

ClubNo	CName	CPurpose	CBudget	CActual
C3	HELPS	SERVICE	$300.00	$330.00

4.4.3 Effect on Aggregate Calculations and Grouping

Null values are ignored in aggregate calculations. Although this statement sounds simple, the results can be subtle. For the COUNT function, COUNT(*) returns a different value than COUNT(column) if the column contains null values. COUNT(*) always returns the number of rows. COUNT(column) returns the number of non-null values in the column. Example 4.34 demonstrates the difference between COUNT(*) and COUNT(column).

EXAMPLE 4.34

COUNT Function with Null Values

List the number of rows in the *Club* table and the number of values in the *CBudget* column.

```
SELECT COUNT(*) AS NumRows,
       COUNT(CBudget) AS NumBudgets
  FROM Club
```

NumRows	NumBudgets
4	3

An even more subtle effect can occur if the SUM or AVG functions are applied to a column with null values. Without regard to null values, the following equation is true: SUM(Column1) + SUM(Column2) = SUM(Column1 + Column2). With null values in at least one of the columns, the equation may not be true because a calculation involving a null value yields a null value. If Column1 has a null value in one row, the plus operation in SUM(Column1 + Column2) produces a null value for that row. However, the value of Column2 in the same row is counted in SUM(Column2). Example 4.35 demonstrates this subtle effect using the minus operator instead of the plus operator.

EXAMPLE 4.35

SUM Function with Null Values

Using the *Club* table, list the sum of the budget values, the sum of the actual values, the difference of the two sums, and the sum of the differences (budget − actual). The last two columns differ because of a null value in the *CBudget* column. Parentheses enclose negative values in the result.

```
SELECT  SUM(CBudget) AS SumBudget,
        SUM(CActual) AS SumActual,
        SUM(CBudget) − SUM(CActual) AS SumDifference,
        SUM(CBudget−CActual) AS SumOfDifferences
  FROM Club
```

SumBudget	SumActual	SumDifference	SumOfDifferences
$1,800.00	$2,030.00	($230.00)	($80.00)

- Mixing inner and outer joins.

Access:

```
SELECT OfferNo, Offering.CourseNo, OffTerm, CrsDesc,
        Faculty.FacSSN, FacFirstName, FacLastName
  FROM ( Faculty RIGHT JOIN Offering
          ON Offering.FacSSN = Faculty.FacSSN )
      INNER JOIN Course
          ON Course.CourseNo = Offering.CourseNo
  WHERE Course.CourseNo LIKE 'IS*' AND OffYear = 2000
```

Oracle:

```
SELECT OfferNo, Offering.CourseNo, OffTerm, CrsDesc,
        Faculty.FacSSN, FacFirstName, FacLastName
  FROM Faculty, Offering, Course
  WHERE Offering.FacSSN = Faculty.FacSSN (+)
    AND Course.CourseNo = Offering.CourseNo
    AND Course.CourseNo LIKE 'IS%' AND OffYear = 2000
```

- Understanding that conditions in the WHERE or HAVING clause can use SELECT statements in addition to scalar (individual) values.
- Identifying Type I nested queries by the IN keyword and the lack of a reference to a table used in an outer query.
- Identifying Type II (correlated) nested queries by a reference to a table used in an outer query.
- Using a Type I nested query to formulate a join.

```
SELECT DISTINCT StdSSN, StdFirstName, StdLastName,
                  StdMajor
  FROM Student
  WHERE Student.StdSSN IN
    ( SELECT StdSSN FROM Enrollment
      WHERE EnrGrade >= 3.5 )
```

- Using a Type I nested query inside a DELETE statement to test conditions on a related table.

```
DELETE FROM Offering
  WHERE Offering.FacSSN IN
    ( SELECT FacSSN FROM Faculty
      WHERE FacFirstName = 'LEONARD'
        AND FacLastName = 'VINCE' )
```

- Not using a Type I nested query for a join when a column from the nested query is needed in the final query result.
- Using a Type II nested query for a difference problem.

```
SELECT FacSSN, FacFirstName, FacLastName, FacDept,
        FacSalary
  FROM Faculty
  WHERE NOT EXISTS
    ( SELECT * FROM Student
      WHERE Student.StdSSN = Faculty.FacSSN )
```

- Noting that division problems often have the word <u>every</u> or <u>all</u> to connect different parts of a problem statement.
- Using the "count" method to formulate division problems.

      SELECT StdNo
        FROM StdClub
        GROUP BY StdNo
        HAVING COUNT(*) = (SELECT COUNT(*) FROM Club)

- Evaluating a simple condition containing a null value in a column expression.
- Using three-valued logic and truth tables to evaluate compound conditions with null values.
- Understanding the result of aggregate calculations with null values.
- Understanding the result of grouping on a column with null values.

QUESTIONS

1. Explain a situation when a one-sided outer join is useful.

2. Explain a situation when a full outer join is useful.

3. How do you interpret the meaning of the LEFT and RIGHT JOIN keywords in the FROM clause?

4. How do you interpret the meaning of the (+) oracle notation in the WHERE clause?

5. What is meant by the "null table" when using the (+) oracle notation?

6. What is a nested query?

7. What is the distinguishing feature about Type I nested queries?

8. What is the distinguishing feature about Type II nested queries?

9. How many times is a Type I nested query executed as part of an outer query?

10. How is a Type I nested query like a procedure in a program?

11. How many times is a Type II nested query executed as part of an outer query?

12. How is a Type II nested query like a nested loop in a program?

13. What is the meaning of the IN comparison operator?

14. What is the meaning of the EXISTS comparison operator?

15. What is the meaning of the NOT EXISTS comparison operator?

16. When can you not use a Type I nested query to perform a join?

17. Why is a Type I nested query a good join method when you need a join in a DELETE statement?

18. How do you detect that a problem involves a division operation?

19. Explain the "count" method for formulating division problems.

20. Why is it sometimes necessary to use the DISTINCT keyword inside the COUNT function for division problems?

21. What is the result of a simple condition when a column expression in the condition evaluates to null?

22. What is a truth table?

23. How many values do truth tables have in the SQL2 standard?

24. How do you use truth tables to evaluate compound conditions?

25. How do null values affect aggregate calculations?

26. Explain why the following equation may not be true if Column1 or Column2 contains null values: SUM(Column1) – SUM(Column2) = SUM(Column1 – Column2)

27. How are null values handled in a grouping column?

PROBLEMS

ORDER

The problems use the tables of the Order Entry database introduced in the Problems section of Chapter 3. When formulating the problems, remember that the *EmpNo* foreign key in the *OrderTbl* table allows null values. An order does not have an associated employee if taken over the Internet.

1. Using a Type I nested query, list the customer number, the name (first and last), and the city of each customer who has a balance greater than $150 and placed an order in February 2000.

2. Using a Type II nested query, list the customer number, the name (first and last), and the city of each customer who has a balance greater than $150 and placed an order in February 2000.

3. Using two Type I nested queries, list the product number, the name, and the price of products with a price greater than $150 that were ordered on January 23, 2000.

4. Using two Type I nested queries and another join style, list the product number, the name, and the price of products with a price greater than $150 that were ordered in January 2000 by customers with balances greater than $400.

5. List the order number, the order date, the employee number, and the employee name (first and last) of orders placed on January 23, 2000. List the order even if there is not an associated employee.

6. List the order number, the order date, the employee number, the employee name (first and last), the customer number, and the customer name (first and last) of orders placed on January 23, 2000. List the order even if there is not an associated employee.

7. List all the people in the database. The resulting table should have all columns of the *Customer* and *Employee* tables. Match the *Customer* and *Employee* tables on first and last names. If a customer does not match any employees, the columns pertaining to the *Employee* table will be blank. Similarly for an employee who does not match any customers, the columns pertaining to the *Customer* table will be blank. (Hint: in Microsoft Access, qualify column names with the table names when using the join operator style.)

8. For each 'Ink Jet' product ordered in January 2000, list the order number, the order date, the customer number, the customer name (first and last), the employee number (if present), the employee name (first and last), the quantity ordered, the product number, and the product name. Include products containing 'Ink Jet' in the product name. Include both internet (no employee) and phone orders (taken by an employee).

9. Using a Type II nested query, list the customer number and the customer name of Colorado customers who have not placed orders in February 2000.

10. Repeat problem 9 using a Type I nested query instead of a nested query.

11. Repeat problem 9 using the MINUS keyword. Note that Access does not support the MINUS keyword.

12. List the order number and the order date of orders containing only one 'Ink Jet' product. An ink jet product contains the words 'Ink Jet' in the product description.

13. List the customer number and the name (first and last) of customers who have ordered only products manufactured by Connex. Only include customers who have ordered at least one product manufactured by Connex. Remove duplicate rows from the result.

14. List the order number and the order date of orders containing every 'Ink Jet' product.

15. List the product number and the name of products contained on every order placed on January 7, 2000, through January 9, 2000.

16. List the customer number and the name (first and last) of customers who have ordered every product manufactured by 'ColorMeg, Inc.' in January 2000.

17. Using a Type I nested query, delete orders placed by customer Betty Wise in January 2000. The CASCADE DELETE action will delete related rows in the *OrdLine* table.

18. Using a Type I nested query, delete orders placed by Colorado customers that were taken by Landi Santos in January 2000. The CASCADE DELETE action will delete related rows in the *OrdLine* table.

19. List the order number and the order date of orders in which any part of the shipping address (street, city, state, and zip) differs from the customer's address.

20. List the employee number and the employee name (first and last) of employees who have taken orders in January 2000 from every Seattle customer.

Null Value Problems

The following problems involve the *Product* table of the Order Entry database. The table is repeated below for your convenience. The *ProdNextShipDate* column contains the next expected shipment date for the product. If the value is null, a new shipment has not been arranged. A shipment may not be scheduled for a variety of reasons, such as the large quantity on hand or unavailability of the product from the manufacturer.

Product					
ProdNo	ProdName	ProdMfg	ProdQOH	ProdPrice	ProdNextShipDate
P0036566	17 inch Color Monitor	ColorMeg, Inc.	12	$169.00	2/20/2000
P0036577	19 inch Color Monitor	ColorMeg, Inc.	10	$319.00	2/20/2000
P1114590	R3000 Color Laser Printer	Connex	5	$699.00	1/22/2000
P1412138	10 Foot Printer Cable	Ethlite	100	$12.00	
P1445671	8-Outlet Surge Protector	Intersafe	33	$14.99	
P1556678	CVP Ink Jet Color Printer	Connex	8	$99.00	1/22/2000
P3455443	Color Ink Jet Cartridge	Connex	24	$38.00	1/22/2000
P4200344	36-Bit Color Scanner	UV Components	16	$199.99	1/29/2000
P6677900	Black Ink Jet Cartridge	Connex	44	$25.69	
P9995676	Battery Back-up System	Cybercx	12	$89.00	2/1/2000

1. Identify the result rows in the following SELECT statement. Both Access and Oracle versions of the statement are shown.

   Access:

   ```
   SELECT *
     FROM Product
     WHERE ProdNextShipDate = #1/22/2000#
   ```

   Oracle:

   ```
   SELECT *
     FROM Product
     WHERE ProdNextShipDate = '22-Jan-2000'
   ```

2. Identify the result rows in the following SELECT statement:

   Access:

   ```
   SELECT *
     FROM Product
     WHERE ProdNextShipDate = #1/22/2000#
       AND ProdPrice < 100
   ```

   Oracle:

   ```
   SELECT *
     FROM Product
     WHERE ProdNextShipDate = '22-Jan-2000'
       AND ProdPrice < 100
   ```

3. Identify the result rows in the following SELECT statement:

   Access:

   ```
   SELECT *
     FROM Product
     WHERE ProdNextShipDate = #1/22/2000#
       OR ProdPrice < 100
   ```

Oracle:

```
SELECT *
  FROM Product
  WHERE ProdNextShipDate = '22-Jan-2000'
    OR ProdPrice < 100
```

4. Calculate the result of the following SELECT statement:

```
SELECT COUNT(*) AS NumRows,
       COUNT (ProdNextShipDate) AS NumShipDates
  FROM Product
```

5. Calculate the result of the following SELECT statement:

```
SELECT ProdNextShipDate, COUNT(*) AS NumRows
  FROM Product
  GROUP BY ProdNextShipDate
```

6. Calculate the result of the following SELECT statement:

```
SELECT ProdMfg, ProdNextShipDate, COUNT(*) AS NumRows
  FROM Product
  GROUP BY ProdMfg, ProdNextShipDate
```

7. Calculate the result of the following SELECT statement:

```
SELECT ProdNextShipDate, ProdMfg, COUNT(*) AS NumRows
  FROM Product
  GROUP BY ProdNextShipDate, ProdMfg
```

REFERENCES FOR FURTHER STUDY

Most textbooks for the business student do not cover query formulation and SQL in as much detail as here. Specialized books on SQL2 such as Bowman, Emerson, and Darnovsky (1996); Cannan and Otten (1992); Date and Darwen (1997); and Melton and Simon (1992) cover a larger subset of SQL but lack the pedagogy found here. Celko (1997) provides many interesting problems and SQL solutions. Groff and Weinberg (1999) cover the various notations for outer joins available in commercial DBMSs. The SQL Server Pro site (http://www.inquiry.com/techtips/thesqlpro/) and the database information center of the *Intelligent Enterprise* magazine (http://www.iemagazine.com/) have plenty of practical advice about SQL.

Appendix 4.A   **Microsoft Access Formulation of Division Problems**

Because Microsoft Access SQL does not support the use of the DISTINCT keyword inside aggregate functions, the solutions in Examples 4.27 and 4.28 will not work. Using stored queries provides a simple remedy in Access SQL. Whenever you need to use DISTINCT inside COUNT, use a stored query with the DISTINCT keyword following the SELECT keyword. In Example 4A.1, the first stored query (Temp4A-1) finds the unique combinations of faculty name and course number. Note the use of the DISTINCT keyword to eliminate duplicates. The second stored query (Temp4A-2) finds the unique course numbers in the *Offering* table. The final query combines the two stored queries. Note that you can use stored queries similar to the way tables are used. Simply use the stored query name in the FROM clause.

EXAMPLE 4A.1   Using Stored Queries Instead of COUNT(DISTINCT . . .)

List the name of faculty who teach in at least one section of all fall 1999 IS courses. The result is identical to that in Example 4.27.

Temp4A-1:

```
SELECT DISTINCT Faculty.FacSSN, FacFirstName,
                FacLastName, CourseNo
  FROM Faculty, Offering
  WHERE Faculty.FacSSN = Offering.FacSSN
    AND OffTerm = 'FALL' AND OffYear = 1999
    AND CourseNo LIKE 'IS*'
```

Temp4A-2:

```
SELECT DISTINCT CourseNo
  FROM Offering
  WHERE OffTerm = 'FALL' AND OffYear = 1999
    AND CourseNo LIKE 'IS*'


SELECT FacSSN, FacFirstName, FacLastName
  FROM [Temp4A-1]
  GROUP BY FacSSN, FacFirstName, FacLastName
  HAVING COUNT(*) =
    ( SELECT COUNT(*) FROM [Temp4A-2]  )
```

Appendix 4.B   **SQL2 Syntax Summary**

This appendix summarizes the SQL2 syntax for nested SELECT statements (subqueries) and outer join operations presented in Chapter 4. For the syntax of other variations of the nested SELECT and outer join operations not presented in Chapter 4, consult an SQL2 reference book such as Groff and Weinberg (1999). Nested SELECT statements can be used in the WHERE clause of the SELECT, UPDATE, and DELETE statements. The conventions used in the syntax notation are identical to those used at the end of Chapter 2.

Expanded Syntax for Row Conditions

```
<Row-Condition>:
  {<Simple-Condition> |—defined in Chapter 3
  <Compound-Condition> |—defined in Chapter 3
  <Exists-Condition> |
  <Element-Condition> }
<Exists-Condition>: [ NOT ] EXISTS <Simple-Select>
<Simple-Select>:—defined in Chapter 3
<Element-Condition>: <Scalar-Expression> <Element-Operator> ( <Simple-Select> )
<Element-Operator>: { = | < | > | >= | <= | <> | [ NOT ] IN }
<Scalar-Expression>:—defined in Chapter 3
```

Expanded Syntax for Group Conditions

```
<Simple-Group-Condition>:—Last choice is new
{ <Column-Expression> ComparisonOperator <Column-Expression> |
  <Column-Expression> [ NOT ] IN ( Constant* ) |
  <Column-Expression> BETWEEN <Column-Expression> AND <Column-Expression> |
  <Column-Expression> IS [NOT] NULL
  ColumnName [ NOT ] LIKE StringPattern
  <Exists-Condition> |
  <Column-Expression> <Element-Operator> <Simple-Select> }
  <Column-Expression>:—defined in Chapter 3
```

Expanded Syntax for Outer Join Operations

```
<Table-Specification>: { <Simple-Table>* | <Join-Operation> | <Outer-Join> }
<Simple-Table>:—defined in Chapter 3
<Join-Operation>:—defined in Chapter 3
<Outer-Join>:
  { TableName LEFT [ OUTER ] JOIN TableName ON <Join-Condition> |
    TableName RIGHT [ OUTER ] JOIN TableName ON <Join-Condition> |
    TableName FULL [ OUTER ] JOIN TableName ON <Join-Condition> |
    ( <Outer-Join > ) }
```

Application Development with Views

This chapter describes concepts underlying views and demonstrates how to use views when developing forms, reports, and other database applications. After this chapter, the student should have acquired the following knowledge and skills:

- Write CREATE VIEW statements.

- Write queries that use views.

- Apply rules to determine if single-table and multiple-table views are updatable.

- Identify the relationship and join column used in a hierarchical form.

- Write queries that provide data for hierarchical forms.

- Formulate queries that provide input for hierarchical reports.

OVERVIEW

Chapters 2, 3, and 4 provided the foundation for understanding relational databases and formulating queries in SQL. Most importantly, you gained practice with a large number of examples, acquired conceptual skills for query formulation, and learned different parts of SQL. This chapter shows you how to apply your query formulation skills to building applications with views.

This chapter emphasizes views as the foundation for building database applications. Before discussing the link between views and database applications, essential background is provided. You will learn the motivation for views, the CREATE VIEW statement in SQL2, and usage of views in SELECT and data manipulation (INSERT, UPDATE, and DELETE) statements. Most view examples in Sections 5.2 and 5.3 are supported in Microsoft Access as stored queries and in Oracle 8 as views. After this background, you will learn about using views to build database applications based on hierarchical forms and reports.

5.1 BACKGROUND

View a table derived from base or physical tables using a query.

A <u>view</u> is a virtual or derived table. Virtual means that a view behaves like a base table but no physical table exists. A view can be used in a query like a base table. However, the rows of a view do not exist until they are derived from base tables. This section describes why views are important and how to define them in SQL.

5.1.1 Motivation

Views provide the external level of the Three Schema Architecture described in Chapter 1. The Three Schema Architecture promotes <u>data independence</u> to reduce the impact of database definition changes on applications that use a database. If an application accesses the database through a view, most changes to the conceptual schema will not affect the application. For example, if a table name used in a view changes, the view definition must be changed but applications using the view do not have to be changed.

<u>Simplification</u> of tasks is another important benefit of views. Many queries can be easier to formulate if a view is used rather than base tables. Without a view, a SELECT statement may involve two, three, or more tables and require grouping if summary data are needed. With a view, the SELECT statement can just reference a view without joins or grouping. Training users to write single table queries is much easier than training them to write multiple table queries with grouping.

Views provide simplification similar to macros in programming languages and spreadsheets. A macro is a named collection of commands. Using a macro removes the burden of specifying the commands just as using a view removes the burden of writing the underlying query.

Views also provide a flexible level of <u>security</u>. Restricting access by views is more flexible than restrictions for fields and tables because a view is any derived part of a database. Data not in the view are hidden from the user. For example, you can restrict a user to selected departments, products, or geographic regions in a view. Security using tables and fields cannot specify conditions and computations, which can be done in a view. A view even can include aggregate calculations to restrict users to row summaries rather than individual rows.

The only drawback to views can be performance. For most views, using the views instead of base tables directly will not involve a significant performance penalty. For some complex views, using the views can involve a significant performance penalty as opposed to using the base tables directly. The performance penalty can vary by DBMS. Before using complex views, you are encouraged to compare performance to using the base tables directly.

5.1.2 View Definition

 Defining a view is no more difficult than writing a query. SQL2 provides the CREATE VIEW statement in which the view name and the underlying SELECT statement must be specified, as shown in Examples 5.1 and 5.2. In Microsoft Access, the SELECT statement part of the examples can be saved as a stored query to achieve the same effect as a view. In Oracle 8, the CREATE VIEW statement executes directly.

EXAMPLE 5.1

Define a Single Table View
Define a view named IS_View consisting of students majoring in IS.

```
CREATE VIEW IS_View AS
    SELECT * FROM Student
        WHERE StdMajor = 'IS'
```

StdSSN	StdFirstName	StdLastName	StdCity	StdState	StdZip	StdMajor	StdClass	StdGPA
123-45-6789	HOMER	WELLS	SEATTLE	WA	98121-1111	IS	FR	3.00
345-67-8901	WALLY	KENDALL	SEATTLE	WA	98123-1141	IS	SR	2.80
567-89-0123	MARIAH	DODGE	SEATTLE	WA	98114-0021	IS	JR	3.60
876-54-3210	CRISTOPHER	COLAN	SEATTLE	WA	98114-1332	IS	SR	4.00
890-12-3456	LUKE	BRAZZI	SEATTLE	WA	98116-0021	IS	SR	2.20
901-23-4567	WILLIAM	PILGRIM	BOTHELL	WA	98113-1885	IS	SO	3.80

EXAMPLE 5.2

Define a Multiple Table View
Define a view named MS_View consisting of offerings taught by faculty in the Management Science department.

```
CREATE VIEW MS_View AS
    SELECT OfferNo, Offering.CourseNo, CrsUnits, OffTerm,
            OffYear, Offering.FacSSN, FacFirstName,
            FacLastName, OffTime, OffDays
        FROM Faculty, Course, Offering
        WHERE FacDept = 'MS'
            AND Faculty.FacSSN = Offering.FacSSN
            AND Offering.CourseNo = Course.CourseNo
```

OfferNo	CourseNo	CrsUnits	OffTerm	OffYear	FacSSN	FacFirstName	FacLastName	OffTime	OffDays
1234	IS320	4	FALL	1999	098-76-5432	LEONARD	VINCE	10:30 AM	MW
3333	IS320	4	SPRING	2000	098-76-5432	LEONARD	VINCE	8:30 AM	MW
4321	IS320	4	FALL	1999	098-76-5432	LEONARD	VINCE	3:30 PM	TTH
4444	IS320	4	WINTER	2000	543-21-0987	VICTORIA	EMMANUEL	3:30 PM	TTH
8888	IS320	4	SUMMER	2000	654-32-1098	LEONARD	FIBON	1:30 PM	MW
9876	IS460	4	SPRING	2000	654-32-1098	LEONARD	FIBON	1:30 PM	TTH
5679	IS480	4	SPRING	2000	876-54-3210	CRISTOPHER	COLAN	3:30 PM	TTH

In the CREATE VIEW statement, a list of column names enclosed in parentheses can follow the view name. A list of column names is required when a column in the view's SELECT statement is renamed or defined with an expression or built-in function. The column list is omitted in MS_View because there are no computed or renamed columns. The column list is required in Example 5.3 because of the aggregate calculation (COUNT(*)). If one column is computed or renamed, the entire list of column names must be given.

EXAMPLE 5.3   Define a View with Renamed Columns

Define a view named Enrollment_View consisting of offering data and the number of students enrolled.

```
CREATE VIEW Enrollment_View
    (OfferNo, CourseNo, Term, Year, Instructor, NumStudents)
    AS
SELECT Offering.OfferNo, CourseNo, OffTerm, OffYear,
        FacLastName, COUNT(*)
    FROM Offering, Faculty, Enrollment
    WHERE Offering.FacSSN = Faculty.FacSSN
        AND Offering.OfferNo = Enrollment.OfferNo
    GROUP BY Offering.OfferNo, CourseNo, OffTerm, OffYear,
        FacFirstName, FacLastName
```

OfferNo	CourseNo	Term	Year	Instructor	NumStudents
1234	IS320	FALL	1999	VINCE	6
4321	IS320	FALL	1999	VINCE	6
5555	FIN300	WINTER	2000	MACON	2
5678	IS480	WINTER	2000	MILLS	5
5679	IS480	SPRING	2000	COLAN	6
6666	FIN450	WINTER	2000	MILLS	2
7777	FIN480	SPRING	2000	MACON	3
9876	IS460	SPRING	2000	FIBON	7

In some DBMSs such as Microsoft Access, a view is merely a stored query. You create a stored query simply by writing it and then supplying a name when saving it.

5.2 USING VIEWS FOR RETRIEVAL

This section shows examples of queries that use views and explains how queries with views are processed. After showing examples in Section 5.2.1, two methods to process queries with views are described in Section 5.2.2.

5.2.1 Using Views in SELECT Statements

Once a view is defined, it can be used in SELECT statements. Simply use the view name in the FROM clause and the view columns in other parts of the statement. You can add other conditions and select a subset of the columns as demonstrated in Examples 5.4 and 5.5.

EXAMPLE 5.4

Query Using a Multiple Table View
List the spring 2000 courses in MS_View.

```
SELECT OfferNo, CourseNo, FacFirstName, FacLastName,
         OffTime, OffDays
    FROM MS_View
    WHERE OffTerm = 'SPRING' AND OffYear = 2000
```

OfferNo	CourseNo	FacFirstName	FacLastName	OffTime	OffDays
3333	IS320	LEONARD	VINCE	8:30 AM	MW
9876	IS460	LEONARD	FIBON	1:30 PM	TTH
5679	IS480	CRISTOPHER	COLAN	3:30 PM	TTH

EXAMPLE 5.5

Query Using a Grouping View (Access)
List the spring 2000 offerings of IS courses in the Enrollment_View. In Oracle, the %
should be used in place of the * for wildcard matching.

```
SELECT OfferNo, CourseNo, Instructor, NumStudents
    FROM Enrollment_View
    WHERE Term = 'SPRING' AND Year = 2000
        AND CourseNo LIKE 'IS*'
```

OfferNo	CourseNo	Instructor	NumStudents
5679	IS480	COLAN	6
9876	IS460	FIBON	7

Both queries are much easier to write than the original queries. A novice user can probably write both queries with just a little training. In contrast, it may take many hours of training for a novice user to write queries with multiple tables and grouping.

According to SQL2, a view can be used in any query. In practice, most DBMSs have some limitations on view usage in queries. For example, some DBMSs do not support the queries[1] shown in Examples 5.6 and 5.7.

EXAMPLE 5.6

Grouping Query Using a View Derived from a Grouping Query
List the average number of students by instructor name using Enrollment_View.

```
SELECT Instructor, AVG(NumStudents) AS AvgStdCount
    FROM Enrollment_View
    GROUP BY Instructor
```

[1]Microsoft Access 97 and 2000 and Oracle 8 both support Examples 5.6 and 5.7.

Instructor	AvgStdCount
COLAN	6
FIBON	7
MACON	2.5
MILLS	3.5
VINCE	6

EXAMPLE 5.7

Joining a Base Table with a View Derived from a Grouping Query

List the offering number, instructor, number of students, and course units using the *Enrollment_View* View and the *Course* table.

```
SELECT OfferNo, Instructor, NumStudents, CrsUnits
    FROM Enrollment_View, Course
    WHERE Enrollment_View.CourseNo = Course.CourseNo
    AND NumStudents < 5
```

OfferNo	Instructor	NumStudents	CrsUnits
5555	MACON	2	4
6666	MILLS	2	4
7777	MACON	3	4

5.2.2 Processing Queries with View References

View Materialization a method to process a query on a view by executing the query defining the view followed by the query using the view. In most cases, materialization is not an efficient way to process a query on a view.

To process queries that reference a view, the DBMS can use either a materialization or modification strategy. <u>Materialization</u> requires that the DBMS execute two queries, as depicted in Figure 5.1. The user submits a query using a view (Query$_v$). The query defin-

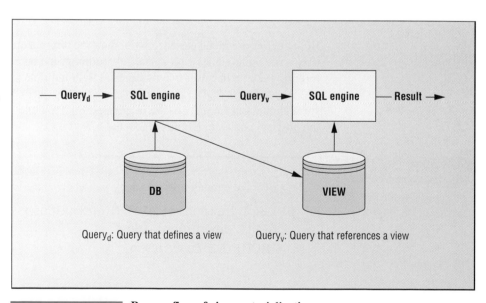

Query$_d$: Query that defines a view   Query$_v$: Query that references a view

Figure 5.1   **Process flow of view materialization.**

ing the view ($Query_d$) is executed and a temporary view table is created. Figure 5.1 depicts this action by the arrow into the view. Then, the query using the view is executed using the temporary view table. Materialization is usually not the preferred strategy because it requires the DBMS to execute two queries. However, on certain queries such as Examples 5.6 and 5.7, materialization may be necessary.

<u>Modification</u> usually provides better performance than materialization because the DBMS only executes one query. Figure 5.2 shows that a query using a view is modified or rewritten as a query using base tables only, then the modified query is executed using the base tables. The modification process happens automatically without any user knowledge or action. In most DBMSs, the modified query cannot be seen even if you want to review it.

As a modification example, consider the transformation shown from Example 5.8 to Example 5.9. When you submit a query using a view, the reference to the view is replaced with the definition of the view. The view name in the FROM clause is replaced by base tables. In addition, the conditions in the WHERE clause are combined using the Boolean AND with the conditions in the query defining the view. The underlined parts in Example 5.9 indicate substitutions made in the modification process.

View Modification a method to process a query on a view involving the execution of only one query. A query using a view is translated into a query using base tables by replacing references to the view with its definition. In most cases, modification provides an efficient way to process a query on a view.

EXAMPLE 5.8   Query Using MS_View

```
SELECT OfferNo, CourseNo, FacFirstName, FacLastName,
OffTime, OffDays
  FROM MS_View
  WHERE OffTerm = 'SPRING' AND OffYear = 2000
```

OfferNo	CourseNo	FacFirstName	FacLastName	OffTime	OffDays
3333	IS320	LEONARD	VINCE	8:30 AM	MW
9876	IS460	LEONARD	FIBON	1:30 PM	TTH
5679	IS480	CRISTOPHER	COLAN	3:30 PM	TTH

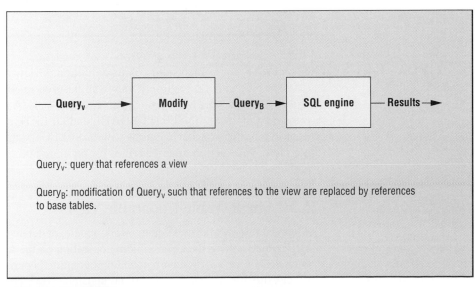

Query$_v$: query that references a view

Query$_B$: modification of Query$_v$ such that references to the view are replaced by references to base tables.

Figure 5.2   **Process flow of view modification.**

EXAMPLE 5.9	Modification of Example 5.8

Example 5.8 is modified by replacing references to MS_View with base table references.

```
SELECT OfferNo, Course.CourseNo, FacFirstName,
         FacLastName, OffTime, OffDays
    FROM Faculty, Course, Offering
    WHERE FacDept = 'MS'
        AND Faculty.FacSSN = Offering.FacSSN
        AND Offering.CourseNo = Course.CourseNo
        AND OffTerm = 'SPRING' AND OffYear = 2000
```

If the DBMS is intelligent, it can sometimes simplify modified queries. For example, the *Course* table is not needed because there are no conditions and columns from the *Course* table in Example 5.9. In addition, the join between the *Offering* and the *Course* tables is not necessary because every *Offering* row is related to a *Course* row (null is not allowed). As a result, the modified query can be simplified by removing the *Course* table. Such simplification will result in a faster execution time, as the most important factor in execution time is the number of tables.

EXAMPLE 5.10	Further Simplification of Example 5.9

Simplify by removing the *Course* table because it is not needed in Example 5.9.

```
SELECT OfferNo, CourseNo, FacFirstName, FacLastName,
         OffTime, OffDays
    FROM Faculty, Offering
    WHERE FacDept = 'MS'
        AND Faculty.FacSSN = Offering.FacSSN
        AND OffTerm = 'SPRING' AND OffYear = 2000
```

5.3 UPDATING USING VIEWS

Depending on its definition, a view can be read-only or updatable. A read-only view can be used in SELECT statements as demonstrated in Section 5.2. All views are at least read-only. A read-only view cannot be used in queries involving INSERT, UPDATE, and DELETE statements. A view that can be used in modification statements as well as SELECT statements is known as an updatable view. This section describes rules for defining both single-table and multiple-table updatable views.

> **Updatable View** a view that can be used in SELECT statements as well as UPDATE, INSERT, and DELETE statements. Views that can be used only with SELECT statements are known as read-only views.

5.3.1 Single-Table Updatable Views

An updatable view allows you to insert, update, or delete rows in the underlying base tables by performing the corresponding operation on the view. Whenever a modification is made to a view row, a corresponding operation is performed on the base table. Intuitively, this means that the rows of an updatable view correspond in a one-to-one manner with rows from the underlying base tables. If a view contains the primary key of the base table, then each view row matches a base table row. A single-table view is updatable if it satisfies the following three rules that include the primary key requirement.

Rules for Single-Table Updatable Views

1. The view includes the primary key of the base table.
2. All required fields (NOT NULL) of the base table are in the view.
3. The view's query does not include GROUP BY or DISTINCT.

Following these rules, *Fac_View1* (Example 5.11) is updatable while *Fac_View2* (Example 5.12) and *Fac_View3* (Example 5.13) are read-only. *Fac_View1* is updatable assuming the missing *Faculty* columns are not required. *Fac_View2* violates Rule 2 while *Fac_View3* violates Rule 3, making them read-only.

EXAMPLE 5.11   Single-Table Updatable View
Create a row and column subset view with the primary key.

```
CREATE VIEW Fac_View1 AS
    SELECT FacSSN, FacFirstName, FacLastName, FacRank,
            FacSalary, FacDept, FacCity, FacState, FacZipCode
    FROM Faculty
    WHERE FacDept = 'MS'
```

FacSSN	FacFirstName	FacLastName	FacRank	FacSalary	FacDept	FacCity	FacState	FacZipCode
098-76-5432	LEONARD	VINCE	ASST	$35,000.00	MS	SEATTLE	WA	98111-9921
543-21-0987	VICTORIA	EMMANUEL	PROF	$120,000.00	MS	BOTHELL	WA	98011-2242
654-32-1098	LEONARD	FIBON	ASSC	$70,000.00	MS	SEATTLE	WA	98121-0094
876-54-3210	CRISTOPHER	COLAN	ASST	$40,000.00	MS	SEATTLE	WA	98114-1332

EXAMPLE 5.12   Single-Table Read-Only View
Create a row and column subset without the primary key.

```
CREATE VIEW Fac_View2 AS
    SELECT FacDept, FacRank, FacSalary
    FROM Faculty
    WHERE FacSalary > 50000
```

FacDept	FacRank	FacSalary
MS	PROF	$120,000.00
MS	ASSC	$70,000.00
FIN	PROF	$65,000.00
FIN	ASSC	$75,000.00

EXAMPLE 5.13   Single-Table Read-Only View
Create a grouping view with faculty department and average salary.

```
CREATE View Fac_View3 (FacDept, AvgSalary) AS
    SELECT FacDept, AVG(FacSalary)
    FROM Faculty
```

```
WHERE FacRank = 'PROF'
GROUP BY FacDept
```

FacDept	AvgSalary
FIN	65000
MS	120000

Because *Fac_View1* is updatable, it can be used in INSERT, UPDATE, and DELETE statements to change the *Faculty* table. In Chapters 3 and 4, you used these statements to change rows in base tables. Examples 5.14 through 5.16 demonstrate that these statements can be used to change view rows and rows of the underlying base tables. Note that modifications to views are subject to the integrity rules of the underlying base table. The insertion in Example 5.14 is rejected if another *Faculty* row has '999-99-8888' as the social security number. When deleting rows in a view or changing the primary key column, the rules on referenced rows apply (Section 2.4). For example, the deletion in Example 5.16 is rejected if the Faculty with *FacSSN* '098-76-5432' has related rows in the *Offering* table and the delete rule for the *Faculty–Offering* relationship is set to RESTRICTED.

EXAMPLE 5.14   Insert Operation on Updatable View

Insert a new faculty row into the MS department.

```
INSERT INTO Fac_View1 (FacSSN, FacFirstName,
                        FacLastName, FacRank, FacSalary,
                        FacDept, FacCity, FacState,
                        FacZipCode)
VALUES ('999-99-8888', 'JOE', 'SMITH', 'PROF', 80000,
        'MS', 'SEATTLE', 'WA', '98011-011')
```

EXAMPLE 5.15   Update Operation on Updatable View

Give assistant professors in Fac_View1 a 10 percent raise.

```
UPDATE Fac_View1
   SET FacSalary = FacSalary * 1.1
   WHERE FacRank = 'ASST'
```

EXAMPLE 5.16   Delete Operation on Updatable View

Delete a specific faculty member from Fac_View1.

```
DELETE FROM Fac_View1
   WHERE FacSSN = '098-76-5432'
```

View Updates with Side Effects

Some modifications to updatable views can be problematic, as demonstrated in Example 5.17 and Tables 5–1 and 5–2. The update statement in Example 5.17 changes the department of the last row (Victoria Emmanuel) in the view and the corresponding row in

TABLE 5–1	Fac_View1 before Update				
FacSSN	FacFirstName	FacLastName	FacRank	FacSalary	FacDept
098-76-5432	LEONARD	VINCE	ASST	$35,000.00	MS
876-54-3210	CRISTOPHER	COLAN	ASST	$40,000.00	MS
654-32-1098	LEONARD	FIBON	ASSC	$70,000.00	MS
543-21-0987	VICTORIA	EMMANUEL	PROF	$120,000.00	MS

TABLE 5–2	Fac_View1 after Example 5.17 Update				
FacSSN	FacFirstName	FacLastName	FacRank	FacSalary	FacDept
098-76-5432	LEONARD	VINCE	ASST	$35,000.00	MS
876-54-3210	CRISTOPHER	COLAN	ASST	$40,000.00	MS
654-32-1098	LEONARD	FIBON	ASSC	$70,000.00	MS

the base table. Upon regenerating the view, however, the changed row disappears (Table 5–2). The update has the side effect of causing the row to disappear from the view. This kind of side effect can occur whenever a column in the WHERE clause of the view definition is changed by an UPDATE statement. Example 5.17 updates the *FacDept* column, the column used in the WHERE clause of the definition of the *Fac_View1* view.

EXAMPLE 5.17

Update Operation on Updatable View with a Side Effect
Change the department of highly paid faculty members to the finance department.

```
UPDATE Fac_View1
   SET FacDept = 'FIN'
   WHERE FacSalary > 100000
```

WITH CHECK OPTION   a clause in the CREATE VIEW statement that prevents side effects when updating a view. The WITH CHECK OPTION clause prevents UPDATE and INSERT statements that violate a view's WHERE clause.

Because this side effect can be confusing to a user, the WITH CHECK OPTION clause can be used to prevent updates with side effects. If the WITH CHECK OPTION is specified in the CREATE VIEW statement (Example 5.18), INSERT or UPDATE statements that violate the WHERE clause are rejected. The update in Example 5.17 would be rejected if *Fac_View1* contained a CHECK OPTION clause because changing *FacDept* to 'FIN' violates the WHERE condition.

EXAMPLE 5.18

Single-Table Updatable View Using the WITH CHECK OPTION
Create a row and column subset view with the primary key.

```
CREATE VIEW Fac_View1_Revised AS
   SELECT FacSSN, FacFirstName, FacLastName, FacRank,
            FacSalary, FacDept, FacCity, FacState, FacZipCode
      FROM Faculty
      WHERE FacDept = 'MS'
   WITH CHECK OPTION
```

5.3.2 Multiple-Table Updatable Views

It may be surprising but some multiple-table views are also updatable. A multiple-table view may correspond in a one-to-one manner with rows from more than one table if the view contains the primary key of each table. Because multiple-table views are more complex than single-table views, there is not wide agreement on updatability rules for multiple-table views. Some DBMSs may not support updatability for any multiple-table views. Other systems support updatability for a large number of multiple-table views. In this section, the updatability rules in Microsoft Access are described as they support a wide range of multiple-table views. Appendix 5.B describes the rules for updatable join views in Oracle 8. The rules for updatable join views in Oracle 8 are similar to Microsoft Access although Oracle is somewhat more restrictive on the allowable manipulation operations.

In Access, multiple-table queries known as 1-M queries are updatable. A 1-M query involves two or more tables with one table playing the role of the 1 table and another table playing the role of the M (many) table. For example, in a query involving the *Course* and the *Offering* tables, *Course* plays the role of the 1 table and *Offering,* the M table. To make a 1-M query updatable, follow these rules:

Rules for Multiple-Table Updatable Queries

1. The query includes the primary key of the M table.
2. The query contains all required fields (NOT NULL) of the M table.
3. The query does not include GROUP BY or DISTINCT.
4. The join field of the 1 table should be unique (either a primary key or a unique specification).
5. The query contains the foreign key column(s) of the M table.
6. The query includes the primary key and required fields of the 1 table if the view supports insert operations on the 1 table. Update operations are supported on the 1 table even if the primary key is omitted in the view.

Using these rules, Course_Offering_View1 (Example 5.19) and Faculty_Offering_View1 (Example 5.21) are updatable. Course_Offering_View2 (Example 5.20) is not updatable because *Offering.CourseNo* (the foreign key of the M table) is missing. In the SELECT statements, the join operator style (INNER JOIN keywords) is used because Microsoft Access requires it for updatable 1-M queries.

EXAMPLE 5.19

Multiple-Table Updatable Query (Access)

Create a 1-M updatable query (saved as Course_Offering_View1) with a join between the *Course* and the *Offering* tables.

Course_Offering_View1:

```
SELECT Course.CourseNo, CrsDesc, CrsUnits,
       Offering.OfferNo, OffTerm, OffYear,
       Offering.CourseNo, OffLocation, OffTime, FacSSN,
       OffDays
  FROM Course INNER JOIN Offering
       ON Course.CourseNo = Offering.CourseNo
```

EXAMPLE 5.20

Multiple-Table Read-Only Query (Access)

This query (saved as Course_Offering_View2) is read-only because it does not contain *Offering.CourseNo.*

Course_Offering View2:
```
SELECT CrsDesc, CrsUnits, Offering.OfferNo,
       Course.CourseNo, OffTerm, OffYear, OffLocation,
       OffTime, FacSSN, OffDays
    FROM Course INNER JOIN Offering
       ON Course.CourseNo = Offering.CourseNo
```

EXAMPLE 5.21

Multiple-Table Updatable View (Access)

Create a 1-M updatable query (saved as Faculty_Offering_View1) with a join between the *Faculty* and the *Offering* tables.

Faculty_Offering_View1:
```
SELECT Offering.OfferNo, Offering.FacSSN, CourseNo,
       OffTerm, OffYear, OffLocation, OffTime, OffDays,
       FacFirstName, FacLastName, FacDept
    FROM Faculty INNER JOIN Offering
       ON Faculty.FacSSN = Offering.FacSSN
```

Inserting Rows in 1-M Updatable Views

Inserting a new row in a 1-M updatable query is more involved than inserting a row in a single-table view. This complication results because there is a choice about the tables that support insert operations. Rows from either both tables (1 and M tables) or only one table can be inserted as a result of a view update. To insert a row into the M table, supply only the values needed to insert a row into the M table as demonstrated in Example 5.22. Note that the value for *Offering.CourseNo* and *Offering.FacSSN* must match existing rows in the *Course* and the *Faculty* tables, respectively.

EXAMPLE 5.22

Inserting a Row into the M Table as a Result of a View Update (Access)

Insert a new row into *Offering* as a result of using Course_Offering_View1.

```
INSERT INTO Course_Offering_View1
   ( Offering.OfferNo, Offering.CourseNo, OffTerm, OffYear,
     OffLocation, OffTime, FacSSN,OffDays )
   VALUES ( 7799, 'IS480', 'SPRING', 2000, 'BLM201',
            #1:30PM#, '098-76-5432', 'MW' )
```

To insert a row into both tables (1 and M tables), the view must include the primary key and the required fields of the 1 table. If the view includes these fields, supplying values for all fields inserts a row into both tables, as demonstrated in Example 5.23. Supplying values for just the 1 table inserts a row only into the 1 table, as demonstrated in Example 5.24. In both examples, the value for *Course.CourseNo* must not match an existing row in *Course*.

EXAMPLE 5.23   Inserting a Row into Both Tables as a Result of a View Update (Access)

Insert a new row into *Course* and *Offering* as a result of using Course_Offering_View1.

```
INSERT INTO Course_Offering_View1
   ( Course.CourseNo, CrsUnits, CrsDesc, Offering.OfferNo,
     OffTerm, OffYear,OffLocation, OffTime, FacSSN,
     OffDays )
VALUES ( 'IS423', 4, 'OBJECT ORIENTED COMPUTING', 8877,
            'SPRING', 2000, 'BLM201', 3:30PM,
            '123-45-6789', 'MW' )
```

EXAMPLE 5.24   Inserting a Row into the 1 Table as a Result of a View Update (Access)

Insert a new row into the *Course* table as a result of using the Course_Offering_View1.

```
INSERT INTO Course_Offering_View1
   ( Course.CourseNo, CrsUnits, CrsDesc)
VALUES ( 'IS481', 4, 'ADVANCED DATABASE' )
```

1-M Updatable Queries with More than Two Tables

Queries involving more than two tables also can be updatable. The same rules apply to 1-M updatable queries with more than two tables. However, you should apply the rules to each join in the query. For example, if a query has three tables (two joins), then apply the rules to both joins. In Faculty_Offering_Course_View1 (Example 5.25), *Offering* is the M table in both joins. Thus, the foreign keys (*Offering.CourseNo* and *Offering.FacSSN*) must be in the query result. In the Faculty_Offering_Course_Enrollment_View1 (Example 5.26), *Enrollment* is the M table in one join and *Offering* is the M table in the other two joins. The primary key of the *Offering* table is not needed in the result unless *Offering* rows can be inserted using the view. In Example 5.26, only the *Enrollment* table is updatable.

EXAMPLE 5.25   1-M Updatable Query with Three Tables (Access)

Faculty_Offering_Course_View1:

```
SELECT CrsDesc, CrsUnits, Offering.OfferNo,
          Offering.CourseNo, OffTerm, OffYear, OffLocation,
          OffTime, Offering.FacSSN, OffDays, FacFirstName,
          FacLastName
FROM ( Course INNER JOIN Offering
          ON Course.CourseNo = Offering.CourseNo )
      INNER JOIN Faculty
          ON Offering.FacSSN = Faculty.FacSSN
```

EXAMPLE 5.26   1-M Updatable Query with Four Tables (Access)

Faculty_Offering_Course_Enrollment_View1:

```
SELECT CrsDesc, CrsUnits, Offering.CourseNo,
          Offering.FacSSN, FacFirstName, FacLastName,
```

```
        OffTerm, OffYear, OffLocation, OffTime, OffDays,
        Enrollment.OfferNo, Enrollment.StdSSN,
        Enrollment.EnrGrade
FROM ( ( Course INNER JOIN Offering
        ON Course.CourseNo = Offering.CourseNo )
    INNER JOIN Faculty
        ON Offering.FacSSN = Faculty.FacSSN )
    INNER JOIN Enrollment
        ON Enrollment.OfferNo = Offering.OfferNo
```

The specific rules about which insert, update, and delete operations are supported on 1-M updatable queries are more complex than what is described here. The purpose here is to demonstrate that multiple-table views can be updatable and the rules can be complex. The Microsoft Access documentation provides a complete description of the rules.

The choices about updatable tables in a multiple-table view can be confusing especially when the view includes more than two tables. Typically, only the M table should be updatable, so the considerations in Examples 5.23 and 5.24 do not apply. The choices are usually dictated by the needs of data entry forms, discussed in the next section.

5.4 USING VIEWS IN HIERARCHICAL FORMS

One of the most important benefits of views is that they are the building blocks for applications. Data entry forms, a cornerstone of most database applications, support retrieval and modification of tables. Data entry forms are formatted so that they are visually appealing and easy to use. In contrast, the plain formatting of base tables may not appeal to most users. This section describes the hierarchical form, a powerful kind of data entry form, and the relationships between views and hierarchical forms.

5.4.1 What Is a Hierarchical Form?

Hierarchical Form a formatted window for data entry and display using a fixed (main form) and variable (subform) part. One record is shown in the main form and multiple, related records are shown in the subform.

A form is a document used in a business process. A form is designed to support a business task such as processing an order, registering for classes, or making an airline reservation. Hierarchical forms support business tasks with a fixed and a variable part. The fixed part of a hierarchical form is known as the main form, while the variable (repeating) part is known as the subform. For example, a hierarchical form for course offerings (Figure 5.3) shows course data in the main form and offering data in the subform. A hierarchical form for class registration (Figure 5.4) shows registration and student data in the main form and enrollment in course offerings in the subform. The billing calculation fields below the subform are part of the main form. In each form, the subform can display multiple records while the main form shows only one record.

Hierarchical forms can be part of a system of related forms. For example, a student information system may have forms for student admissions, grade recording, course approval, course scheduling, and faculty assignments to courses. These forms may be related through updates to the database or by directly sending data between forms. For example, updates to a database made by processing a registration form are used at the end of a term by a grade recording form. This chapter emphasizes the data requirements of individual forms, an important skill of application development. This skill complements other application development skills such as user interface design and workflow design.

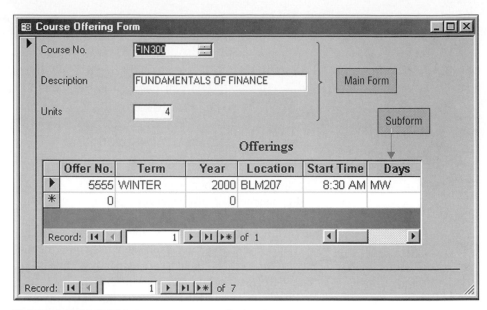

Figure 5.3   Example course offering form.

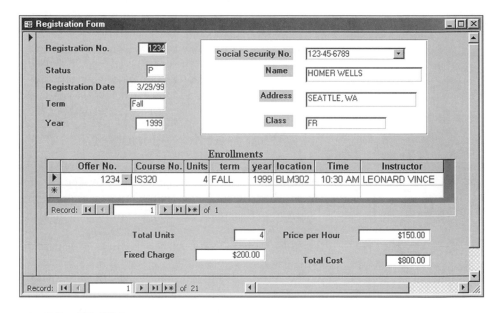

Figure 5.4   Example registration form.

5.4.2 Relationship between Hierarchical Forms and Tables

Hierarchical forms support operations on 1-M (one to many) relationships. A hierarchy or tree is a structure with 1-M relationships. Each <u>1-M relationship</u> has a parent (the 1 table) and a child (the M table). A hierarchical form allows the user to insert, update, delete, and retrieve records in both tables of a 1-M relationship. A hierarchical form is designed to manipulate (display, insert, update, and delete) the 1 table in the main form and the M table in the subform. In essence, a hierarchical form is a nice interface for operations on a 1-M relationship.

As examples, consider the hierarchical forms shown in Figure 5.3 and 5.4. In the Course Offering Form (Figure 5.3), the relationship between the *Course* and the *Offering* tables enables the form to display a *Course* row in the main form and related *Offering* rows in the subform. The Registration Form (Figure 5.4) operates on the *Registration* and the *Enrollment* tables as well as the 1-M relationship between these tables. The *Registration* table is a new table in the university database. Figure 5.5 shows a revised relationship diagram.

To better support a business process, it is often useful to display other information in the main form and subform. Other information (outside of the 1 and the M tables) is usually for display purposes. Although it is possible to design a form to allow fields from other tables to be changed, the requirements of a particular business process may not warrant it. For example, the Registration Form (Figure 5.4) contains fields from the *Student* table so that the user can be authenticated. Likewise, fields from the *Offering,* the *Faculty,* and the *Course* tables are shown in the subform so that the user can make an informed choice. If a business process permits fields from other tables to be changed, this task is usually done using another form.

5.4.3 Query Formulation Skills for Hierarchical Forms

To implement a hierarchical form, you should make decisions for each step listed below. These steps help to clarify the relationship between the form and the database tables. In addition, these steps can be used directly to implement the form in some DBMSs such as Microsoft Access.

1. Identify the 1-M relationship for the form.
2. Identify the join or linking columns for the 1-M relationship.
3. Decide what other tables belong in the main form and the subform.

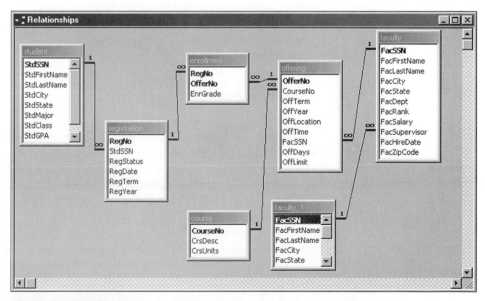

| **Figure 5.5** | **Relationships in the revised university database.** |

4. Decide which tables are updated as a result of using the hierarchical form.
5. Write queries for the main form and the subform.

Step 1: Identify the 1-M Relationship

The most important decision is matching the form to a 1-M relationship in the database. If you are starting from a picture of a form (such as Figure 5.3 or 5.4), look for a relationship that has columns from the 1 table in the main form and columns from the M table in the subform. Usually, the 1 table contains the primary key of the main form. In Figure 5.3, the Course No. field is the primary key of the main form so the *Course* table is the 1 table. In Figure 5.4, the Registration No. field is the primary key of the main form, so the *Registration* table is the 1 table. If you are performing the form design and layout yourself, decide on the 1-M relationship before you sketch the form layout.

Step 2: Identify the Linking Columns

If you can identify the 1-M relationship, identifying the linking columns is usually easy. The linking columns are simply the join columns from both tables in the relationship. In the Course Offering Form, the linking columns are *Course.CourseNo* and *Offering.CourseNo*. In the Registration Form, the linking columns are *Registration.RegNo* and *Enrollment.RegNo*. It is important to remember that the linking columns connect the main form to the subform. With this connection, the subform only shows rows that match the value in the linking column of the main form. Without this connection, the subform does not show rows related to the main form.

Step 3: Determine Other Tables

In addition to the 1-M relationship, other tables can be shown in the main form and the subform to provide a context to the user. If you see columns from other tables, you should note those tables so that you can use them in step 5 when writing queries for the form. For example, the Registration Form includes columns from the *Student* table in the main form. The subform includes columns from the *Offering,* the *Faculty,* and the *Course* tables. Computed columns, such as Total Units, are not a concern until the form is implemented.

Step 4: Determine Updatable Tables

The fourth step requires that you understand the tables that can be changed when using the form. Typically, there is only one table in the main form and one table in the subform that should be changed as the user enters data. In the Registration Form, the *Registration* table is changed when the user manipulates the main form and the *Enrollment* table is changed when the user manipulates the subform. Usually the tables identified in Step 3 are read-only. The *Student,* the *Offering,* the *Faculty,* and the *Course* tables are read-only in the subform.

Sometimes the main form does not support updates to any tables. In the Course Offering Form, the *Course* table is not changed when using the main form. The reason for making the main form read-only is to support the course approval process. Most universities require a separate approval process for new courses using a separate form. The Course Offering Form is designed only for adding offerings to existing courses. If a university does not have this constraint, the main form can be used to change the *Course* table. As part of designing a hierarchical form, you should clearly understand the requirements of the underlying business process. These requirements should then be transformed into decisions about which tables are affected by user actions in the form such as updating a field or inserting a new row.

Step 5: Write Form Queries

The last step integrates decisions made in the other steps. You should write a query for the main form and a query for the subform. These queries must support updates to the tables you identified in step 4. You should follow the rules for formulating updatable views (both single-table and multiple-table) given in Section 5.3. Some DBMSs may require that you use a CREATE VIEW statement for these queries while other DBMSs may allow you to type the SELECT statements directly.

The following examples show queries for the main forms and subforms of Figures 5.3 and 5.4. In Example 5.29, the *Address* form field (Figure 5.4) is derived from the *StdCity* and *StdState* columns. In Example 5.30, the primary key of the *Offering* table is not needed because the query does not support insert operations to the *Offering* table. The query only supports insert operations to the *Enrollment* table. Note that all examples conform to the Access 97/2000 rules for 1-M updatable queries.

EXAMPLE 5.27

Query for the Main Form of the Course Offering Form (Access)

```
SELECT CourseNo, CrsDesc, CrsUnits FROM Course
```

EXAMPLE 5.28

Query for the Subform of the Course Offering Form (Access)

```
SELECT * FROM Offering
```

EXAMPLE 5.29

Query for the Main Form of the Registration Form (Access)

```
SELECT RegNo, RegTerm, RegYear, RegDate,
        Registration.StdSSN, RegStatus, StdFirstName,
        StdLastName, StdClass, StdCity, StdState
    FROM Registration INNER JOIN student
        ON Registration.StdSSN = Student.StdSSN
```

EXAMPLE 5.30

Query for the Subform of the Registration Form (Access)

```
SELECT RegNo, Enrollment.OfferNo, Offer.CourseNo, OffTime,
        OffLocation, OffTerm, OffYear, Offering.FacSSN,
        FacFirstName, FacLastName, CrsDesc, CrsUnits
    FROM ( ( Enrollment INNER JOIN Offering
            ON Enrollment.OfferNo = Offering.OfferNo )
        INNER JOIN Faculty
            ON Faculty.FacSSN = Offering.FacSSN )
        INNER JOIN Course
            ON Course.CourseNo = Offering.CourseNo
```

In the subquery for the Registration Form (Example 5.30), there is one other issue. The subform query will only display an *Offering* row if there is an associated *Faculty* row. If you want the subform to display *Offering* rows regardless of whether there is an associated *Faculty* row, a one-sided outer join should be used, as shown in Example 5.31. You can tell if an outer join is needed by looking at example copies of the form. If you can find offerings listed without an assigned faculty, then you need a one-sided outer join in the query.

EXAMPLE 5.31 Revised Subform Query with a One-Sided Outer Join (Access)

```
SELECT RegNo, Enrollment.OfferNo, Offering.CourseNo,
       OffTime, OffLocation, OffTerm, OffYear,
       Offering.FacSSN, FacFirstName, FacLastName,
       CrsDesc, CrsUnits
   FROM ( ( Enrollment INNER JOIN Offering
           ON Enrollment.OfferNo = Offering.OfferNo)
       INNER JOIN Course
           ON Offering.CourseNo = Course.CourseNo)
       LEFT JOIN Faculty
           ON Faculty.FacSSN = Offering.FacSSN
```

As another example, Table 5–3 summarizes responses to the five query formulation steps for the Faculty Assignment Form shown in Figure 5.6. The goal of this form is to support administrators in assigning Faculty to Course Offerings. The 1-M relationship for the form is the relationship from the *Faculty* table to the *Offering* table. This form cannot be used to insert new *Faculty* rows or change data about *Faculty*. In addition, this form cannot be used to insert new *Offering* rows. The only update operation supported by this form is to change the *Faculty* assigned to teach an existing *Offering*. Examples 5.32 and 5.33 show the main form and the subform queries.

EXAMPLE 5.32 Main Form Query for the Faculty Assignment Form (Access)

```
SELECT FacSSN, FacFirstName, FacLastName, FacDept
   FROM Faculty
```

TABLE 5–3	**Summary of Query Formulation Steps for the Faculty Assignment Form**

Step	Response
1	*Faculty* (1 table), *Offering* (M table)
2	*Faculty.FacSSN, Offering.FacSSN*
3	Only data from the *Faculty* and *Offering* tables
4	Update *Offering.FacSSN*

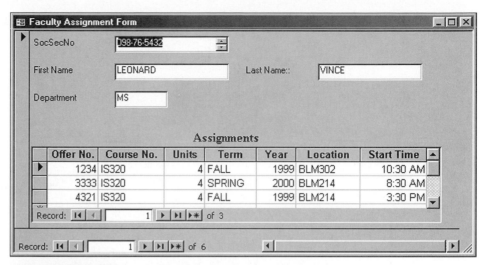

Figure 5.6   **Example faculty assignment form.**

EXAMPLE 5.33   Subform Query for the Faculty Assignment Form (Access)

```
SELECT  OfferNo, Offering.CourseNo, FacSSN, OffTime,
        OffDays, OffLocation, CrsUnits
FROM Offering INNER JOIN Course
        ON Offering.CourseNo = Course.CourseNo
```

5.5 USING VIEWS IN REPORTS

Besides being the building blocks of data entry forms, views are also the building blocks of reports. A <u>report</u> is a stylized presentation of data appropriate to a selected audience. A report is similar to a form in that both use views and present the data much differently than it appears in the base tables. A report differs from a form in that a report does not change the base tables while a form can make changes to the base tables. This section describes the hierarchical report, a powerful kind of report, and the relationship between views and hierarchical reports.

5.5.1 What Is a Hierarchical Report?

Hierarchical Report   a formatted display of a query using indentation to show grouping and sorting.

Hierarchical reports (also known as control break reports) use nesting or indentation to provide a visually appealing format. The Faculty Schedule Report (Figure 5.7) shows data arranged by department, faculty name, and quarter. Each indented field is known as a <u>group</u>. The nesting of the groups indicates the sorting order of the report. The innermost line in a report is known as the <u>detail line</u>. In the Faculty Schedule Report, detail lines show the course number, offering number, and other details of the assigned course. The detail lines also can be sorted. In the Faculty Schedule Report, the detail lines are sorted by course number.

The major advantage of hierarchical reports is that users can grasp more readily the meaning of data that are sorted and arranged in an indented manner. The standard output of a query (a datasheet) is not easy to inspect. For example, compare the Faculty

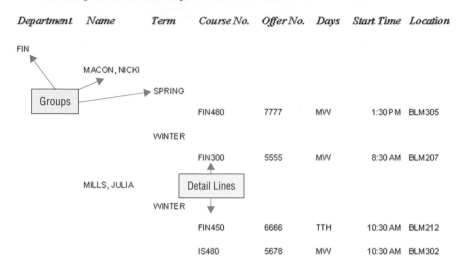

Figure 5.7   Faculty schedule report.

FacDept	FacLastName	FacFirstName	OffTerm	CourseNo	OfferNo	OffLocation	OffTime	OffDays
FIN	MACON	NICKI	SPRING	FIN480	7777	BLM305	1:30 PM	MW
FIN	MACON	NICKI	WINTER	FIN300	5555	BLM207	8:30 AM	MW
FIN	MILLS	JULIA	WINTER	FIN450	6666	BLM212	10:30 AM	TTH
FIN	MILLS	JULIA	WINTER	IS480	5678	BLM302	10:30 AM	MW
MS	COLAN	CHRISTOPHER	SPRING	IS480	5679	BLM412	3:30 PM	TTH
MS	EMMANUEL	VICTORIA	WINTER	IS320	4444	BLM302	3:30 PM	TTH
MS	FIBON	LEONARD	SPRING	IS460	9876	BLM307	1:30 PM	TTH
MS	VINCE	LEONARD	FALL	IS320	4321	BLM214	3:30 PM	TTH
MS	VINCE	LEONARD	FALL	IS320	1234	BLM302	10:30 AM	MW
MS	VINCE	LEONARD	SPRING	IS320	3333	BLM214	8:30 AM	MW

Figure 5.8   Datasheet Showing the Contents of the Faculty Schedule Report.

Schedule Report with the datasheet (Figure 5.8) showing the same information. It can be distracting to see the department, faculty name, and term repeated.

To improve appearance, hierarchical reports can show summary data in the detail lines, computed columns, and calculations after groups. The detail lines in Figure 5.9 show the enrollment (number of students enrolled) in each course offering taught by a professor. In SQL, the number of students is computed with the COUNT function. The columns Percent Full ((Enrollment/Limit) * 100%) and Low Enrollment (a true/false value) are computed. A check box is a visually appealing way to display true/false columns. Many reports show summary calculations after each group. In the Faculty Work Load Report, summary calculations show the total units and students as well as average percentage full of course offerings.

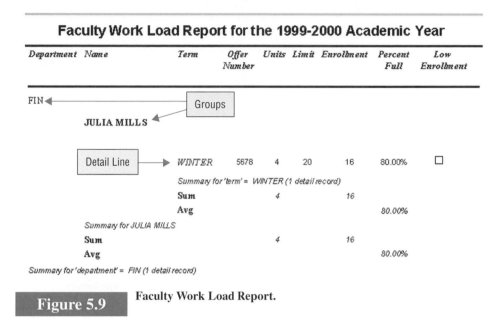

Figure 5.9   **Faculty Work Load Report.**

5.5.2 Query Formulation Skills for Hierarchical Reports

Formulating queries for reports is similar to formulating queries for forms. In formulating a query for a report, you should (1) match fields in the report to database columns, (2) determine the needed tables, and (3) identify the join conditions. Most report queries will involve joins and possibly one-sided outer joins. More difficult queries involving difference and division are not common. These steps can be followed to formulate the query shown in Example 5.34 for the Faculty Schedule Report (Figure 5.7).

EXAMPLE 5.34   Query for a Hierarchical Report, the Faculty Scheduling Report

```
SELECT Faculty.FacSSN, Faculty.FacFirstName, FacLastName,
       Faculty.FacDept, Offering.OfferNo,
       Offering.CourseNo, Offering.OffTerm,
       Offering.OffYear, Offering.OffLocation,
       Offering.OffTime, Offering.OffDays
FROM Faculty, Offering
WHERE Faculty.FacSSN = Offering.FacSSN
   AND ( ( Offering.OffTerm = 'FALL'
   AND Offering.OffYear = 1999 )
   OR ( Offering.OffTerm = 'WINTER'
   AND Offering.OffYear = 2000 )
   OR ( Offering.OffTerm = 'SPRING'
   AND Offering.OffYear = 2000 ) )
```

In some ways, formulating queries for hierarchical reports is easier than for hierarchical forms. Queries for reports do not need to be updatable (they usually are not updatable). In addition, there is only one query for a report as opposed to two or more queries for a hierarchical form.

The major query formulation issue for hierarchical reports is the <u>level</u> of the output. Sometimes there is a choice between whether the query's output contains individual rows or groups of rows. A rule of thumb is that the query should produce data for detail lines on the report. The query for the Faculty Work Load Report (Example 5.35) groups the data and counts the number of students enrolled. The query directly produces data for detail lines on the report. If the query produced one row per student enrolled in a course (a finer level of detail), then the report must calculate the number of students enrolled. With most reporting tools, it is easier to perform aggregate calculations in the query when the detail line of the report shows only summary data.

The other calculations (*PercentFull* and *LowEnrollment*) in Example 5.35 can be performed in the query or report with about the same effort. Note that the field *OffLimit* is a new field in the *Offering* table. It shows the maximum number of students that can enroll in a course offering.

EXAMPLE 5.35   Query for the Faculty Work Load Report with Summary Data in Detail Lines

```
SELECT Offering.OfferNo, FacFirstName, FacLastName,
       FacDept, OffTerm, CrsUnits, OffLimit,
       Count(Enrollment.RegNo) AS NumStds,
       NumStds/OffLimit AS PercentFull,
       (NumStds/Offlimit) < 0.25 As Low Enrollment
FROM Faculty, Offering, Course, Enrollment
WHERE Faculty.FacSSN = Offering.FacSSN
   AND Course.CourseNo = Offering.CourseNo
   AND Offering.OfferNo = Enrollment.OfferNo
   AND ( ( Offering.OffTerm = 'FALL'
   AND Offering.OffYear = 1999 )
     OR ( Offering.OffTerm = 'WINTER'
   AND Offering.OffYear = 2000 )
     OR ( Offering.OffTerm = 'SPRING'
   AND Offering.OffYear = 2000 ) )
   GROUP BY Offering.OfferNo, FacFirstName, FacLastName,
       FacDept, OffTerm, CrsUnits, OffLimit
```

CLOSING THOUGHTS

This chapter has described views, virtual tables derived from base tables with queries. The important concepts about views are the motivation for views and how views can be used to retrieve and change a database. The major benefit of views is data independence. Changes to the definition of base tables usually do not impact applications that use views. Views also can simplify queries written by users as well as provide a flexible security tool. To effectively use views, you need to understand the difference between read-only and updatable views. A read-only view can be used in a query just like a base table. All views are at least read-only, but only some views are updatable. With an updatable view, changes to rows in the view are propagated to the underlying base tables. Both single-table and multiple-table views can be updatable. The most important determinant of updatability is that the view contain primary keys of the underlying base tables.

Views have become the building blocks of database applications because form and report tools use views. Data entry forms support retrieval and changes to a database. Hierarchical forms manipulate 1-M relationships in the database. To define a hierarchical form, you need to identify the 1-M relationship and define updatable views for the fixed (main form) and variable (subform) part of the form. Hierarchical reports provide a visually appealing presentation of data. To define a hierarchical report, you need to identify grouping levels and formulate a query to produce data for detail lines of the report.

This chapter completes Part 1, emphasizing application development with relational databases. In earlier chapters, you gained an understanding of relational databases and developed skills in formulating queries in SQL. This chapter has shown you how to apply your query formulation skills in building applications based on views. To complete your study of Part 1, you need to use a relational DBMS especially to build forms and reports. It is only by applying the concepts to an actual DBMS that you will really learn the concepts.

REVIEW CONCEPTS

- Benefits of views: data independence, simplified query formulation, security.
- View definition in SQL:

      CREATE VIEW IS_Students AS
        SELECT * FROM Student WHERE StdMajor = 'IS'

- Using a view in a query:

      SELECT StdFirstName, StdLastName, StdCity, StdGPA
        FROM IS_Students
        WHERE StdGPA >= 3.7

- Using an updatable view in INSERT, UPDATE, and DELETE statements:

      UPDATE IS_Students
        SET StdGPA = 3.5
        WHERE StdClass = 'SR'

- Rules for defining single-table updatable views: primary key and required columns.
- Rules for defining multiple-table updatable views: primary key and required columns of each updatable table.
- Components of a hierarchical form: main form and subform.
- Relationship of hierarchical forms and 1-M relationships.
- Writing updatable queries for the main form and the subform.
- Hierarchical reports: grouping fields and detail lines.
- Writing queries for hierarchical reports: provide data for detail lines.

QUESTIONS

1. How do views provide data independence?

2. How can views simplify queries written by users?

3. How is a view like a macro in a spreadsheet?

4. What is view materialization?

5. What is view modification?

6. Why do most DBMSs use modification rather than materialization to process view queries?

7. What is an updatable view?

8. Why are some views read-only?

9. What are the rules for single-table updatable views?

10. What are the rules for multiple-table updatable views?

11. What is the purpose of the WITH CHECK clause?

12. What is a hierarchical form?

13. Briefly describe how a hierarchical form can be used in a business process that you know about. For example, if you know something about order processing, describe how a hierarchical form can support this process.

14. What is the difference between a main form and a subform?

15. What is the purpose of linking columns in hierarchical forms?

16. Why should you write updatable queries for a main form and a subform?

17. Why are tables used in a hierarchical form even when the tables cannot be changed as a result of using the form?

18. What is a hierarchical report?

19. How do you identify grouping columns in a report?

20. What is the relationship of grouping columns in a report and columns to sort by?

21. Why is it often easier to write a query for a hierarchical report than for a hierarchical form?

22. What does it mean that a query should produce data for the detail line of a hierarchical report?

PROBLEMS

ORDER

The problems use the extended order entry database depicted in Figure 5P.1 and Table 5P–1. Oracle CREATE TABLE statements for the new tables and the revised *Product* table follow Table 5P–1. This database extends the order entry database used in the problems of Chapters 3 and 4 with three tables: (1) *Supplier,* containing the list of suppliers for products carried in inventory; (2) *Purchase,* recording the general details of purchases to replenish inventory; and (3) *PurchLine,* containing the products requested on a purchase. In addition, the extended order entry database contains a new 1-M relationship (*Supplier* to *Product*) that replaces the *Product.ProdMfg* field in the original database.

In addition to the revisions noted in the previous paragraph, you should be aware of several assumptions made in the design of the extended order entry database:

• The design makes the simplifying assumption that there is only one supplier for each product. This assumption is appropriate for a single retail store that orders directly from manufacturers.

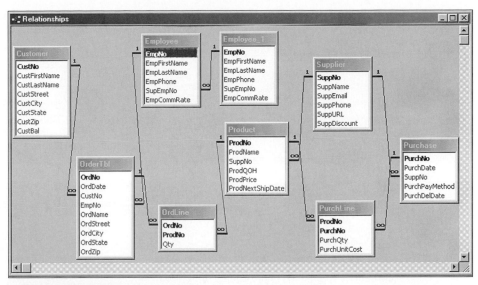

Figure 5P.1	**Relationship diagram for the revised order entry database.**

TABLE 5P–1	Explanations of Selected Columns in the Revised Order Entry Database
Table Name	*Description*
PurchDate	Date of placing the purchase
PurchPayMethod	Payment method for the purchase (Credit, PO, or Cash)
PurchDelDate	Expected delivery date of the purchase
SuppDiscount	Discount provided by the supplier
PurchQty	Quantity of product purchased
PurchUnitCost	Unit cost of the product purchased

- The 1-M relationship from *Supplier* to *Purchase* supports the purchasing process. In this process, a user designates the supplier before selecting items to order from the supplier. Without this relationship, the business process and associated data entry forms would be more difficult to implement.

```
CREATE TABLE Product
ProdNo                    CHAR(8),
ProdName                  VARCHAR2(50) NOT NULL,
SuppNo                    CHAR(8) NOT NULL,
ProdQOH                   INTEGER DEFAULT 0,
ProdPrice                 DECIMAL(12,2) DEFAULT 0,
ProdNextShipDate          DATE,
CONSTRAINT PKProduct      PRIMARY KEY (ProdNo),
CONSTRAINT SuppNoFK1      FOREIGN KEY (SuppNo) REFERENCES Supplier
ON DELETE CASCADE )
```

```
CREATE TABLE Supplier
(       SuppNo CHAR(8),
        SuppName                VARCHAR2(30) NOT NULL,
        SuppEmail               VARCHAR2(50),
        SuppPhone               CHAR(13),
        SuppURL                 VARCHAR2(100),
        SuppDiscount            DECIMAL(3,3),
CONSTRAINT PKSupplier   PRIMARY KEY (SuppNo) )
```

```
CREATE TABLE Purchase
(       PurchNo                 CHAR(8),
        PurchDate               DATE NOT NULL,
        SuppNo                  CHAR(8) NOT NULL,
        PurchPayMethod          CHAR(6) DEFAULT 'PO',
        PurchDelDate            DATE,
CONSTRAINT PKPurchase   PRIMARY KEY (PurchNo) ,
CONSTRAINT SuppNoFK2    FOREIGN KEY (SuppNo) REFERENCES Supplier )
```

```
CREATE TABLE PurchLine
(       ProdNo CHAR(8),
        PurchNo                 CHAR(8),
        PurchQty                INTEGER DEFAULT 1 NOT NULL,
        PurchUnitCost           DECIMAL(12,2),
CONSTRAINT PKPurchLine   PRIMARY KEY (PurchNo, ProdNo),
CONSTRAINT FKPurchNo     FOREIGN KEY (PurchNo) REFERENCES Purchase
  ON DELETE CASCADE,
CONSTRAINT FKProdNo2 FOREIGN KEY (ProdNo) REFERENCES Product )
```

1. Define a view containing products from supplier number S3399214. Include all columns of Product in the view.

2. Define a view containing the details of orders placed in January 2000. Include all *OrderTbl* columns, *OrdLine.Qty,* and the product name in the view.

3. Define a view containing the product number, name, price, and quantity on hand along with the number of orders in which the product appears.

4. Using the view defined in problem 1, write a query to list the products with a price larger than $300. Include all view columns in the result.

5. Using the view defined in problem 2, write a query to list the rows containing the words 'Ink Jet' in the product name. Include all view columns in the result.

6. Using the view defined in problem 3, write a query to list the products in which more than five orders have been placed. Include the product name and number of orders in the result.

7. For the query in problem 4, modify the query so that it uses base tables only.

8. For the query in problem 5, modify the query so that it uses base tables only.

9. For the query in problem 6, modify the query so that it uses base tables only.

10. Is the view in problem 1 updatable? Explain why or why not.

11. Is the view in problem 2 updatable? Explain why or why not. What database tables can be changed by modifying rows in the view?

12. Is the view in problem 3 updatable? Explain why or why not.

13. Define a 1-M updatable query involving the *Customer* and the *OrderTbl* tables. The query should support updates to the *OrderTbl* table. The query should include all columns of the *OrderTbl* table and the name (first and last), street, city, state, and zip of the *Customer* table. Note that this problem is specific to Microsoft Access.

14. Define a 1-M updatable query involving the *Customer,* the *OrderTbl,* and the *Employee* tables. The query should support updates to the *OrderTbl* table. Include all rows in the *OrderTbl* table even if there is a null employee number. The query should include all columns of the *OrderTbl* table; the name (first and last), street, city, state, and zip of the *Customer* table; and the name (first and last) and phone of the *Employee* table. Note that this problem is specific to Microsoft Access.

15. Define a 1-M updatable query involving the *OrdLine* and the *Product* tables. The view should support updates to the *OrdLine* table. The query should include all the columns of the *OrdLine* table and the name, the quantity on hand, and the price of the *Product* table. Note that this problem is specific to Microsoft Access.

16. Define a 1-M updatable query involving the *Purchase* and the *Supplier* tables. The query should support updates to the *Product* and the *Supplier* tables. Include the necessary columns so that both tables are updatable. Note that this problem is specific to Microsoft Access.

17. For the sample Simple Order Form shown in Figure 5P.2, answer the five query formulation questions discussed in Section 5.4.3. The form supports manipulation of the heading and the details of orders.

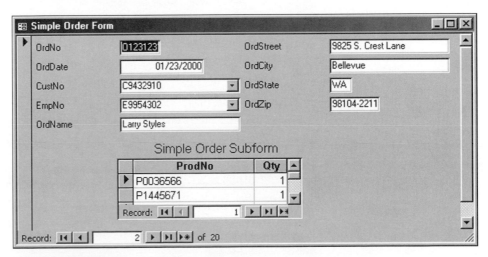

Figure 5P.2   **Simple Order Form.**

18. For the sample Order Form shown in Figure 5P.3, answer the five query formulation questions discussed in Section 5.4.3. Like the Simple Order Form in problem 17, the Order Form supports manipulation of the heading and the details of orders. In addition, the Order Form displays data from other tables to provide a context for the user when completing an order. The Order Form supports both phone (an employee taking the order) and Internet (without an employee taking the order) orders. The subform query should compute the Amount field as Qty*ProdPrice. Do not compute the Total Amount field in either the main form query or the subform query. It is computed in the form.

19. Modify your answer to problem 18 assuming that the Order Form supports only phone orders, not Internet orders.

20. For the sample Simple Purchase Form shown in Figure 5P.4, answer the five query formulation questions discussed in Section 5.4.3. The form supports manipulation of the heading and the details of purchases.

21. For the sample Purchase Form shown in Figure 5P.5, answer the five query formulation questions discussed in Section 5.4.3. Like the Simple Purchase Form in problem 17, the Purchase Form supports manipulation of the heading and the details of purchases. In addition, the Purchase Form displays data from other tables to provide a context for the user when completing a purchase. The subform query should compute the Amount field as PurchQty*PurchUnitCost. Do not compute the Total Amount field in either the main form query or the subform query. It is computed in the form.

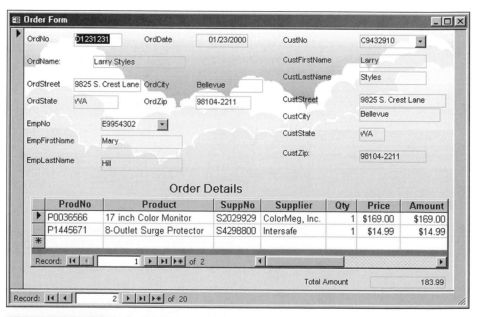

Figure 5P.3   Order Form.

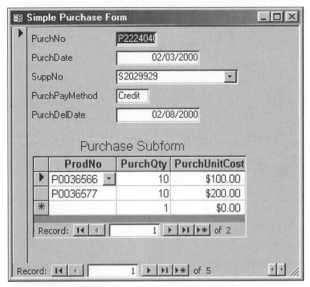

Figure 5P.4 Simple Purchase Form.

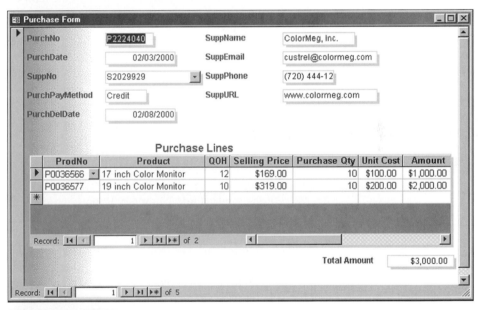

Figure 5P.5 Purchase Form.

22. For the sample Supplier Form shown in Figure 5P.6, answer the five query
    formulation questions discussed in Section 5.4.3. The main form supports
    manipulation of supplier data while the subform supports manipulation of only
    the product number and the product name of products provided by the supplier in
    the main form.

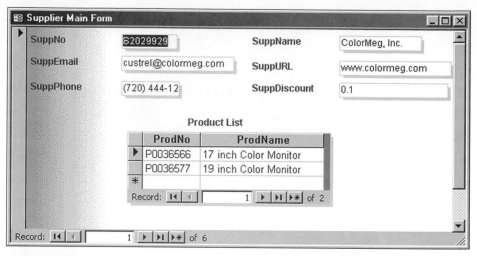

Figure 5P.6   Supplier Form.

23. For the Order Detail Report, write a SELECT statement to produce the data for the detail lines. The grouping column in the report is *OrdNo*. The report should list the orders for customer number O2233457 in January 2000.

Order Detail Report

Order Number	Order Date	Product No	Qty	Price	Amount
O2233457	1/12/2000	P1441567	1	$14.99	$14.99
		P0036577	2	$319.00	$638.00
Total Order Amount					$652.99
O4714645	1/11/2000	P9995676	2	$89.00	$178.00
		P0036566	1	$369.00	$369.00
Total Order Amount					$447.00

24. For the sample Order Summary Report, write a SELECT statement to produce the data for the detail lines. The Zip Code report field is the first five characters of the *CustZip* column. The grouping field in the report is the first five characters of the *CustZip* column. The Order Amount Sum report field is the sum of the quantity times the product price. Limit the report to year 2000 orders. You should also include the month number in the SELECT statement so that the report can be sorted by the month number instead of the Month report field. Use the following expressions to derive columns used in the report:

- In Microsoft Access, the expression left(CustZip, 5) derives the Zip Code report field. In Oracle, the expression substr(CustZip, 1, 5) derives the Zip Code report field.
- In Microsoft Access, the expression format(OrdDate, "mmmm yyyy") derives the Month report field. In Oracle, the expression to_char(OrdDate, 'MONTH YYYY') derives the Month report field.
- In Microsoft Access, the expression month(OrdDate) derives the month. In Oracle, the expression to_number(to_char(OrdDate, 'MM')) derives the month.

Order Summary Report

Zip Code	Month	Order Line Count	Order Amount Sum
80111	January 2000	10	$1,149
	February 2000	21	$2,050
Summary of 80111		31	$3,199
80113	January 2000	15	$1,541
	February 2000	11	$1,450
Summary of 80113		31	$2,191

25. Revise the Order Summary Report to list the number of orders and the average order amount instead of the Order Line Count and Order Amount Sum. You will need two queries to produce the data for the detail lines.

Order Summary Report

Zip Code	Month	Order Count	Average Order Amount
80111	January 2000	4	$287.25
	February 2000	10	$205.00
Summary of 80111		15	$213.27
80113	January 2000	5	$308.20
	February 2000	4	$362.50
Summary of 80113		9	$243.44

REFERENCES FOR FURTHER STUDY

The SQL Server Pro (http://www.inquiry.com/techtips/thesqlpro/) and the database information center of the *Intelligent Enterprise* magazine (http://www.iemagazine.com/) have plenty of practical advice about views and application development. The technical journals of the Advisor.com site (http://www.advisor.com/) provide application development advice for Microsoft SQL Server and Microsoft Access. In Chapter 17, Date (1995) provides additional details of view updatability issues especially related to multiple table views.

Appendix 5.A   **SQL2 Syntax Summary**

This appendix summarizes the SQL2 syntax for the CREATE VIEW statement presented in Chapter 5 and a simple companion statement (DROP VIEW). The conventions used in the syntax notation are identical to those used at the end of Chapter 2.

CREATE VIEW Statement

```
CREATE VIEW ViewName [ ( ColumnName* ) ]
  AS <Select-Statement>
  [ WITH CHECK OPTION ]
<Select-Statement>:—defined in Chapter 3
```

DROP VIEW Statement

```
DROP VIEW ViewName [ { CASCADE | RESTRICT } ]
```

- CASCADE deletes the view and any views that use its definition.
- RESTRICT means that the view is not deleted if any views use its definition.

Appendix 5.B **Rules for Updatable Join Views in Oracle 8**

In Oracle 8, a join view contains one or more tables or views in its defining FROM clause. A join view is updatable if it satisfies the following two conditions:

- It does not contain the DISTINCT keyword, the GROUP BY clause, aggregation functions, and set operations (UNION, MINUS, and INTERSECT).
- It contains the primary key of at least one underlying table in its defining FROM clause.

An updatable join view supports insert, update, and delete operations on one underlying table per manipulation statement. The updatable table is referred to as the <u>key preserving table.</u> An UPDATE statement can modify (in the SET clause) only columns of one key preserving table. An INSERT statement can add values for columns of one key preserved table. Rows can be deleted as long as the join view contains only one key preserving table. Join views with more than one key preserving table do not support DELETE statements.

DATABASE DEVELOPMENT

CHAPTER 6 | *Introduction to Database Development*

CHAPTER 7 | *Data Modeling*

CHAPTER 8 | *Normalization of Relational Tables*

CHAPTER 9 | *View Design and Integration*

CHAPTER 10 | *Physical Database Design*

CHAPTER 11 | *Database Design for Student Loan Limited*

The chapters in Part 2 emphasize practical skills and design processes for each step of the database development process. Chapter 6 introduces the context, objectives, phases, and tools of the database development process. Chapter 7 presents the Crow's Foot notation of the Entity Relationship Model, the practice of data modeling on narrative problems, and conversion of entity relationship diagrams into relational tables. Chapter 8 covers the motivation, functional dependencies, normal forms, and practical considerations of data normalization. Chapter 9 describes view design and view integration, data modeling concepts for large database development efforts. Chapter 10 contains broad coverage of physical database design including the objectives, inputs, file structure and query optimization background, and important design choices. Chapter 11 provides a comprehensive case study that enables students to gain insights about the difficulties of applying the skills to a realistic business database.

Chapter 6

Introduction to Database Development

This chapter provides an overview of the database development process. After this chapter, the student should have acquired the following knowledge and skills:

- List the steps in the information systems life cycle.

- Describe the role of databases in an information system.

- List the goals of database development.

- Understand the relationships among phases in the database development process.

- List functions typically provided by CASE tools for database development.

OVERVIEW

Part 1 of this book provided a foundation for creating applications that use relational databases. You learned about the Relational Data Model, query formulation with SQL, and the link between views and application development. Part 1 assumes that a database already exists. Part 2 explores the issues and skills involved in developing databases. This chapter broadly explains the context, goals, phases, and tools of database development to facilitate learning of specific skills in later chapters of Part 2.

Before learning specific skills, you need to understand the broad context for database development. This chapter discusses a context for databases as part of an information system. You will learn about components of information systems, the life cycle of information systems, and the role of database development as part of information systems development. This information systems context provides a background to understand database development. You will learn the phases of database development, the kind of skills used in database development, and software tools that can help you develop databases.

6.1 INFORMATION SYSTEMS

Databases exist as part of an information system. Before understanding database development, you must understand the larger environment that surrounds a database. This section describes the components of an information system and several strategies to develop information systems.

6.1.1 Components of Information Systems

A system is a set of related components that work together to accomplish some objectives. Objectives are accomplished by interacting with the environment and performing functions. For example, the human circulatory system, consisting of blood, blood vessels, and the heart, makes blood flow to various parts of the body. The circulatory system interacts with other systems of the body to ensure that the right quantity and composition of blood arrives in a timely manner to various body parts.

An information system is similar to a physical system (such as the circulatory system) except that an information system manipulates data rather than a physical object like blood. An information system accepts data from its environment, processes data, and produces output data for decision making. For example, an information system for processing student loans (Figure 6.1) helps a service provider track loans for lending institutions.

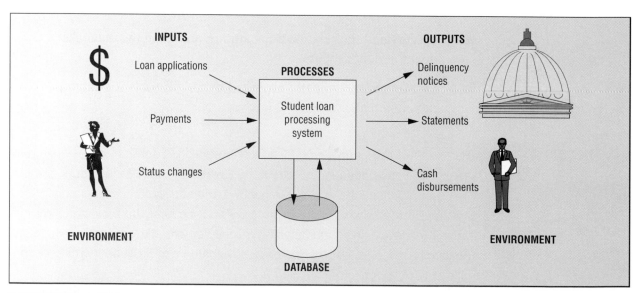

Figure 6.1   Overview of student loan processing system.

The environment of this system consists of lenders, students, and government agencies. Lenders send approved loan applications and students receive cash for school expenses. After graduation, students receive monthly statements and remit payments to retire their loans. If a student defaults, a government agency receives a delinquency notice.

Databases are essential components of many information systems. The role of a database is to provide long-term memory for an information system. The long-term memory contains entities and relationships. For example, the database in Figure 6.1 contains data about students, loans, and payments so that the statements, cash disbursements, and delinquency notices can be generated. Information systems without permanent memory or with only a few variables in permanent memory are not considered in this book because most business information systems have databases with complex structures.

Databases are not the only components of information systems. Information systems also contain people, procedures, input data, output data, software, and hardware. Thus, developing an information system involves more than developing the database, as discussed next.

6.1.2 Information Systems Development Process

Figure 6.2 shows the phases of the traditional systems development life cycle. The particular phases of the life cycle are not standard. Different authors and organizations have proposed from 3 to 20 phases. The traditional life cycle is often known as the waterfall

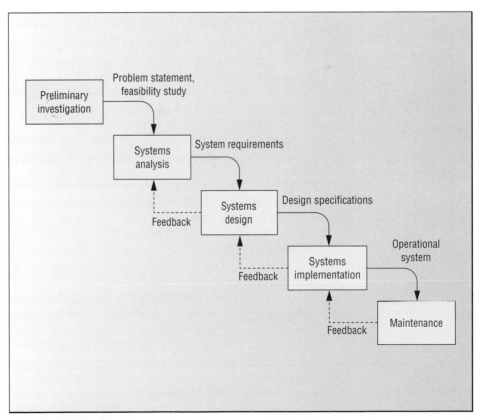

| **Figure 6.2** | Traditional systems development life cycle. |

model or methodology because the result of each phase flows to the next phase. The traditional life cycle is mostly a reference framework. For most systems, the boundary between phases is blurred and there is considerable backtracking between phases. But the traditional life cycle is still useful because it describes the kind of activities and shows addition of detail until an operational system emerges. The following items describe the activities in each phase:

- Preliminary investigation phase: Produces a problem statement and feasibility study. The problem statement includes the objectives, constraints, and scope of the system. The feasibility study identifies the costs and benefits of the system. If the system is feasible, approval is given to begin systems analysis.
- Systems analysis phase: Produces requirements describing processes, data, and environment interactions. Diagramming techniques are used to document processes, data, and environment interactions. To produce the requirements, the current system is studied and users of the proposed system are interviewed.
- Systems design phase: Produces a plan to efficiently implement the requirements. Design specifications are created for processes, data, and environment interaction. The design specifications focus on choices to optimize resources given constraints.
- Systems implementation phase: Produces executable code, databases, and user documentation. To implement the system, the design specifications are coded and tested. Before making the new system operational, a transition plan from the old system to the new system is devised. To gain confidence and experience with the new system, an organization may run the old system in parallel to the new system for a period of time.
- Maintenance phase: Produces corrections, changes, and enhancements to an operating information system. The maintenance phase commences when an information system becomes operational. The maintenance phase is fundamentally different than other phases because it comprises activities from all of the other phases. The maintenance phase ends when developing a new system becomes cost justified. Due to the high fixed costs of developing new systems, the maintenance phase can last decades.

The traditional life cycle has been criticized for several reasons. First, an operating system is not produced until late in the process. By the time a system is operational, the requirements already have changed. Second, there is often a rush to begin implementation so that a product is visible. In this rush, appropriate time may not be devoted to analysis and design.

A number of alternative methodologies have been proposed to alleviate these difficulties. In spiral development methodologies, the life-cycle phases are performed for subsets of a system, progressively producing a larger system until the complete system emerges. Rapid application development methodologies delay producing design documents until requirements are clear. Scaled-down versions of a system known as prototypes are used to clarify requirements. Prototypes can be implemented rapidly using graphical development tools for generating forms, reports, and other code. Implementing a prototype allows users to provide meaningful feedback to developers. Often, users may not understand the requirements unless they can experience a prototype. Thus, prototyping can reduce the risk of developing an information system because it allows earlier and more direct feedback about the system.

In all development methodologies, graphical models of the data, processes, and environment interactions should be produced. The <u>data model</u> describes the kinds of data and relationships. The <u>process model</u> describes relationships among processes. A process can provide input data used by other processes and use the output data of other processes. The <u>environment interaction model</u> describes relationships between events and processes. An event such as the passage of time or an action from the environment can trigger a process to start or stop. The systems analysis phase produces an initial version of these models. The systems design phase adds more details so that the models can be efficiently implemented.

Even though models of data, processes, and environment interactions are necessary to develop an information system, this book emphasizes data models only. In many information systems development efforts, the data model is the most important. For business information systems, the process and environment interaction models are usually produced after the data model. Rather than present notation for the process and environment interaction models, this book emphasizes prototypes to depict connections among data, processes, and the environment. For more details about process and environment interaction models, please consult several references at the end of the chapter.

6.2 GOALS OF DATABASE DEVELOPMENT

Broadly, the goal of database development is to produce a database that provides an important resource for an organization. To fulfill this broad goal, the database should serve a large community of users, support organizational policies, contain high quality data, and allow efficient access. The remainder of this section describes the goals of database development that support these features.

6.2.1 Develop a Common Vocabulary

A database provides a common vocabulary for an organization. Before a common database is implemented, different parts of an organization may have different terminology. For example, there may be multiple formats for addresses, multiple ways to identify customers, and different ways to calculate interest rates. After a database is implemented, communication can improve among different parts of an organization. Thus, a database can unify an organization by establishing a common vocabulary.

Achieving a common vocabulary is not easy. Developing a database requires compromise to satisfy a large community of users. In some sense, a good database designer shares some characteristics with a good politician. A good politician often finds solutions with which everyone finds something to agree or disagree. In establishing a common vocabulary, a good database designer also finds similar imperfect solutions. Forging compromises can be difficult, but the results can improve productivity, customer satisfaction, and other measures of organizational performance.

6.2.2 Define the Meaning of Data

A database contains business rules to support organizational policies. Defining business rules is the essence of defining the semantics or meaning of the database. For example, in an order entry system, an important rule is that an order must precede a shipment. The database can contain an integrity constraint to support this rule. Defining business rules enables the database to actively support organizational policies. This active role contrasts with the more passive role that databases have in establishing a common vocabulary.

In establishing the meaning of data, the database designer must choose appropriate constraint levels. Selecting appropriate constraint levels may require compromise to balance the needs of different groups. Constraints that are too strict may force work-around solutions to handle exceptions. In contrast, constraints that are too loose may allow incorrect data in the database. For example, in a university database, the designer must decide if a course offering can be stored without knowing the instructor. Some user groups may want the instructor to be entered initially to ensure that course commitments can be met. Other user groups may want more flexibility because course catalogs are typically printed well in advance of the beginning of the academic period. Forcing the instructor to be entered at the time a course offering is stored may be too strict. If the database contains this constraint, users may be forced to circumvent it by using a dummy instructor such as TBA (to be announced). The appropriate constraint (forcing entry of the instructor or not) depends on the importance of the needs of the user groups to the goals of the organization.

6.2.3 Ensure Data Quality

The importance of data quality is analogous to the importance of product quality in manufacturing. Poor product quality can lead to loss of sales, lawsuits, and customer dissatisfaction. Because data are the product of an information system, data quality is equally important. Poor data quality can lead to poor decision making about communicating with customers, identifying repeat customers, tracking sales, and resolving customer problems. For example, communicating with customers can be difficult if addresses are outdated or customer names are inconsistently spelled on different orders.

Data quality has many dimensions or characteristics, as depicted in Table 6–1. The importance of data quality characteristics can depend on the part of the database in which they are applied. For example, in the product part of a retail grocery database, important characteristics of data quality may be the timeliness and correctness of prices. For other parts of the database, other characteristics may be more important.

The database design should help achieve adequate data quality. When evaluating alternatives, the database designer should consider data quality characteristics. For example, in a customer database, the database designer should consider the possibility that some customers may not have U.S. addresses. Therefore, the database design may be incomplete if it fails to support non-U.S. addresses.

Achieving adequate data quality may require a cost–benefit trade-off. For example, in a grocery store database, the benefit of timely price updates is reduced consumer

TABLE 6–1	Common Characteristics of Data Quality
Characteristic	*Meaning*
Completeness	Database represents all important parts of the information system.
Lack of ambiguity	Each part of the database has only one meaning.
Correctness	Database contains values perceived by the user.
Timeliness	Business changes are posted to the database without excessive delays.
Reliability	Failures or interference do not corrupt database.
Consistency	Different parts of the database do not conflict.

complaints and less loss in fines from government agencies. Achieving data quality can be costly both in preventative and monitoring activities. For example, to improve the timeliness and accuracy of price updates, automated data entry may be used (preventative activity) as well as sampling the accuracy of the prices charged to consumers (monitoring activity).

The cost–benefit trade-off for data quality should consider long-term as well as short-term costs and benefits. Often the benefits of data quality are long-term, especially data quality issues that cross individual databases. For example, consistency of customer identification across databases can be a crucial issue for strategic decision making. The issue may not be important for individual databases. Chapter 14 on data warehouses addresses issues of data quality related to strategic decision making.

6.2.4 Find an Efficient Implementation

Even if the other design goals are met, a slow-performing database will not be used. Thus, finding an efficient implementation is paramount. However, an efficient implementation should respect the other goals as much as possible. An efficient implementation that compromises the meaning of the database or database quality may be rejected by database users.

Finding an efficient implementation is an optimization problem with an objective and constraints. Informally, the objective is to maximize performance subject to constraints about resource usage, data quality, and data meaning. Finding an efficient implementation can be difficult because of the number of choices available and interaction among choices. In addition, finding an efficient implementation is a continuing effort. Performance should be monitored and design changes should be made if warranted.

6.3 DATABASE DEVELOPMENT PROCESS

This section describes the phases of the database development process and discusses relationships to the information systems development process. The other chapters in Part 2 elaborate on the framework provided here.

6.3.1 Phases of Database Development

The goal of the database development process is to produce an operational database for an information system. To produce an operational database, you need to define the three schemas (external, conceptual, and internal) and populate (supply with data) the database. To create these schemas, you can follow the process depicted in Figure 6.3. The first two phases are concerned with the information content of the database while the last two phases are concerned with efficient implementation. These phases are described in more detail in the remainder of this section.

Conceptual Data Modeling

The conceptual data modeling phase uses data requirements and produces entity relationship diagrams (ERDs) for the conceptual schema and for each external schema. Data requirements can have many formats such as interviews with users, documentation of existing systems, and proposed forms and reports. The conceptual schema should represent all the requirements and formats. In contrast, the external schemas (or views) represent the requirements of a particular usage of the database such as a form or report

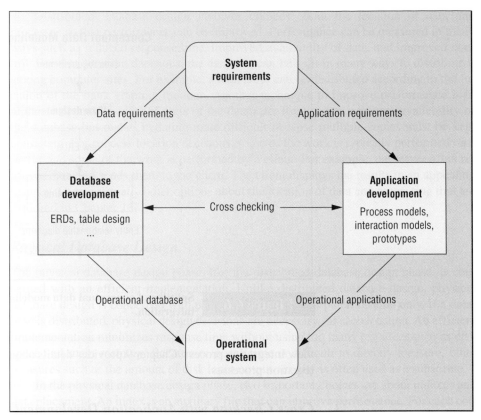

Figure 6.7	Interaction between database and application development.

skills. Soft skills are qualitative, subjective, and people-oriented. Qualitative skills emphasize the generation of feasible alternatives rather than the best alternatives. As a database designer, you want to generate a range of feasible alternatives. The choice among feasible alternatives can be subjective. As a database designer, you want to note the assumptions in which each feasible alternative is preferred. The alternative chosen is often subjective based on the designer's assessment of the most reasonable assumptions. Conceptual data modeling is especially people-oriented. In the role of data modeling, you need to obtain requirements from diverse groups of users. As mentioned earlier, compromise and effective listening are essential skills in data modeling.

Distributed database design and physical database design involve mostly <u>hard</u> skills. Hard skills are quantitative, objective, and data intensive. Background in quantitative disciplines such as statistics and operations management can be useful to understand mathematical models used in these phases. Many of the decisions in these phases can be modeled mathematically using an objective function and constraints. For example, the objective function for index selection is to minimize disk reads and writes with constraints about the amount of disk space and response time limitations. Many decisions cannot be based on objective criteria alone because of uncertainty about database usage. To resolve uncertainty, intensive data analysis can be useful. The database designer should collect and analyze data to understand patterns of database usage and database performance.

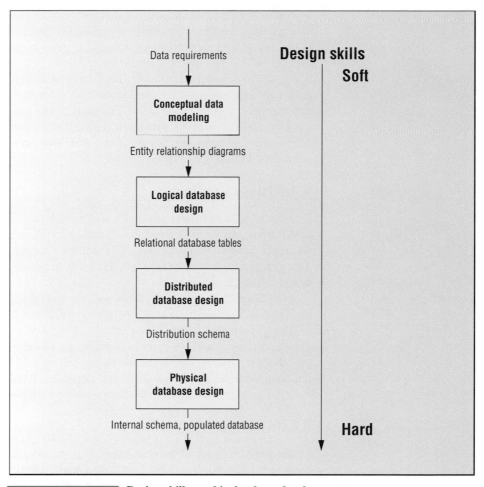

Figure 6.8   **Design skills used in database development.**

Because of the diverse skills and background knowledge required in different phases of database development, role specialization can occur. In large organizations, database design roles are divided between data modelers and database performance experts. Data modelers are mostly involved in the conceptual data modeling and logical database design phases. Database performance experts are mostly involved in the distributed and physical database design phases. Because the skills are different in these roles, the same person will not perform both roles in large organizations. In small organizations, the same person may fulfill both roles.

6.4 TOOLS OF DATABASE DEVELOPMENT

To improve productivity in developing information systems, computer-aided software engineering (CASE) tools have been created. CASE tools can help improve the productivity of information systems professionals working on large projects as well as end users working on small projects. A number of studies suggest that CASE tools facilitate improvements in the early phases of systems development leading to lower cost, higher quality, and faster implementations.

Most CASE tools support the database development process. Some CASE tools support database development as a part of information systems development. Other CASE tools target various phases of database development without supporting other aspects of information systems development.

CASE tools often are classified as front-end and back-end tools. Front-end CASE tools can help designers diagram, analyze, and document models used in the database development process. Back-end CASE tools create prototypes and generate code that can be used to cross check a database with other components of an information system. This section discusses the functions of CASE tools in more detail and demonstrates a commercial CASE tool, Visio Professional.

6.4.1 Diagramming

Diagramming is the most important and widely used function in CASE tools. Most CASE tools provide predefined shapes and connections among the shapes. The connection tools typically allow the shapes to be moved but stay connected as though "glued." This glue feature provides important flexibility because symbols on a diagram may need to be rearranged many times.

For large drawings, CASE tools provide several features. Most CASE tools allow diagrams to span multiple pages. Multiple-page drawings can be printed so that the pages can be pasted together to make a wall display. Layout can be difficult for large drawings. Some CASE tools try to improve the visual appeal of a diagram by performing automatic layout. The automatic layout feature may minimize the number of crossing connections in a diagram. Although automated layout is not typically sufficient by itself, a designer can use it as a first step to improve the visual appearance of a diagram.

6.4.2 Documentation

Documentation is one of the oldest and most valuable functions of CASE tools. CASE tools can store various properties of a data model and link the properties to symbols on the diagram. Example properties stored in a CASE tool include alias names, integrity rules, data types, and owners. In addition to properties, CASE tools can store text describing assumptions, alternatives, and notes. Both the properties and text are stored in the <u>data dictionary,</u> the database of the CASE tool. The data dictionary is also known as the repository or encyclopedia.

To support system evolution, many CASE tools can document versions. A version is a group of changes and enhancements to a system that is released together. Because of the volume of changes, groups of changes rather than individual changes are typically released together. In the life of an information system, many versions can be made. To aid in understanding relationships between versions, many CASE tools support documentation for individual changes and entire versions.

6.4.3 Analysis

CASE tools can provide active assistance to database designers through analysis functions. In documentation and diagramming, CASE tools help make designers more proficient. In analysis functions, CASE tools can perform the work of a database designer. An analysis function is any form of reasoning applied to specifications produced in the database development process. For example, an important analysis function is to convert between an ERD and a table design. Converting from an ERD to a table design is known as <u>forward engineering</u> and converting in the reverse direction is known as <u>reverse engineering</u>.

Analysis functions can be provided in each phase of database development. In the conceptual data modeling phase, analysis functions can reveal conflicts in an ERD. In the logical database design phase, conversion and normalization are common analysis functions. Conversion produces a table design from an ERD. Normalization removes redundancy in a table design. In the distributed database design and physical database design phases, analysis functions can suggest decisions about data location and index selection. In addition, analysis functions for version control can cross database development phases. Analysis functions can convert between versions and show a list of differences between versions.

Because analysis functions are advanced features in CASE tools, availability of analysis functions varies widely. Some CASE tools support little or no analysis functions while others support extensive analysis functions. Because analysis functions can be useful in each phase of database development, no single CASE tool provides a complete range of analysis functions. CASE tools tend to specialize by the phases supported. CASE tools independent of a DBMS typically specialize in analysis functions in the conceptual data modeling phase. In contrast, CASE tools offered by a DBMS vendor often specialize in the distributed database design and physical database design phases.

6.4.4 Prototyping Tools

Prototyping tools provide a link between database development and application development. Prototyping tools can be used to create forms and reports that use a database. Because prototyping tools may generate code (SQL statements and programming language code), they are sometimes known as code generation tools. Prototyping tools are often provided as part of a DBMS. The prototyping tools may feature wizards to aid the designer in quickly creating applications that can be tested by users. Prototyping tools also can create an initial database design by retrieving existing designs from a library of designs. This kind of prototyping tool can be very useful to end users and novice database designers.

6.4.5 Commercial CASE Tools

As shown in Table 6–2, there are a number of CASE tools that provide extensive functionality for database development. Each of the products in Table 6–2 is a complex product that supports the full life cycle of information systems development. Although the features of the products look similar, the quality, the depth, and the breadth of the features may vary across products. In addition, most of the products in Table 6–2 have several different versions that vary in price and features. All of the products are relatively neutral to a particular DBMS despite that companies with major DBMSs offer four of these products. There are a number of other products that specialize in one or more phases of database development, although the products are not listed in Table 6–2.

To provide a flavor for some features of commercial CASE tools, a brief depiction is given of Visio 2000 Professional Edition, an entry-level version of Visio Enterprise. Visio Professional provides excellent drawing capabilities and a number of useful analysis tools. This section depicts Visio Professional because it is an easy-to-use and powerful tool for introductory database courses.

For database development, Visio Professional features several stencils (collections of shapes) and data dictionary support. Visio provides stencils for variations of the entity relationship diagram (Crow's Foot, IDEF1X, Chen, and Martin notations) as well as new object modeling diagrams (Unified Modeling Language). Figure 6.9 depicts the Entity Relationship stencil (on the left) and the drawing window (on the right). If a symbol

TABLE 6–2	Prominent CASE Tools for Database Development		

Tool	Vendor	Innovative Features
PowerDesigner 7	Sybase	Forward and reverse engineering for relational databases and Java; model management support for comparing and merging models; application code generation
Oracle Designer	Oracle	Forward and reverse engineering for relational databases; reverse engineering of forms; application code generation
Visio 2000 Enterprise Edition	Microsoft	Forward and reverse engineering for relational databases and the Unified Modeling Language; model management support for comparing and merging models; generation of data models from natural language descriptions
ERWin	Computer Associates	Forward and reverse engineering for relational databases; application code generation; model management support for comparing and merging models
ER/Studio	Embarcadero Technologies	Forward and reverse engineering for relational databases; Java code generation; model management support for comparing and merging models
Visible Analyst	Visible Systems Corporation	Forward and reverse engineering for relational databases; model management support for comparing and merging models

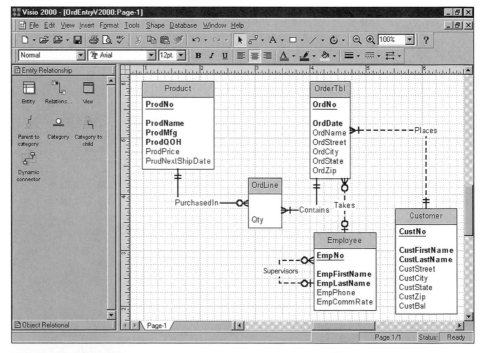

| Figure 6.9 | Stencil and canvas windows in Visio Professional. |

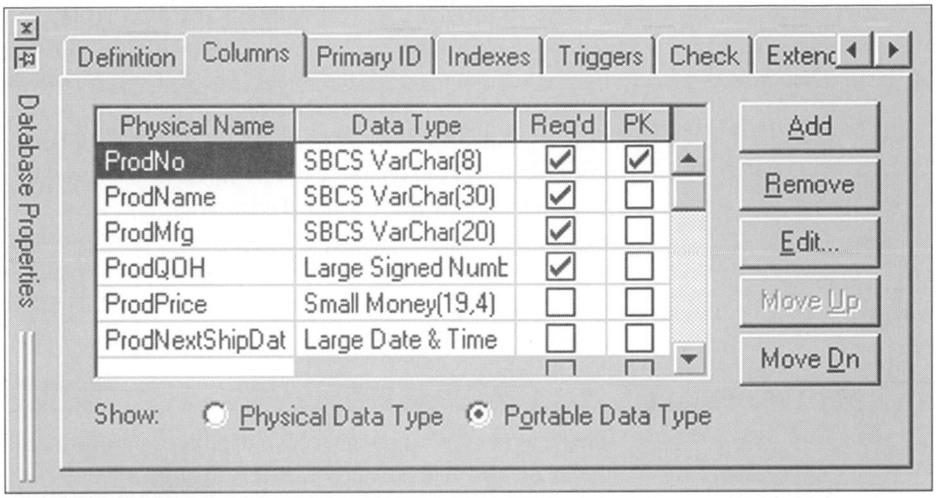

Physical Name	Data Type	Req'd	PK
ProdNo	SBCS VarChar(8)	☑	☑
ProdName	SBCS VarChar(30)	☑	☐
ProdMfg	SBCS VarChar(20)	☑	☐
ProdQOH	Large Signed Numt	☑	☐
ProdPrice	Small Money(19,4)	☐	☐
ProdNextShipDat	Large Date & Time	☐	☐

Figure 6.10   Database Properties window in Visio Professional for the *Product* entity type.

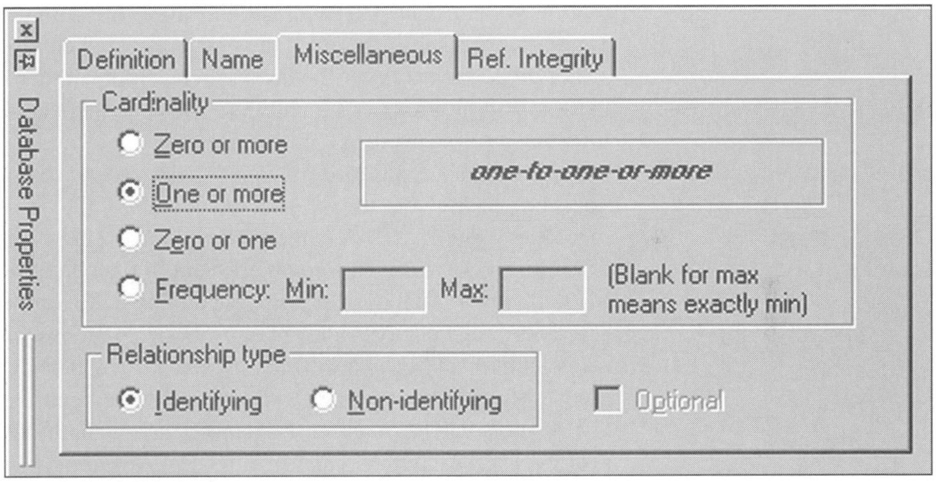

Figure 6.11   Database Properties window in Visio Professional for the *Contains* relationship.

is moved, it stays connected to other symbols because of a feature known as "glue." For example, if the Product rectangle is moved, it stays connected to the OrdLine rectangle through the PurchasedIn line. Visio Professional can automatically lay out the entire diagram if requested.

Visio provides a data dictionary to accompany the Entity Relationship stencil. For entity types (rectangle symbols), Visio supports the name, data type, required, and primary key properties as shown in the Columns tab of Figure 6.10 as well as many other properties in the nonselected tabs. For relationships (connecting line symbols), Visio supports properties about the definition, name, cardinality, and referential integrity as shown in Figure 6.11. For additional data dictionary support, custom properties and properties specific to a DBMS can be added.

Visio provides several analysis and prototyping tools beyond its stencil and data dictionary features. The analysis tools primarily support the schema conversion task in the logical database design phase. The Refresh Model Wizard detects and resolves differences between a Visio database diagram and an existing relational database. The Reverse Engineer Wizard performs the reverse task of converting a relational database definition into a Visio database diagram. Visio also supports various error checks to ensure consistent database diagrams. For prototyping, Visio can store shapes in relational databases. This feature can be particularly useful for providing a visual interface for hierarchical data such as organization charts and bill of material data. For more powerful prototyping, Visio supports the Visual Basic with Applications (VBA) language, an event-driven language integrated with Microsoft Office.

CLOSING THOUGHTS

This chapter described the role of databases in information systems and the nature of the database development process. Information systems are collections of related components that produce data for decision making. Databases provide the permanent memory for information systems. Development of an information system involves a repetitive process of analysis, design, and implementation. Database development occurs in all phases of systems development. Because a database is often a crucial part of an information system, database development can be the dominant part of information systems development. Development of the processing and environment interaction components are often performed after the database development. Cross checking between the database and applications is the link that connects the database development process to the information systems development process.

This chapter described the goals, phases, and tools of database development. The goals emphasize both the information content of the database as well as efficient implementation. The phases of database development first establish the information content of the database and then find an efficient implementation. The conceptual data modeling and logical database design phases involve the information content of the database. The distributed database design and physical database design phases involve efficient implementation. Because developing databases can be a challenging process, computer-aided software engineering (CASE) tools have been created to improve productivity. CASE tools can be essential in helping the database designer to draw, document, and prototype the database. In addition, some CASE tools provide active assistance with analyzing a database design.

This chapter provides a context for the other chapters in Part 2. You might want to reread this chapter after completing other chapters in Part 2. The other chapters in Part 2 provide details about the phases of database development. Chapters 7 and 9 describe the conceptual data modeling phase. Chapter 7 presents details of the Entity Relationship Model and discusses data modeling skills. Chapter 9 presents view design and view integration for managing large conceptual data modeling efforts. Chapter 8 presents normalization techniques for relational tables. Chapter 10 presents physical database design techniques. Chapter 11 discusses a case study to demonstrate the techniques studied in Part 2.

REVIEW CONCEPTS

- System: related components that work together to accomplish objectives.
- Information system: system that accepts, processes, and produces data.
- Waterfall model of information systems development: reference framework for activities in the information systems development process.

- Role of databases in information systems: provide permanent memory.
- Define a common vocabulary to unify an organization.
- Define the meaning of data to support organizational processes.
- Ensure data quality to improve quality of decision making.
- Find an efficient implementation to ensure that the database can be used.
- Conceptual data modeling to represent the information content independent of a target DBMS.
- View design and view integration to manage the complexity of large data modeling efforts.
- Logical database design to refine a conceptual data model to a target DBMS.
- Distributed database design to find locations of data and processing to achieve an efficient implementation.
- Physical database design to achieve efficient implementations on each computer site.
- Develop prototype forms and reports to cross check among the database and applications using the database.
- Soft skills for conceptual data modeling: qualitative, subjective, and people-oriented.
- Hard skills for finding an efficient implementation: quantitative, objective, and data intensive.
- Computer-aided software engineering (CASE) tools to improve productivity in the database development process.
- Fundamental assistance of CASE tools: drawing and documenting.
- Active assistance of CASE tools: analysis and prototyping.

QUESTIONS

1. What is the relationship between a system and an information system?

2. Provide an example of a system that is not an information system.

3. For an information system of which you are aware, describe some of the components (input data, output data, people, software, hardware, and procedures).

4. Briefly describe some of the kinds of data in the database for the information system in question 3.

5. Describe the phases of the waterfall model.

6. Why is the waterfall model considered only a reference framework?

7. What is the relationship of the database development process to the information systems development process?

8. What is a data model? Process model? Environment interaction model?

9. What is the purpose of prototyping in the information systems development process?

10. How is a database designer like a politician in establishing a common vocabulary?

11. Why should a database designer establish the meaning of data?

12. Why is data quality important?

13. Provide examples of data quality problems according to two characteristics mentioned in Section 6.2.3.

14. Why is it important to find an efficient implementation?

15. What are the inputs and the outputs of the conceptual data modeling phase?

16. What are the inputs and the outputs of the logical database design phase?

17. What are the inputs and the outputs of the distributed database design phase?

18. What are the inputs and the outputs of the physical database design phase?

19. What does it mean to say that the conceptual data modeling phase and the logical database design phase are concerned with the information content of the database?

20. Why are there two phases (conceptual data modeling and logical database design) that involve the information content of the database?

21. What is the relationship of view design and view integration to conceptual data modeling?

22. What is a soft skill?

23. What is a hard skill?

24. What kind of background is appropriate for hard skills?

25. Why do large IS organizations sometimes have different people performing design phases dealing with information content and efficient implementation?

26. Why are software tools useful in the database development process?

27. What kinds of support can a software tool provide for drawing a database diagram?

28. What kinds of support can a software tool provide for documenting a database design?

29. What kinds of support can a software tool provide for analyzing a database design?

30. What kinds of support can a software tool provide for prototyping?

31. Should you expect to find one software vendor providing a full range of functions (drawing, documenting, analyzing, and prototyping) for the database development process? Why or why not?

PROBLEMS

Because of the introductory nature of this chapter, there are no problems in this chapter. Problems appear at the end of other chapters in Part 2.

REFERENCES FOR FURTHER STUDY

For a more detailed description of the database development process, you can consult specialized books on database design such as Batini, Ceri, and Navathe (1992) and Teorey (1999). For more details on the systems development process, you can consult books on systems analysis and design such as Whitten and Bentley (2001). For more details about data quality, consult Kimball (1996), Redman (1992), and Strong, Lee, and Wang (1997).

Data Modeling

This chapter describes the practice of data modeling, an important skill for designing databases. After this chapter, the student should have acquired the following knowledge and skills:

■ Understand the Crow's Foot notation for entity relationship diagrams.

■ Understand important relationship patterns.

■ Use generalization hierarchies to represent similar entity types.

■ Refine and document entity relationship diagrams.

■ Appreciate the diversity of notation for entity relationship diagrams.

■ Convert an ERD to tables using mapping rules.

OVERVIEW

Chapter 6 provided a broad presentation on the database development process. You learned about the relationship between database development and information systems development, the phases of database development, and the kinds of skills you need to master. This chapter describes data modeling using entity relationship diagrams, an important skill in the conceptual data modeling phase.

To become a good data modeler, you need to understand the notation in entity relationship diagrams and get plenty of practice building diagrams. To help you master the notation, this chapter presents the symbols used in entity relationship diagrams and compares entity relationship diagrams to relational database diagrams that you have seen in earlier chapters. This chapter then probes deeper into relationships, the most distinguishing part of entity relationship diagrams. You will learn about identification dependency, relationship patterns, and an equivalence between two kinds of relationships. Next, you will learn how to represent similarities among entities using generalization hierarchies.

With this background, you are ready to build entity relationship diagrams for small problems. You will learn to analyze a narrative problem, refine a design through transformations, and document important design decisions. This chapter concludes with rules to convert an entity relationship diagram into relational tables.

7.1 INTRODUCTION TO ENTITY RELATIONSHIP DIAGRAMS

Gaining an initial understanding of entity relationship diagrams (ERDs) requires careful study. This section introduces the Crow's Foot notation for ERDs, a popular notation supported by many CASE tools. To get started, this section begins with the basic symbols of entity types, relationships, and attributes. This section then explains cardinalities and their appearance in the Crow's Foot notation. This section concludes by comparing the Crow's Foot notation to relational database diagrams. If you are covering Part 2 before Part 1, you may want to skip this subsection.

7.1.1 Basic Symbols

Entity Type   a collection of entities (persons, places, events, or things) of interest in an application, represented by a rectangle in an entity relationship diagram.

ERDs have three basic elements: entity types, relationships, and attributes. <u>Entity types</u> (also known as object types) are collections of things of interest (entities) in an application. Entity types can represent physical objects such as books, people, and places, as well as events such as payments. Entities are uniquely identified to allow tracking across business processes. For example, customers have a unique identification to support order processing, shipment, and product warranty processes. In the Crow's Foot notation as well as most other notations, rectangles denote entity types. In Figure 7.1, the *Course* entity type represents the set of courses in the database.

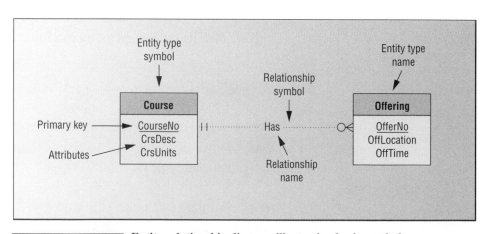

Figure 7.1   **Entity relationship diagram illustrating basic symbols.**

Attributes are properties of entity types or relationships. An entity type should have a primary key as well as other descriptive attributes. Attributes are shown inside an entity type rectangle. If there are many attributes, the attributes can be suppressed and listed on a separate page. Some ERD drawing tools show attributes in a zoomed view, separate from the rest of the diagram. Underlining indicates that the attribute(s) serves as the primary key of the entity type.

Relationships are named associations among entity types. In the Crow's Foot notation, relationship names appear on the line connecting the entity types involved in the relationship. In Figure 7.1, the *Has* relationship shows that the *Course* and *Offering* entity types are directly related. Relationships store associations in both directions. For example, the *Has* relationship shows what offerings exist for a given course and what course corresponds to a given offering. The *Has* relationship is binary because it involves two entity types. Section 7.2 presents examples of more complex relationships involving only one entity type (unary relationships) and more than two entity types (M-way relationships).

In a loose sense, ERDs have a natural language correspondence. Entity types can correspond to nouns and relationships to verbs or prepositional phrases connecting nouns. In this sense, one can read an entity relationship diagram as a collection of sentences. For example, the ERD in Figure 7.1 can be read as "course has offerings." Note that there is an implied direction in relationships. In the other direction, one could write, "offering is given for a course." If practical, it is a good idea to use active rather than passive verbs for relationships. Therefore, *Has* is preferred as the relationship name. You should use the natural language correspondence as a guide rather than strict rule. For large ERDs, you will not always find a good natural language correspondence for all parts of the diagrams.

Attribute a property of an entity type or relationship. Each attribute has a data type that defines the kind of values and permissible operations on the attribute.

Relationship a named association among entity types. A relationship represents a two-way or bidirectional association among entities. Most relationships involve two entity types.

7.1.2 Relationship Cardinality

Cardinality a constraint on the number of entities that participate in a relationship. In an ERD, the minimum and maximum number of entities are specified for both directions of a relationship.

Cardinalities constrain the number of objects that participate in a relationship. To depict the meaning of cardinalities, an object or instance diagram is useful. Figure 7.2 shows a set of courses ({Course1, Course2, Course3}), a set of offerings ({Offering1, Offering2, Offering3, Offering4}), and connections between the two sets. In Figure 7.2,

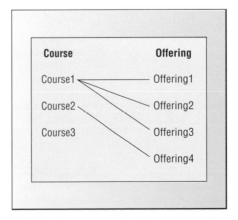

Figure 7.2   **Instance diagram for the *Has* relationship.**

Course1 is related to Offering1, Offering2, and Offering3, Course2 is related to Offering4, and Course3 is not related to any *Offering* objects. Likewise, Offering1 is related to Course1, Offering2 is related to Course1, Offering3 is related to Course1, and Offering4 is related to Course2. From this instance diagram, we might conclude that each offering is related to exactly one course. In the other direction, each course is related to 0 or more offerings.

Crow's Foot Representation of Cardinalities

The Crow's Foot notation uses three symbols to represent cardinalities. The Crow's Foot symbol (two angled lines and one straight line) denotes the many cardinality. In Figure 7.3, the Crow's Foot symbol near the *Offering* entity type means that a course can be related to many offerings. The circle means a cardinality of zero, while a single line means a cardinality of one.

To depict minimum and maximum cardinalities, the cardinality symbols are placed adjacent to each entity type in a relationship. The minimum cardinality symbol appears toward the relationship name while the maximum cardinality symbol appears toward the entity type. In Figure 7.3, a course is related to a minimum of zero offerings (circle in the inside position) and a maximum of many offerings (Crow's Foot in the outside position). Similarly, an offering is related to exactly one (one and only one) course as shown by the single vertical lines in both inside and outside positions.

Classification of Cardinalities

Cardinalities are classified by common values for minimum and maximum cardinality. Table 7–1 shows two classifications for minimum cardinalities. A minimum cardinality of one or more indicates a <u>mandatory relationship.</u> For example, participation in the *Has* relationship is mandatory for each *Offering* entity due to the minimum cardinality of one. A mandatory relationship makes the entity type <u>existence dependent</u> on the relationship. The *Offering* entity type depends on the *Has* relationship because an *Offering* object cannot be stored without a related *Course* object. In contrast, a minimum cardinality of 0 indicates an <u>optional</u> relationship. For example, the *Has* relationship is optional to the *Course* entity type because a *Course* object can be stored without being re-

---

Existence Dependency
an entity that cannot exist unless another related entity exists. A mandatory relationship produces an existence dependency.

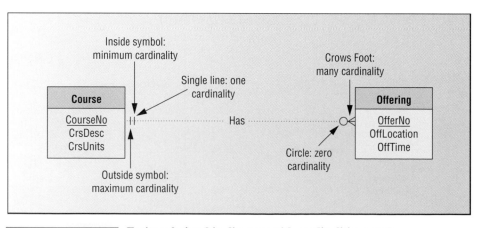

| **Figure 7.3** | **Entity relationship diagram with cardinalities noted.** |

lated to an *Offering* object. Figure 7.4 shows that the *Teaches* relationship is optional for both entity types.

Table 7–1 also shows several classifications for maximum cardinalities. A maximum cardinality of one means the relationship is <u>single-valued</u> or <u>functional.</u> For example, the *Has* and *Teaches* relationships are functional for *Offering* because an *Offering* object can be related to a maximum of one *Course* and one *Faculty* object. The word "function" comes from mathematics where a function gives one value. A relationship that has a maximum cardinality of one in one direction and more than one (many) in the other direction is called a <u>1-M</u> (read one-to-many) relationship. Both the *Has* and *Teaches* relationships are 1-M.

Similarly, a relationship that has a maximum cardinality of more than one in both directions is known as an <u>M-N</u> (many-to-many) relationship. In Figure 7.5, the *TeamTeaches* relationship allows multiple professors to jointly teach the same offering, as shown in the instance diagram of Figure 7.6. M-N relationships are common in business databases. For example, M-N relationships usually represent the connection between parts and suppliers, authors and books, and skills and employees. A part can be supplied by many suppliers and a supplier can supply many parts.

TABLE 7–1	Summary of Cardinality Classifications
Classification	*Cardinality Restrictions*
Mandatory	Minimum cardinality $\geq$ 1
Optional	Minimum cardinality $=$ 0
Functional or single-valued	Maximum cardinality $=$ 1
1-M	Maximum cardinality $=$ 1 in one direction and Maximum cardinality $>$ 1 in the other direction.
M-N	Maximum cardinality is $>$ 1 in both directions.
1-1	Maximum cardinality $=$ 1 in both directions.

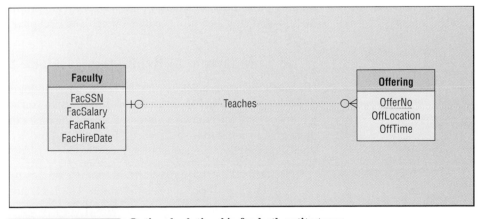

Figure 7.4   **Optional relationship for both entity types.**

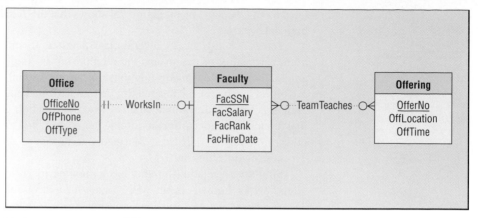

Figure 7.5   **M-N and 1-1 relationship examples.**

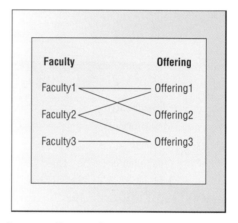

Figure 7.6   **Instance diagram for the M-N TeamTeaches relationship.**

Less common are 1-1 relationships in which the maximum cardinality equals one in both directions. For example, the *WorksIn* relationship in Figure 7.5 allows a faculty to be assigned to one office and an office to be occupied by at most one faculty.

7.1.3 Comparison to Relational Database Diagrams

To finish this section, let us compare the notation in Figure 7.3 with the relational database diagrams (from Microsoft Access) with which you are familiar. It is easy to become confused between the two notations. Some of the major differences are listed below.[1] To help you visualize these differences, Figure 7.7 shows a relational database diagram for the *Course-Offering* example.

1. Relational database diagrams do not use names for relationships. Instead foreign keys represent relationships. The ERD notation does not use foreign

---

[1]Section 7.6 presents conversion rules that describe the differences more precisely.

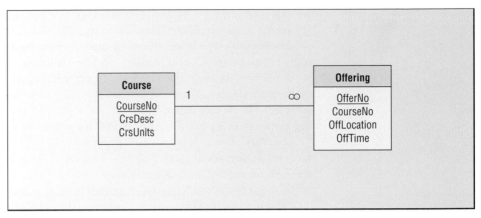

Figure 7.7   **Relational database diagram for the Course-Offering example.**

keys. For example, *Offering.CourseNo* is a column in Figure 7.7 but not an attribute in Figure 7.3.

2. Relational database diagrams show only maximum cardinalities.
3. Some ERD notations (including the Crow's Foot notation) allow both entity types and relationships to have attributes. Relational database diagrams only allow tables to have columns.
4. Relational database diagrams allow a relationship between two tables. Some ERD notations (although not the Crow's Foot notation) allow M-way relationships involving more than two entity types. The next section shows how to represent M-way relationships in the Crow's Foot notation.
5. In some ERD notations (although not the Crow's Foot notation), the position of the cardinalities is reversed.

7.2 UNDERSTANDING RELATIONSHIPS

This section explores the entity relationship notation in more depth by examining important aspects of relationships. The first subsection describes identification dependency, a specialized kind of existence dependency. The second subsection describes three important relationship patterns: (1) relationships with attributes, (2) self-referencing relationships, and (3) associative entity types representing multi-way (M-way) relationships. The final subsection describes an important equivalence between M-N and 1-M relationships.

7.2.1 Identification Dependency (Weak Entities and Identifying Relationships)

Weak Entity   an entity type that borrows all or part of its primary key from another entity type. Identifying relationships indicate the entity types that supply components of the borrowed primary key.

In an ERD, some entity types may not have their own primary key. Entity types without their own primary key must borrow part (or all) of their primary key from other entity types. Entity types that borrow part or their entire primary key are known as <u>weak entities.</u> The relationship(s) that provides components of the primary key is known as an <u>identifying relationship.</u> Thus, an identification dependency involves a weak entity and one or more identifying relationships.

Identification dependency occurs because some entities are closely associated with other entities. For example, a room does not have a separate identity from its building a room is physically contained in a building. You can reference a room only by providing its associated building identifier. In the ERD for buildings and rooms (Figure 7.8), the *Room* entity type is identification dependent on the *Building* entity type in the *Contains* relationship. A solid relationship line indicates an identifying relationship. For weak entities, the underlined attribute (if present) is part of the primary key, but not the entire primary key. Thus, the primary key of *Room* is a combination of *BldgID* and *RoomNo*. As another example, Figure 7.9 depicts an identification dependency involving the weak entity *State* and the identifying relationship *Holds*.

Identification dependency is a specialized kind of existence dependency. Recall that an existent-dependent entity type has a mandatory relationship (minimum cardinality of one). Weak entities are existent dependent on the identifying relationships. In addition to the existence dependency, weak entities borrow part or their entire primary key.

The next section shows several additional examples of identification dependency in the discussion of associative entity types and M-way relationships. The use of identification dependency is necessary for associative entity types.

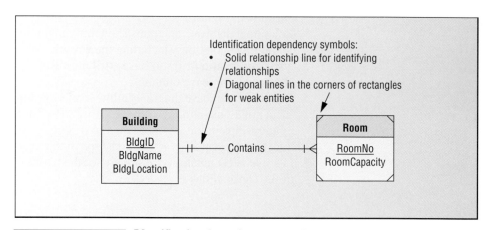

Figure 7.8   **Identification dependency example.**

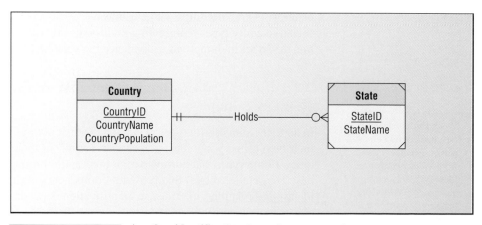

Figure 7.9   **Another identification dependency example.**

7.2.2 Relationship Patterns

This section discusses three patterns for relationships that you will encounter in database development efforts: (1) M-N relationships with attributes, (2) self-referencing (unary) relationships, and (3) associative entity types representing M-way relationships. Although these relationship patterns do not dominate ERDs, they are important when they occur. You need to study these patterns carefully to correctly apply them in database development efforts.

M-N Relationships with Attributes

As briefly mentioned in Section 7.1, relationships can have attributes. This situation typically occurs with M-N relationships. In an M-N relationship, attributes are associated with the combination of entity types, not just one of the entity types. If an attribute is associated with only one entity type, then it should be part of that entity type, not the relationship. Figures 7.10 and 7.11 depict M-N relationships with attributes. In Figure 7.10,

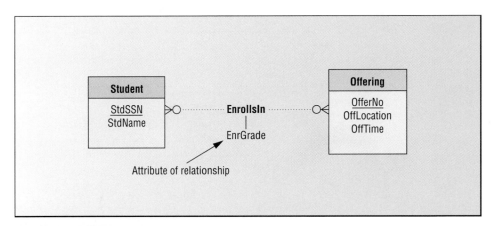

Figure 7.10   **M-N relationship with an attribute.**

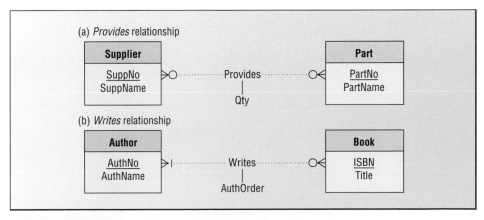

Figure 7.11   **Additional M-N relationships with attributes.**

the attribute *EnrGrade* is associated with the combination of a student and offering, not either one alone. For example, the *EnrollsIn* relationship records the fact that the student with social security number 123-77-9993 has a grade of 3.5 in the offering with offer number 1256. In Figure 7.11(a), the attribute *Qty* represents the quantity of a part supplied by a given supplier. In Figure 7.11(b), the attribute *AuthOrder* represents the order in which the author's name appears in the title of a book. To reduce clutter on a large diagram, the attributes of relationships may not be shown.

1-M relationships also can have attributes, but 1-M relationships with attributes are much less common than M-N relationships with attributes. In Figure 7.12, the *Commission* attribute is associated with the *Lists* relationship, not with either the *Agent* or *Home* entity type. A home will only have a commission if an agent lists it.

Self-Referencing (Unary) Relationships

A self-referencing (unary) relationship involves connections among members of the same set. Self-referencing relationships are sometimes called reflexive relationships because they are like a reflection in a mirror. Figure 7.13 displays two self-referencing re-

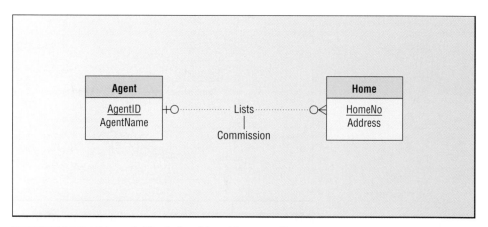

Figure 7.12   **1-M relationship with an attribute.**

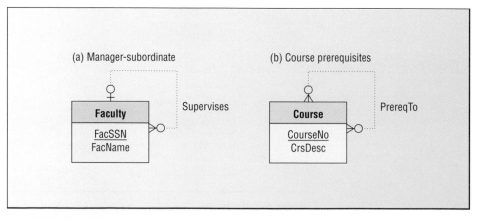

Figure 7.13   **Examples of self-referencing (unary) relationships.**

lationships involving the *Faculty* and *Course* entity types. Both relationships involve two entity types that are the same (*Faculty* for *Supervises* and *Course* for *PreReqTo*). These relationships depict important concepts in a university database. The *Supervises* relationship depicts an organizational chart, while the *PreReqTo* relationship depicts dependencies among courses that can affect a student's course planning.

For self-referencing relationships, it is important to distinguish between 1-M and M-N relationships. An instance diagram can help you understand the difference. Figure 7.14(a) shows an instance diagram for the *Supervises* relationship. Notice that each faculty can have at most one superior. For example, Faculty2 and Faculty3 have Faculty1 as a superior. Therefore, *Supervises* is a 1-M relationship because each faculty can have at most one supervisor. In contrast, there is no such restriction in the instance diagram for the *PreReqTo* relationship [Figure 7.14(b)]. For example, both IS480 and IS460 are prerequisites to IS461. Therefore, *PreReqTo* is an M-N relationship because a course can be a prerequisite to many courses, and a course can have many prerequisites.

Self-referencing relationships occur in a variety of business situations. Any data that can be visualized like Figure 7.14 can be represented as a self-referencing relationship. Typical examples include hierarchical charts of accounts, genealogical charts, part designs, and transportation routes. In these examples, self-referencing relationships are an important part of the database.

There is one other noteworthy aspect of self-referencing relationships. Sometimes a self-referencing relationship is not needed. For example, if you only want to know whether an employee is a supervisor, a self-referencing relationship is not needed. Rather, an attribute can be used to indicate whether an employee is a supervisor.

Self-Referencing Relationship a relationship involving the same entity type. Self-referencing relationships represent associations among members of the same set.

Associative Entity Types Representing Multiway (M-Way) Relationships

Some ERD notations support relationships involving more than two entity types, known as M-way (multiway) relationships where the M means more than two. For example, the Chen[2] ERD notation (with diamonds for relationships) allows relationships to connect more than two entity types, as depicted in Figure 7.15. The *Uses* relationship lists sup-

---

[2]The Chen notation is named after Dr. Peter Chen, who published the paper defining the Entity Relationship Model in 1976.

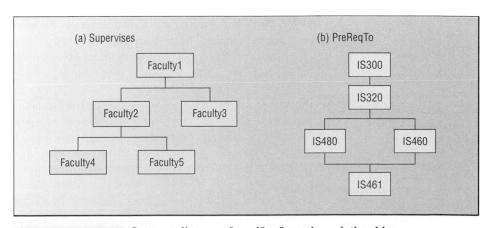

Figure 7.14   **Instance diagrams for self-referencing relationships.**

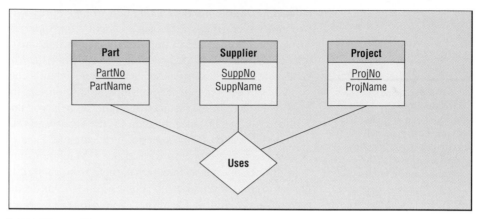

Figure 7.15   M-way (ternary) relationship using Chen notation.

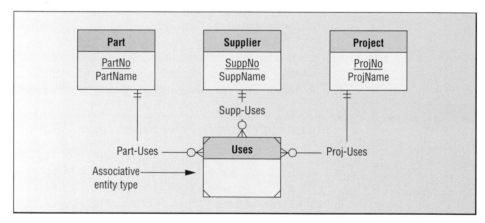

Figure 7.16   Associative entity type to represent a ternary relationship.

pliers and parts used on projects. For example, a relationship instance involving Supplier1, Part1, and Project1 means that Supplier1 Supplies Part1 on Project1. An M-way relationship involving three entity types is called a <u>ternary relationship.</u>

Although you cannot directly represent M-way relationships in the Crow's Foot notation, you should understand how to indirectly represent them. You use an <u>associative entity type</u> and a collection of binary relationships to represent an M-way relationship. In Figure 7.16, three 1-M relationships link the associative entity type, *Uses,* to the *Part, Supplier,* and *Project* entity types. The *Uses* entity type is associative because its role is to connect other entity types. Because associative entity types provide a connecting role, they are sometimes given names using active verbs. In addition, associative entity types are always weak as they must borrow the entire primary key. For example, the *Uses* entity type obtains its primary key through the three identifying relationships.

As another example, Figure 7.17 shows the associative entity type *Provides* that connects the *Employee, Skill,* and *Project* entity types. An example instance of the *Provides* entity type contains Employee1 providing Skill1 on Project1.

Associative Entity Type
a weak entity that replaces an M-way relationship. An associative entity type depends on two or more entity types for its primary key.

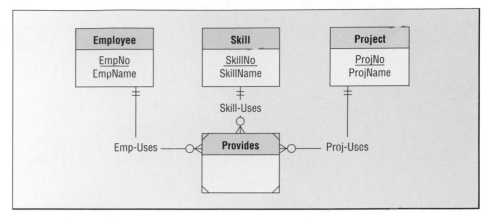

Figure 7.17 **Associative entity type connecting Employee, Skill, and Project**

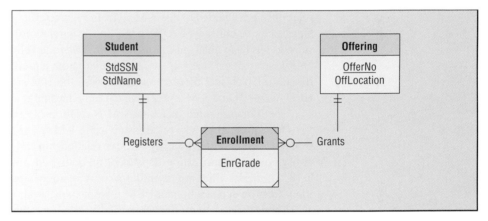

Figure 7.18 *EnrollsIn* **M-N relationship (Figure 7.10) transformed into 1-M relationships.**

The issue of when to use an associative entity type representing an M-way relationship can be difficult to understand. If a database only needs to record pairs of facts, an associative entity type is not needed. For example, if a database only needs to record who supplies a part and what projects use a part, then an associative entity type should not be used. In this case, there should be binary relationships between *Supplier* and *Part* and between *Project* and *Part*. You should use an associative entity type when the database should record combinations of three (or more) objects rather than just combinations of two objects. For example, if a database needs to record which supplier provides parts on specific projects, an associative entity type is needed. Because M-way relationships are an advanced topic, Chapters 8 and 9 provide more rigorous ways to reason about M-way relationships.

7.2.3 Equivalence between 1-M and M-N Relationships

To improve your understanding of M-N relationships, you should know an important equivalence for M-N relationships. An M-N relationship can be replaced by an associative entity type and two 1-M relationships. Figure 7.18 shows the *EnrollsIn* (Figure 7.10)

Relationship Equivalence an M-N relationship can be replaced by an associative entity type and two identifying 1-M relationships.

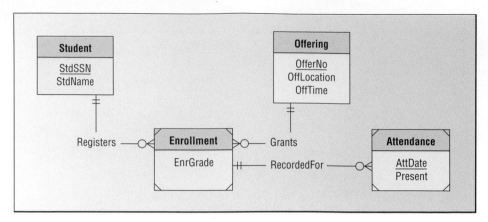

Figure 7.19   **Attendance entity type added to the ERD of Figure 7.18.**

relationship converted to this 1-M style. In Figure 7.18, two identifying relationships and an associative entity type replace the *EnrollsIn* relationship. The relationship name (*EnrollsIn*) has been changed to a noun (*Enrollment*) to follow the convention of nouns for entity type names. The 1-M style is similar to the representation in a relational database diagram. If you feel more comfortable with the 1-M style, then use it. In terms of the ERD, the M-N and 1-M styles have the same meaning.

The transformation of a binary M-N relationship into 1-M relationships is similar to representing an M-way relationship using 1-M relationships. Whenever an M-N relationship is represented as an associative relationship and two 1-M relationships, the new entity type is identification dependent on both 1-M relationships, as shown in Figure 7.18. Similarly, when representing M-way relationships, the associative entity type is identification dependent on all 1-M relationships, as shown in Figures 7.16 and 7.17.

There is one situation when the 1-M style is preferred to the M-N style. When an M-N relationship must be related to other entity types in another relationship, use the 1-M style. For example, assume that in addition to enrollment in a course offering, attendance in each class session should be recorded. In this situation, the 1-M style is preferred because it is necessary to link an enrollment with attendance records. Figure 7.19 shows the *Attendance* entity type added to the ERD of Figure 7.18. Note that an M-N relationship between the *Student* and *Offering* entity types would not have allowed another relationship with *Attendance*.

Figure 7.19 provides other examples of identification dependencies. The solid line by *Attendance* means that *Attendance* is identification dependent on *Enrollment* in the *RecordedFor* relationship. The primary key of *Attendance* consists of *AttDate* along with the primary key of *Enrollment*. Similarly, *Enrollment* is identification dependent on both *Student* and *Offering*. The primary key of *Enrollment* is a combination of *StdSSN* and *OfferNo*.

7.3 CLASSIFICATION IN THE ENTITY RELATIONSHIP MODEL

People classify objects to better understand their environment. For example, animals are classified into mammals, reptiles, and other categories to understand the similarities and differences among different species. In business, classification is also pervasive. Classification can be applied to investments, employees, customers, loans, parts, and so on. For example, when applying for a home mortgage, an important distinction is between fixed- and adjustable-rate mortgages. Within each kind of mortgage, there are many variations distinguished by features such as repayment period, prepayment penalties, and amount of loan.

This section describes ERD notation to support classification. You will learn to use generalization hierarchies, specify cardinality constraints for generalization hierarchies, and use multiple-level generalization hierarchies for complex classifications.

7.3.1 Generalization Hierarchies

Generalization hierarchies allow entity types to be related by the level of specialization. Figure 7.20 depicts a generalization hierarchy to classify employees as salaried versus hourly. Both salaried and hourly employees are specialized kinds of employees. The *Employee* entity type is known as the <u>supertype</u> (or parent). The entity types, *SalaryEmp* and *HourlyEmp,* are known as the <u>subtypes</u> (or children). Because each subtype object <u>is a</u> supertype object, the relationship between a subtype and a supertype is known as ISA. For example, a salaried employee is an employee. Because the relationship name (ISA) is always the same, it is not shown on the diagram.

<u>Inheritance</u> supports sharing between a supertype and its subtypes. Because every subtype object is also a supertype object, the attributes of the supertype also apply to all subtypes. For example, every entity of *SalaryEmp* has an employee number, name, and hiring date because it is also an entity of *Employee.* Inheritance means that the attributes of a supertype are automatically part of its subtypes. That is, each subtype inherits the attributes of its supertype. For example, the attributes of the *SalaryEmp* entity type are its direct attribute (*EmpSalary*) and its inherited attributes from *Employee* (*EmpNo, EmpName, EmpHireDate,* etc.). Inherited attributes are not shown in an ERD. Whenever you have a subtype, assume that it inherits the attributes from its supertype.

7.3.2 Disjointness and Completeness Constraints

Generalization hierarchies do not show cardinalities because they are always the same. Rather, disjointness and completeness constraints can be shown. <u>Disjointness</u> means that subtypes in a generalization hierarchy do not have any entities in common. In Figure 7.21, the generalization hierarchy is disjoint because a security cannot be both a stock and a bond. In contrast, the generalization hierarchy in Figure 7.22 is not disjoint because teaching assistants can be considered both students and faculty. Thus, the set of students

Generalization Hierarchy a collection of entity types arranged in a hierarchical structure to show similarity in attributes. Each subtype or child entity represents a subset of its supertype or parent entity.

Inheritance a data modeling feature that supports sharing of attributes between a supertype and a subtype. Subtypes inherit attributes from their supertype.

| **Figure 7.20** | **Generalization hierarchy for employees.** |

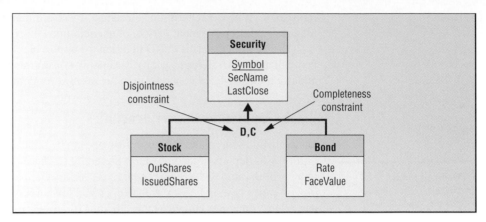

Figure 7.21   **Generalization hierarchy for securities.**

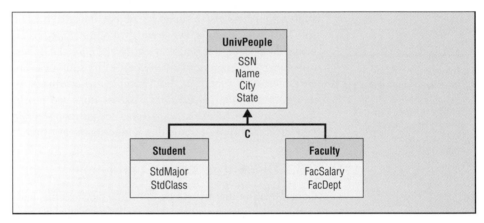

Figure 7.22   **Generalization hierarchy for university people.**

overlaps with the set of faculty. <u>Completeness</u> means that every entity of a supertype must be an entity in one of the subtypes in the generalization hierarchy. The completeness constraint in Figure 7.21 means that every security must be either a stock or a bond.

Some generalization hierarchies lack both disjointness and completeness constraints. In Figure 7.20, the lack of a disjointness constraint means that some employees can be both salaried and hourly. The lack of a completeness constraint indicates that some employees are not paid by salary or the hour (perhaps by commission).

7.3.3 Multiple Levels of Generalization

Generalization hierarchies can be extended to more than one level. This practice can be useful in disciplines such as investments where knowledge is highly structured. In Figure 7.23, there are two levels of subtypes beneath securities. Inheritance extends to all subtypes, direct and indirect. Thus, both the *Common* and *Preferred* entity types inherit the attributes of *Stock* (the immediate parent) and *Security* (the indirect parent). Note that disjointness and completeness constraints can be made for each group of subtypes.

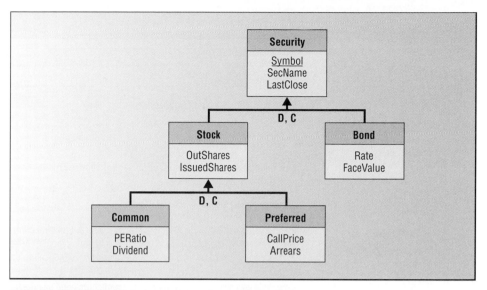

Figure 7.23   **Multiple levels of generalization hierarchies.**

7.4 REVIEW OF NOTATION AND COMPARISON TO OTHER NOTATIONS

You have seen a lot of ERD notation in the previous sections of this chapter. It is easy to become overwhelmed without a review to depict the most important points. To help you recall the notation introduced in the earlier sections, Table 7–2 presents a summary.

7.4.1 Comprehensive ERD Example

Figure 7.24 demonstrates most of the ERD notation for the university database of Chapter 3. Some of the attributes are omitted for brevity. Note that the *Enrollment* entity type (associative) and the identifying relationships (*Registers* and *Grants*) could appear as an M-N relationship as previously shown in Figure 7.10.

7.4.2 Diagram Variations

The ERD notation presented in this chapter is similar but not identical to what you may encounter later. There is no standard notation for ERDs. There are perhaps four to six reasonably popular ERD notations, each having its own small variations that appear in practice. The notation in this chapter comes from the Crow's Foot stencil in Visio Professional 5 with the addition of the generalization notation. Appendix A presents the class diagram notation of the Unified Modeling Language, an emerging notation for data modeling. The notations that you encounter in practice will depend on factors such as the data modeling tool (if any) used in your organization and the industry. One thing is certain: you should be prepared to adapt to the notation in use.

Symbol Variations

Because there is no widely accepted ERD standard, different symbols can be used to represent the same concept. Relationship cardinalities are a source of wide variation. You

TABLE 7–2 | **Summary of Crow's Foot Notation**

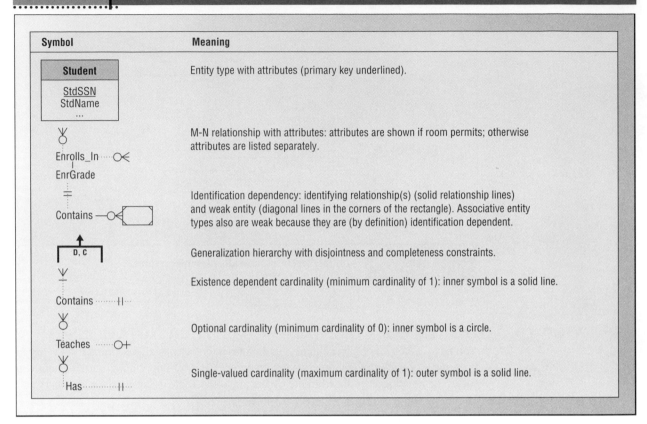

Symbol	Meaning
Student / StdSSN / StdName / ...	Entity type with attributes (primary key underlined).
Enrolls_In / EnrGrade	M-N relationship with attributes: attributes are shown if room permits; otherwise attributes are listed separately.
Contains	Identification dependency: identifying relationship(s) (solid relationship lines) and weak entity (diagonal lines in the corners of the rectangle). Associative entity types also are weak because they are (by definition) identification dependent.
D, C	Generalization hierarchy with disjointness and completeness constraints.
Contains	Existence dependent cardinality (minimum cardinality of 1): inner symbol is a solid line.
Teaches	Optional cardinality (minimum cardinality of 0): inner symbol is a circle.
Has	Single-valued cardinality (maximum cardinality of 1): outer symbol is a solid line.

should pay attention to the placement of the cardinality symbols. The notation in this chapter places the symbols close to the "far" entity type, while other notations place the cardinality symbols close to the "near" entity type. The notation in this chapter uses a visual representation of cardinalities with the minimum and maximum cardinalities given by three symbols. Other notations use a text representation with letters and integers instead of symbols. For example, Figure 7.25 shows a Chen ERD of Figure 7.3 with the position of cardinalities reversed, cardinalities depicted with text, and relationships denoted by the diamonds.

Other symbol variations are visual representations for certain kinds of entity types. In some notations, weak entities and M-N relationships have special representations. Weak entities are sometimes enclosed in double rectangles. Identifying relationships are sometimes enclosed in double diamonds. M-N relationships with attributes are sometimes shown as a rectangle with a diamond inside denoting the dual qualities (both relationship and entity type).

Rule Variations

In addition to symbol variations, there are also rule variations, as shown in the following list. In each restriction, there is a remedy. For example, if only binary relationships are supported, M-way relationships must be represented as an associative entity type with 1-M relationships.

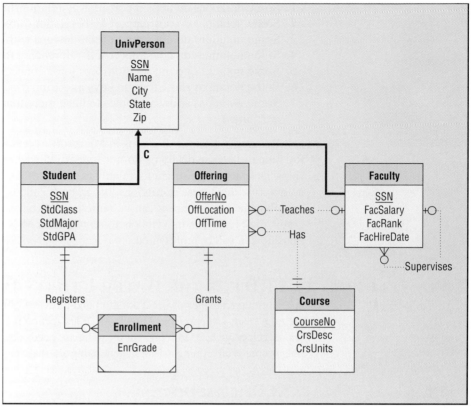

Figure 7.24   **ERD for the university database.**[3]

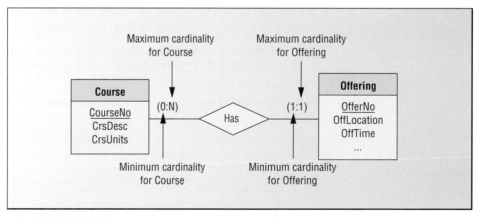

Figure 7.25   **Chen notation for the course-offering ERD.**

---

[3]The inherited primary key (SSN) is shown for emphasis.

1. Some notations do not support M-way relationships.
2. Some notations do not support M-N relationships.
3. Some notations do not support relationships with attributes.
4. Some notations do not support self-referencing (unary) relationships.
5. Some notations permit relationships to be connected to other relationships.
6. Some notations show foreign keys as attributes.
7. Some notations allow attributes to have more than one value (multivalued attributes).

Relational database diagrams in Microsoft Access have most of these restrictions. Relational database diagrams do not support M-way relationships and M-N relationships. Despite these restrictions, relational database diagrams are no less expressive than notations without these restrictions. In certain situations, you may need additional symbols, but the same concept can be represented. For example, relational database diagrams may require more symbols to represent an M-N relationship, but an M-N relationship can still be represented.

7.5 DEVELOPING AN ERD FOR THE WATER UTILITY DATABASE

After seeing examples of ERD notation and a review of the most significant points, you are now ready to apply your knowledge. This section presents a small narrative problem and develops an ERD to represent the database needs described in the narrative. The emphasis here is on refining a design, generating alternatives, and justifying design decisions.

7.5.1 Database Description

Let's begin with a brief description of a customer database for a municipal water utility. You can assume that this description is the result of an initial investigation with appropriate personnel at the water utility. The database should support recording of water usage and billing for water usage. To support these functions, the database should contain data about customers, rates, water usage, and bills. Other functions such as payment processing and customer service are omitted from this description for brevity. The following list describes the data requirements in more detail.

- Customer data include a unique customer number, a name, a billing address, a type (commercial or residential), an applicable rate, and a collection (one or more) of meters.
- Meter data include a unique meter number, address, size, and model.
- An employee periodically reads each meter on a scheduled date. When a meter is read, a meter reading document is created containing a unique meter reading number, an employee number, a meter number, a time stamp (includes date and time), and a consumption level.
- The water utility bills customers based on their most recent meter readings and applicable rates. A bill consists of a heading part and a list of detail lines. The heading part contains a customer number, preparation date, payment due date, and date range for the consumption period. Each detail line contains a meter number, water consumption, and amount.
- A rate includes a unique rate code, description, fixed dollar amount, consumption threshold, and variable amount (dollars per cubic foot). Consumption up to the threshold is billed at the fixed amount. Consumption

above the threshold is billed at the variable amount. Customers are assigned rates using a number of factors such as customer type, address, and adjustment factors.

7.5.2 Initial ERD

Let us begin by identifying potential entity types. Recall that nouns describing people, things, places, and events can represent entity types in an ERD. Prominent nouns in the narrative are customer, meter, bill, reading, and rate. For each of these nouns, the narrative describes associated attributes. Figure 7.26 shows a preliminary ERD with entity types for nouns and associated attributes. Note that collections of things are not attributes. For example, the fact that a customer has a collection of meters will be shown as a relationship rather than as an attribute of the *Customer* entity type. In addition, references between these entity types will be shown as relationships rather than attributes. For example, the fact that a reading contains a meter number will be recorded as a relationship.

Adding Relationships

After identifying preliminary entity types and attributes, let us continue by connecting entity types with relationships. A good place to start is with references in the narrative among entity types. The relationships in Figure 7.27, *Assigned, Uses,* and *ReadBy* follow from the narrative. For example, a meter reading contains a meter number. There is no relationship between the *Customer* and *Bill* entity types because the relationship can be derived from the relationships *Includes, ReadBy,* and *Uses.* To reduce the size of the ERD, only the primary keys are shown in Figure 7.27.

The *Includes* relationship between the *Bill* and *Reading* entity types is more subtle. Each detail line on a bill shows the consumption of water through a meter during the most recent billing period. To compute the consumption through a meter, you subtract the reading level in the previous period from the reading level in the most recent period. The *Includes* relationship connects a bill to its most recent meter readings, thus supporting the consumption calculation.

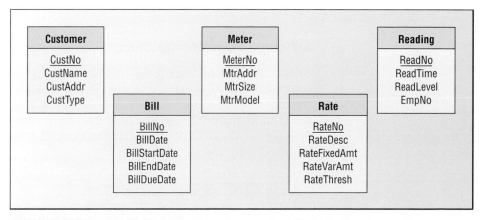

Figure 7.26   **Preliminary entity types and attributes in the water utility database.**

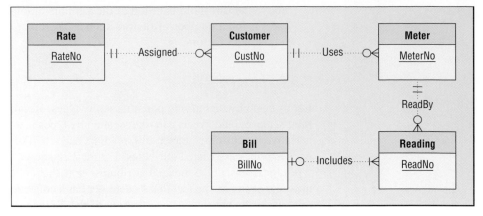

Figure 7.27   **Entity types connected by relationships.**

7.5.3 Refinements to the Initial ERD

Data modeling is usually an iterative or repetitive process. You construct a preliminary data model and then refine it many times. In refining a data model, you should generate feasible alternatives and evaluate them according to user requirements. You typically need to gather additional information from users to evaluate alternatives. This process of refinement and evaluation can continue many times for large databases. To depict the iterative nature of data modeling, this section describes several refinements to the initial ERD design.

Transforming Attributes into Entity Types

A common refinement is to transform an <u>attribute into an entity type.</u> When the database should contain more than just the identifier of an entity, this transformation is useful. In the water utility ERD, the *Reading* entity type contains the *EmpNo* attribute. If other data about an employee are needed, *EmpNo* can be expanded into an entity type, as shown in Figure 7.28.

Splitting Compound Attributes

Another common refinement is to split <u>compound attributes into smaller attributes.</u> A compound attribute contains multiple kinds of data. For example, the *Customer* entity type has an address attribute containing data about a customer's street, city, state, and postal code. Splitting compound attributes can facilitate search of the embedded data. Splitting the address attribute as shown in Figure 7.29 supports searches by street, city, state, and postal code.

Adding Generalization Hierarchies

A third transformation is to make an <u>entity type into a generalization hierarchy.</u> If there are attributes that do not apply to all entities and there is an accepted classification of entities, a generalization hierarchy may be useful. For example, water utility customers can be classified as commercial or residential. The attributes specific to commercial customers (*Tax-*

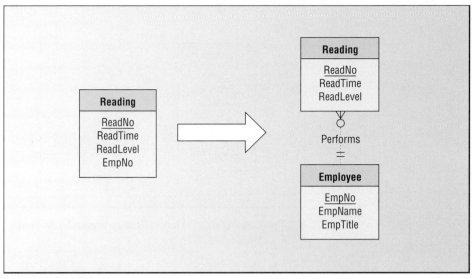

Figure 7.28   Transformation of an attribute into an entity type.

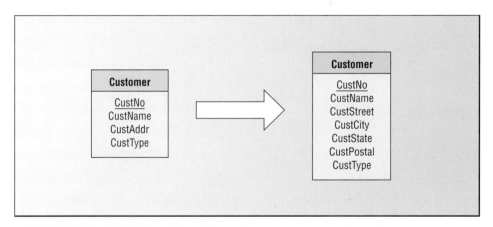

Figure 7.29   Split of *CustAddr* attribute into component attributes.

PayerID and *EnterpriseZone*) do not apply to residential customers and vice versa. In Figure 7.30, the attributes specific to commercial and residential customers have been moved to the subtypes. An additional benefit of this transformation is the avoidance of null values. For example, entities in the *Commercial* and *Residential* entity types will not have null values. Some entities in the original *Customer* entity type would have had null values. Residential customers would have had null values for *TaxPayerID* and *EnterpriseZone*.

Expanding Entity Types

A fourth transformation is to make an entity type into two <u>entity types and a relationship.</u> This transformation can be useful to record a finer level of detail about an entity. For example, rates in the water utility database apply to all levels of consumption beyond an initial level. It can be useful to allow different rates depending on the con-

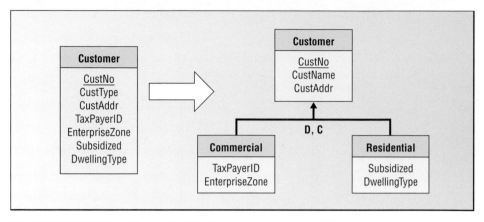

Figure 7.30 Generalization hierarchy for water utility customers.

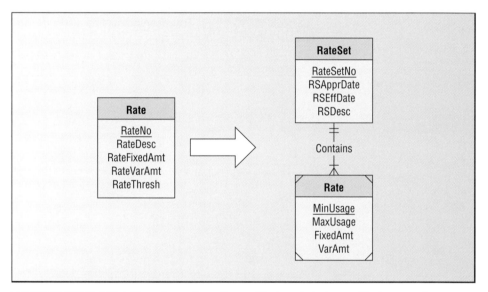

Figure 7.31 Transformation of an entity type into two entity types and a relationship.

sumption level. Figure 7.31 shows a transformation to the *Rate* entity type to allow rates to vary by consumption. The *RateSet* entity type represents a set of rates approved by the utility's governing commission. The primary key of the *Rate* entity type borrows from the *RateSet* entity type. Identification dependency is not required when transforming an entity type into two entity types and a relationship. In this situation, identification dependency is useful, but in other situations it may not be appropriate.

When designing a database, you should carefully explore alternative designs. The transformations discussed in this section can help you consider alternative designs. The possible transformations are not limited to those discussed in this section. You can reverse most of these transformations. For example, you can add a supertype to depict similarities among entity types. Check the references at the end of this chapter for books on database design that describe more possible transformations.

7.5.4 Finalizing the ERD

After considering alternative designs, you will eventually decide on a final ERD. To allow others to evaluate and understand your ERD, you should justify important design decisions. In addition, you should check your final ERD for consistency and completeness. This section depicts design decisions and consistency and completeness checks for the water utility database.

Documenting Design Decisions

You should document decisions in which there is more than one feasible choice. For example, both 0 and 1 are feasible choices for the minimum cardinality from the *Meter* entity type to the *Customer* entity type in Figure 7.27. To choose among these cardinalities, you should explain the consequences of each choice to appropriate users. A minimum cardinality of 0 allows a free-standing meter not associated with a customer such as for a new home. A minimum cardinality of one means that a meter must always be associated with a customer. Document your decision by recording who recommended the alternative and why.

You also should document decisions that might be unclear to others. For example, the minimum cardinality of 0 from the *Reading* entity type to the *Bill* entity type might be unclear. You should document the need for this cardinality because of the time difference between the creation of a bill and its associated readings. A meter is read sometimes days before an associated bill is created.

Design decisions should be incorporated into your final ERD. If you are using an ERD tool that has a data dictionary, include design justifications as documentation in the data dictionary. Otherwise, you can list the justifications on a separate page and annotate your ERD, as shown in Figure 7.32. The circled numbers in Figure 7.32 refer to explanations in Table 7–3. Note that some of the refinements shown previously were not used in the final ERD.

Completeness and Consistency Checks

In addition to documenting your final ERD, you should check it for consistency and completeness. The checks in Table 7–4 ensure that there are no obvious errors in your ERD. These checks do not ensure that you have considered multiple alternatives, correctly represented user requirements, and properly documented your design.

7.6 CONVERTING AN ERD TO RELATIONAL TABLES

Conversion from the ERD notation to relational tables is important because of industry practice. Computer-aided software engineering (CASE) tools support some kind of entity relationship notation. It is common practice to use a CASE tool as an aid in developing an ERD. Because most commercial DBMSs use the Relational Model, you must convert your ERD into relational tables to implement your database design.

This section describes the conversion process in two parts. First, the basic rules to convert entity types, relationships, and attributes are described. Second, specialized rules to convert optional 1-M relationships, generalization hierarchies, and 1-1 relationships are shown.

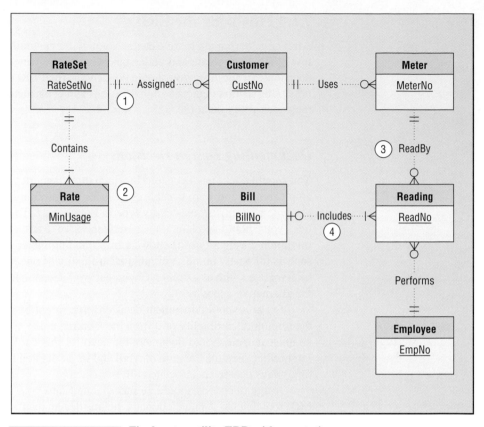

Figure 7.32

Final water utility ERD with annotations.

TABLE 7–3 | **List of Design Justifications for the Final ERD**

1. A rate set is a collection of rates approved by the governing commission of the utility.

2. Rates are similar to lines on a tax table. An individual rate is identified by the rate set identifier along with the minimum consumption level of the rate.

3. The minimum cardinality indicates that a meter must always be associated with a customer. For new property, the developer is initially responsible for the meter. If a customer forecloses on property, the financial institution holding the deed will be responsible.

4. A reading is not associated with a bill until the bill is prepared. A reading may be created several days before the associated bill.

7.6.1 Basic Conversion Rules

The rules that follow convert everything on an ERD except generalization hierarchies. You should apply these rules until everything in your ERD is converted. The first two rules should be used before the other rules. As you apply these rules, you can use a check mark to indicate what parts of your ERD have been converted.

TABLE 7–4	Completeness and Consistency Checks

Type of Check	*Description*
Completeness	1. All entity types have a primary key (direct or borrowed).
	2. All entity types participate in at least one relationship.
	3. All relationships are named.
	4. Cardinality is given for all entity types in a relationship.
Consistency	1. All relationships connect two entity types (not necessarily distinct).
	2. Entity type and relationship names are unique.
	3. Attribute names are unique within entity types and relationships.
	4. Relationships are not connected to other relationships.

1. **Entity Type Rule:** Each entity type (except subtypes) becomes a table. The primary key of the entity type (if not weak) becomes the primary key of the table. The attributes of the entity type become columns in the table. This rule should be used first before the relationship rules.
2. **1-M Relationship Rule:** Each 1-M relationship becomes a foreign key in the table corresponding to the many entity type (the entity type near the Crow's Foot symbol). If the minimum cardinality is one, the foreign key cannot accept null values.
3. **M-N Relationship Rule:** Each M-N relationship becomes a separate table. The primary key of the table is a combined key consisting of the primary keys of the entity types participating in the M-N relationship.
4. **Identification Dependency Rule:** Each identifying relationship (denoted by a solid relationship line) adds a column to a primary key. The primary key of the table corresponding to the weak entity type consists of (i) the underlined local key (if any) in the weak entity type and (ii) the primary key(s) of the entity type(s) connected by the identifying relationship(s).

To understand these rules, you can apply them to some of the ERDs given earlier in the chapter. Using Rules 1 and 2, you can convert Figure 7.33 into the CREATE TABLE statements shown in Figure 7.34. Rule 1 is applied to convert the *Course* and *Offering* entity types to tables. Then, Rule 2 is applied to convert the *Has* relationship to a foreign key (*Offering.CourseNo*). The *Offering* table contains the foreign key because the *Offering* entity type has the maximum cardinality of one.

Next, you can apply the M-N relationship rule (Rule 3) to convert the ERD in Figure 7.35. Following this rule leads to the *Enrolls_In* table in Figure 7.36. The primary key of *Enrolls_In* is a combination of the primary keys of the *Student* and the *Offering* entity types.

To gain practice with the identification dependency rule (Rule 4), you can use it to convert the ERD in Figure 7.37. The result of converting Figure 7.37 is identical to Figure 7.34 except that the *Enrolls_In* table is renamed *Enrollment*. The ERD in Figure 7.37 requires two applications of the identification dependency rule. Each application of the identification dependency rule adds a component to the primary key of the *Enrollment* table.

You also can apply the rules to convert self-referencing relationships. For example, you can apply the 1-M and M-N relationship rules to convert the self-referencing

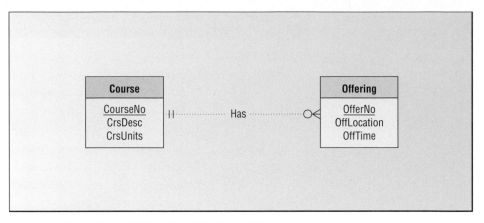

Figure 7.33   ERD with 1-M relationship.

```
CREATE TABLE Course
     ( CourseNo      CHAR(6)        NOT NULL,
       CrsDesc       VARCHAR,
       CrsUnits      SMALLINT
CONSTRAINT PKCourse PRIMARY KEY (CourseNo) )

CREATE TABLE Offering
     ( OfferNo       LONG           NOT NULL,
       OffLocation   CHAR(20),
       CourseNo      CHAR(6)        NOT NULL,
       OffTime       TIME,
       ...,
CONSTRAINT PKOffering PRIMARY KEY (OfferNo),
CONSTRAINT FKCourseNo FOREIGN KEY (CourseNo) REFERENCES Course  )
```

Figure 7.34   Conversion of Figure 7.33.

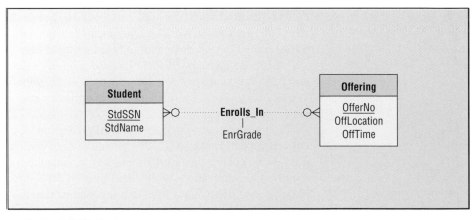

Figure 7.35   M-N relationship with an attribute.

```
CREATE TABLE Student
(      StdSSN          CHAR(11)        NOT NULL,
       StdName         VARCHAR,
       ...
CONSTRAINT PKStudent PRIMARY KEY (StdSSN)            )

CREATE TABLE Offering
(      OfferNo         LONG            NOT NULL,
       OffLocation     VARCHAR,
       OffTime         TIME,
       ...
CONSTRAINT PKOffering PRIMARY KEY (OfferNo) )

CREATE TABLE Enrolls_In
(      OfferNo         LONG            NOT NULL,
       StdSSN          CHAR(11)        NOT NULL,
       EnrGrade        DECIMAL(2,1),
CONSTRAINT PKEnrolls_In PRIMARY KEY (OfferNo, StdSSN),
CONSTRAINT FKOfferNo FOREIGN KEY (OfferNo) REFERENCES Offering,
CONSTRAINT FKStdSSN FOREIGN KEY (StdSSN) REFERENCES Student    )
```

Figure 7.36   **Conversion of Figure 7.35.**

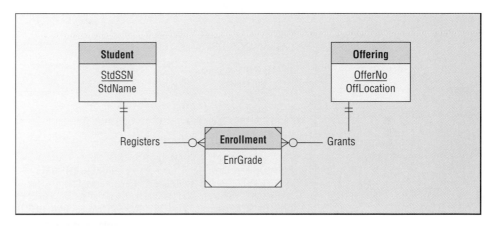

Figure 7.37   *Enrolls_in* **M-N relationship transformed into 1-M relationships.**

relationships in Figure 7.38. Using the 1-M relationship rule, the *Supervises* relationship converts to a foreign key in the *Faculty* table, as shown in Figure 7.39. Using the M-N relationship rule, the *Prereq_To* relationship converts to the *Prereq_To* table with a combined primary key of the course number of the prerequisite course and the course number of the dependent course.

You also can apply conversion rules to more complex identification dependencies, as depicted in Figure 7.40. The first part of the conversion is identical to the conversion of Figure 7.37. Application of the 1-M rule makes the combination of *StdSSN* and *OfferNo* foreign keys in the *Attendance* table (Figure 7.41). Note that the foreign keys in *Attendance* refer to *Enrollment,* not to *Student* and *Offering.* Finally, one application of the identification dependency rule makes the combination of *StdSSN, OfferNo,* and *AttDate* the primary key of the *Attendance* table.

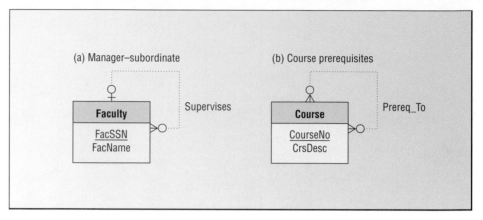

Figure 7.38   Examples of 1-M and M-N self-referencing relationships.

```
CREATE TABLE Faculty
(      FacSSN          CHAR(11)         NOT NULL,
       FacName         VARCHAR,
       FacSupervisor   CHAR(11),
       ...
CONSTRAINT PKFaculty PRIMARY KEY (FacSSN),
FOREIGN KEY (FacSupervisor) REFERENCES Faculty  )

CREATE TABLE Course
(      CourseNo        CHAR(6)          NOT NULL,
       CrsDesc         VARCHAR,
       CrsUnits        SMALLINT,
CONSTRAINT PKCourse PRIMARY KEY (CourseNo) )

CREATE TABLE Prereq_To
(      Prereq_CNo      CHAR(6)          NOT NULL,
       Depend_CNo                       CHAR(6)  NOT NULL,
CONSTRAINT PKPrereq_To PRIMARY KEY (Prereq_CNo, Depend_CNo),
CONSTRAINT FKPrereq_CNo FOREIGN KEY (Prereq_CNo) REFERENCES Course,
CONSTRAINT FKDepend_CNo FOREIGN KEY (Depend_CNo) REFERENCES Course   )
```

Figure 7.39   Conversion of Figure 7.38.

7.6.2 Converting Optional 1-M Relationships

Using the 1-M relationship rule results in null values when converting optional relationships. Recall that a relationship with a minimum cardinality of 0 is optional. For example, the *Teaches* relationship (Figure 7.42) is optional to *Offering* because an *Offering* object can be stored without being related to a *Faculty* object. Converting Figure 7.42 results in two tables (*Faculty* and *Offering*) as well as a foreign key (*FacSSN*) in the *Offering* table. The foreign key should allow null values because the minimum cardinality of the *Offering* entity type in the relationship is optional (0). However, null values can lead to complications in evaluating the results of queries.

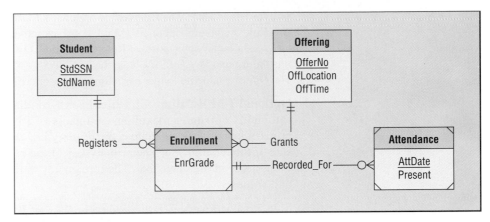

Figure 7.40   ERD with two weak entity types.

```
CREATE TABLE Attendance
(       OfferNo         LONG            NOT NULL,
        StdSSN          CHAR(11)        NOT NULL,
        AttDate         DATE            NOT NULL,
        Present         BOOL,
CONSTRAINT PKAttendance PRIMARY KEY (OfferNo, StdSSN, AttDate),
CONSTRAINT FKOfferNoStdSSN FOREIGN KEY (OfferNo, StdSSN) REFERENCES Enrollment   )
```

Figure 7.41   Conversion of *Attendance* entity type in Figure 7.40.

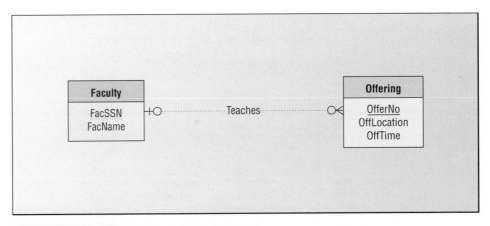

Figure 7.42   Optional 1-M relationship.

To avoid null values when converting optional 1-M relationships, you can apply Rule 5 below. Rule 5 converts optional 1-M relationships into a table instead of a foreign key. Figure 7.43 shows an application of Rule 5 to the ERD in Figure 7.42. The *Teaches* table contains the foreign key *FacSSN*. Note that the *FacSSN* column does not permit null values. The *Offering* table no longer has a foreign key referring to the *Faculty* table.

5. **Optional 1-M Relationship Rule:** Each 1-M relationship with a minimum cardinality of 0 and a maximum cardinality of 1 becomes a new table. The primary key of the new table is the primary key of the entity type on the many side of the relationship. The primary key of the other entity type becomes a foreign key in the new table. The foreign key in the new table does not permit null values.

Rule 5 is controversial. Using Rule 5 in place of Rule 2 (1-M Relationship Rule) avoids null values in foreign keys. However, using Rule 5 results in more tables. Query formulation can be more difficult with additional tables. In addition, query execution can be slower due to extra joins. The choice of using Rule 5 in place of Rule 2 depends on the importance of avoiding null values versus avoiding extra tables. In many databases, avoiding extra tables may be more important than avoiding null values.

7.6.3 Converting Generalization Hierarchies

The approach to convert generalization hierarchies mimics the entity relationship notation as much as possible. Rule 6 converts each entity type of a generalization hierarchy into a table. The only column appearing in a table that is different from the ERD is the inherited primary key. In Figure 7.44, *EmpNo* is a column in the *SalaryEmp* and *HourlyEmp* tables because it is the primary key of the parent entity type (*Employee*). In addition, the *SalaryEmp* and *HourlyEmp* tables have a foreign key constraint referring to the *Employee* table. The CASCADE delete option is set in both foreign key constraints (see Figure 7.45).

```
CREATE TABLE Faculty
(      FacSSN          CHAR(11)        NOT NULL,
       FacName         VARCHAR,
       ... ,
CONSTRAINT PKFaculty PRIMARY KEY (FacSSN)         )


CREATE TABLE Offering
(      OfferNo         LONG            NOT NULL,
       OffLocation     VARCHAR,
       OffTime         TIME,
       ... ,
CONSTRAINT PKOffering PRIMARY KEY (OfferNo)  )


CREATE TABLE Teaches
(      OfferNo         LONG            NOT NULL,
       FacSSN          CHAR(11)        NOT NULL,
CONSTRAINT PKTeaches PRIMARY KEY (OfferNo),
CONSTRAINT FKFacSSN FOREIGN KEY (FacSSN) REFERENCES Faculty   )
```

Figure 7.43 Conversion of Figure 7.42.

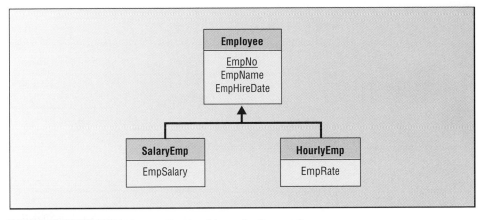

Figure 7.44   **Generalization hierarchy for employees.**

```
CREATE TABLE Employee
(       EmpNo           LONG            NOT NULL,
        EmpName         VARCHAR,
        EmpHireDate     DATE,
CONSTRAINT PKEmployee PRIMARY KEY (EmpNo)       )

CREATE TABLE SalaryEmp
(       EmpNo           LONG            NOT NULL,
        EmpSalary       DECIMAL(10,2),
CONSTRAINT PKSalaryEmp PRIMARY KEY (EmpNo) ,
CONSTRAINT FKSalaryEmp FOREIGN KEY (EmpNo) REFERENCES Employee ON DELETE CASCADE  )

CREATE TABLE HourlyEmp
(       EmpNo           LONG            NOT NULL,
        EmpRate         DECIMAL(10,2),
CONSTRAINT PKHourlyEmp PRIMARY KEY (EmpNo) ,
CONSTRAINT FKHourlyEmp FOREIGN KEY (EmpNo) REFERENCES Employee ON DELETE CASCADE  )
```

Figure 7.45   **Conversion of generalization hierarchy in Figure 7.44.**

6. **Generalization Hierarchy Rule:** Each entity type of a generalization hierarchy becomes a table. The columns of a table are the attributes of the corresponding entity type plus the primary key of the parent entity type. For each table representing a subtype, define a foreign key constraint that references the table corresponding to the parent entity type. Use the CASCADE option for deletions of referenced rows.

Rule 6 also applies to generalization hierarchies of more than one level. To convert the generalization hierarchy of Figure 7.46, five tables are produced (see Figure 7.47). In each table, the primary key of the parent (*Security*) is included. In addition, foreign key constraints are added in each table corresponding to a subtype.

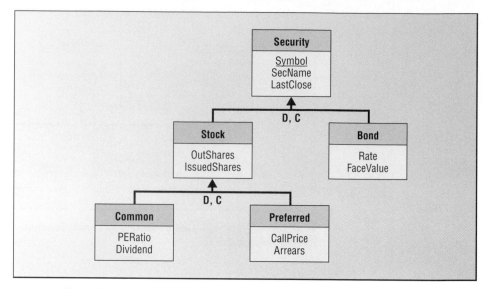

Figure 7.46   **Multiple levels of generalization hierarchies.**

```
CREATE TABLE Security
(      Symbol        CHAR(6)         NOT NULL,
       SecName       VARCHAR,
       LastClose     DECIMAL(10,2),
CONSTRAINT PKSecurity PRIMARY KEY (Symbol)   )

CREATE TABLE Stock
(      Symbol        CHAR(6)         NOT NULL,
       OutShares     INTEGER,
       IssuedShares  INTEGER,
CONSTRAINT PKStock PRIMARY KEY (Symbol),
CONSTRAINT FKStock FOREIGN KEY (Symbol) REFERENCES Security ON DELETE CASCADE  )

CREATE TABLE Bond
(      Symbol        CHAR(6)         NOT NULL,
       Rate          DECIMAL(12,4),
       FaceValue     DECIMAL(10,2),
CONSTRAINT PKBond PRIMARY KEY (Symbol),
CONSTRAINT FKBond FOREIGN KEY (Symbol) REFERENCES Security ON DELETE CASCADE  )

CREATE TABLE Common
(      Symbol        CHAR(6)         NOT NULL,
       PE/Ratio      DECIMAL(12,4),
       Dividend      DECIMAL(10,2),
CONSTRAINT PKCommon PRIMARY KEY (Symbol),
CONSTRAINT FKCommon FOREIGN KEY (Symbol) REFERENCES Stock ON DELETE CASCADE)

CREATE TABLE Preferred
(      Symbol        CHAR(6)         NOT NULL,
       CallPrice     DECIMAL(12,2),
       Arrears       DECIMAL(10,2),
CONSTRAINT PKPreferred PRIMARY KEY (Symbol),
CONSTRAINT FKPreferred FOREIGN KEY (Symbol) REFERENCES Stock ON DELETE CASCADE)
```

Figure 7.47   **Conversion of generalization hierarchy in Figure 7.46.**

Because the Relational Model does not directly support generalization hierarchies, there are several other ways to convert generalization hierarchies. The other approaches vary depending on the number of tables and the placement of inherited columns. Rule 6 may result in extra joins to gather all data about an entity, but there are no null values and only small amounts of duplicate data. For example, to collect all data about a common stock, you should join the *Common, Stock,* and *Security* tables. Other conversion approaches may require fewer joins but result in more redundant data and null values. The references at the end of this chapter discuss the pros and cons of several approaches to convert generalization hierarchies.

You also should note that generalization hierarchies are directly supported in SQL3, the emerging standard for object relational databases presented in Chapter 16. Using SQL3 avoids loss of semantic information when converting generalization hierarchies.

7.6.4 Converting 1-1 Relationships

Outside of generalization hierarchies, 1-1 relationships are not common. They can occur when entities with separate identifiers are closely related. For example, Figure 7.48 shows the *Employee* and *Office* entity types connected by a 1-1 relationship. Separate entity types seem intuitive but a 1-1 relationship connects the entity types. Rule 7 converts 1-1 relationships into two foreign keys unless many null values will result. In Figure 7.48, most employees will not manage offices. Thus, the conversion in Figure 7.49 eliminates the foreign key (*OfficeNo*) in the employee table.

7. **1-1 Relationship Rule:** The 1-1 relationship is converted into two foreign keys. If the relationship is optional with respect to one of the entity types, the corresponding foreign key may be dropped to eliminate null values.

7.6.5 Comprehensive Conversion Example

This section presents a larger example to integrate your knowledge of the conversion rules. Figure 7.50 shows an ERD similar to the final ERD for the water utility problem discussed in Section 7.5. For brevity, some attributes have been omitted. Figure 7.51 shows the relational tables derived through the conversion rules. Table 7–5 lists the conversion rules used along with brief explanations.

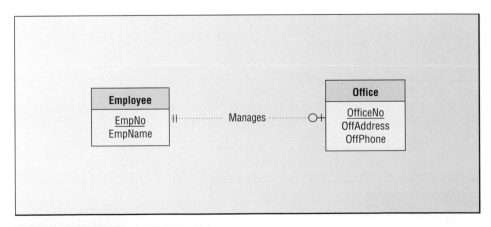

Figure 7.48   **1-1 Relationship.**

```
CREATE TABLE Employee
(       EmpNo           LONG            NOT NULL,
        EmpName         VARCHAR,
CONSTRAINT PKEmployee PRIMARY KEY (EmpNo)  )

CREATE TABLE Office
(       OfficeNo        LONG            NOT NULL,
        OffAddress      VARCHAR,
        OffPhone        CHAR(10),
        EmpNo           LONG,
CONSTRAINT PKOffice PRIMARY KEY (OfficeNo) ,
CONSTRAINT FKEmpNo FOREIGN KEY (EmpNo) REFERENCES Employee
CONSTRAINT EmpNoUnique UNIQUE (EmpNo) )
```

Figure 7.49   **Conversion of the 1-1 relationship in Figure 7.48.**

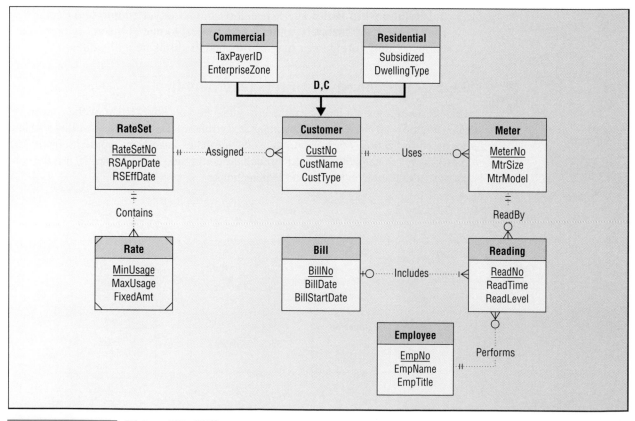

Figure 7.50   **Water utility ERD.**

```
CREATE TABLE Customer
(       CustNo          LONG            NOT NULL,
        CustName        VARCHAR,
        CustType        CHAR(6),
        RateSetNo       LONG            NOT NULL,
CONSTRAINT PKCustomer PRIMARY KEY (CustNo),
CONSTRAINT FKRateSetNo FOREIGN KEY (RateSetNo) REFERENCES RateSet )

CREATE TABLE Commercial
(       CustNo          LONG            NOT NULL,
        TaxPayerID      CHAR(20)        NOT NULL,
        EnterpiseZone   BOOL,
CONSTRAINT PKCommercial PRIMARY KEY (CustNo),
CONSTRAINT FKCommercial FOREIGN KEY (CustNo) REFERENCES Customer
  ON DELETE CASCADE )

CREATE TABLE Residential
(       CustNo          LONG            NOT NULL,
        Subsidized                      BOOL,
        DwellingType                    CHAR(6),
CONSTRAINT PKResidential PRIMARY KEY (CustNo),
CONSTRAINT FKResidential FOREIGN KEY (CustNo) REFERENCES Customer
  ON DELETE CASCADE )

CREATE TABLE RateSet
(       RateSetNo       LONG            NOT NULL,
        RSApprDate      DATE,
        RSEffDate       DATE,
CONSTRAINT PKRateSet PRIMARY KEY (RateSetNo) )

CREATE TABLE Rate
(       RateSetNo       LONG            NOT NULL,
        MinUsage        LONG,
        MaxUsage        LONG,
        FixedAmt        DECIMAL(10,2),
CONSTRAINT PKRate PRIMARY KEY (RateSetNo, MinUsage),
CONSTRAINT FKRateSetNo FOREIGN KEY (RateSetNo) REFERENCES RateSet )

CREATE TABLE Meter
(       MeterNo         LONG            NOT NULL,
        MtrSize         INTEGER,
        MtrModel        CHAR(6),
        CustNo          LONG            NOT NULL,
CONSTRAINT PKMeter PRIMARY KEY (MeterNo),
CONSTRAINT FKCustNo FOREIGN KEY (CustNo) REFERENCES Customer )
```

Figure 7.51   **Conversion of the ERD in Figure 7.50**

```
CREATE TABLE Reading
(        ReadNo          LONG              NOT NULL,
         ReadTime        TIME,
         ReadLevel       INTEGER,
         MeterNo         LONG              NOT NULL,
         EmpNo           LONG              NOT NULL,
         BillNo          LONG,
CONSTRAINT PKReading PRIMARY KEY (ReadNo),
CONSTRAINT FKEmpNo FOREIGN KEY (EmpNo) REFERENCES Employee,
CONSTRAINT FKMeterNo FOREIGN KEY (MeterNo) REFERENCES Meter,
CONSTRAINT FKBillNo FOREIGN KEY (BillNo) REFERENCES Bill )

CREATE TABLE Bill
(        BillNo          LONG              NOT NULL,
         BillDate        DATE,
         BillStartDate   DATE,
CONSTRAINT PKBill PRIMARY KEY (BillNo) )

CREATE TABLE Employee
(        EmpNo           LONG              NOT NULL,
         EmpName         CHAR(50),
         EmpTitle        CHAR(20),
CONSTRAINT PKEmployee PRIMARY KEY (EmpNo) )
```

Figure 7.51   Conversion of the ERD in Figure 7.50 (Continued).

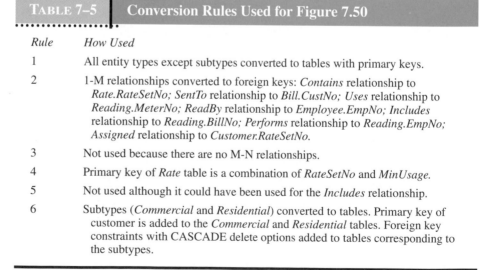

TABLE 7–5	Conversion Rules Used for Figure 7.50

Rule	How Used
1	All entity types except subtypes converted to tables with primary keys.
2	1-M relationships converted to foreign keys: *Contains* relationship to *Rate.RateSetNo; SentTo* relationship to *Bill.CustNo; Uses* relationship to *Reading.MeterNo; ReadBy* relationship to *Employee.EmpNo; Includes* relationship to *Reading.BillNo; Performs* relationship to *Reading.EmpNo; Assigned* relationship to *Customer.RateSetNo.*
3	Not used because there are no M-N relationships.
4	Primary key of *Rate* table is a combination of *RateSetNo* and *MinUsage.*
5	Not used although it could have been used for the *Includes* relationship.
6	Subtypes (*Commercial* and *Residential*) converted to tables. Primary key of customer is added to the *Commercial* and *Residential* tables. Foreign key constraints with CASCADE delete options added to tables corresponding to the subtypes.

CLOSING THOUGHTS

This chapter has described data modeling, an important database development skill. To master data modeling, you need to understand the notation used in entity relationship diagrams (ERDs) and get plenty of practice building ERDs. Using the Crow's Foot ERD notation, this chapter described the basic symbols, important relationship patterns, and generalization hierarchies. The basic symbols are entity types, relationships, attributes, and cardinalities to depict the number of entities participating in a relationship. Four important relationship patterns were described: many-to-many (M-N) relationships with attributes, associative relationships representing M-way relationships, identifying relationships providing primary keys to weak entities, and self-referencing (unary) relationships. Generalization hierarchies allow classification of entity types to depict similarities among entity types. To help you recall the notation, a convenient summary was presented.

To help you apply your knowledge of the ERD notation, a practice problem was presented. This chapter described how to derive an initial ERD for a narrative problem, refine the ERD through transformations, and document important design decisions. You are encouraged to apply this same process using the problems at the end of the chapter.

The final part of this chapter presented rules to convert an ERD into relational tables. These rules will help you convert modest-size ERDs into tables. For large problems, you should use a good CASE tool. Even if you use a CASE tool, understanding the conversion rules provides insight into the differences between the Entity Relationship and Relational Models.

This chapter emphasized data modeling skills, constructing ERDs, refining ERDs, and converting ERDs into relational tables. The next chapter presents normalization, a technique to remove redundancy from relational tables. Together, data modeling and normalization are fundamental skills for database development.

REVIEW CONCEPTS

- Basic concepts: entity types, relationships, and attributes.
- Minimum and maximum cardinalities to constrain relationship participation.
- Self-referencing (unary) relationships to represent associations among objects of the same entity type.
- Identification dependency involving weak entities and identifying relationships to support entity types that borrow part of the primary key.
- M-N relationships with attributes: attributes are associated with the combination of entity types, not one of the entity types.
- Equivalence between an M-N relationship and an associative entity type with identifying 1-M relationships.
- Associative entity types to represent M-way relationships among more than two entity types.
- Generalization hierarchies to show similarities among entity types.
- Transformations to generate alternative ERDs.
- Documentation practices for important design decisions.
- Basic rules to convert entity types and relationships.
- Specialized conversion rules to convert optional 1-M relationships, generalization hierarchies, and 1-1 relationships.

QUESTIONS

1. What is an entity type? attribute? relationship? How does an entity type differ from an attribute?

2. What is the natural language correspondence for entity types and relationships?

3. What is the difference between an ERD and an instance diagram?

4. What symbols are the ERD counterparts of foreign keys in the Relational Model?

5. What cardinalities indicate functional, optional, and mandatory relationships?

6. When is it important to convert an M-N relationship into 1-M relationships?

7. How can an instance diagram help to determine whether a self-referencing relationship is a 1-M or an M-N relationship?

8. When should an ERD contain weak (identification-dependent) entity types?

9. What is the difference between an existence-dependent and a weak entity type?

10. Why is classification important in business?

11. What is inheritance in generalization hierarchies?

12. What is the purpose of disjointness and completeness constraints for a generalization hierarchy?

13. What does it mean to say that constructing an ERD is an iterative process?

14. Why decompose a compound attribute into smaller attributes?

15. When is it appropriate to transform an attribute into an entity type?

16. Why transform an entity type into two entity types and a relationship?

17. Why transform an entity type into a generalization hierarchy?

18. What symbols are used for cardinality in the Crow's Foot notation?

19. List some differences in ERD notation that you may experience in your career.

20. How is an M-N relationship converted to the Relational Model?

21. How is a 1-M relationship converted to the Relational Model?

22. What is the difference between the 1-M relationship rule and the optional 1-M relationship rule?

23. How is a weak entity type converted to the Relational Model?

24. How is a generalization hierarchy converted to the Relational Model?

25. How is a 1-1 relationship converted to the Relational Model?

PROBLEMS

The problems are divided between data modeling problems and conversion problems. Additional conversion problems are found in Chapter 8, where conversion is followed by normalization. Besides the problems presented here, the case study in Chapter 11 provides additional practice.

Data Modeling Problems

ORDER

1. Define an ERD for the following narrative. The database should track homes and owners. A home has a unique home identifier, a street address, a city, a state, a zip, a number of bedrooms, a number of bathrooms, and square feet. A home is either owner-occupied or rented. An owner has a social security number, a name, an optional spouse name, a profession, and an optional spouse profession. An owner can possess one or more homes. Each home has only one owner.

2. Refine the ERD from problem 1 by adding an agent entity type. Agents represent owners in the sale of a home. An agent can list many homes but only one agent can list a home. An agent has a unique agent identifier, a name, a office identifier, and a phone number. When an owner agrees to list a home with an agent, a commission (percentage of the sales price) and selling price are determined.

3. In the ERD from problem 2, transform the attribute office identifier into an entity type. Data about an office include the phone number, the manager name, and the address.

4. In the ERD from problem 3, add a buyer entity type. A buyer entity type has a social security number, a name, a phone, preferences for the number of bedrooms and bathrooms, and a price range. An agent can work with many buyers, but a buyer works with only one agent.

5. Refine the ERD from problem 4 with a generalization hierarchy to depict similarities between buyers and owners.

6. Revise the ERD from problem 5 by adding an offer entity type. A buyer makes an offer on a home for a specified sales price. The offer starts on the submission date and time and expires on the specified date and time. A unique offer number identifies an offer. A buyer may submit multiple offers for the same home.

7. Construct an ERD to represent accounts in a database for personal financial software. The software supports checking accounts, credit cards, and two kinds of investments (mutual funds and stocks). No other kinds of accounts are supported and every account must fall into one of these account types. For each kind of account, the software provides a separate data entry screen. The following list describes the fields on the data entry screens for each kind of account.

    • For all accounts, the software requires the unique account identifier, the account name, the date established, and the balance.

    • For checking accounts, the software supports attributes for the bank name, the bank address, the checking account number, and the routing number.

    • For credit cards, the software supports attributes for the credit card number, the expiration date, and the credit card limit.

    • For stocks, the software supports attributes for the stock symbol, the stock type (common or preferred), the last dividend amount, the last dividend date, the exchange, the last closing price, and the number of shares (a whole number).

    • For mutual funds, the software supports attributes for the mutual fund symbol, the share balance (a real number), the fund type (stock, bond, or mixed), the last closing price, the region (domestic, international, or global), and tax-exempt status (yes or no).

8. Construct an ERD to represent categories in a database for personal financial software. A category has a unique category identifier, a name, a type (expense, asset, liability, or revenue), and a balance. Categories are organized hierarchically so that a category can have a parent category and one or more subcategories. For example, the category "household" can have subcategories for "cleaning" and "maintenance." A category can have any number of levels of subcategories. Make an instance diagram to depict the relationships among categories.

9. Design an ERD for a part entity type. A part has a unique part identifier, a name, and a color. A part can have multiple subparts and multiple parts that use it. The quantity of each subpart should be recorded. Make an instance diagram to depict relationships among parts.

10. Design an ERD to represent a credit card statement. The statement has two parts: a heading containing the unique statement number, the account number of the credit card holder, and the statement date; and a detail section containing a list of zero or more transactions for which the balance is due. Each detail line contains a line number, a transaction date, a merchant name, and the amount of the transaction. The line number is unique within a statement.

11. Modify your ERD from problem 10. Everything is the same except that each detail line contains a unique transaction number in place of the line number. Transaction numbers are unique across statements.

12. Define a generalization hierarchy for students. Students can be classified as graduate or undergraduate. All students have a unique student identifier, a name, a gender, a date of birth, and an admittance date. Undergraduate students have a major, a minor, and a class (freshman, sophomore, junior, senior). Graduate students have a thesis advisor, a thesis title, and assistantship status (research, teaching, none).

13. Design an ERD with entity types for projects, specialties, and contractors. Add relationships and/or entity types as indicated in the following description. Each contractor has exactly one specialty, but many contractors can provide the same specialty. A contractor can provide the same specialty on multiple projects. A project can use many specialties, and a specialty can be used on many projects. Each combination of project and specialty should have at least two contractors.

14. For the following problem, define an ERD for the initial requirements and then revise the ERD for the new requirements. Your solution should have an initial ERD, a revised ERD, and a list of design decisions for each ERD. In performing the problem, you may want to follow the process shown in Section 7.5.
    The database supports the placement office of a leading graduate school of business. The primary purpose of the database is to schedule interviews and facilitate searches by students and companies. Consider the following requirements in your initial ERD:

    • Student data include a unique student identifier, a name, a phone number, an e-mail address, a web address, a major, a minor, and a GPA.

    • The placement office maintains a standard list of positions based on the Labor Department's list of occupations. Position data include a unique position identifier and a position description.

- Company data include a unique company identifier, a company name, and a list of positions and interviewers. Each company must map its positions into the position list maintained by the placement office. For each available position, the company lists the cities in which positions are available.

- Interviewer data include a unique interviewer identifier, a name, a phone, an e-mail address, and a web address. Each interviewer works for one company.

- An interview includes a unique interview identifier, a date, a time, a location (building and room), an interviewer, and a student.

After reviewing your initial design, the placement office decides to revise the requirements. Make a separate ERD to show your refinements. Refine your original ERD to support the following new requirements:

- Allow companies to use their own language to describe positions. The placement office will not maintain a list of standard positions.

- Allow companies to reserve blocks of interview time. The interview blocks will not specify times for individual interviews. Rather a company will request a block of X hours during a specified week. Companies reserve interview blocks before the placement office schedules individual interviews. Thus the placement office needs to store interviews as well as interview blocks.

- Allow students to submit bids for interview blocks. Students receive a set amount of bid dollars that they can allocate among bids. The bid mechanism is a pseudo market approach to allocating interviews, a scarce resource. A bid contains a unique bid identifier, a bid amount, and a company. A student can submit many bids and an interview block can receive many bids.

15. For the following problem, define an ERD for the initial requirements and then revise the ERD for the new requirements. Your solution should have an initial ERD, a revised ERD, and a list of design decisions for each ERD. In performing the problem, you may want to follow the process shown in Section 7.5. Design a database for managing the task assignments on a work order. A work order records the set of tasks requested by a customer at a specified location.

    - A customer has a unique customer identifier, a name, and a billing address (street, city, state, zip).

    - A work order has a unique work order number, a creation date, a date required, a completion date, an optional supervising employee, a work address (street, city, state, zip), and a set of tasks.

    - Each task has a unique task identifier, a task name, an hourly rate, and estimated hours. Tasks are standardized across work orders so that the same task may be performed on many work orders.

    - Each task on a work order has a status (not started, in progress, or completed), actual hours, and a completion date. The completion date is not entered until the status changes to complete.

    After reviewing your initial design, the company decides to revise the requirements. Make a separate ERD to show your refinements. Refine your original ERD to support the following new requirements:

- The company wants to maintain a list of materials. The data about materials include a unique material identifier, a name, and an estimated cost.

- Each work order also has a collection of material requirements. Material requirements include a material, an estimated quantity of the material, and the actual quantity of the material used.

- The estimated number of hours for a task depends on the work order and the task, not on the task alone. Each task of a work order includes an estimated number of hours.

16. For the following problem, define an ERD for the initial requirements and then revise the ERD for the new requirements. Your solution should have an initial ERD, a revised ERD, and a list of design decisions for each ERD. In performing the problem, you may want to follow the process shown in Section 7.5.

    Design a database to assist physical plant personnel in managing assignments of keys to employees. The primary job of the database is to ensure proper accounting for all keys.

- An employee has a unique employee number, a name, a position, and an optional office number.

- A building has a unique building number, a name, and a location within the campus.

- A room has a room number, a size (physical dimensions), a capacity, a number of entrances, and a description of equipment in the room. Because each room is located in exactly one building, the identification of a room depends on the identification of a building.

- Key types (also known as master keys) are designed to open one or more rooms. A room may have one or more key types that open it. A key type has a unique key type number, a date designed, and the employee authorizing the key type. A key type must be authorized before it is created.

- A copy of a key type is known as a key. Keys are assigned to employees. Each key is assigned to exactly one employee, but an employee can hold multiple keys. The key type number plus a copy number uniquely identify a key. The date the copy was made should be recorded in the database.

    After reviewing your initial design, the physical plant supervisor decides to revise the requirements. Make a separate ERD to show your refinements. Refine your original ERD to support the following new requirements:

- The physical plant needs to know not only the current holder of a key but the past holders of a key. For past key holders, the date range that a key was held should be recorded.

- The physical plant needs to know the current status of each key: in use by an employee, in storage, or reported lost. If lost, the date reported lost should be stored.

17. Define an ERD that supports the generation of product explosion diagrams, assembly instructions, and part lists. These documents are typically included in hardware products sold to the public. Your ERD should represent the final products as well as the parts comprising final products. The following points provide more details about the documents.

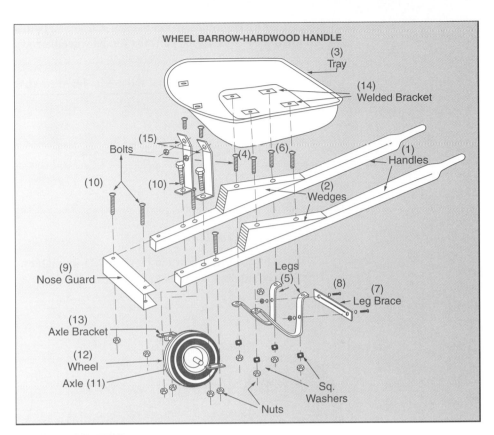

Figure 7P.1   Product explosion diagram.

- Your ERD should support the generation of product explosion diagrams as shown in Figure 7P.1 for a wheelbarrow with a hardwood handle. Your ERD should store the containment relationships along with the quantities required for each subpart. For the line drawings and geometric position specifications, assume that you have image and position data types to store attribute values.

- Your ERD should support the generation of assembly instructions. Each product can have a set of ordered steps for instruction. The following table shows some of the assembly instructions for a wheelbarrow. The numbers in the instructions refer to the parts diagram.

Sample Assembly Instructions for the Wheelbarrow

Step	Instructions
1	Assembly requires a few hand tools, screwdriver, box, or open wrench to fit the nuts.
2	Do NOT wrench tighten nuts until entire wheelbarrow has been assembled.
3	Set the handles (1) on two boxes or two saw horses (one at either end).
4	Place a wedge (2) on top of each handle and align the bolt holes in the wedge with corresponding bolt holes in the handle.

• Your ERD should support the generation of a parts list for each product. The following table shows the parts list for the wheelbarrow.

Partial Parts List for the Wheelbarrow	
Quantity	Part Description
1	Tray
2	Hardwood handle
2	Hardwood wedge
2	Leg

Conversion Problems

1. Convert the ERD shown in Figure 7CP.1 into tables. List the conversion rules used and the resulting changes to the tables.

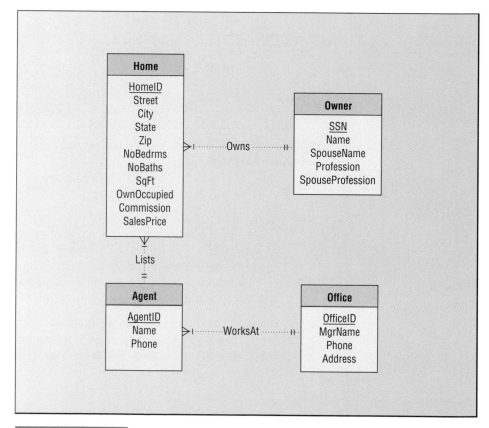

Figure 7CP.1

2. Convert the ERD shown in Figure 7CP.2 into tables. List the conversion rules used and the resulting changes to the tables.

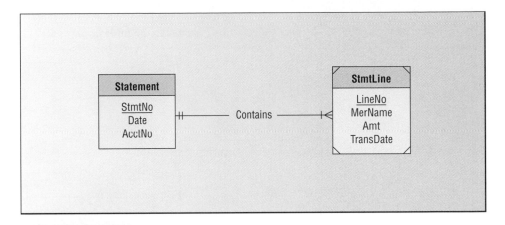

Figure 7CP.2

3. Convert the shown ERD in Figure 7CP.3 into tables. List the conversion rules used and the resulting changes to the tables.

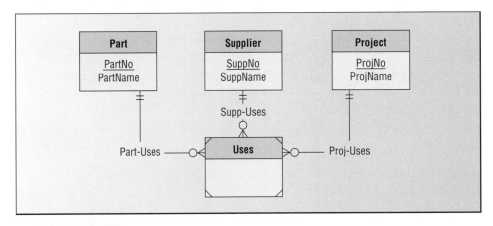

Figure 7CP.3

4. Convert the shown ERD in Figure 7CP.4 into tables. List the conversion rules used and the resulting changes to the tables.

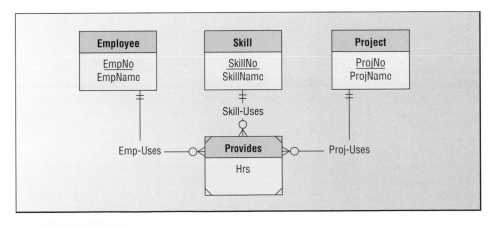

Figure 7CP.4

5. Convert the shown ERD in Figure 7CP.5 into tables. List the conversion rules used and the resulting changes to the tables.

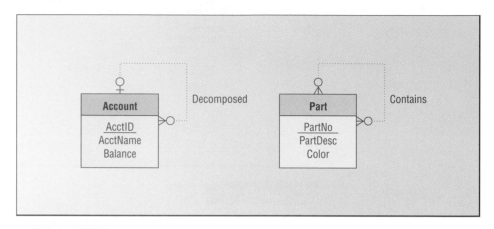

Figure 7CP.5

6. Convert the shown ERD in Figure 7CP.6 into tables. List the conversion rules used and the resulting changes to the tables.

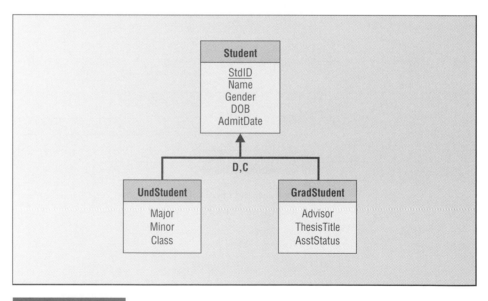

Figure 7CP.6

7. Convert the shown ERD in Figure 7CP.7 into tables. List the conversion rules used and the resulting changes to the tables.

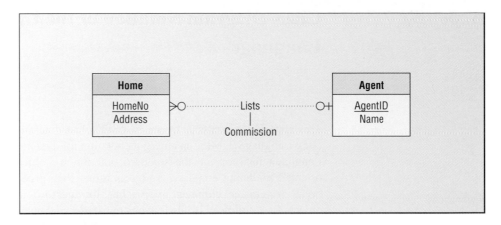

Figure 7CP.7

8. Convert the shown ERD in Figure 7CP.8 into tables. List the conversion rules used and the resulting changes to the tables.

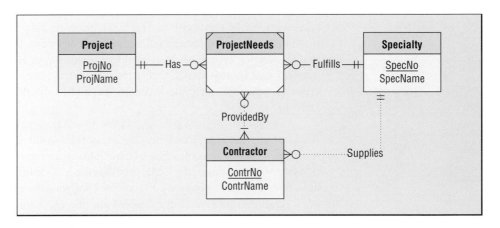

Figure 7CP.8

REFERENCES FOR FURTHER STUDY

Three specialized books on database design are Batini, Ceri, and Navathe (1992); Nijssen and Halpin (1989), and Teorey (1999). Chapter 3 of Batini, Ceri, and Navathe and Chapter 10 of Nijssen and Halpin provide more details on transformations to refine an ERD. For more details about conversion of generalization hierarchies, consult Chapter 11 of Batini, Ceri, and Navathe. The database information center of the *Intelligent Enterprise* magazine (http://www.iemagazine.com/) has plenty of practical advice about data modeling.

Appendix 7.A **Class Diagram Notation of the Unified Modeling Language**

This appendix presents an overview of the class diagram notation of the Unified Modeling Language (UML), an emerging notation for data modeling. The Unified Modeling Language has become the standard notation for object-oriented modeling. Object-oriented modeling emphasizes objects rather than processes, as emphasized in traditional systems development approaches. In object-oriented modeling, one defines the objects first, followed by the features (attributes and operations) of the objects, and then the dynamic interaction among objects. The UML contains class diagrams, interface diagrams, and interaction diagrams to support object-oriented modeling. The class diagram notation provides an alternative to the ERD notations presented in this chapter.

Class diagrams show classes (collections of objects), associations (binary relationships) among classes, and object features (attributes and operations). Figure 7A.1 shows a simple class diagram containing the *Offering* and *Faculty* classes. The diagram was drawn with the UML template in Visio Professional 5. The association in Figure 7A.1 represents a 1-M relationship. The UML supports role names and cardinalities (minimum and maximum) for each direction in an association. The 0 . . 1 cardinality means that an offering object can be related to a minimum of zero faculty objects and a maximum of one faculty object. Operations are listed below the attributes. Each operation contains a parenthesized list of parameters along with the data type returned by the operation.

Associations in the UML are similar to relationships in the Crow's Foot notation. Associations can represent binary or unary relationships. To represent an M-way relationship, a class and a collection of associations are required. To represent an M-N relationship with attributes, the UML provides the association class to allow associations to have attributes and operations. Figure 7A.2 shows an association class that represents an M-N relationship between the *Student* and the *Offering* classes. The association class contains the relationship attributes.

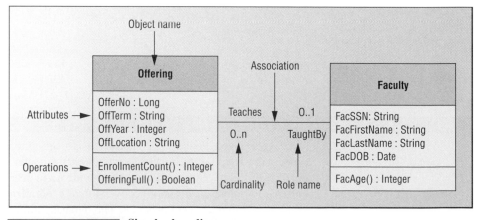

Figure 7A.1   **Simple class diagram.**

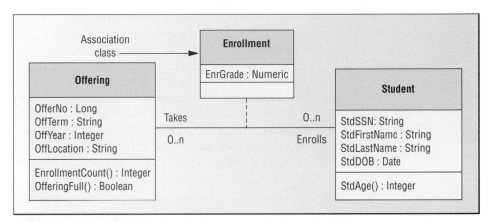

Figure 7A.2   Association class representing an M-N relationship with attributes.

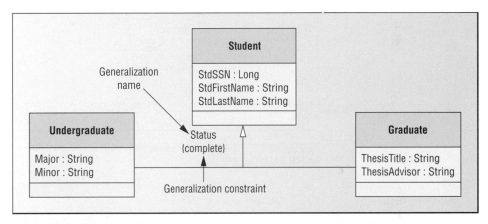

Figure 7A.3   Class diagram with a generalization relationship.

Unlike most ERD notations, support for generalization was built into the UML from its inception. In most ERD notations, generalization was added as an additional feature after a notation was well-established. In Figure 7A.3, the large empty arrow denotes a classification of the *Student* class into *Undergraduate* and *Graduate* classes. The UML supports generalization names and constraints. In Figure 7A.3, the *status* generalization is complete, meaning that every student must be an undergraduate or a graduate student.

The UML also provides a special symbol for composition relationships, similar to identification dependencies in ERD notations. In a composition relationship, the objects in a child class belong only to objects in the parent class. In Figure 7A.4, each *OrdLine* object belongs to one *Order* object. Deleting a parent object cascades to delete the related child objects. As a consequence, the child objects usually borrow part of their primary key from the parent object. However, the UML does not require this identification dependency.

UML class diagrams provide many other features not presented in this brief overview. The UML supports different kinds of classes to integrate programming language concerns with data modeling concerns. Other kinds of classes include value classes, stereotype classes, parameterized classes, and abstract classes. For generalization, the UML supports additional constraints such as static and dynamic classification and different interpretations of generalization relationships (subtype and subclass). For data integrity, the UML supports the specification of constraints in a class diagram.

You should note that class diagrams are just one part of the UML. To some extent, class diagrams must be understood in the context of object-oriented modeling and the entire UML. You should expect to devote an entire academic term to understanding object-oriented modeling and the UML. If you would like more details about the UML, consult a specialized book on the topic such as the description by its developers, Booch, Jacobson, and Rumbaugh (1998); Fowler and Scott (1997); and Muller (1999).

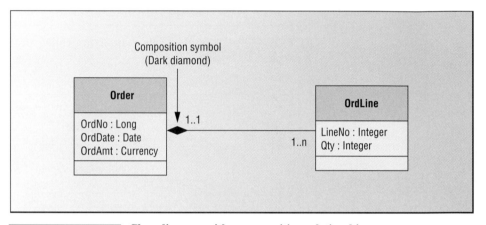

Figure 7A.4   Class diagram with a composition relationship.

Chapter 8

Normalization of Relational Tables

This chapter describes normalization, a technique to eliminate unwanted redundancy in relational tables. After this chapter, the student should have acquired the following knowledge and skills:

■ Identify modification anomalies in tables with excessive redundancies.

■ Define functional dependencies among columns of a table.

■ Normalize tables by detecting violations of normal forms and applying normalization rules.

■ Analyze M-way relationships using the concept of independence.

■ Appreciate the usefulness and limitations of normalization.

OVERVIEW

Chapter 7 provided the tools for data modeling, a fundamental skill for database development. You learned about the notation used in entity relationship diagrams, important data modeling patterns, and conversion of entity relationship diagrams (ERDs) into relational tables. You applied this knowledge to construct ERDs for small, narrative problems. This chapter extends your database design skills by presenting normalization techniques to remove redundancy in relational tables.

Redundancies can cause insert, update, and delete operations to produce unexpected side effects known as modification anomalies. This chapter prescribes normalization techniques to remove modification anomalies caused by redundancies. You will learn about functional dependencies, several normal forms, and a procedure to generate tables without redundancies. In addition, you will learn how to analyze M-way relationships for redundancies. This chapter concludes by briefly presenting additional normal forms and discussing the usefulness and limitations of normalization techniques in the database development process.

8.1 Overview of Relational Database Design

After converting an ERD to relational tables, your work is not yet finished. You need to analyze the tables for redundancies that can make the tables difficult to use. This section describes why redundancies can make a table difficult to use and presents an important kind of constraint to analyze redundancies.

8.1.1 Avoidance of Modification Anomalies

Modification Anomaly
an unexpected side effect that occurs when changing the data in a table with excessive redundancies.

A good database design ensures that users can change the contents of a database without unexpected side effects. For example, with a university database, a user should be able to insert a new course without having to simultaneously insert a new offering of the course and a new student enrolled in the course. Likewise, when a student is deleted from the database due to graduation, course data should not be inadvertently lost. These problems are examples of modification anomalies, unexpected side effects that occur when changing the contents of a table with excessive redundancies. A good database design avoids modification anomalies by eliminating excessive redundancies.

To understand more precisely the impact of modification anomalies, let us consider a poorly designed database. Imagine that a university database consists of the single table shown in Table 8–1. Such a poor design[1] makes it easy to identify anomalies. The following list describes some of the problems with this design.

- This table has insertion anomalies. An insertion anomaly occurs when extra data beyond the desired data must be added to the database. For example, to insert a course, it is necessary to know a student and an offering because the

---

[1]This single-table design is not as extreme as it may seem. Users without proper database training often design a database using a single table.

TABLE 8–1	Sample Data for the Big University Database Table							
StdSSN	*StdCity*	*StdClass*	*OfferNo*	*OffTerm*	*OffYear*	*Grade*	*CourseNo*	*CrsDesc*
S1	SEATTLE	JUN	O1	FALL	2000	3.5	C1	DB
S1	SEATTLE	JUN	O2	FALL	2000	3.3	C2	VB
S2	BOTHELL	JUN	O3	WINTER	2000	3.1	C3	OO
S2	BOTHELL	JUN	O2	FALL	2000	3.4	C2	VB

combination of *StdSSN* and *OfferNo* is the primary key. Remember that a row cannot exist with null values for part of its primary key.

- This table has update anomalies. An <u>update anomaly</u> occurs when it is necessary to change multiple rows to modify only a single fact. For example, if we change the *StdClass* of student S1, two rows must be changed. If S1 was enrolled in 10 classes, 10 rows must be changed.

- This table has deletion anomalies. A <u>deletion anomaly</u> occurs whenever deleting a row inadvertently causes other data to be deleted. For example, if we delete the enrollment of S2 in O3 (third row), we lose the information about offering O3 and course C3.

To deal with these anomalies, users may circumvent them (such as using a dummy primary key to insert a new course) or database programmers may write code to prevent inadvertent loss of data. A better solution is to modify the table design to remove the redundancies that cause the anomalies.

8.1.2 Functional Dependencies

Functional dependencies are important tools when analyzing a table for excessive redundancies. A functional dependency is a constraint about the database contents. Constraints can be characterized as value-based versus value-neutral (Figure 8.1). A <u>value-based</u> constraint involves a comparison of a column to a constant using a comparison operator such as $<$, $=$, or $>$. For example, age ≥ 21 is an important value-based constraint in a database used to restrict sales of alcohol to minors. A <u>value-neutral</u> constraint involves a comparison of columns. For example, a value-neutral constraint is that retirement age should be greater than current age in a database for retirement planning.

Primary key (PK) and foreign key (FK) constraints are important kinds of value-neutral constraints. A primary key can take any value as long as it does not match an existing primary key value. A foreign key constraint requires that the value of a column in one table match the value of a column in another table.

A functional dependency is another important kind of value-neutral constraint. A <u>functional dependency</u> (FD) is a constraint about two or more columns of a table. X determines Y ($X \rightarrow Y$) if there exists at most one value of Y for every value of X. The word

Functional Dependency
a constraint about two or more columns of a table. X determines Y ($X \rightarrow Y$) if there exists at most one value of Y for every value of X.

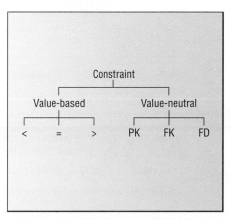

Figure 8.1   **Classification of database constraints.**

"function" comes from mathematics where a function gives one value. For example, social security number determines city (*StdSSN* → *StdCity*) in the university database table if there is at most one city value for every social security number. A column appearing on the left-hand side of an FD is called a <u>determinant</u> or, alternatively, an <u>LHS</u>, for left-hand side. In this example, *StdSSN* is a determinant.

You also can think about functional dependencies as identifying <u>potential</u> primary keys for other tables. By stating that *X* → *Y*, if *X* and *Y* are placed together in a table without other columns, *X* is the primary key. Every determinant (LHS) is a potential primary key if placed in a table with the other columns that it determines. For example, if *StdSSN*, *StdCity*, and *StdClass* are placed in a table together and *StdSSN* → *StdCity, StdClass* then *StdSSN* is the primary key.

> **Determinant** the column(s) appearing on the left-hand side (LHS) of a functional dependency.

Functional Dependency Diagrams and Lists

A functional dependency diagram compactly displays the functional dependencies of a particular table. You should arrange FDs so that one can visually group columns sharing the same determinant. In Figure 8.2, it is easy to spot the dependencies where *StdSSN* is the determinant. By the position and height of lines, you also can see the dependencies where the combination of *StdSSN* and *OfferNo* is the determinant. A good visual arrangement can facilitate the normalization process described in the next section.

If you prefer, you can list FDs rather than arrange them in a diagram. With many FDs, you might find it difficult to make a diagram. If you list FDs, you can group them by LHS, as shown in Table 8–2.

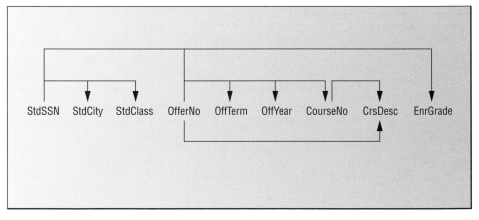

Figure 8.2   Dependency diagram for the "big" university database table.

TABLE 8–2	**List of FDs for the University Database Table**

StdSSN → StdCity, StdClass

OfferNo → OffTerm, OffYear, CourseNo, CrsDesc

CourseNo → CrsDesc

StdSSN, OfferNo → EnrGrade

Asserting Functional Dependencies

Functional dependencies are important business rules that are asserted during the database development process. The database designer interacts with users to understand the functional dependencies that exist for a table. For example, a user may state that each course offering has a unique offering number along with the year and term of the offering. From this statement, the designer can assert that the *OfferNo* column determines the *OffYear* and *OffTerm* columns. Database designers must understand the meaning of functional dependencies so that functional dependencies can be identified during the database development process.

A functional dependency cannot be proven to exist by examining the rows of a table. However, examining the contents of a table can prove that a functional dependency does not hold. For example in the university database table, we can conclude that *StdClass* does not determine *StdCity* because there are two rows with the same value for *StdClass* but a different value for *StdCity*. Thus, it is sometimes helpful to examine sample rows in a table to see what functional dependencies do not hold. There are several commercial database design tools that automate the process of eliminating dependencies through examination of sample rows. Ultimately, the database designer must make the final decision about what functional dependencies exist in a table.

In recording functional dependencies, it is also important to distinguish when one column alone is the determinant versus a combination of columns. Part of this confusion is due to the meaning of columns in the left-hand versus right-hand side of a dependency. To record that student social security number determines city and class, you can write either *StdSSN* → *StdCity, StdClass* (more compact) or *StdSSN* → *StdCity* and *StdSSN* → *StdClass* (less compact). If you assume that the e-mail address is also unique for each student, then you can write *Email* → *StdCity, StdClass*. You should not write *StdSSN, Email* → *StdCity, StdClass* because these FDs imply that the combination of *StdSSN* and *Email* is the determinant. Thus, you should write FDs so that the LHS does not contain unneeded columns.[2]

8.2 NORMAL FORMS

Normalization is the process of removing redundancy in a table so that the table is easier to modify. A number of normal forms have been developed to remove redundancies. A normal form is a rule about allowable dependencies. Each normal form removes certain kinds of redundancies. As shown in Figure 8.3, first normal form (1NF) is the starting point. All tables without repeating groups are in 1NF. 2NF is stronger than 1NF. Only a subset of the 1NF tables is in 2NF. Each successive normal form refines the previous normal form to remove additional kinds of redundancies. Because BCNF (Boyce-Codd normal form) is a revised (and stronger) definition for 3NF, 3NF and BCNF are shown in the same part of Figure 8.3.

2NF and 3NF/BCNF are rules about functional dependencies. If the functional dependencies for a table match the specified pattern, the table is in the specified normal form. 3NF/BCNF is the most important in practice because higher normal forms involve other kinds of dependencies that are less common and more difficult to understand. Therefore, most emphasis is given to 3NF/BCNF. Section 8.3 presents 4NF as a way to reason about M-way relationships. Section 8.4 presents 5NF and DKNF (domain key

---

[2]This concept is more properly known as "full functional dependence." Full functional dependence means that the LHS is minimal.

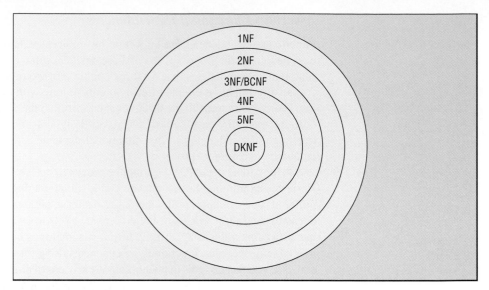

	Figure 8.3	Relationship of normal forms.

TABLE 8–3		Unnormalized University Database Table						
StdSSN	*StdCity*	*StdClass*	*OfferNo*	*OffTerm*	*OffYear*	*Grade*	*CourseNo*	*CrsDesc*
S1	SEATTLE	JUN	O1	FALL	2000	3.5	C1	DB
			O2	FALL	2000	3.3	C2	VB
S2	BOTHELL	JUN	O3	WINTER	2000	3.1	C3	OO
			O2	FALL	2000	3.4	C2	VB

normal form) to show that higher normal forms have been proposed. DKNF is the ultimate normal form, but it remains an ideal rather than a practical normal form.

8.2.1 First Normal Form

1NF prohibits nesting or repeating groups in tables. A table not in 1NF is unnormalized or nonnormalized. In Table 8–3, the university table is unnormalized because the two rows contain repeating groups. To convert an unnormalized table into 1NF, you replace each value of a repeating group with a row. In a new row, you copy the nonrepeating columns. You can see the conversion by comparing Table 8–3 with Table 8–1 (two rows with repeating groups versus four rows without repeating groups).

Because most commercial DBMSs require 1NF tables, you do not normally need to convert tables into 1NF. However, you often need to perform the reverse process (1NF tables to unnormalized tables) for report generation. As discussed in Chapter 5, reports use nesting to show relationships. However, the underlying tables do not have nesting.

8.2.2 Second and Third Normal Form

The definitions of 2NF and 3NF distinguish between key and nonkey columns.[3] A column is a key column if it is part of a candidate key or a candidate key by itself. Recall that a <u>candidate key</u> is a minimal set of column(s) that has unique values in a table. Minimality means that none of the columns can be removed without removing the uniqueness property. Nonkey columns are any other columns. In Table 8–1, the combination of (*StdSSN, OfferNo*) is the only candidate key. Other columns such as *StdCity* and *StdClass* are nonkey columns.

> **Combined Definition of 2NF and 3NF** a table is in 3NF if every nonkey column is dependent on a candidate key, the whole candidate key, and nothing but candidate keys.[4]

The goal of 2NF and 3NF is to produce tables in which every key determines the other columns. An easy way to remember the definitions of both 2NF and 3NF is shown in the margin.

Second Normal Form

> **2NF Definition** a table is in 2NF if every nonkey column is dependent on the whole key, not part of the key.

To understand this definition, let us break it down to the 2NF and 3NF parts. The 2NF definition uses the first part of the definition as shown in the margin.

To see if a table is in 2NF, you should look for FDs that violate the definition. An FD in which part of a key determines a nonkey column violates 2NF. If the key contains only one column, the table is in 2NF. Looking at the dependency diagram in Figure 8.2, you can easily detect violations of 2NF. For example, *StdCity* is a nonkey column but *StdSSN*, not the entire primary key (combination of *StdSSN* and *OfferNo*), determines it. The only FDs that satisfy the 2NF definition are *StdSSN, OfferNo → EnrGrade* and *CourseNo → CrsDesc*.

To place the table into 2NF, split the original table into smaller tables that satisfy the 2NF definition. In each smaller table, the entire primary key (not part of the primary key) should determine the nonkey columns. The splitting process involves the project operator of relational algebra. For the university database table, three projection operations split it so that the underlined primary key determines the nonkey columns in each table below.

UnivTable1 (<u>StdSSN</u>, StdCity, StdClass)

UnivTable2 (<u>OfferNo</u>, OffTerm, OffYear, CourseNo, CrsDesc)

UnivTable3 (<u>StdSSN</u>, <u>OfferNo</u>, EnrGrade)

The splitting process should preserve the original table in two ways. First, the original table should be recoverable by using natural join operations on the smaller tables. Second, the FDs in the original table should be derivable from the FDs in the smaller tables. Technically, the splitting process is known as a nonloss, dependency-preserving decomposition. Some of the references at the end of this chapter explain the theory underlying the splitting process.

After splitting the original table into smaller tables, you should add referential integrity constraints to connect the tables. Whenever a table is split, the splitting attribute becomes a foreign key in the table in which it is not a primary key. For example, *StdSSN* is a foreign key in *UnivTable3* because the original university table was split on this column. Therefore, define a referential integrity constraint stating that *UnivTable3.StdSSN*

---

[3]In the literature, key columns are known as prime and nonkey columns as nonprime.

[4]You can remember this definition by its analogy to the traditional justice oath: "Do you swear to tell the truth, the whole truth, and nothing but the truth . . ."

refs to *UnivTable1.StdSSN*. The *UnivTable3* table is repeated below with its referential integrity constraints.

> **UnivTable3** (<u>StdSSN</u>, <u>OfferNo</u>, EnrGrade)
> FOREIGN KEY (StdSSN) REFERENCES UnivTable1
> FOREIGN KEY (OfferNo) REFERENCES UnivTable2

Third Normal Form

UnivTable2 still has modification anomalies. For example, you cannot add a new course unless the *OfferNo* column value is known. To eliminate the modification anomalies, the definition of 3NF should be applied.

An FD in which one nonkey column determines another nonkey column violates 3NF. In *UnivTable2* above, the FD (*CourseNo* → *CrsDesc*) violates 3NF because both columns, *CourseNo* and *CrsDesc* are nonkey. To fix the violation, split *UnivTable2* into two tables, as shown below, and add a foreign key constraint.

> **UnivTable2-1** (<u>OfferNo</u>, OffTerm, OffYear, CourseNo)
> FOREIGN KEY (CourseNo) REFERENCES UnivTable2-2
> **UnivTable2-2** (<u>CourseNo</u>, CrsDesc)

An equivalent way to define 3NF is that 3NF prohibits <u>transitive dependencies</u>. A transitive dependency is a functional dependency derived by the law of transitivity. The law of transitivity says that if an object A is related to B, and B is related to C, then conclude that A is related to C. For example, the < operator obeys the transitive law: A < B and B < C implies that A < C. Functional dependencies, like the < operator, obey the law of transitivity: A → B, B → C, then A → C. In Figure 8.2, *OfferNo* → *CrsDesc* is a transitive dependency derived from *OfferNo* → *CourseNo* and *CourseNo* → *CrsDesc*.

Because transitive dependencies are easy to overlook, the preferred definition of 3NF does not use transitive dependencies. In addition, you will learn in Section 8.2.4 that you should omit derived dependencies such as transitive dependencies in your analysis.

Combined Example of 2NF and 3NF

The big patient table as depicted in Table 8–4 provides another example for applying your knowledge of 2NF and 3NF. The big patient table contains facts about patients, health care providers, patient visits to a clinic, and diagnoses made by health care providers. The big patient table contains a combined primary key consisting of the combination of *VisitNo* and *ProvNo* (provider number). Like the big university database table

---

3NF Definition a table is in 3NF if it is in 2NF and every nonkey column is dependent only on the key.

Transitive Dependency an FD derived by the law of transitivity. Transitive FDs should not be recorded as input to the normalization process.

TABLE 8–4	Sample Data for the Big Patient Table

VisitNo	VisitDate	*PatNo*	PatAge	PatCity	PatZip	*ProvNo*	ProvSpecialty	Diagnosis
V10020	1/13/2000	P1	35	DENVER	80217	D1	INTERNIST	EAR INFECTION
V10020	1/13/2000	P1	35	DENVER	80217	D2	NURSE PRACTIONER	INFLUENZA
V93030	1/20/2000	P3	17	ENGLEWOOD	80113	D2	OBGYN	PREGNANCY
V82110	1/18/2000	P2	60	BOULDER	85932	D3	CARDIOLOGIST	MURMUR

depicted in Table 8–1, the big patient table reflects a poor table design with many redundancies. Table 8–5 lists the associated FDs. You should verify that the FDs do not violate the sample data in Table 8–4.

As previously discussed, FDs that violate 2NF involve part of a key determining a nonkey. Many of the FDs in Table 8–5 violate the 2NF definition because the combination of *VisitNo* and *ProvNo* is the primary key. Thus, the FDs with only *VisitNo* or *ProvNo* in the LHS violate 2NF. To alleviate the 2NF violations, split the big patient table so that the violating FDs are associated with separate tables. In the revised list of tables, *PatientTable1* and *PatientTable2* contain the violating FDs. *PatientTable3* retains the remaining columns.

> **PatientTable1** (<u>ProvNo</u>, ProvSpecialty)
>
> **PatientTable2** (<u>VisitNo</u>, VisitDate, PatNo, PatAge, PatCity, PatZip)
>
> **PatientTable3** (<u>VisitNo</u>, <u>ProvNo</u>, Diagnosis)
>   FOREIGN KEY (VisitNo) REFERENCES PatientTable2
>   FOREIGN KEY (ProvNo) REFERENCES PatientTable1

PatientTable1 and *PatientTable3* are in 3NF because there are no nonkey columns that determine other nonkey columns. However, *PatientTable2* violates 3NF because the FDs *PatNo → PatZip, PatAge* and *PatZip → PatCity* involve nonkey columns that determine other nonkey columns. To alleviate the 3NF violations, split *PatientTable2* into three tables as shown in the revised table list. In the revised list of tables, *PatientTable2-1* and *PatientTable2-2* contain the violating FDs, while *PatientTable2-3* retains the remaining columns.

> **PatientTable2-1** (<u>PatNo</u>, PatAge, PatZip)
>   FOREIGN KEY (PatZip) REFERENCES PatientTable2-2
>
> **PatientTable2-2** (<u>PatZip</u>, PatCity)
>
> **PatientTable2-3** (<u>VisitNo</u>, PatNo, VisitDate)
>   FOREIGN KEY (PatNo) REFERENCES PatientTable2-1

Using 2NF and 3NF requires two normalization steps. The normalization process can be performed in one step using Boyce-Codd normal form, as presented in the next subsection.

8.2.3 Boyce-Codd Normal Form

BCNF Definition a table is in BCNF if every determinant is a candidate key.

The revised 3NF definition, known as Boyce-Codd normal form (BCNF), is a better definition because it is simpler and covers a special case omitted by the original 3NF definition. The BCNF definition is simpler because it does not refer to 2NF.

TABLE 8–5	List of FDs for the Big Patient Table

PatNo → PatAge, PatCity, PatZip

PatZip → PatCity

ProvNo → ProvSpecialty

VisitNo → PatNo, VisitDate, PatAge, PatCity, PatZip

VisitNo, ProvNo → Diagnosis

Violations of BCNF involve FDs in which the determinant (LHS) is not a candidate key. In a poor table design such as the big university database table (sample data in Table 8–1 and FD list in Table 8–2), you can easily detect violations of BCNF. For example, *StdSSN* is a determinant but not a candidate key (it is part of a candidate key but not a candidate key itself). The only FD in Table 8–2 that does not violate BCNF is *StdSSN, OfferNo → EnrGrade*.

For another example, let us apply the BCNF definition to the FDs of the big patient table shown in Table 8–5. All of the FDs in Table 8–5 violate the BCNF definition except the last FD (*VisitNo, ProvNo → Diagnosis*). All of the other FDs have determinants that are not candidate keys (part of a candidate key in some cases but not an entire candidate key). To alleviate the BCNF violations, split the big patient table into smaller tables. Each determinant should be placed into a separate table along with the columns that it determines. The result is identical to the split for 3NF (see the result of the last 3NF example) with the *PatientTable1, PatientTable3, PatientTable2-1, PatientTable2-2,* and *PatientTable2-3* tables.

Relationship between 3NF and BCNF

Although BCNF and 3NF usually produce the same result, BCNF is a stronger definition than 3NF. BCNF covers two special cases not covered by 3NF: (1) part of a key determines part of a key and (2) a nonkey column determines part of a key. These situations are only possible if there are multiple candidate keys and each candidate key contains more than one column.

UnivTable4 depicts a table in 3NF but not in BCNF. *UnivTable4* (see Figure 8.4) has two candidate keys: combination of *StdSSN* and *OfferNo* (the primary key) and the combination of *Email* and *OfferNo*. *UnivTable4* contains a redundancy because *Email* is repeated for each *StdSSN*. In the FDs for *UnivTable4*, note that *StdSSN* and *Email* determine each other. *UnivTable4* is in 3NF because every candidate key determines the nonkey column (*EnrGrade*). However, the dependencies between *StdSSN* and *Email* violate BCNF. Both *StdSSN* and *Email* are determinants, but neither is a candidate key by itself. To eliminate the redundancy, you can split *UnivTable4* into two tables, as shown in Figure 8.4.

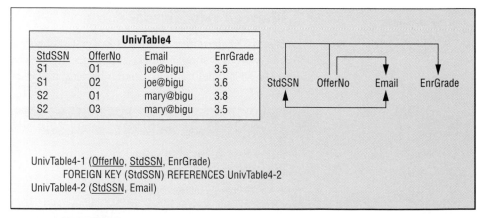

UnivTable4			
StdSSN	OfferNo	Email	EnrGrade
S1	O1	joe@bigu	3.5
S1	O2	joe@bigu	3.6
S2	O1	mary@bigu	3.8
S2	O3	mary@bigu	3.5

UnivTable4-1 (<u>OfferNo</u>, <u>StdSSN</u>, EnrGrade)
        FOREIGN KEY (StdSSN) REFERENCES UnivTable4-2
UnivTable4-2 (<u>StdSSN</u>, Email)

Figure 8.4   **Sample rows, dependency diagram, and normalized tables for *UnivTable4*.**

UnivTable5 is another example of a table in 3NF but not in BCNF. This table has two candidate keys: the combination of *StdSSN* and *AdvisorNo* (the primary key) and the combination of *StdSSN* and *Major*. *UnivTable5* has a redundancy as *Major* is repeated for each row with the same *AdvisorNo*. The dependency diagram (Figure 8.5) shows that *AdvisorNo* is a determinant but not a candidate key by itself. To eliminate the redundancy, split *UnivTable5* into two tables as shown in Figure 8.5.

Do not let these examples deceive you. These examples were purposely constructed to depict the difference between 3NF and BCNF. In practice, most tables in 3NF are also in BCNF. The importance of BCNF is that it is a simpler definition and can be applied in the procedure described in the next section.

8.2.4 Simple Synthesis Procedure

The simple synthesis procedure can be used to generate tables satisfying BCNF starting with a list of functional dependencies. The word "synthesis" means that the individual functional dependencies are combined to form tables. This usage is similar to other disciplines such as music where synthesis involves combining individual sounds to form larger units such as melodies, scores, and so on.

Figure 8.6 depicts the steps of the simple synthesis procedure. The first two steps ensure that the FDs are not redundant. The last three steps produce tables for collections of FDs. The tables produced in the last three steps may not be correct if the FDs are redundant.

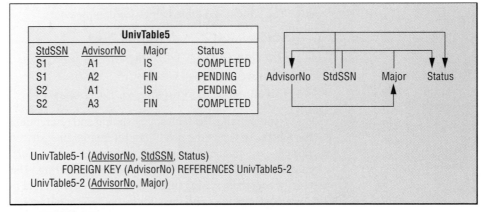

UnivTable5-1 (AdvisorNo, StdSSN, Status)
      FOREIGN KEY (AdvisorNo) REFERENCES UnivTable5-2
UnivTable5-2 (AdvisorNo, Major)

Figure 8.5   **Sample rows, dependency diagram, and normalized tables for** *UnivTable5*.

1. Eliminate extraneous columns from the LHS of FDs.

2. Remove derived FDs from the FD list.

3. Arrange the FDs into groups with each group having the same determinant.

4. For each FD group, make a table with the determinant as the primary key.

5. Merge tables in which one table contains all columns of the other table.

Figure 8.6   **Steps of the simple synthesis procedure.**

To understand this procedure, you can apply it to the FDs of the university database table (Table 8–2). In the first step, there are no extraneous columns in the determinants. To demonstrate an extraneous column, suppose there was the FD *StdSSN, StdCity* → *StdClass*. In this FD, if *StdCity* is removed from the left-hand side, then the FD *StdSSN* → *StdClass* still holds. The *StdCity* column is redundant in the FD and should be removed.

To apply the second step, you need to know how FDs can be derived from other FDs. Although there are a number of ways to derive FDs, the most prominent way is through the law of transitivity as stated in the discussion of 3NF (Section 8.2.2). For our purposes here, we will only eliminate transitively derived FDs in step 2. For details about the other ways to derive FDs, consult references at the end of the chapter.

In the second step, the FD *OfferNo* → *CrsDesc* is a transitive dependency because *OfferNo* → *CourseNo* and *CourseNo* → *CrsDesc* implies *OfferNo* → *CrsDesc*. Therefore, you should delete this dependency from the list of FDs.

In the third step, you should group the FDs by determinant. From Table 8–2, you can make the following FD groups:

- *StdSSN* → *StdCity, StdSSN* → *StdClass*
- *OfferNo* → *OffTerm, OfferNo* → *OffYear, OfferNo* → *CourseNo*
- *CourseNo* → *CrsDesc*
- *StdSSN, OfferNo* → *EnrGrade*

In the fourth step, you replace each FD group with a table having the common determinant as the primary key. Thus you have four resulting BCNF tables as shown below. You should add table names for completeness.

> **Student**(*StdSSN, StdCity, StdClass*)
> **Offering**(*OfferNo, OffTerm, OffYear, CourseNo*)
> **Course**(*CourseNo, CrsDesc*)
> **Enrollment**(*StdSSN, OfferNo, EnrGrade*)

After defining the tables, you should add referential integrity constraints to connect the tables. To detect the need for a referential integrity constraint, you should look for a primary key in one table appearing in other tables. For example, *CourseNo* is the primary key of *Course* but it also appears in *Offering*. Therefore, define a referential integrity constraint stating that *Offering.CourseNo* refers to *Course.CourseNo*. The tables are repeated below with the addition of referential integrity constraints.

> **Student**(*StdSSN, StdCity, StdClass*)
> **Offering**(*OfferNo, OffTerm, OffYear, CourseNo*)
>   FOREIGN KEY (CourseNo) REFERENCES Course
> **Course**(*CourseNo, CrsDesc*)
> **Enrollment**(*StdSSN, OfferNo, EnrGrade*)
>   FOREIGN KEY (StdSSN) REFERENCES Student
>   FOREIGN KEY (OfferNo) REFERENCES OFFER

The fifth step is not necessary because the FDs for this problem are simple. When there are multiple candidate keys for a table, the fifth step is necessary. For example, if *Email* is added as a column, then the FDs *Email* → *StdSSN* and *StdSSN* → *Email* should be added to the list. Note that the FDs *Email* → *StdCity, StdClass* should not be added to the list because they can be transitively derived from the other FDs. As a result of step 3, another group of FDs is added. In step 4, a new table (*Student2*) is added with *Email* as the primary key. Because the *Student* table contains the columns of the *Student2* table, the tables (*Student* and *Student2*) are merged in step 5. One of the candidate keys (*StdSSN* or *Email*) is chosen as the primary key.

> *Email → StdSSN, StdSSN → Email*
> **Student2**(*Email, StdSSN, StdCity, StdClass*)

You can use the synthesis procedure to analyze simple dependency structures. Most tables resulting from a conversion of an ERD should have simple dependency structures because the data modeling process has already done much of the normalization process. Most tables should be nearly normalized after the conversion process.

For complex dependency structures, you should use a commercial design tool to perform normalization. To make the synthesis procedure easy to use, some of the details have been omitted. In particular, step 2 can be rather involved because there are more ways to derive dependencies than transitivity. Even checking for transitivity can be difficult with many columns. The full details of step 2 can be found in references cited at the end of the chapter. Even if you understand the complex details, step 2 cannot be done by hand for complex dependency structures. For complex dependency structures, you need to use a CASE tool even if you are an experienced database designer.

Another Simple Synthesis Example

To gain more experience with the simple synthesis procedure, you can follow along on another example. This example describes a database to track reviews of papers submitted to an academic conference. Prospective authors submit papers for review and possible acceptance in the published conference proceedings. Here are more details about authors, papers, reviews, and reviewers:

- Author information includes a unique author number, a name, a mailing address, and a unique but optional electronic address.
- Paper information includes the primary author, the paper number, the title, the abstract, and review status (pending, accepted, rejected).
- Reviewer information includes the reviewer number, the name, the mailing address, and a unique but optional electronic address.
- A completed review includes the reviewer number, the date, the paper number, comments to the authors, comments to the program chairperson, and ratings (overall, originality, correctness, style, and relevance).

Before beginning the procedure, you must identify the FDs in the problem. The following is a list of FDs for the problem:

> *AuthNo → AuthName, AuthEmail, AuthAddress*
> *AuthEmail → AuthNo*
> *PaperNo → Primary-AuthNo, Title, Abstract, Status*
> *RevNo → RevName, RevEmail, RevAddress*
> *RevEmail → RevNo*
> *RevNo, PaperNo → Auth-Comm, Prog-Comm, Date, Rating1, Rating2, Rating3, Rating4, Rating5.*

Because the LHS is minimal in each FD, the first step is finished. The second step is not necessary because there are no transitive dependencies. Note that the FDs *AuthEmail → AuthName, AuthAddress* and *RevEmail → RevName, RevAddress* can be transitively derived. If any of these FDs were part of the original list, they should be removed. For each of the six FD groups, you can list a table. In the last step, combine the FD groups with *AuthNo* and *AuthEmail* and *RevNo* and *RevEmail* as determinants.

Author(<u>AuthNo,</u> AuthName, AuthEmail, AuthAddress)

Paper(<u>PaperNo,</u> Primary-Auth, Title, Abstract, Status)
   FOREIGN KEY (Primary-Auth) REFERENCES Author

Reviewer(<u>RevNo,</u> RevName, RevEmail, RevAddress)

Review(<u>PaperNo, RevNo,</u> Auth-Comm, Prog-Comm, Date, Rating1, Rating2, Rating3, Rating4, Rating5)
   FOREIGN KEY (PaperNo) REFERENCES Paper
   FOREIGN KEY (RevNo) REFERENCES Reviewer

8.3 REFINING M-WAY RELATIONSHIPS

Beyond BCNF, a remaining concern is the analysis of M-way relationships. Recall that M-way relationships are represented by associative entity types in the Crow's Foot ERD notation. In the conversion process, an associative entity type converts into a table with a combined primary key consisting of three or more components. The concept of independence, underlying 4NF, is an important tool to analyze M-way relationships. Using the concept of independence, you may find that an M-way relationship should be split into two or more binary relationships to avoid redundancy. In Chapter 9, you will use forms to analyze the need for M-way relationships. The following sections describe the concept of relationship independence and 4NF.

8.3.1 Relationship Independence

Before you study how independence can influence a database design, let us discuss the meaning of independence in statistics. Two variables are statistically independent if knowing something about one variable tells you nothing about another variable. More precisely, two variables are independent if the probability of both variables (the joint probability) can be derived from the probability of each variable alone. For example, one variable may be the age of a rock and another variable may be the age of the person holding the rock. Because the age of a rock and the age of a person holding the rock are unrelated, these variables are considered independent. However, the age of a person and a person's marital status are related. Knowing a person's age tells us something about the probability of being single, married, or divorced. If two variables are independent, it is redundant to store data about how they are related. You can use probabilities about individual variables to derive joint probabilities.

Relationship Independence a relationship that can be derived from two independent relationships.

The concept of <u>relationship independence</u> is similar to statistical independence. If two relationships are independent (that is, not related), it is redundant to store data about a third relationship. You can derive the third relationship by combining the two essential relationships through a join operation. If you store the derived relationship, modification anomalies can result. Thus, the essential idea of relationship independence is not to store relationships that can be derived by joining other (independent) relationships.

Relationship Independence Example

To clarify relationship independence, consider the associative entity type *Enroll* (Figure 8.7) representing a three-way relationship among students, offerings, and textbooks. The *Enroll* entity type converts to the *Enroll* table (Table 8–6) that consists only of a combined primary key: *StdSSN, OfferNo,* and *TextNo.*

The design question is whether the *Enroll* table has redundancies. If there is redundancy, modification anomalies may result. The *Enroll* table is in BCNF so there are no anomalies due to functional dependencies. However, the concept of independence leads to the discovery of redundancies. The *Enroll* table can be divided into three combinations of columns representing three binary relationships: *StdSSN–OfferNo,* representing the relationship between students and offerings; *OfferNo–TextNo,* representing the relationship between offerings and textbooks; and *StdSSN–TextNo,* representing the relationship between students and textbooks. If any of the binary relationships can be derived from the other two, there is a redundancy.

- The relationship between students and offerings (*StdSSN–OfferNo*) cannot be derived from the other two relationships. For example, suppose that textbook T1 is used in two offerings, O1 and O2, and by two students, S1 and S2. Knowing these two facts, you do not know the relationship between students and offerings. For example, S1 could be enrolled in O1 or perhaps O2.

- Likewise, the relationship between offerings and textbooks (*OfferNo–TextNo*) cannot be derived. A professor's choice for a collection of

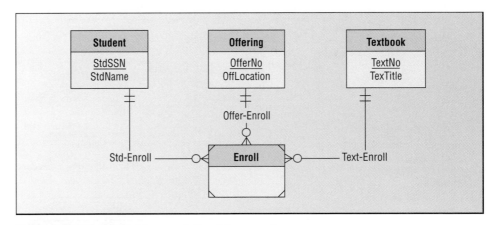

Figure 8.7   **M-way relationship example.**

TABLE 8–6	Sample Rows of the *Enroll* Table	
StdSSN	*OfferNo*	*TextNo*
S1	O1	T1
S1	O2	T2
S1	O1	T2
S1	O2	T1

textbooks cannot be derived by knowing who enrolls in an offering and what textbooks a student uses.

- However, the relationship between students and textbooks (*StdSSN–TextNo*) can be derived by the other two relationships. For example, if student S1 is enrolled in offering O1 and offering O1 uses textbook T1, then you can conclude that student S1 uses textbook T1 in offering O1. Because the *Student–Offering* and *Offering–Textbook* relationships are independent, you know the textbooks used by a student without storing the relationship instances.

Because of this independence, the *Enroll* table and the related associative entity type *Enroll* have redundancy. To remove the redundancy, replace the *Enroll* entity type with two binary relationships (Figure 8.8). Each binary relationship converts to a table as shown in Tables 8–7 and 8–8. The *Enroll* and *Orders* tables have no redundancies. For example, to delete a student's enrollment in an offering (say S1 in O1), only one row must be deleted from Table 8–7. In contrast, two rows must be deleted from Table 8–6.

If the assumptions change slightly, an argument can be made for an associative entity type representing a three-way relationship. Suppose that the bookstore wants to record textbook purchases by offering and student. Then, the relationship between students and textbooks is no longer independent of the other two relationships. Even though a student is enrolled in an offering and the offering uses a textbook, the student may not purchase the textbook (perhaps borrow it) for the offering. In this situation, there is no independence and a three-way relationship is needed. In addition to the M-N relationships in Figure 8.8, there should be a new associative entity type and three 1-M rela-

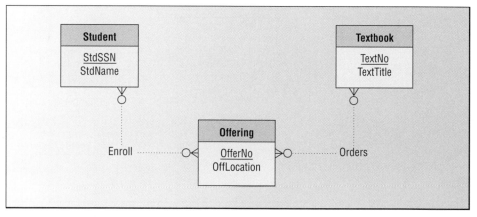

| **Figure 8.8** | Decomposed relationships example. |

TABLE 8–7	Sample Rows of the Binary *Enroll* Table

StdSSN	*OfferNo*
S1	O1
S1	O2

TABLE 8–8	Sample Rows of the Binary *Orders* Table

OfferNo	*TextNo*
O1	T1
O1	T2
O2	T1
O2	T2

tionships, as shown in Figure 8.9. You need the *Enroll* relationship to record student selections of offerings and the *Orders* relationship to record professor selections of textbooks. The *Purchase* entity type records purchases of textbooks by students in a course offering. However, a purchase cannot be known from the other relationships.

8.3.2 Multivalued Dependencies and Fourth Normal Form (4NF)

In relational database terminology, a relationship that can be derived from other relationships is known as a multivalued dependency (MVD). An MVD involves three columns as described in the marginal definition.

MVDs are generalizations of functional dependencies (FDs). Every FD is an MVD but not every MVD is an FD. An MVD in which an *A* value is associated with only one value of *B* and one value of *C* is also an FD. In this section, we are interested only in MVDs that are <u>not</u> also FDs. An MVD that is not an FD is known as a <u>nontrivial MVD</u>.

MVDs can lead to redundancies because of independence among columns. You can see the redundancy by using a table to depict an MVD, as shown in Figure 8.10. If the two rows above the line exist and the MVD $A \rightarrow \rightarrow B \mid C$ is true, then the two rows below the line will exist. The two rows below the line will exist because *B* and *C* are independent. In Figure 8.10, A1 is associated with two *B* values (B1 and B2) and two *C* values (C1 and C2). Because of independence, A1 will be associated with every combination of its related *B* and *C* values. The two rows below the line are redundant because they can be derived.

To apply this concept to the *Enroll* table, consider the possible MVD *OfferNo* $\rightarrow \rightarrow$ *StdSSN* | *TextNo*. In the first two rows of Figure 8.11, offering O1 is associated with stu-

> **MVD Definition**   the multivalued dependency (MVD) $A \rightarrow \rightarrow B \mid C$ (read *A* multidetermines *B* or *C*) means that
> 1. A given *A* value is associated with a collection of *B* and *C* values and
> 2. *B* and *C* are independent, given the relationships between *A* and *B* and *A* and *C*.

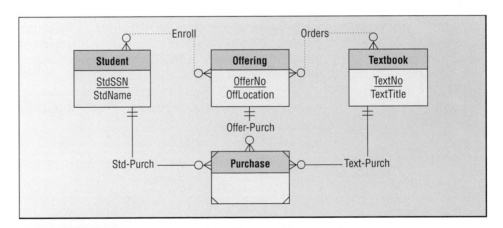

Figure 8.9   **M-way and binary relationships example.**

A	*B*	*C*
A1	B1	C1
A1	B2	C2
A1	B2	C1
A1	B1	C2

Figure 8.10   Table representation of an MVD.

OfferNo	*StdSSN*	*TextNo*
O1	S1	T1
O1	S2	T2
O1	S2	T1
O1	S1	T2

Figure 8.11   Representation of the MVD in the *Enroll* table.

dents S1 and S2 and textbooks T1 and T2. If the MVD is true, then the two rows below the line will exist. The last two rows do not need to be stored if you know the first two rows and the MVD exist.

4NF

4NF Definition   a table is in 4NF if it does not contain any MVDs that are not also FDs.[5]

Fourth normal form (4NF) prohibits redundancies caused by multivalued dependencies. As an example, the table *Enroll*(*StdSSN, OfferNo, TextNo*) (Table 8–6) is not in 4NF if the MVD *OfferNo* → → *StdSSN* | *TextNo* exists. To eliminate the MVD, split the M-way table *Enroll* into the binary tables *Enroll* (Table 8–7) and *Orders* (Table 8–8).

The ideas of MVDs and 4NF are somewhat difficult to understand. The ideas are somewhat easier to understand if you think of an MVD as a relationship that can be derived by other relationships because of independence. Chapter 9 presents another way to reason about M-way relationships using patterns in data entry forms.

8.4 HIGHER-LEVEL NORMAL FORMS

The normalization story does not end with 4NF. Other normal forms have been proposed, but their practicality has not been demonstrated. This section briefly describes two higher normal forms to complete your normalization background.

8.4.1 Fifth Normal Form (5NF)

5NF applies to M-way relationships like 4NF. Unlike 4NF, 5NF involves situations when a three-way relationship should be replaced with three binary relationships, not two binary relationships as for 4NF. Because situations in which 5NF applies (as opposed to 4NF) are rare, 5NF is generally not considered a practical normal form. Understanding the details of 5NF requires a lot of intellectual investment, but the return on your study time is rarely applicable.

The example in Figure 8.12 demonstrates a situation in which 5NF could apply. The *Authorization* entity type represents authorized combinations of employees, worksta-

---

[5]Equivalently, a table is in 4NF if it does not contain any nontrivial MVDs.

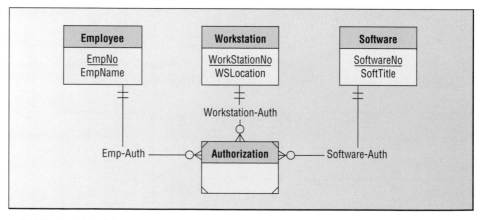

Figure 8.12   **Associative entity type.**

tions, and software. This associative entity has redundancy because it can be divided into three binary relationships as shown in Figure 8.13. If you know employees authorized to use workstations, software licensed for workstations, and employees trained to use software, then you know the valid combinations of employees, workstations, and software. Thus, it is necessary to record the three binary combinations (employee–workstation, software–workstation, and employee–software), not the three-way combination of employee, workstation, and software.

Whether the situation depicted in Figure 8.13 is realistic is debatable. For example, if software is licensed for servers rather than workstations, the *Software-Auth* relationship may not be necessary. Even though it is possible to depict situations in which 5NF applies, these situations may not exist in real organizations.

8.4.2 Domain Key Normal Form (DKNF)

After reading about so many normal forms, you may be asking questions such as "Where does it stop?" and "Is there an ultimate normal form?" Fortunately, the answer to the last question is yes. In a 1981 paper, Dr. Ronald Fagin proposed domain key normal form (DKNF) as the ultimate normal form. In DKNF, <u>domain</u> refers to a data type: a set of values with allowable operations. A set of values is defined by the kind of values (e.g., whole numbers versus floating-point numbers) and the integrity rules about the values (e.g., values greater than 21). <u>Key</u> refers to the uniqueness property of candidate keys. A table is in DKNF if every constraint on a table can be derived from keys and domains. A table in DKNF cannot have modification anomalies.

Unfortunately, DKNF remains an ideal rather than a practical normal form. There is no known algorithm for converting a table into DKNF. In addition, it is not even known what tables can be converted to DKNF. As an ideal, you should try to define tables in which most constraints result from keys and domains. These kinds of constraints are easy to test and understand.

8.5 PRACTICAL CONCERNS ABOUT NORMALIZATION

After reading this far, you should be well acquainted with the tools of relational database design. Before you are ready to use these tools, some practical advice is useful. This section discusses the role of normalization in the data-

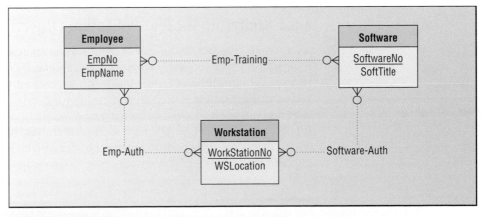

Figure 8.13   **Replacement of associative entity type with three binary relationships.**

base development process and the importance of thinking carefully about the objective of eliminating modification anomalies.

8.5.1 Role of Normalization in the Database Development Process

There are two opposite ways to use normalization in the database development process: (i) as a refinement tool or (ii) as an initial design tool. In the <u>refinement approach</u>, you perform conceptual data modeling using the Entity Relationship Model. If the design is large, you can design ERDs for individual views and then integrate them as described in Chapter 9. After you achieve a conceptual database design, the logical design step follows. In logical design, you transform the ERD into tables using the conversion rules. Then, you apply normalization techniques to analyze each table: identify FDs, use the simple synthesis procedure to remove redundancies, and analyze a table for independence if the table represents an M-way relationship.

In the <u>initial design approach</u>, you use normalization techniques in conceptual data modeling. Instead of drawing an ERD, you identify functional dependencies and apply a normalization procedure like the simple synthesis procedure. After defining the tables, you identify the referential integrity constraints and construct a relational model diagram such as that available in Microsoft Access. If needed, an ERD can be generated from the relational database diagram.

This book clearly favors using normalization as a refinement tool, not as an initial design tool. Through development of an ERD, you intuitively group related fields. Much normalization is accomplished in an informal manner without the tedious process of recording functional dependencies. As a refinement tool, there is usually less normalization to perform. The purpose is to ensure that you have not overlooked any redundancies. Normalization provides a rigorous way to reason about the quality of the design.

Another reason for favoring the refinement approach is that M-N relationships can be overlooked when using normalization as the initial design approach. If an M-N relationship has no attributes, there will not be any functional dependencies that show the need for a table. For example, in a design about textbooks and course offerings, if the relationship between them has no attributes, there are no functional dependencies that relate textbooks and course offerings.[6] In drawing an ERD, however, the need for an M-N relationship becomes clear.

8.5.2 Analyzing the Normalization Objective

As a design criterion, avoidance of modification anomalies is biased toward database changes. As you have seen, removing anomalies usually results in a database with many tables. A design with many tables makes the database easier to change but more difficult to query. If a database is used predominantly for queries, avoiding modification anomalies may not be an appropriate design goal. Chapter 14 describes databases for decision support in which the primary use is query rather than modification. In this situation, a design that is not fully normalized may be appropriate. <u>Denormalization</u> is the process of combining tables so that they are easier to query. In addition, physical design goals

---

[6]An FD can be written with a null right-hand side to represent M-N relationships. The FD for the offering–textbook relationship can be expressed as *TextId, OfferNo* $\rightarrow \varnothing$. However, this kind of FD is awkward to state. It is much easier to define an M-N relationship.

may conflict with logical design goals. Chapter 10 describes physical database design goals and the use of denormalization as a technique to improve query performance.

Another time to consider denormalization is when an FD is not important. The classic example contains the FDs *Zip → City, State* in a customer table where *City* means the post office city. In some databases, these dependencies may not be important to maintain. If there is not a need to manipulate zip codes independent of customers, the FDs can be safely ignored. However, there are databases in which it is important to maintain a table of zip codes independent of customer information. For example, if a retailer does business in many states and countries, a zip code table is useful to record sales tax rates.[7] If you ignore an FD in the normalization process, you should note that it exists but will not lead to any significant anomalies. Proceed with caution: most FDs will lead to anomalies if ignored.

CLOSING THOUGHTS

This chapter described how redundancies could make a table difficult to change, causing modification anomalies. Avoiding modification anomalies is the goal of normalization techniques. As a prerequisite to normalizing a table, you should list the functional dependencies (FDs). This chapter described three normal forms (2NF, 3NF, and BCNF) based on functional dependencies. The simple synthesis procedure was presented to analyze functional dependencies and produce tables in BCNF. Providing a complete list of FDs is the most important part of the normalization process. Even if you do not understand the normal forms, you can purchase a CASE tool to perform normalization. CASE tools are not capable of providing a complete list of FDs, however.

This chapter also described an approach to analyze M-way relationships (represented by associative entity types) using the concept of independence. If two relationships are independent, a third relationship can be derived from them. There is no need to store the third relationship. The independence concept is equivalent to a multivalued dependency. 4NF prohibits redundancy caused by multivalued dependencies.

This chapter and Chapter 7 emphasized data modeling and normalization, fundamental skills for database development. To facilitate your learning, the examples in these chapters were of modest size. To help you manage larger problems, Chapter 9 describes techniques that provide a way to divide a large problem into smaller problems and then combine the results of the smaller problems into a complete design.

REVIEW CONCEPTS

- Redundancies in a table cause modification anomalies.
- Modification anomalies: unexpected side effects when inserting, updating, or deleting.
- Functional dependencies: a value-neutral constraint similar to a primary key.
- 2NF: nonkey columns dependent on the entire key, not a subset of the key.
- 3NF: nonkey columns dependent only on the key, not on other nonkey columns.
- BCNF: every determinant is a candidate key.
- Simple synthesis procedure: analyze FDs and produce tables in BCNF.
- Use the simple synthesis procedure to analyze simple dependency structures.
- Use commercial design software to analyze complex dependency structures.

---

[7]A former database student made this comment about the database of a large computer retailer.

- Use relationship independence as a criterion to split M-way relationships into smaller relationships.
- MVD: association with collections of values and independence among columns.
- MVDs cause redundancy because rows can be derived using independence.
- 4NF: no redundancies due to MVDs.
- Use normalization techniques as a refinement tool rather than as an initial design tool.
- Denormalize a table if FDs do not cause modification anomalies.

QUESTIONS

1. What is an insertion anomaly?

2. What is an update anomaly?

3. What is a deletion anomaly?

4. What is the cause of modification anomalies?

5. What is a functional dependency?

6. How is a functional dependency like a candidate key?

7. Can a software design tool identify functional dependencies? Briefly explain your answer.

8. What kinds of FDs are not allowed in 2NF?

9. What kinds of FDs are not allowed in 3NF?

10. What kinds of FDs are not allowed in BCNF?

11. What is the relationship between BCNF and 3NF? Is BCNF a stricter normal form than 3NF? Briefly explain your answer.

12. Why is the BCNF definition preferred to the 3NF definition?

13. What is the goal of the simple synthesis procedure?

14. What is a limitation of the simple synthesis procedure?

15. What is a transitive dependency?

16. Are transitive dependencies permitted in 3NF tables? Explain why or why not.

17. Why eliminate transitive dependencies in the simple synthesis procedure?

18. How is relationship independence similar to statistical independence?

19. What kind of redundancy is caused by relationship independence?

20. What is a multivalued dependency (MVD)?

21. What is the relationship between MVDs and FDs?

22. What is the goal of 4NF?

23. What are the advantages of using normalization as a refinement tool rather than as an initial design tool?

24. Why is 5NF not considered a practical normal form?

25. Why is DKNF not considered a practical normal form?

26. When is denormalization useful? Provide an example to depict when it may be beneficial for a table to violate 3NF.

PROBLEMS

ORDER

Besides the problems presented here, the case study in Chapter 11 provides additional practice. To supplement the examples in this chapter, Chapter 11 provides a complete database design case including conceptual data modeling, schema conversion, and normalization.

1. For the big university database table, list FDs with the column *StdCity* as the determinant that are <u>not</u> true due to the sample data. With each FD that does not hold, show the sample data that violate it. Remember that it takes two rows to demonstrate a violation of an FD. The sample data are repeated in Table 8P–1 for your reference.

2. Following on problem 1, list FDs with the column *StdCity* as the determinant that the sample data do not violate. For each FD, add one or more sample rows and then identify the sample data that violate the FD. Remember that it takes two rows to demonstrate a violation of an FD.

3. For the big patient table, list FDs with the column *PatZip* as the determinant that are <u>not</u> true due to the sample data. Exclude the FD *PatZip → PatCity* because it is a valid FD. With each FD that does not hold, show the sample data that violate it. Remember that it takes two rows to demonstrate a violation of an FD. The sample data are repeated in Table 8P–2 for your reference.

4. Following on problem 3, list FDs with the column *PatZip* as the determinant that sample data do not violate. Exclude the FD *PatZip → PatCity* because it is a valid FD. For each FD, add one or more sample rows and then identify the sample data that violate the FD. Remember that it takes two rows to demonstrate a violation of an FD.

TABLE 8P–1	Sample Data for the Big University Database Table							
StdSSN	*StdCity*	*StdClass*	*OfferNo*	*OffTerm*	*OffYear*	*Grade*	*CourseNo*	*CrsDesc*
S1	SEATTLE	JUN	O1	FALL	2000	3.5	C1	DB
S1	SEATTLE	JUN	O2	FALL	2000	3.3	C2	VB
S2	BOTHELL	JUN	O3	WINTER	2000	3.1	C3	OO
S2	BOTHELL	JUN	O2	FALL	2000	3.4	C2	VB

TABLE 8P–2	Sample Data for the Big Patient Table							
VisitNo	*VisitDate*	*PatNo*	*PatAge*	*PatCity*	*PatZip*	*ProvNo*	*ProvSpecialty*	*Diagnosis*
V10020	1/13/2000	P1	35	DENVER	80217	D1	INTERNIST	EAR INFECTION
V10020	1/13/2000	P1	35	DENVER	80217	D2	NURSE PRACTIONER	INFLUENZA
V93030	1/20/2000	P3	17	ENGLEWOOD	80113	D2	OBGYN	PREGNANCY
V82110	1/18/2000	P2	60	BOULDER	85932	D3	CARDIOLOGIST	MURMUR

5. Apply the simple synthesis procedure to the FDs of the big patient table. The FDs are repeated in Table 8P–3 for your reference. Show the result of each step in the procedure. Include the primary keys and the foreign keys in the final list of tables.

6. The FD diagram in Figure 8P.1 depicts relationships among columns in an order entry database. Figure 8P.1 shows FDs with determinants *CustNo, OrderNo, ItemNo,* the combination of *OrderNo* and *ItemNo,* the combination of *ItemNo* and *PlantNo,* and the combination of *OrderNo* and *LineNo.* In the bottom FDs, the combination of *LineNo* and *OrderNo* determines *ItemNo* and the combination of *OrderNo* and *ItemNo* determines *LineNo.* There are two candidate keys for the underlying table: the combination of *OrderNo, ItemNo,* and *PlantNo* and the combination of *OrderNo, LineNo,* and *PlantNo.* Using the FD diagram as a guide, make a table with sample data. Using the sample data, identify insertion, update, and deletion anomalies in the table.

7. Following on problem 6, derive 2NF tables for the FD diagram in Figure 8P.1.

8. Following on problem 6, derive 3NF tables for the FD diagram in Figure 8P.1.

9. Following on problem 6, apply the simple synthesis procedure to produce BCNF tables using the FD diagram in Figure 8P.1.

10. Modify your table design in problem 9 if the shipping address (*ShipAddr*) column determines customer number (*CustNo*). Do you think that this additional FD is reasonable? Briefly explain your answer.

TABLE 8P–3	**List of FDs for the Big Patient Table**

PatNo → PatAge, PatCity, PatZip

PatZip → PatCity

ProvNo → ProvSpecialty

VisitNo → PatNo, VisitDate, PatAge, PatCity, PatZip

VisitNo, DocNo → Diagnosis

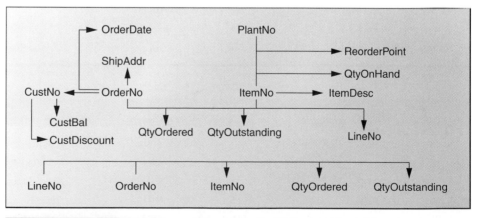

Figure 8P.1	**Dependency diagram for the big order entry table.**

11. Go back to the original FD diagram in which *ShipAddr* does not determine *CustNo*. How does your table design change if you want to keep track of a master list of shipping addresses for each customer? Assume that you do not want to lose a shipping address when an order is deleted.

12. Convert the ERD in Figure 8P.2 into tables and perform further normalization as needed. After converting to tables, write down FDs for each table. If a table is not in BCNF, explain why and split it into two or more tables that are in BCNF.

13. Convert the ERD in Figure 8P.3 into tables and perform further normalization as needed. After the conversion, write down FDs for each table. If a table is not in BCNF, explain why and split it into two or more tables that are in BCNF. Note that in the *Owner* and *Buyer* entity types, the primary key (*SSN*) is included although it is inherited from the *Person* entity type.

14. Extend the solution to the problem described in Section 8.2.4 about a database to track submitted conference papers. In the description, underlined parts are new. Write down the new FDs. Using the simple synthesis algorithm, design a collection of tables in BCNF. Note dependencies that are not important to the problem and relax your design from BCNF as appropriate. Justify your reasoning.

- Author information includes a unique author number, a name, a mailing address, and a unique but optional electronic address.

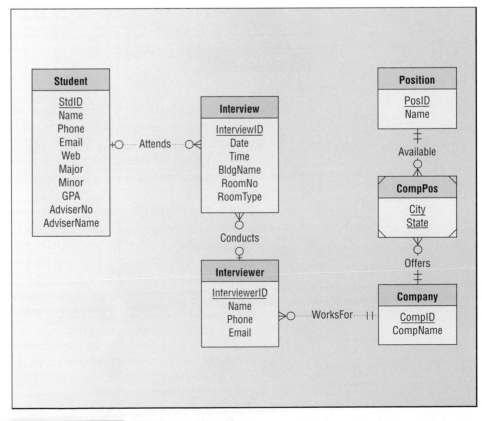

Figure 8P.2   ERD for problem 12.

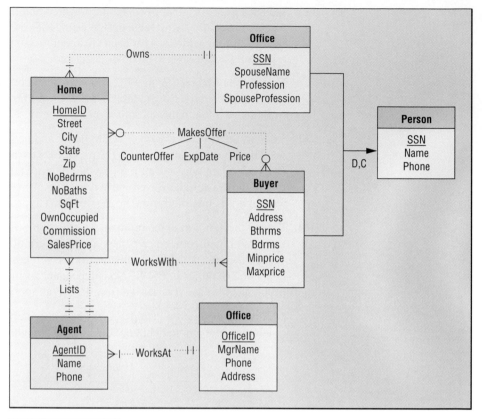

Figure 8P.3 ERD for problem 13.

- Paper information includes the list of authors, the primary author, the paper number, the title, the abstract, review status (pending, accepted, rejected), and a list of subject categories.
- Reviewer information includes the reviewer number, the name, the mailing address, a unique but optional electronic address, and a list of expertise categories.
- A completed review includes the reviewer number, the date, the paper number, comments to the authors, comments to the program chairperson, and ratings (overall, originality, correctness, style, and relevance).
- Accepted papers are assigned to sessions. Each session has a unique session identifier, a list of papers, a presentation order for each paper, a session title, a session chairperson, a room, a date, a start time, and a duration. Note that each accepted paper can be assigned to only one session.

15. For the following description of an airline reservation database, identify functional dependencies and construct normalized tables. Using the simple synthesis algorithm, design a collection of tables in BCNF. Note dependencies that are not important to the problem and relax your design from BCNF as appropriate. Justify your reasoning.

   The Fly by Night Operation is a newly formed airline aimed at the burgeoning market of clandestine travelers (fugitives, spies, con artists, scoundrels, deadbeats, cheating spouses, politicians, etc.). The Fly by Night Operation needs a database to track flights, customers, fares, airplane performance, and personnel assignment. Since the Fly by Night Operation is touted as a "fast way out of town," individual seats are not assigned, and flights of other carriers are not tracked. More specific notes about different parts of the database are listed below:

- Information about a flight includes its unique flight number, its origin, its (supposed) destination, and (roughly) estimated departure and arrival times. To reduce costs, the Fly by Night Operation only has nonstop flights with a single origin and destination.
- Flights are scheduled for one or more dates with an airplane and a crew assigned to each flight, and the remaining capacity (seats remaining) noted. In a crew assignment, the employee number and the role (e.g., captain, flight attendant) are noted.
- Airplanes have a unique serial number, a model, a capacity, and a next-scheduled-maintenance date.
- The maintenance record of an airplane includes a unique maintenance number, a date, a description, the serial number of the plane, and the employee responsible for the repairs.
- Employees have a unique employee number, a name, a phone, and a job title.
- Customers have a unique customer number, a phone number, and a name (typically an alias).
- A record is maintained of flight reservations including a unique reservation number, a flight number, a customer number, a date, a fare, and the payment method (usually cash but occasionally someone else's check or credit card). If the payment is by credit card, a credit card number and an expiration date are part of the reservation record.

16. For the following description of an accounting database, identify functional dependencies and construct normalized tables. Using the simple synthesis algorithm, design a collection of tables in BCNF. Note dependencies that are not important to the problem and relax your design from BCNF as appropriate. Justify your reasoning.

- The primary function of the database is recording of entries into a register. A user can have multiple accounts and there is a register for each account.
- Information about users includes a unique user number, a name, a street address, a city, a state, a zip, and an e-mail address (optional).
- Accounts have attributes including a unique number, a unique name, a start date, a last check number, a type (Checking, Investment, etc.), a user number, and a current balance (computed). For checking accounts, the bank number (unique), the bank name, and the bank address also are recorded.
- An entry contains a unique number, a type, an optional check number, a payee, a date, an amount, a description, an account number, and a list of entry lines. The type can have various values including ATM, Next Check Number, Deposit, and Debit Card.
- In the list of entry lines, the user allocates the total amount of the entry to categories. An entry line includes a category name, a description of the entry line, and an amount.
- Categories have other attributes not shown in an entry line: a unique category number (the name is also unique), a description, a type (asset, expense, revenue, or liability), and tax-related status (yes or no).

- Categories are organized in hierarchies. For example, there is a category Auto with subcategorizes Auto:fuel and Auto:repair. Categories can have multiple levels of subcategories.

17. For the ERDs in Figure 8P.4, describe assumptions under which the ERDs correctly depict the relationships among operators, machines, and tasks. In each case, choose an appropriate name for the relationship(s) and describe the meaning of the relationship(s). In part (b) you should also choose the name for the new entity type.

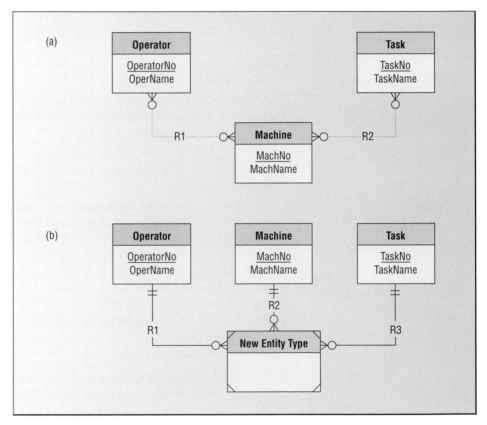

Figure 8P.4   ERD for problem 17.

REFERENCES FOR FURTHER STUDY

The subject of normalization can be much more detailed than described in this chapter. For a more detailed description of normalization, consult computer science books such as Date (1995), ElMasri and Navathe (1994), and Teorey (1999). The simple synthesis procedure was adapted from Hawryszkiewycz (1984). For a classic tutorial on normalization, consult Kent (1983). Fagin (1981) describes domain key normal form, the ultimate normal form. In addition, the database information center of the *Intelligent Enterprise* magazine (http://www.iemagazine.com/) has plenty of practical advice about normalization.

Chapter 9

View Design and Integration

This chapter describes the practice of designing user views and combining user views into a complete conceptual design. After this chapter, the student should have acquired the following knowledge and skills:

- Understand the motivation for view design and integration.

- Analyze a form and construct an ERD to represent it.

- Determine an integration strategy for a database development effort.

- Perform both incremental and parallel integration approaches.

- Recognize and resolve synonyms and homonyms in the view integration process.

OVERVIEW

Chapters 7 and 8 provided the tools for data modeling and normalization, fundamental skills for database design. You applied this knowledge to construct entity relationship diagrams (ERDs) for modest-size problems, convert ERDs into relational tables, and normalize the tables. This chapter extends your database design skills by showing you how to analyze views and integrate user views into a complete, conceptual schema.

To become a good database designer, you need to extend your skills to larger problems. To motivate you about the importance of extending your skills, this chapter describes the nature of large database development projects. This chapter then presents a methodology for view design with an emphasis on constructing an ERD to represent a data entry form. Forms can provide important sources of requirements for database design. You will learn to analyze individual forms, construct an ERD, and check the ERD for consistency against the form.

This chapter then describes the process of view integration, combining ERDs derived from individual views. You will learn about the incremental and parallel integration approaches, determination of an integration strategy by analyzing relationships among forms, and application of the integration process using both the incremental and parallel approaches.

9.1 MOTIVATION FOR VIEW DESIGN AND INTEGRATION

The complexity of a database reflects the complexity of the underlying organization and the functions that a database supports. Many factors can contribute to the complexity of an organization. Size is certainly an important determinant of complexity. Size can be measured in many ways such as by sales volume, the number of employees, the number of products, and the number of countries in which the organization is operating. Size alone is not the only determinant, however. Other factors that contribute to organizational complexity are the regulatory environment, the competitive environment, and the organizational structure. For example, the areas of payroll and personnel can be tremendously complex because of the number of employee types, details of compensation packages, union agreements, and government regulations.

Large organizations have many databases with individual databases supporting groups of functions such as payroll, personnel, accounting, material requirements, and so on. These individual databases can be very complex, as measured by the size of the ERDs. An ERD for a large database can have hundreds of entity types and relationships. When converted to a relational database, the database can have hundreds to perhaps thousands of tables. A large ERD is difficult to visually inspect because it can fill an entire wall. Other measures of complexity involve the use of the database through forms, reports, computer programs, and validation rules. A large database can have hundreds to thousands of forms, reports, computer programs, and validation rules.

Designing large databases is a time-consuming and labor-intensive process. The design effort often involves collecting requirements from many different groups of users. Requirements can be notoriously difficult to capture. Users often need to experience the database to clarify their requirements. Because of the volume of requirements and the difficulty of capturing requirements, a large database design effort can involve a team of designers. Coordination among designers is an important part of the database design effort.

To manage complexity, the "divide and conquer" strategy is used in many areas of computing. Dividing a large problem allows smaller problems to be independently solved. The solutions to the smaller problems are then combined into a solution for the entire problem.

View design and integration (Figure 9.1) is an approach to managing the complexity of the database design effort. In view design, an ERD is constructed for each group

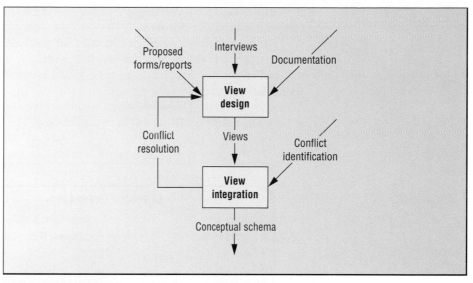

| **Figure 9.1** | **Overview of view design and integration.** |

of users. The requirements can come in many formats such as interviews, documentation of an existing system, and proposed forms and reports. A view is typically small enough for a single person to design. Multiple designers can work on views covering different parts of the database. The view integration process merges the views into a complete, conceptual schema. Integration involves recognizing and resolving conflicts. To resolve conflicts, it is sometimes necessary to revise the conflicting views. Compromise is an important part of conflict resolution in the integration process.

The remaining sections of this chapter provide details about the view design and integration activities. A special emphasis is given to data entry forms as a source of requirements.

9.2 VIEW DESIGN WITH FORMS

Forms can provide an important source of requirements for database design. Because of familiarity, users can effectively communicate many requirements through the forms they use. To aid you in using forms as database requirements, this section describes a procedure to design views using data entry forms. The procedure enables you to analyze the data requirements of a form. After the form analysis procedure, application of the procedure to forms with M-way relationships is discussed.

9.2.1 Form Analysis

In using forms for database design, you reverse the process described in the first part of the book. Earlier, you were given a database and then you defined forms to meet certain information processing needs. With a form-driven approach to database design, forms are defined before the database is designed. Forms often may exist in paper format or as part of an existing system. The form definition does not need to be as complete as required after the database is defined. For example, the entire set of events defining user interaction with the form need not be defined. Instead, form definition can involve a sketch on a word processor (Figure 9.2) or drawing tool. In addition, you may need several sample instances of a form.

The use of forms in view design does not preclude requirements in other formats such as interviews and documentation of an existing system. You should use all kinds of requirements in the view design process. As an important source of requirements, forms should be analyzed carefully.

In form analysis (Figure 9.3), you create an entity relationship diagram to represent a form. The resulting ERD is a view of the database. The ERD should be general enough

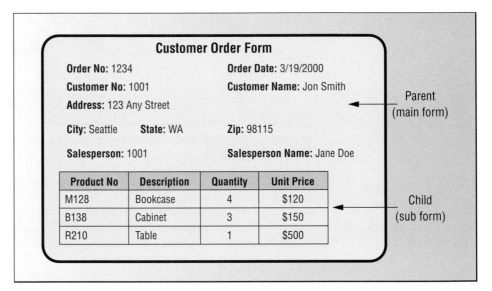

| Figure 9.2 | Sample Customer Order Form. |

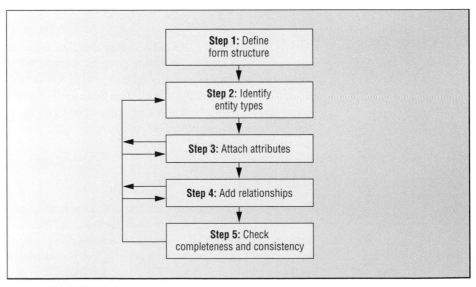

| Figure 9.3 | Steps in the form analysis process. |

to support the form and perhaps other anticipated processing. The backtracking in Figure 9.3 shows that the form analysis process can return to previous steps. It is not necessary to perform the steps sequentially. In particular, if any problems are found in the last step, other steps must be repeated to correct the problems. The remainder of this section explains the form analysis steps in more detail and applies the form analysis process to example forms.

Step 1: Define Form Structure

In the first step, you construct a hierarchy that depicts the form structure. Most forms consist of a simple hierarchy where the main form is the parent and the subform is the child. For example, Figure 9.4 depicts the structure of the customer order form in Figure 9.2. A box (parent or child) in the hierarchy diagram is called a node. Complex forms can have more nodes (parallel subforms) and more levels (subforms inside subforms) in the hierarchy. For example, an automotive service order form may have a subform (child) showing part charges and another subform (child) showing labor charges. Complex forms such as a service order form are not as common because they can be difficult for users to understand.

As part of making the form structure, you should identify keys within each node in the hierarchy. In Figure 9.4, node keys are underlined. In the parent node, the <u>node key</u> value is unique among all form instances. In the child node, the node key value is unique within the parent node. For example, a product number is unique on an order. However, two orders may use the same product number.

Step 2: Identify Entity Types

In the second step, you may split each node in the hierarchical structure into one or more entity types. Typically, each node in the hierarchical structure represents more than one entity type. You should look for form fields that can be primary keys of an entity type in

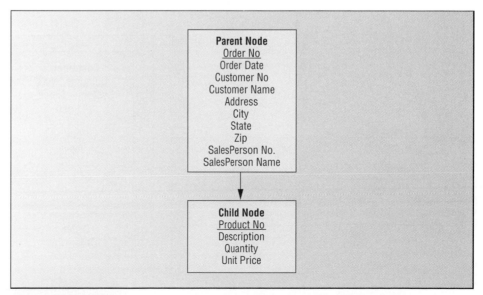

Figure 9.4   **Hierarchical structure for the Customer Order Form.**

the database. Make an entity type if the form field is a potential primary key and there are other associated fields in the form. Equivalently, you group form fields into entity types using functional dependencies (FDs). All form fields determined by the same field(s) should be placed together in the same entity type.

As an example of step 2, there are three entity types in the parent node of Figure 9.4, as shown in Figure 9.5: *Customer* identified by *Customer No, Order* identified by *Order No,* and *Salesperson* identified by *Salesperson No.* The parent node key (*Order No*) usually designates an entity type. *Customer No* and *Salesperson No* are good choices because there are other associated fields (*Customer Name* and *Salesperson Name*). In the child node, there is one entity type: *Product* designated by *Product No* because *Product No* can be a primary key with other associated fields.

Step 3: Attach Attributes

In the third step, you attach attributes to the entity types identified in the previous step. It is usually easy to associate form fields with the entity types. Group together fields that are associated with the primary keys found in step 2. Sometimes the proximity of fields can provide clues to their grouping: form fields close together often belong in the same entity type. In this example, group the fields as shown in Figure 9.6. *Order* with *Order No* and *Order Date, Customer* with *Customer No, Customer Name, Address, City, State,* and *Zip, SalesPerson* with *SalesPerson No* and *SalesPerson Name,* and *Product* with *Product No, Description,* and *Unit Price.*

If you are clever, you might notice that *Quantity* does not seem to belong to *Product* because the combination of *Order No* and *Product No* determine *Quantity.* You can create a new entity type (*OrderLine*) with *Quantity* as an attribute. If you miss this entity type, *Quantity* can be made an attribute of a relationship in the next step. In addition, the *Unit Price* attribute can be considered an attribute of the *OrderLine* entity type if the historical price rather than the current price of a product is tracked.

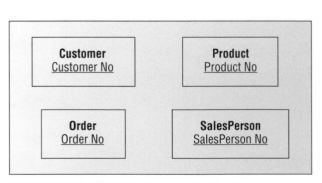

Figure 9.5 Entity types for the Customer Order Form.

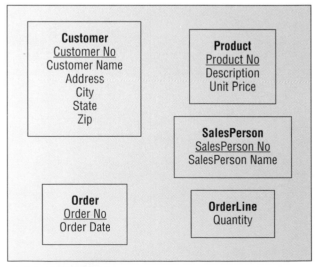

Figure 9.6 Attributes added to the entity types of Figure 9.5.

Step 4: Add Relationships

In the fourth step, you connect entity types with relationships and specify cardinalities. Table 9–1 summarizes rules about connecting entity types. You should begin with the entity type containing the primary key of the form. Let us call this the form entity type. Make the form entity type the center of the ERD. Typically, many relationships are between the form entity type and other entity types derived from the parent and the child nodes. In Figure 9.5, *Order* is the form entity type.

After identifying the form entity type, add 1-M relationships with other entity types derived from fields in the main form. This leaves us with *Order* connected to *Customer* and *SalesPerson* through 1-M relationships as shown in Figure 9.7. You should verify that the same customer can make many orders and the same salesperson can take many orders by examining additional form instances and talking to knowledgeable users.

Next connect the entity types derived from fields in the subform. *Product* and *OrderLine* can be connected by a 1-M relationship. An order line contains one product, but the same product may appear in order lines of different forms.

To finish the relationships, you need to connect an entity type derived from the main form fields with an entity type derived from subform fields. Typically, the relationship

TABLE 9–1	Rules to Connect Entity Types

1. Place the form entity type in the center of the ERD.

2. Add relationships between the form entity type and other entity types derived from the parent node. The relationships are usually 1-M.

3. Add a relationship to connect the form entity type to an entity type in the child node.

4. Add relationships to connect entity types derived from the child node if not already connected.

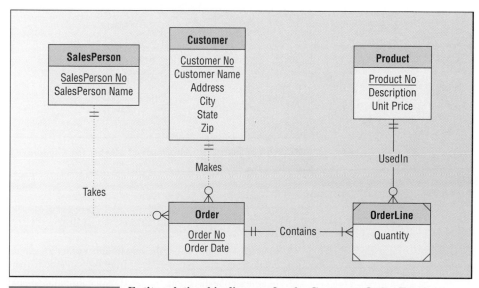

Figure 9.7	**Entity relationship diagram for the Customer Order Form.**

will connect the form entity type (*Order*) with an entity type derived from the child node. This relationship can be 1-M or M-N. In Figure 9.7, you can assume that an order can be associated with many products. If you examine other order form instances, you could see the same product associated with different orders. Therefore, a product can be associated with many orders. Here, it is important to note that *Quantity* is not associated with either *Product* or *Order* but with their combination. The combination can be considered a relationship or entity type. In Figure 9.7, *OrderLine* is an entity type. Figure 9.8 shows an alternative representation as an M-N relationship.

Step 5: Check Completeness and Consistency

In the fifth step, you check the ERD for consistency and completeness with the form structure. The ERD should be complete and consistent as defined in Chapter 7 (Section 7.5). For example, the ERD should contain minimum and maximum cardinalities for all relationships, a primary key for all entity types, and a name for all relationships.

For consistency, the form structure provides several constraints on the relationship cardinalities as summarized in Table 9–2. The first rule is necessary because only one value is displayed on the form. For example, there is only one value displayed for the customer number, name, and so on. As an example of the first rule, the maximum cardinality is one in the relationship from *Order* to *Customer* and from *Order* to *SalesPerson*. The second rule ensures that there is a 1-M relationship from the parent to the child

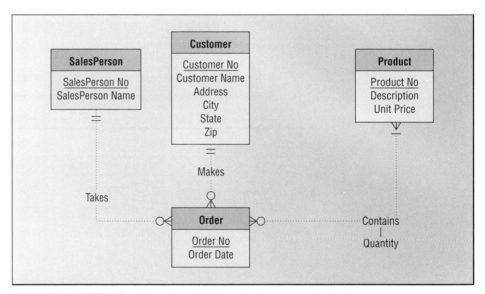

Figure 9.8 **Alternative ERD for the Customer Order Form.**

TABLE 9–2	Consistency Rules for Relationship Cardinalities

1. In at least one direction, the maximum cardinality should be one for relationships connecting entity types derived from the same node (parent or child).

2. In at least one direction, the maximum cardinality should be greater than one for relationships connecting entity types derived from nodes on different levels of the form hierarchy.

node. A given record in the parent node can be related to many records in the child node. As an example of the second rule, the relationship from *Order* to *OrderLine* has a maximum cardinality of M. In the alternative ERD (Figure 9.8), the maximum cardinality is M from *Order* to *Product*.

After following the steps of form analysis, you also can explore transformations as discussed in Chapter 7 (Section 7.5). The attribute to entity type transformation is often useful. If the form only displays a primary key, you may not initially create an entity type. For example, if only the salesperson number is displayed, you may not create a separate salesperson entity type. You can ask the user whether other data about a salesperson should be maintained. If yes, transform the salesperson number into an entity type.

Another Form Analysis Example

The Invoice Form (Figure 9.9) provides another example. A customer receives an invoice form along with the products ordered. In the main form, an invoice contains fields to identify the customer and the order. In the subform, an invoice identifies the products and the quantities shipped, ordered, and back ordered. The quantity back ordered equals the quantity ordered less the quantity shipped. Corresponding to this form, Figure 9.10 shows the hierarchical structure.

Figure 9.11 shows the result of steps 2 and 3 for the Invoice Form. The asterisks denote computed fields. *Invoice, Customer,* and *Order* are derived from the parent node. *Product* and *ShipLine* are derived from the child node. If you miss *ShipLine,* you can add it later as a relationship.

Figure 9.12 displays the ERD for the customer Invoice Form. The *SentTo* and *ShipFor* relationships connect entity types from the parent node. The *ShipsIn* relationship connects an entity type in the parent node (*Invoice*) with an entity type in the child node (*ShipLine*). Figure 9.13 shows an alternative ERD with the *ShipLine* entity type replaced by an M-N relationship.

9.2.2 Analysis of M-Way Relationships Using Forms

Chapter 8 described the concept of relationship independence as a way to reason about the need for M-way relationships. This section describes a more application-oriented

INVOICE FORM

Customer No.: 1273
Name: Contemporary Designs
Address: 123 Any Street
City: Seattle State: WA

Invoice No.: 06389
Date: 3/28/2000
Order No.: 61384
Zip: 98105

Product No.	Description	Qty. Ord.	Qty. Ship	Qty. Back.	Unit Price	Total Price
B381	Cabinet	2	2		150.00	300.00
R210	Table	1	1		500.00	500.00
M128	Bookcase	4	2	2	200.00	400.00

Total Amount	$1200.00
Discount	60.00
Amount Due	$1140.00

Figure 9.9 Sample Invoice Form.

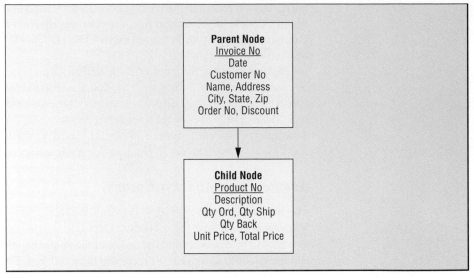

Figure 9.10   Hierarchical structure for the Invoice Form.

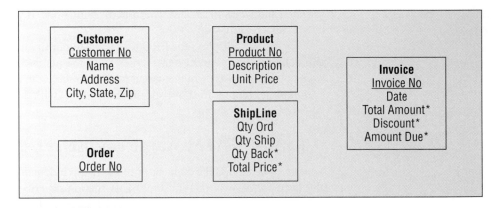

Figure 9.11   Entity types for the Invoice Form.

way to reason about M-way relationships. You can use data entry forms to help determine if an associative entity type representing an M-way relationship is needed in an ERD. M-way relationships can be difficult to understand because they involve three or more entity types. Data entry forms provide a context to understand M-way relationships. Without the context of a form, it can be difficult to determine that an M-way relationship is necessary as opposed to binary relationships.

An M-way relationship may be needed if a form shows a data entry pattern involving three entity types. Typically, one entity type resides on the main form and the other two entity types reside on the subform. Figure 9.14 shows a form with a project in the main form and part–supplier combinations (two entity types) in the subform. This form can be used to purchase parts for a particular project (localized purchasing). Because purchasing decisions are made by projects, both Part No. and Supplier No. can be updated in the subform. Figure 9.15 shows an ERD for this form. An associative entity type

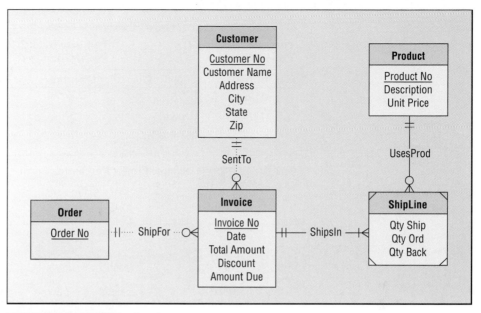

Figure 9.12   **ERD for the Invoice Form.**

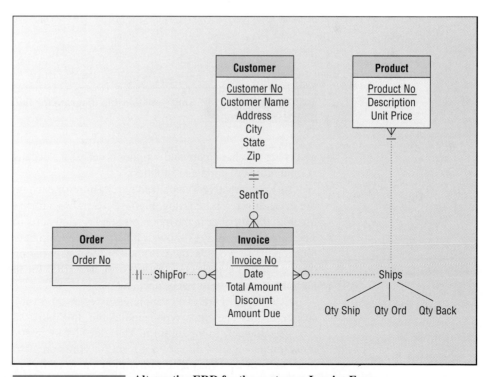

Figure 9.13   **Alternative ERD for the customer Invoice Form.**

Project Purchasing Form			
Purchase No.: P1234		**Purchase Date:** 3/19/2000	
Project No.: PR1		**Project Manager:** Jon Smith	
Part No.	**Supplier No.**	**Quantity**	**Unit Price**
M128	S100	4	$120
M129	S101	3	$150
R210	S102	1	$500

Figure 9.14   Sample Project Purchasing Form.

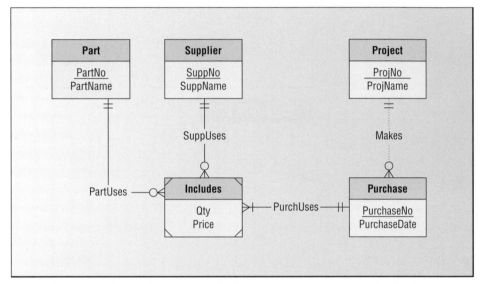

Figure 9.15   Entity relationship diagram for the Project Purchasing Form.

involving purchase, part, and supplier is necessary because a purchase can involve many combinations of parts and suppliers.

As an alternative to localized purchasing for each project, some organizations may prefer centralized purchasing. Figure 9.16 shows a form to support centralized purchasing with the supplier in the main form and related parts (one entity type) in the subform. The ERD in Figure 9.17 shows a binary relationship between *Purchase* and *Part.* To allocate parts to projects, there is another form with the project in the main form and the parts used by the project in the subform. The ERD for the other form would need a binary relationship between project and part.

Even if there are two or more entity types in a subform, binary relationships may suffice if only one entity type is updatable. In Figure 9.14, both Supplier No. and Part No. are updatable in the subform. Thus, an M-way relationship is necessary. As a counterexample, Figure 9.18 shows a form for course registration. The subform shows primary keys of the *Offering, Faculty,* and *Course* entity types, but only *Offering* is updatable in the subform. Faculty No and Course No are read only. The selection of a faculty member and the course corresponding to the offering are made in other forms. Thus, the ERD only contains binary relationships as Figure 9.19 shows.

Purchasing Form

Purchase No.: P1234   **Purchase Date:** 3/19/2000
Supplier No.: S101   **Supplier Name:** Anytime Supply

Part No.	Quantity	Unit Price
M128	4	$120
M129	3	$150
R210	1	$500

Figure 9.16   Sample Purchasing Form.

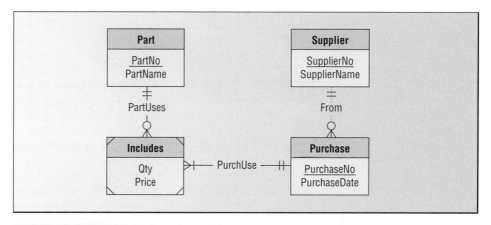

Figure 9.17   Entity relationship diagram for the Purchasing Form.

Registration No.: 1273   **Date:** 5/15/2000
Quarter: Fall   **Year:** 2000
Student No.: 123489   **Student Name:** Sue Thomas

Offer No	Course No	Days	Time	Location	Faculty No	Faculty Name
1234	IS480	MW	10:30	BLM211	1111	Sally Hope
3331	IS460	MW	8:30	BLM411	2121	George Jetstone
2222	IS470	MW	1:30	BLM305	1111	Sally Hope

Figure 9.18   Registration form.

9.3 VIEW INTEGRATION

With a large database project, even skilled database designers need a way to manage the complexity of the design process. Together, view design and integration can help you manage a large database design project by providing a way to break a large effort into smaller parts. In the last section, you studied how to design an ERD that represents the data requirements of a form. This section describes how to combine individual views into a complete database design. Two approaches for view integration are presented along with an example of each approach.

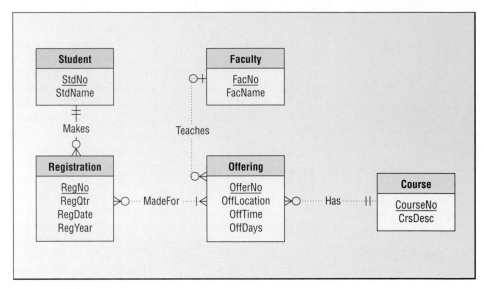

Figure 9.19   **Entity relationship diagram for the Registration form.**

9.3.1 Incremental and Parallel Integration Approaches

The incremental and parallel approaches are opposite ways to perform view integration. In the incremental approach (Figure 9.20), a view and a partially integrated ERD are merged in each integration step. Initially, the designer chooses a view and constructs an ERD for it. For subsequent views, the designer performs integration while analyzing the next view. The view design and integration processes are performed jointly for each view after the first one. This approach is incremental as a partially integrated ERD is produced after each step. This approach is also binary as the current view is analyzed along with the partially integrated ERD.

In the parallel approach (Figure 9.21), ERDs are produced for each view and then the view ERDs are merged. The integration occurs in one large step after all views are analyzed. This approach is parallel because different designers can perform view designs at the same time. Integration can be more complex in the parallel approach because integration is postponed until the end when all views are integrated to produce the final ERD.

Both approaches have advantages and disadvantages. The incremental approach has more integration steps, but each integration step is smaller. The parallel approach postpones integration until the end when a large integration effort may be necessary. The incremental approach is well suited to closely related views. For example, the order and the invoice forms are closely related because an order precedes an invoice. The parallel approach works well on large projects with views that are not closely related. Independent teams can work on different parts of a design in parallel. On a large project with many database designers, the parallel approach supports more independent work.

Determining an Integration Strategy

The incremental and the parallel approaches are typically combined in a large database design project. An integration strategy (Figure 9.22) specifies a mix of incremental and

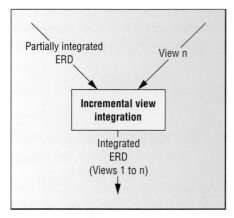

Figure 9.20   Incremental integration process.

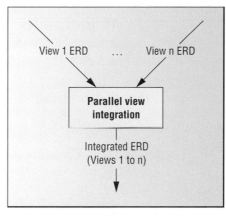

Figure 9.21   Parallel integration process.

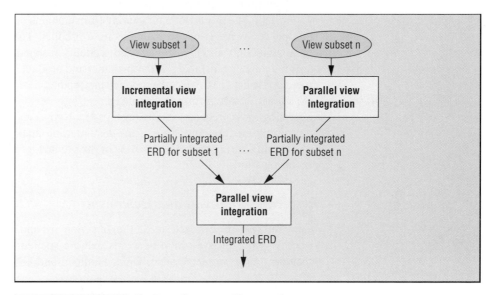

Figure 9.22   Outline of a general integration strategy.

parallel approaches to integrate a set of views. To choose an integration strategy, you divide the views into subsets (say *n* subsets). For each subset of views, the incremental approach is followed. You should choose subsets of views so that views in a subset are closely related. Views in diffcrent subsets should not be closely related. Incremental integration across subsets of views can proceed in parallel. After an integrated ERD is produced for each subset of views, a parallel integration produces the final, integrated ERD. If the ERDs from each subset of views do not overlap much, the final integration should not be difficult. If there is significant overlap among the subsets of views, incremental integration can be used to combine the ERDs from the view subsets.

As an example, consider a database to support a consulting firm. The database should support marketing to potential customers, billing on existing projects, and conducting work on projects. The database design effort can be divided into three parts (marketing, billing, and working). A separate design team may work incrementally on each part. If the marketing part has requirements for customer contacts and promotions, two incremental ERDs should be produced. After working independently, the teams can perform a parallel integration to combine their work.

Precedence Relationships among Forms

To help determine an integration strategy, you can identify precedence relationships among forms. Form A precedes form B if form A must be complete before form B is used. Form A typically provides some data used in form B. For example, the invoice form (Figure 9.9) uses the quantity of each product ordered (from the order form) to determine the quantity to ship. A good rule of thumb is to place forms with precedence relationships in the same view subset. Thus, the invoice and order forms should be in the same subset of views.

To further depict the use of precedence relationships, let us extend the order and invoice example. Figure 9.23 shows precedence relationships among forms for a custom manufacturing company. The product design form contains data about the components of a product. The product manufacturing form contains data about the sequence of physical operations necessary to manufacture a product. The customer and product forms contain data only about customers and products, respectively. The precedence relationships indicate that instances of the customer and product forms must be complete before an order is taken. Likewise, the product and product design forms must be complete before a manufacturing form is completed.

Using these precedence relationships, the forms can be divided into two groups: (i) an ordering process consisting of the customer, product, order, and invoice forms and (ii) a manufacturing process consisting of the product, product design, and product manufacturing forms.

Resolving Synonyms and Homonyms

In any integration approach, resolution of synonyms and homonyms is a very important issue. A <u>synonym</u> is a group of words that are spelled differently but have the same meaning. For example, OrdNo, Order Number, and ONO are likely synonyms. Syn-

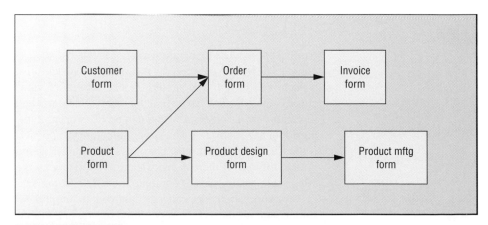

Figure 9.23   **Precedence relationships among forms.**

onyms often occur because different parts of an organization may use different vocabulary to describe the same things. This situation is especially likely if a common database did not exist before.

A <u>homonym</u> is a group of words that have the same sound and often the same spelling but have different meanings. In database design, homonyms arise because of context of usage. For example, two forms may show an address field. In one form, the address may only represent the street address while in the other form, it represents the street, city, state, and zip. Even when both address fields represent the street address, they may not be the same. One form might contain the billing address while the other form contains the shipping address.

Resolving synonyms and homonyms is a major part of standardizing a vocabulary that is a large part of database development. The use of naming standards and a corporate data dictionary can aid in the identification and resolution of synonyms and homonyms. A corporate data dictionary can be created and maintained with a CASE tool. Some CASE tools help with enforcement of naming standards. Even with these tools, recognizing synonyms and homonyms can be difficult. The most important point is to be alert for their existence. Resolving them is easier: rename synonyms the same (or establish an official list of synonyms) and rename homonyms differently.

9.3.2 View Integration Examples

This section depicts the incremental and parallel approaches to view integration using the customer order and invoice forms. The final result is identical with both approaches, but the path to this result is different.

Incremental Integration Example

To demonstrate the incremental integration approach, let us integrate the customer invoice form (Figure 9.9) with the ERD from Figure 9.7. The hierarchical structure of the invoice form is shown in Figure 9.10. You can start by adding an entity for invoice with invoice number and date. As steps 2 and 3 are performed (Figure 9.11), it is useful to see how the entity types should be merged into the existing ERD (Figure 9.7). The other form fields that match existing entity types are listed below.

- *Order No* matches the *Order* entity type.
- *Customer No, Customer Name, Address, City, State,* and *Zip* match the *Customer* entity type.
- *Product No, Description,* and *Unit Price* match the *Product* entity type.

As you match form fields to existing entity types, you should check for synonyms and homonyms. For example, it is not clear that *Address, City, State,* and *Zip* fields have the same meaning in the two forms. Certainly these fields have the same general meaning. However, it is not clear whether a customer might have a different address for ordering purposes than for shipping purposes. You may need to conduct additional interviews and examine additional form instances to resolve this issue. If you determine that the two sets of fields are homonyms (an order may be billed to one address and shipped to another), there are a number of data modeling alternatives, as listed below.

- Revise the *Customer* entity type with two sets of address fields: billing address fields and shipping address fields. This solution restricts the customer to having only a single shipping address. If more than one shipping address is possible, this solution is not feasible.

- Add shipping address fields to the *Invoice* entity type. This solution supports multiple shipping addresses per customer. However, if an invoice is deleted, the shipping address is lost.

- Create a new entity type (*ShipAddress*) with the shipping address fields. This solution supports multiple shipping addresses per customer. It may require overhead to gather the shipping addresses. If shipping addresses are maintained separate from invoices, this solution is the best.

The integrated ERD in Figure 9.24 uses the second alternative. In a real problem, more information should be gathered from the users before making the decision.

In the incremental integration process, the usual process of connecting entity types (step 4 of Figure 9.3) should be followed. For example, there is an M cardinality relating an entity type derived from the parent node with an entity type derived from the child node. The maximum cardinality in *ShipsIn* from *Invoice* to *ShipLine* satisfies this constraint. Note that *ShipLine* could be represented as an M-N relationship instead of as an entity type with two 1-M relationships.

As another point of interest from Figure 9.24, there is no relationship from *Invoice* to *Customer.* At first thought, a relationship may seem necessary because customer data appear on the main form of an invoice. If the invoice customer can be different than the order customer, a relationship between *Invoice* and *Customer* is needed. If the customer on an order is the same as the customer on the related invoice, a relationship is not

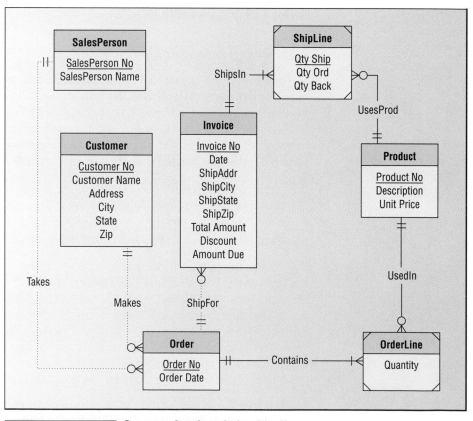

Figure 9.24   **Integrated entity relationship diagram.**

needed. The customer for an invoice can be found by navigating from *Invoice* to *Order* and *Order* to *Customer.* In Figure 9.24, the assumption is that the order customer and the invoice customer are identical.

Parallel Integration Example

To demonstrate the parallel integration process, let us integrate the customer invoice form (Figure 9.9) with the order form (Figure 9.2). The major difference between the parallel and the incremental approaches is that integration occurs later in the parallel approach. Thus, the first step is to construct an ERD for each form using the steps of form analysis described earlier. In the ERD for the invoice form (Figure 9.12), *Invoice* is directly connected to both *Customer* and *Order.* The direct connection follows the practice of making the form entity type (*Invoice*) the center of the diagram.

The integration process merges the order form ERD (Figure 9.7) with the invoice form ERD (Figure 9.12) to produce the ERD shown in Figure 9.24. The final ERD should be the same whether an incremental or parallel approach is used.

Again, a major integration issue is the resolution of homonyms for the address fields. In the two ERDs (Figures 9.7 and 9.12), the *Customer* entity type contains the address fields. Working independently on the two forms, it is easy to overlook the two uses of the address fields: billing and shipping. Unless you note that the address fields in the invoice form are for shipping purposes, you may not notice that the fields are homonyms.

Another integration issue is the connections among *Invoice, Order,* and *Customer.* In Figure 9.7, *Customer* is directly connected to *Order,* but in Figure 9.12, *Order* and *Customer* are not directly connected by a relationship. The integration process must resolve this difference. The relationship between *Order* and *Customer* is needed because orders precede invoices. A relationship between *Invoice* and *Customer* is not needed if the customer shown on an invoice is the same customer shown on the associated order. Assuming that the customer on an order is identical to the customer on the associated invoices, *Invoice* is not directly connected to *Customer* in Figure 9.24.

These two integration examples depict the advantage of the incremental integration approach over the parallel approach. Conflicts due to different uses of fields and timing (orders precede invoices) are resolved sooner in the incremental approach. In the parallel approach, such conflicts are not detected until the final step. This discussion conveys the sentiment discussed earlier: incremental integration is most appropriate when integrating closely related views.

CLOSING THOUGHTS

This chapter has described view design and integration, an important skill for designing large databases. Large databases can involve ERDs with hundreds of entity types and relationships. In addition to the large size of the ERDs, there are often hundreds of forms, reports, and computer programs that will use the database. View design and integration helps manage the complexity of such large database design efforts.

This chapter emphasized forms in the view design process. Forms are an important source of requirements because they are common and easily communicated. A five-step procedure was given to analyze a form. The result of the form analysis process is an ERD that captures the data requirements of the form. This chapter also described how the form analysis process could help detect the need for M-way relationships in an ERD.

This chapter described two approaches to view integration. In the incremental approach, a view and the partially integrated ERD are merged in each integration step. In the parallel approach, ERDs are produced for each view and then the individual ERDs are merged. The incremental approach works well for closely related views, while the parallel approach works well for unrelated views. This chapter discussed how to determine an integration strategy to combine the incremental and parallel approaches. In any integration approach, resolving synonyms and homonyms is critical. This chapter demonstrated how forms provide a context to resolve synonyms and homonyms.

This chapter concludes the first two phases (conceptual data modeling and logical database design) of database development. After completing these steps, you should have a high-quality relational database design: a design that represents the needs of the organization and is free of redundancies. To achieve an efficient design, Chapter 10 describes physical design concepts and techniques. Chapter 11 provides a detailed case study to apply the ideas in Part 2 of this book.

REVIEW CONCEPTS

- Characteristics of large database design efforts.
- Importance of forms as sources of database requirements.
- Five steps of form analysis.
- Form structure: nodes and node keys.
- Rules for adding relationships in form analysis.
- Rules to check cardinalities for consistency in form analysis.
- Using form analysis to detect the need for M-way relationships.
- Using the incremental and parallel integration approaches.
- Determining an integration strategy by combining incremental and parallel approaches.
- Detection of synonyms and homonyms in view integration.

QUESTIONS

1. What factors influence the size of a conceptual schema?
2. How does the view design and integration process help to manage the complexity of large database design efforts?
3. What is the goal of form analysis?
4. What are node keys in a form structure?
5. How do nodes in a form structure correspond to main forms and subforms?
6. What is the form entity type?
7. Why does the ERD for a form often have a different structure than the form?
8. Why is it recommended to place the form entity type in the center of the ERD?
9. Explain the first consistency rule in Table 9–2.
10. Explain the second consistency rule in Table 9–2.
11. How many integration steps are necessary to perform incremental integration with 10 views?
12. How many view design steps are necessary to perform parallel integration with 10 views?
13. In the incremental integration approach, why are view design and integration performed together?

14. When is the incremental integration approach appropriate?

15. When is the parallel integration approach appropriate?

16. What is an integration strategy?

17. When does a form depend on another form?

18. What criteria can you use to decide how to group views in an integration strategy?

19. What is a synonym in view integration? A homonym?

20. How can using forms in database design help you to detect synonyms and homonyms?

PROBLEMS

ORDER

Besides the problems presented here, the case studies in this book's website provide additional practice. To supplement the examples in this chapter, Chapter 11 provides a complete database design case including view design and integration.

1. Perform form analysis for the Simple Order Form (problem 17 of Chapter 5). Your solution should include a hierarchical structure for the form, an ERD that represents the form, and design justifications. Ignore the database design in Chapter 5 when performing the analysis. In your analysis, you can assume that an order must contain at least one product.

2. Perform form analysis for the Order Form (problem 18 of Chapter 5). Your solution should include a hierarchical structure for the form, an ERD that represents the form, and design justifications. Ignore the database design in Chapter 5 when performing the analysis. Here are a number of additional points to supplement the sample form shown in problem 18 of Chapter 5:
   • In all additional form instances, customer data appears on the main form.
   • In some additional form instances, the employee data does not appear on the main form.
   • In some additional form instances, the price for the same product varies. For example, the price for product P0036566 is $169.00 on some instances and $150.00 on other instances.
   • The supplier number cannot be updated on the subform. In addition, the supplier number and name are identical for all instances of the subform with the same product number.

3. Perform form analysis for the Simple Purchasing Form (problem 20 of Chapter 5). Your solution should include a hierarchical structure for the form, an ERD that represents the form, and design justifications. Ignore the database design in Chapter 5 when performing the analysis. Here are a number of additional points to supplement the sample form shown in problem 20 of Chapter 5:
   • The purchase unit price can vary across form instances containing the same product number.
   • A purchase must contain at least one product.

4. Perform form analysis for the Purchasing Form (problem 21 of Chapter 5). Your solution should include a hierarchical structure for the form, an ERD that represents the form, and design justifications. Ignore the database design in Chapter 5 when performing the analysis. Here are a number of additional points to supplement the sample form shown in problem 21 of Chapter 5:

- In all additional form instances, supplier data appears on the main form.
- The selling price can vary across form instances containing the same product number.
- The unit cost and QOH are identical across subform instances for a given product.

5. Perform form analysis for the Supplier Form (problem 22 of Chapter 5). Your solution should include a hierarchical structure for the form, an ERD that represents the form, and design justifications. Ignore the database design in Chapter 5 when performing the analysis. In analyzing the form, you can assume that a given product only appears on one Supplier Form instance.

6. Perform parallel integration using the ERDs that you created in problems 2, 4, and 5. Ignore the database design in Chapter 5 when performing the analysis. In performing the integration, you should assume that every product on a purchase form must come from the same supplier. In addition, you should assume that a Supplier Form instance must be completed before products can be ordered or purchased.

7. Perform form analysis on the Project Staffing Form below. Projects have a manager, a start date, an end date, a category, a budget (hours and dollars), and a list of staff assigned. For each staff assigned, the available hours and assigned hours are shown.

<table>
<tr><td colspan="4" align="center">**Project Staffing Form**</td></tr>
<tr>
<td colspan="2">**Project ID:** PR1234
Category: Auditing
Budget Hours: 170
Begin Date: 6/1/2000</td>
<td colspan="2">**Project Name:** A/P testing
Manager: Scott Jones
Budget Dollars: $10,000
End Date: 6/30/2000</td>
</tr>
<tr><th>Staff ID</th><th>Staff Name</th><th>Avail Hours</th><th>Assigned Hours</th></tr>
<tr><td>S128</td><td>Rob Scott</td><td>10</td><td>10</td></tr>
<tr><td>S129</td><td>Sharon Store</td><td>20</td><td>5</td></tr>
<tr><td>S130</td><td>Sue Kendall</td><td>20</td><td>15</td></tr>
</table>

8. Perform incremental integration using the ERD from problem 7 and the Program Form below. A project is divided into a number of programs. Each program is assigned to one employee. An employee can be assigned to a program only if the employee has been assigned to the project.

<table>
<tr><td colspan="4" align="center">**Program Form**</td></tr>
<tr>
<td colspan="2">**Staff ID:** S128
Project ID: PR1234</td>
<td colspan="2">**Name:** Rob Scott
Project Manager: Scott Jones</td>
</tr>
<tr><th>Program ID</th><th>Hours</th><th>Status</th><th>Due Date</th></tr>
<tr><td>PR1234-1</td><td>10</td><td>Completed</td><td>6/25/2000</td></tr>
<tr><td>PR1234-2</td><td>10</td><td>Pending</td><td>6/27/2000</td></tr>
<tr><td>PR1234-3</td><td>20</td><td>Pending</td><td>6/15/2000</td></tr>
</table>

9. Perform incremental integration using the ERD from problem 8 and the Timesheet Form below. The Timesheet Form allows an employee to record hours worked on various programs during a time period.

<table>
<tr><td colspan="4" align="center">**Timesheet Form**</td></tr>
<tr><td colspan="2">**Timesheet ID:** TS100
Total Hours: 18
Staff ID: S128
Begin Date: 5/1/2000</td><td colspan="2">**Time Period No:** 5

Name: Rob Scott
End Date: 5/31/2000</td></tr>
<tr><td>**Program ID**</td><td>**Hours**</td><td>**Pay Type**</td><td>**Date**</td></tr>
<tr><td>PR1234-1</td><td>4</td><td>Regular</td><td>5/2/2000</td></tr>
<tr><td>PR1234-1</td><td>6</td><td>Overtime</td><td>5/2/2000</td></tr>
<tr><td>PR1234-2</td><td>8</td><td>Regular</td><td>5/3/2000</td></tr>
</table>

10. Define an integration strategy for the Work Order, Program, and Timesheet forms. Briefly justify your integration strategy.

REFERENCES FOR FURTHER STUDY

View design and integration is covered in more detail in specialized books on database design. The best reference on view design and integration is Batini, Ceri, and Navathe (1992). Other database design books such as Nijssen and Halpin (1989) and Teorey (1999) also cover view design and integration. More details about the methodology for form analysis and view integration can be found in Choobineh, Mannino, Konsynski, and Nunamaker (1988) and Choobineh, Mannino, and Tseng (1992). A recent update to this work on form analysis is by Batra (1997).

Physical Database Design

This chapter describes physical database design, the final phase of the database development process. Physical database design transforms a table design from the logical design phase into an efficient implementation that supports all applications using the database. After this chapter, the student should have acquired the following knowledge and skills:

- Describe the inputs, outputs, and objectives of physical database design.

- List characteristics of sequential, Btree, and hash file structures.

- Appreciate the difficulties of performing physical database design and the need for periodic review of physical database design choices.

- Understand the trade-offs in index selection and denormalization decisions.

- Understand the need for good tools to help make physical database design decisions.

OVERVIEW

Chapter 9 extended your data modeling skills to larger problems. You learned about the motivation for view design and integration, how to analyze the data requirements of forms, and how to combine views into a complete, conceptual schema. This chapter extends your database design skills by showing you how to achieve an efficient implementation of your table design.

To become proficient in physical database design, you need to understand the process and environment. This chapter describes the process of physical database design including the inputs, outputs, and objectives along with two critical parts of the environment, file structures and query optimization. Most of the choices in physical database design relate to characteristics of file structures and query optimization decisions.

After understanding the process and environment, you are ready to perform physical database design. In performing physical database design, you should provide good inputs and make choices to balance the needs of retrieval and update applications. This chapter describes table profiles and application profiles as important but sometimes difficult-to-define inputs. Index selection is the most important choice of physical database design. This chapter describes trade-offs in index selection and provides index selection rules that you can apply to moderate-size databases. In addition to index selection, this chapter presents denormalization, record formatting, and parallel processing as techniques to improve database performance.

10.1 OVERVIEW OF PHYSICAL DATABASE DESIGN

Decisions in the physical database design phase involve the storage level of a database. Collectively, the storage-level decisions are known as the internal schema. This section describes the storage level as well as the objectives, inputs, and outputs used in physical database design.

10.1.1 Storage Level of Databases

The storage level is closest to the hardware and operating system. At the storage level, a database consists of physical records (also known as blocks or pages) organized into files. A <u>physical record</u> is a collection of bytes that are transferred between volatile storage in main memory and stable storage on a disk. Main memory is considered volatile storage because the contents of main memory may be lost if a failure occurs. A <u>file</u> is a collection of physical records organized for efficient access. Figure 10.1 depicts relationships between logical records (rows of a table) and physical records stored in a file. Typically, a physical record contains multiple logical records. The size of a physical record is a power of two such as 1024 bytes (2^{10}) or 4096 (2^{12}). A large logical record may be split over multiple physical records. Another possibility is that logical records from more than one table are stored in the same physical record.

The DBMS and the operating system work together to satisfy requests for logical records made by applications. Figure 10.2 depicts the process of transferring physical and logical records between a disk, DBMS buffers, and application buffers. Normally, the DBMS and the application have separate memory areas known as buffers. When an application makes a request for a logical record, the DBMS locates the physical record containing it. In the case of a read operation, the operating system transfers the physical

Physical Record
collection of bytes that are transferred between volatile storage in main memory and stable storage on a disk. The number of physical record accesses is an important measure of database performance.

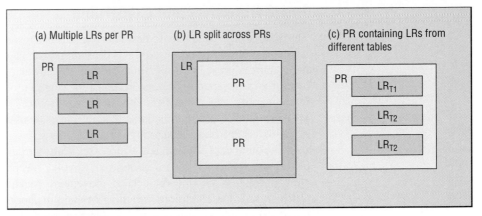

(a) Multiple LRs per PR	(b) LR split across PRs	(c) PR containing LRs from different tables

Figure 10.1   Relationships between logical records (LR) and physical records (PR).

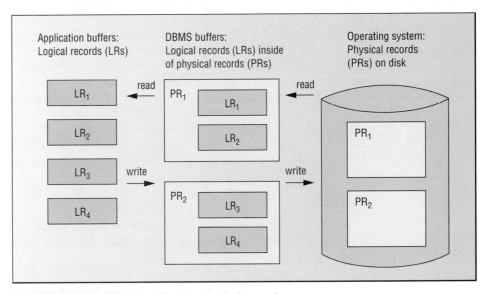

Figure 10.2   Transferring physical records.

record from disk to the memory area of the DBMS. The DBMS then transfers the logical record to the application's buffer. In the case of a write operation, the transfer process is reversed.

A logical record request may not result in a physical record transfer because of buffering. The DBMS tries to anticipate the needs of applications so that corresponding physical records already reside in the buffers of the DBMS. A significant concern about predicting database performance is knowing when a logical record request leads to a physical record transfer. For example, if multiple applications are accessing the same logical records, the corresponding physical records may reside in the DBMS buffers. Consequently, the uncertainty about the contents of DBMS buffers can make physical database design difficult.

10.1.2 Objectives and Constraints

The goal of physical database design is to minimize response time to access and change a database. Because response time is difficult to estimate directly, minimizing computing resources is used as a substitute measure. The resources that are consumed by database processing are physical record transfers, central processing unit (CPU) operations, main memory, and disk space. The latter two resources (main memory and disk space) are considered as constraints rather than resources to minimize. Minimizing main memory and disk space can lead to high response times.

The number of physical record accesses limits the performance of most database applications. A physical record access may involve mechanical movement of a disk including rotation and magnetic head movement. Mechanical movement is generally much slower than electronic switching of main memory. The speed of a disk access is measured in milliseconds (thousandths of a second) whereas a memory access is measured in nanoseconds (billionths of a second). Thus, a physical record access may be many times slower than a main memory access. Reducing the number of physical record accesses will usually improve response time.

CPU usage also can be a factor in some database applications. For example, sorting requires a large number of comparisons and assignments. These operations, performed by the CPU, are many times faster than a physical record access, however. To accommodate both physical record accesses and CPU usage, a weight can be used to combine them into one measure. The weight is usually close to 0 to reflect that many CPU operations can be performed in the time to perform one physical record transfer.

The objective of physical database design is to minimize the combined measure for all applications using the database. Generally, improving performance on retrieval applications comes at the expense of update applications and vice versa. Therefore, an important theme of physical database design is to balance the needs of retrieval and update applications.

The measures of performance are too detailed to estimate by hand except for simple situations. Complex optimization software calculates estimates using detailed cost formulas. The optimization software is usually part of the SQL compiler. Understanding the nature of the performance measure helps one to interpret choices made by the optimization software.

For most choices in physical database design, the amounts of main memory and disk space are usually fixed. In other words, main memory and disk space are constraints of the physical database design process. As with constraints in other optimization problems, you should consider the effects of changing the given amounts of main memory and disk space. Increasing the amounts of these resources can improve performance. The amount of performance improvement may depend on many factors such as the DBMS, table design, and applications using the database.

> **Combined Measure of Database Performance**
> $PRA + W * CPU\text{-}OP$, where PRA is the number of physical record accesses, $CPU\text{-}OP$ is the number of CPU operations such as comparisons and assignments, and W is a weight, a real number between 0 and 1.

10.1.3 Inputs, Outputs, and Environment

Physical database design consists of a number of different inputs and outputs as depicted in Figure 10.3 and summarized in Table 10–1. The starting point is the table design from the logical database design phase. The table and application profiles are used specifically for physical database design. Because these inputs are so critical to the physical database design process, they are discussed in more detail in Section 10.2. The most important outputs are decisions about file structures and data placement. Section 10.5 discusses these decisions in more detail. For simplicity, decisions about other outputs are made separately even though the outputs can be related. For example, file structures are

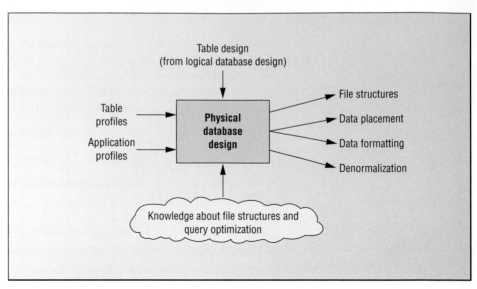

Figure 10.3   Inputs, outputs, and environment of physical database design.

TABLE 10–1	Summary of Inputs, Outputs, and Environment of Physical Database Design

Item	*Description*
Inputs	
Table profiles	Statistics for each table such as the number of rows and unique column values
Application profiles	Statistics for each form, report, and query such as the tables accessed/updated and the frequency of access/update
Outputs	
File structures	Method of organizing physical records for each table
Data placement	Criteria for arranging physical records in close proximity
Data formatting	Usage of compression and derived data
Denormalization	Combining separate tables into a single table
Environment Knowledge	
File structures	Characteristics such as kind of access supported and cost formulas
Query optimization	Access decisions made by the optimization component for each query

usually selected separately from denormalization decisions even though denormalization decisions can affect file structure decisions. Thus, physical database design is better characterized as a series of decision-making processes rather than one large process.

Knowledge about file structures and query optimization is in the environment of physical database design rather than being an input. The knowledge can be embedded in database design tools. If database design tools are not available, a designer informally uses knowledge about the environment to make physical database decisions. Acquiring the knowledge can be difficult because much of it is specific to each DBMS. Because knowledge of the environment is so crucial in the physical database design process, Sections 10.3 and 10.4 discuss it in more detail.

10.1.4 Difficulties

Before proceeding to more details about physical database design, it is important to understand why physical database design is difficult. The difficulty is due to the number of decisions, relationships among decisions, detailed inputs, complex environment, and uncertainty in predicting physical record accesses. These factors are briefly discussed below. In the remainder of this chapter, keep these difficulties in mind.

• The number of possible choices available to the designer can be large. For databases with many fields, the number of possible choices can be too large to evaluate even on large computers.

• The decisions cannot be made in isolation of each other. For example, file structure decisions for one table can influence the decisions for other tables.

• The quality of decisions is limited to the precision of the table and application profiles. However, these inputs can be large and difficult to collect. In addition, the inputs change over time so that periodic collection is necessary.

• The environment knowledge is specific to each DBMS. Much of the knowledge is either a trade secret or too complex to fully know.

• The number of physical record accesses is difficult to predict because of uncertainty about the contents of DBMS buffers. The uncertainty arises because the mix of applications accessing the database is constantly changing.

10.2 INPUTS OF PHYSICAL DATABASE DESIGN

Physical database design requires inputs specified in sufficient detail. Inputs specified without enough detail can lead to poor decisions in physical database design and query optimization. This section describes the level of detail recommended for both table profiles and application profiles.

10.2.1 Table Profiles

A table profile summarizes a table as a whole, the columns within a table, and the relationships between tables, as shown in Table 10–2. Because table profiles are tedious to construct manually, many DBMSs provide statistics programs to construct them automatically. The designer may need to periodically run the statistics program so that the profiles do not become obsolete. For large databases, table profiles may be estimated on samples of the database. Using the entire database can be too time consuming and disruptive.

For column and relationship summaries, the distribution conveys the number of rows and related rows for column values. The distribution of values can be specified in a number of ways. A simple way is to assume that the column values are uniformly distributed. Uniform distribution means that each value has an equal number of rows. If the uniform value assumption is made, only the minimum and maximum values must be specified.

TABLE 10–2	Typical Components of a Table Profile
Component	Statistics
Table	Number of rows and physical records
Column	Number of unique values; distribution of values
Relationship	Distribution of the number of related rows

A more detailed way to specify a distribution is to use a histogram. A <u>histogram</u> is a two-dimensional graph where the *x*-axis represents column ranges and the *y*-axis represents the number of rows containing the range of values. For example, the first bar in Figure 10.4 means that 1,500 rows have a salary greater than or equal to 0 and less than or equal to 20,000. The number of ranges to encode a distribution depends on the column and the method of choosing ranges. References at the end of the chapter describe methods to choose ranges.

Table profiles are used to calculate estimates of the combined measure of performance presented in Section 10.1.2. For example, the number of physical records is used to calculate the physical record accesses to retrieve all rows of a table. The distribution of column values is needed to estimate the fraction of rows that satisfy a condition in a query. For example, to estimate the fraction of rows that satisfy the condition, Salary < 45,000, you would sum the number of rows in the first three bars of Figure 10.4 and use linear interpolation in the fourth bar.

It is sometimes useful to store more detailed data about columns. If columns are related, errors can be made when estimating the fraction of rows that satisfy conditions connected by Boolean operators. For example, if the salary and age columns are related, the fraction of rows satisfying the Boolean expression Salary > 45,000 AND Age < 25 cannot be accurately estimated by knowing the distribution of salary and age alone. Data about the statistical relationship between salary and age are also necessary. Because summaries about column relationships are costly to collect and store, many DBMSs assume that columns are independent.

10.2.2 Application Profiles

Application profiles summarize the queries, forms, and reports that access a database, as shown in Table 10–3. For forms, the frequency of using the main form and the subform for each kind of operation (insert, update, delete, and retrieval) should be specified. For queries and reports, the distribution of parameter values encodes the number of times the query/report is executed with various parameter values. Unfortunately, DBMSs are not as

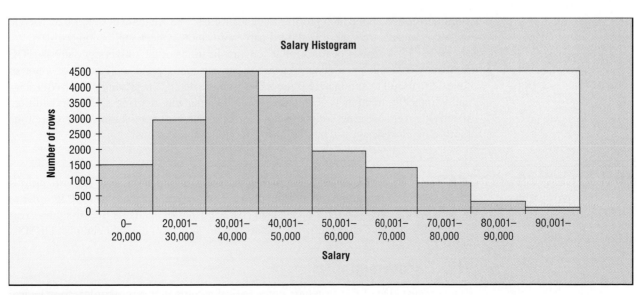

Figure 10.4   **Example histogram for salary column.**

TABLE 10–3	Typical Components of an Application Profile

Application Type	Statistics
Query	Frequency, distribution of parameter values
Form	Frequency of insert, update, delete, and retrieval operations to the main form and the subform
Report	Frequency, distribution of parameter values

TABLE 10–4	Example Application Profiles

Application Name	Tables	Operation	Frequency
Enrollment Query	Course, Offering, Enrollment	Retrieval	100 per day during the registration period; 50 per day during the drop/add period
Registration Main Form	Registration	Insert	1,000 per day during the registration period
Registration Subform	Enrollment	Insert	5,000 per day during the registration period; 1,000 per day during drop/add period
Registration Main Form	Registration	Delete	100 per day during the registration period; 10 per day during the drop/add period
Registration Subform	Enrollment	Delete	1,000 per day during the registration period; 500 per day during the drop/add period
Registration Main Form	Registration, Student	Retrieval	6,000 per day during the registration period; 1,500 per day during the drop/add period
Registration Subform	Enrollment, Course, Offering, Faculty	Retrieval	6,000 per day during the registration period; 1,500 per day during the drop/add period
Faculty Workload Report	Faculty, Course, Offering, Enrollment	Retrieval	50 per day during the last week of the academic period; 10 per day otherwise; typical parameters: current year and academic period

helpful to collect application profiles as table profiles. The database designer may need to write specialized software or find third-party software to collect application profiles.

Table 10–4 depicts profiles for several applications of the university database. The frequency data are specified as an average per unit time period such as per day. Sometimes it is useful to summarize frequencies in more detail. Specifying peak frequencies and variance in frequencies can help avoid problems with demand spikes. In addition, specifying response time limits indicates the importance of applications. Response time limits can allow designs to be tilted toward critical applications.

10.3 FILE STRUCTURES

As mentioned in Section 10.1, selecting among alternative file structures is one of the most important choices in physical database design. In order to choose intelligently, you must understand characteristics of available file structures. This section describes the characteristics of common file structures available in most DBMSs.

10.3.1 Sequential Files

The simplest kind of file structure stores logical records in insertion order. New logical records are appended to the last physical record in the file, as shown in Figure 10.5. Unless logical records are inserted in a particular order and no deletions are made, the file

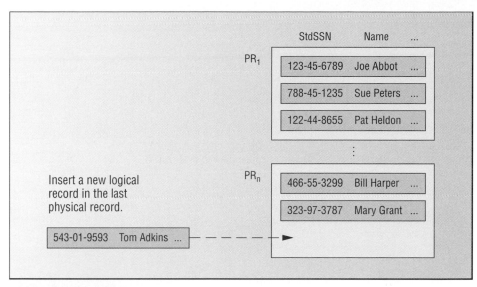

Figure 10.5   Inserting a new logical record into an unordered sequential file.

Sequential File   a simple file organization in which records are stored in insertion order or by key value. Sequential files are simple to maintain and provide good performance for processing large numbers of records.

becomes unordered. Unordered files are sometimes known as heap files because of the lack of order.

The primary advantage of unordered sequential files is fast insertion. However, when logical records are deleted, insertion becomes more complicated. For example, if the second logical record in PR$_1$ is deleted, space is available in PR$_1$. A list of free space must be maintained to tell if a new record can be inserted into the empty space instead of into the last physical record. Alternately, new logical records can always be inserted in the last physical record. However, periodic reorganization to reclaim lost space due to deletions is necessary.

Because ordered retrieval is sometimes needed, ordered sequential files can be preferable to unordered sequential files. Logical records are arranged in key order where the key can be any column, although it is often the primary key. Ordered sequential files are faster when retrieving in key order, either the entire file or a subset of records. The primary disadvantage to ordered sequential files is slow insertion speed. Figure 10.6 demonstrates that records must sometimes be rearranged during the insertion process. The rearrangement process can involve movement of logical records between blocks and maintenance of an ordered list of physical records.

10.3.2 Hash Files

Hash File   a specialized file structure that supports search by key. Hash files transform a key value into an address to provide fast access.

Hash files, in contrast to sequential files, support fast access of records by primary key value. The basic idea behind hash files is a function that converts a key value into a physical record address. The mod function (remainder division) is a simple hash function. Table 10–5 applies the mod function to the *StdSSN* column values in Figure 10.6. For simplicity, assume that the file capacity is 100 physical records. The divisor for the mod function is 97, a large prime number close to the file capacity. The physical record number is the result of the hash function result plus the starting physical record number, assumed to be 150. Figure 10.7 shows selected physical records of the hash file.

Hash functions may assign more than one key to the same physical record address. A <u>collision</u> occurs when two keys hash to the same physical record address. As long as

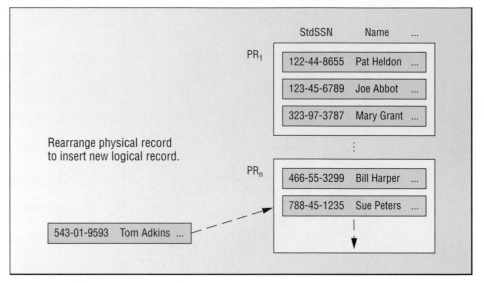

| **Figure 10.6** | Inserting a new logical record into an ordered sequential file. |

TABLE 10–5	**Hash Function Calculations for *StdSSN* Values**	
StdSSN	*StdSSN Mod* 97	*PR Number*
122448655	26	176
123456789	39	189
323973787	92	242
466553299	80	230
788451235	24	174
543019593	13	163

the physical record has free space, a collision is no problem. However, if the original or home physical record is full, a collision-handling procedure locates a physical record with free space. Figure 10.8 demonstrates the linear probe procedure for collision handling. In the linear probe procedure, a logical record is placed in the next available physical record if its home address is occupied. To retrieve a record by its key, the home address is initially searched. If the record is not found in its home address, a linear probe is initiated.

The existence of collisions highlights a potential problem with hash files. If collisions do not occur often, insertions and retrievals are very fast. If collisions occur often, insertions and retrievals can be slow. The likelihood of a collision depends on how full the file is. Generally, if the file is less than 70 percent full, collisions do not occur often. However, maintaining a hash file that is only 70 percent full can be a problem if the table grows. If the hash file becomes too full, a reorganization is necessary. A reorganization can be time consuming and disruptive because a larger hash file is allocated and all logical records are inserted into the new file.

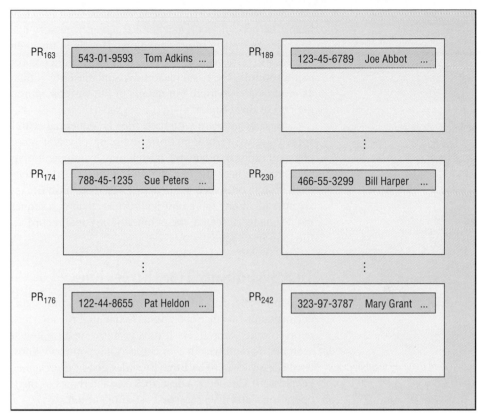

Figure 10.7   Hash file after insertions.

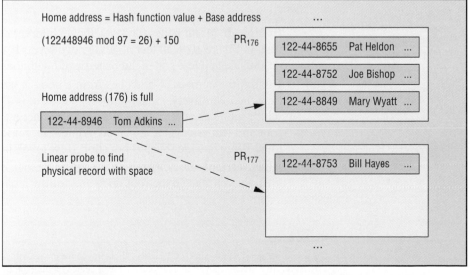

Figure 10.8   Linear probe collision handling during an insert operation.

To eliminate reorganizations, dynamic hash files have been proposed. In a dynamic hash file, periodic reorganization is never necessary and search performance does not degrade after many insert operations. However, the average number of physical record accesses to retrieve a record may be slightly higher as compared to a static hash file that is not too full. The basic idea in dynamic hashing is that the size of the hash file grows as records are inserted. For details of the various approaches, consult the references at the end of this chapter.

Another problem with hash files is sequential search. Good hash functions tend to spread logical records uniformly among physical records. Because of gaps between physical records, sequential search may examine empty physical records. For example, to search the hash file depicted in Figure 10.7, 100 physical records must be examined even though only six contain data. Even if the hash file is reasonably full, logical records are spread among more physical records than in a sequential file. Thus, when performing a sequential search, the number of physical record accesses may be higher in a hash file than in a sequential file.

10.3.3 Multiway Tree (Btree) Files

Sequential files and hash files provide good performance on some operations but poor performance on other operations. Sequential files perform well on sequential search but poorly on key search. Hash files perform well on key search but poorly on sequential search. The multiway tree, or Btree as it is popularly known, is a compromise and widely used file structure. The Btree provides good performance on both sequential search and key search. This section describes characteristics of the Btree, shows examples of Btree operations, and discusses the cost of operations.

Btree Characteristics: What's in a Name?

Btree File   a popular file structure supported by most DBMSs because it provides good performance both on key search as well as sequential search. A Btree file is a balanced, multiway tree.

A Btree is a special kind of tree, as depicted in Figure 10.9. A tree is a structure in which each node has at most one parent except for the root or top node. The Btree structure possesses a number of characteristics, discussed in the following list, that make it a useful file structure. Some of the characteristics are possible meanings for the letter "B"[1] in the name.

- **Balanced:** all leaf nodes (nodes without children) reside on the same level of the tree. In Figure 10.9, all leaf nodes are two levels beneath the root. A balanced tree ensures that all leaf nodes can be retrieved with the same access cost.
- **Bushy:** the number of branches from a node is large, perhaps 10 to 100 branches. Multiway, meaning more than two, is a synonym for bushy. The width (number of arrows from a node) and height (number of nodes between root and leaf nodes) are inversely related: increase width, decrease height. The ideal Btree is wide (bushy) but short (few levels).
- **Block-Oriented:** each node in a Btree is a block or physical record. To search a Btree, you start in the root node and follow a path to a leaf node containing

---

[1]Another possible meaning for the letter "B" is Bayer, for the inventor of the Btree, Professor Rudolph Bayer. In a private conversation, Professor Bayer denied naming the Btree after himself or for his employer at the time, Boeing. When pressed, Professor Bayer only said that the B represents the B.

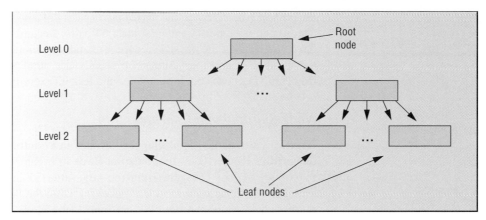

Figure 10.9   Structure of a Btree of height 3.

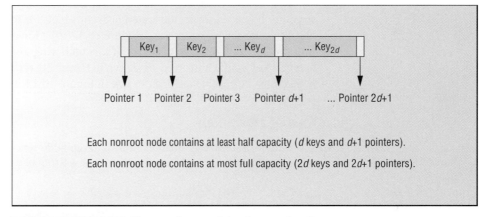

Figure 10.10   Btree node containing keys and pointers.

data of interest. The height of a Btree is important because it determines the number of physical record accesses for searching.

- **Dynamic:** the shape of a Btree changes as logical records are inserted and deleted. Periodic reorganization is never necessary for a Btree. The next subsection describes node splitting and concatenation, the ways that a Btree changes as records are inserted and deleted.
- **Ubiquitous:** the Btree is a widely implemented and used file structure.

Before studying the dynamic nature, let us look more carefully at the contents of a node as depicted in Figure 10.10. Each node consists of pairs with a key value and a pointer (physical record address), sorted by key value. The pointer identifies the physical record that contains the logical record with the key value. Other data in a logical record, besides the key, do not usually reside in the nodes. The other data may be stored in separate physical records or in the leaf nodes.

An important property of a Btree is that each node, except the root, must be at least half full. The physical record size, the key size, and the pointer size determine node capacity. For example, if the physical record size is 1,024 bytes, the key size is 4 bytes, and the pointer size is 4 bytes, the maximum capacity of a node is 128 <key, pointer> pairs. Thus, each node must contain at least 64 pairs. Because the designer usually does not have control over the physical record size and the pointer size, the key size determines the number of branches. Btrees are usually not good for large key sizes due to less branching per node and, hence, taller and less-efficient Btrees.

Node Splitting and Concatenation

Insertions are handled by placing the new key in a nonfull node or by splitting nodes, as depicted in Figure 10.11. In the partial Btree in Figure 10.11(a), each node contains a maximum of four keys. Inserting the key value 55 in Figure 10.11(b) requires re-arrangement in the right-most leaf node. Inserting the key value 58 in Figure 10.11(c) requires more work because the right-most leaf node is full. To accommodate the new value, the node is split into two nodes and a key value is moved to the root node. In Figure 10.11(d), a split occurs at two levels because both nodes are full. When a split occurs at the root, the tree grows another level.

Deletions are handled by removing the deleted key from a node and repairing the structure if needed, as demonstrated in Figure 10.12. If the node is still at least half full, no additional action is necessary [Figure 10.12(b)]. However, if the node is less than half full, the structure must be changed. If a neighboring node contains more than half capacity, a key can be borrowed, as shown in Figure 10.12(c). If a key cannot be borrowed, nodes must be concatenated, as shown in Figure 10.12(d).

Cost of Operations

The height of a Btree is small even for a large table when the branching factor is large. An upper bound or limit on the height (h) of a Btree is

$$h \leq ceil(\log_d n/2)$$

where

> $ceil$ is the ceiling function ($ceil(x)$ is the smallest integer $\geq x$)
>
> d is the minimum number of keys in a node
>
> n is the number of keys to store in the index
>
> Example: $h \leq 4$ for $n = 1,000,000$ and $d = 42$

The height dominates the number of physical record accesses in Btree operations. The cost in terms of physical record accesses to find a key is less than or equal to the height. If the row data are not stored in the tree, another physical record access is necessary to retrieve the row data after finding the key. The cost to insert a key includes the cost to locate the nearest key plus the cost to change nodes. In the best case [Figure 10.11(b)], the additional cost is one physical record access to change the index record and one physical record access to write the row data. The worst case occurs when a new level is added to the tree, as depicted in Figure 10.11(d). Even in the worst case, the height of the tree still dominates. Another $2h$ write operations are necessary to split the tree at each level.

B+tree

Sequential searches can be a problem with Btrees. To perform a range search, the search procedure must travel up and down the tree. For example, to retrieve keys in the range

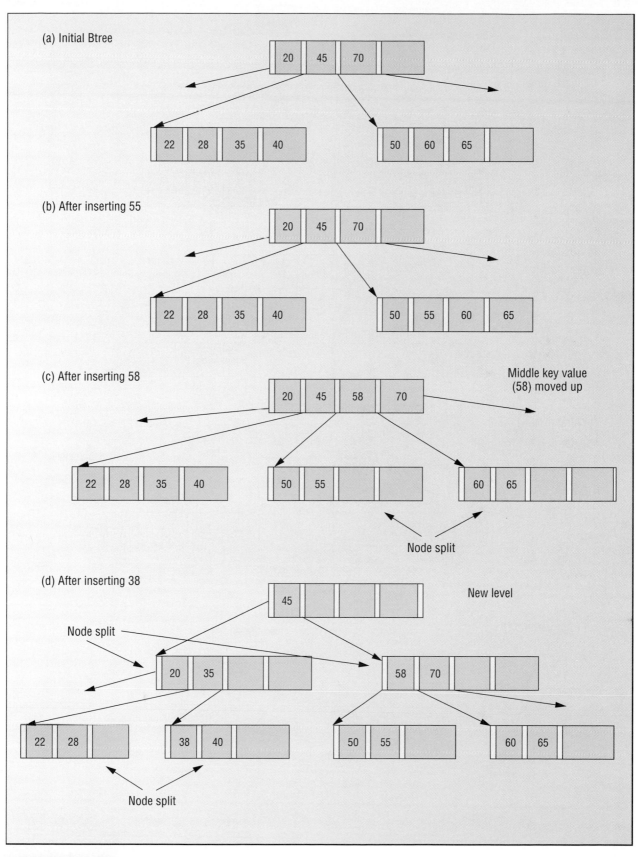

(a) Initial Btree

(b) After inserting 55

(c) After inserting 58

Middle key value
(58) moved up

Node split

(d) After inserting 38

New level

Node split

Node split

Node split

Figure 10.11   **Btree insertion examples.**

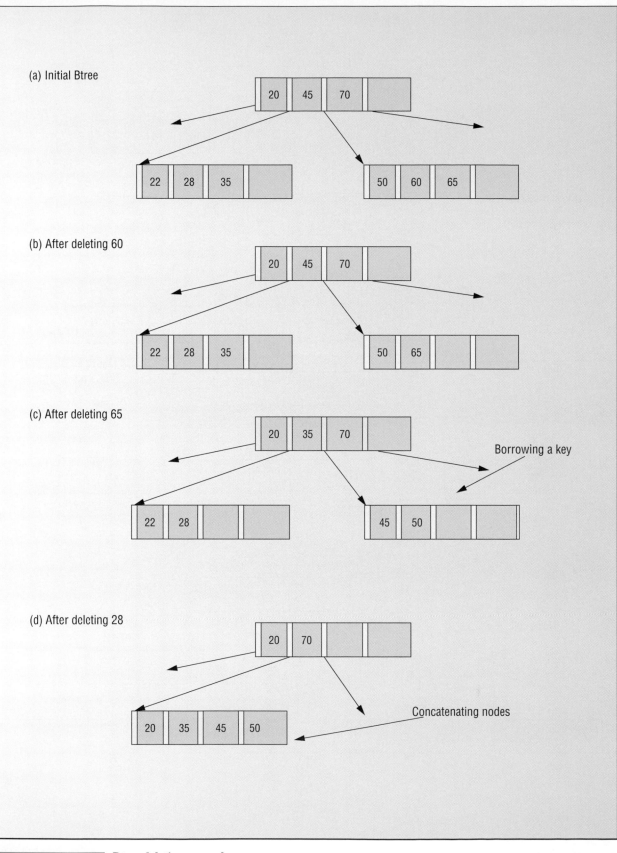

Figure 10.12 Btree deletion examples.

B+tree File the most popular variation of the Btree. In a B+tree, all keys are redundantly stored in the leaf nodes. The B+tree provides improved performance on sequential and range searches.

28 to 60 in Figure 10.12(a), the search process starts in the root, descends to the left leaf node, returns to the root, and then descends to the right leaf node. This procedure has problems with retention of physical records in memory. Operating systems may replace physical records if there have not been recent accesses. Because some time may elapse before a parent node is accessed again, the operating system may replace it with another physical record if main memory becomes full. Thus, another physical record access may be necessary when the parent node is accessed again.

To ensure that physical records are not replaced, the B+tree variation is usually implemented. Figure 10.13 shows the two parts of a B+tree. The triangle (index set) represents a normal Btree index. The lower part (sequence set) contains the leaf nodes. All keys reside in the leaf nodes even if a key appears in the index set. The leaf nodes are connected together so that sequential searches do not need to move up the tree. Once the initial key is found, the search process accesses only nodes in the sequence set.

10.3.4 Summary of File Structures

To help you recall the file structures, Table 10–6 summarizes their major characteristics. In the first row, hash files can be used for sequential access but there may be extra physical records because keys are evenly spread among physical records. In the second row, unordered and ordered sequential files must examine on average half the physical

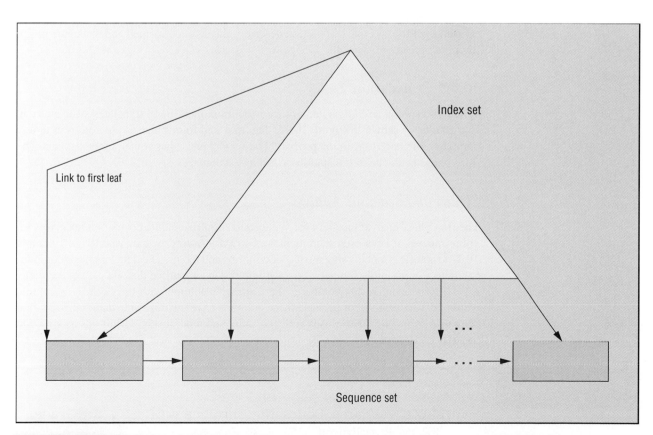

Figure 10.13   **B+tree structure.**

TABLE 10–6	Summary of File Structures			
	Unordered	*Ordered*	*Hash*	*B+tree*
Sequential search	Y	Y	Extra PRs	Y
Key search	Linear	Linear	Constant time	Logarithmic
Range search	N	Y	N	Y
Usage	Primary only	Primary only	Primary or secondary	Primary or secondary

records (linear). Hash files examine a constant number (usually close to 1) of physical records assuming that the file is not too full. Btrees have logarithmic search costs because of the relationship between the height, the log function, and search cost formulas. File structures can store all the data of a table (primary file structure) or store only key data. A secondary file structure or index provides an alternative path to the data.

10.4 QUERY OPTIMIZATION

In most relational DBMSs, you do not have the choice of how queries are implemented on the physical database. The query optimization component assumes this responsibility. Your productivity increases because you do not need to make these tedious decisions. However, you can sometimes improve the optimization process if you understand it. To provide you with an understanding of the optimization process, this section describes the tasks performed and discusses tips to improve optimization results.

10.4.1 Translation Tasks

When you submit an SQL statement for execution, the DBMS translates your query in four phases as shown in Figure 10.14. The first and fourth phases are common to any computer language translation process. The second phase has some unique aspects. The third phase is unique to translation of database languages.

Syntax and Semantic Analysis

The first phase analyzes a query for syntax and simple semantic errors. Syntax errors involve misuse of keywords such as if the FROM keyword was misspelled in Example 10.1. Semantic errors involve misuse of columns and tables. The data language compiler can detect only simple semantic errors involving incompatible data types. For example, a WHERE condition that compares the *CourseNo* column with the *FacSalary* column results in a semantic error because these columns have incompatible data types. To find semantic errors, the DBMS uses table, column, and relationship definitions as stored in the data dictionary.

EXAMPLE 10.1 (ORACLE)	Joining Three Tables

```
SELECT FacName, CourseNo, Enrollment.OfferNo, EnrGrade
  FROM Enrollment, Offering, Faculty
  WHERE CourseNo LIKE 'IS%' AND OffYear = 1999
```

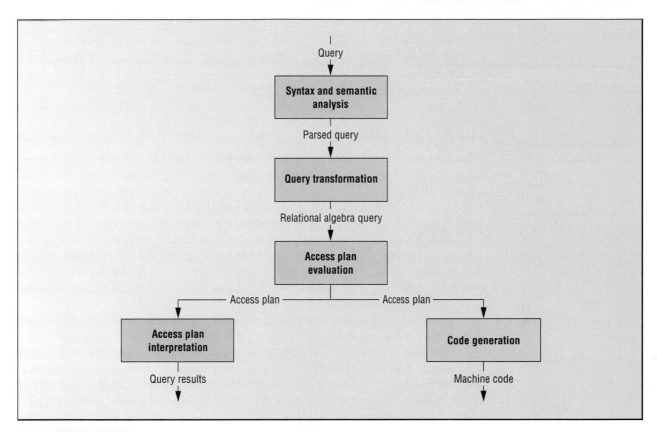

Figure 10.14   **Tasks in database language translation.**

```
AND OffTerm = 'Fall'
AND Enrollment.OfferNo = Offering.OfferNo
AND Faculty.FacSSN = Offering.FacSSN
```

Query Transformation

The second phase transforms a query into a simplified and standardized format. As with optimizing programming language compilers, database language translators can eliminate redundant parts of a logical expression. For example, the logical expression (OffYear = 1999 AND OffTerm = 'WINTER') OR (OffYear = 1999 AND OffTerm = 'SPRING') can be simplified to OffYear = 1999 AND (OffTerm = 'WINTER' OR OffTerm = 'SPRING'). Join simplification is unique to database languages. For example, if Example 10.1 contained a join with the *Student* table, this table could be eliminated if no columns or conditions involving the *Student* table are used in the query.

The standardized format is usually based on relational algebra. The relational algebra operations are rearranged so that the query can be executed faster. Typical rearrangement operations are described on the following page. Because the query optimization component performs this rearrangement, you do not have to be careful about writing your query in an efficient way.

- Restriction operations are combined so that they can be tested together.
- Projection and restriction operations are moved before join operations to eliminate unneeded columns and rows before expensive join operations.
- Cross product operations are transformed into join operations if a join condition exists in the WHERE clause.

Access Plan Evaluation

Access Plan a tree that encodes decisions about file structures to access individual tables, the order of joining tables, and the algorithm to join tables.

The third phase determines how to implement the rearranged relational algebra expression as an access plan. An access plan indicates how to implement the query as operations on files, as depicted in Figure 10.15. In an access plan, the leaf nodes are individual tables in the query, and the arrows point upwards to indicate the flow of data. The nodes above the leaf nodes indicate decisions about accessing individual tables. In Figure 10.15, Btree indexes are used to access individual tables. The first join combines the *Enrollment* and the *Offering* tables. The Btree file structures provide the sorting needed for the merge join algorithm. The second join combines the result of the first join with the *Faculty* table. The intermediate result must be sorted on *FacSSN* before the merge join algorithm can be used.

The query optimization component evaluates a large number of access plans. Access plans vary by join orders, file structures, and join algorithms. For example, Figure 10.16 shows a variation of the access plan in Figure 10.15 in which the join order is changed. The query optimization component can evaluate many more access plans than you can by hand. Typically, the query optimization component evaluates thousands of access plans. Evaluating access plans can involve a significant amount of time when the query contains more than four tables.

The query optimization component uses cost formulas to evaluate access plans. Each operation in an access plan has a corresponding cost formula that estimates the physical record accesses and CPU operations. The cost formulas use table profiles to estimate the number of rows in a result. For example, the number of rows resulting from

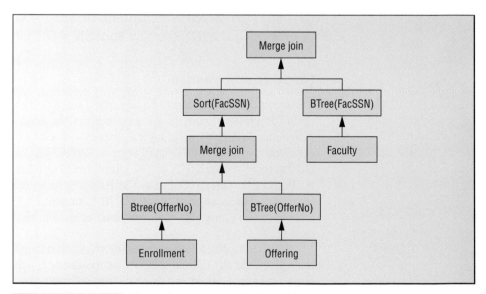

Figure 10.15 Example access plan for Example 10.1.

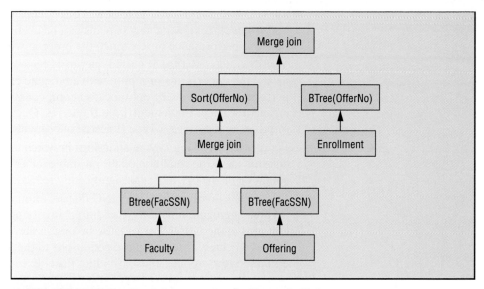

Figure 10.16 **Another access plan for Example 10.1.**

a WHERE condition can be estimated using distribution data such as a histogram. The query optimization component chooses the access plan with the lowest cost.

Access Plan Execution

The last phase executes the selected access plan. The query optimization component either generates machine code or interprets the access plan. Execution of machine code results in faster response than interpreting an access plan. However, most DBMSs interpret access plans because of the variety of hardware supported. The performance difference between interpretation and machine code execution is usually not significant for most users.

10.4.2 Optimization Tips

Even though the query optimization component performs its role automatically, the database designer also has a role to play. In some situations, you can influence the quality of solutions produced and improve the speed of the optimization process. Perhaps the largest impact is to choose a DBMS with a good optimization component. Here is a list of choices available to the database designer to improve the optimization process:

- The query optimization component needs detailed and current statistics to evaluate access plans. Statistics that are not detailed enough or outdated can lead to the choice of poor access plans.
- The optimization process can be time consuming, especially for queries containing more than four tables. To reduce optimization time, some DBMSs save access plans to avoid the time-consuming phases of the translation process. Query binding is the process of associating a query with an access plan. Some DBMSs rebind automatically if a query changes or the database changes (file structures, table profiles, data types, etc.).

- Some DBMSs allow you to review access plans. For queries with poor performance, reviewing access plans can be useful to see if an index might improve performance or to change the order in which tables are joined.
- You should avoid Type II nested queries (Chapter 4), especially when the nested query performs grouping with aggregate calculation. Many DBMSs perform poorly as query optimization components often do not consider efficient ways to implement Type II queries. Query execution speed can improve by replacing a Type II nested query with a separate query.
- For queries involving 1-M relationships in which there is a condition on the join column, make the condition on the one table rather than the many table. The condition on the one table can significantly reduce the effort in joining the tables.
- For queries involving the HAVING clause, eliminate conditions that do not involve aggregate functions. Conditions involving simple comparisons of columns in the GROUP BY clause belong in the WHERE clause, not the HAVING clause. Moving these conditions to the WHERE clause will eliminate rows sooner, thus providing faster execution.

The first point about detailed statistics needs further elaboration. Optimizers using the uniform value assumption often choose sequential file access rather than Btree access. For example, consider a query to list employees with salaries greater than $100,000. If the salary range is $10,000 to $2,000,000, about 95 percent of the employee table should satisfy this condition using the uniform value assumption. For most companies, however, few employees would have a salary greater than $100,000. Using the estimate from the uniform value assumption, the optimizer will choose a sequential file instead of a Btree to access the employee table. Using a histogram instead of the uniform value assumption should provide a more accurate estimate.

Beyond manipulating inputs of the optimization process, you should thoroughly benchmark a query optimization component before purchasing it. Benchmarking allows you to compare performance of multiple DBMSs as well as reveal weaknesses of a specific DBMS. It is recommended to use industry standard benchmarks as well as organization-specific benchmarks. The end of this chapter provides references to industry standard benchmarks. If you do not have the resources to run standard benchmarks, you can use published results that are available for a variety of platforms.

10.5 INDEX SELECTION

Index selection is the most important decision available to the physical database designer. However, it also can be one of the most difficult decisions. As a designer, you need to understand why index selection is difficult and the limitations of performing index selection without an automated tool. This section helps you gain this knowledge by defining the index selection problem, discussing trade-offs in selecting indexes, and presenting index selection rules for moderate-size databases.

Index a secondary file structure that provides an alternative path to the data. In a clustering index, the order of the data records is close to the index order. In a nonclustering index, the order of the data records is unrelated to the index order.

10.5.1 Problem Definition

Index selection involves two kinds of indexes, clustered and nonclustered. In a <u>clustering</u> index, the order of the rows is close to the index order. Close means that physical records containing rows will not have to be accessed more than one time if the index is accessed sequentially. Figure 10.17 shows the sequence set of a B+tree index pointing to associated rows inside physical records. Note that for a given node in the sequence set, most associated rows are clustered inside the same physical record. Ordering the row data by the index field is a simple way to make a clustered index.

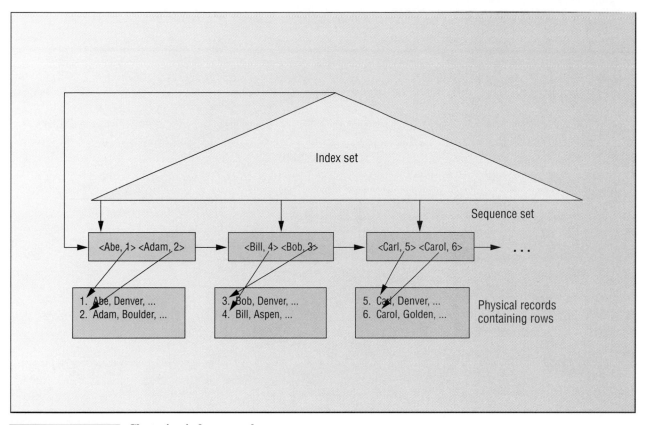

Figure 10.17   **Clustering index example.**

In contrast, a <u>nonclustering</u> index does not have this closeness property. In a non-clustered index, the order of the rows is not related to the index order. Figure 10.18 shows that the same physical record may be repeatedly accessed when using the sequence set. The pointers from the sequence set nodes to the rows cross many times, indicating that the index order is different than the row order.

Index Selection Problem for each table, select at most one clustering index and zero or more nonclustering indexes.

Index selection involves choices about clustered and nonclustered indexes, as shown in Figure 10.19. It is usually assumed that each table is stored in one file. The SQL statements indicate the database work to be performed by applications. The weights should combine the frequency of a statement with its importance. The table profiles must be specified in the same level of detail as required for query optimization.

Usually, the index selection problem is restricted to Btree indexes and separate files for each table. The references at the end of the chapter provide details about using other kinds of indexes (such as hash indexes) and placing data from multiple tables in the same file. However, these extensions make the problem more difficult without adding much performance improvement. The extensions are useful only in specialized situations.

10.5.2 Trade-offs and Difficulties

The best selection of indexes balances faster retrieval with slower updates. A nonclustering index can improve retrievals by providing fast access to selected records. In Example 10.2, a nonclustering index on either the *OffYear, OffTerm,* or *CourseNo* columns may be useful if relatively few rows satisfy the associated condition in the query. Usually, less

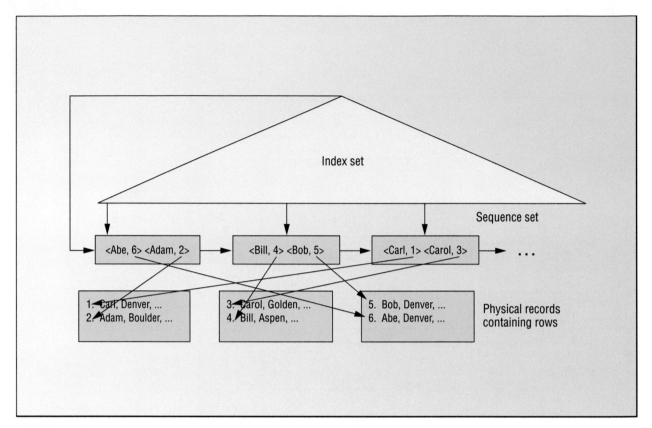

Figure 10.18 Nonclustering index example.

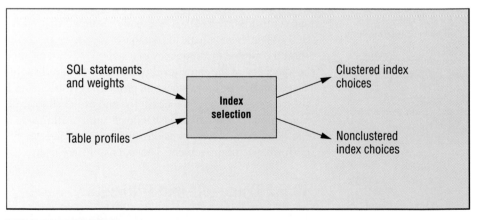

Figure 10.19 Inputs and outputs of index selection.

than 5 percent of the rows must satisfy a condition for a nonclustering index to be useful. It is unlikely that any of the conditions in Example 10.2 will yield such a small fraction of the rows.

A nonclustering index also can be useful in a join if a small number of rows result in one table. For example, if only a few *Offering* rows meet all three conditions in Example 10.2, a nonclustering index on the *Faculty.FacSSN* column may be useful when joining the *Faculty* and *Offering* tables.

EXAMPLE 10.2
(ORACLE)

Join of the Faculty and Offering Tables

```
SELECT FacName, CourseNo, OfferNo
  FROM Offering, Faculty
  WHERE CourseNo LIKE 'IS%' AND OffYear = 1999
    AND OffTerm = 'FALL'
    AND Faculty.FacSSN = Offering.FacSSN
```

A clustering index can improve retrievals under more situations than a nonclustering index. A clustering index is useful in the same situations as a nonclustering index except that the number of resulting rows can be larger. For example, a clustering index on either the *CourseNo, OffYear,* or *OffTerm* columns may be useful if perhaps 20 percent of the rows satisfy the associated condition in the query.

A clustering index also can be useful on joins because it avoids the need to sort. For example, using clustering indexes on the *Offering.FacSSN* and *Faculty.FacSSN* columns, the *Offering* and *Faculty* tables can be joined by merging the rows from each table. Merging rows is often a fast way to join tables if the tables do not need to be sorted (clustered indexes exist).

The cost to maintain indexes as a result of INSERT, UPDATE, and DELETE statements balances retrieval improvements. INSERT and DELETE statements affect all indexes of a table. Thus, many indexes on a table are not preferred if the table has frequent insert and delete operations. UPDATE statements affect only the columns listed in the SET clause. If UPDATE statements on a column are frequent, the benefit of an index is usually lost.

Clustering index choices are more sensitive to maintenance than nonclustering index choices. Clustering indexes are more expensive to maintain than nonclustering indexes because the data file must be changed similar to an ordered sequential file. For nonclustering indexes, the data file can be maintained as an unordered sequential file.

Difficulties of Index Selection

Index selection is difficult to perform well for a variety of reasons:

- Application weights are difficult to specify. Judgments that combine frequency and importance can make the result subjective.
- Distribution of parameter values is sometimes needed. Many SQL statements in reports and forms use parameter values. If parameter values vary from being highly selective to not very selective, selecting indexes is difficult.
- The behavior of the query optimization component must be known. Even if an index appears useful for a query, the query optimization component must use it. There may be subtle reasons why the query optimization component does not use an index, especially a nonclustering index.

- The number of choices is large. Even if indexes on combinations of columns are ignored, the theoretical number of choices is exponential in the number of columns (2^{NC}, where *NC* is the number of columns). Although many of these choices can be easily eliminated, the number of practical choices is still quite large.

- Index choices can be interrelated. The interrelationships can be subtle, especially when choosing indexes to improve join performance.

An index selection tool can help with the last three problems. A good tool should use the query optimization component to derive cost estimates for each application under a given choice of indexes. However, a good tool cannot help alleviate the difficulty of specifying application weights and parameter value distributions.

10.5.3 Selection Rules

Despite the difficulties previously discussed, you usually can avoid poor index choices by following some simple rules. You also can use the rules as a starting point for a more careful selection process.

Rule 1: A primary key is a good candidate for a clustering index.

Rule 2: To support joins, consider indexes on foreign keys. A nonclustering index on a foreign key is a good idea when there are important queries with highly selective conditions on the related primary key table. A clustering index is a good choice when most joins use a related table with a clustering index on its primary key and there are not highly selective conditions on the related table.

Rule 3: A column with many values may be a good choice for a nonclustering index if it is used in equality conditions. The term "many values" means that the column is almost unique.

Rule 4: A column used in highly selective range conditions is a good candidate for a nonclustering index.

Rule 5: A frequently updated column is not a good index candidate.

Rule 6: Volatile tables (lots of insertions and deletions) should not have many indexes.

Applying the Selection Rules

Let us apply these rules to the *Student, Enrollment,* and *Offering* tables of the university database. Table 10–7 lists SQL statements and frequencies for these tables. The names beginning with $ represent parameters supplied by the user. The frequencies assume a student population of 4,000 in which students enroll in an average of four offerings per term. Table 10–8 lists summaries of the table profiles. More detail about column and relationship distributions can be encoded in histograms.

Table 10–9 lists index choices according to the index selection rules. Only a few indexes are recommended because of the frequency of maintenance statements and the absence of highly selective conditions on columns other than the primary key. In queries 9 and 10, the conditions on *OffTerm* and *OffYear* are not likely to be highly selective. There is an index on *StdGPA* because parameter values should be very high or low, providing high selectivity. A more detailed study of the *StdGPA* index may be necessary because

TABLE 10–7	**Statements and Frequencies for Several University Database Tables**

SQL Statement	Frequency	Comments
1. INSERT INTO Student . . .	1,000/year	Beginning of year
2. INSERT INTO Enrollment . . .	16,000/term	During registration
3. INSERT INTO Offering . . .	1,000/year	Just before scheduling deadline
4. DELETE Student WHERE StdSSN = $X	1,100/year	After graduation
5. DELETE Offering WHERE OfferNo = $X	1,000/year	End of year
6. DELETE Enrollment WHERE OfferNo = $X AND StdSSN = $Y	10,000/year	End of year
7. SELECT * FROM Student WHERE StdGPA > $X	300/year	$X is usually very large or small
8. SELECT * FROM Student WHERE StdSSN = $X	16,000/term	

9. SELECT * FROM Offering
   WHERE OffTerm = $X AND OffYear = $Y
      AND CourseNo LIKE $Z
	4,000/term	Few rows in result

10. SELECT * FROM Offering, Enrollment
   WHERE StdSSN = $X AND OffTerm = $Y AND OffYear = $Z
      AND Offer.OfferNo = Enrollment.OfferNo
	4,000/term	Few rows in result

11. UPDATE Student SET StdGPA = $X WHERE StdSSN = $Y	4,000/term	Updated at end of reporting form
12. UPDATE Enrollment SET EnrGrade = $X WHERE StdSSN = $Y AND OfferNo = $Z	16,000/term	Part of grade reporting form
13. UPDATE OfferNo SET FacSSN = $X WHERE OfferNo = $Y	500/year	
14. UPDATE OfferNo SET OffLimit = OffLimit − 1 WHERE OfferNo = $Y	16,000/term	Part of registration form

TABLE 10–8	**Table Profiles**

Table	Number of Rows	Column (Number of Unique Values)
Student	30,000	StdSSN (PK), StdName (29,000), StdAddress (20,000), StdCity (500), StdZip (1,000), StdState (50), StdMajor (100), StdGPA (400)
Enrollment	300,000	StdSSN (30,000), OfferNo (2,000), EnrGrade (400)
Offering	10,000	OfferNo (PK), CourseNo (900), OffTime (20), OffLocation (500), FacSSN (1,500), OffTerm (4), OffYear (10), OffDays (10)
Course	1,000	CourseNo (PK), CrsDesc (1,000), CrsUnits (6)
Faculty	2,000	FacSSN (PK), FacName (1,900), FacAddress (1,950), FacCity (50), FacZip (200), FacState (3), FacHireDate (300), FacSalary (1,500)

TABLE 10–9	Index Selections for the University Database Tables		
Column	Index Kind	Rule	
Student.StdSSN	Clustering	1	
Student.StdGPA	Nonclustering	4	
Offering.OfferNo	Clustering	1	
Enrollment.OfferNo	Clustering	2	

it has a considerable amount of update activity. Even though not suggested by the SQL statements, the *StdName* and *FacName* columns also may be good index choices because they are almost unique (a few duplicates) and reasonably stable. If there are additional SQL statements that use these columns in conditions, nonclustered indexes should be considered.

To create the indexes, the CREATE INDEX statement can be used as shown in the examples below. The word following the INDEX keyword is the name of the index. The CREATE index statement also can be used to create an index on a combination of columns by listing multiple columns in the parentheses. The SQL2 CREATE INDEX statement does not support designation of an index as clustering or nonclustering. This designation is vendor specific in an extension of the CREATE INDEX statement or a window-based program to define indexes.

```
CREATE UNIQUE INDEX StdSSNIndex ON Student (StdSSN)
CREATE INDEX StdGPAIndex ON Student (StdGPA)
CREATE UNIQUE INDEX OfferNoIndex ON Offering (OfferNo)
CREATE INDEX EnrollOfferNoIndex ON Enrollment (OfferNo)
```

10.6 ADDITIONAL CHOICES IN PHYSICAL DATABASE DESIGN

Although index selection is the most important decision of physical database design, there are other decisions that can significantly improve performance. This section discusses two decisions, denormalization and record formatting, that can improve performance in selected situations. Next, this section presents parallel processing to improve database performance, an increasingly popular alternative. Finally, several ways to improve performance related to specific kinds of processing are briefly discussed.

10.6.1 Denormalization

Normalized Designs
- Have better update performance.
- Require less coding to enforce integrity constraints.
- Support more indexes to improve query performance.

Denormalization combines tables so that they are easier to query. After combining tables, the new table may violate a normal form such as BCNF. Although some of the denormalization techniques do not lead to violations in a normal form, they still make a design easier to query and more difficult to update. Denormalization should always be done with extreme care because a normalized design has important advantages. Chapter 8 described one situation for denormalization: ignoring a functional dependency if it does not lead to significant modification anomalies. This section describes additional situations under which denormalization may be justified.

Repeating Groups

A repeating group is a collection of associated values such as sales history, lines of an order, or payment history. The rules of normalization force repeating groups to be stored in an M table separate from an associated one table. For example, the lines of an order are stored in an order line table, separate from a related order table. If a repeating group is always accessed with its associated one table, denormalization may be a reasonable alternative.

Figure 10.20 shows a denormalization example of quarterly sales data. Although the denormalized design does not violate BCNF, it is less flexible for updating than the normalized design. The normalized design supports an unlimited number of quarterly sales as compared to only four quarters of sales results for the denormalized design. However, the denormalized design does not require a join to combine territory and sales data.

Generalization Hierarchies

Following the conversion rule for generalization hierarchies in Chapter 7 can result in many tables. If queries often need to combine these separate tables, it may be reasonable to store the separate tables as one table. Figure 10.21 demonstrates denormalization of the *Emp, HourlyEmp,* and *SalaryEmp* tables. They have 1-1 relationships because they represent a generalization hierarchy. Although the denormalized design does not violate BCNF, the combined table may waste much space because of null values. However, the denormalized design avoids the outer join operator to combine the tables.

Codes and Meanings

Normalization rules require that foreign keys be stored alone to represent 1-M relationships. If a foreign key represents a code, the user often requests an associated name or description in addition to the foreign key value. For example, the user may want to see the state name in addition to the state code. Storing the name or description column along with the code violates BCNF, but it eliminates some join operations. If the name

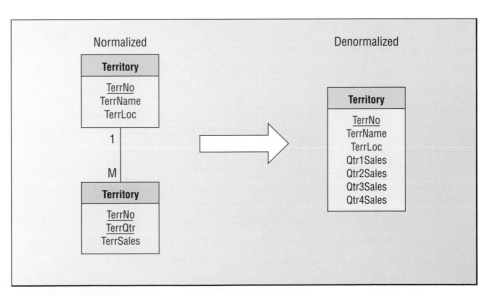

Figure 10.20   **Denormalizing a repeating group.**

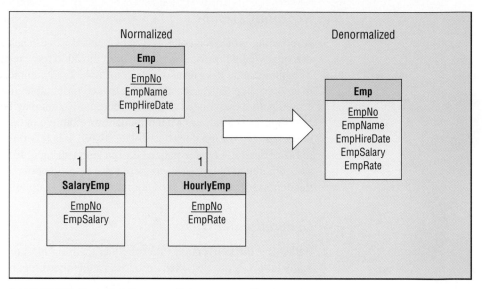

Figure 10.21 Denormalizing a generalization hierarchy.

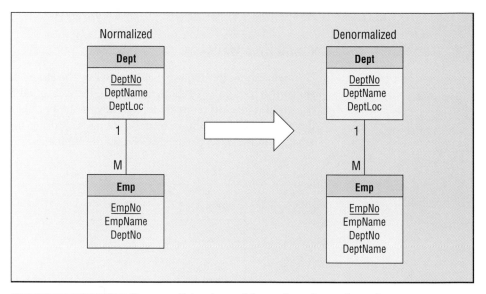

Figure 10.22 Denormalizing to combine code and meaning columns.

or description column is not changed often, denormalization may be a reasonable choice. Figure 10.22 demonstrates denormalization for the *Dept* and *Emp* tables. In the denormalized design, the *DeptName* column has been added to the *Emp* table.

10.6.2 Record Formatting

Record formatting decisions involve compression and derived data. With an increasing emphasis on storing complex data types such as audio, video, and images, compression is becoming an important issue. In some situations, there are multiple compression al-

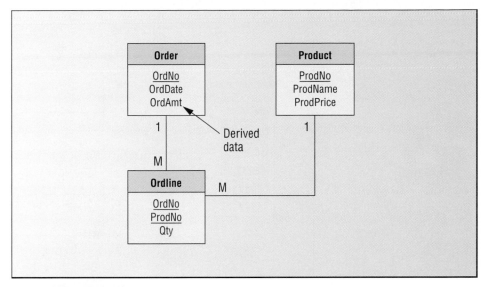

Figure 10.23   **Storing derived data to improve query performance.**

ternatives available. Compression is a trade-off between input–output and processing effort. Compression reduces the number of physical records transferred but may require considerable processing effort to compress and decompress the data.

Decisions about derived data involve trade-offs between query and update operations. For query purposes, storing derived data reduces the need to retrieve data needed to calculate the derived data. However, updates to the underlying data require additional updates to the derived data. Storing derived data to reduce join operations may be reasonable. Figure 10.23 demonstrates derived data in the *Order* table. If the total amount of an order is frequently requested, storing the derived column *OrdAmt* may be reasonable. Calculating order amount requires a summary or aggregate calculation of related *OrdLine* and *Product* rows to obtain the *Qty* and *ProdPrice* columns. Storing the *OrdAmt* column avoids two join operations.

10.6.3 Parallel Processing

Retrieval and modification performance can be improved significantly through parallel processing. Retrievals involving many records can be improved by reading physical records in parallel. For example, a report to summarize daily sales activity may read thousands of records from several tables. Parallel reading of physical records can reduce significantly the execution time of the report. In addition, performance can be improved significantly for batch applications with many write operations and read/write of large logical records such as images.

As a response to the potential performance improvements, many DBMSs provide parallel processing capabilities. These capabilities require hardware and software support for Redundant Arrays of Independent Disks (RAID).[2] The RAID controller (Figure 10.24)

RAID   a collection of disks (a disk array) that operates as a single disk. RAID storage supports parallel read and write operations with high reliability.

---

[2]RAID originally was an acronym for Redundant Arrays of Inexpensive Disks. Because prices of disk drives have fallen dramatically since the invention of the RAID idea (1988), *inexpensive* has been replaced by *independent*.

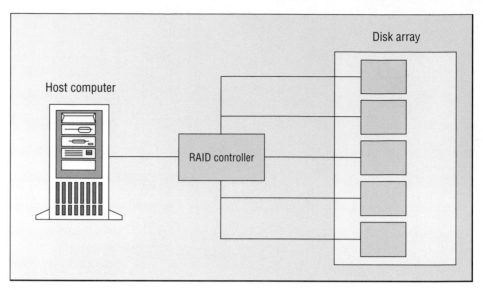

Disk array

Host computer

RAID controller

Figure 10.24   **Components of a RAID storage system.**

enables an array of disks to appear as one large disk to the DBMS. For very high performance, a RAID controller can control as many as 90 disks. Because of the controller, RAID storage requires no changes in applications and queries. However, the query optimization component may be changed to account for the effect of parallel processing on access plan evaluation.

Striping is an important concept for RAID storage. Striping involves the allocation of physical records to different disks. A stripe is the set of physical records that can be read or written in parallel. Normally, a stripe contains a set of adjacent physical records. Figure 10.25 depicts an array of four disks that allows the reading or writing of four physical records in parallel.

To utilize RAID storage, a number of architectures have emerged. The architectures, known as RAID-0 through RAID-6, support parallel processing with varying amounts of performance and reliability. Reliability is an important issue because the mean time between failures (a measure of disk drive reliability) decreases as the number of disk drives increases. To combat reliability concerns, RAID architectures incorporate redundancy and error-correcting codes. For most purposes, two RAID architectures dominate the other architectures:

- **RAID-1:** involves a full mirror or redundant array of disks to improve reliability. Each physical record is written to both disk arrays in parallel. Read operations from separate queries can access a disk array in parallel to improve performance across queries. RAID-1 involves the most storage overhead as compared to other RAID architectures.

- **RAID-5:** uses both data and error-correcting pages (known as parity pages) to improve reliability. Read operations can be performed in parallel on stripes. Write operations involve a data page and an error-correcting page on another disk. To reduce disk contention, the error-correcting pages are randomly located across disks. RAID-5 uses storage space more efficiently than RAID-1 but can involve slower write times because of the error-correcting pages. Thus, RAID-1 is often preferred for highly volatile parts of a database.

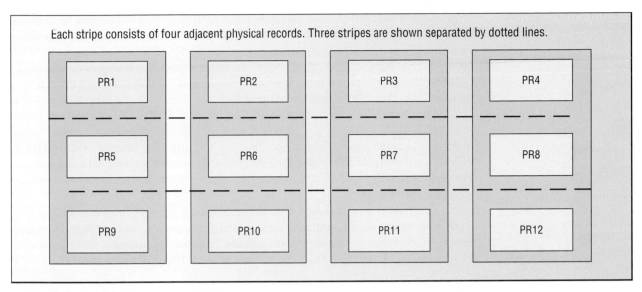

Each stripe consists of four adjacent physical records. Three stripes are shown separated by dotted lines.

Figure 10.25   **Striping in RAID storage systems.**

10.6.4 Other Ways to Improve Performance

There are a number of other ways to improve database performance that are related to a specific kind of processing. For transaction processing (Chapter 13), you can add computing capacity (faster and more processors, memory, and hard disk) and make trade-offs in transaction design. For data warehouses (Chapter 14), you can add computing capacity and design new tables with derived data. For distributed database processing (Chapter 15), you can allocate processing and data to various computing locations. Data can be allocated by partitioning a table vertically (column subset) and horizontally (row subset) to locate data close to its usage. These design choices are discussed in the respective chapters in Part 3.

In addition to tuning performance for specific processing requirements, you also can improve performance by utilizing options specific to a DBMS. For example, most DBMSs have options for file structures that can improve performance. You must carefully study the specific DBMS to understand these options. It may take several years of experience and specialized education to understand options of a particular DBMS. However, the payoff of increased salary and demand for your knowledge can be worth the study.

CLOSING THOUGHTS

This chapter has described the nature of the physical database design process and details about the inputs, environment, and design decisions. Physical database design involves details closest to the operating system such as movement of physical records. The objective of physical database design is to minimize certain computing resources (physical record accesses and processing effort) without compromising the meaning of the database. Physical database design is a difficult process because the inputs can be difficult to specify, the environment is complex, and the number of choices can be overwhelming.

To improve your proficiency in performing physical database design, this chapter described details about the inputs and the environment of physical database design. This chapter described table profiles and application profiles as inputs that must be specified in sufficient detail to achieve an efficient design. The environment consists of file structures and the query optimization component of the DBMS. For file structures, this chapter described characteristics of sequential, hash, and Btree file structures used by many DBMSs. For query optimization, this chapter described the tasks of query optimization and tips to produce better optimization results.

After establishing the background for the physical database design process, the inputs, and the environment, this chapter described decisions about index selection, denormalization, and record formatting. For index selection, this chapter described trade-offs between retrieval and update applications and presented rules for selecting indexes. For denormalization and data formatting, this chapter presented a number of situations when they are useful.

This chapter concludes the database development process. After completing these steps, you should have an efficient table design that represents the needs of an organization. To complete your understanding of the database development process, Chapter 11 provides a detailed case study to apply the ideas in Part 2 of this book.

REVIEW CONCEPTS

- Relationship between physical records and logical records.
- Objective of physical database design.
- Difficulties of physical database design.
- Level of detail in table and application profiles.
- Histograms to specify column distributions.
- Characteristics of sequential, hash, and Btree file structures.
- Possible meanings of the letter "B" in the name Btree: balanced, bushy, block-oriented.
- Tasks of data language translation.
- The usage of cost formulas and table profiles to evaluate access plans.
- The importance of table profiles with sufficient detail for access plan evaluation.
- The difference between clustered and nonclustered indexes.
- Trade-offs in selecting indexes.
- Index selection rules to avoid poor index choices.
- Denormalization to improve join performance.
- Record formatting to reduce physical record accesses and improve query performance.
- RAID storage to provide parallel processing for retrievals and updates.
- RAID architectures to provide parallel processing with high reliability.

QUESTIONS

1. What is the difference between a physical record access and a logical record access?

2. Why is it difficult to know when a logical record access results in a physical record access?

3. What is the objective of physical database design?

4. What computing resources are constraints rather than being part of the objective of physical database design?

5. What are the contents of table profiles?

6. What are the contents of application profiles?

7. Describe two ways to specify distributions of columns used in table and application profiles.

8. What is a file structure?

9. What is the difference between a primary and a secondary file structure?

10. Describe the uses of sequential files for sequential search, range search, and key search.

11. What is the purpose of a hash function?

12. Describe the uses of hash files for sequential search, range search, and key search.

13. What is the difference between a static hash file and a dynamic hash file?

14. Define the terms balanced, bushy, and block-oriented as they relate to Btree files.

15. Briefly explain the use of node splits and concatenations in the maintenance of Btree files.

16. What does it mean to say that Btrees have logarithmic search cost?

17. What is the difference between a Btree and a B+tree?

18. What happens in the query transformation phase of database language translation?

19. What is an access plan?

20. How are access plans evaluated in query optimization?

21. Why does the uniform value assumption sometimes lead to poor access plans?

22. What does it mean to bind a query?

23. What is the difference between a clustered and a nonclustered index?

24. When is a nonclustered index useful?

25. When is a clustered index useful?

26. What is the relationship of index selection to query optimization?

27. What are the trade-offs in index selection?

28. Why is index selection difficult?

29. When should you use the index selection rules?

30. Why should you be careful about denormalization?

31. Identify two situations when denormalization may be useful.

32. What is RAID storage?

33. For what kinds of applications can RAID storage improve performance?

34. What is striping in relation to RAID storage?

35. What are the advantages and disadvantages of RAID-1 versus RAID-5?

36. What are trade-offs in storing derived data?

37. What processing environments also involve physical database design decisions?

PROBLEMS

ORDER

Besides the problems presented here, the case study in Chapter 11 provides additional practice. To supplement the examples in this chapter, Chapter 11 provides a complete database design case including physical database design.

1. Use the following data to perform the indicated calculations. Show formulas that you used to perform the calculations.

> Row size = 100 bytes
> Number of rows = 100,000
> Primary key size = 6 bytes
> Physical record size = 4,096 bytes
> Pointer size = 4 bytes
> Floor(X) is the largest integer less than or equal to X.
> Ceil(X) is the smallest integer greater than or equal to X.

1.1. Calculate the number of rows that can fit in a physical record. Assume that only complete rows can be stored (use the Floor function).

1.2. Calculate the number of physical records necessary for a sequential file. Assume that physical records are filled to capacity except for perhaps the last physical record (use the Ceil function).

1.3. If an unordered sequential file is used, calculate the number of physical record accesses on the average to retrieve a row with a specified key value.

1.4. If an ordered sequential file is used, calculate the number of physical record accesses on the average to retrieve a row with a specified key value. Assume that the key exists in the file.

1.5. Calculate the average number of physical record accesses to find a key that does not exist in an unordered sequential file and an ordered sequential file.

1.6. Calculate the number of physical records for a static hash file. Assume that each physical record of the hash file is 70 percent full.

1.7. Calculate the maximum branching factor on a node in a Btree. Assume that each record in a Btree consists of <key value, pointer> pairs.

1.8. Using your calculation from problem 1.7, calculate the maximum height of a Btree index.

1.9. Calculate the maximum number of physical record accesses to find a node in the Btree with a specific key value.

2. Answer query optimization questions for the following SQL statement:

```
SELECT * FROM Customer
  WHERE CustCity = 'Denver' AND CustBalance > 5000
    AND CustState = 'CO'
```

2.1. Show four access plans for this query assuming that nonclustered indexes exist on the columns *CustCity, CustBalance,* and *CustState.* There is also a clustered index on the primary key column, *CustNo.*

2.2. Using the uniform value assumption, estimate the fraction of rows that satisfy the condition on *CustBalance.* The smallest balance is 0 and the largest balance is $10,000.

2.3. Using the following histogram, estimate the fraction of rows that satisfy the condition on *CustBalance.*

Histogram for *CustBalance*

Range	Rows
0–100	1,000
101–250	950
251–500	1,050
501–1,000	1,030
1,001–2,000	975
2,001–4,500	1,035
4,501–	1,200

3. Answer query optimization questions for the following SQL statement:

```
SELECT OrdNo, OrdDate, Vehicle.ModelNo
  FROM Customer, Order, Vehicle
  WHERE CustBalance > 5000
    AND Customer.CustNo = Vehicle.CustNo
    AND Vehicle.SerialNo = Order.SerialNo
```

3.1. List the possible orders to join the *Customer, Order,* and *Vehicle* tables.

3.2. For one of these join orders, make an access plan. Assume that Btree indexes exist for only the primary keys, *Customer.CustNo, Order.OrdNo,* and *Vehicle.SerialNo.*

4. For the following tables and SQL statements, select indexes that balance retrieval and update requirements. For each table, justify your choice using the rules discussed in Section 10.5.3.

Customer(<u>CustNo,</u> CustName, CustCity, CustState, CustZip, CustBal)
Order(<u>OrdNo,</u> OrdDate, CustNo)
    FOREIGN KEY CustNo REFERENCES Customer
OrdLine(<u>OrdNo, ProdNo,</u> OrdQty)
    FOREIGN KEY OrdNo REFERENCES Order
    FOREIGN KEY ProdNo REFERENCES Product
Product(<u>ProdNo,</u> ProdName, ProdColor, ProdPrice)

SQL Statement	Frequency
1. INSERT INTO Customer . . .	100/day
2. INSERT INTO Product . . .	100/month
3. INSERT INTO Order . . .	3,000/day
4. INSERT INTO OrdLine . . .	9,000/day
5. DELETE Product WHERE ProdNo = $X	100/year
6. DELETE Customer WHERE CustNo = $X	1,000/year
7. SELECT * FROM Order, Customer WHERE OrdNo = $X AND Order.CustNo = Customer.CustNo	300/day
8. SELECT * FROM OrdLine, Product WHERE OrdNo = $X AND OrdLine.ProdNo = Product.ProdNo	300/day

9. SELECT * FROM Customer, Order, OrdLine, Product
   WHERE CustName = $X AND OrdDate = $Y AND Customer.CustNo = Order.CustNo
   AND Order.OrdNo = OrdLine.OrdNo AND Product.ProdNo = OrdLine.ProdNo
	500/day

10. UPDATE OrdLine SET OrdQty = $X WHERE OrdNo = $Y	300/day
11. UPDATE Product SET ProdPrice = $X WHERE ProdNo = $Y	300/month

4.1. For the *Customer* table, what columns are good choices for the clustered index? Nonclustered indexes?

4.2. For the *Product* table, what columns are good choices for the clustered index? Nonclustered indexes?

4.3. For the *Order* table, what columns are good choices for the clustered index? Nonclustered indexes?

4.4. For the *OrdLine* table, what columns are good choices for the clustered index? Nonclustered indexes?

5. Indexes on combinations of columns are not as useful as indexes on individual columns. Consider a combination index on two columns, *CustState* and *CustCity*, where *CustState* is the primary ordering and *CustCity* is the secondary ordering. For what kinds of conditions can the index be used? For what kinds of conditions is the index not useful?

6. For query 9 in problem 4, list the possible join orders considered by the query optimization component.

7. For the following tables of a financial planning database, identify possible uses of denormalization and derived data to improve performance. In addition, identify denormalization and derived data already appearing in the tables. The tables track financial assets held and trades made by customers. A trade involves a purchase or sale of a specified quantity of an asset by a customer. Assets include stocks and bonds. The *Holding* table contains the <u>net</u> quantity of each asset held by a customer. For example, if a customer has purchased 10,000 shares of IBM and sold 4,000, the *Holding* table shows a net quantity of 6,000. A frequent query is to list the most recent valuation for each asset held by a customer. The most recent valuation is the net quantity of the asset times the most recent price.

Customer(<u>CustNo,</u> CustName, CustAddress, CustCity, CustState, CustZip, CustPhone)

Asset(<u>AssetNo,</u> SecName, LastClose)

Stock(<u>AssetNo,</u> OutShares, IssShares)

Bond(<u>AssetNo,</u> BondRating, FacValue)

PriceHistory(<u>AssetNo,</u> <u>PHistDate,</u> PHistPrice)

　　FOREIGN KEY AssetNo REFERENCES Asset

Holding(<u>CustNo,</u> <u>AssetNo,</u> NetQty)

　　FOREIGN KEY CustNo REFERENCES Customer

　　FOREIGN KEY AssetNo REFERENCES Asset

Trade(<u>TradeNo,</u> CustNo, AssetNo, TrdQty, TrdPrice, TrdDate, TrdType, TrdStatus)

　　FOREIGN KEY CustNo REFERENCES Customer

　　FOREIGN KEY AssetNo REFERENCES Asset

8. Rewrite the following SQL statement to improve its performance on most DBMSs. Use the tips in Section 10.4.2 to rewrite the statement. The Access SQL statement uses the financial trading database shown in problem 7. The purpose of the statement is to list the customer number and the name of customers and the sum of the amount of their completed October 1999 buy trades. The amount of a trade is the quantity (number of shares) times the price per share. A customer should be in the result if the sum of the amount of his/her completed October 2000 buy trades exceeds by 25 percent the sum of the amount of his/her completed September 2000 buy trades.

```
SELECT Customer.CustNo, CustName,
       SUM(TrdQty * TrdPrice) AS SumTradeAmt
  FROM Customer, Trade
  WHERE Customer.CustNo = Trade.CustNo
    AND TrdType = 'BUY'
    AND TrdDate BETWEEN #10/1/2000# AND
        #10/31/2000#
  GROUP BY Customer.CustNo, CustName
  HAVING SUM(TrdQty * TrdPrice) >
    ( SELECT 1.25 * SUM(TrdQty * TrdPrice) FROM Trade
       WHERE TrdDate BETWEEN #9/1/2000# AND
             #9/30/2000#
         AND TrdType = 'BUY'
         AND Trade.CustNo = Customer.CustNo )
```

REFERENCES FOR FURTHER STUDY

The subject of physical database design can be much more detailed and mathematical than described in this chapter. For a more detailed description of file structures and physical database design, consult computer science books such as Elmasri and Navathe (1999) and Teorey and Fry (1982). For detailed tutorials about query optimization, consult Jarke and Koch (1984) and Mannino, Chu, and Sager (1988). Finkelstein, Schkolnick, and Tiberio (1988) describe DBDSGN, an index selection tool for SQL/DS, an IBM relational DBMS. For practical descriptions of physical database design, consult Gibson, Hughes, and Remington (1989), Rodgers (1989), Schumacher (1994), and Viehman (1994). Books on physical database design for specific DBMSs include Ensor and Stevenson (1997) and Gillette, Muench, and Tabaka (1996). Benchmarks of DBMSs and related products can be found at http://www.segue.com/ and http://www.csrad.com/.

Appendix 10.A   **SQL2 Syntax Summary**

This appendix summarizes the SQL2 syntax for the CREATE INDEX statement presented in the chapter. The conventions used in the syntax notation are identical to those used at the end of Chapter 2.

CREATE INDEX and DROP INDEX Statements

```
CREATE [ UNIQUE ] INDEX IndexName ON TableName
<Sort-Specification>: Column Name [ { ASC | DESC } ]
DROP INDEX Index Name
```

Chapter 11

Database Design for Student Loan Limited

Learning Objectives

This chapter applies the knowledge and skills described in the other chapters of Part 2 to a moderate-size case. After this chapter, the student should have acquired the following knowledge and skills:

- Perform view modeling and view integration for a comparable case.

- Refine an ERD using conversion and normalization for a comparable case.

- Estimate a workload on a table design of moderate size.

- Perform index selection for a comparable case.

OVERVIEW

The other chapters of Part 2 have provided knowledge and techniques about the phases of the database development process. You learned about the Entity Relationship Model (Chapter 7), refining a conceptual schema through conversion and normalization (Chapters 7 and 8), the view modeling and view integration processes for large conceptual data modeling efforts (Chapter 9), and finding an efficient implementation (Chapter 10). In addition, you learned about the broad context of database development (Chapter 6). This chapter applies the specific design techniques of other chapters to a moderate-size case. By carefully following the case and its solution, you should reinforce your design skills, gain insights about the database development process, and obtain a model for database development of comparable cases.

This chapter presents a case derived from discussions with information systems professionals of a large commercial processor of student loans. Servicing student loans is a rather complex business due to the many different kinds of loans, changing government regulations, and numerous billing conditions. To adapt the case for this chapter, many details have been omitted. The database for the actual information system is more than 150 tables. The case presented here preserves the essential concepts of student loan processing but is understandable in one chapter. You should find the case challenging and informative. You might even learn how to have your student loans forgiven!

11.1 CASE DESCRIPTION

This section describes the purpose and environment of student loan processing as well as the work flow of a proposed system for Student Loan Limited. In addition to the details in this section, Appendix 11.A contains a glossary of fields contained in the forms and reports.

11.1.1 Overview

The Guaranteed Student Loan (GSL) program was created to help students pay for their college education. GSL loans are classified according to subsidy status: (1) <u>subsidized,</u> in which the federal government pays interest accruing during school years, and (2) <u>unsubsidized,</u> in which the federal government does not pay interest accruing during school years. On unsubsidized loans, the interest accruing during school years is added to the principal when repayment begins. Repayment of loans begins about six months after separation from school. A given student can receive multiple GSL loans with each loan possibly having a different interest rate and subsidy status.

To support the GSL program, different organizations may play the role of lender, guarantor, and service provider. Students apply for loans from <u>lenders,</u> including banks, savings and loans, and credit unions. The U.S. Department of Education makes loans possible by guaranteeing repayment if certain conditions are met. Lenders ensure that applicants are eligible for the GSL program. The <u>service provider</u> tracks student status, calculates repayment schedules, and collects payments. The <u>guarantor</u> ensures that loans are serviced properly by monitoring the work of the service provider. If a loan enters claim (nonpayment status) and the loan has not been serviced according to Department of Education guidelines, the guarantor can become liable. To reduce risk, lenders usually do not service or guarantee their loans. Instead, lenders typically contract with a service provider and guarantor.

Student Loan Limited is a leading service provider for GSL and other types of student loans. Student Loan Limited currently uses a legacy system with older file technology. They want to switch to a client–server architecture using a relational DBMS. The new architecture should allow them to respond to new regulations easier as well as to pursue new business such as the direct lending program.

11.1.2 Flow of Work

Processing of student loans follows the pattern shown in Figure 11.1. Students apply for a loan from a lender. In the approval process, the lender usually identifies a guarantor. If the loan is approved, the student signs a promissory note that describes the interest rate and the repayment terms. After the promissory note is signed, the lender sends a loan

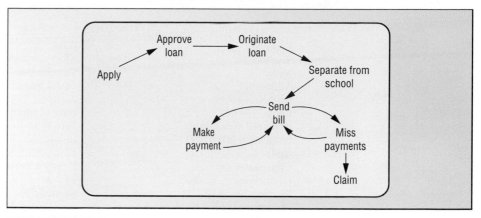

Figure 11.1　Loan processing work flow.

origination form to Student Loan Limited. Student Loan Limited then disburses funds as specified in the loan origination form. Typically, funds are disbursed in each period of an academic year.

Upon separating from school (graduation or leaving school), the repayment process begins. Shortly after a student separates from school, Student Loan Limited sends a disclosure letter. A disclosure letter provides an estimate of the monthly payment required to repay an outstanding loan by the end of the payment period. The student receives one disclosure letter per note except if the notes have been consolidated into a single note. Notes are consolidated if the interest rate, subsidy status, and repayment period are similar.

About six months after separation, Student Loan Limited sends the first bill. For convenience, Student Loan Limited sends one consolidated statement even if the student has multiple outstanding loans. With most students, Student Loan Limited processes periodic bills and payments until all loans are repaid. If a student becomes delinquent, collection activities begin. If collection is successful, the student returns to the billing-payment cycle. Otherwise, the loan enters claim (default) and may be given to a collection agency.

Loan Origination Form

The Loan Origination Form, an electronic document sent from a lender, triggers involvement of Student Loan Limited. Figures 11.2 and 11.3 show sample forms with student, loan, and disbursement data. An origination form only includes one loan identified by a unique loan number. Each time a loan is approved, the lender sends a new loan origination form. The disbursement method can be electronic funds transfer (EFT) or check. If the disbursement method is EFT (Figure 11.2), the routing number, the account number, and the financial institution must be given. The disbursement plan shows the date of disbursement, the amount, and any fees. Note that the total amount of the loan is the sum of the amounts disbursed plus the fees. Fees typically amount to 6 percent of the loan.

Disclosure Letter

After a student graduates but before repayment begins, Student Loan Limited is required to send disclosure letters for each outstanding loan. Typically, disclosure letters are sent about 60 days after a student separates from school. In some cases, more than one disclosure letter per loan may be sent at different times. A disclosure letter includes fields

Loan Origination Form

Loan No. L101
Student No.
Name
Address
City, State, Zip
Phone (341) 555-2222
Expected Graduation
Institution ID: U100
Address
City, State, Zip
Disbursement Method
Routing No. R10001
Disbursement Bank
Lender No. LE100
Guarantor No. G100
Note Value: $10000

Date   6 Sept. 2001
S100
Sam Student
15400 Any Street
Anytown, USA 00999
Date of Birth 11/11/1981
May 2002
Institution Name: University of Colorado
1250 14th Street, Suite 700
Denver CO 80217
EFT **X**   *Check*
Account No.   A111000
Any Student Bank USA
Lender Name Any Bank USA
Guarantor Name Any Guarantor USA
Subsidized: Yes   **Rate:** 8.5%

Disbursement Plan

Date	Amount	Origination Fee	Guarantee Fee
30 Sept 2001	$3,200	$100	$100
30 Dec 2001	$3,200	$100	$100
30 Mar 2002	$3,000	$100	$100

Figure 11.2   Sample Loan Origination Form.

Loan Origination Form

Loan No. L100
Student No.
Name
Address
City, State, Zip
Phone (341) 555-2222
Expected Graduation
Institution ID: U100
Address
City, State, Zip
Disbursement Method
Routing No. —
Disbursement Bank
Lender No. LE100
Guarantor No. G100
Note Value: $10000

Date   7 Sept. 2000
S100
Sam Student
15400 Any Street
Anytown, USA 00999
Date of Birth 11/11/1981
May 2002
Institution Name: University of Colorado
1250 14th Street, Suite 700
Denver CO 80217
EFT   *Check* **X**
Amount No. —
—
Lender Name Any Bank USA
Guarantor Name   Any Guarantor USA
Subsidized: No   **Rate:** 8.0%

Disbursement Plan

Date	Amount	Origination Fee	Guarantee Fee
29 Sept 2000	$3,200	$100	$100
30 Dec 2000	$3,200	$100	$100
28 Mar 2001	$3,000	$100	$100

Figure 11.3   Sample Loan Origination Form.

for the amount of the loan, amount of the monthly payment, number of payments, interest rate, total finance charge, and due date of the first and last payments. In the sample disclosure letter (Figure 11.4), the fields in the form letter are underlined. Student Loan Limited is required to retain copies of disclosure letters in case the guarantor needs to review the loan processing of a student.

Statement of Account

About six months after a student separates, Student Loan Limited sends the first bill. For most students, additional bills follow monthly. In Student Loan Limited vocabulary, a bill is known as a statement of account. Figures 11.5 and 11.6 show sample statements. The top half of a statement contains the unique statement number, amount due, due date, amount paid, and payment method (EFT or check). If the payment method is check (Figure 11.5), the student returns the statement to Student Loan Limited with the

---

Disclosure Letter

1 July 2002
Subject: Loan L101

Dear Mr. Student,

According to our records, your guaranteed student loan enters repayment status in September 2002. The total amount that you borrowed was $10,000. Your payment schedule includes 120 payments with an interest rate of 8.5%. Your estimated finance charge is $4,877.96. Your first payment will be due on October 31, 2002. Your monthly payment will be $246.37. Your last payment is due September 30, 2012.

Sincerely,

Anne Administrator, Student Loan Limited

Figure 11.4   Sample disclosure letter.

Statement of Account

Statement No.	B100	**Date**	1 Oct. 2002
Student No.	S100	**Name**	Sam Student
Street	123 Any Street	**Zip**	00011
City	Any City	**State**	Any State
Amount Due	$246.37	**Due Date**	31 Oct 2002
Payment Method	*Check* **X** *EFT*	**Amount Enclosed**	

Loan Summary

Loan No.	**Balance**	**Rate**
L100	$10,000	8.5%
L101	$10,000	8.2%

For Office Use Only

Date Paid:

Figure 11.5   Sample statement of account for check payment.

Statement of Account

Statement No.	B101	**Date**	1 Nov. 2002
Student No.	S100	**Name**	Sam Student
Street	123 Any Street	**Zip**	00011
City	Any City	**State**	Any State
Amount Due	$246.37	**Due Date**	30 Nov. 2002
Payment Method	*Check* *EFT* **X**	**Amount Enclosed**	

Note: $246.37 will be deducted from your account on 30 Nov 2002

Loan Summary

Loan No.	**Balance**	**Rate**
L100	$9,946.84	8.5%
L101	$9,944.34	8.2%

For Office Use Only

Date Paid:

Figure 11.6   Sample statement of account for EFT payment.

check enclosed. In this case, the amount paid is completed either by the student when the bill is returned or by data entry personnel of Student Loan Limited when the statement is processed. If the payment method is EFT (Figure 11.6), the amount paid is shown on the statement along with the date that the transfer will be made. The date paid is completed by Student Loan Limited when a payment is received. The lower half of a statement lists the status of each loan. For each loan, the loan number, outstanding balance, and interest rate are shown.

After a payment is received, Student Loan Limited applies the principal amount of the payment to outstanding loan balances. The payment is apportioned among each outstanding loan according to an associated payment schedule. If a student pays more than the specified amount, the extra amount may be applied in a number of ways such as the loan with highest interest rate is reduced first or all outstanding loans are reduced equally. The method of applying extra amounts is determined by Department of Education policy. As with most government policies, it is subject to change. Applications of a payment to loan balances can be seen by comparing two consecutive statements. Figures 11.5 and 11.6 show that $53.16 of the October 2002 payment was applied to loan L100.

Loan Activity Report

After the end of each year, Student Loan Limited sends each student a report summarizing all loan activity. For each loan, the report (Figure 11.7) shows the total payments received, the amount applied to reduce the principal, and the interest paid. Student Loan Limited is required to retain copies of loan activity reports in case the guarantor needs to review the loan processing of a student.

New Technology

To reduce paper, Student Loan Limited is interested in imaging the documents (disclosure letters and loan activity reports) required by guarantors. After imaging the documents, they would like to store recent documents in the student loan database and nonrecent documents in archival storage.

Loan Activity Report

		Date	1 Feb. 2003
Student No.	S100	Name	Sam Student
Street	123 Any Street	Zip	00011
City	Any City	State	Any State

Payment Summary for 2002

Loan No.	Beg. Balance	Principal	Interest	End Balance
L100	$10,000	160.60	211.37	9839.40
L101	$10,000	168.12	203.85	9831.88

For Office Use Only

Date Paid:

Figure 11.7   Sample loan activity report.

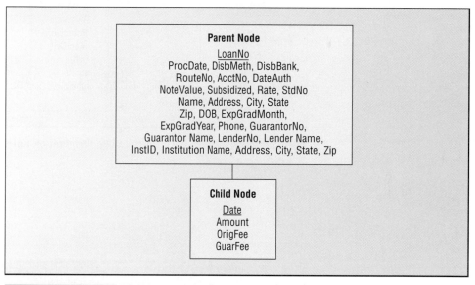

Figure 11.8   Structure of the Loan Origination Form.

11.2 CONCEPTUAL DATA MODELING

The conceptual data modeling phases use the incremental integration approach because the case is not too large and the forms are related. Incremental integration begins with the loan origination form because it triggers involvement of Student Loan Limited with a loan.

11.2.1 ERD for the Loan Origination Form

The Loan Origination Form contains two nodes, as shown in Figure 11.8. The child node contains the repeating disbursement fields. The *Loan* entity type is the center of the ERD, as shown in Figure 11.9. The surrounding entity types (*Guarantor, Lender, Institution,* and *Student*) and associated relationships are derived from the parent node. The minimum cardinality is 0 from *Loan* to *Guarantor* because some loans do not have a guarantor (lender

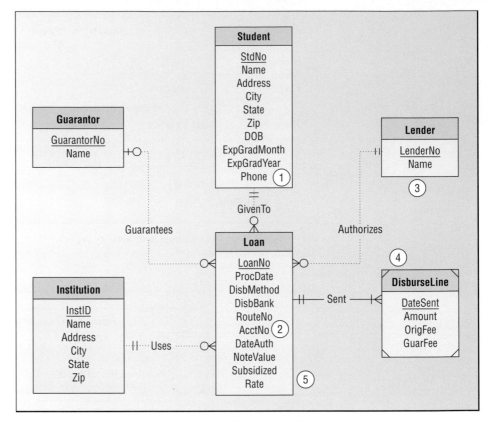

| Figure 11.9 | ERD for the Loan Origination Form. |

| TABLE 11–1 | Assumptions for the ERD in Figure 11.9 |

Annotation Number	Explanation
1	The expected graduation fields can be combined into one field or kept as two fields.
2	Routing number (*RouteNo*), account number (*AcctNo*), and disbursement bank (*DisbBank*) are required if the disbursement method is EFT. Otherwise, they are not used.
3	There would probably be other data about lenders and guarantors that is stored. Because the form only shows the identifying number and name, the ERD does not include extra fields.
4	*DisburseLine* is identification dependent on *Loan*. Because *DisburseLine.DateSent* is a local key, there cannot be two disbursements of the same loan on the same date. The primary key of *DisburseLine* is a concatenation of *LoanNo* and *DateSent*.
5	The sum of the amount, the origination fee, and the guarantee fee in the disbursement plan should equal the note value.

performs role). The *DisburseLine* entity type and associated relationship are derived from the child node. Table 11–1 shows assumptions corresponding to the annotations in Figure 11.9.

11.2.2 Incremental Integration after Adding the Disclosure Letter

The disclosure letter contains only a single node (Figure 11.10) because it has no repeating groups. Figure 11.11 shows the integrated ERD, with corresponding assump-

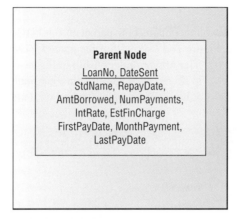

Figure 11.10   **Structure of the disclosure letter.**

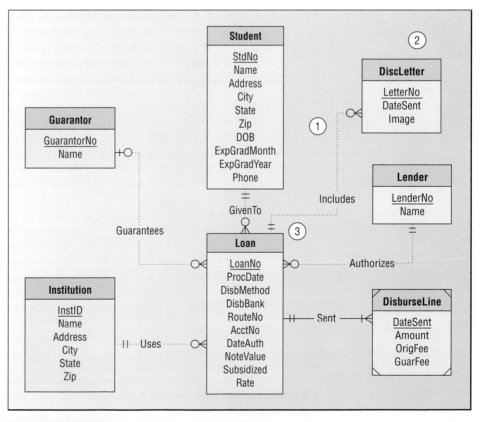

Figure 11.11   **ERD after adding the disclosure letter.**

tions shown in Table 11–2. The ERD in Figure 11.11 assumes that images can be stored in the database. Therefore, the particular fields of a disclosure letter are not stored. The unique *LetterNo* field has been added as a convenient identifier of a disclosure letter. If images cannot be stored in the database, some of the fields in the disclosure letter may need to be stored because they are difficult to compute.

11.2.3 Incremental Integration after Adding the Statement of Account

The statement of account contains both parent and child nodes (Figure 11.12) because it has a repeating group. Figure 11.13 shows the integrated ERD with corresponding assumptions shown in Table 11–3. The *Applied* relationship in Figure 11.13 represents the parent-child relationship in the form hierarchy. The minimum cardinality is 0 from *Loan* to *Statement* because a loan does not have any amounts applied until after it enters payment status.

TABLE 11–2	Assumptions for the ERD in Figure 11.11

Annotation Number	Explanation
1	The relationship between *DiscLetter* and *Loan* allows multiple letters per loan. As stated in the case, multiple disclosure letters may be sent for the same loan.
2	The *Image* field contains a scanned image of the letter. The guarantor may require a copy of the letter if the loan is audited. As an alternative to storing the image, an indicator of the physical location could be stored if imaging technology is not used.
3	The minimum cardinality of 0 is needed because a payment plan is not created until a student has separated from school.

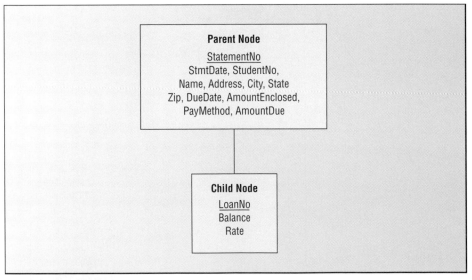

Parent Node

StatementNo
StmtDate, StudentNo,
Name, Address, City, State
Zip, DueDate, AmountEnclosed,
PayMethod, AmountDue

Child Node

LoanNo
Balance
Rate

Figure 11.12 Structure of the statement of account.

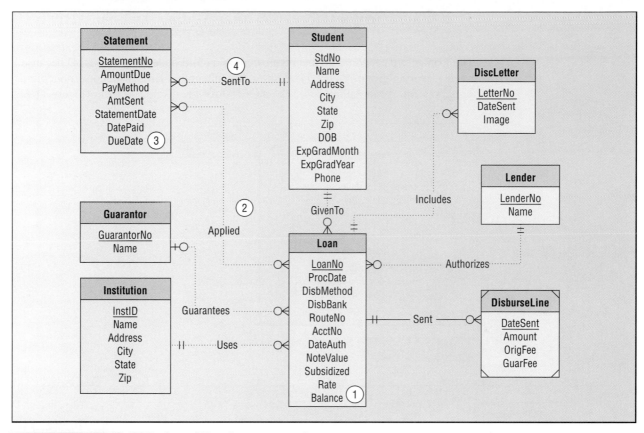

Figure 11.13	ERD after adding the statement of account.

TABLE 11–3 | Assumptions for the ERD in Figure 11.13

Annotation Number	Explanation
1	*Balance* is added as a field to reflect the loan summary on a statement. The balance reflects the last payment made on a loan.
2	The *Applied* relationship is created at the same time as the statement. However, the principal and interest fields are not updated until after a payment is received. The attributes (*Principal* and *Interest*) of the applied relationship are not shown in the diagram to reduce clutter.
3	If the payment method is EFT, other attributes such as routing number and account number might be needed in *Statement*. Since these attributes are not shown in a statement, they are omitted from the *Statement* entity type.
4	The *SentTo* relationship is redundant. It can be derived from the *Applied* and *GivenTo* relationships. If time to derive the *SentTo* relationship is not onerous, it can be dropped.

11.2.4 Incremental Integration after Adding the Loan Activity Report

The loan activity report contains both parent and child nodes (Figure 11.14) because it has a repeating group. Figure 11.15 shows the integrated ERD with corresponding assumptions shown in Table 11–4. Like the ERD for the disclosure letter (Figure 11.11),

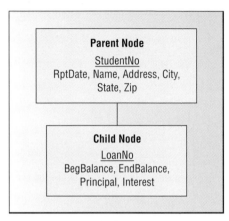

Figure 11.14   **Structure of the loan activity report.**

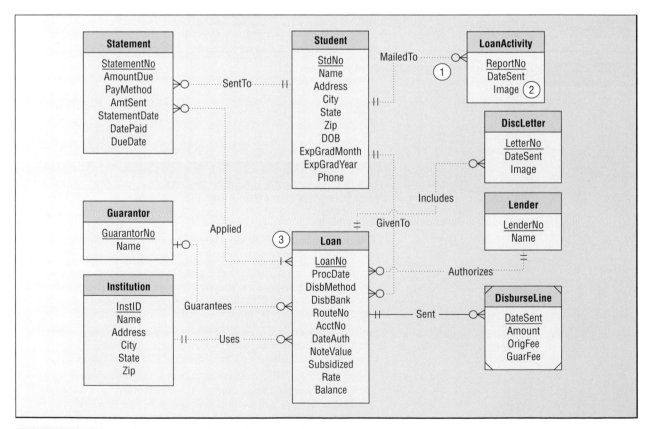

Figure 11.15   **ERD after adding the loan activity report.**

the ERD in Figure 11.15 assumes that images can be stored in the database. Therefore, the particular fields of a loan activity report are not stored. The unique *ReportNo* field has been added as a convenient identifier of an activity report. If images cannot be stored in the database, some of the fields in the loan activity report may need to be stored because they are difficult to compute.

11.3 REFINING THE CONCEPTUAL SCHEMA

After building a conceptual ERD, you refine it by applying conversion rules to produce an initial table design and using normalization rules to remove excessive redundancies from your initial table design. This section describes refinements of the conceptual ERD that produce a good table design for Student Loan Limited.

11.3.1 Schema Conversion

The conversion can be performed using the first four rules (Chapter 7) as depicted in Table 11–5. The optional 1-M relationship rule (Rule 5) could be applied to the *Guarantees* relationship. However, the number of loans without guarantors appears small so the

TABLE 11–4	Assumptions for the ERD in Figure 11.15

Annotation Number	Explanation
1	The *LoanActivity* entity type is not directly related to the *Loan* entity type because it is assumed that an activity report summarizes all loans of a student.
2	The *Image* field contains a scanned image of the report. The guarantor may require a copy of the report if the loan is audited. As an alternative to storing the image, an indicator of the physical location could be stored if imaging technology is not used.
3	To make the calculations easier, fields for annual principal and interest could be added to the *Loan* entity type. These fields would be updated after every payment is received. These fields should be considered during physical database design.

TABLE 11–5	Rules Used to Convert the ERD of Figure 11.15

Conversion Rule	Objects	Comments
Entity type rule	*Student, Statement, Loan, DiscLetter, LoanActivity, Lender, Guarantor, Institution, DisburseLine* tables	Primary keys in each table are identical to entity types except for *DisburseLine*
1-M relationship rule	*Loan.StdNo, Loan.GuarantorNo, Loan.LenderNo, LoanActivity.StdNo, DiscLetter.LoanNo, Statement.StdNo, DisburseLine.LoanNo, Loan.InstID,*	Foreign key columns and referential integrity constraints added
M-N relationship rule	*Applies* table	Combined primary key: *StatementNo, LoanNo*
Identification dependency rule	Primary key (*LoanNo, DateSent*)	*LoanNo* added to primary key of *DisburseLine* table

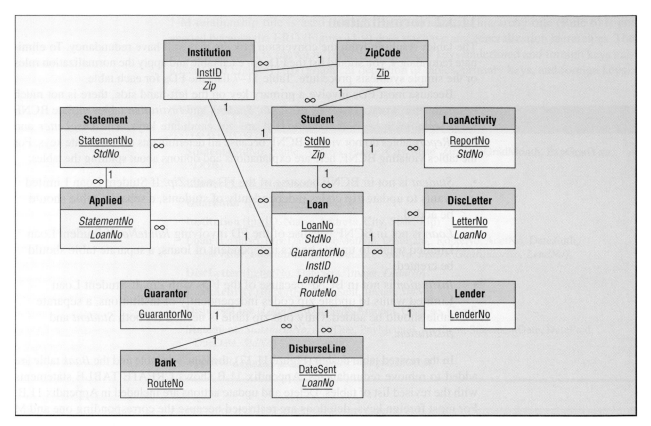

Figure 11.17 **Relational model diagram for the revised table design.**

meaning without the statement. The update action of most foreign keys was set to cascade to allow easy changing of primary key values.

11.4 PHYSICAL DATABASE DESIGN

After producing a good table design, you are ready to implement the database. This section describes physical database design decisions including index selection, derived data, and denormalization for the Student Loan Limited database. Before describing these decisions, table and application profiles are defined.

11.4.1 Application and Table Profiles

To clarify anticipated usage of the database, the documents described in Section 11.1 are split into database access applications as summarized in Table 11–8. Three separate applications are associated with the Loan Origination Form. Verifying data involves retrievals to ensure that the student, lender, institution, and guarantor exist. If a student does not exist, a new row is added. Creating a loan involves inserting a row in the *Loan* table and multiple rows in the *DisburseLine* table. For the other documents, there is an application to create the document and retrieve the document. For statements of account, there is also an application to update the *Applied* and *Loan* tables when payments are received.

To make physical database design decisions, the relative importance of applications must be specified. The frequencies in Table 11–9 assume 100,000 new loans per year

TABLE 11–8	**Application Characteristics**

Application	Tables	Conditions
Verify data (for loan origination)	Student, Lender, Institution, Guarantor	StdNo = $X; LenderNo = $Y; InstID = $Z; GuarantorNo = $W
Create loan (for loan origination)	Loan, DisburseLine	1 row inserted in Loan; multiple rows inserted in DisburseLine
Create student (for loan origination)	Student	1 row inserted
Create disclosure letter	Student, Loan, DiscLetter	Insert row in DiscLetter; retrieve rows from Student and Loan (LoanNo = $X)
Display disclosure letter	DiscLetter	LoanNo = $X
Create loan activity report	Student, Loan, LoanActivity, Applied, Statement	Insert row in LoanActivity; retrieve rows from Student (StdNo = $X) and Statement (DatePaid in past year)
Display loan activity report	LoanActivity	StdNo = $X
Create statement of account	Statement	1 row inserted in Statement; multiple rows inserted in Applied
Display statement of account	Statement, Student, Applied, Loan	StdNo = $X AND DateSent = $Y; sometimes using StatementNo = $Z
Apply payment	Applied, Statement, Loan	Applied rows updated; LoanNo = $X AND StatementNo = $Y; Balance updated in Loan table

TABLE 11–9	**Application Frequencies**

Application	Frequency	Comments
Verify data	100,000/year	Most activity at beginning of term
Create loan	100,000/year	Most activity at beginning of term
Create student	20,000/year	Most students are repeat
Create disclosure letter	50,000/year	Spread evenly throughout year
Display disclosure letter	5,000/year	Spread evenly throughout year
Create loan activity report	30,000/year	End-of-year processing
Display loan activity report	5,000/year	Spread evenly throughout year
Create statement of account	100,000/year	Once per month
Display statement of account	10,000/year	Spread evenly throughout year
Apply payment	100,000/year	Spread evenly throughout month

and 100,000 students in repayment per year. The loan origination applications and the statement of account applications dominate the workload. The coarse frequencies (per year) are sufficient to indicate the relative importance of applications. A finer specification (e.g., by month or day) may be needed to schedule work such as to arrange for batch processing instead of on-line processing. For example, applications involving loan origination forms may be processed in batch instead of on-line.

After defining the application profiles, table profiles can be defined. The volume of modification activity (inserts, updates, deletes) can help in the estimation of table profiles. In addition, you should use statistics from existing systems and interviews with key application personnel to help make the estimates. Table 11–10 provides an overview of the profiles. More detail about column distributions and relationship distributions can be added after the system is partially populated.

11.4.2 Index Selection

You can select indexes using the application profiles and the rules described in Chapter 10. To clarify the selection process, let us consider retrieval needs before manipulation needs. Recall that Rules 1 through 4 (Chapter 10) involve selection of indexes for retrieval needs. The following list discusses useful index choices for retrieval purposes.

- Indexes on the primary keys of the *Student, Lender, Guarantor, Institution, DiscLetter, LoanActivity, Statement,* and *Bank* tables support the verify loan, display disclosure letter, display activity report, and display statement of account applications.
- A nonclustering index on student name may be a good choice to support retrieval of the statements of account and the loan activity reports.
- To support joins, nonclustering indexes on foreign keys *Loan.StdNo, Statement.StdNo, Applied.LoanNo,* and *Applied.StatementNo* may be useful. For example, an index on *Loan.StdNo* facilitates joining the *Student* and the *Loan* tables when given a specific *StdNo* value.

TABLE 11–10	Table Profiles	

Table	Number of Rows	Column (Number of Unique Values)
Student	100,000	StdNo (PK), Name (99,000), Address (90,000), City (1,000), Zip (1,000), DOB (365), ExpGradMonth (12), ExpGradYear (10)
Loan	300,000	LoanNo (PK), ProcDate (350), DisbMethod (3), DisbBank (3,000), RouteNo (3,000), AcctNo (90,000), DateAuth (350), NoteValue (1,000), Subsidized (2), Rate (1,000), Balance (10,000), StdNo (100,000), InstID (2,000), GuarantorNo (100), LenderNo (2,000)
Institution	2,000	InstID (PK), Name (2,000), Address (2,000), City (500), State (50), Zip (500)
DiscLetter	1,000,000	LetterNo (PK), DateSent (350), Image (1,000,000), LoanNo (300,000)
Statement	2,000,000	StatementNo (PK), AmtDue (100,000), PayMethod (3), AmtSent (200,000), StatementDate (350), DatePaid (350), DueDate (350), StdNo (100,000)
Guarantor	100	GuarantorNo (PK), Name (100)
Bank	3,000	RouteNo (PK), DisbBank (3,000)
DisburseLine	900,000	LoanNo (300,000), DateSent (350), Amount (5,000), OrigFee (5,000), GuarFee (5,000)
Applied	6,000,000	LoanNo (300,000), StatementNo (2,000,000), Principal (100,000), Interest (1,000,000)
ZipCode	1,000	Zip (PK), State (50)
Lender	2,000	LenderNo (PK), Name (2,000)

Because the *Applied* and *Loan* tables have lots of modifications, you should proceed with caution about indexes on the component fields. Some mitigating factors may offset the impact of the modification activity, however. The updates in the apply payment application do not affect the foreign key fields in these tables. Batch processing can reduce the impact of the insertions on the *Loan* and the *Applied* tables. The create loan and create statement of account applications may be performed in batch because loan origination forms are received in batch and statements of account can be produced in batch. If the indexes are too much of a burden for batch processing, it may be possible to destroy the indexes before batch processing and recreate them after finishing.

Table 11–11 shows index choices based on the previous discussion. The choices assume that foreign key indexes on the *Applied* and the *Loan* tables do not impede the insertion activity. Further investigation is probably necessary to determine the impact of indexes on insertions in the *Loan* and the *Applied* tables.

11.4.3 Derived Data and Denormalization Decisions

There are some derived data in the revised table design. The *NoteValue* column in the *Loan* table can be derived from columns in related rows of the *DisburseLine* table. The *DiscLetter* and the *LoanActivity* tables have lots of derived data in the *Image* columns. In all of these cases, the derived data seem justified because of the difficulty of computing it.

Denormalization may be useful for some foreign keys. If users frequently request the name along with the foreign key, denormalization may be useful for the foreign keys in the *Loan* table. For example, storing both *LenderNo* and *Lender.Name* in the *Loan* table violates BCNF, but it may reduce joins between the *Loan* and the *Lender* tables. The usage of the database should be monitored carefully to determine whether the *Loan*

TABLE 11–11	Index Selections for the Revised Table Design	
Column	*Index Kind*	*Rule*
Student.StdNo	Clustering	1
Student.Name	Nonclustering	3
Statement.StatementNo	Clustering	1
DiscLetter.LetterNo	Clustering	1
Loan.LoanNo	Clustering	1
Institution.InstID	Clustering	1
Guarantor.GuarantorNo	Clustering	1
Lender.LenderNo	Clustering	1
LoanActivity.ReportNo	Clustering	1
ZipCode.Zip	Clustering	1
Bank.RouteNo	Clustering	1
Statement.StdNo	Nonclustering	2
Loan.StdNo	Nonclustering	2
Applied.StatementNo	Clustering	2
Applied.LoanNo	Nonclustering	2

table should be denormalized by adding name columns in addition to the *LenderNo, GuarantorNo, InstID,* and *RouteNo* columns. If performance can be significantly improved, denormalization is a good idea because the *Lender, Guarantor, Institution,* and *Bank* tables are relatively static.

11.4.4 Other Implementation Decisions

There are a number of implementation decisions that involve the database development process. Because these decisions can have a large impact on the success of the loan servicing system, they are highlighted in this section.

• Smooth conversion from the old system to the new system is an important issue. One impediment to smooth conversion is processing volumes. Sometimes processing volumes in a new system can be much larger than in the old system. One way to alleviate potential performance problems is to execute the old and the new systems in parallel with more work shifted to the new system over time.

• An important part of the conversion process involves the old data. Converting the old data to the new format is not usually difficult except for data quality concerns. Sometimes, the poor quality of old data causes many rejections in the conversion process. The conversion process needs to be sensitive to rejecting poor-quality data because rejections can require extensive manual corrections.

• The size of the image data (loan activity reports and disclosure letters) can impact the performance of the database. Archival of the image data can improve performance for images that are infrequently retrieved.

CLOSING THOUGHTS

This chapter presented a moderate-size case study as a capstone of the database development process. The Student Loan Limited case described a significant subset of commercial student loan processing including accepting loans from lenders, notifying students of repayment, billing and processing payments, and reporting loan status. The case solution integrated techniques presented in the other chapters of Part 2. The solution depicted models and documentation produced in the conceptual modeling, logical database design, and physical database design phases.

After careful reading of this chapter, you are ready to tackle database development for a real organization. You are encouraged to work cases available through the textbook's website to solidify your understanding of the database development process. This case, although presenting you with a larger, more integrated problem than the other chapters in Part 2, is still not comparable to performing database development for a real organization. For a real organization, requirements are often open-ended, unclear, and continuous. Deciding on the database boundary and modifying the database design in response to requirement changes are crucial to long-term success. Monitoring the operation of the database allows you to improve performance as dictated by database usage. These challenges make database development a stimulating intellectual activity.

QUESTIONS

1. Why is the student application process not considered in the conceptual design phase?

2. Why is the incremental integration approach used to analyze the requirements?

3. Why is the Loan Origination Form analyzed first?

4. How is the note value field on the Loan Origination Form related to other data on the form?

5. Explain how the 1-M relationship in the Loan Origination Form is represented in the ERD of Figure 11.9.

6. What is the primary key of the *DisburseLine* entity type in Figure 11.9?

7. What data are contained in the image field of the *DiscLetter* entity type in Figure 11.11?

8. Explain how the 1-M relationship in the statement of account is represented in the ERD of Figure 11.13.

9. Why is the optional 1-M relationship rule (Rule 5 of Chapter 9) not used to convert the ERD of Figure 11.15?

10. Explain how the *Authorizes* relationship in Figure 11.15 is converted in Figure 11.16.

11. Explain how the identification dependency in Figure 11.15 is converted in Figure 11.16.

12. Explain how the *Applied* relationship in Figure 11.15 is converted in Figure 11.16.

13. Explain why the *DiscLetter* table is in BCNF.

14. Discuss a possible justification for violating BCNF with the *Student* table depicted in Table 11–7.

15. Why decompose the documents into multiple database applications as depicted in Table 11–8?

16. Explain the difference between batch and on-line processing of loan origination forms. Why is batch processing feasible for loan origination forms?

17. How can batch processing reduce the impact of maintaining indexes?

18. Explain why a clustered index is recommended for the *Applied.StatementNo* column.

19. Explain why a nonclustered index is recommended for the *Applied.LoanNo* column.

20. Why is it reasonable to store the *NoteValue* column in the *Loan* table rather than compute it when needed?

PROBLEMS

ORDER

The following problems involve extensions to the Student Loan Limited case. For additional cases of similar complexity, visit this book's website.

1. Use the optional 1-M relationship rule to convert the *Guarantees* relationship in Figure 11.15. Modify the relational model diagram in Figure 11.16 with the conversion change.

2. Simplify the ERD for the Loan Origination Form (Figure 11.9) by combining the *Loan* entity type with entity types associated with a loan (*Lender* and *Guarantor*).

What transformation (see Chapter 7) is used to combine the entity types? What transformation can be used to split bank attributes (*RouteNo* and *DisbBank*) into a separate entity type?

3. Modify the ERD in Figure 11.15 to reflect a change in the relationship between an activity report and associated loans of a student. The assumption in the case is that an activity report summarizes all of a student's loans. The new assumption is that an activity report may summarize only a subset of a student's loans.

4. Explain how denormalization can be used to combine the *LoanActivity* and the *Student* tables. The *DiscLetter* and the *Loan* tables.

5. Student Loan Limited has decided to enter the direct lending business. A direct lending loan is similar to a guaranteed student loan except there is neither a lender nor a guarantor for a direct lending loan. Due to the lack of a lender and a guarantor, there are no origination and guarantee fees. However, there is a service fee of about 3 percent per note value. In addition, a student may choose income-contingent repayment after separating from school. If a student chooses income-contingent repayment, the term of the loan and the payment amount are revised.

   (*a*) Modify the ERD in Figure 11.15 to reflect these new requirements.

   (*b*) Convert the ERD changes to a table design. Show your conversion result as a modification to the relational database diagram in Figure 11.16.

6. Student Loan Limited cannot justify the expense of imaging software and hardware. Therefore, the database design must be modified. The *Image* columns in the *DiscLetter* and the *LoanActivity* tables cannot be stored. Instead, the data stored in the image fields have to be stored or computed on demand.

   (*a*) Make recommendations for storing or computing the underlined fields in a disclosure letter. Modify the table design as necessary. Consider update and retrieval trade-offs in your recommendation.

   (*b*) Make recommendations for storing or computing the fields in a loan activity report. Modify the table design as necessary. Consider update and retrieval trade-offs in your recommendation.

Appendix 11.A   **Glossary of Form and Report Fields**

Appendix A provides a brief description of the fields found on the documents presented in Section 11.1. The field names are the captions from the associated document.

Loan Origination Form

- *Loan No.:* unique alphanumeric value that identifies a Loan Origination Form.
- *Date:* date that the Loan Origination Form was completed.
- *Student No.:* unique alphanumeric value that identifies a student.
- *Name:* name of student applying.
- *Address:* street address of student applying.
- *City, State, Zip:* concatenation of the student's city, state, and zip code.
- *Phone:* phone number including area code of the student applying.
- *Date of Birth:* birth date of student applying.
- *Expected Graduation:* month and year of expected graduation.
- *Institution ID:* federal identification number of the university or school.
- *Institution Name:* name of the university or school.
- *Address:* street address of the university or school.
- *City, State, Zip:* concatenation of the institution's city, state, and zip code.
- *Disbursement Method:* the method used to distribute funds to the student applicant; the values can be EFT (electronic funds transfer) or check.
- *Routing No.:* unique alphanumeric value that identifies a bank to disburse the funds; only used if disbursement method is EFT.
- *Account No.:* unique alphanumeric value that identifies an account of the student applicant; Account No. is only guaranteed to be unique within the student's bank (identified by routing number).
- *Disbursement Bank:* name of the bank from which the funds are disbursed; used only if the disbursement method is EFT.
- *Lender No.:* unique alphanumeric value that identifies the financial institution lending funds to the student applicant.
- *Lender Name:* name of the financial institution lending to the student applicant.
- *Guarantor No.:* unique alphanumeric value that identifies the financial institution ensuring the loan is properly serviced.
- *Guarantor Name:* name of the guaranteeing financial institution.
- *Note Value:* amount (in dollars) borrowed by the student applicant; note value is equal to the sum of the disbursement amounts and the fees (origination and guarantee).
- *Subsidized:* yes/no value indicating whether the government pays the interest while the student is in school.
- *Rate:* interest rate on the loan.
- *Date:* disbursement date; this is the Date field under Disbursement Plan.

- *Amount:* disbursement amount in dollars.
- *Origination Fee:* fee (in dollars) charged by the lending institution.
- *Guarantee Fee:* fee (in dollars) charged by the guarantor.

Disclosure Letter

- *Date:* date (1 July 2002) that the letter was sent to the student applicant.
- *Loan No.:* loan number of the associated loan.
- *Last Name:* title and last name (Mr. Student) of student applicant.
- *Repayment Starting:* month and year (September 2002) when loans enter repayment status.
- *Amount Borrowed:* sum of amounts ($10,000) borrowed in all loans covered by the payment plan.
- *Number of Payments:* estimated number of scheduled payments (120) to retire the amount borrowed.
- *Interest Rate:* weighted average percentage rate (8.28%) of loans covered by the payment plan.
- *Finance Charge:* estimated finance charge ($4,877.96) if amount borrowed is repaid according to the payment plan.
- *Payment Amount:* amount of payment ($246.37) required for each month (except perhaps for the last month). If a student does not pay this amount each month, the student will be in arrears unless other arrangements are made.
- *First Payment Date:* date (October 31, 1998) when the first payment is due if the payment plan is followed.
- *Last Payment Date:* date (September 30, 2012) when the last payment is due if the payment plan is followed.

Statement of Account

- *Statement No.:* unique alphanumeric value (B100) that identifies the statement of account form.
- *Date:* date that the statement was sent.
- *Student No.:* unique alphanumeric value that identifies a student.
- *Name:* name of student applying.
- *Address:* street address of student applicant (part of the mailing address).
- *City:* city of the student applicant (part of the mailing address).
- *State:* two-letter state abbreviation of the student applicant (part of the mailing address).
- *Zip:* five- or nine-digit zip code of the student applicant (part of the mailing address).
- *Amount Due:* amount (in dollars) that the student should remit.
- *Due Date:* date when repayment should be received by Student Loan Limited. A late penalty may be assessed if the amount is received at a later date.
- *Payment Method:* either check or EFT.
- *Amount Enclosed:* amount (in dollars) sent with the payment. If payment method is EFT, the applicant does not complete this field.
- *Loan No.:* unique alphanumeric value that identifies a loan of the applicant.
- *Balance:* outstanding loan balance (in dollars) before repayment.

- *Rate:* percentage interest rate applying to the loan.
- *Date Paid:* date when the payment is received; this field should be completed by staff at Student Loan Limited.

Loan Activity Report
- *Date:* date that the report was prepared.
- *Student No.:* unique alphanumeric value that identifies a student.
- *Name:* name of student applying.
- *Street:* street address of student applicant (part of the mailing address).
- *City:* city of the student applicant (part of the mailing address).
- *State:* two-letter state abbreviation of the student applicant (part of the mailing address).
- *Zip:* five- or nine-digit zip code of the student applicant (part of the mailing address).
- *Loan No.:* unique alphanumeric value that identifies a loan of the applicant.
- *Beg. Balance:* outstanding loan balance (in dollars) at beginning of year.
- *Principal:* amount of payments applied to principal.
- *Interest:* amount of payments applied to interest.
- *End Balance:* outstanding loan balance (in dollars) at end of year after applying payments.

Appendix 11.B   **CREATE TABLE Statements**

Appendix B contains CREATE TABLE statements for the tables resulting from the conversion and normalization process described in Section 11.3.

```
CREATE TABLE Student
        ( StdNo          CHAR(10)       NOT NULL,
          Name           CHAR(30)       NOT NULL,
          Address        VARCHAR        NOT NULL,
          Phone          CHAR(9),
          City           CHAR(30)       NOT NULL,
          Zip            CHAR(9)        NOT NULL,
          ExpGradMonth   SMALLINT,
          ExpGradYear    INTEGER,
          DOB            DATE           NOT NULL,
CONSTRAINT FKZip FOREIGN KEY (Zip) REFERENCES ZipCode
    ON DELETE NO ACTION
    ON UPDATE CASCADE,
CONSTRAINT PKStudent PRIMARY KEY (StdNo) )
```

```
CREATE TABLE Lender
        ( LenderNo       LONGINT        NOT NULL,
          Name           CHAR(30)       NOT NULL,
        CONSTRAINT PKLender PRIMARY KEY (LenderNo) )
```

```
CREATE TABLE Guarantor
        ( GuarantorNo    CHAR(10)       NOT NULL,
          Name           CHAR(30)       NOT NULL,
        CONSTRAINT PKGuarantor PRIMARY KEY (GuarantorNo) )
```

```
CREATE TABLE Institution
        ( InstID         CHAR(10)       NOT NULL,
          Name           CHAR(30)       NOT NULL,
          Address        VARCHAR        NOT NULL,
          City           CHAR(30)       NOT NULL,
          Zip            CHAR(9)        NOT NULL,
CONSTRAINT FKZip FOREIGN KEY (Zip) REFERENCES ZipCode
    ON DELETE NO ACTION
    ON UPDATE CASCADE,
CONSTRAINT PKInstitution PRIMARY KEY (InstID) )
```

```
CREATE TABLE ZipCode
        ( Zip              CHAR(9)          NOT NULL,
          State            CHAR(2)          NOT NULL,
     CONSTRAINT PKZipCode PRIMARY KEY (Zip) )
```

```
CREATE TABLE Loan
        ( LoanNo           CHAR(10)         NOT NULL,
          ProcDate         DATE             NOT NULL,
          DisbMethod       CHAR(6)          NOT NULL,
          RouteNo          CHAR(10),
          AcctNo           CHAR(10),
          DateAuth         INTEGER          NOT NULL,
          NoteValue        DECIMAL(10,2)    NOT NULL,
          Subsidized       BOOLEAN          NOT NULL,
          Rate             FLOAT            NOT NULL,
          Balance          DECIMAL(10,2),
          StdNo            CHAR(10)         NOT NULL,
          InstID           CHAR(10)         NOT NULL,
          GuarantorNo      CHAR(10),
          LenderNo         CHAR(10)         NOT NULL,
CONSTRAINT FKStdNo FOREIGN KEY (StdNo) REFERENCES Student
   ON DELETE NO ACTION
   ON UPDATE CASCADE,
CONSTRAINT FKInstID FOREIGN KEY (InstID) REFERENCES Institution
   ON DELETE NO ACTION
   ON UPDATE CASCADE,
CONSTRAINT FKGuarantorNo FOREIGN KEY (GuarantorNo) REFERENCES Guarantor
   ON DELETE NO ACTION
   ON UPDATE CASCADE,
CONSTRAINT FKLenderNo FOREIGN KEY (LenderNo) REFERENCES Lender
   ON DELETE NO ACTION
   ON UPDATE CASCADE,
CONSTRAINT FKRouteNo FOREIGN KEY (RouteNo) REFERENCES Bank
   ON DELETE NO ACTION
   ON UPDATE CASCADE,
CONSTRAINT PKLoanPRIMARY KEY (LoanNo) )
```

```
CREATE TABLE Bank
        ( RouteNo          CHAR(10)         NOT NULL,
          Narne            CHAR(30)         NOT NULL,
     CONSTRAINT PKBank PRIMARY KEY (RouteNo) )
```

```
CREATE TABLE DisburseLine
        ( LoanNo          CHAR(10)          NOT NULL,
          DateSent        DATE              NOT NULL,
          Amount          DECIMAL(10,2)     NOT NULL,
          OrigFee         DECIMAL(10,2)     NOT NULL,
          GuarFee         DECIMAL(10,2)     NOT NULL,
CONSTRAINT FKLoanNo FOREIGN KEY (LoanNo) REFERENCES Loan
    ON DELETE CASCADE
    ON UPDATE CASCADE,
CONSTRAINT PKDisburseLine PRIMARY KEY (LoanNo, DateSent) )
```

```
CREATE TABLE DiscLetter
        ( LetterNo        LONGINT           NOT NULL,
          DateSent        DATE              NOT NULL,
          Image           BITMAP            NOT NULL,
          LoanNo          CHAR(10)          NOT NULL,
CONSTRAINT FKLoanNo FOREIGN KEY (LoanNo) REFERENCES Loan
    ON DELETE NO ACTION
    ON UPDATE CASCADE,
CONSTRAINT PKDiscLetter PRIMARY KEY (LetterNo) )
```

```
CREATE TABLE LoanActivity
        ( ReportNo        LONGINT           NOT NULL,
          DateSent        DATE              NOT NULL,
          Image           BITMAP            NOT NULL,
          StdNo           CHAR(10)          NOT NULL,
CONSTRAINT FKStdNo FOREIGN KEY (StdNo) REFERENCES Student
    ON DELETE NO ACTION
    ON UPDATE CASCADE,
CONSTRAINT PKLoanActivity PRIMARY KEY (ReportNo) )
```

```
CREATE TABLE Statement
        ( StatementNo     CHAR(10)          NOT NULL,
          StatementDate   DATE              NOT NULL,
          PayMethod       CHAR(6)           NOT NULL,
          StdNo           CHAR(10)          NOT NULL,
          AmtDue          DECIMAL(10,2)     NOT NULL,
          DueDate         DATE              NOT NULL,
          AmtSent         DECIMAL(10,2),
          DatePaid        DATE,
CONSTRAINT FKStdNo FOREIGN KEY (StdNo) REFERENCES Student
    ON DELETE NO ACTION
    ON UPDATE CASCADE,
CONSTRAINT PKStatement PRIMARY KEY (StatementNo) )
```

```
CREATE TABLE Applied
        ( LoanNo          CHAR(10)            NOT NULL,
          StatementNo     CHAR(10)            NOT NULL,
          Principal       DECIMAL(10,2)       NOT NULL,
          Interest        DECIMAL(10,2)       NOT NULL,
CONSTRAINT FKLoanNo FOREIGN KEY (LoanNo) REFERENCES Loan
    ON DELETE NO ACTION
    ON UPDATE CASCADE,
CONSTRAINT FKStatementNo FOREIGN KEY (StatementNo) REFERENCES Statement
    ON DELETE CASCADE
    ON UPDATE CASCADE,
CONSTRAINT PKApplied PRIMARY KEY (LoanNo, StatementNo) )
```

MANAGING DATABASE ENVIRONMENTS

CHAPTER 12 | *Data and Database Administration*

CHAPTER 13 | *Transaction Management*

CHAPTER 14 | *Data Warehouse Technology and Management*

CHAPTER 15 | *Client–Server Processing and Distributed Databases*

CHAPTER 16 | *Object Database Management Systems*

The chapters in Part 3 emphasize the role of database specialists and the details of managing databases in various operating environments. Chapter 12 provides a context for the other chapters through coverage of the responsibilities, tools, and processes used by database administrators and data administrators. The other chapters in Part 3 provide a foundation for managing databases in important environments: Chapter 13 on transaction processing, Chapter 14 on data warehouses, Chapter 15 on distributed processing and data, and Chapter 16 on object database management. These chapters emphasize concepts, architectures, and design choices important to database specialists.

Chapter 12

Data and Database Administration

Learning Objectives

This chapter provides an overview of the responsibilities and tools of database specialists known as data administrators and database administrators. After this chapter, the student should have acquired the following knowledge and skills:

■ Compare and contrast the responsibilities of database administrators and data administrators.

■ Manage databases using SQL statements for security and integrity.

■ Understand the roles of data dictionary tables and the information resource dictionary.

■ Describe the data planning process.

■ Understand the process to select and evaluate DBMSs.

■ Perceive the processing environments in which database technology exists.

OVERVIEW

Part 2 of this book provided a foundation for database development. You learned about data modeling, schema conversion, normalization, view integration, and physical database design concepts. Utilizing the knowledge and skills in Parts 1 and 2, you should be able to develop databases and implement applications that use the databases. Part 3 explores the issues and skills involved in managing databases in different processing environments. This chapter describes the responsibilities and tools of data specialists (data administrators and database administrators) and provides an introduction to the different processing environments for databases.

Before learning the details of the processing environments, you need to understand the organizational context in which databases exist and learn tools and processes for managing databases. This chapter first discusses an organizational context for databases. You will learn about database support for management decision making, the goals of information resource management, and the responsibilities of data and database administrators. After explaining the organizational context, this chapter presents new tools and processes to manage databases. You will learn new SQL statements for security and integrity, concepts about triggers, stored procedures, and data dictionary manipulation as well as processes for data planning and DBMS selection. This chapter concludes with an introduction to the different processing environments that will be presented in more detail in the other chapters of Part 3.

12.1 ORGANIZATIONAL CONTEXT FOR MANAGING DATABASES

This section reviews management decision-making levels and discusses database support for decision making at all levels. After this background, this section describes the function of information resource management and the responsibilities of data specialists to manage information resources.

12.1.1 Database Support for Management Decision-Making

Operational Database
a database to support the daily functions of an organization.

Databases support business operations and management decision making at various levels. Most large organizations have developed many operational databases to help conduct business efficiently. Operational databases directly support major functions such as order processing, manufacturing, accounts payable, and product distribution. The reasons for investing in an operational database are typically faster processing, larger volumes of business, and reduced personnel costs.

As organizations achieve improved operations, they begin to realize the decision-making potential of their databases. Operational databases provide the raw materials for management decision making as depicted in Figure 12.1. Lower-level management can obtain exception and problem reports directly from operational databases. However, much value must be added to leverage the operational databases for middle and upper management. The operational databases must be summarized and integrated to provide value for tactical and strategic decision making. Integration is necessary because operational databases often are developed in isolation without regard for the information needs of tactical and strategic decision making.

Table 12–1 provides examples of management decisions and data requirements. Lower-level management deals with short-term problems related to individual transactions. Periodic summaries of operational databases and exception reports assist operational management. Middle management relies on summarized data that are integrated across operational databases. Middle management may want to integrate data across dif-

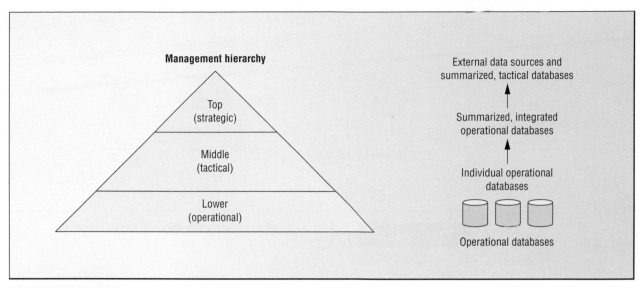

Figure 12.1	**Database support for management levels.**

TABLE 12–1	**Examples of Management Decision Making**

Level	*Example Decisions*	*Data Requirements*
Top	Identify new markets and products; plan growth; reallocate resources across divisions	Economic and technology forecasts; news summaries; industry reports; medium-term performance reports
Middle	Choose suppliers; forecast sales, inventory, and cash; revise staffing levels; prepare budgets	Historical trends; supplier performance; critical path analysis; short-term and medium-term plans
Lower	Schedule employees; correct order delays; find production bottlenecks; monitor resource usage	Problem reports; exception reports; employee schedules; daily production results; inventory levels

ferent departments, manufacturing plants, and retail stores. Top management relies on the results of middle management analysis and external data sources. Top management needs to integrate data so that customers, products, suppliers, and other important entities can be tracked across the entire organization. In addition, external data must be summarized and then integrated with internal data.

12.1.2 Information Resource Management to Knowledge Management

Information Life Cycle the stages of information transformation in an organization. Each entity has its own information life cycle that should be managed and integrated with the life cycles of other entities.

As a response to the challenges of leveraging operational databases and information technology for management decision making, the philosophy of information resource management has arisen. Information resource management involves processing, distributing, and integrating information throughout an organization. A key element of information resource management is the control of information life cycles (Figure 12.2). Each level of management decision making and business operations has its own information life cycle. For effective decision making, the life cycles must be integrated to

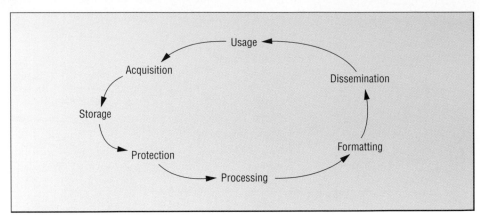

Figure 12.2   **Typical stages of an information life cycle.**

provide timely and consistent information. For example, information life cycles for operations provide input to life cycles for management decision making.

Data quality is a particular concern for information resource management because of the impact of data quality on management decision making. As discussed in Chapter 6, data quality involves a number of dimensions such as correctness, timeliness, consistency, completeness, and reliability. Often the level of data quality that suffices for business operations may be insufficient for decision making at upper levels of management. This conflict is especially true for the consistency dimension. For example, inconsistency of customer identification across operational databases can impair decision making at the upper management level. Information resource management emphasizes a long-term perspective on data quality to ensure support for management decision making.

In recent years, there has been a movement to extend information resource management into knowledge management. Traditionally, information resource management has emphasized technology to support predefined recipes for decision making rather than the ability to react to a constantly changing business environment. To succeed in today's business environment, organizations must emphasize fast response and adaptation rather than planning. To meet this challenge, Dr. Yogesh Malhotra, a well-known management consultant, argues that organizations should develop systems that facilitate knowledge creation rather than information management. For knowledge creation, he advocates a greater emphasis on human information processing and organization dynamics to balance the technology emphasis, as shown in Figure 12.3.

This vision for knowledge management provides a context for the use of information technology to solve business problems. The best information technology will fail if not aligned with the human and organization elements. Information technology should amplify individual intellectual capacity, compensate for limitations in human processing, and support positive organization dynamics.

Knowledge Management applying information technology with human information processing capabilities and organization processes to support rapid adaptation to change.

12.1.3 Responsibilities of Data Administrators and Database Administrators

As part of controlling information resources, new management responsibilities have arisen. The data administrator (DA) is a middle- or upper-management position with broad responsibilities for information resource management. The database administrator

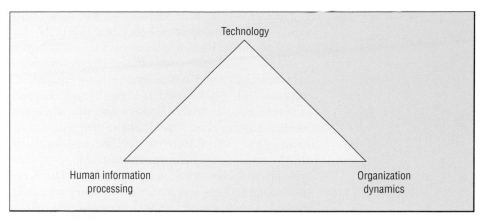

Figure 12.3   **Three pillars of knowledge management.**

TABLE 12– 2	Responsibilities of Data Administrators and Database Administrators

Position	Responsibilities
Data administrator	Develops an enterprise data model
	Establishes interdatabase standards and policies about naming, data sharing, and data ownership
	Negotiates contractual terms with information technology vendors
	Develops long-range plans for information technology
Database administrator	Develops detailed knowledge of individual DBMSs
	Consults on application development
	Performs data modeling and logical database design
	Enforces data administration standards
	Monitors database performance
	Performs technical evaluation of DBMSs
	Creates security, integrity, and rule-processing statements
	Devises standards and policies related to individual databases and DBMSs

(DBA) is a support role with responsibilities related to individual databases and DBMSs. Table 12–2 compares the responsibilities of data administrators and database administrators. The data administrator views the information resource in a broader context than the database administrator. The data administrator considers all kinds of data whether stored in relational databases, files, web pages, or external sources. The database administrator typically considers only data stored in databases.

Development of the <u>enterprise data model</u> is one of the most important responsibilities of the data administrator. An enterprise data model provides an integrated model of all databases of an organization. Because of its scope, an enterprise model is less detailed than the individual databases that it encompasses. The enterprise model concentrates on the major subjects in operational databases rather than the full details. An enterprise data model can be developed for data planning (what databases to develop) or decision support (how

Enterprise Data Model a conceptual data model of an organization. An enterprise data model can be used for data planning and decision support.

to integrate and summarize existing databases). Section 12.3 describes the details of data planning while Chapter 14 describes the details of developing an enterprise data model for decision support. The data administrator is usually heavily involved in both efforts.

Large organizations may offer much specialization in data administration and database administration. For data administration, specialization can occur by task and environment. On the task side, data administrators can specialize in planning versus policy establishment. On the environment side, data administrators can specialize in environments such as decision support, transaction processing, and nontraditional data such as images, text, and video. For database administration, specialization can occur by DBMS, task, and environment. Because of the complexities of learning a DBMS, DBAs typically specialize in one or a few products. Task specialization is usually divided between data modeling and performance evaluation. Environment specialization is usually divided between transaction processing and data warehouses.

In small organizations, the boundary between data administration and database administration is fluid. There may not be separate positions for data administrators and database administrators. The same people may perform duties from both positions. As organizations grow, specialization usually develops so that separate positions are created.

12.2 TOOLS OF DATABASE ADMINISTRATION

To fulfill the responsibilities mentioned in the previous section, database administrators use a variety of tools. You already have learned about tools for data modeling, logical database design, view creation, and physical database design. Some of the tools are SQL statements (CREATE VIEW and CREATE INDEX) while others are part of CASE tools for database development. This section presents additional tools for security, integrity, rule processing, stored procedures, and data dictionary access.

12.2.1 Security

Database Security
protecting databases from unauthorized access and malicious destruction.

Security involves protecting a database from unauthorized access and malicious destruction. Because of the value of data in corporate databases, there is strong motivation for unauthorized users to gain access. Competitors have strong motivation to access sensitive information about product development plans, cost-saving initiatives, and customer profiles. Lurking criminals want to steal unannounced financial results, business transactions, and sensitive customer data such as credit card numbers. Social deviants can wreak havoc by intentionally destroying database records. With growing use of the World Wide Web to conduct business, competitors, criminals, and social deviants have even more opportunity to compromise database security.

Security is a broad subject involving many disciplines. There are legal and ethical issues about who can access data and when data can be disclosed. There are network, hardware, operating system, and physical controls that augment the controls provided by DBMSs. There are also operational problems about passwords, authentication devices, and privacy enforcement. These issues are not further addressed because they are beyond the scope of DBMSs and database specialists. The remainder of this subsection emphasizes access control approaches and SQL statements for authorization rules.

Authorization Rules
define authorized users, allowable operations, and accessible parts of a database. The database security system stores authorization rules and enforces them for each database access.

For access control, DBMSs support creation and storage of authorization rules and enforcement of authorization rules when users access a database. Figure 12.4 depicts the interaction of these elements. Database administrators create authorization rules that define who can access what parts of a database for what operations. Enforcement of authorization rules involves authenticating the user and ensuring that authorization rules are not violated by access requests (database retrievals and modifications). Authentica-

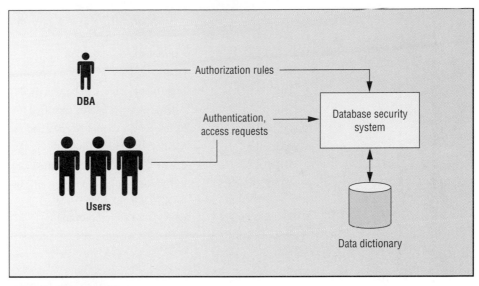

Figure 12.4 Database security system.

tion occurs when a user first connects to a DBMS. Authorization rules must be checked for each access request.

The most common approach to authorization rules is known as <u>discretionary access control.</u> In discretionary access control, users are assigned access rights or privileges to specified parts of a database. For precise control, privileges are usually specified for views rather than tables or fields. Users can be given the ability to read, update, insert, and delete specified parts of a database. To simplify the maintenance of authorization rules, privileges can be assigned to groups rather than individual users. Because groups are usually more stable than individual users, authorization rules that reference groups require less maintenance than rules referencing individual users. Users are assigned to groups and given passwords. During the database login process, the database security system authenticates users and notes the groups to which they belong.

SQL2 supports discretionary authorization rules using the GRANT statement. In a GRANT statement, you specify the privileges (see Table 12–3), the object (table, column, or view), and the list of authorized users (or groups). In Example 12.1, SELECT access is given to three groups (ISFaculty, ISAdvisor, ISAdministrator) while UPDATE access is given only to the ISAdministrator. Individual users must be assigned to the groups before they can access the *ISStudentGPA* view. To remove an access privilege, the REVOKE statement is used. In Example 12.2, the SELECT privilege is removed from ISFaculty.

Discretionary Access Control users are assigned access rights or privileges to specified parts of a database. Discretionary access control is the most common kind of security control supported by commercial DBMSs.

EXAMPLE 12.1 View Definition and GRANT Statements

```
CREATE VIEW ISStudentGPA AS
  SELECT StdSSN, StdFirstName, StdLastName, StdGPA
    FROM Student
    WHERE StdMajor = 'IS'
GRANT SELECT ON ISStudentGPA
  TO ISFaculty, ISAdvisor, ISAdministrator
GRANT UPDATE ON ISStudentGPA.StdGPA TO ISAdministrator
```

TABLE 12–3	Explanation of SQL2 Privileges

Privilege	Explanation
SELECT	Query the object; cannot be specified for individual columns
UPDATE	Modify the value; can be specified for individual columns
INSERT	Add a new row; can be specified for individual columns
DELETE	Delete a row; cannot be specified for individual columns
ALTER	Modify the table definition
INDEX	Create an index on the specified table
REFERENCES	Reference columns of the given table in integrity constraints such as foreign key constraints
EXECUTE	Execute the stored procedure

EXAMPLE 12.2   Remove Access Privileges Using the REVOKE Statement

REVOKE SELECT ON ISStudentGPA FROM ISFaculty

In addition to granting the privileges in Table 12–3, a user can be authorized to pass privileges to other users using the WITH GRANT OPTION keyword. This option should be used with great care because it is more difficult to track authorizations. A better approach is to grant privileges to groups rather than individual users.

Most DBMSs allow authorization restrictions by application objects such as forms and reports in addition to the database objects permissible in the GRANT statement. These additional security constraints are usually specified in the application development tools, rather than in SQL. For example, Microsoft Access 97 allows definition of authorization rules through the User and Group Permissions window, as shown in Figure 12.5. Permissions for database objects (tables and stored queries) as well as application objects (forms and reports) can be specified using this window.

Mandatory access controls are less flexible than discretionary access controls. In mandatory control approaches, each object is assigned a classification level and each user is given a clearance level. A user can access an object if the user's clearance level provides access to the classification level of the object. Typical clearance and classification levels are confidential, secret, and top secret. Mandatory access control approaches have primarily been applied to highly sensitive and static databases for national defense and intelligence gathering. Because of the limited flexibility of mandatory access controls, only a few DBMSs support them. DBMSs that are used in national defense and intelligence gathering must support mandatory controls, however.

In addition to access controls, DBMSs support encryption of databases. Encryption involves the encoding of data to obscure their meaning. An encryption algorithm changes the original data (known as the plaintext). To decipher the data, the user supplies an encryption key to restore the encrypted data (known as the ciphertext) to its original (plaintext) format. Two of the most popular encryption algorithms are the Data Encryption Standard and the Public-Key Encryption algorithm. Because the Data Encryption Standard can be broken by massive computational power, the Public-Key Encryption algorithm has become the preferred approach.

Mandatory Access Control   a database security approach for highly sensitive and static databases. A user can access a database element if the user's clearance level provides access to the classification level of the element.

Figure 12.5   **User and Group Permissions window in Microsoft Access 97.**

 ## 12.2.2 Integrity Constraints

You already have seen integrity constraints presented in previous chapters. In Chapter 2, you were introduced to primary keys, foreign keys, candidate keys, and non-null constraints along with the corresponding SQL syntax. In Chapter 7, you studied cardinality constraints and generalization hierarchy constraints. In Chapter 8, you studied functional and multivalued dependencies as part of the normalization process. In addition, Chapter 10 described indexes that can be used to efficiently enforce primary and candidate key constraints. This subsection describes additional kinds of integrity constraints and the corresponding SQL syntax.

SQL Domains

In Chapter 2, standard SQL data types were defined. A data type indicates the kind of data (character, numeric, yes/no, etc.) and permissible operations (numeric operations, string operations, etc.) for columns using the data type. SQL2 provides a limited ability to define new data types using the CREATE DOMAIN statement. A domain can be created as a subset of a standard data type. Example 12.3 demonstrates the CREATE DOMAIN statement along with usage of the new domains in place of standard data types.

EXAMPLE 12.3   CREATE DOMAIN Statements and Usage of the Domains

```
CREATE DOMAIN StudentClass AS CHAR(2)
   CHECK (VALUE IN ('FR', 'SO', 'JR', 'SR') )
CREATE DOMAIN CourseUnits AS SMALLINT
   CHECK (VALUE BETWEEN 1 AND 9 )
```

In the CREATE TABLE for the *Student* table, the domain can be referenced in the *StdClass* column.

```
StdClass  StudentClass  NOT NULL
```

In the CREATE TABLE for the *Course* table, the domain can be referenced in the *CrsUnits* column.

```
CrsUnits  CourseUnits  NOT NULL
```

SQL3, the emerging new standard, provides a more powerful capability than the CREATE DOMAIN statement. In SQL3, user-defined data types can be defined with new operators and functions. In addition, user-defined data types can be defined using other user-defined data types. Chapter 16 describes user-defined data types as part of the presentation of SQL3.

SQL Assertions

SQL assertions are more powerful than constraints about domains, columns, primary keys, and foreign keys. An assertion can involve a SELECT statement of arbitrary complexity. Thus, assertions can be used for constraints involving multiple tables and statistical calculations, as demonstrated in Examples 12.4 through 12.6. However, complex assertions should be used sparingly because they can be inefficient to enforce. There are often more efficient ways to enforce assertions such as through event conditions in a form and stored procedures. As a DBA, you are advised to investigate the event programming capabilities of application development tools before using complex assertions.

EXAMPLE 12.4

Create Assertion Statement

This assertion statement ensures that no faculty has a course load of less than three units or more than nine units.

```
CREATE ASSERTION FacultyWorkLoad
  CHECK (NOT EXISTS
    ( SELECT Faculty.FacSSN, OffTerm, OffYear
        FROM Faculty, Offering, Course
        WHERE Faculty.FacSSN = Offering.FacSSN
          AND Offering.CourseNo = Course.CourseNo
        GROUP BY Faculty.FacSSN, OffTerm, OffYear
        HAVING SUM(CrsUnits) < 3 OR SUM(CrsUnits) > 9 ) )
```

EXAMPLE 12.5

Create Assertion Statement

This assertion statement ensures that no two courses are offered at the same time and place. The conditions involving the *OffTime* and *OffDays* columns should be refined to check for any overlap, not just equality. Because these refinements would involve string and date functions specific to a DBMS, they are not shown.

```
CREATE ASSERTION OfferingConflict
  CHECK (NOT EXISTS
    ( SELECT O1.OfferNo
        FROM Offering O1, Offering O2
```

```
WHERE O1.OfferNo <> O2.OfferNo
   AND O1.OffTerm = O2.OffTerm
   AND O1.OffYear = O2.OffYear
   AND O1.OffDays = O2.OffDays
   AND O1.OffTime = O2.OffTime
   AND O1.OffLocation = O2.OffLocation ) )
```

EXAMPLE 12.6   Create Assertion Statement

This assertion statement ensures that no course offering exceeds its enrollment limit.

```
CREATE ASSERTION EnrollmentExceedingLimit
   CHECK (NOT EXISTS
      ( SELECT Enrollment.OfferNo, OffLimit
         FROM Offering, Enrollment
         WHERE Offering.OfferNo = Enrollment.OfferNo
         GROUP BY Enrollment.OfferNo, OffLimit
         HAVING COUNT(*) > OffLimit ) )
```

Usually, assertions are checked after a related modification operation completes. For example, the OfferingConflict constraint in Example 12.5 would be checked for each insertion of an *Offering* row and for each change to one of the columns in the WHERE clause of the assertion. In some cases, an assertion should be delayed until other statements complete. The keyword DEFERRABLE can be used to allow an assertion to be tested at a later time. Deferred checking is an issue with transaction design discussed in Chapter 13.

Domains and assertions can be deleted using the DROP DOMAIN and DROP ASSERTION statements. In each case, you only need to specify the name of the domain or assertion to remove.

CHECK Constraints in the CREATE TABLE Statement

When a constraint involves row conditions on columns of the same table, a CHECK constraint should be used instead of an ASSERTION. CHECK constraints are easier to write and more efficient to enforce than ASSERTIONS. CHECK constraints are specified as part of the CREATE TABLE statement as shown in Example 12.7.

EXAMPLE 12.7   CHECK Constraint Clauses

Here is a CREATE TABLE statement with CHECK constraints for the valid GPA range and upper-class students (juniors and seniors) having a declared (non-null) major. Note that the GPA constraint could have been specified in a CREATE DOMAIN statement instead.

```
CREATE TABLE Student
   ( StdSSN        CHAR(11)       NOT NULL,
     StdFirstName  VARCHAR(50)    NOT NULL,
     StdLastName   VARCHAR(50)    NOT NULL,
     StdCity       VARCHAR(50)    NOT NULL,
```

```
StdState        CHAR(2)              NOT NULL,
StdZip          CHAR(9)              NOT NULL,
StdMajor        CHAR(6),
StdClass        CHAR(6),
StdGPA          DECIMAL (3,2),
CONSTRAINT PKStudent PRIMARY KEY (StdSSN),
CONSTRAINT ValidGPA CHECK ( StdGPA BETWEEN 0 AND 4 ),
CONSTRAINT MajorDeclared CHECK
    ( StdClass IN ('FR','SO') OR StdMajor IS NOT NULL ) )
```

12.2.3 Triggers and Stored Procedures

Triggers and stored procedures are two nonstandard tools. Neither is part of SQL2 although they will be standardized in SQL3. Because of the utility of these tools, many DBMSs have developed them as proprietary extensions of SQL. This subsection discusses the purpose of these tools and presents simple examples to depict their usage.

Triggers

Trigger a rule that is stored and executed by the database rule system. Because triggers typically involve an event, a condition, and an action, they are sometimes known as event–condition–action rules.

Triggers are part of a rule-processing capability in a DBMS. Rule processing provides automation of routine tasks such as to update related tables and send alerts when exceptional conditions occur. For example, a trigger can update an inventory table when a shipment record is created. Triggers can be important tools in workflow management, as discussed in Chapter 13. In addition, expert system capability can be coded through triggers. For example, triggers can be used to classify customers as good or bad credit risks.

Although no standard syntax exists, triggers typically involve an event, a condition, and an action. For this reason, they are sometimes known as event–condition–action rules. For example, a trigger can specify that one should decrement the number-of-seats-remaining column when a student enrolls in a course offering. The three components of this trigger are listed below:

- **Event:** insertion of a row in the *Enrollment* table.
- **Condition:** seats remaining column is greater than 0.
- **Action:** decrement the seats-remaining column in the *Offering* table.

In Transact-SQL, the extended SQL of Microsoft SQL Server, a trigger is defined with the CREATE TRIGGER statement, as shown in Example 12.8. The ON and FOR clauses together define the event. The AS clause defines the condition and action parts. The UPDATE statement specifies the action (change the value of the *OffSeatsRemain* column) and the condition (matching *OfferNo* values). The keyword INSERTED refers to the row of the table mentioned in the ON clause.

EXAMPLE 12.8

CREATE TRIGGER Statement
Here is the Transact-SQL trigger to change the seats remaining in an *Offering* row when a row is inserted in the *Enrollment* table.

```
CREATE TRIGGER UpdateSeatsRemaining
    ON Enrollment
```

```
FOR INSERT
AS UPDATE Offering
   SET OffSeatsRemain = OffSeatsRemain - 1
   WHERE Offering.OfferNo = INSERTED.OfferNo
```

Triggers can be more complex than this example. The condition of a trigger can involve a time reference for exception handling. For example, a payment can be considered delinquent if it is not received by 20 days after the corresponding statement was sent. The action part can involve SQL statements, execution of stored procedures, and statements in the proprietary procedural language of the DBMS. To support complex actions, most DBMSs provide proprietary SQL extensions. For example, Microsoft SQL Server provides a number of conditional statements, looping statements, and input–output functions.

Trigger processing involves more complex processing than assertion processing. Triggers must be stored in the data dictionary through something like a DEFINE TRIGGER statement. The DBMS needs a rule-processing subsystem to check triggers after each database event. In addition, the DBA needs to check carefully the consistency and completeness of triggers. An assertion is a limited kind of trigger with an implicit condition and action. Because assertions are simpler than triggers, they are usually easier to create and more efficient to execute. Because of efficiency issues, triggers should not be used for integrity checking.

Stored Procedures

Stored Procedure a collection of statements that are managed by a DBMS. Stored procedures extend the capabilities of SQL. Most DBMSs provide a proprietary language in which to write stored procedures.

Stored procedures extend the computational ability of SQL. SQL2 is limited in the kinds of database retrievals performed on structured data such as organization charts and part compositions. For example, a stored procedure can list all subparts (direct and indirect) used to make a given part. This retrieval cannot be performed in SQL2. Stored procedures also can perform custom operations on data types not supported by SQL. For example, a stored procedure can perform operations on time series data (arrays) that cannot be done in SQL. In building business information systems, the need for stored procedures arises often.

To depict the capabilities of stored procedures, Example 12.9 shows a simple stored procedure written in PL/SQL, the procedural language of Oracle. In the first part of the procedure, the parameters are declared. The statements to execute appear after the BEGIN keyword. In Example 12.9, SQL statements are used along with references to parameters. Much more complex procedures can be defined as PL/SQL supports variable declarations, conditional statements, and looping statements. This procedure can be invoked by using the procedure name along with parameter values such as DeleteEnrollment('123456789', 4567).

EXAMPLE 12.9   Stored Procedure

This PL/SQL procedure deletes an enrollment of a student in a course offering and increases the number of remaining seats in the associated course offering.

```
CREATE PROCEDURE DeleteEnrollment (
   aStdSSN IN CHAR(11), anOfferNo IN INTEGER )
AS BEGIN
   DELETE FROM Enrollment
      WHERE StdSSN = aStdSSN and OfferNo = anOfferNo;
```

```
       UPDATE Offering
          SET OffSeatsRemain = OffSeatsRemain + 1
          WHERE Offering.OfferNo = anOfferNo;
    END
```

Unlike triggers, stored procedures must be explicitly executed. Stored procedures are often executed as an event in a data entry form or as the action of a trigger. In some proprietary extensions of SQL, stored procedures can be called in an SQL statement. SQL3 provides the ability to define stored procedures and use them in SQL statements.

Stored procedures are stored either in the data dictionary or in a procedure library. To be stored in the data dictionary, procedures must be written in the proprietary procedural language of the DBMS such as PL/SQL. Procedures written in programming languages such as Visual Basic and COBOL are stored in procedure libraries. Storing a procedure in the data dictionary provides more flexibility for client–server processing than does storing in procedure libraries. Chapter 15 discusses issues about storage of procedures for client–server database processing. In addition, procedures stored in the data dictionary can be controlled through the database security system.

12.2.4 Data Dictionary Manipulation

Metadata data that describe other data including the source, use, value, and meaning of the data.

The data dictionary is a special database that describes individual databases and the database environment. The data dictionary contains data descriptors called <u>metadata</u> that define the source, use, value, and meaning of data. DBAs typically deal with two kinds of data dictionaries to track the database environment. Each DBMS provides a data dictionary to track tables, columns, assertions, indexes, and other objects managed by the DBMS. Independent CASE tools provide a data dictionary known as the information resource dictionary that tracks a broader range of objects relating to information systems development. This subsection provides details about both kinds of data dictionaries.

Catalog Tables Used by DBMSs

Most DBMSs provide a large collection of catalog tables that comprise the data dictionary. SQL2 does not standardize the composition of the data dictionary, although it does provide a list of recommended catalog tables. It would have been impossible to obtain approval of standard catalog tables because most DBMSs already had proprietary catalogs before the SQL2 standard. Because the recommended catalog tables have few implementations, they are not listed here. Instead, Table 12–4 lists some of the most important catalog tables of Oracle.

A DBA implicitly modifies catalog tables when using data definition commands such as CREATE TABLE. The DBMS uses the catalog tables to process queries, authorize users, check integrity constraints, and perform other database processing. The DBMS consults the catalog tables before performing almost every action. Thus, the integrity of the catalog tables is crucial to the operation of the DBMS. Only the most-authorized users should be permitted to modify the catalog tables. To improve security and reliability, the data dictionary is usually a separate database stored independently of user databases.

A DBA can query the catalog tables through proprietary interfaces and SELECT statements. Proprietary interfaces such as the Table Definition window of Microsoft Access 97 are easier to use than SQL but not portable across DBMSs. SELECT statements provide more control over the information retrieved than do proprietary interfaces.

TABLE 12–4	Common Catalog Tables for Oracle
Table Name	*Contents*
USER_CATALOG	Contains basic data about each table and view defined by a user.
USER_OBJECTS	Contains data about each object (functions, procedures, indexes, triggers, assertions, etc.) defined by a user. This table contains the time created and the last time changed for each object.
USER_TABLES	Contains extended data about each table such as space allocation and statistical summaries.
USER_TAB_COLUMNS	Contains basic and extended data for each column such as the column name, the table reference, the data type, and a statistical summary.
USER_VIEWS	Contains the SQL statement defining each view.

Information Resource Dictionary

Information Resource Dictionary a database of metadata that describes the entire information systems life cycle. The information resource dictionary system manages access to an IRD.

An information resource dictionary contains a much broader collection of metadata than does a data dictionary for a DBMS. An information resource dictionary (IRD) contains metadata about individual databases, computerized and human processes, configuration management, version control, human resources, and the computing environment. Conceptually, an IRD defines metadata used throughout the information systems life cycle. Both DBAs and DAs can use an IRD to manage information resources. In addition, other information systems professionals can use an IRD during selected tasks in the information systems life cycle.

Because of its broader role, an IRD is not consulted by a DBMS to conduct operations. Rather, an information resource dictionary system (IRDS) manages an IRD. Many CASE tools can use the IRDS to access an IRD, as depicted in Figure 12.6. CASE tools can access an IRD directly through the IRDS or indirectly through the import/export feature. The IRD has an open architecture so that CASE tools can customize and extend its conceptual schema.

There are two primary proposals for the IRD and the IRDS. The IRD and the IRDS are currently standards developed by the International Standards Organization (ISO). The implementation of the standards, however, is not widespread. Microsoft and Texas Instruments have jointly developed the Microsoft Repository, which supports many of the goals of the IRD and the IRDS although it does not conform to the standard. However, the Microsoft Repository is gaining widespread acceptance among CASE tool vendors. At this point, it appears to be the de facto standard for the IRD and the IRDS.

12.3 PROCESSES FOR DATABASE SPECIALISTS

This section describes processes conducted by data administrators and database administrators. Data administrators perform data planning as part of the information systems planning process. Both data administrators and database administrators may perform tasks in the process of selecting and evaluating DBMSs. This section presents the details of both processes.

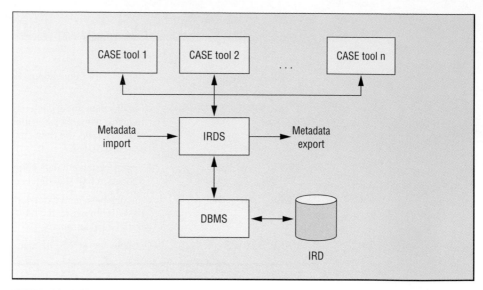

Figure 12.6   IRDS architecture.

12.3.1 Data Planning

Despite the vast sums of money spent on information technology, many organizations feel disappointed in the payoff. Many organizations have created islands of automation that support local objectives but not the global objectives for the organization. The islands-of-automation approach can lead to a misalignment of the business and information technology objectives. One result of the misalignment is the difficulty in extracting the decision-making value from operational databases.

As a response to problems with islands of automation, many organizations perform a detailed planning process for information technology and systems. The planning process is known under various names such as information systems planning, business systems planning, information systems engineering, and information systems architecture. All of these approaches provide a process to achieve the following objectives:

- Evaluation of current information systems with respect to the goals and objectives of the organization.
- Determination of the scope and the timing of the development of new information systems and utilization of new information technology.
- Identification of opportunities to apply information technology for competitive advantage.

Information Systems Planning   the process of developing enterprise models of data, processes, and organizational roles. Information systems planning evaluates existing systems, identifies opportunities to apply information technology for competitive advantage, and plans new systems.

The information systems planning process involves the development of enterprise models of data, processes, and organizational roles, as depicted in Figure 12.7. In the first part of the planning process, broad (nondetailed) models are developed. Table 12–5 shows the initial level of detail for the data, process, and organization models. Because the enterprise data model is usually more stable than the process model, it is developed first. To integrate these models, interaction models are developed, as shown in Table 12–5. If additional detail is desired, the process and the data models are further expanded. These models should reflect the current information systems infrastructure as well as the planned future direction.

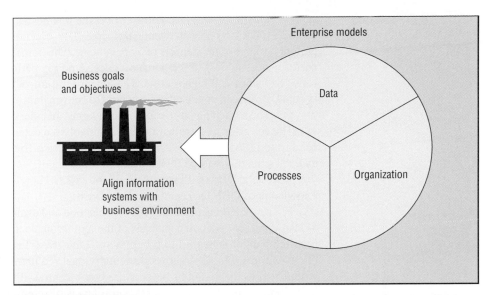

| **Figure 12.7** | **Enterprise models developed in the information systems planning process.** |

TABLE 12–5	**Level of Detail of Enterprise Models**
Model	*Levels of Detail*
Data	Subject model (initial level), entity model (detailed level)
Process	Functional areas and business processes (initial level), activity model (detailed level)
Organization	Role definitions and role relationships
Data–process interaction	Matrix and diagrams showing data requirements of processes
Process–organization interaction	Matrix and diagrams showing role responsibilities
Data–organization	Matrix and diagrams showing usage of data by roles

Data administrators play an important part in the development of information system plans. Data administrators conduct numerous interviews to develop the enterprise data model and coordinate with other planning personnel to develop the interaction models. To improve the likelihood that plans will be accepted and used, data administrators should involve senior management. By emphasizing the decision-making potential of integrated information systems, senior management will be motivated to support the planning process.

12.3.2 Selection and Evaluation of Database Management Systems

Selection and evaluation of DBMS software can be a very important task of an organization. DBMSs provide an important part of the computing infrastructure. As organizations strive to conduct electronic commerce over the Internet and extract value from operational databases, DBMSs play an even greater role. The selection and evaluation process is important because of the impacts of a poor choice. The immediate impacts are slow database performance and loss of the purchase price. A poorly performing information system can cause lost sales and higher costs. The longer-term impacts are high switching costs. To switch DBMSs, an organization may need to convert data, recode software, and retrain employees. The switching costs can be much larger than the original purchase price.

The selection and evaluation process involves a detailed assessment of organization needs and DBMS features. The goal of the process is to determine a small set of candidate systems that will be investigated in more detail. Because of the detailed nature of the process, a DBA performs most of the tasks. Therefore, a DBA needs a thorough knowledge of DBMSs to perform the process.

Figure 12.8 depicts the steps of the selection and evaluation process. In the first step, a DBA conducts a detailed analysis of the requirements. Because of the large number of requirements, it is helpful to group them. Table 12–6 lists major groupings of requirements while Table 12–7 shows some individual requirements in one group. Each individual requirement should be classified as essential, desirable, or optional to the requirement group. In some cases, several levels of requirements may be necessary. For individual requirements, a DBA should be able to objectively measure them in the candidate systems.

After determining the groupings, the DBA should assign weights to the major requirement groups and score candidate systems. With more than a few major requirement groups, assigning consistent weights is very difficult. The DBA needs a tool to help assign consistent weights and to score candidate systems. Unfortunately, no analytical method for weight assignment and system scoring has achieved widespread usage. To encourage the use of analytical methods for weight assignment and scoring, one promising approach is depicted.

The <u>Analytic Hierarchy Process</u> provides a simple approach that achieves a reasonable level of consistency. Using the Analytic Hierarchy Process, the DBA assigns

Analytic Hierarchy Process a decision theory technique to evaluate problems with multiple objectives. The process can be used to select and evaluate DBMSs by allowing a systematic assignment of weights to requirements and scores to features of candidate DBMSs.

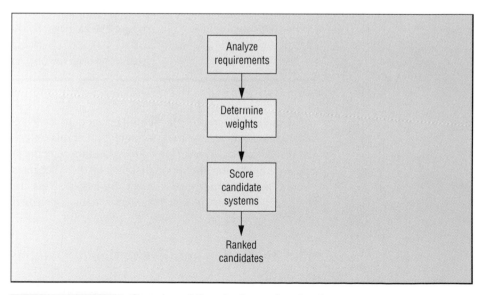

| Figure 12.8 | **Overview of the selection and evaluation process.** |

TABLE 12–6	Some Major Requirement Groups

Category

Data definition (conceptual)

Nonprocedural retrieval

Data definition (internal)

Application development

Procedural language

Concurrency control

Recovery management

Distributed processing and data

Vendor support

Query optimization

TABLE 12–7	Some Detailed Requirements for the Conceptual Data Definition Category

Requirement (Importance)	*Explanation*
Entity integrity (essential)	Declaration and enforcement of primary keys
Candidate keys (desirable)	Declaration and enforcement of candidate keys
Referential integrity (essential)	Declaration and enforcement of referential integrity
Referenced rows (desirable)	Declaration and enforcement of rules for referenced rows
Standard data types (essential)	Support for whole numbers (several sizes), floating-point numbers (several sizes), fixed-point numbers, fixed-length strings, variable-length strings, and dates (date, time, and timestamp)
User-defined data types (desirable)	Support for new data types or a menu of optional data types
User interface (optional)	Graphical user interface to augment SQL CREATE statements
General assertions (optional)	Declaration and enforcement of multitable constraints

weights to pairwise combinations of requirement groups. For example, the DBA should assign a weight that represents the importance of conceptual data definition as compared to nonprocedural retrieval. The Analytic Hierarchy Process provides a nine-point scale with interpretations shown in Table 12–8. Table 12–9 applies the scale to rank some of the requirement groups in Table 12–6. For consistency, if entry $A_{ij} = x$, then $A_{ji} = 1/x$. In addition, the diagonal elements in Table 12–9 should always be 1. Thus, it is necessary to complete only half the rankings in Table 12–9.

Scoring candidate DBMSs can be complex because of the number of individual requirements and the need to combine individual requirements into an overall score for the requirement group. As the first part of the scoring process, the DBA should carefully investigate the features of each candidate DBMS. For each individual requirement, a binary indicator (available or not), rank, or numeric weight should be assigned.

Many ways have been proposed to combine the individual feature scores into an overall score for the requirement group. The Analytic Hierarchy Process supports pairwise comparisons among candidate DBMSs using the rating values in Table 12–8. The

TABLE 12–8	**Interpretation of Rating Values for Pairwise Comparisons**

Ranking Value of A_{ij}	Meaning
1	Requirements i and j are equally important.
3	Requirement i is slightly more important than requirement j.
5	Requirement i is significantly more important than requirement j.
7	Requirement i is very significantly more important than requirement j.
9	Requirement i is absolutely more important than requirement j.

TABLE 12–9	**Sample Weights for Some Requirement Groups[1]**			
	Data Definition (Conceptual)	Nonprocedural Retrieval	Application Development	Concurrency Control
Data Definition (Conceptual)	1	⅕	⅕	½
Nonprocedural Retrieval	5	1	⅓	⅕
Application Development	5	3	1	⅓
Concurrency Control	7	5	3	1

interpretations change slightly to reflect the comparison among candidate DBMSs rather than importance of requirement groups. The DBA subjectively uses the individual feature scores to assign ranking values for each pairwise comparison. Other methods such as the Logic Scoring of Preferences involve a numerical combination of the individual feature weights. Because of the complexity of other methods, you should consult the chapter references for details.

After the selection and evaluation process completes, the top two or three candidate DBMSs should be evaluated in more detail. The DBA may want to evaluate the DBMSs on a trial basis. Application-specific benchmarks can be created to gauge the efficiency of a DBMS for its intended usage. In addition, the user interface and application development capabilities can be evaluated by building small applications.

The final phase of the selection process may involve nontechnical considerations performed by data administrators along with senior management and legal staff. Assessment of each vendor's future prospects is important because information systems can have a long life. If the underlying DBMS does not advance with the industry, it may not support future initiatives and upgrades to the information systems that use it. Because of the high fixed and variable costs (maintenance fees) of a DBMS, negotiation is often a critical element of the final selection process. The final contract terms along with one or two key advantages often make the difference in the final selection.

---

[1]The Analytic Hierarchy Process requires normalization of the weights. See the references for complete details.

12.4 MANAGING DATABASE ENVIRONMENTS

DBMSs operate in several different processing environments. Data specialists must understand the environments to ensure adequate database performance and set standards and policies. This section provides an overview of the processing environments with an emphasis on the tasks performed by database administrators and data administrators. The other chapters in Part 3 provide the details of the processing environments.

12.4.1 Transaction Processing

Transaction processing involves the daily operations of an organization. Every day, organizations process large volumes of orders, payments, cash withdrawals, airline reservations, insurance claims, and other kinds of transactions. DBMSs provide essential services to perform transactions in an efficient and reliable manner. Organizations such as banks with automatic tellers, airlines with on-line reservation systems, and universities with on-line registration could not function without reliable and efficient transaction processing. With exploding interest to conduct business over the Internet, the importance of transaction processing will grow even larger.

Data specialists have many responsibilities for transaction processing, as listed in Table 12–10. Data administrators may perform planning responsibilities involving infrastructure and disaster recovery. Database administrators usually perform the more detailed tasks such as consulting on transaction design and monitoring performance. Because of the importance of transaction processing, database administrators often must be on call to troubleshoot problems. Chapter 13 presents the details of transaction processing for concurrency control and recovery management. After you read Chapter 13, you may want to review Table 12–10 again.

12.4.2 Data Warehouse Processing

Data warehousing involves the decision support side of databases. Because many organizations have not been able to use operational databases directly to support management decision making, the idea of a data warehouse was conceived. A data warehouse is a central database where enterprisewide data are stored to support decision support activities by user departments. Data from operational databases and external sources are extracted, cleaned, summarized, and then loaded into a data warehouse. Because the data warehouse contains historical data, most activity involves retrievals of highly summarized data.

TABLE 12–10	Responsibilities of Database Specialists for Transaction Processing
Area	*Responsibilities*
Transaction design	Consult about design to balance integrity and performance; educate about design issues and DBMS features
Performance monitoring	Monitor transaction performance and troubleshoot performance problems; modify resource levels to improve performance
Transaction processing infrastructure	Determine resource levels for efficiency (disk, memory, and CPU) and reliability (RAID level)
Disaster recovery	Provide contingency plans for various kinds of database failures

TABLE 12–11	Responsibilities of Database Specialists for Data Warehouses
Area	*Responsibilities*
Data warehouse usage	Educate and consult about application design and DBMS features for data warehouse processing
Performance monitoring	Monitor data warehouse loading performance and troubleshoot integrity problems; modify resource levels to improve performance
Data warehouse architecture	Determine architecture to support decision-making needs; select database products to support architecture; determine resource levels for efficient processing
Enterprise data model	Provide expertise about operational database content; determine conceptual data model for the data warehouse; promote data quality to support data warehouse development

Data specialists have many responsibilities for data warehouses, as listed in Table 12–11. Data administrators may perform planning responsibilities involving the data warehouse architecture and the enterprise data model. Database administrators usually perform the more detailed tasks such as performance monitoring and consulting. To support a large data warehouse, a software product separate from a DBMS may be necessary. A selection and evaluation process should be conducted to choose the most appropriate product. Chapter 14 presents the details of data warehouses. After you read Chapter 14, you may want to review Table 12–11 again.

12.4.3 Distributed Environments

DBMSs can operate in distributed environments to support both transaction processing and data warehouses. In distributed environments, DBMSs can provide the ability to distribute processing and data among computers connected by a network. For distributed processing, a DBMS may allow the distribution of functions provided by the DBMS as well as application processing to be distributed among different computers in a network. For distributed data, a DBMS may allow tables to be stored and possibly replicated at different computers in a network. The ability to distribute processing and data provides the promise of improved flexibility, scalability, performance, and reliability. However, these improvements only can be obtained through careful design.

Data specialists have many responsibilities for distributed database environments, as shown in Table 12–12. Data administrators usually perform planning responsibilities involving setting goals and determining architectures. Because distributed environments do not increase functionality, they must be justified by improvements in the underlying applications. Database administrators perform more detailed tasks such as performance monitoring and distributed database design. To support distributed environments, other software products along with major extensions to a DBMS may be necessary. A selection and evaluation process should be conducted to choose the most appropriate products. Chapter 15 presents the details of distributed processing and distributed data. After you read Chapter 15, you may want to review Table 12–12 again.

12.4.4 Object Database Management

Object DBMSs support additional functionality for transaction processing and data warehouse applications. Many information systems use a richer set of data types than provided by relational DBMSs. For example, many financial databases need to manip-

TABLE 12–12	Responsibilities of Database Specialists for Distributed Environments

Area	*Responsibilities*
Application development	Educate and consult about impacts of distributed environment for transaction processing and data warehouses
Performance monitoring	Monitor performance and troubleshoot problems with a special emphasis on distributed environments
Distributed environment architectures	Identify goals for distributed environments; choose distributed processing and distributed database architectures to meet goals; select additional software products to support architectures
Distributed environment design	Design distributed databases; determine resource levels for efficient processing

TABLE 12–13	Responsibilities of Database Specialists for Object Databases

Area	*Responsibilities*
Application development	Educate and consult about using new data types and creating functions for new data types
Performance monitoring	Monitor performance and troubleshoot problems with new data types
Object database architectures	Identify goals for object DBMSs; choose object database architectures
Object database design	Design object databases; select data types; create new data types

ulate time series, a data type not provided by most relational DBMSs. With the ability to convert any kind of data to a digital format, the need for new data types is even more pronounced. Business databases often need to integrate traditional data with nontraditional data based on new data types. For example, information systems for processing insurance claims must manage traditional data such as account numbers, claim amounts, and accident dates as well as nontraditional data such as images, maps, and drawings. Because of these needs, existing relational DBMSs have been extended with object capabilities and new object DBMSs have been developed.

Data specialists have many responsibilities for distributed database environments, as shown in Table 12–13. Data administrators usually perform planning responsibilities involving setting goals and determining architectures. Database administrators perform more detailed tasks such as performance monitoring, consulting, and object database design. An object DBMS can be a major extension to an existing relational DBMS or a new DBMS. A selection and evaluation process should be conducted to choose the most appropriate product. Chapter 16 presents the details of object DBMSs. After you read Chapter 16, you may want to review Table 12–13 again.

CLOSING THOUGHTS

This chapter has described the responsibilities, tools, and processes used by database specialists to manage databases and support management decision making. Many organizations provide two roles for managing information resources. Data administrators perform broad planning and policy setting, while database administrators perform detailed oversight of individual databases and DBMSs. To provide a context to understand the responsibilities of these positions, this chapter discussed the philosophy of information resource management that emphasizes information technology as a tool for processing, distributing, and integrating information throughout an organization.

This chapter described a number of tools to support database administrators. Database administrators use security rules to restrict access and integrity constraints to improve data quality. This chapter described conceptual aspects of security rules and integrity constraints along with associated SQL syntax. Triggers and stored procedures extend the capabilities of DBMSs for rule processing and complex operations. This chapter described the conceptual aspects of triggers and stored procedures along with simple examples. The data dictionary is an important tool for managing individual databases as well as integrating database development with information systems development. This chapter presented two kinds of data dictionaries: catalog tables used by DBMSs and the information resource dictionary used by CASE tools.

Database specialists need to understand two important processes to manage information technology. Data administrators participate in a detailed planning process that determines new directions for information systems development. This chapter described the data planning process as an important component of the information systems planning process. Both data administrators and database administrators participate in the selection and evaluation of DBMSs. Database administrators perform the detailed tasks while data administrators often make final selection decisions using the detailed recommendations. This chapter described the steps of the selection and evaluation process and the tasks performed by database administrators and data administrators in the process.

This chapter provides a context for the other chapters in Part 3. Those chapters provide details about different database environments including transaction processing, data warehouses, distributed environments, and object DBMSs. This chapter has emphasized the responsibilities, tools, and processes of database specialists for managing these environments. After completing the other chapters in Part 3, you are encouraged to reread this chapter to help you integrate the details with the management concepts and techniques.

REVIEW CONCEPTS

- Information resource management: management philosophy to control information resources and apply information technology to support management decision making.
- Database administrator: support position for managing individual databases and DBMSs.
- Data administrator: management position with planning and policy responsibilities for information technology.
- Discretionary access controls for assigning access rights to groups and users.
- Mandatory access controls for highly sensitive and static databases used in intelligence gathering and national defense.
- SQL GRANT and REVOKE statements for discretionary authorization rules.

```
GRANT SELECT ON ISStudentGPA
    TO ISFaculty, ISAdvisor, ISAdministrator
REVOKE SELECT ON ISStudentGPA FROM ISFaculty
```

- SQL CREATE DOMAIN statement for data type constraints.

```
CREATE DOMAIN StudentClass AS CHAR(2)
    CHECK (VALUE IN ('FR', 'SO', 'JR', 'SR') )
```

- SQL CREATE ASSERTION statement for complex integrity constraints.

```
CREATE ASSERTION EnrollmentExceedingLimit
  CHECK (NOT EXISTS
    ( SELECT Enrollment.OfferNo, OffLimit
        FROM Offering, Enrollment
        WHERE Offering.OfferNo = Enrollment.OfferNo
        GROUP BY Enrollment.OfferNo, OffLimit
        HAVING COUNT(*) > OffLimit ) )
```

- CHECK constraints in the CREATE TABLE statement for constraints involving row conditions on columns of the same table.

```
CREATE TABLE Student
      ( StdSSN         CHAR(11)       NOT NULL,
        StdFirstName   VARCHAR(50)    NOT NULL,
        StdLastName    VARCHAR(50)    NOT NULL,
        StdCity        VARCHAR(50)    NOT NULL,
        StdState       CHAR(2)        NOT NULL,
        StdZip         CHAR(9)        NOT NULL,
        StdMajor       CHAR(6),
        StdClass       CHAR(6),
        StdGPA         DECIMAL(3,2),
CONSTRAINT PKStudent PRIMARY KEY (StdSSN),
CONSTRAINT ValidGPA CHECK ( StdGPA BETWEEN 0 AND 4 ),
CONSTRAINT MajorDeclared CHECK
  ( StdClass IN ('FR','SO') OR StdMajor IS NOT NULL ) )
```

- Triggers as part of a rule processing system for exception reporting, workflow management, and expert classifications.
- Trigger components: event, condition, and action.
- Stored procedures for complex retrievals and calculations that cannot be performed in SQL.
- Catalog tables for tracking the objects managed by a DBMS
- Information resource dictionary for managing the information systems development process.
- Development of an enterprise data model as an important part of the information systems planning process.
- Selection and evaluation process for analyzing organization needs and DBMS features.
- Responsibilities of database specialists for managing transaction processing, data warehouses, distributed environments, and object DBMSs.

QUESTIONS

1. Why is it difficult to use operational databases for management decision making?

2. How must operational databases be transformed for management decision making?

3. What are the phases of the information life cycle?

4. What does it mean to integrate information life cycles?

5. What data quality dimension is important for management decision making but not for operational decision making?

6. How does knowledge management differ from information resource management?

7. What are the three pillars of knowledge management?

8. What kind of position is the data administrator?

9. What kind of position is the database administrator?

10. Which position (data administrator versus database administrator) takes a broader view of information resources?

11. What is an enterprise data model?

12. For what reasons is an enterprise data model developed?

13. What kinds of specialization are possible in large organizations for data administrators and database administrators?

14. What is discretionary access control?

15. What is mandatory access control?

16. What kind of database requires mandatory access control?

17. What are the purposes of the GRANT and REVOKE statements in SQL?

18. Why should authorization rules reference groups instead of individual users?

19. Why do authorization rules typically use views rather than tables or columns?

20. What other disciplines does computer security involve?

21. What is the purpose of the CREATE DOMAIN statement?

22. What additional capabilities (beyond SQL2) does SQL3 add for domains?

23. What is the purpose of assertions in SQL?

24. What does it mean to say that an assertion is deferrable?

25. What are alternatives to SQL assertions? Why would you use an alternative to an assertion?

26. For what purposes should a trigger be used?

27. Why should triggers normally not be used for integrity constraints?

28. What are the three parts of a trigger? Briefly explain what each part contains.

29. For what purposes would you write a stored procedure?

30. What are the advantages of writing a stored procedure in the proprietary language of the DBMS?

31. What kind of metadata does a data dictionary contain?

32. What are catalog tables? What kind of catalog tables are managed by DBMSs?

33. What is the purpose of an information resource dictionary?

34. What functions does an information resource dictionary system perform?

35. What are the purposes of information systems planning?

36. Why is the enterprise data model developed before the process model?

37. Why is the selection and evaluation process important for DBMSs?

38. What are some complexities in the selection and evaluation process for a complex product like a DBMS?

39. What are the steps in the selection and evaluation process?

40. How is the Analytic Hierarchy Process used in the selection and evaluation process?

41. What responsibilities does the database administrator play in the selection and evaluation process?

42. What responsibilities does the data administrator play in the selection and evaluation process?

43. What are the responsibilities of database administrators for transaction processing?

44. What are the responsibilities of database administrators for managing data warehouses?

45. What are the responsibilities of database administrators for managing databases in distributed environments?

46. What are the responsibilities of database administrators for managing object databases?

47. What are the responsibilities of data administrators for transaction processing?

48. What are the responsibilities of data administrators for managing data warehouses?

49. What are the responsibilities of data administrators for managing databases in distributed environments?

50. What are the responsibilities of data administrators for managing object databases?

PROBLEMS

Because of the introductory nature of this chapter, there are no problems in this chapter. Problems appear at the end of other chapters in Part 3.

REFERENCES FOR FURTHER STUDY

The book by Jay Louise Weldon (1981) remains the classic book on database administration despite its age. Davenport and Prusak (1997) and Prusak (1997) describe the concept of knowledge management and provide case studies to demonstrate its application. Specialized books such as Bowman, Emerson, and Darnovsky (1996); Cannan and Otten (1992); Date and Darwen (1997); Groff and Weinberg (1999); and Melton and Simon (1992) provide more details about the security and integrity features of SQL2. Inmon

(1986) and Martin (1982) have written detailed descriptions of information systems planning. Hackathorn and Karimi (1988) compare approaches to information systems planning. Fernandez, Summers, and Wood (1981) wrote a classic book on database security and integrity. For more details about the Analytic Hierarchy Process mentioned in Section 12.3.2, consult Saaty (1988) and Zahedi (1986). Su et al. (1987) describe the Logic Scoring of Preferences, an alternative approach to DBMS selection.

Appendix 12.A   SQL2 Syntax Summary

This appendix summarizes the SQL2 syntax for the GRANT, REVOKE, CREATE DOMAIN, and CREATE ASSERTION statements as well as the CHECK constraint clause presented in the chapter. The conventions used in the syntax notation are identical to those used at the end of Chapter 2.

GRANT and REVOKE Statements

```
GRANT { <Privilege>* | ALL PRIVILEGES }ON TableName
  TO UserName [ WITH GRANT OPTION ]
<Privilege>:
  { SELECT |
    DELETE |
    INSERT [ (ColumnName*) ] |
    REFERENCES [ (ColumnName*) ] |
    UPDATE [ (ColumnName*) ] }
REVOKE [ GRANT OPTION FOR ] <Privilege>*
  ON TableName TO UserName [ { CASCADE | RESTRICT } ]
```

CREATE DOMAIN and DROP DOMAIN Statements

```
CREATE DOMAIN DomainName DataType
  [ CHECK ( <Domain-Condition> ) ]
<Domain-Condition>:
  { VALUE <Comparison-Operator> Constant |
    VALUE BETWEEN Constant AND Constant |
    VALUE IN ( Constant* ) }
<Comparison-Operator>: { = | < | > | <= | >= | <> }
DROP DOMAIN DomainName { CASCADE | RESTRICT }
```

CREATE ASSERTION and DROP ASSERTION Statements

```
CREATE ASSERTION AssertionName
  CHECK ( <Group-Condition> )
  <Group-Condition>: —initially defined in Chapter 3 and extended in Chapter 4
DROP ASSERTION AssertionName { CASCADE | RESTRICT }
```

CHECK Constraint Clause in the CREATE TABLE Statement

```
CREATE TABLE TableName
  ( <Column-Definition>* [, <Table-Constraint>* ] )
<Column-Definition>: ColumnName DataType
  [ DEFAULT { DefaultValue | USER | NULL } ] [ <Column-Constraint> ]
```

```
<Column-Constraint>: [ CONSTRAINT ConstraintName ]
  { NOT NULL |
    <Foreign-Key-Constraint> |—defined in Chapter 2
    <Uniqueness-Constraint> | —defined in Chapter 2
    <Check-Constraint> }
<Table-Constraint>: [ CONSTRAINT ConstraintName ]
  { <Primary-Key-Constraint> |—defined in Chapter 2
    <Foreign-Key-Constraint> |—defined in Chapter 2
    <Uniqueness-Constraint> | —defined in Chapter 2
    <Check-Constraint> }
<Check-Constraint>: CHECK ( <Row-Condition> )
<Row-Condition>: —defined in Chapter 3
```

Transaction Management

This chapter describes transaction management features to support concurrent usage of a database and recovery from failures. After this chapter, the student should have acquired the following knowledge and skills:

- Explain the ACID transaction properties and the concepts of recovery and concurrency transparency.

- Understand the role of locking to prevent interference problems among multiple users.

- Understand the role of recovery tools to deal with database failures.

- Understand transaction design issues that improve performance.

- Describe the relationship of workflow management to transaction management.

OVERVIEW

Chapter 12 presented a context for managing databases and an overview of the different processing environments for databases. You learned about the responsibilities of database specialists and the tools and processes used by database specialists. The most prevalent and important database environment is transaction processing that supports the daily operations of an organization. This chapter begins the details of Part 3 by describing how DBMSs support transaction processing.

This chapter presents a broad coverage of transaction management. Before you can understand how DBMSs support transaction processing, you need a more detailed understanding of transaction concepts. This chapter describes properties of transactions, SQL statements to define transactions, and properties of transaction processing. After learning about transaction concepts, you are ready to study concurrency control and recovery management, two major services to support transaction processing. For concurrency control, this chapter describes the objective, interference problems, and tools of concurrency control. For recovery management, this chapter describes failure types, recovery tools, and recovery processes.

Besides knowing the transaction management services provided by a DBMS, you should understand issues of transaction design. This chapter describes important issues of transaction design including hot spots, transaction boundaries, isolation levels, and integrity constraint enforcement. To broaden your background, you should understand how database transactions fit into the larger context of collaborative work. The final section describes workflow management and contrasts it with transaction management in DBMSs.

13.1 BASICS OF DATABASE TRANSACTIONS

Transaction: a unit of work that should be processed reliably. DBMSs provide recovery and concurrency control services to process transactions efficiently and reliably.

Transaction processing involves the operating side of databases. Whereas operations management describes how physical goods are produced, transaction management describes how information goods or transactions are controlled. Transaction management, like management of physical goods, is enormously important to modern organizations. Organizations such as banks with automatic tellers, airlines with on-line reservation systems, and universities with on-line registration could not function without reliable and efficient transaction processing. Large organizations now conduct tens to thousands of transactions per second. With growing interest in electronic commerce, the importance of transaction processing will grow even larger.

In common discourse, a transaction is an interaction among two or more parties for the conduct of business such as buying a car from a dealership. Transactions for DBMSs have a more precise meaning. A database transaction involves a collection of operations that must be processed as one unit of work. Transactions should be processed reliably so that there is no loss of data due to multiple users and system failures. To help you grasp this more precise meaning, this section presents examples of transactions and defines properties of transactions.

13.1.1 Transaction Examples

A transaction is a user-defined concept. For example, making an airline reservation may involve reservations for the departure and return. To the user, the combination of the departure and the return is a transaction, not the departure and the return separately. Most travelers do not want to depart without returning. The implication for DBMSs is that a transaction is a user-defined set of database operations. A transaction can involve any number of reads and writes to a database. To provide the flexibility of user-defined transactions, DBMSs cannot restrict transactions to only a specified number of reads and writes to a database.

An information system may have many different kinds of transactions. Table 13–1 depicts transactions of an order entry system. At any point in time, users may be conducting business with each of these kinds of transactions. For example, many customers may be placing an order while other customers check on the status of their orders.

SQL Statements to Define Transactions

To define a transaction, you can use some additional SQL statements. Figure 13.1 depicts additional SQL statements to define the prototypical automatic teller machine (ATM) transaction. The BEGIN TRANSACTION[1] and COMMIT statements define the statements in a transaction. Any other SQL statements between them are part of the transaction. Typically, a transaction involves a number of SELECT, INSERT, UPDATE, and DELETE statements. In Figure 13.1, an actual transaction would have valid SQL statements for the lines beginning with SELECT, UPDATE, and INSERT.

---

[1]SQL2 specifies the COMMIT statement. Another transaction begins following the next COMMIT statement. Some DBMSs add a BEGIN TRANSACTION statement to more explicitly show transaction boundaries.

TABLE 13–1	Typical Transactions in an Order Entry System

Transaction Kind	Description
Add order	Customer places a new order.
Update order	Customer changes details of an existing order.
Check status	Clerk reports the status of an order to customer.
Payment	Payment received from customer.
Shipment	Goods sent to customer.

```
BEGIN TRANSACTION
    Display greeting
    Get account number, pin, type, and amount
    SELECT account number, type, and balance
    If balance is sufficient then
          UPDATE account by posting debit
          UPDATE account by posting credit
          INSERT history record
          Display final message and issue cash
    Else
          Write error message
    End If
    On Error: ROLLBACK
COMMIT
```

Figure 13.1   Pseudo code for an airline reservation transaction.

Besides the BEGIN TRANSACTION and COMMIT statements, the ROLLBACK statement may be used. ROLLBACK is like an undo command in a word processor. ROLLBACK causes all effects of a transaction to be removed. The database is restored to the state before the transaction was executed. One situation for issuing a ROLLBACK statement is to allow the user to cancel a transaction. The ROLLBACK statement also can be used as part of exception-handling statements such as the "On Error" line in Figure 13.1. Exception-handling statements are part of programming languages such as COBOL and Visual Basic. Exception handling allows unanticipated errors such as communication errors to be processed separately from the normal logic of the transaction.

Transactions can be defined within embedded or standalone SQL. Embedded SQL means using SQL inside a host programming language such as COBOL or Visual Basic. Figure 13.1 depicts pseudo code for a transaction embedded inside a host programming language. Valid programming language statements would be substituted for lines with pseudo code such as "Display greeting." When a transaction is used in stand-alone SQL, the BEGIN TRANSACTION and COMMIT statements are often omitted. In this case, each SQL statement defaults to a separate transaction.

Other Transaction Examples

Figures 13.2 and 13.3 depict transactions for an airline reservation and product order. In both examples, the transaction consists of more than one database action (read or write).

13.1.2 Transaction Properties

DBMSs ensure that transactions obey certain properties. The most important and widely known properties are the ACID properties (atomic, consistent, isolated, and durable) as discussed below.

- **Atomic** means that a transaction cannot be subdivided. Either all the work in the transaction is completed or nothing is done. For example, the ATM transaction will not debit an account without also crediting a corresponding account.

```
BEGIN TRANSACTION
   Display greeting
   Get reservation preferences from user
   SELECT departure and return flight records
   If reservation is acceptable then
        UPDATE seats remaining of departure flight record
        UPDATE seats remaining of return flight record
        INSERT reservation record
        Print ticket if requested
   End If
   On Error: ROLLBACK
COMMIT
```

| **Figure 13.2** | Pseudo code for an airline reservation transaction. |

```
BEGIN TRANSACTION
   Display greeting
   Get order request
   SELECT product record
   If product is available then
        UPDATE QOH of product record
        INSERT order record
        Send message to shipping department
   End If
   On Error: ROLLBACK
COMMIT
```

| **Figure 13.3** | Pseudo code for a product order transaction. |

- **Consistent** means that if applicable constraints are true before the transaction starts, the constraints will be true after the transaction terminates. For example, if a user's account is balanced before a transaction, then the account is balanced after the transaction. Otherwise, the transaction is rejected and no changes take effect.

- **Isolated** means that changes resulting from a transaction are not revealed to other users until the transaction terminates. For example, your significant other will not know that you are withdrawing money until your ATM transaction completes.

- **Durable** means that any changes resulting from a transaction are permanent. No failure will erase any changes after a transaction terminates. For example, if a bank's computer experiences a failure five minutes after your transaction completes, the results of your transaction are still recorded on the bank's database.

To ensure that transactions meet the ACID properties, DBMSs provide certain services that are transparent to database developers (programmers and analysts). In common usage, transparency means that you can see through an object, rendering its inner details invisible. For DBMSs, transparency means that the inner details of transaction services are invisible. Transparency is very important because services that ensure ACID transactions are difficult to implement. By providing these services, DBMSs improve productivity of database programmers and analysts.

DBMSs provide two services, recovery transparency and concurrency transparency, to ensure that transactions obey the ACID properties. Recovery involves actions to deal with failures such as communication errors and software crashes. Concurrency involves actions to control interference among multiple, simultaneous users of the database. The following discussion provides details about transparency for recovery and concurrency.

- <u>Recovery transparency</u> means that the DBMS automatically restores a database to a consistent state after a failure. For example, if a communication failure occurs during an ATM transaction, the effects of the transaction are automatically removed from the database. On the other hand, if the DBMS crashes three seconds after an ATM transaction is completed, the effects of the transaction still remain on the database.

- <u>Concurrency transparency</u> means that users perceive the database as a single-user system even though there may be many simultaneous users. For example, even though many users may try to reserve a popular flight using a reservation transaction, the DBMS ensures that users do not overwrite each other's work.

Even though the inner details of concurrency and recovery are not visible to a user, these services are not free. Recovery and concurrency involve overhead that may adversely impact performance or require additional resources to reach an acceptable level of performance. The database designer must be aware of the resource implications of these services. More computing resources such as memory or hard disk space may be useful to improve performance. In addition, the purchase price of a DBMS may depend on how efficiently these services can be performed. DBMSs that perform transaction processing very efficiently can be costly.

Transaction design is another reason for understanding details of concurrency control and recovery. Even if the database designer devotes adequate resources to transaction processing, poor transaction design can lead to performance problems. To achieve a satisfactory transaction design, you should have background about the details of concurrency control and recovery, as discussed in the following sections.

13.2 CONCURRENCY CONTROL

Most organizations cannot function without multiuser databases. For example, airline, retail, banking, and help desk databases can have thousands of users simultaneously trying to conduct business. Multiple users can access these databases concurrently, that is, at the same time. If access was restricted to only one user at a time, little work would be accomplished and most users would take their business elsewhere. However, concurrent users cannot be permitted to interfere with each other. This section defines the objective, problems, and tools for concurrency control.

13.2.1 Objective of Concurrency Control

The objective of concurrency control is to maximize transaction throughput while preventing interference among multiple users. Transaction throughput, the number of transactions processed per time unit, is a measure of the amount of work performed by a DBMS. Typically, transaction throughput is reported in transactions per minute. In a high-volume environment such as order entry, DBMSs may need to process thousands of transactions per minute. From the perspective of the user, transaction throughput is related to response time. Higher transaction throughput means lower response times. Users are typically unwilling to wait more than a few seconds for completion of a transaction.

If there is no interference, the result of executing concurrent transactions is the same as executing the same transactions in some sequential order. Sequential execution means that one transaction completes before another one executes, thus ensuring no interference. Executing transactions sequentially would result in low throughput and high waiting times. Thus, DBMSs allow transactions to execute simultaneously while ensuring the results are the same as though executed sequentially.

Transactions executing simultaneously cannot interfere unless they are manipulating common data. Most concurrent transactions manipulate only small amounts of common data. For example, in an airline reservation, two users can simultaneously enter new reservation records because the reservation records are unique for each customer. However, interference can occur on the seats-remaining field of a flight table. For popular flights, many users may want to decrement the value of the seats-remaining field. It is critical that the DBMS control concurrent updating of this field in popular flight records.

A hot spot is common data that multiple users try to change simultaneously. Essentially, a hot spot represents a scarce resource that users must queue to access. Typical hot spots are the seats remaining for popular flights, the quantity on hand of popular inventory items, and the seats taken in popular course offerings. In an ideal world, DBMSs would only track hot spots. Unfortunately, hot spots can be difficult to know in advance so DBMSs typically track access to all parts of a database.

Interference on hot spots can lead to lost data and poor decision making. The following sections describe interference problems and the tools to prevent them.

13.2.2 Interference Problems

There are three problems that can result because of simultaneous access to a database: (1) lost update, (2) uncommitted dependency, and (3) incorrect summary. This section defines each problem and presents examples of their occurrence.

Lost Update

Lost update is the most serious interference problem because changes to a database are inadvertently lost. In a lost update, one user's update overwrites another user's update, as depicted by the timeline of Figure 13.4. The timeline shows two concurrent transac-

---

Transaction Throughput the number of transactions processed per time interval. It is an important measure of transaction processing performance.

Hot Spot common data that multiple users try to change. Without adequate concurrency control, users may interfere with each other on hot spots.

Lost Update a concurrency control problem in which one user's update overwrites another user's update.

Transaction A	Time	Transaction B
Read SR (10)	T_1	
	T_2	Read SR (10)
If SR > 0 then SR = SR − 1	T_3	
	T_4	If SR > 0 then SR = SR − 1
Write SR (9)	T_5	
	T_6	Write SR (9)

Figure 13.4   **Example lost update problem.**

tions trying to update the seats remaining (*SR*) field of the same flight record. Assume that the value of *SR* is 10 before the transactions begin. After time T_2, both transactions have stored the value of 10 for *SR* in local buffers as a result of the read operations. After time T_4, both transactions have made changes to their local copy of *SR*. However, each transaction changes the value to 9, unaware of the activity of the other transaction. After time T_6, the value of *SR* on the database is 9. But the value after finishing both transactions should be 8, not 9! One of the changes has been lost.

Some students become confused about the lost update problem because of the actions performed on local copies of the data. The calculations at times T_3 and T_4 are performed in memory buffers specific to each transaction. Even though transaction A has changed the value of *SR,* transaction B performs the calculation with its own local copy of *SR* having a value of 10. The write operation performed by transaction A is not known to transaction B unless transaction B reads the value again.

A lost update involves two or more transactions trying to change (write to) the same part of the database. As you will see in the next two subsections, two transactions also can conflict if only one is changing the database.

Uncommitted Dependency

Uncommitted Dependency a concurrency control problem in which one transaction reads data written by another transaction before the other transaction commits.

An uncommitted dependency occurs when one transaction reads data written by another transaction before the other transaction commits. An uncommitted dependency is also known as a dirty read because it is caused by one transaction reading dirty (uncommitted) data. In Figure 13.5, transaction A reads the *SR* field, changes its local copy of the *SR* field, and writes the new value back to the database. Transaction B then reads the changed value. Before transaction A commits, however, an error is detected and transaction A issues a rollback. The rollback could have been issued as a result of the user canceling the transaction or as a result of a failure. The value used by transaction B is now a phantom value. The real *SR* value is now 10 because A's change was not permanent. Transaction B may use its value (9) to make an erroneous decision. For example, if *SR*'s value was 1 before transaction A began, transaction B might be denied a reservation.

Because data are not permanent until a transaction commits, a conflict can occur even though only one transaction writes to the database. An uncommitted dependency involves one transaction writing and another transaction reading the same part of the database. However, an uncommitted dependency will not occur unless there is a rollback. The next problem shows another conflict when only one transaction writes to a database.

Transaction A	Time	Transaction B
Read SR (10)	T_1	
SR = SR − 1	T_2	
Write SR (9)	T_3	
	T_4	Read SR (9)
Rollback	T_5	

Figure 13.5   **Example dirty read problem.**

Incorrect Summary

> **Incorrect Summary** a concurrency control problem in which a transaction reads several values, but another transaction updates some of the values while the first transaction is still executing.

The third problem, <u>incorrect summary,</u> is the least serious of the interference problems. An incorrect summary[2] occurs when a transaction calculating a summary function reads some values before another transaction changes the values but reads other values after another transaction changes the values. In Figure 13.6, transaction B reads SR_1 after transaction A changes the value but reads SR_2 before transaction A changes the value. For consistency, transaction B should use all the values either before or after they are changed by another transaction. An incorrect summary involves one transaction reading and the second transaction changing the same part of the database.

A variation of the incorrect summary problem is known as the phantom read problem. The <u>phantom read problem</u> occurs when a transaction executes a query with record conditions. Then another transaction inserts or modifies data that the query would retrieve. Finally, the original transaction executes the same query again. The second query execution retrieves different records than the first execution. The new and changed records are phantom because they did not exist in the result of the first query execution.

13.2.3 Concurrency Control Tools

This section describes two tools (locks and the two-phase locking protocol) used by most DBMSs to prevent the three interference problems discussed in the previous section. In addition to the two tools, the deadlock problem is presented because it can result through the use of locks. This section closes by briefly discussing optimistic concurrency control approaches that do not use locks.

Locks

> **Lock** a fundamental tool of concurrency control. A lock on a database item prevents other transactions from performing conflicting actions on the same item.

Locks provide a way to prevent other users from accessing part of the database being used. Before accessing part of the database, a lock must be obtained. Other users must wait if trying to obtain a conflicting lock on the same part of the database. Table 13–2 shows conflicts for two kinds of locks. A <u>shared</u> (S) <u>lock</u> must be obtained before reading part of the database, while an <u>exclusive</u> (X) <u>lock</u> must be obtained before writing. As shown in Table 13–2, any number of users can hold a shared lock on the same part of the database. However, only one user can hold an exclusive lock.

---

[2]An incorrect summary is also known as an inconsistent analysis and a nonrepeatable read.

Transaction A	Time	Transaction B
Read SR_1 (10)	T_1	
$SR_1 = SR_1 - 1$	T_2	
Write SR_1 (9)	T_3	
	T_4	Read SR_1 (9)
	T_5	Sum = Sum + SR_1
	T_6	Read SR_2 (5)
	T_7	Sum = Sum + SR_2
Read SR_2 (5)	T_8	
$SR_2 = SR_2 - 1$	T_9	
Write SR_2 (4)	T_{10}	

Figure 13.6   **Example incorrect summary problem.**

TABLE 13–2	**Locking Conflicts**	

	User 2 Requests	
	S Lock	X Lock
User 1 Holds		
S Lock	Lock granted	User 2 waits
X Lock	User 2 waits	User 2 waits

The concurrency control manager is the part of the DBMS responsible for managing locks. The concurrency control manager maintains a hidden[3] table to record locks held by various transactions. A lock record contains a transaction identifier, a record identifier, a kind, and a count, as explained in Table 13–3. In the simplest scheme, the kind is either shared or exclusive, as discussed previously. Most DBMSs have other kinds of locks to improve efficiency and allow for more concurrent access. The concurrency control manager can perform two actions on lock records. The lock action adds a record to the lock table. Likewise, the unlock or release action deletes a record from the lock table.

Locking granularity is one complication about locks. Granularity refers to the size of the database item locked. The previous discussion assumed that locks are held for records. Most DBMSs can hold locks for different granularities, as depicted in Figure 13.7. The entire database is the coarsest lock that can be held. If an exclusive lock is held on the entire database, no other users can access the database until the lock is released. On the other extreme, an individual field is the finest lock that can be held. Locks also can be held on parts of the database not generally seen by users. For example, locks can be held on indexes and pages (physical records).

Locking Granularity
the size of the database item locked. Locking granularity is a trade-off between waiting time (amount of concurrency permitted) and overhead (number of locks held).

---

[3]The lock table is hidden from all users except the internal concurrency control manager. Under special circumstances, the database administrator can access the lock table.

TABLE 13–3	Fields in a Lock Record
Field Name	*Description*
Transaction identifier	Unique identifier for transaction
Record identifier	Identifies the record to be locked
Kind	Indicates the intended usage of the locked record
Count	Number of other users holding this kind of lock

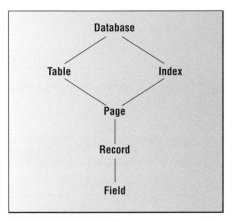

Figure 13.7   **Typical levels of locking granularity.**

Intent Lock a lock on a large database item (such as a table) that indicates that the user intends to lock smaller items contained in the larger item. Intent locks conflict with shared or exclusive locks on the large database item but do not conflict with locks on smaller contained items.

Locking granularity is a trade-off between overhead and waiting. Holding locks at a fine level decreases waiting among users but increases system overhead because more locks must be obtained. Holding locks at a coarser level reduces the number of locks but increases the amount of waiting. In some DBMSs, the concurrency control manager tries to detect the pattern of usage and promotes locks if needed. For example, the concurrency control manager initially can grant record locks to a transaction in anticipation that only a few records will be locked. If the transaction continues to request locks, the concurrency control component can promote the record locks to a lock on the entire table.

To alleviate the blocking caused by locking coarse items as shared or exclusive, intent locks can be used. Intent locks support more concurrency on coarse items than shared or exclusive locks. A transaction requests an intent lock if it intends to lock items of finer granularity. For example, a transaction should request an intent lock on a table for which it intends to lock records of the table. The intent lock on the table does not conflict with other intent locks on the table but conflicts with shared or exclusive locks on the table.

Deadlocks

Deadlock a problem of mutual waiting that can occur when using locks. If a deadlock is not resolved, the involved transactions will wait forever.

Using locks to prevent interference problems can lead to deadlocks. A deadlock is a problem of mutual waiting. One transaction has a resource that another transaction needs, and a second transaction holds a resource that the first transaction needs. Figure 13.8 depicts a deadlock among two transactions trying to reserve seats on a flight in-

Transaction A	Time	Transaction B
XLock SR$_1$	T$_1$	
	T$_2$	XLock SR$_2$
XLock SR$_2$ (wait)	T$_3$	
	T$_4$	XLock SR$_1$ (wait)

Figure 13.8   Example deadlock problem.

volving more than one part. Transaction A acquires an exclusive lock on the first part (say from Denver to Chicago) followed by transaction B acquiring a lock on the second part (say from Chicago to New York). Transaction A tries to lock the second part but is blocked because transaction B holds an exclusive lock. Likewise, transaction B must wait to obtain a lock on the first part. Deadlocks can involve more than two transactions, but the pattern is more complex.

The concurrency control manager can either prevent deadlocks or detect deadlocks. To prevent deadlocks, the concurrency control manager aborts transactions. Most DBMSs use a time-out policy to select transactions to abort. The concurrency control manager aborts (with a ROLLBACK statement) any transaction waiting for more than a specified time. Note that a time-out policy may abort transactions that are not deadlocked. The time-out interval should be set large enough so that few nondeadlocked transactions will wait that long. Some DBMSs try to detect deadlocks by looking for patterns of mutual waiting. Because detecting deadlocks can involve significant computation time, most DBMSs do not try to detect them.

Two Phase Locking Protocol

Definition of 2PL
(1) Before reading or writing to a part of the database, the transaction must acquire the applicable lock to that part of the database.
(2) After releasing a lock, the transaction does not acquire any new locks.

To ensure that lost update problems do not occur, the concurrency control manager requires that all transactions follow the Two Phase Locking (2PL) protocol. Protocol is a fancy word for a group behavior rule. A protocol binds all members of a group to behave in a specified manner. For human communication, Robert's Rules of Order require all members of a meeting to follow certain rules. For data communication, protocols ensure that messages have a common format that both sender and receiver can process. For concurrency control, all transactions must follow the 2PL protocol to ensure that no interference problems occur. Two phase locking has two conditions, as shown in the margin.

The first condition follows from the usage of locks as previously explained. The second condition is subtler. If new locks are acquired after releasing locks, a group of transactions can operate on different states of a data item, leading to lost update problems.

The second condition is usually simplified[4] so that at least exclusive locks are held until the end of the transaction. At the commit point, locks of a transaction are released. Figure 13.9 graphically depicts the 2PL with the simplified second condition. At the beginning of the transaction (BOT), a transaction has no locks. A growing phase ensues in

---

[4]Strict 2PL, the most popular variation of 2PL, does not release exclusive locks until end of transaction. Rigorous 2PL, another 2PL variation, does not release any locks until end of transaction. Because strict 2PL allows more concurrency and involves fewer deadlocks than rigorous 2PL, it is more widely implemented.

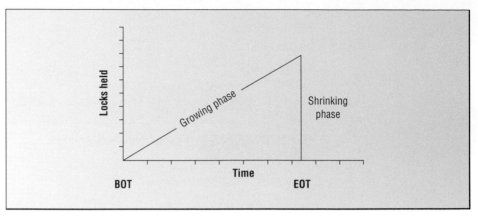

Figure 13.9 Growing and shrinking phases of 2PL.

which the transaction acquires locks but never releases any locks. At the end of the transaction (EOT), the shrinking phase occurs in which all locks are released together.

Simplifying the definition of 2PL makes the protocol easier to enforce and prevents the other concurrency control problems (uncommitted dependency and incorrect summary). Holding locks until end of transaction obviates the difficult problem of predicting when a transaction may release locks. Holding locks until end of transaction also prevents the uncommitted dependency and incorrect summary problems because changes are not exposed to other transactions until permanent (after commit).

Optimistic Approaches

The use of locks and 2PL is a pessimistic approach to concurrency control. Locking assumes that every transaction conflicts. If contention is only for relatively few hot spots, then locking may require excessive overhead.

Optimistic concurrency control approaches assume that conflicts are rare. If conflicts are rare, it is more efficient to check for conflicts rather than use locks to force waiting. In optimistic approaches, transactions are permitted to access the database without acquiring locks. Instead, the concurrency control manager checks whether a conflict has occurred. The check can be performed either just before a transaction commits or after each read and write. By reviewing the relative time of reads and writes, the concurrency control manager can determine whether a conflict has occurred. If a conflict occurs, the concurrency control manager issues a rollback and restarts the offending transaction.

Despite the appeal of optimistic approaches, most DBMSs use 2PL. Although Oracle provides a kind of optimistic concurrency control known as versioning, it does not appear widely used. The performance of optimistic approaches depends on the frequency of conflicts. If conflicts increase, the performance of optimistic approaches decreases. Even if conflicts are rare, optimistic approaches can have more variability because the penalty for conflicts is larger in optimistic approaches. Pessimistic approaches resolve conflicts by waiting. Optimistic approaches resolve conflicts by rolling back and restarting. Restarting a transaction may delay a transaction more than waiting for a resource to be released.

13.3 RECOVERY MANAGEMENT

Recovery management is a service to restore a database to a consistent state after a failure. This section describes the kinds of failures to prevent, the tools of recovery management, and the recovery processes that use the tools.

13.3.1 Data Storage Devices and Failure Types

From the perspective of database failures, volatility is an important characteristic of data storage devices. Main memory is <u>volatile</u> because it loses its state if power is lost. In contrast, a hard disk is <u>nonvolatile</u> because it retains its state if power is lost. This distinction is important because DBMSs cannot depend on volatile memory to recover data after failures. Even nonvolatile devices are not completely reliable. For example, certain failures make the contents of a hard disk unreadable. To achieve high reliability, DBMSs may replicate data on several kinds of nonvolatile storage media such as a hard disk, magnetic tape, and an optical disk. Using a combination of nonvolatile devices improves reliability because different kinds of devices usually have independent failure rates.

Some failures affect main memory only, while others affect both volatile and nonvolatile memory. Table 13–4 shows four kinds of failures along with their effect and frequency. The first two kinds of failures affect memory of one executing transaction. When writing code, one often checks for error conditions such as an invalid account number or cancellation of the transaction by the user. A program-detected failure usually leads to aborting the transaction with a specified message to the user. The SQL ROLLBACK statement is used to abort a transaction if an abnormal condition occurs. Recall that the ROLLBACK statement causes all changes made by the transaction to be removed from the database. Program-detected failures are usually the most common and least harmful.

Abnormal termination has an effect similar to a program-detected failure but a different cause. The transaction aborts, but the error message is often unintelligible to the user. Abnormal termination can be caused by events such as transaction time-out, communication line failure, or programming error (for example, dividing by zero). The On Error statement in Figure 13.1 detects abnormal termination. A ROLLBACK statement removes any effects of the terminated transaction on the database.

The last two kinds of failures have more serious consequences but are usually far less common. A system failure is an abnormal termination of the operating system. An operating system failure affects all executing transactions. A device failure such as a disk crash affects all executing transactions and all committed transactions whose work is recorded on the disk. A device failure can take hours to recover while a system crash can take minutes.

TABLE 13–4	Failure Types, Effects, and Frequency	
Type	*Effect*	*Frequency*
Program-detected	Local (1 transaction)	Most frequent
Abnormal termination	Local (1 transaction)	Moderate frequency
System failure	Global (all active transactions)	Not frequent
Device failure	Global (all active and past transactions)	Least frequent

13.3.2 Recovery Tools

The recovery manager uses redundancy and control of the timing of database writes to restore a database after a failure. Three tools discussed in this section—transaction log, checkpoint, and database backup—are forms of redundancy. The last tool—force writing—allows the recovery manager to control when database writes are recorded. This section explains the nature of these tools, while the next section explains how these tools are used in recovery processes.

Transaction Log

Transaction Log   a table that contains a history of all database changes. The recovery manager uses its log table to recover from failures.

A transaction log is like a shadow following a database. Any change to the database is also recorded in the log. A typical log (Table 13–5) contains a transaction identifier, the database action, the time, a row identifier, a column name, and values (old and new). The old and new values are sometimes called the before and after images, respectively. If the database action is insert, the log only contains the new value. Similarly, if the database action is delete, the log only contains the old value. Besides insert, update, and delete actions, log records are created for the begin and the end of a transaction. The log is usually stored as a hidden database table not available to normal users.

The recovery manager can perform two operations on the log. In an undo operation, the database reverts to a previous state by substituting the old value for whatever value is stored in the database. In a redo operation, the recovery component reestablishes a new state by substituting the new value for whatever value is stored in the database. To undo (redo) a transaction, the undo (redo) operation is applied to all log records of a specified transaction except for the begin and commit records.

A log can add considerable storage overhead. In an environment of large transaction volumes, 10,000 megabytes of log records can be generated each day. Because of this large size, many organizations have both an on-line log stored on disk and an archive log stored on magnetic tape. In addition to the size, the integrity of the log is crucial. Some DBMSs can maintain redundant logs to provide nonstop processing in case of a log failure.

Checkpoint Table

Checkpoint Table   a hidden table that contains the current position of the log at specified intervals. The checkpoint table is used to reduce the time to recover from failures.

The checkpoint table is another hidden table used by the recovery manager. The purpose of the checkpoint table is to reduce the time to recover from failures. At periodic times, a record is written to the checkpoint table to record the current log position. In addition, a checkpoint record is added to the log to record all active transactions and all log buffers

TABLE 13–5	Example Transaction Log for an ATM Transaction

TransNo	Action	Time	Table	Row	Column	Old	New
T101	BEGIN	10:29					
T101	Update	10:30	Acct	A10	Bal	100	200
T101	Update	10:30	Acct	A25	Bal	500	400
T101	Insert	10:32	Hist	H100	CustNo		C100
T101	END	10:33					

are written to disk. At restart time, the recovery manager consults the checkpoint table to commence the restoration process.

The checkpoint interval is defined as the period between writing to the checkpoint table. The interval can be expressed as a time (such as five minutes) or as a number of committed transactions. The checkpoint interval is a design parameter. A small interval reduces restart work but causes more overhead to record checkpoints. A large interval reduces checkpoint overhead but increases restart work. A typical checkpoint interval might be five minutes for large transaction volumes.

The implementation of the checkpoint process depends on the DBMS. In most DBMSs, all transaction activity must cease while a checkpoint occurs. Other systems permit concurrent transaction processing while a checkpoint occurs. The checkpoint interval should be larger (less frequent) if the DBMS requires all transaction activity to cease until a checkpoint completes.

Force Writing

Force Writing the ability to control when data are transferred to nonvolatile storage. This ability is fundamental to recovery management.

The ability to control when data are transferred to nonvolatile storage is known as force writing. Without the ability to control the timing of write operations to nonvolatile storage, recovery is not possible. Force writing means that the DBMS, not the operating system, controls when data are written to nonvolatile storage. Normally, when a program issues a write command, the operating system puts the data in a buffer. For efficiency, the data are not written to disk until the buffer is full. Typically, there is some small delay between the arrival of data in a buffer and the transferring of the buffer to disk. With force writing, the operating system allows the DBMS to transfer the data directly to disk without the intermediate use of the buffer.

The recovery manager uses force writing at checkpoint time and the end of a transaction. At checkpoint time, in addition to inserting a checkpoint record, all log and sometimes all database buffers are force written to disk. This force writing can add considerable overhead to the checkpoint process. At the end of a transaction, the recovery manager force writes any log records of a transaction remaining in memory.

Database Backup

A backup is a copy of all or part of a disk. The backup is used when the disk containing the database or log is damaged. A backup is usually made on magnetic tape because it is less expensive and more reliable than disk. Periodically, a backup should be made for both the database and the log. To save time, most backup schedules include less frequent massive backups to copy the entire contents of a disk and more frequent incremental backups to copy only the changed part.

13.3.3 Recovery Processes

The recovery process depends on the kind of failure. Recovery from a device failure is simple but can be time consuming, as listed below:

- The database is restored from the most recent backup.
- Then, the recovery manager applies the redo operator to all committed transactions after the backup. Because the backup may be several hours to days old, the log must be consulted to restore transactions committed after the backup.
- The recovery process finishes by restarting incomplete transactions.

For local failures and system failures, the recovery process depends on when database changes are recorded on disk. Database changes can be recorded before the commit (immediate update) or after the commit (deferred update). The amount of work and the use of log operations (undo and redo) depend on the timing of database updates. The remainder of this section describes recovery processes for local and system failures under each scenario.

Immediate Update

Immediate Update Approach database updates are written to the disk when they occur but after corresponding log updates. To restore a database, both undo and redo operations may be needed.

In the immediate update approach, database updates are written to the disk when they occur. Database writes occur at checkpoint time and when buffers are full. However, it is essential that database writes occur after writes of the corresponding log records. This usage of the log is known as the write ahead log protocol. If log records were written after corresponding database records, recovery would not be possible if a failure occurred between the time of writing the database records and the log records.

Recovery from a local failure is easy because only a single transaction is affected. All log records of the transaction are found. The undo operation is then applied to each log record of the transaction. If a failure occurs during the recovery process, the undo operation is applied again. The effect of applying the undo operator multiple times is the same as applying undo one time. After completing the undo operations, the recovery manager may offer the user the chance to restart the aborted transaction.

Recovery from a system failure is more difficult because all active users are affected. To help you understand recovery from a system failure, Figure 13.10 shows the progress of a number of transactions with respect to the end of a transaction, the most recent checkpoint, and the failure. Each transaction represents a class of transactions. For example, transaction class T1 represents transactions started and finished before the checkpoint (and the failure). There are no other kinds of transactions possible.

The immediate update approach may involve both undo and redo operations, as summarized in Table 13–6. To understand the amount of work necessary, remember that

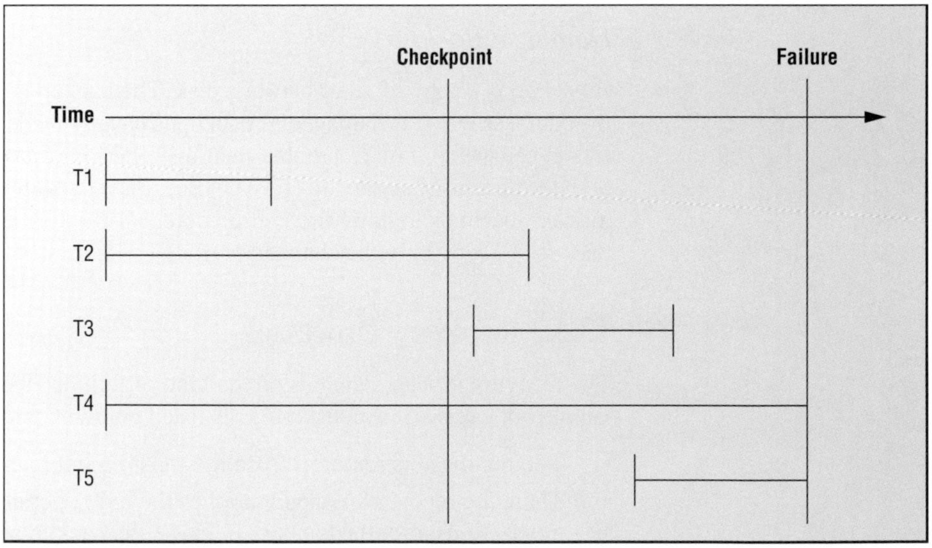

Figure 13.10 Transaction timeline.

TABLE 13–6	Summary of Restart Work for the Immediate Update Approach

Class	Description	Restart Work
T1	Finished before CP	None
T2	Started before CP; finished before failure	Redo forward from checkpoint
T3	Started after CP; finished before failure	Redo forward from checkpoint
T4	Started before CP; not yet finished	Undo backwards from most recent log record
T5	Started after CP; not yet finished	Undo backwards from most recent log record

log records are stable at checkpoint time and end of transaction and database changes are stable at checkpoint time. Although other database writes occur when a buffer fills, the timing of other writes is unpredictable. T1 transactions require no work because both log and database changes are stable before the failure. T2 transactions must be redone from the checkpoint because only database changes prior to the checkpoint are stable. T3 transactions must be redone entirely because database changes are not guaranteed to be stable even though some changes may be recorded on disk. T4 and T5 transactions must be undone entirely because some database changes after the checkpoint may be recorded on disk.

After a system failure, the checkpoint table and the log are used to restore transactions to a consistent state. Using the most recent checkpoint record, the recovery manager locates the log record written at the time of the checkpoint. Active transactions are classified, as specified in Table 13–6. The recovery manager applies the undo operator to all T4 and T5 transactions and the redo operator to all T2 and T3 transactions. Finally, all T4 and T5 transactions are restarted.

Deferred Update

Deferred Update Approach database updates are written only after a transaction commits. To restore a database, only redo operations are used.

In the deferred update approach, database updates are written to disk only after a transaction commits. No database writes occur at checkpoint time except for already committed transactions. The advantage of the deferred update approach is that undo operations are not necessary. However, it may be necessary to perform more redo operations than in the immediate update approach.

Local failures are handled without any restart work in the deferred update approach. Because no database changes occur until after a transaction commits, the transaction is aborted without any undo work. The recovery manager may still provide the user with the option of restarting the transaction.

System failures also can be handled without undo operations as depicted in Table 13–7. T4 and T5 transactions (not yet committed) do not require undo operations because no database changes are written to disk until after a transaction commits. T2 and T3 transactions (committed after the checkpoint) require redo operations because it is not known whether all database changes are stable. T2 transactions (started before the checkpoint) must be redone from their first log record rather than just from the checkpoint as in the immediate update approach. Thus, the deferred update approach requires

TABLE 13-7	Summary of Restart Work for the Deferred Update Approach	
Class	Description	Restart Work
T1	Finished before CP	None
T2	Started before CP; finished before failure	Redo forward from first log record
T3	Started after CP; finished before failure	Redo forward from first log record
T4	Started before CP; not yet finished	None
T5	Started after CP; not yet finished	None

more restart work for T2 transactions than does the immediate update approach. However, the deferred update approach requires no restart work for T4 and T5 transactions, while the immediate update approach must undo T4 and T5 transactions.

13.4 TRANSACTION DESIGN ISSUES

With DBMSs providing recovery and concurrency transparency, it is surprising that the database programmer still has important design decisions. The decisions made by database programmers can have a significant impact on the performance of transactions. Knowledge of the details of concurrency control and recovery can make you a better transaction designer. This section describes design decisions available to database programmers to improve transaction performance.

13.4.1 Transaction Boundary and Hot Spots

The database programmer is typically faced with developing an application to accomplish some database processing. For example, a database programmer may develop an application to enable a user to withdraw cash from an ATM, order a product, or register for classes. To build the application, the database programmer uses the transaction defining statements of SQL and the concurrency control and recovery services of the DBMS. The database programmer has at least several alternatives about where to use the transaction defining statements of SQL. This decision is called the transaction boundary.

The database programmer typically has the option of making one large transaction with all SQL statements or dividing the SQL statements into multiple, smaller transactions. For example, the SQL statements in the ATM transaction can be considered one transaction, as shown in Figure 13.1. Another option is to make each SQL statement a separate transaction. When transaction boundary statements (BEGIN TRANSACTION and COMMIT) are not used, each SQL statement defaults to a separate transaction.

Transaction Boundary
an important decision of transaction design in which an application consisting of a collection of SQL statements is divided into one or more transactions.

Trade-offs in Choosing Transaction Boundaries

When choosing a transaction's boundary, the objective is to minimize the duration of the transaction while ensuring that critical constraints are satisfied. DBMSs are designed for transactions of short duration because locking can force other transactions to wait. The duration includes not only the number of reads and writes to the database but the time spent waiting for user responses. Generally, the transaction boundary should not involve user interaction. In the ATM, airline reservation, and product order transactions (Figures 13.1, 13.2 and 13.3, respectively), the BEGIN TRANSACTION and COMMIT statements could be moved to surround just the SQL part of the pseudo code.

Duration should not compromise constraint checking. Because constraint checking must occur by the end of a transaction, it may be difficult to check some constraints if a transaction is decomposed into smaller transactions. For example, an important constraint in accounting transactions is that debits equal credits. If the SQL statements to post a debit and a credit are placed in the same transaction, then the DBMS can enforce the accounting constraint at the end of a transaction. If they are placed in separate transactions, constraint checking cannot occur until after both transactions are committed.

Hot Spots

To understand how transaction boundaries can affect users, hot spots should be identified. Recall that hot spots are common data that multiple users try to change simultaneously. If a selected transaction boundary eliminates (creates) a hot spot, it may be a good (poor) design.

Hot spots can be classified as system independent and system dependent. System-independent hot spots are parts of a table that many users simultaneously may want to change. Rows, fields, and the entire table can be system-independent hot spots. For example, in the airline reservation transaction (Figure 13.2), the seats-remaining field of popular flight records is a system-independent hot spot. The seats-remaining field is a hot spot on any DBMS executing this transaction.

System-dependent hot spots depend on the DBMS. Usually, system-dependent hot spots involve parts of the database hidden to normal users. Pages (physical records) containing database rows or index file records often can be system-dependent hot spots. For example, some DBMSs lock the next available page when inserting a record into a table. When inserting a new history record in the ATM transaction (Figure 13.1), the next available page of the history table is a system-dependent hot spot. On those DBMSs that lock just the individual record, there is no hot spot. There are also typically hot spots with certain commonly accessed nodes of indexes.

13.4.2 Example Transaction Boundary Design

To depict the transaction boundary choice, hierarchical forms provide a convenient context. A hierarchical form represents an application that reads and writes to a database. For example, the registration form of the university database (Figure 13.11) manipulates the *Registration* table in the main form and the *Enrollment* and *Offering* tables in the subform. When using the registration form to enroll in courses, a record is inserted in the *Registration* table after completing the main form. After completing each line in the subform, a record is inserted into the *Enrollment* table and the *OffSeatsRemain* field of the associated *Offering* row is updated.

When designing a hierarchical form, the database programmer has three reasonable choices for the transaction boundary:

1. The entire form.
2. The main form as one transaction and *all* subform lines as a second transaction.
3. The main form as one transaction and *each* subform line as separate transactions.

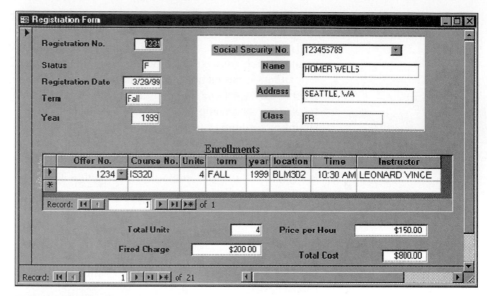

Figure 13.11   **Example of the registration form.**

The third choice is usually preferred because it provides transactions with the shortest duration. However, constraint checking may force the choice to (1) or (2). In the registration form, there are constraints that involve an entire registration such as a minimum number of hours for financial aid and prerequisites for a course. However, these constraints are not critical to check at end of a transaction. Most universities check these constraints at a later point before the next academic period begins. Thus, choice (3) is the best choice for the transaction boundary.

There are several hot spots common for each transaction boundary choice. The *OffSeatsRemain* field in popular *Offering* rows is a system-independent hot spot in any transaction involving the subform lines. The *OffSeatsRemain* field must be updated after each enrollment. The next page in the *Enrollment* table is a system-dependent hot spot in some DBMSs. After each subform line, a row is inserted in the *Enrollment* table. If the database locks the next available page rather than just the new row, all subform line transactions must obtain an exclusive lock on the next available physical record. However, if the DBMS can lock at the row level, there is no hot spot because each transaction will insert a different row.

Choice (3) provides another advantage due to reduced deadlock possibilities. In choices (1) and (2), deadlocks are possible because the transactions involve multiple course enrollments. For example, one transaction could obtain a lock on a data communications offering (IS470) and another transaction on a database offering (IS480). The first transaction may then wait for a lock on the IS480 offering, and the second transaction may wait for a lock on the IS470 offering. Choice (3) will be deadlock free if the hot spots are always obtained in the same order by every transaction. For example, if every transaction first obtains a lock on the next available page of *Enrollment* and then obtains a lock on an *Offering* row, then deadlock will not occur.

13.4.3 Isolation Levels

Two phase locking prevents the three concurrency control problems described in Section 12.2.2 if all locks are held until end of transaction. However, some transactions may not need this level of concurrency control. The lost update problem is the most serious problem and should always be prevented. Some transactions may be able to tolerate conflicts caused by the uncommitted dependency and inconsistent analysis problems. Transactions that do not need protection from these problems can relax conditions of the 2PL protocol and achieve faster execution speed.

The isolation level specifies the degree to which a transaction is separated from actions of other transactions. A transaction designer can balance concurrency control overhead with interference problems prevented by specifying the appropriate isolation level. The most common isolation levels are discussed below:

> **Isolation Level** defines the degree to which a transaction is separated from actions of other transactions. A transaction designer can balance concurrency control overhead with interference problems prevented by specifying the appropriate isolation level.

- **Serializable:** This isolation level prevents all three concurrency control problems but involves the most overhead and waiting. All locks must be held until end of transaction to ensure that none of the concurrency control problems occurs. You should use this level for transactions that cannot tolerate any concurrency problems.

- **Read Stability:** This isolation level prevents uncommitted dependency problems and nonrepeatable read problems involving retrieved records. Thus, a transaction can read a record more than one time and obtain the same value each time. Nonrepeatable reads involving queries (phantom reads) are not prevented. Thus, if a transaction executes the same query more than once, different records may be retrieved. You should use this level for transactions that will not execute the same query multiple times.

- **Cursor Stability:** This isolation level prevents uncommitted dependency problems but permits nonrepeatable read problems. Transactions using this isolation level can release read locks immediately rather than hold them to end of transaction. You should use this level for transactions that can tolerate changing data and for transactions that will not read the same data more than once.

- **Uncommitted Read:** This isolation level prevents lost update problems but permits uncommitted dependencies and nonrepeatable read problems. Transactions using this isolation level can access uncommitted changes of other transactions. Since this isolation level permits uncommitted dependencies, it is usually appropriate for retrievals only. If a transaction is sensitive to operating data that may be undone, this isolation level is not appropriate.

In SQL2, you can specify isolation levels using the SET TRANSACTION statement, as shown in Example 13.1. The SET TRANSACTION statement is usually placed just after the BEGIN TRANSACTION statement before any data manipulation statements. In this example, the READ COMMITTED keywords denote the cursor stability level. The other possible keywords are SERIALIZABLE for the serializable level, REPEATABLE READ for the read stability level, and READ UNCOMMITTED for the uncommitted read level. Some vendors do not support all of these levels while other vendors support additional levels.

EXAMPLE 13.1

SET TRANSACTION Statement to Set the Isolation Level of a Transaction

```
BEGIN TRANSACTION
SET TRANSACTION ISOLATION LEVEL READ COMMITTED
. . .
COMMIT
```

13.4.4 Timing of Integrity Constraint Enforcement

Besides setting the isolation level, SQL2 allows control of the timing of integrity constraint enforcement. By default, constraints are enforced immediately after each INSERT, UPDATE, and DELETE statement. For most constraints such as primary and foreign keys, immediate enforcement is appropriate. If a constraint is violated, the DBMS issues a rollback operation on the transaction. The rollback restores the database to a consistent state as the ACID properties ensure consistency at the end of a transaction.

For complex constraints, immediate enforcement may not be appropriate. For example, a faculty workload constraint ensures that each faculty member teaches between three and nine units each semester. If a transaction assigns an entire workload, checking of the constraint should be deferred until end of transaction. For these kinds of complex constraints, constraint timing should be specified.

In SQL2, constraint timing involves constraint definition and transaction definition. SQL2 provides an optional constraint timing clause that applies to primary key constraints, foreign key constraints, uniqueness constraints, check constraints, and assertions. A database administrator typically uses the constraint timing clause for constraints that may need deferred checking. Constraints that never need deferred checking do not need the timing clause as the default is NOT DEFERRABLE. The timing clause defines whether a constraint is deferrable and the default enforcement if deferrable, as shown in Examples 13.2 and 13.3.

Deferred Constraint Checking enforcing integrity constraints at end of transaction rather than immediately after each manipulation statement. Complex constraints may benefit from deferred checking.

EXAMPLE 13.2   Timing Clause for the *FacultyWorkLoad* Assertion

The constraint is deferrable and the default enforcement is deferred.

```
CREATE ASSERTION FacultyWorkLoad
  CHECK (NOT EXISTS
    ( SELECT Faculty.FacSSN, OffTerm, OffYear
        FROM Faculty, Offering, Course
        WHERE Faculty.FacSSN = Offering.FacSSN
          AND Offering.CourseNo = Course.CourseNo
        GROUP BY Faculty.FacSSN, OffTerm, OffYear
        HAVING SUM(CrsUnits) < 3 OR SUM(CrsUnits) > 9 ) )
  DEFERRABLE INITIALLY DEFERRED
```

EXAMPLE 13.3   Timing Clause for the *OfferingConflict* Assertion

The constraint is deferrable and the default enforcement is immediate.

```
CREATE ASSERTION OfferingConflict
  CHECK (NOT EXISTS
    ( SELECT O1.OfferNo
        FROM Offering O1, Offering O2
        WHERE O1.OfferNo <> O2.OfferNo
          AND O1.OffTerm = O2.OffTerm
          AND O1.OffYear = O2.OffYear
          AND O1.OffDays = O2.OffDays
```

```
                  AND O1.OffTime = O2.OffTime
                  AND O1.OffLocation = O2.OffLocation ) )
DEFERRABLE INITIALLY IMMEDIATE
```

For each transaction, the database programmer may specify whether deferrable constraints are deferred or immediately enforced using the SET CONSTRAINTS statement. Normally the SET CONSTRAINTS statement is placed just after the BEGIN TRANSACTION statement, as shown in Example 13.4. The SET CONSTRAINTS statement is not necessary for deferrable constraints that use the default enforcement. For example, if the *FacultyWorkLoad* assertion is deferred, no SET CONSTRAINTS statement is necessary because its default enforcement is deferred.

EXAMPLE 13.4   SET CONSTRANTS Statements for Several Transactions

```
BEGIN TRANSACTION
SET CONSTRAINTS FacultyWorkLoad IMMEDIATE
. . .
COMMIT

BEGIN TRANSACTION
SET CONSTRAINTS OfferingConflict DEFERRED
. . .
COMMIT
```

Implementation of the constraint timing part of SQL2 is highly variable. Most DBMSs do not support the constraint timing part exactly as specified in the standard. Many DBMSs have different syntax and proprietary language extensions for constraint timing.

13.5 WORKFLOW MANAGEMENT

Transaction management is part of a much larger area known as workflow management. Workflow management supports business processes, both automated and human performed. In contrast, transaction management supports properties of automated database processing. This section presents workflow management to provide a broader perspective for transaction management. This section first describes workflows, a broader notion than a database transaction. This section then discusses enabling technologies for workflow management, showing how transaction management is an important component.

13.5.1 Characterizing Workflows

Workflow A collection of related tasks structured to accomplish a business process.

Workflows support business processes such as providing phone service, obtaining a loan, and ordering a product. Workflows consist of tasks that can be performed by computers (software and hardware), humans, or a combination. For example, in providing phone service, software determines the time of a service appointment and updates a scheduling database, while a technician inspects the phone box to determine whether a problem exists. A workflow defines the order of performing the tasks, the conditions for tasks to be performed, and the results of performing tasks. For example, providing phone service involves an initial customer contact, an optional service visit, billing, and payment collection. Each of these tasks may have conditions under which they are performed and may result in actions such as database updates and invocation of other tasks.

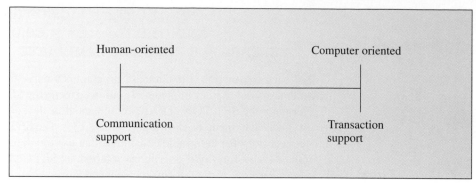

Figure 13.12 **Classification of workflow by task performance.**
Adapted from Sheth, Georgakopoulos, and Hornrick (1995).

Many different kinds of workflows exist. Sheth, Georgakopoulos, and Hornrick (1995) classify workflows as human-oriented versus computer-oriented, as depicted in Figure 13.12. In <u>human-oriented</u> workflows, humans provide most of the judgment to accomplish work. The computer has a passive role to supply data to facilitate human judgment. For example, in processing a loan, loan officers often determine the status of loans when the customer does not meet standard criteria about income and debt. Consultation with underwriters and credit personnel may be necessary. To support human-oriented workflows, electronic communication software such as e-mail, chat, and document annotation may be useful. In <u>computer-oriented</u> tasks, the computer determines the processing of work. For example, software for an ATM transaction determines whether a customer receives cash or is denied the request. To support computer-oriented workflows, transaction management is a key technology.

Another way to classify workflows is by task complexity versus task structure, as depicted in Figure 13.13. <u>Task complexity</u> involves the difficulty of performing individual tasks. For example, the decision to grant a loan may involve complex reasoning using many variables. In contrast, processing a product order may only involve requesting the product data from the customer. <u>Task structure</u> involves the relationships among tasks. Workflows with complex conditions have high structure. For example, processing an insurance claim may have conditions about denying the claim, litigating the claim, and investigating the claim.

13.5.2 Enabling Technologies

To support the concept of a workflow discussed in the previous section, three enabling technologies are important: (i) distributed object management, (ii) workflow specification, and (iii) customized transaction management. Transaction management as described in earlier sections fits as part of the third technology. The remainder of this section elaborates on each technology.

Distributed Object Management

Workflows can involve many types of data in remote locations. For example, data can include photos of an insurance claim, x-rays supporting a diagnosis, and an appraisal documenting a property for a loan application. These types of data are not traditionally managed by DBMSs. A new class of DBMSs known as object DBMSs has been developed to manage diverse types of data. Chapter 16 describes this new class of DBMSs.

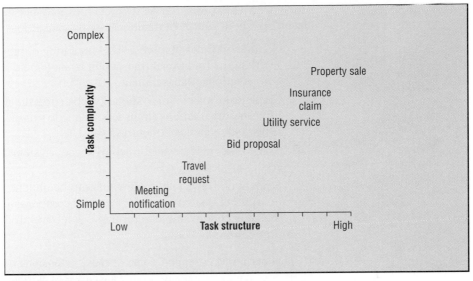

Figure 13.13   **Classification of workflow by task structure and complexity.**
Adapted from Sheth, Georgakopoulos, and Hornrick (1995).

In addition to new types of data, the data are typically not stored at one location and may be controlled by different DBMSs. For example, to support a loan application, a loan officer uses a credit report from a credit bureau, an appraisal from a certified appraiser, and loan processing guidelines from government agencies. Accessing and controlling distributed data can be difficult. Chapter 15 describes important principles of managing distributed data. Difficulties also can arise because the data may be controlled by different systems, some of which may not support SQL.

Workflow Specification and Implementation

To support workflows, the structure of tasks must be properly represented and implemented. Representing a workflow involves identifying the tasks and specifying the relationships among tasks. A complex task can involve a hierarchy of subtasks. A complex workflow can involve many tasks with numerous relationships. Constraints, rules, and graphical notation can be used to depict the order of tasks and task completion. One use of task relationships is to define constraints among transactions. For example, workflow specification can indicate that a student should be denied financial aid unless enrolling for a minimum number of hours by a specified date.

After a workflow is specified, it must be efficiently implemented. The implementation may involve diverse hardware, software, and people. A major challenge is to make diverse components communicate efficiently. Optimizing workflows through reengineering has become an important concern in many organizations. Optimization may involve removing duplicate tasks and increasing the amount of parallel work.

A number of software systems have been developed to support workflow specification. The main function of software under the name "workflow management" is to support workflow specification and implementation.

Customized Transaction Management

The earlier sections of this chapter described how DBMSs support ACID transactions. The ACID properties are indeed important and widely supported by DBMSs. However, to support workflows, the ACID properties may not be sufficient. The following list identifies shortcomings of traditional ACID transactions for workflow management:

- Some workflows involve tasks with a long duration because of user interaction. Traditional transaction management may not work well for these conversational transactions.

- Some tasks may involve subtasks, changing the notion of atomicity. The idea of nested transactions (transactions inside transactions) has been proposed for tasks with complex structures.

- Some tasks may be performed by legacy systems that do not support the ACID properties.

- Some workflows may require tasks to be undone after they are complete. In accounting systems, it is common for compensating transactions to correct mistakes. For example, returning a defective product removes the effect of the original product order.

Some DBMSs support some of these extensions now. For example, Sybase SQL Server provides save points so that a ROLLBACK statement can undo only part of the transaction. This extension can reduce the amount of work lost when a long transaction fails. Because of the utility of save points, the new SQL3 standard provides a SAVE-POINT statement and an extended ROLLBACK statement that can undo work to a specified save point.

To more fully support workflow management, some industry leaders have proposed that transaction management should be customized according to workflow requirements. The transaction properties supported for a workflow should be part of the workflow specification, not hardwired into the software supporting workflow management. DBMSs supporting workflow management may need to be more flexible. DBMSs might support different kinds of transactions or even allow transaction properties to be specified. Event processing in DBMSs can be used to support some features such as compensating transactions. Most DBMSs would need a major extension to support customized transaction management.

CLOSING THOUGHTS

This chapter has described the concept of database transactions, the services provided by the DBMS to support transactions, and transaction design skills for database programmers. A transaction is a user-defined unit of work with any number of reads and writes to a database. To define a transaction, several new SQL statements were introduced including BEGIN TRANSACTION, COMMIT, and ROLLBACK. DBMSs ensure that transactions are atomic (all or nothing), consistent (satisfy integrity constraints after completion), isolated (no interference from concurrent users), and durable (survive failures). To ensure these properties of transactions, DBMSs provide services for concurrency transparency (making a database seem like a single-user system) and recovery transparency (automatically restoring a database after a failure). These powerful services are not free as they can consume large amounts of computing resources and add to the purchase price of a DBMS.

Even though the concurrency and recovery services provided by a DBMS are transparent, you should understand some details of these services. Knowledge of these services can help you allocate computing resources, select a DBMS that provides the appropriate level of transaction support, and design efficient transactions. For concurrency control, you should understand the objective, interference problems, and the two phase locking protocol. For recovery management, you should understand the kinds of failures, the redundant storage needed for recovery, and the amount of work to restore a database after a failure.

To apply your knowledge of transaction management, this chapter demonstrated principles of transaction design. The most important choice in transaction design is the selection of a transaction boundary. The objective of choosing a transaction boundary is to minimize duration subject to the need for constraint checking. Critical constraints such as debit–credit in accounting systems may dictate that an application remain as one transaction rather than be split into smaller transactions. Other important decisions involve the degree of interference permitted, known as the isolation level, and the timing of constraint enforcement. SQL2 syntax for both decisions was shown in the chapter.

As either a database programmer or database administrator, you should remember that database transactions are only one kind of support for organizational work. Workflow management addresses issues beyond transaction management such as dependencies among transactions, different kinds of transactions, and annotation of work.

This chapter has described services of DBMSs to support transaction processing, the operating side of databases. Other chapters in Part 3 examine services to support other kinds of database processing such as data warehousing in Chapter 14. You should contrast the requirements to support transaction processing (operating decision making) as compared to data warehousing (tactical and strategic decision making).

REVIEW CONCEPTS

- Transactions containing a user-specified collection of database reads and writes.
- SQL statements to define transactions:

  BEGIN TRANSACTION and COMMIT
  ROLLBACK

- ACID properties of transactions: atomic, consistent, isolated, durable.
- Transparent services to hide inner details of transaction management.
- Concurrency transparency to support simultaneous usage of a database.
- Recovery transparency to restore a database to a consistent state after a failure.
- Concurrency control objective: maximizing transaction throughput while preventing interference problems.
- Interference on hot spots, common data manipulated by concurrent users.
- Effect of interference problems: lost update, uncommitted dependency, incorrect summary.
- Concurrency control manager to grant, release, and analyze locks.
- Growing and shrinking phases of two phase locking (2PL).
- Resolution of deadlocks with time-out and transaction restarting.
- Optimistic concurrency control approaches when interference is rare.
- Volatile versus nonvolatile storage.
- Effect of local, system, and media failures.
- Force writing to ensure nonvolatility of database writes.
- Redundant storage for recovery: log, checkpoint, backup.
- Amount of restart work in immediate update and deferred update recovery approaches.
- Selecting a transaction boundary to minimize duration while enforcing critical integrity constraints.
- Identifying system-independent and system-dependent hot spots in transactions.

- Transaction boundaries for hierarchical forms.
- Isolation levels for balancing the kinds of interference permitted against the corresponding overhead of concurrency control to prevent interference.
- Constraint timing specification to defer enforcement of integrity constraints until end of transaction.
- Workflow management to support collaborative work.

QUESTIONS

1. What does it mean to say that a transaction is a user-defined concept? Why is it important that transactions are user defined?

2. List transactions with which you have interacted in the last week.

3. Explain the purpose of the SQL statements for transaction management. What happens when you do not use the transaction management statements?

4. Briefly explain the meaning of the ACID properties. How do concurrency control and recovery management support the ACID properties?

5. Briefly explain the meaning of transparency as it relates to computer processing. Why is transparency important for concurrency control and recovery management?

6. What costs are associated with concurrency transparency and recovery transparency? In what role, database administrator or database programmer, would you assess these costs?

7. What is the objective of concurrency control? How is the measure used in the objective related to waiting time?

8. What is a hot spot? How are hot spots related to interference problems?

9. Discuss the consequences of each kind of interference problem. Which problem seems to be the most serious?

10. Explain how using locks prevents the lost update problem.

11. Explain how using locks and 2PL prevents the uncommitted dependency problem.

12. Explain how using locks prevents the incorrect summary problem.

13. What is locking granularity? What are the trade-offs of holding locks at a finer level versus a coarser level of granularity?

14. What is an intent lock? Why are intent locks used on items of coarse granularity?

15. Why is the second condition of 2PL typically simplified so that locks are released at the end of a transaction?

16. What is the appeal of optimistic concurrency control approaches? Why might optimistic concurrency control approaches not be used even if they provide better-expected performance?

17. Explain the difference between volatile and nonvolatile storage.

18. Explain the effects of local, system, and device failures on active and past transactions.

19. Why is force writing the most fundamental tool of recovery management?

20. What kind of redundant data is stored in logs, checkpoints, and backups?

21. Why is management of the log critical to recovery?

22. What restart work is necessary for a media failure?

23. What restart work is necessary for local and system failures under the immediate update approach?

24. What restart work is necessary for local and system failures under the deferred update approach?

25. What is a transaction boundary? Why can an inappropriate choice for transaction boundary lead to poor performance?

26. What criteria should be used in selecting a transaction boundary?

27. Why must constraints such as the debit–credit constraint be enforced as part of a transaction rather than between transactions?

28. Explain the difference between system-independent and system-dependent hot spots. Why is it useful to identify hot spots?

29. Explain the three choices for transaction boundary of a hierarchical form.

30. How can deadlock possibility be influenced by the choice of a transaction boundary?

31. Why should you consider relaxing the conditions of the 2PL protocol for a given transaction?

32. What are the SQL isolation levels and how do they relax the conditions of the 2PL protocol?

33. Provide an example of a constraint for which deferred enforcement may be appropriate.

34. What SQL statements and clauses involve constraint timing specification?

35. What is the role of the DBA in specification of constraint timing?

36. What is the role of the database programmer in specification of constraint timing?

37. What is a workflow and how is it related to database transactions?

38. What are the differences between human-oriented and computer-oriented workflows?

39. Provide examples of workflows with high task complexity. High task structure.

40. Discuss the enabling technologies for workflow management. What role does transaction management play in workflow management?

41. What are limitations of transaction management to support workflows?

PROBLEMS

ORDER

The problems provide practice using transaction-defining SQL statements, testing your knowledge of concurrency control and recovery management, and analyzing design decisions about transaction boundaries and hot spots.

1. Think of two transactions that you have encountered recently. Define pseudo code for the transactions in the style of Figures 13.1, 13.2, and 13.3.

2. Identify hot spots in your transactions from problem 1.

3. Using a timeline, depict a lost update problem using your transactions from problem 1 if no concurrency control is used.

4. Using a timeline, depict an uncommitted dependency problem using your transactions from problem 1 if no concurrency control is used.

5. Using a timeline, depict an incorrect summary problem using your transactions from problem 1 if no concurrency control is used.

6. Explain whether deadlock would be a problem using your transactions from problem 1 if locking is used. If a deadlock is possible, use a timeline to demonstrate deadlock with your transactions.

7. Use the Accounting Database tables and the Accounting Register (shown below) to answer problems 7.1 to 7.7. Comments are listed after the tables and the form.

> **Account**(<u>AcctNo</u>, Name, Address, Balance, LastCheck, StartDate)
> **Entry**(<u>EntryNo</u>, *AcctNo*, Date, Amount, Desc)
> **Category**(<u>CatNo</u>, Name, Description)
> **EntryLine**(<u>EntryNo</u>, <u>CatNo</u>, Amount, Description)

Accounting Register for Wells Fargo Credit Line

Entry No.	E101		**Date:**	3/11/2001
Description:	Purchases at OfficeMax		**Amount:**	$442.00
Invoice No.	I101			

Category	*Description*	*Amount*
Office supplies	Envelopes	25.00
Equipment	Fax machine	167.00
Computer software	MS Office upgrade	250.00

- The primary keys in the tables are underlined. The foreign keys are italicized.
- The Accounting Register records activities on an account, such as a line of credit or accounts receivable. The Accounting Register is designed for use by the accounting department of moderate-size businesses. The sample form shows one recorded entry, but a register contains all recorded entries since the opening of the account.
- The main form is used to insert a record into the *Entry* table and update the *Balance* field of the *Account* table. Accounts have a unique name (Wells Fargo Credit Line) that appears in the title of the register. Accounts have other attributes not shown on the form: a unique number (name is also unique), start date, address, type (Receivable, Investment, Credit, etc.), and current balance.
- In the subform, the user allocates the total amount of the entry to categories. The *Category* field is a combo box. When the user clicks on the category field, the category number and name are displayed. Entering a new subform line inserts a row into the *EntryLine* table.
- The *Description* field in the subform describes a row in the *EntryLine* table rather than the *Category* table.

7.1 What are the possible transaction boundaries for the Accounting Register form?

7.2 Select a transaction boundary from your choices in problem 7.1. Justify your choice using the criteria defined in Section 13.4.1.

7.3 Identify system-independent hot spots that result from concurrent usage (say, many clerks in the accounting department) of the Accounting Register. For each hot spot, explain why it is a hot spot.

7.4 Identify system-dependent hot spots that result from concurrent usage (say, many clerks in the accounting department) of the Accounting Register. You may assume that the DBMS cannot lock finer than a database page.

7.5 Describe a lost update problem involving one of your hot spots that could occur with concurrent usage of the Accounting Register. Use a timeline to depict your example.

7.6 Describe a dirty read situation involving one of your hot spots that could occur with concurrent usage of the Accounting Register. Use a timeline to depict your example.

7.7 Is deadlock likely to be a problem with concurrent usage of the Accounting Register? Consider the case where locks are held until all subform lines are complete. Why or why not? If deadlock is likely, provide an example as justification. Would there still be a deadlock problem if locks were held only until completion of each line on the subform? Why or why not?

8. Use the Patient tables and the Patient Billing Form (shown below) to answer problems 8.1 to 8.4. Comments are listed after the tables and the form.

Patient(PatSSN, PatName, PatCity, PatAge)
Doctor(DocNo, DocName, DocSpecialty)
Bill(BillNo, PatSSN, BillDate, AdmitDate, DischargeDate)
Charge(ChgNo, BillNo, ItemNo, ChgDate, ChgQty, DocNo)
Item(Itemno, ItemDesc, ItemUnit, ItemRate, ItemQty)

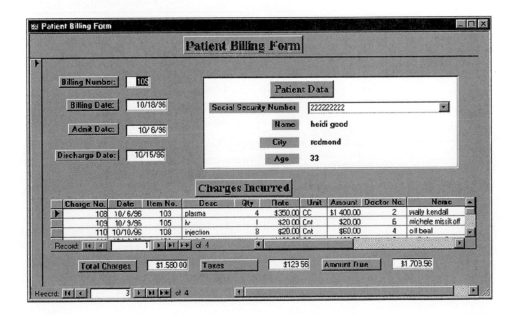

- The main form is used to insert a record into the *Bill* table. Fields from the *Patient* table are read-only in the main form.
- The subform can be used to insert a new row into the *Charge* table. Fields from the *Doctor* and the *Item* tables are read-only.
- When a subform line is entered, the associated item row is updated. The form field *Qty* is subtracted from the current value in the field *ItemQty* (item quantity on hand).

8.1 What are the possible transaction boundaries for the Patient Billing Form?

8.2 Select a transaction boundary from your choices in problem 8.1. Justify your choice using the criteria defined in Section 13.4.1.

8.3 Identify system-independent hot spots that result from concurrent usage (say, many health providers) of the Patient Billing Form. For each hot spot, explain why it is a hot spot.

8.4 Identify system-dependent hot spots that result from concurrent usage of the Patient Billing Form. You may assume that the DBMS cannot lock finer than a database page.

9. Use the Airline Reservation database tables and the Flight Reservation Form (shown below) to answer problems 9.1 to 9.4. Comments are listed after the tables and the form.

> **Flight**(<u>FlightNo</u>, DepCityCode, ArrCityCode, DepTime, ArrTime, FlgDays)
> **FlightDate**(<u>FlightNo, FlightDate,</u> RemSeats)
> **Reservation**(<u>ResNo</u>, CustNo, ResDate, Amount, CrCardNo)
> **ReserveFlight**(<u>ResNo, FlightNo, FlightDate</u>)
> **Customer**(<u>CustNo</u>, CustName, Custstreet, CustCity, CustState, CustZip)
> **City**(<u>CityCode</u>, CityName, Altitude, AirportConditions)

Flight Reservation Form

Reservation No.	R101	Today's Date:	8/26/2001
Credit Card No.	CC101	Amount:	$442.00
Customer No.	C101	Customer Name	Jill Horn

Flight Schedule

Flight No.	Date	Dep City	Dep Time	Arr City	Arr Time
F101	8/26/2001	DNV	10:30AM	CHG	11:45AM
F201	8/31/2001	CHG	10:00AM	DNV	1:20PM

- The primary keys in the tables are underlined. The foreign keys are italicized. Note that the combination of *ResNo, FlightNo,* and *FlightDate* is the primary key of the *ReserveFlight* table. The combination of *FlightNo* and *FlightDate* is a foreign key in the *ReserveFlight* table. The foreign key refers to the *FlightDate* table.
- The Flight Reservation Form is somewhat simplified as it accommodates only a single class of seating, no reserved seats, and no meals. However, commuter and low-cost airlines often have these restrictions.
- The main form is used to insert a record into the *Reservation* table. The fields from the *Customer* table are read-only.

• The subform is used to insert new rows in the *ReserveFlight* table and update the field *RemSeats* in the *FlightDate* table. The fields from the *Flight* table are read-only.

9.1 Select a transaction boundary for the Flight Reservation Form. Justify your choice using the criteria defined in Section 13.4.1.

9.2 Identify system-independent hot spots that result from concurrent usage (say, many reservation agents) of the Flight Reservation Form. For each hot spot, explain why it is a hot spot.

9.3 Identify system-dependent hot spots that result from concurrent usage of the Flight Reservation Form. You may assume that the DBMS cannot lock finer than a database page.

9.4 Is deadlock likely to be a problem with concurrent usage of the Flight Reservation Form? If deadlock is likely, provide an example as justification.

10. The following timeline shows the state of transactions with respect to the most recent backup, checkpoint, and failure. Use the timeline when solving the problems in subparts of this problem.

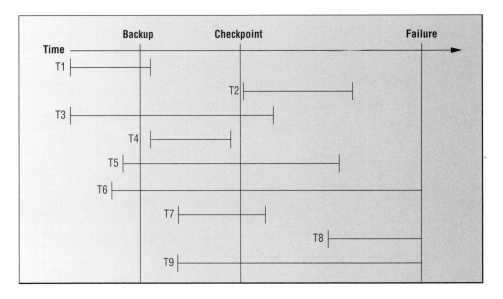

10.1 Describe the restart work if transaction T3 is aborted (with a ROLLBACK statement) after the checkpoint but prior to the failure. Assume that the recovery manager uses the deferred update approach.

10.2 Describe the restart work if transaction T3 is aborted (with a ROLLBACK statement) after the checkpoint but prior to the failure. Assume that the recovery manager uses the immediate update approach.

10.3 Describe the restart work if a system failure occurs. Assume that the recovery manager uses the deferred update approach.

10.4 Describe the restart work if a system failure occurs. Assume that the recovery manager uses the immediate update approach.

10.5 Describe the restart work if a device failure occurs.

11. Use the World Wide Web to review transaction processing benchmarks. Why has the debit–credit benchmark been superseded by other benchmarks? How many transactions per minute are reported for various DBMSs? Inspect the code for one or more benchmark transactions. Can you identify hot spots in the transactions?

REFERENCES FOR FURTHER STUDY

This chapter, although providing a broad coverage of transaction management, has only covered the basics. Transaction management is a detailed subject for which entire books have been written. Specialized books on transaction management include Bernstein, Hadzilacos, and Goodman (1988) and Gray and Reuter (1993). Peinl, Reuter, and Sammer (1988) provide a stock-trading case study on transaction design that elaborates on the ideas presented in Section 13.4. For details about transaction processing performance, consult the home page of the Transaction Processing Performance Council (http://www.tpc.org/). This group maintains many industry standard benchmarks. For more details about workflow management, Sheth, Georgakopoulos, and Hornrick (1995) provide a good overview and numerous references.

Appendix 13.A   SQL2 Syntax Summary

This appendix summarizes the SQL2 syntax for the constraint timing clause, the SET CONSTRAINTS statement, and the SET TRANSACTION statement shown in the chapter. The conventions used in the syntax notation are identical to those used at the end of Chapter 2.

Constraint Timing Clause

```
CREATE TABLE TableName
  ( <Column-Definition>* [ , <Table-Constraint>* ] )

<Column-Definition>: ColumnName DataType
  [ DEFAULT { DefaultValue | USER | NULL } ] [ <Column-Constraint> ]

<Column-Constraint>: [ CONSTRAINT ConstraintName ]
  { NOT NULL |
     <Foreign-Key-Constraint>  |— defined in Chapter 2
     <Uniqueness-Constraint>  |— defined in Chapter 2
     <Check-Constraint> }— defined in Chapter 12
  [ <Timing-Clause> ]

<Table-Constraint>: [ CONSTRAINT ConstraintName ]
  { <Primary-Key-Constraint>  |— defined in Chapter 2
     <Foreign-Key-Constraint>  |— defined in Chapter 2
     <Uniqueness-Constraint>  |— defined in Chapter 2
     <Check-Constraint>} — defined in Chapter 12
  [ <Timing-Clause> ]

<Timing-Clause>:
   { NOT DEFERRABLE |
     DEFERRABLE { INITIALLY IMMEDIATE | INITIALLY DEFERRED } }

CREATE ASSERTION AssertionName
  CHECK ( <Group-Condition> ) [ <Timing-Clause> ]

  <Group-Condition>:— defined in Chapter 3
```

SET CONSTRAINTS Statement

```
SET CONSTRAINTS {  ALL | ConstraintName*  } {  IMMEDIATE | DEFERRED  }
```

SET TRANSACTION Statement

```
SET TRANSACTION ISOLATION LEVEL <Isolation-Level> [ <Intent-Level> ]
<Isolation-Level>:
  { SERIALIZABLE |
    REPEATABLE READ |
    READ COMMITTED |
    READ UNCOMMITTED }

<Intent-Level>: { READ WRITE | READ ONLY }
```

Data Warehouse Technology and Management

This chapter provides the foundation for a new and emerging form of databases, called data warehouses, being used increasingly for decision support. After this chapter, the student should have acquired the following knowledge and skills:

- Understand conceptual differences between operational databases and data warehouses.

- Define terms and concepts used in data warehousing applications.

- Understand architectures to apply data warehouse technology in organizations.

- Apply operators to manipulate data cubes.

- Learn data modeling techniques for building and maintaining multidimensional data cubes.

- Describe the processes to build and manage data warehouses.

OVERVIEW

Imagine a corporate executive of a national soda bottler asking the question, "What was the total diet soda sales during the past 12 months in the Northeast, and how does this number compare with the national average?" Follow-up questions may include, "What was the breakup of diet soda sales in the Northeast by states and cities" and "Is there any cyclical trend in diet soda sales over the last

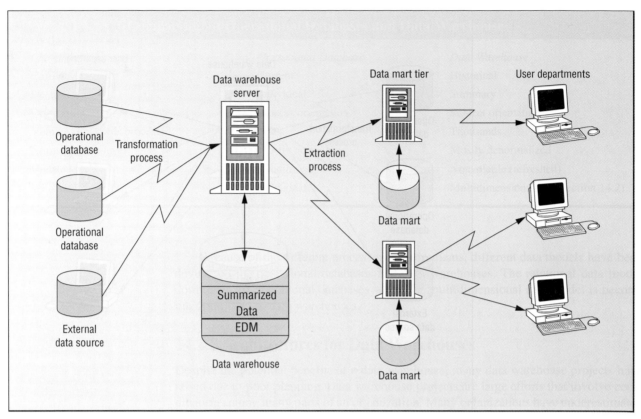

Figure 14.2   **Three-tier data warehouse architecture.**

Data mining is best considered as an adjunct to a mature data warehouse. Data mining needs more detailed data than traditional data warehouses provide. The volumes of data and the dimensionality of data can be much greater for data mining techniques than other data warehouse analysis tools. Data mining techniques thrive with clean, high-dimensional, transaction data. Because data warehouses have more summarized data, there is often a need to extend data warehouses with more detailed data for data mining purposes.

Data mining requires a collection of tools that extend beyond traditional statistical analysis tools. Traditional statistical analysis tools are not well suited to high-dimensional data with a mix of numeric and categorical data. In addition, traditional statistical techniques do not scale well to large amounts of data. Data mining typically includes the following kinds of tools:

- Data access tools to extract and sample transaction data according to complex criteria from multiple-source databases.
- Data visualization tools that enable a decision maker to gain a deeper, intuitive understanding of data.
- A rich collection of models to cluster, predict, and determine association rules from large amounts of data. The models involve neural networks, genetic algorithms, decision tree induction, rule discovery algorithms, probability networks, and other expert system technologies.

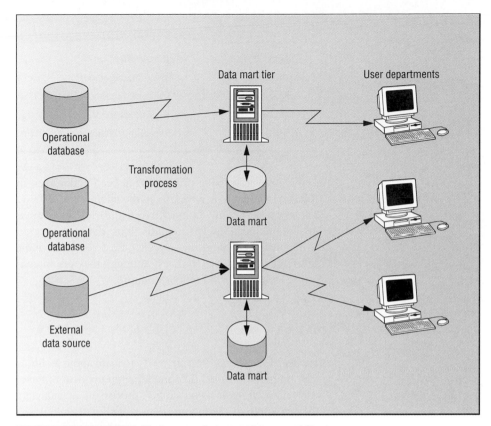

Figure 14.3   **Bottom-up data warehouse architecture.**

- An architecture that provides optimization, client–server processing, and parallel queries to scale to large amounts of data.

As a complement to data warehousing, data mining provides insights that may elude traditional techniques. Data mining holds the promise of more effectively leveraging data warehouses by providing the ability to identify hidden relationships in the data stored there. It facilitates a data-driven discovery, using techniques such as building association rules (e.g., between advertising budget and seasonal sales), generating profiles (e.g., buying patterns for a specific customer segment), and so forth. This knowledge can be used to improve business operations in critical areas, enabling target marketing efforts, better customer service, and improved fraud detection.

14.1.5 Applications of Data Warehouses

Data warehousing projects are usually undertaken for competitive reasons: to achieve strategic advantage or to stay competitive. In many industries, a few organizations typically pioneer data warehousing technology to gain competitive advantage. Often a data warehousing project is undertaken as part of a corporate strategy to shift from a product focus to a customer focus. A successful data warehouse can help identify new markets, focus resources on profitable customers, improve retention of customers, and reduce inventory costs. After success by the pioneering organizations, other organizations quickly follow to stay competitive.

TABLE 14–2	Data Warehousing Applications by Industry
Industry	*Key Applications*
Airline	Yield management, route assessment
Telecommunications	Customer retention, network design
Insurance	Risk assessment, product-design, fraud detection
Retail	Target marketing, supply-chain management

Data warehousing projects have been undertaken in a wide range of industries. A few key applications have driven the adoption of data warehousing projects as listed in Table 14–2. Highly competitive industries such as retail, insurance, airlines, and telecommunications (particularly long distance service) have invested early in data warehouse technology and projects. Less competitive industries such as regulated utilities have been slower to invest although they are increasing investments as data warehouse technology and practice mature.

14.2 MULTIDIMENSIONAL REPRESENTATION OF DATA

After understanding the unique data requirements for decision support, you are ready to learn about technology to satisfy the requirements. The multidimensional data model supports data representation and operations specifically tailored for decision support processing in data warehouses. This section describes the terminology, operations, data modeling techniques, and technology approaches for multidimensional databases.

14.2.1 Example of a Multidimensional Data Cube

Consider a company that sells soda products in different parts of the United States. In particular, the company markets four different soda products (i.e., soda, diet soda, lime soda, and orange soda) in five different regions of the country (i.e., Northeast, Midwest, West, Southwest, and Southeast). Each region consists of several states, and each state consists of several cities. In order to store daily sales data for each product and each region in a relational database, you need Table 14–3, consisting of three fields (*PRODUCT, LOCATION,* and *SALES*) and 20 records (four instances of *PRODUCT* times five instances of *LOCATION*).

The above data representation can be complex and unwieldy. First, imagine that the company wishes to add a fifth product (say, caffeine-free soda). In order to track sales by regions for this new product, you need to add five rows, one each for each region. Second, note that the data in Table 14–3 represent sales data for a particular day (say, January 1, 2000). In order to store the same data for all 365 days of 2000, you need to add a fourth column to store the sales date, and duplicate the twenty rows for each date 365 times to yield a total of 7,300 rows. By the same token, if you wish to store historic data for a period of 10 years, you need 73,000 rows. In each of the above cases, the relational database increases dramatically in magnitude, while becoming more difficult to understand and manage.

An examination of the data in Table 14–3 reveals that there are two fundamental dimensions in the table, namely *PRODUCT* and *LOCATION* (region). The above table can therefore be conceptually simplified by clearly identifying these dimensions in a multidimensional table (Table 14–4).

TABLE 14–3	Relational Representation of Sales Data	
PRODUCT	**LOCATION**	**SALES**
Soda	Northeast	80
Soda	Midwest	40
Soda	West	70
Soda	Southwest	75
Soda	Southeast	65
Diet soda	Northeast	110
Diet soda	Midwest	90
Diet soda	West	55
Diet soda	Southwest	85
Diet soda	Southeast	45
Lime soda	Northeast	60
Lime soda	Midwest	50
Lime soda	West	60
Lime soda	Southwest	45
Lime soda	Southeast	85
Orange soda	Northeast	25
Orange soda	Midwest	30
Orange soda	West	35
Orange soda	Southwest	45
Orange soda	Southeast	60

TABLE 14–4	Multidimensional Representation of Sales Data			
	PRODUCT			
LOCATION	*Soda*	*Diet soda*	*Lime soda*	*Orange soda*
Northeast	80	110	60	25
Midwest	40	90	50	30
West	70	55	60	35
Southwest	75	85	45	45
Southeast	65	45	85	60

The multidimensional data representation is simple to understand and extend. For example, adding a fifth product category requires an additional column to the right of Table 14–4. Adding dates requires a third dimension called *TIME*, resulting in a three-dimensional cube as shown in Figure 14.4. You can conceptually think of this three-dimensional table as a book consisting of 365 pages, each page storing sales data by product and region for a specific date of the year. In addition, the multidimensional form is more compact and requires less disk space because common field values are not duplicated (e.g., diet soda, Northeast), as in Table 14–3.

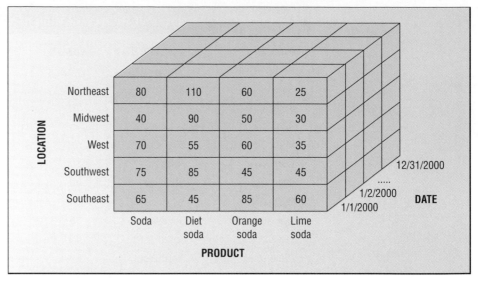

Figure 14.4   **A three-dimensional data cube**

The multidimensional data representation can provide for more efficient query processing than the relational representation. Consider the query to determine total unit sales for diet soda countrywide. Using the relational representation (Table 14–3), the DBMS must browse the entire table to locate the five records containing the diet soda value in the *PRODUCT* field. An index on the *PRODUCT* column may not improve performance if a large fraction of rows contain the diet soda value. Using the multidimensional model (Table 14–4), the DBMS searches the *PRODUCT* column corresponding to PRODUCT = "diet soda" prior to reading the five sales values across this row and summing them. Although optimization techniques can be applied to both representations, the multidimensional representation provides an inherent advantage. As the number of dimensions and the size of each dimension increase, the query processing advantage of the multidimensional approach increases.

In summary, a multidimensional database has two advantages over traditional relational databases. First, it is conceptually easy to understand and visualize if the underlying data model has more than two dimensions. Second, multidimensional databases can offer significant performance improvements in query processing especially as the number of dimensions and dimension sizes increase.

14.2.2 Key Terminology

Data Cube   a multidimensional format in which cells contain numeric data called measures organized by subjects called dimensions. A data cube is sometimes known as a hypercube because conceptually it can have an unlimited number of dimensions.

A <u>data cube</u> or hypercube generalizes the two-dimensional (Table 14–4) and three-dimensional (Figure 14.4) representations shown in the previous section. A data cube consists of cells containing <u>measures</u> (numeric values such as sales amounts) and <u>dimensions</u> to group numeric data (e.g., *PRODUCT, LOCATION,* and *TIME*). Each dimension contains several <u>members</u> that may be predefined (input member) or computed from other members (derived member). For instance, the *LOCATION* dimension has five input members (i.e., Northeast, Midwest, etc.). As shown in Figure 14.4, it does not have any derived member, but you can add Total as a derived member to store the total sales by *LOCATION* (imagine the total sales being stored in an additional row at the bottom of Figure 14.4). Storing a derived member alleviates the need to calculate totals for every query execution.

Dimension Details

Dimensions may have subdimensions or hierarchies. For instance, the *LOCATION* dimension may have a hierarchy of state (e.g., Midwest consisting of the states Ohio, Illinois, Michigan, and so forth), which in turn may have further hierarchies by counties or cities (e.g., Ohio consisting of Cleveland, Columbus, Cincinnati, and so forth). Likewise, the *TIME* dimension can have hierarchies by year, quarter, month, and date (day of month). Hierarchies can be used to drill down from higher levels of detail (e.g., region) to lower levels (e.g., states and cities) and to roll up in the reverse direction. Although hierarchies are not essential, they allow a convenient and efficient representation. Without hierarchies, the *LOCATION* dimension must contain the most detailed level (cities) of members. However, this representation can be difficult to compute aggregates across the dimension. Alternatively, the *LOCATION* dimension can be divided into separate dimensions for regions, states, and cities, resulting in a larger data cube.

Dimensions can sometimes be grouped into classes. For example, the *PRODUCT* dimension may have a class called size, referring to whether the product is available in a 12-oz. can, a 20-oz. bottle, a 1-liter bottle, or a 2-liter bottle. Classes and hierarchies differ by sharing of members. Classes support sharing of members (e.g., both diet soda and orange soda can be offered in 12-oz. cans). In contrast, hierarchies do not support sharing of members (e.g., Ohio is in the Midwest region and not in any other region). Classes allow a more compact representation when members are shared.

The selection of dimensions has an influence on the sparsity of the data cube. Sparsity indicates the extent of empty cells in a data cube. Sparsity can be a problem if two or more dimensions are related. For example, if certain products are sold only in selected regions, cells may be empty. If a large number of cells are empty, the data cube can waste space and be slow to process. Special compression techniques can be used to reduce the size of sparse data cubes.

Measure Details

Cells in a data cube contain measures such as the sales values in Figure 14.4. Measures support numeric operations such as simple arithmetic, statistical calculations, and simultaneous equations. A cell may contain one or more measures. For example, the number of units can be another measure for the sales data cube. The number of cells in a multidimensional cube should equal the number of records in the corresponding relational table (Table 14–4 contains 20 cells corresponding to 20 records in Table 14–3).

Derived measures are not stored inside the data cube but are computed from other measures at run-time. For example, you can calculate total dollar sales as total unit sales times unit price. If parallel processing is available, derived measure calculations can combine entire planes of a data cube as opposed to computing values one cell at a time.

Other Data Cube Examples

As this section has indicated, data cubes can extend beyond the three-dimensional example in Figure 14.4. Table 14–5 lists common data cubes to support human resource management and financial analysis. The dimensions with slashes indicate hierarchical dimensions. The *TIME* and *LOCATION* dimensions are also hierarchical, but since the hierarchy depends on the organization, possible subdimensions are not listed.

TABLE 14–5	Data Cubes to Support Human Resource Management and Financial Analysis

Data Cube	Typical Dimensions	Typical Measures
Turnover analysis	Company/line of business/department, location, salary range, position classification, time	Head count for hires, transfers, terminations, and retirements
Employee utilization	Company/line of business/department, location, salary range, position classification, time	Full time equivalent (FTE) hours, normal FTE hours, overtime FTE hours
Asset analysis	Asset type, years in service band, time, account, company/line of business/department, location	Cost, net book value, market value
Vendor analysis	Vendor, location, account, time, business unit	Total invoice amount

14.2.3 Time-Series Data

One kind of measure of particular interest to multidimensional databases is the time series. Time is, in fact, one of the most common dimensions in a data warehouse, and is useful for capturing trends, making forecasts, and so forth. A time series allows users to store all historic data in one cell, instead of specifying a separate time dimension. The structure of a measure becomes more complex with a time series, but the number of dimensions is reduced. A major advantage is that a number of statistical functions can operate directly on time-series data.

A time series is an array data type with a number of special properties as listed below. The array supports a collection of values, one for each time period. Examples of time-series measures include sales figures (over time), historic stock quotes, and so forth. The following list shows the properties that a time series can have:

- Data Type: This property denotes the kind of data stored in the data points. Data type is usually numeric such as single precision numbers, double precision numbers, or integer.
- Start Date: This property denotes the starting date of the first data point, for example, 1/1/2000.
- Calendar: This property contains the calendar year appropriate for the time series, for example, 2000 fiscal year. An extensive knowledge of calendar rules such as determining leap years and dates of holidays embedded in the calendar property provides considerable savings in time and effort in data warehouse development.
- Periodicity: This property specifies the interval between data points. Periodicity can be daily, weekly, monthly, quarterly, yearly (calendar or fiscal years), hourly, 15-minute intervals, 4-4-5 accounting periods, custom periodicity, and so forth.
- Conversion: This property specifies how to convert unit data into aggregate data. For instance, aggregating daily sales into weekly sales requires summing daily data points, while aggregating daily stock prices into weekly prices requires an averaging operation.

14.2.4 Data Cube Operations

A number of decision support operations have been proposed for the data cube. This section discusses the most commonly used operations. A standard set of data cube operations is still under development, and not all data warehouse tools currently support all operations.

Slice

Because a data cube can contain a large number of dimensions, users often need to focus on a subset of the dimensions to gain insights. The slice operator retrieves a subset of a data cube similar to the restriction operator of relational algebra. In a slice operation, one or more dimensions are set to specific values and the remaining data cube is displayed. For example, Figure 14.5 shows the data cube resulting from the slice operation on the data cube in Figure 14.4 where TIME = 1/1/2000 and the other two dimensions (*LOCATION* and *PRODUCT*) are shown.

A variation of the slice operator allows a decision maker to summarize across members rather than to focus on just one member. The slice summarize operator replaces one or more dimensions with summary calculations. The summary calculation often indicates the total value across members or the central tendency of the dimension such as the average or median value. For example, Figure 14.6 shows the result of a slice summarize operation where the *PRODUCT* dimension is replaced by the sum of sales across all products. A new column called Total Sales can be added to store overall product sales for the entire year (i.e., over all days).

Dice

Because individual dimensions can contain a large number of members, users need to focus on a subset of members to gain insights. The dice operator replaces a dimension with a subset of values of the dimension. For example, Figure 14.7 shows the result of a dicing operation to display sales for the Midwest region for January 1, 2000. Dicing typically follows a slicing operation and returns a subset of the values displayed in the

LOCATION	Soda	Diet soda	Orange soda	Lime soda
Northeast	80	110	60	25
Midwest	40	90	50	30
West	70	55	60	35
Southwest	75	85	45	45
Southeast	65	45	85	60

PRODUCT

(LOCATION × PRODUCT slice for TIME = 1/1/2000)

Figure 14.5   **Example slice operation.**

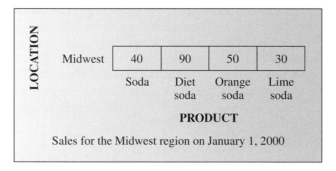

Figure 14.6   Example slice summarize operation.

Figure 14.7   Example dice operation.

preceding slice. It helps focus attention on one or more rows or columns of numbers from a slice.

Drill-Down

Users often want to navigate among the levels of hierarchical dimensions. The drill-down operator allows users to navigate from a more general level to a more specific level. For example, Figure 14.8 shows a drill-down operation on the Midwest region of the *LOCATION* dimension. The plus sign by the Midwest region indicates a drill-down operation.

Roll-Up

Roll-up (also called drill-up) is the opposite of drill-down. Roll-up involves moving from a specific level to a more general level of a hierarchical dimension. For example, a decision maker may roll up sales figures from daily to quarterly level for end-of-quarter reporting needs. In the soda sales example, Figure 14.5 shows a roll-up of the Midwest region from Figure 14.7.

LOCATION	PRODUCT: Soda	Diet soda	Orange soda	Lime soda
Northeast	80	110	60	25
+ Midwest				
Illinois	20	20	10	15
Indiana	5	30	10	5
Ohio	15	40	30	10
West	70	55	60	35
Southwest	75	85	45	45
Southeast	65	45	85	60

Figure 14.8 **Drill-down operation for the Midwest region in Figure 14.5.**

TABLE 14–6 Summary of Data Cube Operators

Operator	*Purpose*	*Description*
Slice	Focus attention on a subset of dimensions	Replace a dimension with a single member value or with a summary of its measure values
Dice	Focus attention on a subset of member values	Replace a dimension with a subset of members
Drill-down	Obtain more detail about a dimension	Navigate from a more general level to a more specific level of a hierarchical dimension
Roll-up	Summarize details about a dimension	Navigate from a more specific level to a more general level of a hierarchical dimension
Pivot	Allow a data cube to be presented in a visually appealing order	Rearrange the dimensions in a data cube

Pivot

The pivot operator supports rearrangement of the dimensions in a data cube. For example, in Figure 14.8, the position of the *PRODUCT* and the *LOCATION* dimensions can be reversed so that *PRODUCT* appears on the rows and *LOCATION* on the columns. The pivot operator allows a data cube to be presented in the most appealing visual order.

Summary of Operators

To help you recall the data cube operators, Table 14–6 summarizes the purpose of each operator.

SQL Support for Data Cube Operations

Before finishing this section, there should be a word about SQL support for data cube operations. Since SQL2 provides little support for data cube operations, proprietary SQL extensions have begun to flourish. Most of the extensions do not directly support data cube operations. Rather, the extensions provide improved summarization capabilities beyond the GROUP BY clause. Most of these capabilities are already part of report-writing tools so their inclusion in SQL may not be significant. Some of the typical extensions are listed below:

- Ranking supports requests for the top or the bottom percentage of results.
- Subtotals allow the result to contain multiple levels of totals, similar to hierarchical reports.
- Ratios simplify the formulation of queries that compare individual values to group totals.
- Moving totals and averages allow smoothing of data for time-series analysis.

SQL3, the just-approved new SQL standard, provides new summarization capabilities. These features are an attempt to unify the proliferation of proprietary data cube extensions although they probably will not obviate the need for visual tools that directly support data cube operations. In addition, it may be a number of years before these new features become widely implemented because of the size and the complexity of the new SQL3 standard. The following list briefly summarizes new summarization features in SQL3:

- The ROLLUP operator in the GROUP BY clause produces a summary of each value in a grouped column.
- The CUBE operator in the GROUP BY clause produces a complete matrix covering each grouped column.
- The GROUPING SETS operator in the GROUP BY clause allows nested groupings in a result.

14.2.5 Relational Data Modeling for Multidimensional Data

When using a relational database for a data warehouse, a new data modeling technique is needed to represent multidimensional data. A star schema is a relational data modeling representation for data cubes. The star schema diagram looks like a star with one large central table, called the <u>fact table,</u> at the center of the star that is linked to multiple <u>dimension tables</u> in a radial manner using primary and foreign keys. The fact table stores numeric data (facts) such as sales figures, while the dimension tables store descriptive data corresponding to individual dimensions of the data cube such as product, location, and time. There is a 1-M relationship from each dimension table to the fact table. The star schema of the earlier soda sales example is shown in Figure 14.9. This schema consists of three dimension tables, namely *PRODUCT, STORE* (a lower hierarchical level than city in the *LOCATION* dimension), and *TIME,* and one fact table called *SALES.*

Note that the star schema in Figure 14.9 represents only a single business process, namely, tracking sales. Additional star schemas may be required for other processes, such as forecasting and inventory management. Some of the dimension tables may overlap across these additional schemas. However, each schema will have its own fact tables. For example, the fact table for the forecasting process may be *FORECASTED_SALES,*

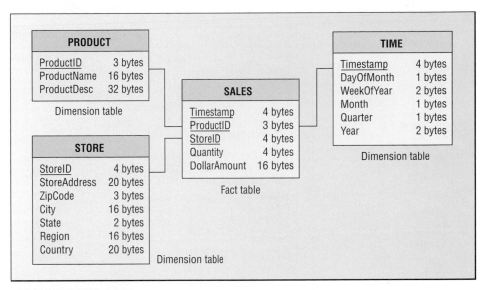

Figure 14.9   Star schema for the soda sales example.

as opposed to the *SALES* table for the sales tracking process, though they may share the same dimension tables, *PRODUCT, STORE,* and *TIME.*

For each fact table, careful consideration should be devoted to its grain or summary level. For instance, if you wish to store sales data for each soda category by individual store, the fact table should have the store identifier as a foreign key. Likewise, if you intend to store daily sales data, the fact table should have the date as a foreign key. Using week as the foreign key will not provide the daily sales data.

Fact tables are usually normalized while dimension tables are often not in third normal form. Normalizing dimension tables to avoid storage anomalies is generally not necessary because they are usually stable and small. The nature of a data warehouse indicates that dimension tables be designed for retrieval, not update. Retrieval performance is improved by eliminating the join operations that would be needed to combine fully normalized dimension tables.

When the dimension tables are structured and large, it may be necessary to split dimension and fact tables. For example, if the *STORE* table in Figure 14.9 contains thousands of stores structured in regions and districts, the *STORE* dimension table can be split into three dimension tables, as shown in Figure 14.10. In addition, two fact tables have been added. This variation is known as the snowflake schema because the dimension tables cluster around multiple fact tables, not just a single fact table.

14.2.6 Multidimensional Database Technologies

Several competing technologies have been developed to provide multidimensional data capabilities. Vendors of relational DBMSs have extended their products with additional query features to support operations on data cubes. These products are collectively known as ROLAP, for Relational On-line Analytic Processing. On-line Analytical Processing (OLAP) is the general name of technology to support multidimensional databases. Vendors of decision support software have developed a

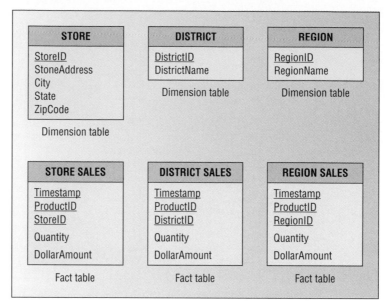

STORE	DISTRICT	REGION
StoreID StoneAddress City State ZipCode	DistrictID DistrictName	RegionID RegionName
Dimension table	Dimension table	Dimension table

STORE SALES	DISTRICT SALES	REGION SALES
Timestamp ProductID StoreID Quantity DollarAmount	Timestamp ProductID DistrictID Quantity DollarAmount	Timestamp ProductID RegionID Quantity DollarAmount
Fact table	Fact table	Fact table

Figure 14.10   Snowflake schema for the soda sales example.

new architecture that directly manipulates data cubes. These products are collectively known as MOLAP, for Multidimensional OLAP. A third technology approach, known as HOLAP (Hybrid OLAP), has been developed to combine the ROLAP and MOLAP approaches. A fourth product group, known as DOLAP (Desktop OLAP), has been developed to support small-scale data marts and end-user query capabilities. This section describes the features of these technology approaches and the structure of the market for OLAP products.

ROLAP (Relational OLAP)

ROLAP   a relational database implementation of a multidimensional database in which data cubes (or parts of data cubes) are dynamically constructed from relational tables when requested in queries.

In this approach, standard relational databases are used to store logical multidimensional data. Data modeling is done using the star or snowflake schemas as described in the previous section. Data cubes are dynamically constructed from data in the underlying tables. Typically, only a subset of a data cube must be constructed as specified in a user's query. Extensions to SQL allow users to manipulate the dimensions and measures in virtual data cubes.

This approach leverages existing investments in relational databases and their capability to handle extremely large tables. However, the dynamic calculation of data cubes can place a heavy burden on a database server. ROLAP is best suited for simple analysis of large volumes of data or where close integration with relational production databases provides significant benefit.

MOLAP (Multidimensional OLAP)

MOLAP   an implementation approach for a multidimensional database in which data cubes are precalculated and managed by a specially designed DBMS for data cubes.

In contrast to ROLAP systems, MOLAP systems manipulate stored data cubes. The storage engines of MOLAP systems are optimized for the unique characteristics of multidimensional data such as sparsity and complex aggregation across thousands of cells. Be-

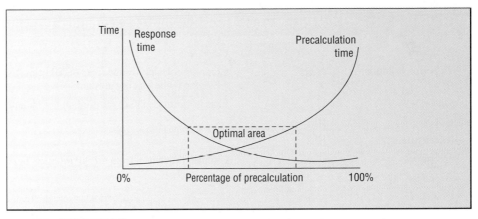

Figure 14.11 Trade-off between precalculation and response time.

cause data cubes are precomputed, MOLAP query performance is generally better than ROLAP. Even with techniques to deal with sparsity, MOLAP systems can be overwhelmed by the size of data cubes. A fully calculated data cube may expand many times as compared to the raw input data, resulting in a "data explosion." For instance, a 200 MB source file can expand to over 50 GB. This data explosion problem limits the size of data cubes that MOLAP systems can manipulate.

HOLAP (Hybrid OLAP)

Ideally, the data warehouse designer should attempt to balance precalculation time with response time. As shown in Figure 14.11, there is a trade-off between response time and precalculation time. The optimum approach may include partial precalculation while leaving less frequently requested calculations until run time. While precalculation improves data access speeds, large precalculation times make MOLAP unsuitable for applications where the data warehouse must be refreshed frequently. In addition, storage limitations of MOLAP systems preclude storage of some data cubes. Thus, the ideal approach balances precalculation and response time needs.

Because of the trade-off between response time and precalculation time, the HOLAP (Hybrid OLAP) approach has been developed. HOLAP supports both MOLAP and ROLAP approaches. HOLAP approaches allow a data warehouse to be divided between precomputed and dynamically generated data cubes. When an OLAP query is submitted, the HOLAP system can combine data from both precomputed and dynamically generated data cubes. The major disadvantage of the HOLAP approach is that two vendors (ROLAP and MOLAP) may be required.

DOLAP (Desktop OLAP)

In response to the need for desktop query tools and small data marts, DOLAP systems also have been developed. These systems can be used as stand-alones for small data marts or in conjunction with ROLAP and MOLAP tools. In the latter case, DOLAP systems support customized views of large data warehouses.

TABLE 14–7	1999 Market Shares[1] by Revenue of Companies Providing OLAP Products	
Company	*Market Share*	*Comments*
Hyperion Solutions	27.8%	Company formed from merger of Arbor Software and Hyperion Software; Essbase is the leading product
Oracle	11.2	Express product; Discover product not included in market share
Cognos	10.9	
Micro Strategy	10.2	
Microsoft	7.5	Estimated revenues from OLAP products bundled with SQL Server
Business Objects	5.2	
Comshare	3.1	
Applix	3.0	
IBM	2.9	DB2 OLAP Server; reseller of Essbase
Other	18.2	Includes Sterling, PWC, SAS Institute, Seagate, Brio Technology, Pilot Software, Gentia, and Informix

Structure of the Market for OLAP Products

According to data compiled by Business Intelligence Ltd., the sales of OLAP products reached $2.5 billion in 1999, a 25 percent gain over 1998. Business Intelligence Ltd. projects sales of OLAP products to reach $4 billion by 2002. The OLAP market is relatively young as it did not reach any significant sales until the early 1990s. Because of its youth, the market is rapidly changing with new products, companies, and consolidation of existing products and companies. Table 14–7 lists the leading companies as of 1999. Only a few of the companies in Table 14–7 are leading suppliers of traditional DBMSs. Although Hyperion appears as the market leader, the market is so volatile that no company can be considered dominant.

14.3 BUILDING A DATA WAREHOUSE

Building a data warehouse involves a life cycle similar to the systems development process. This section describes the process of building a data warehouse with a focus on the unique aspects of data warehouses as compared to other information system projects.

14.3.1 Requirements Specification

Building a data warehouse is a process of matching decision support needs to the realities of available data. Hence, users and database administrators (DBAs) must both be consulted in the requirements specification process. Though this process can be done using a series of interviews with user groups and DBAs, a better approach is to bring both parties to a series of joint application requirements (JAR) sessions. The intent of these sessions is to collectively understand what data are currently available from production systems and what data are required to support users' decision support needs. Secondary

---

[1]Market shares according to a 1999 study by Business Intelligence Ltd.

that required by the fact table. The trade-off between hierarchical details and data warehouse performance should be evaluated. Low-level hierarchies enhance drill-down options but may involve a significantly larger database and commensurate performance degradation. If time is an important dimension, the team should investigate the trade-off between a time dimension and a time-series measure. The result of the third step is a logical representation of each data cube that can be implemented through various technologies.

On completion of the logical design, the data warehouse team then can turn its attention to physical design issues. Physical design involves a number of capacity-planning issues such as disk space, server requirements, and personnel resources. Estimating the size of the data warehouse determines the disk capacity required. The frequency of updating the warehouse data determines the currency of the data stored as well as provides personnel and resource estimates required for maintaining the data warehouse after its implementation. Decisions about storage versus computation of derived measures affect the performance and the size of the data warehouse.

Data warehouse size depends on the number of fact and dimension tables, the record size for each table, and the historical duration of data being stored. Table 14–9 shows the approximate data warehouse size for the logical model shown in Figure 14.9. The size calculation assumes daily sales data for each of the four soda categories by individual stores with 20,000 stores, and a historic duration of 10 years of data. The total estimated size of the data warehouse is more than 9 GB, most of which is occupied by the fact table. Note that the above estimation did not factor in any growth in the number of stores selling soda products over the 10-year period; if such increase in stores is warranted, appropriate modification must be made to the *STORE* dimension and *SALES* fact estimates.

The last step involves the selection of the implementation technology: ROLAP, MOLAP, or HOLAP. Usually, the DOLAP architecture is appropriate only for small data marts or as a component of a larger data warehouse. The data warehouse team should conduct a careful evaluation process. The team should identify features of the alternative products, list data warehouse needs, and evaluate how well each alternative system satisfies the needs. Benchmarks, both industry standard and organization specific, can be useful to evaluate performance. The data warehouse team should even consider using a few products for a short time to better understand their strengths and weaknesses.

After choosing an implementation technology, the DBA should implement the data cubes. If ROLAP technology is chosen, the data cubes will be transformed into star or snowflake schemas. Since MOLAP systems directly support data cubes, no transformation is necessary. A HOLAP system provides the additional burden of deciding how to represent the different parts of a data warehouse as stored or virtual data cubes.

TABLE 14–9	Data Warehouse Size Estimation Example

PRODUCT dimension table:
  4 products $\times$ (3 + 16 + 32) bytes = 84 bytes

TIME dimension table:
  (365 $\times$ 10) days $\times$ (4 + 1 + 2 + 1 + 1 + 2) bytes = 3661 bytes

STORE dimension table:
  20,000 stores $\times$ (4 + 20 + 3 + 16 + 2 + 16 + 20) bytes = 1.30 Mbytes

SALES fact table:
  4 products $\times$ 3650 days $\times$ 20,000 stores $\times$ (4 + 3 + 4 + 4 + 16) bytes = 9.052 GB

TABLE 14–8	Steps in Data Warehouse Design

1. Identify the data cubes.

2. Identify the grains and the data sources for each measure.

3. Identify the members, the hierarchies, and the classes of each dimension.

4. Conduct physical design: historical duration, storage of derived measures, frequency of update.

5. Choose the implementation technology: ROLAP, MOLAP, or HOLAP.

goals of these meetings may involve scheduling the implementation of the data ware house and seeking ways of funding it.

During the JAR sessions, the data warehouse team should try to identify subjects business processes. Existing production systems and their shortcomings may be used a starting point for identifying data utilized by each process. Sources of the subject da (typically, production systems) and individuals or groups responsible for managing th data (data stewards) should then be identified. Subsequent JAR sessions also should i clude the data stewards in an effort to better define availability and use of corporate dat

The success of a data warehouse depends critically on the accuracy and complete ness of process and data specifications identified in the requirements phase. Successful requirements specification, in turn, depends on active involvement and feedback of a constituent groups in the data warehouse building process. Realistic expectations shoul be set regarding the capabilities of the data warehouse and conveyed as such to all par ties involved.

14.3.2 Logical and Physical Design

Five steps, outlined in Table 14–8, should be followed to design a data warehouse. Collectively, these five steps serve as the basis for logical modeling of the data warehouse and its physical implementation.

The first step identifies the data cubes that will be stored (either logically or physically) in the data warehouse. For each data cube, the DBA should identify the dimensions and the measures. For example, the DBA might identify a sales data cube consisting of dimensions product, store, and time along with measures sales and units sold. Additional details about the dimensions and the measures should be provided in later steps.

The next step is to identify the grain, or lowest level of facts, for each data cube. Typical grains are individual transaction, individual line item, daily snapshot, weekly snapshot, and so forth. Determining the appropriate grain is important because a data warehouse will not support decision making at any level lower than the fact table grain. For each measure, the data warehouse team should document how it can be extracted from production databases. Derived measures and their frequency of use also should be documented. The decision to store or compute derived measures should be postponed until the physical design step.

After analyzing the measures, the DBA identifies the details of each dimension including the members, the hierarchies, and the classes. The choice of dimensions should be based on business processes and data required by these processes and should not be derived from fact tables. Some dimensions may include hierarchical levels finer than

14.3.3 Data Extraction

Following the design process, the next phase in data warehouse building is to select required data from production systems, organize and reformat them (data cleansing), aggregate them, and load them into the data warehouse. While some of these activities can be performed by off-the-shelf software packages, most often, the data warehouse team must build a software program called a production data extract system for extracting data, during both the initial data warehouse implementation and its subsequent updating during the maintenance phase.

It is important to understand the importance of data cleansing in the data extraction process. Data stored from multiple legacy databases are typically dirty, meaning that they may not conform to each other or to enterprisewide data quality standards. If directly implemented, dirty data may result in data inconsistency and integrity problems. In addition, since legacy databases typically have limited (sometimes departmental) views of data, attempting to integrate them may lead to the data quality concerns outlined in Table 14–10. Since many transaction systems draw data from single databases, these inconsistencies are invisible to those systems. However, the problems are magnified when attempting to integrate data across multiple databases.

Data Extraction Steps

Extracting data from production databases and loading them to the data warehouse involves a sequence of 10 steps as shown in Table 14–11. Some or all of these steps can be automated by a production data extract system. The remainder of this section describes the steps in more detail.

- Extract primary data from production systems: Data to be stored in the data warehouse first must be selected (i.e., extracted) from appropriate production databases. The extracted data are typically a daily, weekly, or monthly snapshot of data that can be loaded to the fact table. If production data are stored in relational databases, extraction is a relatively simple process involving a few SQL queries. The query results can be stored in a file or streamed one record at a time to the requesting application. However, if the data are stored in legacy systems with unknown file formats, extracting such data are considerably more difficult and may require running a report or creating a utility dump file. Many third-party data extract tools provide such functionality.

TABLE 14–10	Data Quality Problems Involving Integration

Multiple identifiers: some databases may use different primary keys for the same entity such as different customer numbers, regions, etc.

Multiple names: the same field may be represented using different field names

Different units: measures and dimensions may have different units and granularities

Missing values: data may not exist in some databases

Orphaned transactions: some transactions may be missing important parts such as an order without a customer

TABLE 14–11	Steps in Data Extraction

1. Extract primary data from production systems.
2. Build indexes for dimension tables.
3. Transform dimension data into load record images.
4. Load dimension data.
5. Sort and build fact aggregates.
6. Build indexes for fact aggregates.
7. Load fact data.
8. Process exceptions.
9. Perform quality assurance.
10. Publish.

- Dimension tables and indexes: Dimension tables, although generally stable, may require periodic insertions and deletions. For instance, a new row should be inserted into the STORE dimension when a new store is opened. Any change in a dimension table should be accompanied by updating its index so that its link to the fact table is current. The data warehouse team must therefore institute an administrative process for posting changes to dimension tables.

- Transform dimension data into load record images: This step refers to arranging the production data into proper rows and columns, with appropriate integer, floating-point, and date conversions, for direct loading into the data warehouse. These conversions are better done in the legacy production environment (source) than in the destination data warehouse environment because the source system is more familiar with the formatting and organization of the production data.

- Load dimension data: Appropriately formatted dimension data from production systems (load images) are now transferred to the data warehouse system using a bulk loading program or SQL INSERT statements. A bulk loading program is desirable when large amounts of data are loaded because it is usually faster than SQL INSERT statements.

- Sort and build fact aggregates: Since a data warehouse stores only aggregate data, the production data now must be sorted and aggregated for storage. Depending on the scale and the magnitude of the sort, dedicated sorting packages may be employed. Data sorted by an appropriate dimensional attribute are then aggregated to represent individual rows in the fact table.

- Build indexes for fact aggregates: One or more indexes should be created or updated for aggregate data to be added to the fact tables. These indexes will help when joining data from fact and dimension tables.

- Load fact data: Aggregate data are loaded into the fact table using a bulk loading operation, and referential integrity between tables is checked. A combined primary key is most desirable since only the portion of the key for the most recent time period is dropped and rebuilt when new data are loaded (instead of dropping and rebuilding the entire key). Using parallel processors generally improves the speed of the load process.

- Process exceptions: Unforeseen problems may arise while loading dimension or fact table data because of the data volume, the number of indexes, or other reasons. In cases where the bulk load is unsuccessful, fact and/or dimension table data have to be entered manually.

- Perform quality assurance: On completion of the loading process, a data quality assurance manager should make a global assessment of the status of the load. A quick but powerful way of checking load integrity is to check totals across the production and data warehouse systems. In addition, completeness checks and reasonable checks should be performed. A completeness check counts the number of reporting units, such as stores, and sees whether they all reported during a given period. A reasonableness check determines whether key facts fall in reasonable bounds and are a reasonable extrapolation of previous history. In extreme cases, where the load process is incomplete or data are corrupted, the entire load needs to be backed out and retried later.

- Publish: The final step in the production extract process is to alert users to the status of the last load. The completeness of the load and the portions of data to avoid should be indicated so that users can revise their decision support models.

14.3.4 Practical Considerations

Not all multidimensional DBMSs are equal, particularly with storage capacity. These limitations should be taken into account when selecting a tool for data warehouse implementation. The most significant issues are discussed next.

- Cell limit: Multidimensional databases typically support only a finite number of cells. Though the cell limit may be a few trillion cells, it may be inadequate for certain organizations. The problem is even greater for databases that do not support time-series data. Many multidimensional database vendors try to overcome cell limitations by providing run-time joins or consolidations among multiple tables, which may cause performance degradation.

- Sparsity: Cells containing repeated or no data (i.e., sparse cells) may lead to a disk space problem for a large data warehouse. As more dimensions are added to a data cube, the sparsity increases. For example, a sales table with 32 million cells and 98 percent sparsity will contain only 640,000 populated cells.

- Dimensional hierarchies: Some multidimensional databases support hierarchies within dimensions, others don't. In general, as the number of dimensions increases, the number of cells (i.e., database size) increases exponentially. Most commercial databases reach the cell limit well before they run out of dimensions. For example, a particular server may support 32 dimensions and have a limit of two billion cells. For example, a 20-dimension data cube with three members per dimension requires about 3.5 billion cells (3^{20}), well beyond the cell limit.

- Dimension limits: Some multidimensional DBMSs have an absolute maximum number of dimensions. Other systems have a maximum number of dimensions per data cube or fact table. The latter is usually more flexible because a data warehouse may contain many data cubes.

- <u>Classes within dimensions:</u> Some multidimensional database systems require that subsets of dimension members such as product size, product color, and so on (belonging to the *PRODUCT* dimension) be defined as separate dimensions. Other systems allow them to be combined within classes for the same *PRODUCT* dimension, eliminating the need for additional dimensions.

- <u>Capacity versus processing:</u> A multidimensional database with a large capacity but slow query processing may be no more useful than a database with limited capacity.

- <u>Drilling to relational data:</u> Many organizations already have standardized their production databases on relational databases. Duplicating all detailed data in a multidimensional data warehouse may not be desired under such circumstances. It may be more reasonable to retain detailed data in relational production databases while storing only summary-level data in a multidimensional database. In Figure 14.12, the relational database contains store-level sales data while the multidimensional database contains sales aggregates by city, state, and region rolled into 556 values. The multidimensional database can provide aggregate sales data for decision support purposes, while drilling down to the underlying relational database can quickly retrieve sales data for individual stores.

14.4 MAINTAINING A DATA WAREHOUSE

Most data warehouses are generally used in two modes. In query mode, they are typically used 16 to 22 hours per day supporting decision support needs. In refresh mode, they go offline for two to eight hours per day, week, or month (depending on the desired level of data currency). The downtime usually occurs in late evenings or early mornings for data updating, indexing, and quality assurance.

14.4.1 Query Phase

In this phase, the entire user community is connected to the data warehouse via query tools. A query tool is generally a client application residing on a desktop that maintains

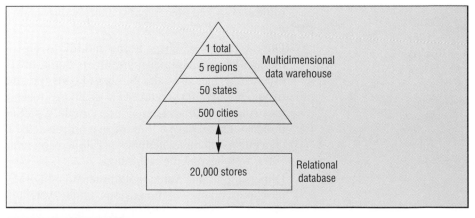

Figure 14.12   Drilling down to a relational database.

a network connection to back-end databases for purposes of sending SQL queries and receiving answer sets. The desktop may include ad-hoc query tools as well as canned queries and report writers. The returned answer set may contain several hundred to several thousand rows of data. The network and the query tools should be powerful enough to import and display such data volumes.

Generally, about 80 percent of these queries are browses involving single-table selects, while the remaining 20 percent require multiple table joins. Browse queries usually touch a single field in a dimension table. Users can browse by selecting specific fields from pull-down menus on a graphical interface. Appropriate SQL statements are generated by the query tool and are transparent to the user. Users also may wish to drill down dimensional hierarchies to narrow their search to fewer records. This narrowing process is done via a progressive browse process, by adding additional constraints to an earlier query.

Multiple table join queries involve the fact table and one or more dimension tables, linked together via their primary and foreign keys. Theoretically, multiple fact tables also can be combined, but this approach is not recommended given the size of fact tables. Parallel hardware and special algorithms not available in relational databases often are used to support joins in multidimensional databases. Predicting query performance and load on a data warehouse is difficult, however, because they depend on the number of users, the query mix, and the sparsity of the stored data.

14.4.2 Refresh Phase

In this phase, all or part of the data warehouse is taken off-line while new data are loaded. The new data are typically an extract from one or more production systems and are delivered via the production data extract system described earlier. The overall system should be optimized to minimize downtime due to data loading. Disk mirroring provides one way to minimize downtime. In disk mirroring, one disk mirror supports queries while the other supports loading. Mirroring also increases reliability in the query phase by providing additional redundancy in the event of a disk failure.

The speed of loading large tables can be increased significantly using segmentable fact table indexes if supported by the data warehouse vendor. In this approach, the index on the fact table is dropped and recreated only for the most recent time period, rather than for the entire table. The load executes quickly because most data loads append data at the end of the time series (i.e., the most recent day, week, or month).

CLOSING THOUGHTS

This chapter provided an introduction to the concepts and practice of data warehousing. The chapter began by examining conceptual differences between relational databases, traditionally used for supporting transaction processing, and multidimensional databases, suggested for the new generation of decision support applications. The unique characteristics of decision support data were outlined, followed by a discussion of data warehouses, data marts, and data mining.

The chapter next examined the new multidimensional form of data representation by comparing it with the relational form for a soda sales example. The terminology and operations used in multidimensional representation were described next. The star and snowflake schemas were presented as ways of modeling multidimensional databases as a set of fact and dimension tables linked via primary and foreign keys. Several DBMS architectures were described that provide multidimensional data representation and operations.

The process of building a data warehouse was discussed next. This process starts with determination of user requirements (via a sequence of JAR sessions), logical and physical design of the warehouse, and finally building of the production extract system. Subsequent maintenance of the data warehouse involves building query tools (or buying them from third-party vendors) to facilitate single-table or join queries and rerunning the production extract system on a timed basis (daily, weekly, or monthly) to update the warehouse data.

REVIEW CONCEPTS

- Data needs for transaction processing versus decision support applications.
- Multidimensional data cube: dimensions, measures, hierarchies, classes, time-series data type.
- Multidimensional operators: slice, dice, drill-down, roll-up, pivot.
- Star schema: fact table, dimension table, grains, hierarchies.
- Snowflake schema for splitting large dimension tables.
- Multidimensional DBMS architectures: ROLAP, MOLAP, HOLAP, and DOLAP.
- Five steps in designing a data warehouse.
- Ten steps to build a production extract system.
- Process of data warehouse building and maintenance.

QUESTIONS

1. What are operational databases not particularly suited for decision support applications?

2. How is a data warehouse different from a data mart?

3. When is the three-tier data warehouse architecture more appropriate than the two-tier data warehouse architecture?

4. What are the components of an enterprise data model?

5. What are some causes for failures in data warehouse projects?

6. Does a bottom-up data warehouse architecture use an enterprise data model?

7. What are the differences between the ROLAP, the MOLAP, and the HOLAP architectures?

8. What are the advantages of multidimensional representation over relational representation for data used for decision support?

9. Explain the differences between dimension hierarchies and dimension classes.

10. What are the advantages of using time-series data in a cell instead of time as a dimension?

11. How is slicing a data cube different from dicing?

12. What are the differences between drilling down a data cube and slicing or dicing it?

13. How is a pivot operation useful for multidimensional databases?

14. Explain the significance of sparsity in a data cube.

15. How is the star schema described in this chapter different from entity relationship diagrams?

16. What are the differences between fact tables and dimension tables?

17. Explain the significance of indexing fact and dimension tables in a data warehouse.

18. Why is data cleaning an important issue in building data warehouses?

19. What is the utility of creating a production extract system?

20. How is quality assurance performed in the data warehouse implementation process?

PROBLEMS

ORDER

Consider the database shown below used by an automobile insurance provider to perform two processes: (1) policy transaction: create and maintain customer policies and (2) claims transaction: process claims made by other parties. The policy transaction utilizes the five tables *POLICY, COVERED_ITEM, INSURED_PARTY, INSURED_AUTO,* and *AGENT,* while the claims transaction uses the six tables *CLAIM, CLAIMANT, POLICY, AGENT, INSURED_PARTY,* and *THIRD_PARTY.* The eight tables in this database are shown below, along with their primary and foreign keys. For each table, you may assume field formats of your own choice.

Table: POLICY

Policy _Num	Policy _Date	Covered_ Item_Num	Insured_ Party_SSN	Insured _Auto	Agent _SSN	Policy_ Amount	Effective _Date

Primary key: Policy_Num

Foreign keys: Covered_Item_Num, Insured_Party_SSN, Insured_Auto, Agent_SSN

Table: COVERED_ITEM

Covered_ Item_Num	Covered_ Item_Desc	Covered_ Item_Cost

Primary key: Covered_Item_Num
Foreign keys: None

Table: INSURED_PARTY

Insured_ Party_SSN	Drivers_ Lic_Num	Drivers_ Lic_State	Name	Address	Phone	Age	Risk Category	Insurance _Category

Primary key: Insured_Party_SSN
Foreign keys: None

Table: INSURED_AUTO

Policy _Num	Lic_Plate _Num	Lic_Plate _State	VIN	Make	Model	Year	Mileage	Options	Safety_ Rating	Principal Driver_SSN

Primary key: Lic_Plate_Num, Lic_Plate_State
Foreign keys: Policy_Num, Principal_Driver_SSN

Table: AGENT

Agent _SSN	Agent _Name	Agent _Phone	Agent _Dept	Agent _Type	Agent _Address

Primary key: Agent_SSN
Foreign keys: None

Table: CLAIM

Claim _Num	Policy _Num	Insured _Party _SSN	Claimant _SSN	Third _Party _SSN	Claim _Desc	Claim_ Estimate	Claim_ Amount	Agent _SSN	Insured _Party _Desc

Primary key: Claim_Num
Foreign keys: Policy_Num, Insured_Party_SSN, Claimant_SSN, Third_Party_SSN, Agent_SSN

Table: CLAIMANT

Claimant _SSN	Claimant _Name	Claimant _Address	Claimant _Phone	Claimant _Policy_Num	Claimant_Ins Company	Claimant _Desc

Primary key: Claimant_SSN
Foreign keys: None

Table: THIRD_PARTY

Third _Party _SSN	Third _Party _Name	Third _Party _Address	Third _Party _Phone	Third _Party _Desc

Primary key: Third_Party_SSN
Foreign keys: None

1. Identify the different dimension and fact tables and the component columns from the data provided above.

2. Identify primary and foreign keys that can be used to link these tables.

3. Draw a star schema representing a customer policy maintenance transaction.

4. Draw a second star schema to represent a claims transaction.

5. In the customer policy schema, how can the data be divided between a production database and a data warehouse? What should be the finest level grain in a data cube?

6. Identify hierarchies in the dimensions in the data cube for the policy transaction.

7. In the claims schema, how can the data be divided between a production database and a data warehouse? What should be the finest level grain in a data cube?

8. Identify hierarchies in the dimensions in the data cube for the claims transaction.

9. If you slice the data cube for the policy transaction to view all insurance records created by a certain agent, what tables and/or fields will you see?

10. If you now dice the result of the slice operation in problem 9 above to view all automobiles insured by a particular person (insured party), what tables and/or fields would you see?

11. Begin with a data cube with four dimensions (*Insured_Party, Insured_Auto, Covered_Item,* and *Agent*) and one measure (policy amount) in the cells. From this data cube, describe the operation to generate a new data cube with three dimensions (*Insured_Party, Covered_Item,* and *Agent*) and one measure (average auto policy amount).

REFERENCES FOR FURTHER STUDY

This chapter should only be considered an introduction to data warehouses because of the importance and the scope of the subject. Numerous books and articles have been written about data warehouses that provide more depth than this chapter. Devlin (1997); Inmon (1996), the father of data warehousing; and Kimball (1996) have written widely read books on data warehouses. The *Communications of the ACM* devoted an entire issue (September 1998) to data warehousing. See the bibliography entries for Bontempo and Zagelow, Claudio, Gardner, Scott, Sigal, Sutter, and Watson and Haley. The *Journal of Data Warehousing* from the Data Warehousing Institute (http://www.dw-institute.com/) and the DM Review (http://www.dmreview.com/) provide timely and unbiased reporting on data warehousing trends, vendors, and issues. You also can find additional information in websites under the topics "Data Warehouses" and "Data Mining" in the list of URLs.

Client–Server Processing and Distributed Databases

Learning Objectives

This chapter describes how database management systems utilize computer networks and remote computers to support client–server processing and distributed databases. After this chapter, the student should have acquired the following knowledge and skills:

- List reasons for distributed processing and distributed data.

- Describe two-tier, three-tier, and multiple-tier client–server database architectures.

- Compare and contrast approaches for Web database connectivity.

- Describe differences between technology for tightly integrated and loosely integrated distributed databases.

- Compare the different kinds of distributed database transparency.

- Understand the nature of query processing and transaction processing for distributed databases.

OVERVIEW

Chapters 13 and 14 described database processing for transactions and decision support. As both chapters explained, transaction and decision support processing are vital to modern organizations. In this chapter, you will learn how computer networks, remote computers, and remote data storage can improve reliability and performance for both kinds of processing.

This chapter explains how DBMSs utilize computer networks, remote computers, and remote data storage. Before understanding the details, you should understand the motivation for utilizing these resources. This chapter discusses the pros and cons of both distributed processing and distributed data. After grasping the motivation, you are ready to learn how DBMSs allow work to be distributed among computers in a client–server manner. This chapter describes client–server architectures and the use of the architectures for Web database connectivity. Distributing data in addition to distributing processing allows more flexibility but also involves more complexity. To depict the trade-off between flexibility and complexity, this chapter explains distributed database architectures, levels of transparency for distributed data, and distributed database processing for queries and transactions.

15.1 OVERVIEW OF DISTRIBUTED PROCESSING AND DISTRIBUTED DATA

To understand the issues, it is easier to separate distributed processing from distributed data. Both areas have distinct architectures, design problems, and processing technologies. After learning them separately, you can understand how to combine them. This section begins your study by discussing the historical development and motivations behind distributed processing and data.

15.1.1 Evolution of Distributed Processing and Distributed Data

The technologies available for distributed processing and data have evolved from previous technologies. Even in the early days of computing, there was widespread recognition of the need to share resources across a network. <u>Timesharing</u> was a popular way to share resources in the 1970s. In a timesharing network, computer terminals are connected to a mainframe computer as in Figure 15.1. Computing time is shared among users typing on character-based terminals. Timesharing networks support only small amounts of data transmitted between a mainframe computer and terminals. Thus, graphical interfaces were not feasible given the data transmission limitations and the limited intelligence of the terminals.

The advent of personal computers and local area networks spurred changes in distributed processing in the 1980s. Local area networks support high-speed data transfer while personal computers support rich graphical interfaces. Thus, larger amounts of data can be transmitted and computer graphics can be supported by a personal computer, not a mainframe computer. File sharing and remote procedure calls augmented timesharing. In <u>file sharing</u> [Figure 15.2(a)], a personal computer requests a file from another computer on a network. In a <u>remote procedure call</u> [Figure 15.2(b)], a personal computer invokes a stored procedure on another computer in a network. File sharing and remote procedure calls are simple ways to share processing and data in a network.

Because of limitations with file sharing and remote procedure calls, distributed processing and distributed data have evolved again in the 1990s. Recall that Chapter 1

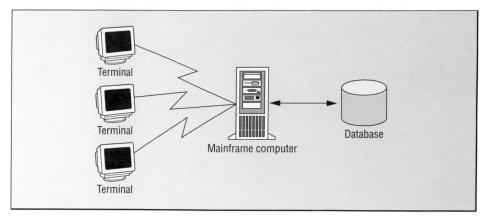

| Figure 15.1 | **Timesharing network.** |

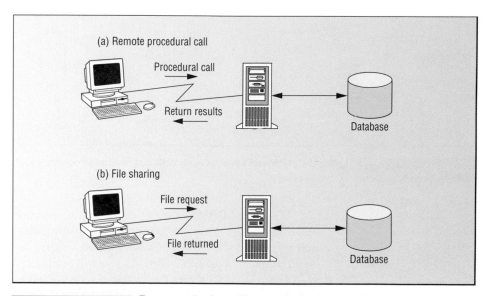

| Figure 15.2 | **Resource sharing with a network of personal computers.** |

(Section 1.4.2) introduced the idea of the client–server approach for utilizing computer networks, remote computers, and remote data. A <u>client</u> is a program that makes requests to a server. The <u>server</u> performs the request and communicates the result to the client.

The client–server approach supports the use of remote computing resources. In Figure 15.3(a), different computers contain the client and the server software. In this arrangement, processing power is spread among various computers that are connected by a network. In Figure 15.3(b), both the processing resources and the data resources are dispersed across multiple locations or sites. The processing capabilities of a server computer can range from a workstation to a powerful mainframe. The client–server approach provides the flexibility to use the capacity that matches the task. The client and the server software can even be deployed on the same computer if the task requirements do not require separate computers.

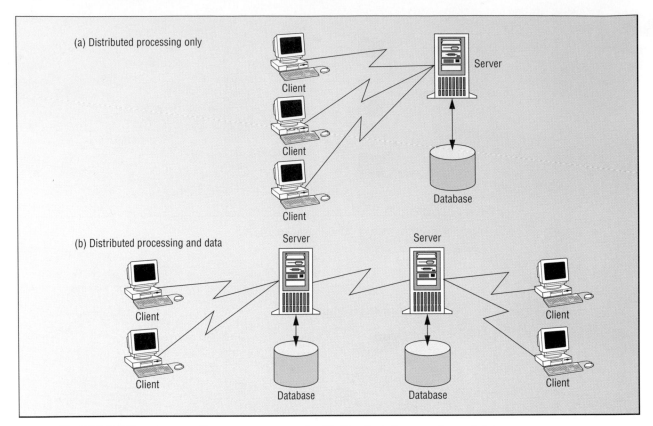

Figure 15.3 **Using the client–server approach with distributed processing and data.**

Distributed DBMSs and the client–server approach provide more flexibility than file sharing and remote procedure calls. For sharing data, <u>distributed DBMSs</u> allow subsets of a table to be distributed among computers in a network. Users submit queries instead of requests for entire files. As you will see in the second half of this chapter, the distributed DBMS assumes the burden of locating and assembling data when requested. For sharing processing, the client–server approach can distribute work among any number of computers in a network. When requesting work, a client can submit a request and continue (asynchronous) instead of waiting for the remote procedure to finish (synchronous). In addition, the client–server approach supports more intelligence in a message than in a procedure call.

15.1.2 Motivation for Distributed Processing

Distributed processing with the client–server approach offers a number of advantages related to flexibility, scalability, and interoperability. <u>Flexibility</u> refers to the ease of maintaining and adapting a system. Maintenance costs often dominate the cost of initially developing an information system because of long life and system revisions. The client–server approach promotes flexibility because volatile sections of code can be isolated from more stable sections. For example, user interface code can be separated from the business rules and the data access code. If a new interface is deployed, other parts of the code remain unchanged. In addition, the client–server approach is ideally suited for object-oriented programming to support reusability. Chapter 16 describes object-oriented databases and programming.

The client–server approach supports scalable growth of hardware and software capacity. Scalability refers to the ability to add and remove capacity in small units. On the server side, work from an overloaded server may be moved to a new server to alleviate a bottleneck or handle new demand from additional workstations. The new server can have just the level of additional computing capacity necessary. On the client side, work can be moved from clients to a server to allow the use of inexpensive client hardware (thin clients). Work also may move in the opposite direction (from server to client) to alleviate server processing loads and take advantage of client computing capabilities.

Scalable growth also can lead to improved performance. For example, adding middleware can reduce contention problems caused by many users accessing a database. The next section describes middleware that can efficiently manage many simultaneous users accessing a database. In addition, specialized servers can be employed to handle work that would otherwise slow all users. For example, multimedia servers can handle requests for images, thus freeing other servers from this time-consuming task.

Client–server systems based on open standards support interoperability. Interoperability refers to the ability of two or more systems to exchange and use software and data. Open standards promote a marketplace of suppliers, leading to lower costs and higher quality. Software components in the marketplace are interoperable if they conform to the standards. The most heavily standardized area is the Internet, where client–server databases are becoming increasingly important, as discussed in Section 15.3.

Despite the advantages of distributed processing, some significant pitfalls may occur. Developing client–server software may be more complex because of architectural choices. A client–server architecture specifies an arrangement of components and a division of processing among the components. Section 15.2 presents several possible architectures for client–server database processing. The choice of an inappropriate architecture can lead to poor performance and maintenance problems. In addition to architectural issues, the designer may face a difficult decision about building a client–server database on proprietary methods versus open standards. Proprietary methods allow easier resolution of problems because one vendor is responsible for all problems. Proprietary methods also may have better performance because they are not as general as open standards. In the long run, proprietary methods can be expensive and inflexible, however. If the vendor does not grow with the industry, a client–server database may become outdated and expensive to upgrade.

15.1.3 Motivation for Distributed Data

Distributed data offer a number of advantages related to data control, communication costs, and performance. Distributing a database allows the location of data to match an organization's structure. For example, parts of a customer table can be located close to customer processing centers. Decisions about sharing and maintaining data can be set locally to provide control closer to the data usage. Often, local employees and management understand issues related to data better than management at remote locations.

Distributed data can lead to lower communication costs and improved performance. Data should be located so that 80 percent of the requests are local. Local requests incur little or no communication costs and delays compared to remote requests. Increased data availability also can lead to improved performance. Data are more available because there is no single computer responsible for controlling access. In addition, data can be replicated so that they are available at more than one site.

TABLE 15–1	Summary of Distributed Processing and Data	
	Distributed Processing	*Distributed Data*
Advantages	Flexibility, interoperability, scalability	Local control of data, improved performance, reduced communication costs
Disadvantages	High complexity, high development cost, possible interoperability problems	High complexity, additional security concerns

Despite the advantages of distributed data, some significant pitfalls may occur. Distributed database design issues are very difficult. A poor design can lead to higher communication costs and poor performance. Distributed database design is difficult because of the lack of tools, the number of choices, and the relationships among choices. Distributed transaction processing can add considerable overhead, especially for replicated data. Distributed data involve more security concerns because many sites can manage data. Each site must be properly protected from unauthorized access.

15.1.4 Summary of Advantages and Disadvantages

Before moving forward, you should take a moment to compare distributed processing and distributed data. Table 15–1 summarizes the advantages and the disadvantages of distributed processing and distributed data as separate technologies. To gain maximum leverage, the technologies can be combined. At this time, distributed processing with the client–server approach is the more mature and widely deployed technology. As distributed database technology matures and gains acceptance, organizations will deploy both technologies.

15.2 CLIENT–SERVER DATABASE ARCHITECTURES

The design of a client–server database affects the advantages and the disadvantages cited in the previous section. A good design tends to magnify advantages and reduce disadvantages relative to an organization's requirements. A poor design may exacerbate disadvantages and diminish advantages. Proper design of a client–server database may make the difference between success and failure of an information system project. To help you achieve good designs, this section discusses design issues of client–server databases and describes how these issues are addressed in various architectures.

Client–Server Architecture an arrangement of components (clients and servers) among computers connected by a network. A client–server architecture supports efficient processing of messages (requests for service) between clients and servers.

15.2.1 Design Issues

Two design issues, division of processing and process management, affect the design of a client–server database. Division of processing refers to the allocation of tasks to clients and servers. Process management involves interoperability among clients and servers and efficiently processing messages between clients and servers. Software for process management is known as "middleware" because of its mediating role. This section describes these issues so that you will understand how various architectures address them in the next section.

Division of Processing

In a typical client–server database, there are a number of tasks that can be performed locally on a client or remotely on a server. The following list briefly describes these tasks.

- Presentation: code to maintain the graphical user interface. The presentation code displays objects, monitors events, and responds to events. Events include user-initiated actions with the mouse and the keyboard as well as external events initiated by timers and other users.
- Validation: code to ensure the consistency of the database and user inputs. Validation logic often is expressed as integrity rules that are stored in a database.
- Business logic: code to perform business functions such as payroll calculations, eligibility requirements, and interest calculations. Business logic may change as the regulatory and the competitive environments change.
- Workflow: code to ensure completion of business processes. Workflow code may route forms, send messages about a deadline, and notify users when a business process is completed.
- Data access: code to extract data to answer queries and modify a database. Data access code consists of SQL statements and translation code that is usually part of the DBMS. If multiple databases are involved, some translation code may reside in software separate from a DBMS.

Parts of these tasks can be divided between clients and servers. For example, some validation can be performed on a PC client and some can be performed on a database server. Thus, there is a lot of flexibility about how processing tasks can be divided. Section 15.2.2 describes several popular ways to divide processing tasks.

Middleware

Middleware a software component in a client–server architecture that performs process management. Middleware allows servers to efficiently process messages from a large number of clients. In addition, middleware can allow clients and servers to communicate across heterogeneous platforms. To handle large processing loads, middleware often is located on a dedicated computer.

Interoperability is an important function of middleware. Clients and servers can exist on platforms with different hardware, operating systems, DBMSs, and programming languages. Figure 15.4 depicts middleware allowing clients and servers to communicate without regard to the underlying platforms of the clients and the servers. The middleware enables a client and a server to communicate without knowledge of each other's platform.

Efficient message control is another important function of middleware. In a typical client–server environment, there are many clients communicating with a few servers. A server can become overloaded just managing the messages that it receives rather than completing the requests. Middleware frees servers to concentrate on completing requests rather than managing requests. Middleware can perform queuing, scheduling, and routing of messages, allowing clients and servers to perform work at different speeds and times.

Based on the functions of interoperability and message control, several kinds of middleware are commercially available, as described in the following list:

- Transaction-processing monitors are the oldest kind of middleware. Traditionally, transaction-processing monitors relieve the operating system of managing database processes. A transaction-processing monitor can switch control among processes much faster than an operating system. In this role, a

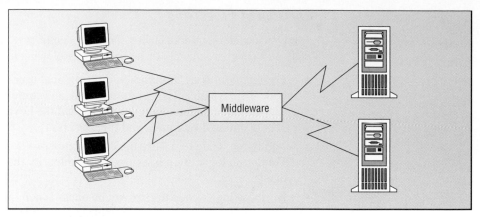

| Figure 15.4 | **Client–server computing with middleware.** |

transaction-processing monitor receives transactions, schedules them, and manages them to completion. Recently, transaction-processing monitors have taken additional tasks such as updating multiple databases in a single transaction.

- Message-oriented middleware maintains a queue of messages. A client process can place a message on a queue and a server process can remove a message from a queue. Message-oriented middleware differs from transaction-processing monitors primarily in the intelligence of the messages. Transaction-processing monitors provide built-in intelligence but use simple messages. In contrast, message-oriented middleware provides much less built-in intelligence but supports more complex messages.

- Object-request brokers provide a high level of interoperability and message intelligence. To use an object-request broker, messages must be encoded in a standard interface description language. An object-request broker resolves platform differences between a client and a server. In addition, a client can communicate with a server without knowing the location of the server.

15.2.2 Description of Architectures

The design issues are addressed in a number of architectures. For each architecture, this section describes typical division of processing, message management approaches, and trade-offs among architectures.

Two-Tier Architecture

Two-Tier Architecture
a client–server architecture in which a PC client and a database server interact directly to request and transfer data. The PC client contains the user interface code, the server contains the data access logic, and the PC client and the server share the validation and business logic.

The two-tier architecture features a PC client and a database server as shown in Figure 15.5. The PC client contains the presentation code and SQL statements for data access. The database server processes the SQL statements and sends query results back to the PC client. In addition, the database server performs process management functions. The validation and business logic code can be split between the PC client and the database server. The PC client can invoke stored procedures on the database server for business logic and validation. Typically, much of the business logic code resides on the client. PC

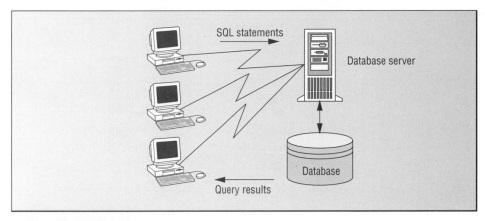

Figure 15.5   Two-tier architecture.

clients in a two-tier architecture are sometimes called "fat clients" because of the large amount of business logic they contain.

The two-tier architecture is a good approach for systems with stable requirements and a moderate number of clients. On the positive side, the two-tier architecture is the simplest to implement due to the number of good commercial development environments. On the negative side, software maintenance can be difficult because PC clients contain a mix of presentation, validation, and business logic code. To make a significant change in business logic, code must be modified on many PC clients. In addition, utilizing new technology may be difficult because two-tier architectures often rely on proprietary software rather than open standards. To lessen reliance on a particular database server, the PC client can connect to intermediate database drivers such as the Open Database Connectivity (ODBC) drivers instead of directly to a database server. The intermediate database drivers then communicate with the database server.

Performance can be poor when a large number of clients submit requests because the database server may be overwhelmed with managing messages. Several sources report that two-tier architectures are limited to about 100 simultaneous clients. With a larger number of simultaneous clients, a three-tier architecture may be necessary. In addition, connecting to intermediate drivers rather than directly to a database server can slow performance.

Three-Tier Architecture

Three-Tier Architecture a client–server architecture with three layers: a PC client, a backend database server, and either a middleware or an application server.

To improve performance, the three-tier architecture adds another server layer, as depicted in Figure 15.6. One way to improve performance is to add a middleware server [Figure 15.6(a)] to handle process management. The middleware usually consists of a transaction-processing monitor or message-oriented middleware. A transaction-processing monitor may support more simultaneous connections than message-oriented middleware. However, message-oriented middleware provides more flexibility in the kinds of messages supported. A second way to improve performance is to add an application server for specific kinds of processing such as report writing. In either approach, the additional server software can reside on a separate computer, as depicted in Figure 15.6. Alternatively, the additional server software can be distributed between the database server and the PC clients.

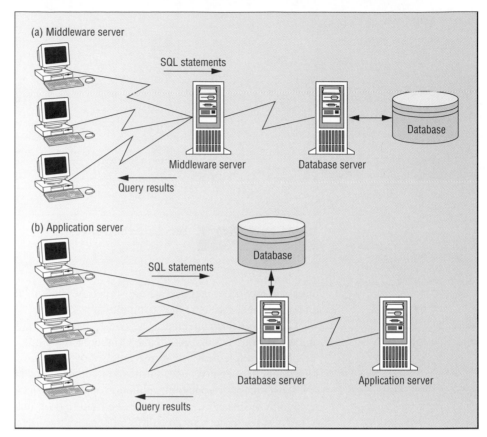

(a) Middleware server

SQL statements

Query results

Middleware server   Database server   Database

(b) Application server

Database

SQL statements

Query results

Database server   Application server

Figure 15.6   **Three-tier architecture.**

Although the three-tier architecture addresses performance degradations of the two-tier architecture, it does not address division-of-processing concerns. The PC clients and the database server still contain the same division of code although the tasks of the database server are reduced. Multiple-tier architectures provide more flexibility on division of processing.

Multiple-Tier Architecture

Multiple-Tier Architecture a client–server architecture with more than three layers: a PC client, a backend database server, an intervening middleware server, and application servers. The application servers perform business logic and manage specialized kinds of data such as images.

To improve performance and provide flexible division of processing, multiple-tier architectures support additional layers of servers, as depicted in Figure 15.7. The application servers can be invoked from PC clients, middleware, and database servers. The additional server layers provide a finer division of processing than a two- or a three-tier architecture. The additional server layers also can improve performance because both middleware and application servers can be deployed.

Software buses provide a flexible and standard approach for multiple-tier architectures, as shown in Figure 15.8. A software bus resolves differences among server and client platforms. Software units of code or objects can be located on any server, even replicated on multiple servers to improve reliability. PC clients can request objects without knowing the platform, location, or implementation details of the object. Currently,

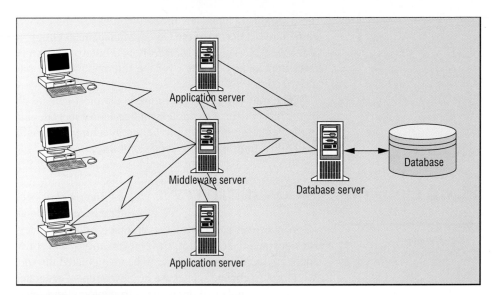

Figure 15.7   **Multiple-tier architecture.**

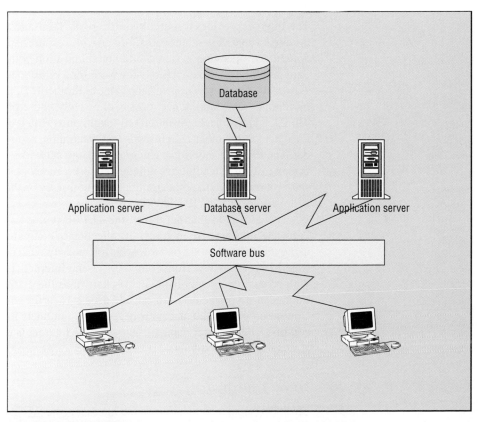

Figure 15.8   **Multiple-tier architecture with software bus.**

there are three candidates for software buses: the Common Object Request Broker Architecture (CORBA) of the Object Management Group, the Distributed Component Object Model (COM+) of Microsoft, and Enterprise Java Beans of Sun Microsystems. All three approaches operate over the Internet and corporate intranets, as described in the next section.

The multiple-tier architecture is the most general client–server architecture. It can be the most difficult to implement because of its generality. However, a good design and implementation of a multiple-tier architecture can provide the most benefits in terms of scalability, interoperability, and flexibility.

15.3 WEB DATABASE CONNECTIVITY

Web Database Connectivity
client–server architectures that allow a Web page to query and update remote databases managed by servers on the Internet.

As the Internet has become wildly popular, so has the need for accessing databases through World Wide Web (WWW or Web) pages. Internet commerce depends heavily on database access for websites devoted to book sales, travel reservations, and software distribution. Web database connectivity allows a database to be manipulated through a web page. A user may use a Web form to change a database or view a report generated from a database. This section discusses a number of approaches to deploy client–server databases through the Web. Before discussing these approaches, a brief tutorial about the Internet and the World Wide Web is provided.

15.3.1 Internet Basics

The Internet provides resource sharing among thousands of networks. For this reason it is called a "network of networks." To provide resource sharing among different kinds of computers, operating systems, and communication equipment, the Internet uses standard protocols. A protocol is a fancy word for a rule about group behavior or interaction. The Internet uses the Transmission Control Protocol (TCP) and the Internet Protocol (IP) to communicate among networks. Collectively, these protocols are known as TCP/IP. The TCP splits messages into fixed-length units called datagrams or packets, reassembles them at the other end, resends lost datagrams, and rearranges them in the right order. The IP routes individual datagrams among networks. Routing can be a complex task because of incompatibilities among networks, many possible routes, and the changing status of routes. To facilitate routing, each computer on the Internet has a unique numeric address known as an IP address.

In addition to Internet usage, the TCP/IP protocols are used for private networks known as intranets. An intranet is a collection of computers and communication devices using the TCP/IP protocol. However, for security reasons, computers in an intranet are usually not accessible from computers on the Internet. The combination of the Internet with accessible intranet computers is known as the extranet. For added security, an intranet can be protected from outside access by a firewall, as depicted in Figure 15.9. Client–server database access is necessary in intranets for internal computing needs. In contrast, client–server database access in the Internet is usually for outside parties such as customers and suppliers.

World Wide Web

The most popular application on the Internet is the World Wide Web (WWW). Using the WWW, you can browse pages located on any computer on the Internet. Another set of standards provides the foundation for the WWW. The Hypertext Transfer Protocol

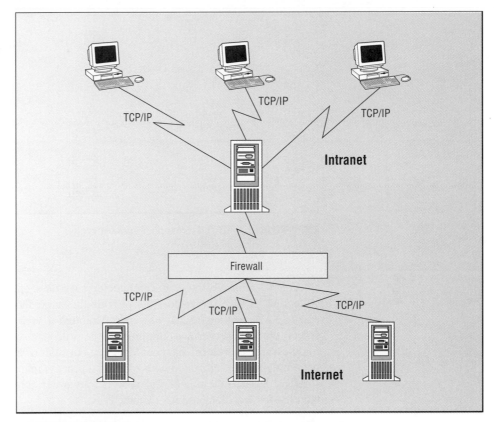

Figure 15.9	**Intranet and Internet relationship.**

(HTTP) establishes a session between a browser and a Web server. During the session, the browser and the server interact to send and receive files containing Web pages. Each page has a unique address known as a Uniform Resource Locator (URL). The first part of a URL specifies the protocol of a service. The second part of a URL specifies a computer on the Internet containing the file. Communication devices such as routers and gateways translate the second part into a numeric IP address. The third part of a URL specifies a path to a file containing the page. For example in the URL http://www.microsoft.com/products/default.html, "http" indicates the service, "www.microsoft.com" indicates the computer, and "products/default.html" indicates the directory and the file name of the page.

The browser and the server work together to send and receive pages. Web pages are written in a language called the Hypertext Markup Language (HTML). A browser displays pages on a PC by interpreting HTML code in the file sent by a server. Part of the HTML code can contain hyperlinks or requests for other pages. When a user clicks on a hyperlink, the browser sends a request to a server to retrieve the page, as depicted in Figure 15.10. The server locates the file containing the page and sends it to the requesting browser. The user then sees the requested page after the browser interprets the HTML code in the file.

To access databases, additional servers and interactions augment the browser (client) and the Web server actions of Figure 15.10. Since a Web server mediates almost

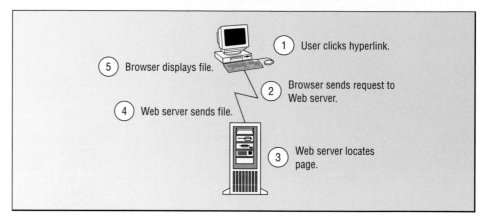

①　User clicks hyperlink.

⑤　Browser displays file.

②　Browser sends request to Web server.

④　Web server sends file.

③　Web server locates page.

Figure 15.10   **Web page request cycle.**

all requests from a browser, the architectures would seem to fit at least the three-tier architecture. A Web server does not provide the same services as database middleware, discussed in Section 15.2.1, however. Although a Web server can invoke a database server, the Web server does not provide the process management services of database middleware. Therefore, this book does not consider a Web server as database middleware unless it is augmented with additional process management capabilities. The next sections describe the role of Web servers in two-tier, three-tier, and multiple-tier architectures for Web database interconnectivity.

XML and XSL

HTML has a number of limitations that have become more pronounced as the Web explosively grows. In HTML, the content, the structure, and the formatting of a page are mixed together. This mixture makes it difficult to search Web pages, display web pages in different formats for different devices, and standardize the content of Web pages. To support the rapid growth of the Web, the ability to search, display, and standardize Web pages must improve.

These limitations have led to the development of the eXtensible Markup Language (XML) and the eXtensible Style Language (XSL). In contrast to HTML, XML provides a clean separation between the structure and the content of a document. The Document Type Declaration section of an XML document provides field names, field properties, and the structure of fields. In this sense, the Document Type Declaration provides a standard way to express view definitions (although not view mappings).[1] XSL supports transformation of XML documents into HTML and other display languages. Both languages are extensible in that they support the development of industry-specific standards for document content, structure, and display.

In terms of the Web page request cycle of Figure 15.10, the server and/or the browser may be capable of processing XML and XSL in addition to HTML. If the

---

[1] In the future, schemas may replace document type declarations. Schemas provide a number of advantages over document type declarations. Schemas have not been officially approved by the official governing board of the Web as of the writing of this chapter.

browser contains XML and XSL processors, the server can send XML and XSL to the browser instead of HTML. The browser then can transform the XML and XSL into HTML and then display the HTML. If the browser does not contain XML and XSL processors, the server can process the XML and XSL and send HTML to the browser. In the near future, the major browsers will contain XML and XSL processors.

15.3.2 Common Gateway Interface

Common Gateway Interface (CGI) an interface that allows a Web server to invoke an external program on the same computer. CGI was the earliest and still is the most universal way to achieve Web database connectivity.

The Common Gateway Interface (CGI) allows a Web server to communicate with an external program. The Web server can pass parameters to the external program. The external program uses the parameters to produce output that is sent back to the browser. Usually, the output contains HTML so that the browser can display it properly. The CGI approach is portable across most Web servers, although the external program may not be portable. The external program can be written in a compiled language like C or an interpreted language like PERL.

The CGI provides several ways to facilitate database connectivity, as depicted in Figure 15.11. In the straight CGI approach, the external program sends SQL statements to the database server and encodes the results in HTML or XML format. In the hybrid CGI approach, the external program sends SQL statements to a partner program that interacts with a database server. The hybrid CGI approach usually provides better performance

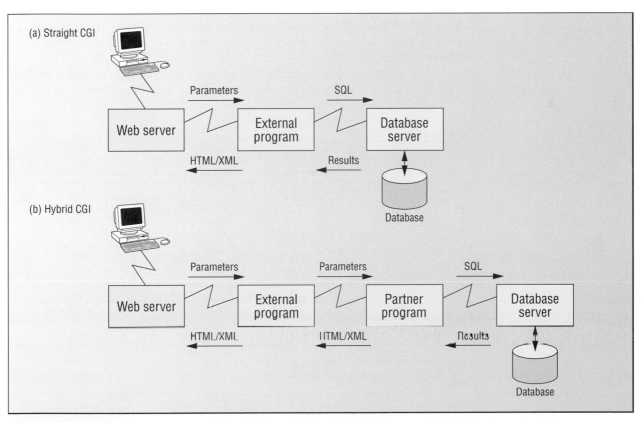

Figure 15.11   **CGI approaches to Web database connectivity.**

because the partner program manages database connections among multiple CGI processes. In effect, the partner program performs some middleware functions.

The hybrid CGI approach, although more efficient than the straight CGI approach, may not scale to many simultaneous users. A more efficient approach is to add additional process management functions in the Web server so that the Web server directly communicates with the database server. The next section describes several approaches to direct communication between a Web server and a database server.

15.3.3 Server-Side Connectivity

Server-Side Connectivity an approach to Web database connectivity in which a browser communicates with a database server without invoking an external program. Although server-side connectivity is more scalable than the Common Gateway Interface, it requires a specialized Web server or a separate middleware server.

Server-side connectivity bypasses the external program needed with the CGI approaches. The Web server directly communicates with the database server without invoking an external program. However, a specialized Web server (Figure 15.12) may be needed to provide the direct connection between the Web server and the database server. The specialized Web server supports tasks such as management of simultaneous users, support for transactions that span Web pages, and message queuing.

To utilize server-side connectivity, the programmer writes SQL statements and associated database-processing logic in a Web page or external file. To insulate the client from the database logic, the database code can execute stored procedures on the database server. The database code is enclosed in special symbols to indicate that it executes on the server, not the client. For example, Microsoft provides server-side technology known as Active Server Pages. In an Active Server Page, code surrounded by the special characters $<\%$ and $\%>$ executes on the server, not the client. Database code can be used in an Active Server Page to query and update remote databases. After the database server processes the request, the Web server sends the database results back to the browser as HTML or XML.

A limitation of server-side database connectivity is the need for a specialized Web server. A middleware server can eliminate the need for a specialized Web server, as de-

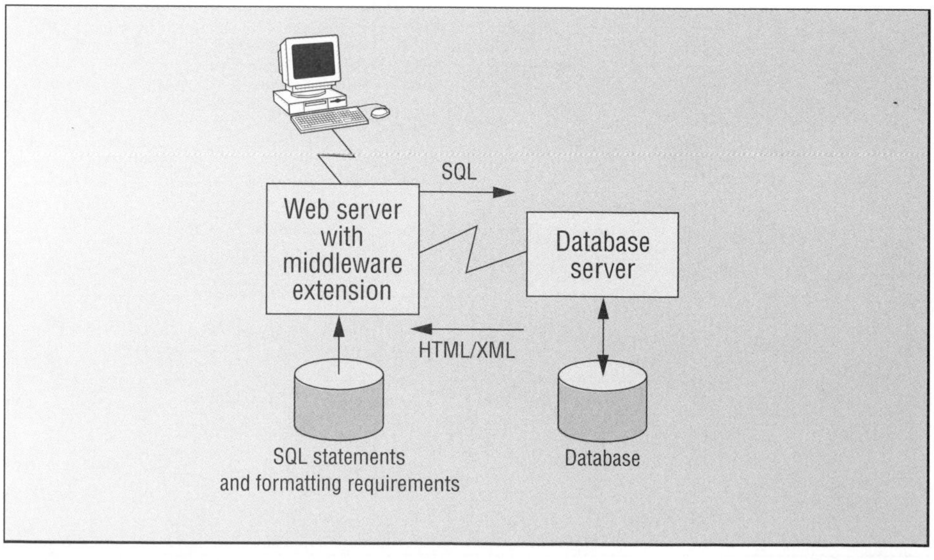

Figure 15.12   **Server-side connectivity approach.**

picted in Figure 15.13. The middleware contains a listener component that routes database requests to the middleware server. The middleware server provides transaction management and message queuing services.

The server-side approaches provide robust services for transaction processing as well as a software bus for utilizing remote objects. The specialized Web servers and the middleware servers can support hundreds to thousands of simultaneous users. The software bus built into specialized Web servers and middleware servers provides transparent access to objects distributed across the Internet. The software bus fulfills the promise of a multiple-tier architecture for Web database connectivity.

15.3.4 Client-Side Connectivity

Client-Side Connectivity
a style of computing on the World Wide Web in which client computing capacity can be more fully utilized without storing code on the client. Client-side connectivity can enhance database connectivity by providing a more customized interface than permitted by HTML and by allowing data buffering by the client.

Although server-side connectivity supports a multiple-tier architecture, it does not fully exploit client computing capabilities. In the server-side approaches, the browser is limited to interpretation of HTML. Even with the scripting capabilities in the new versions of HTML (DHTML), client computing capabilities can be underutilized. The client-side approaches utilize available computing capabilities without storing the code on the client.

Figure 15.14 depicts two approaches to enhance client interfaces for database processing. Java is a language intended for embedded applications. A Java applet is a special kind of program that executes inside a virtual machine located in a Web browser. The virtual machine prevents an applet from damaging the resources of a PC. A Web server sends a Java applet to a requesting Web browser inside a PC client. After receiving the applet, the Web browser executes it to produce specified effects on the browser.

ActiveX differs from Java in that an ActiveX object is a binary file that can be executed directly on a PC client. No virtual machine is used for ActiveX objects. Like Java applets, a Web server sends an ActiveX object as a result of a request by a PC client. Unlike Java applets, ActiveX objects can execute inside a browser or as separate processes.

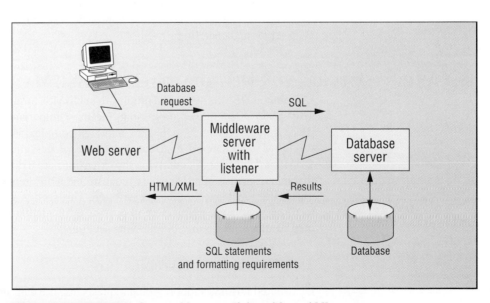

| **Figure 15.13** | **Server-side connectivity with a middleware server.** |

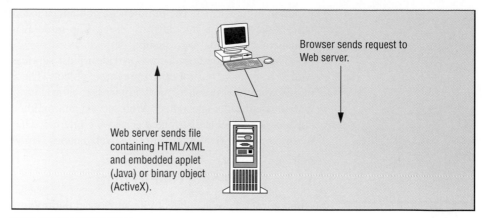

Browser sends request to
Web server.

Web server sends file
containing HTML/XML
and embedded applet
(Java) or binary object
(ActiveX).

| **Figure 15.14** | **Web page request cycle with client-side connectivity.** |

The client-side approaches can be integrated with the server-side approaches described in the previous section. This combination provides the advantages of a multiple-tier client–server architecture with a customized interface on a PC client. PC clients remain thin because the customization code (Java applets and ActiveX objects) resides on a remote server. In addition, PC clients can execute remote code on other servers through Java or ActiveX code.

15.3.5 Summary of Web Database Connectivity Approaches

To help you compare and contrast database connectivity approaches, Table 15–2 provides a convenient summary. For websites attracting a modest number of hits, the CGI approaches work well. For large commercial sites, the server-side connectivity approaches are needed. The middleware-server approach works well with existing Web servers. The extended-Web-server approach may require a commitment to a specific Web server and operating system.

15.4 ARCHITECTURES FOR DISTRIBUTED DATABASE MANAGEMENT SYSTEMS

Distributed DBMSs are more complex than DBMSs to support client–server processing. To support client–server processing, the most important extension is middleware for process management. Middleware, although complex, is often a separate product from the DBMS. To support distributed database processing, fundamental extensions to a DBMS are necessary. Underlying the extensions are a different component architecture that manages distributed database requests and a different schema architecture that provides additional layers of data description. This section describes the component architecture and schema architecture to provide a foundation for more details about distributed database processing in following sections.

15.4.1 Component Architecture

Distributed DBMSs support global requests that use data stored at more than one site. A site is any computer with a unique network address such as an IP address. Sites are often geographically distributed, although the definition supports sites located in close

TABLE 15–2	Summary of Web Connectivity Approaches		
Approach	*Architecture*	*Example Product*	*Comments*
Straight CGI	Two-tier	Apache Web server with external PERL program	Inexpensive; portability only limited by external program; limited scalability
Hybrid CGI	Two-tier	Apache Web server with Cold Fusion server extensions	More expensive than straight CGI; portability depends on partner program; scalable to modest loads
Extended Web server (server-side connectivity)	Three-tier and multiple-tier	Internet Information Server with Microsoft Transaction Server	Expensive; Web server dependent; highly scalable
Middleware server (server-side connectivity)	Three-tier and multiple-tier	Oracle Application Server	Expensive; Web server independent; highly scalable
Client-side connectivity	Two- and multiple-tier	Microsoft Remote Data Service, Java Relational Model Interface	Customized client interface; efficient data buffering; usually works with server-side connectivity approaches

proximity. Global requests include queries that combine data from more than one site and transactions that update data at more than one site. If all requests require only data from one site, distributed database processing capabilities are not required.

To depict global requests, you need to begin with a distributed database. Distributed databases are potentially useful for organizations that operate in multiple locations. Figure 15.15 depicts a distributed database for an electronic retail company. The company performs customer processing at Boise and Tulsa and manages warehouses at Seattle and Denver. The distribution of the database follows the geographical locations of the business. The *Customer, Order,* and *OrderLine* tables (customer-order data) are split between Boise and Tulsa, while the *Product* and *Inventory* tables (product data) are split between Seattle and Denver. An example of a global query is to check both warehouse sites for sufficient quantity of a product to satisfy a shipment invoice. An example of a global transaction is an order-entry form that inserts records into the *Order* and *Order-Line* tables at one location and updates the *Product* table at the closest warehouse site.

To support global queries and transactions, distributed DBMSs contain additional components as compared to traditional, nondistributed DBMSs. Figure 15.16 depicts a possible arrangement of the components of a distributed DBMS. Each server with access to the distributed database is known as a site. If a site contains a database, a local data manager (LDM) controls it. The local data managers provide complete features of a DBMS as described in other chapters. The distributed data manager (DDM) optimizes query execution across sites, coordinates concurrency control and recovery across sites, and controls access to remote data. In performing these tasks, the distributed database manager uses the global dictionary (GD) to locate parts of the database. The global dictionary can be distributed to various sites similar to the way that data are distributed. Because of the complexity of the distributed database manager, Section 15.6 presents more details about distributed query processing and transaction processing.

In the component architecture, the local database managers can be homogeneous or heterogeneous. A distributed DBMS with homogeneous local DBMSs is <u>tightly integrated.</u> The distributed database manager can call internal components and access the internal state of local data managers. The tight integration allows the distributed DBMS to

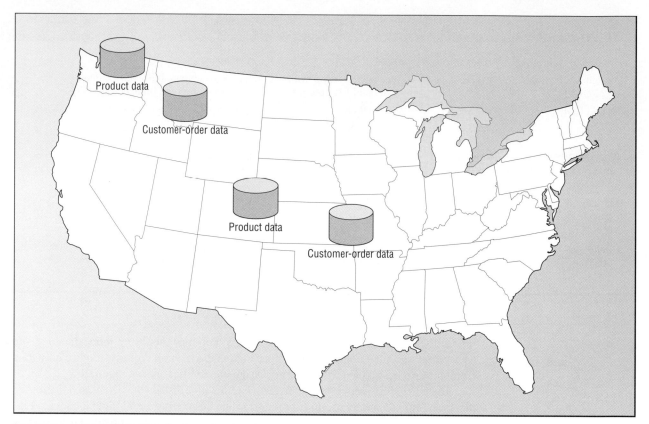

Figure 15.15   Distribution of order-entry data.

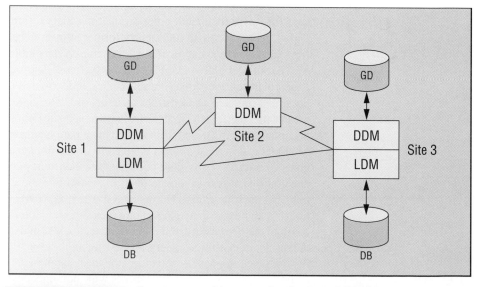

Figure 15.16   Component architecture of a distributed DBMS.

efficiently support both distributed queries and transactions. However, the homogeneity requirement precludes integration of existing databases.

A distributed DBMS with heterogeneous local data managers is <u>loosely integrated.</u> The distributed database manager acts as middleware to coordinate local data managers. SQL often provides the interface between the distributed data manager and the local data managers. The loose integration supports data sharing among legacy systems and independent organizations. However, the loosely integrated approach may not be able to support transaction processing in a reliable and efficient manner.

15.4.2 Schema Architectures

To accommodate distribution of data, additional layers of data description are necessary. However, there is no widely accepted schema architecture for distributed databases like the widely accepted Three Schema Architecture for traditional DBMSs. This section depicts possible schema architectures for tightly integrated distributed DBMSs and loosely integrated distributed DBMSs. The architectures provide a reference about the kinds of data description necessary and how the data description can be compartmentalized.

The schema architecture for a tightly integrated distributed DBMS contains additional layers for fragmentation and allocation, as depicted in Figure 15.17. The fragmentation schema contains the definition of each fragment while the allocation schema

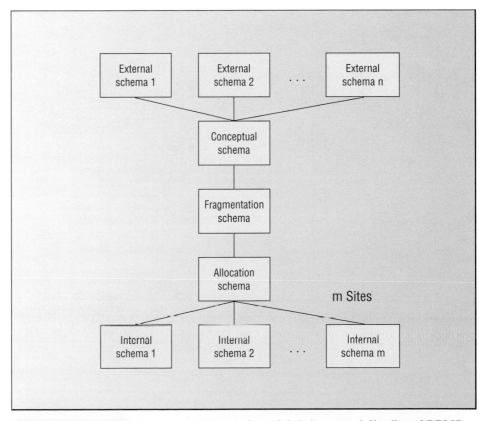

Figure 15.17   **Schema architecture for a tightly integrated distributed DBMS.**

contains the location of each fragment. A <u>fragment</u> can be defined as a vertical subset (project operation), a horizontal subset (restrict operation), or a mixed fragment (combination of project and restrict operations). A fragment is allocated to one site but sometimes to multiple sites. If the distributed DBMS supports replication, a fragment can be allocated to multiple sites. In some distributed DBMSs that support replication, one copy of a fragment is considered the primary copy and the other copies are secondary. Only the primary copy is guaranteed to be current.

The schema architecture for a loosely integrated distributed DBMS supports more autonomy of local database sites in addition to data sharing. Each site contains the traditional three schema levels, as depicted in Figure 15.18. To support data sharing, the distributed DBMS provides a local mapping schema for each site. The local mapping schemas describe the exportable data at a site and provide conversion rules to translate data from a local format into a global format. The global conceptual schema depicts all of the kinds of data and relationships that can be used in global requests. Some distributed DBMSs do not have a global conceptual schema. Instead, global external schemas provide views of shared data in a common format.

There can be many differences among the local data formats. Local sites may use different DBMSs, each with a different set of data types. The data models of the local DBMSs can be different, especially if legacy systems are being integrated. Legacy systems might use file interfaces and navigational data models (network and hierarchical)

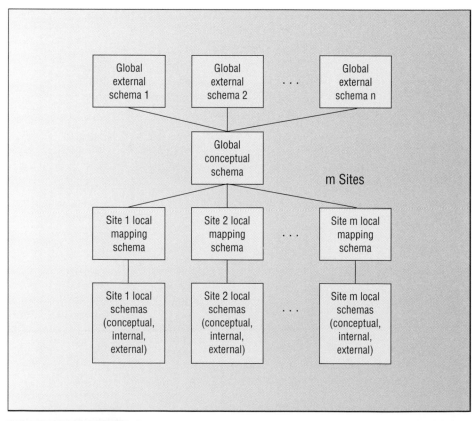

| **Figure 15.18** | **Schema architecture for a loosely integrated distributed DBMS.** |

that do not support SQL. Even if local sites support a common SQL standard, there can be many differences such as different data types, scales, units of measure, and codes. The local mapping schemas resolve these differences by providing conversion rules that transform data from a local format into a global format.

The tightly integrated and loosely integrated architectures represent two extreme possibilities. Many variations between these two architectures have been proposed and implemented. For example, to provide additional local autonomy but more efficiency for global requests, a loosely integrated system can require that all local sites support a common SQL interface. The tightly and loosely integrated approaches also can be combined. Networks of tightly integrated distributed databases can be loosely integrated to share selective data in global requests. In this case the loosely integrated distributed DBMS acts as a gateway between tightly integrated distributed databases.

15.5 TRANSPARENCY FOR DISTRIBUTED DATABASE PROCESSING

Recall from Chapter 13 that transparency refers to whether the inner details of a service are visible or hidden. In transaction processing, concurrency and recovery services are transparent, or hidden from database users. In distributed database processing, transparency is related to data independence. If database distribution is transparent, users can write queries with no knowledge of the distribution. In addition, distribution changes will not cause changes to existing queries and transactions. If the database distribution is not transparent, users must reference some distribution details in queries and distribution changes can lead to changes in existing queries.

This section describes common levels of transparency and provides examples of query formulation with each level. Before discussing transparency levels, a motivating example is presented.

15.5.1 Motivating Example

To depict the levels of transparency, more details about the order-entry database are provided. The order-entry database consists of five tables, as shown in the relationship diagram of Figure 15.19. Assume that customers are located in two regions (East and West) and products are stored in two warehouses (1: Denver, 2: Seattle).

One collection of fragments can be defined using the customer region field as shown in Table 15–3. The *Western-Customers* fragment consists of customers with a region equal to West. There are two related fragments: the *Western-Orders* fragment, consisting of orders for western customers, and the *Western-OrderLines* fragment, consisting of order lines matching western orders. Similar fragments are defined for rows involving eastern customers.

The order and order line fragments are derived from a customer fragment using the semi-join operator. A <u>semi-join</u> is half of a join: the rows of one table that match the rows of another table. For example, a semi-join operation defines the *Western-Orders* fragment as the rows of the *Order* table matching customer rows with a region of West. A fragment defined with a semi-join operation is sometimes called a derived horizontal fragment. Because some fragments should have rows related to other fragments, the semi-join operator is important for defining fragments.

Warehouse fragments are defined using the *WareHouseNo* field as shown in Table 15–4. In the fragment definitions, warehouse number 1 is assumed to be located in Denver and warehouse number 2 in Seattle. The *Product* table is not fragmented because the entire table is replicated at multiple sites.

Semi-Join   an operator of relational algebra that is especially useful for distributed database processing. A semi-join is half of a join: the rows of one table that match with at least one row of another table. Only the rows of the first table appear in the result.

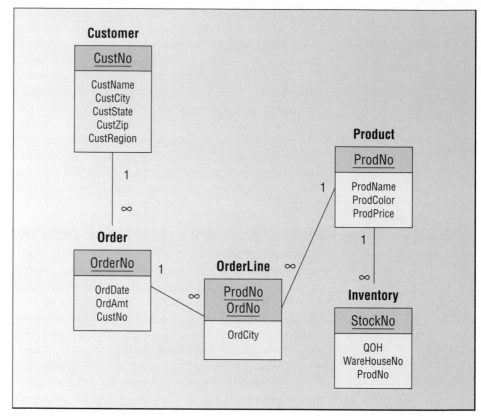

Figure 15.19 Relationship diagram for the order-entry database.

TABLE 15–3 **Fragments Based on the *CustRegion* Field**[2]

```
CREATE FRAGMENT Western-Customers AS
  SELECT * FROM Customer WHERE CustRegion = 'West'

CREATE FRAGMENT Western-Orders AS
  SELECT Order.* FROM Order, Customer
    WHERE Order.CustNo = Customer.CustNo AND CustRegion = 'West'

CREATE FRAGMENT Western-OrderLines AS
  SELECT OrderLine.* FROM Customer, OrderLine, Order
    WHERE OrderLine.OrdNo = Order.OrdNo
      AND Order.CustNo = Customer.CustNo AND CustRegion = 'West'

CREATE FRAGMENT Eastern-Customers AS
  SELECT * FROM Customer WHERE CustRegion = 'East'

CREATE FRAGMENT Eastern-Orders AS
  SELECT Order.* FROM Order, Customer
    WHERE Order.CustNo = Customer.CustNo AND CustRegion = 'East'

CREATE FRAGMENT Eastern-OrderLines AS
  SELECT OrderLine.* FROM Customer, OrderLine, Order
    WHERE OrderLine.OrdNo = Order.OrdNo
      AND Order.CustNo = Customer.CustNo AND CustRegion = 'East'
```

---

[2]The syntax in Table 15–3 is not official SQL syntax.

TABLE 15–4	Fragments Based on the *WareHouseNo* Field

```
CREATE FRAGMENT Denver-Inventory AS
  SELECT * FROM Inventory WHERE WareHouseNo = 1
CREATE FRAGMENT Seattle-Inventory AS
  SELECT * FROM Inventory WHERE WareHouseNo = 2
```

TABLE 15–5	Allocation of Fragments of the Order-Entry Database

Fragments	Site
Western-Customers, Western-Orders, Western-OrderLines	Boise
Eastern-Customers, Eastern-Orders, Eastern-OrderLines	Tulsa
Denver-Inventory, Product	Denver
Seattle-Inventory, Product	Seattle

Fragmentation can be more complex than described in the order-entry database. There can be many additional fragments to accommodate a business structure. For example, if there are additional customer processing centers and warehouses, additional fragments can be defined. In addition, vertical fragments can be defined as projection operations in addition to the horizontal fragments using restriction and semi-join operations. A fragment can even be defined as a combination of projection, selection, and semi-join operations. The only restriction is that the fragments must be disjoint. Disjointness means that horizontal fragments do not contain common rows and vertical fragments do not contain common columns except for the primary key.

After fragments are defined, they are allocated to sites. Fragments are sometimes defined based on where they should be allocated. The allocation of order-entry fragments follows this approach, as shown in Table 15–5. The Boise site contains the western customer fragments, while the Tulsa site contains the eastern customer fragments. Similarly, the inventory fragments are split between the Denver and the Seattle sites. The *Product* table is replicated at the Denver and the Seattle sites because each warehouse stocks every product.

In practice, the design and the allocation of fragments is much more difficult than depicted here. Designing and allocating fragments is similar to index selection. Data about the frequency of queries, the frequency of parameter values in queries, and the behavior of the global query optimizer are needed. In addition, data about the frequency of originating sites for each query are needed. The originating site for a query is the site in which the query is stored. Just as for index selection, optimization models and tools can aid decision making about fragment design and allocation. The details of the optimization models and the tools are beyond the scope of this book. The references at the end of the chapter provide details about fragment design and allocation.

Fragmentation Transparency a level of independence in distributed DBMSs in which queries can be formulated without knowledge of fragments.

15.5.2 Fragmentation Transparency

Fragmentation transparency provides the highest level of data independence. Users formulate queries and transactions without knowledge of fragments, locations, or local formats. If fragments, locations, or local formats change, queries and transactions are not affected. In essence, users perceive the distributed database as a centralized database. Fragmentation transparency involves the least work for users but the most work for distributed DBMSs.

To contrast the transparency levels, Table 15–6 lists some representative queries and transactions that use the order-entry database. In these queries, the parameters $X and $Y are used rather than individual values. With fragmentation transparency, queries and transactions can be submitted without change regardless of the fragmentation of the database.

15.5.3 Location Transparency

Location Transparency
a level of independence in distributed DBMSs in which queries can be formulated without knowledge of locations. However, knowledge of fragments is necessary.

Location transparency provides a lesser level of data independence than fragmentation transparency. Users need to reference fragments in formulating queries and transactions. However, knowledge of locations and local formats is not necessary. Even though site knowledge is not necessary, users are indirectly aware of a database's distribution because many fragments are allocated to a single site. Users may make an association between fragments and sites.

Location transparency involves more work in formulating requests, as shown in Table 15–7. In the Find queries, the union operator collects rows from all fragments. The Update Inventory query involves about the same amount of coding. The user substitutes a fragment name in place of the condition on *WareHouseNo* because this condition defines the fragment.

In the Customer Move request, much more coding is necessary. An update operation cannot be used because the field to update defines the fragment. Instead, rows must be inserted in the new fragments and deleted from the old fragments. For the customer fragment, the SELECT . . . INTO statement stores field values in variables that are used in the subsequent INSERT statement. The deletions are performed in the stated order if referenced rows must be deleted last. If deletions completely cascade, only one DELETE statement on the *Western-Customers* fragment is necessary.

The SQL statements for the first two requests do not reveal the number of union operations that may be required. With two fragments, only one union operation is necessary. With n fragments, $n-1$ union operations are necessary, however.

TABLE 15–6	Representative Requests Using the Order-Entry Database

Find Order
```
SELECT * FROM Order, Customer
   WHERE Order.Custno = $X
      AND Order.CustNo = Customer.CustNo
```

Find Product Availability
```
SELECT * FROM Inventory
   WHERE ProdNo = $X
```

Update Inventory
```
UPDATE Inventory SET QOH = QOH - 1
   WHERE ProdNo = $X AND WareHouseNo = $Y
```

Customer Move
```
UPDATE Customer SET CustRegion = $X
   WHERE CustNo = $Y
```

TABLE 15–7	Requests Written with Location Transparency

Find Order
```
SELECT * FROM Western-Orders, Western-Customers
   WHERE  Western-Orders.CustNo = $X
      AND  Western-Orders.CustNo = Western-Customers.CustNo
UNION
SELECT * FROM Eastern-Orders, Eastern-Customers
   WHERE  Eastern-Orders.CustNo = $X
      AND  Eastern-Orders.Custno = Eastern-Customers.CustNo
```

Find Product Availability
```
SELECT * FROM Denver-Inventory
   WHERE ProdNo = $X
UNION
SELECT * FROM Seattle-Inventory
   WHERE ProdNo = $X
```

Update Inventory (Denver)
```
UPDATE Denver-Inventory SET QOH = QOH - 1
   WHERE ProdNo = $X
```

Customer Move (West to East)
```
SELECT CustName, CustCity, CustState, CustZip
   INTO $CustName, $CustCity, $CustState, $CustZip
   FROM Western-Customers WHERE CustNo = $Y

INSERT INTO Eastern-Customers
     (CustNo, CustName, CustCity, CustState, CustZip, CustRegion)
   VALUES ($Y, $CustName, $CustCity, $CustState, $CustZip, 'East')

INSERT INTO Eastern-Orders
   SELECT * FROM Western-Orders WHERE CustNo = $Y

INSERT INTO Eastern-OrderLines
   SELECT * FROM Western-OrderLines
     WHERE OrdNo IN
       (SELECT OrdNo FROM Western-Orders WHERE CustNo = $Y)

DELETE FROM Western-OrderLines
   WHERE OrdNo IN
       (SELECT OrdNo FROM Western-Orders WHERE CustNo = $Y)

DELETE Western-Orders WHERE CustNo = $Y

DELETE Western-Customers WHERE CustNo = $Y
```

To some extent, views can shield users from some of the fragment details. For example, using a view defined with union operations would obviate the need to write the union operations in the query. However, views may not simplify manipulation statements. If the DBMS does not support fragmentation transparency, it seems unlikely that updatable views could span sites. Thus, the user would still have to write the SQL statements for the Customer Move request.

15.5.4 Local Mapping Transparency

Local Mapping Transparency a level of independence in distributed DBMSs in which queries can be formulated without knowledge of local formats. However, knowledge of fragments and fragment allocations is necessary.

Local mapping transparency provides a lesser level of data independence than location transparency. Users need to reference fragments at sites in formulating queries and transactions. However, knowledge of local formats is not necessary. If sites differ in formats as in loosely integrated distributed databases, local mapping transparency still relieves the user of considerable work.

Location transparency may not involve much additional coding effort from that shown in Table 15–7. The only changes between Tables 15–7 and 15–8 are the addition of the site names in Table 15–8. If fragments are replicated, additional coding is necessary in transactions. For example, if a new product is added, two INSERT statements (one for each site) are necessary with local mapping transparency. With location trans-

---

TABLE 15–8 | **Requests Written with Local Mapping Transparency**

Find Order
```
SELECT *
  FROM Western-Orders@Boise, Western-Customers@Boise
  WHERE Western-Orders@Boise.CustNo = $X
    AND Western-Orders@Boise.CustNo =
          Western-Customers@Boise.CustNo
UNION
SELECT *
  FROM Eastern-Orders@Tulsa, Eastern-Customers@Tulsa
  WHERE Eastern-Orders@Tulsa.CustNo = $X
    AND Eastern-Orders@Tulsa.CustNo =
          Eastern-Customers@Tulsa.CustNo
```

Find Product Availability
```
SELECT * FROM Denver-Inventory@Denver
  WHERE ProdNo = $X
UNION
SELECT * FROM Seattle-Inventory@Seattle
  WHERE ProdNo = $X
```

Update Inventory (Denver)
```
UPDATE Denver-Inventory@Denver SET QOH = QOH - 1
  WHERE ProdNo = $X
```

Customer Move (West to East)
```
SELECT CustName, CustCity, CustState, CustZip
  INTO $CustName, $CustCity, $CustState, $CustZip
  FROM Western-Customers@Boise WHERE CustNo = $Y

INSERT INTO Eastern-Customers@Tulsa
    (CustNo, CustName, CustCity, CustState, CustZip, CustRegion)
    VALUES ($Y, $CustName, $CustCity, $CustState, $CustZip, 'East')

INSERT INTO Eastern-Orders@Tulsa
  SELECT * FROM Western-Orders@Boise WHERE CustNo = $Y

INSERT INTO Eastern-OrderLines@Tulsa
  SELECT * FROM Western-OrderLines@Boise
    WHERE OrdNo IN
      (SELECT OrdNo FROM Western-Orders@Boise
        WHERE CustNo = $Y)

DELETE FROM Western-OrderLines@Boise
  WHERE OrdNo IN
    (SELECT OrdNo FROM Western-Orders@Boise
      WHERE CustNo = $Y)

DELETE Western-Orders@Boise WHERE CustNo = $Y

DELETE Western-Customers@Boise WHERE CustNo = $Y
```

parency, only one INSERT statement is necessary. The amount of additional coding depends on the amount of replication.

From the discussion in this section, you falsely may assume that fragmentation transparency is preferred to the other levels of transparency. Fragmentation transparency provides the highest level of data independence but is the most complex to implement. Many distributed DBMSs cannot achieve this level of data independence. In addition, fragmentation transparency may encourage excessive resource consumption because users do not perceive the underlying distributed database processing. With location and local mapping transparency, users perceive the underlying distributed database processing at least to some extent. The amount and the complexity of distributed database processing can be considerable as described in the next section.

15.6 DISTRIBUTED DATABASE PROCESSING

Just as distributed data can add complexity for query formulation, it adds considerable complexity to query processing and transaction processing. Distributed database processing involves movement of data, remote processing, and site coordination that are absent from centralized database processing. Although the details of distributed database processing can be hidden from programmers and users, performance implications sometimes cannot be hidden. This section presents details about distributed query processing and distributed transaction processing to make you aware of complexities that can affect performance.

15.6.1 Distributed Query Processing

Distributed query processing is more complex than centralized query processing for several reasons. Distributed query processing involves both local (intrasite) and global (intersite) optimization. Global optimization involves data movement and site selection decisions that are absent in centralized query processing. For example, to perform a join of distributed fragments, one fragment can be moved, both fragments can be moved to a third site, or just the join values of one fragment can be moved. If the fragments are replicated, then a site for each fragment must be chosen.

Distributed query processing is also more complex because multiple optimization objectives exist. In a centralized environment, minimizing resource (input–output and processing) usage is consistent with minimizing response time. In a distributed environment, minimizing resources may conflict with minimizing response time because of parallel processing opportunities. Parallel processing can reduce response time but increase the overall amount of resources consumed (input–output, processing, and communication). In addition, the weighting of communication costs versus local costs (input–output and processing) depends on network characteristics. For wide area networks, communication costs can dominate local costs. For local area networks, communication costs are more equally weighted with local costs.

The increased complexity makes optimization of distributed queries even more important than optimization of centralized queries. Because distributed query processing involves both local and global optimization, there are many more possible access plans for a distributed query than a corresponding centralized query. Variance in performance among distributed access plans can be quite large. The choice of a bad access plan can lead to extremely poor performance. In addition, distributed access plans sometimes need to adjust for site conditions. If a site is unavailable or overloaded, a distributed access plan should dynamically choose another site. Thus, some of the optimization process may need to be performed dynamically (during run-time) rather than statically (during compile-time).

To depict the importance of distributed query optimization, access plans for a sample query are presented. To simplify the presentation, a wide area network with relatively slow communication times is used. Only communication times (*CT*) are shown for each access plan. Communication time consists of a fixed message delay (*MD*) and a variable transmission time (*TT*). Each record is transmitted as a separate message.

$$CT = MD + TT$$

where

MD = Number of messages * Delay per message

TT = Number of bits / Data rate

Global Query: List the order number, the order date, the product number, the product name, the product price, and the order quantity for eastern orders with a specified customer number, date range, and product color. Table 15–9 lists statistics for the query and the network.

```
SELECT * EO.OrdNo, OrdDate, P.ProdNo, QtyOrd, ProdName, ProdPrice
   FROM Eastern-Orders EO, Eastern-Orderlines EOL, Product P
   WHERE EO.CustNo = $X AND EO.OrdNo = EOL.OrdNo AND P.Color = 'Red'
   AND EOL.ProdNo = P.ProdNo and OrdDate BETWEEN $Y AND $Z
```

1. Move the *Product* table to Tulsa site where the query is processed.

   CT = 1,000 * 0.1 + (1,000 * 1,000) / 100,000 = 110 seconds

2. Restrict the *Product* table at the Denver site, then move the result to Tulsa where the remainder of the query is processed.

   CT = 200 * 0.1 + (200 * 1,000) / 100,000 = 22 seconds

3. Perform join and restrictions of *Eastern-Orders* and *Eastern-OrderLines* fragments at the Tulsa site. Move the result to the Denver site to join with the *Product* table.

   CT = 25 * 0.1 + (25 * 2,000) / 100,000 = 3 seconds

TABLE 15–9   **Statistics for the Query and the Network**

Record length is 1,000 bits for each table.

Customer has 5 orders in the specified date range.

Each order contains on the average 5 products.

Customer has 3 orders in the specified date range and color.

200 "red" products.

10,000 orders, 50,000 order lines, and 1,000 products in the fragments.

Fragment allocation given in Table 15–6.

Delay per message is 0.1 second.

Data rate is 100,000 bits per second.

4. Restrict the *Product* table at the Denver site. Move only the resulting product numbers (32 bits) to Tulsa. Perform joins and restrictions at Tulsa. Move the results back to Denver to combine with the *Product* table.

CT (Denver to Tulsa) $= 200 * 0.1 + (200 * 32) / 100,000 = 20.064$ seconds

CT (Tulsa to Denver) $= 15 * 0.1 + (15 * 2,000) / 100,000 = 1.8$ seconds

$CT = CT$ (Denver to Tulsa) $+ CT$ (Tulsa to Denver) $= 21.864$ seconds

These access plans show a wide variance in communication times. Even more variance would be shown if the order fragments were moved from Tulsa to Denver. The third access plan dominates the others because of its low message delay. Additional analysis of the local processing costs would be necessary to determine the best access plan.

15.6.2 Distributed Transaction Processing

Distributed transaction processing follows the principles described in Chapter 13. Transactions obey the ACID properties and the distributed DBMS provides concurrency and recovery transparency. However, a distributed environment makes the implementation of the principles more difficult. Independently operating sites must be coordinated. In addition, new kinds of failures exist because of the communication network. To deal with these complexities, new protocols are necessary. This section presents an introduction to the problems and solutions of distributed concurrency control and recovery management.

Distributed Concurrency Control

Distributed concurrency control can involve more overhead than centralized concurrency control because local sites must be coordinated through messages over a communication network. The simplest scheme involves centralized coordination, as depicted in Figure 15.20. At the beginning of a transaction, the coordinating site is chosen and the

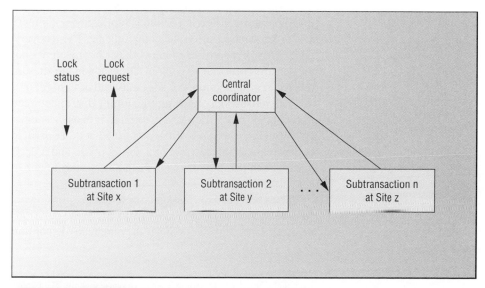

Figure 15.20   Centralized concurrency control.

Primary Copy Protocol
a protocol for
concurrency control of
distributed transactions.
Each replicated fragment
is designated as either the
primary copy or a
secondary copy. During
distributed transaction
processing, only the
primary copy is
guaranteed to be current
at end of transaction.
Updates may be
propagated to secondary
copies after end of
transaction.

transaction is divided into subtransactions performed at other sites. Each site hosting a subtransaction submits lock and release requests to the coordinating site using the normal two phase locking rules.

Centralized coordination involves the fewest messages and the simplest deadlock detection. However, reliance on a centralized coordinator may make transaction processing less reliable. To alleviate reliance on a centralized site, lock management can be distributed among sites. The price for higher reliability is more message overhead and more complex deadlock detection. The number of messages can be twice as much in the distributed coordination scheme as compared to the centralized coordination scheme.

With both centralized and distributed coordination, replicated data are a problem. Updating replicated data involves extra overhead because a write lock must be obtained on all copies before any copy is updated. Obtaining write locks on multiple copies can cause delays and even rollbacks if a copy is not available.

To reduce overhead with locking multiple copies, the primary copy protocol can be used. In the primary copy protocol, one copy of each replicated fragment is designated as the primary copy, while the other copies are secondary. Write locks are necessary only for the primary copy. After a transaction updates the primary copy, updates are propagated to the secondary copies. However, secondary copies may not be updated until after the transaction commits. The primary copy protocol provides improved performance but at the cost of noncurrent secondary copies. Because reduced overhead is often more important than current secondary copies, many distributed DBMSs use the primary copy protocol.

Distributed Recovery Management

Distributed DBMSs must contend with failures of communication links and sites, failures that do not affect centralized DBMSs. Detecting failures involves coordination among sites. If a link or site fails, any transaction involving the site must be aborted. In addition, the site should be avoided in future transactions until it is resolved.

Failures can be more complex than just a single site or communication link. A number of sites and links can fail simultaneously, leaving a network partitioned. In a partitioned network, different partitions (collections of sites) cannot communicate although sites in the same partition can communicate. The recovery manager must ensure that different parts of a partitioned network act in unison. It should not be possible for sites in one partition to decide to commit a transaction but sites in another partition to decide not to commit a transaction. All sites must either commit or abort.

**Two Phase Commit
Protocol (2PC)** a rule to
ensure that distributed
transactions are atomic.
2PC uses a voting and a
decision phase to
coordinate commits of
local transactions.

The most widely known protocol for distributed recovery is the two phase commit protocol.[3] For each transaction, one site is chosen as the coordinator and the transaction is divided into subtransactions performed at other participant sites. The coordinator and the participant sites interact in a voting phase and a decision phase. At the end of both phases, each participant site has acted in unison to either commit or abort its subtransaction.

The voting and decision phases require actions on both the coordinator and the participant sites, as depicted in Figure 15.21. In the decision phase, the coordinator sends a message to participants asking if they are ready to commit. If all participants vote ready,

---

[3]Do not confuse two phase commit with two phase locking. The two phase commit protocol is used only for distributed database recovery. Two phase locking can be used for centralized and distributed concurrency control.

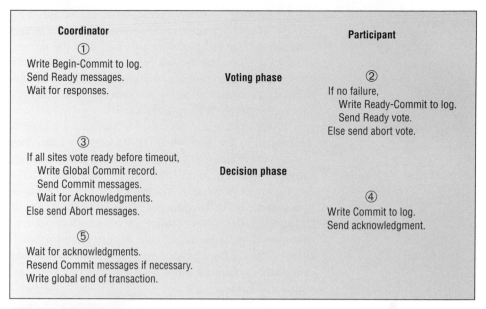

Figure 15.21   **Two phase commit processing for coordinator and participants.**

the coordinator begins the decision phase. The coordinator writes the global commit records and asks each participant to commit its subtransaction. When the coordinator receives acknowledgment from all participants, the coordinator writes the global end-of-transaction record. If a failure occurs in either the voting or the decision phase, the coordinator sends an abort message to all participating sites.

In practice, the two phase commit protocol presented in Figure 15.21 is just the basic protocol. Other complications such as a failure during recovery complicate the protocol. In addition, modifications to the basic protocol can reduce the number of messages needed to enforce the protocol. Because these extensions are beyond the scope of this book, you should consult the references at the end of the chapter for more details.

The two phase commit protocol can use a centralized or a distributed coordinator. The trade-offs are similar to centralized versus distributed coordination for concurrency control. Centralized coordination is simpler than distributed coordination but can be less reliable.

The two phase commit protocol does not handle any conceivable kind of failure. For example, the two phase commit protocol may not work correctly if log records are lost. There is no known protocol guaranteeing that all sites act in unison to commit or abort in the presence of arbitrary failures. Because the two phase commit protocol efficiently handles common kinds of failures, it is widely used in distributed DBMSs.

CLOSING THOUGHTS

This chapter has described the motivation, the architectures, and the services of DBMSs that support distributed processing and distributed data. Utilizing distributed processing and data can significantly improve DBMS services but at the cost of new design challenges. Distributed processing can improve scalability, interoperability, and flexibility while distributed data can improve data control, communication costs, and system performance. To realize these benefits, significant challenges caused by the complexity of distributed processing and data must be overcome.

Choosing an appropriate architecture is one way to overcome additional complexity. This chapter described several client–server architectures to utilize distributed processing. The two-tier, three-tier, and multiple-tier architectures provide alternatives among cost, complexity, and benefit levels. Implementing a client–server architecture on the Internet can provide additional advantages because the open standards of the Internet promote a competitive marketplace. This chapter described several architectures that support Web database connectivity.

This chapter also described architectures and processing for distributed DBMSs. Architectures for distributed DBMSs differ in the integration of the local databases. Tightly integrated systems provide both query and transaction services but require uniformity in the local DBMSs. Loosely integrated systems support data sharing among a mix of modern and legacy DBMSs. An important part of the data architecture is the level of data independence. This chapter described several levels of data independence that differ by the level of data distribution knowledge required to formulate global requests. To provide an introductory understanding to the complexity of distributed database processing, this chapter described distributed query processing and transaction processing. Both services involve complex issues not present in centralized DBMSs.

REVIEW CONCEPTS

- Timesharing, file sharing, and remote procedure calls as early forms of distributed processing and distributed data.
- Motivations for distributed processing: scalability, interoperability, and flexibility.
- Motivations for distributed data: increased local control, reduced communication costs, improved performance.
- Design issues in distributed processing: division of processing and process management.
- Kinds of code to distribute between a client and a server.
- Process management tasks performed by database middleware.
- Differences between transaction-processing monitors, message-oriented middleware, and software buses.
- Characteristics of two-tier, three-tier, and multiple-tier architectures.
- Characteristics of CGI, extended server, and middleware server approaches for Web database connectivity.
- Role of client-side approaches in Web database connectivity.
- Global queries and transactions.
- Role of the local database manager, the distributed database manager, and the global dictionary in the component architecture of a distributed DBMS.
- Schema architectures for tightly integrated and loosely integrated distributed DBMSs.
- Relationship of distributed database transparency levels and data independence.
- Kinds of fragmentation: horizontal, vertical, and derived horizontal.
- Complexity of fragment design and allocation.
- Query formulation for fragmentation transparency, location transparency, and local mapping transparency.
- Performance measures and objectives for distributed query processing.

- Use of two phase locking for distributed concurrency control.
- Use of the primary copy protocol to reduce update overhead with replicated data.
- Additional kinds of failures in a distributed database environment.
- Two phase commit protocol for distributed recovery.
- Trade-offs between centralized and distributed coordination for distributed concurrency control and recovery.

QUESTIONS

1. What is the role of clients and servers in distributed processing?

2. Briefly define the terms flexibility, interoperability, and scalability. How does distributed processing support interoperability, flexibility, and scalability?

3. Discuss some of the pitfalls of developing client–server systems.

4. How can a distributed database improve data control?

5. How can a distributed database reduce communication costs and improve performance?

6. Discuss some of the pitfalls when developing distributed databases.

7. Discuss why distributed processing is more mature and more widely implemented than distributed databases.

8. Why are division of processing and process management important in client–server architectures?

9. Explain how two-tier architectures address division of processing and process management.

10. Explain how three-tier architectures address division of processing and process management.

11. Explain how multiple-tier architectures address division of processing and process management.

12. What is a thin client? How does a thin client relate to division of processing in client–server architectures?

13. List some reasons for choosing a two-tier architecture.

14. List some reasons for choosing a three-tier architecture.

15. List some reasons for choosing a multiple-tier architecture.

16. What is a software bus? How does a software bus differ from other kinds of middleware such as a transaction-processing monitor and message-oriented middleware?

17. Is a Web server middleware? Explain why or why not.

18. Why is there widespread interest in database connectivity over the Internet and intranets?

19. What is the Common Gateway Interface (CGI) and how is it used for Web database connectivity?

20. List some reasons to use an extended Web server for Web database connectivity.

21. List some reasons to use a middleware server for Web database connectivity instead of an extended Web server.

22. How does client-side connectivity enhance server-side processing for database connectivity?

23. What is a global request?

24. How does the integration level of the distributed DBMS affect the component architecture?

25. When is a tightly integrated distributed DBMS appropriate? When is a loosely integrated distributed DBMS appropriate?

26. Discuss the differences in the schema architecture for tightly and loosely integrated distributed DBMSs.

27. How is distributed database transparency related to data independence?

28. Is a higher level of distribution transparency always preferred? Briefly explain why or why not.

29. What is a derived horizontal fragment and why is it useful? What is the relationship of the semi-join operator and derived horizontal fragmentation?

30. What is the larger difference in query formulation: (1) fragmentation transparency to location transparency or (2) location transparency to local mapping transparency? Justify your answer.

31. Why is fragment design and allocation a complex task?

32. Why is global query optimization important?

33. What are differences between global and local optimization in distributed query processing?

34. Why are there multiple objectives in distributed query processing? Which objective seems to be more important?

35. What are the components of performance measures for distributed query processing? What factors influence how these components can be combined into a performance measure?

36. How does two phase locking for distributed databases differ from two phase locking for centralized databases?

37. Why is the primary copy protocol widely used?

38. What kinds of additional failures occur in a distributed database environment? How can these failures be detected?

39. What is the difference between the voting and the decision phases of the two phase commit protocol?

40. Discuss the trade-offs between centralized and distributed coordination in distributed concurrency control and recovery.

PROBLEMS

ORDER

The problems provide practice with defining fragments, formulating queries at various transparency levels, and defining strategies for distributed query processing. The questions use the revised university database tables listed below. This database is similar to the database used in Chapter 3 except for the additional campus columns in the *Student, Offering,* and *Faculty* tables.

Student(<u>StdNo,</u> StdName, StdCampus, StdCity, StdState, StdZip, StdMajor, StdYear)

Course(<u>CourseNo,</u> CrsDesc, CrsCredits)
    FOREIGN KEY CustNo REFERENCES Customer

Offering(<u>OfferNo,</u> CourseNo, OffCampus, OffTerm, OffYear, OffLocation, OffTime, OffDays, FacNo)
    FOREIGN KEY CourseNo REFERENCES Course
    FOREIGN KEY FacNo REFERENCES Faculty

Enrollment(<u>OfferNo, StdNo,</u> EnrGrade)
    FOREIGN KEY OfferNo REFERENCES Offering
    FOREIGN KEY StdNo REFERENCES Student

Faculty(<u>FacNo,</u> FacName, FacCampus, FacDept, FacPhone, FacSalary, FacRank)

1. Write SQL SELECT statements to define two horizontal fragments as students who attend (1) the Boulder campus and (2) the Denver campus.

2. Write SQL SELECT statements to define two horizontal fragments as faculty who teach at (1) the Boulder campus and (2) the Denver campus.

3. Write SQL SELECT statements to define two horizontal fragments as offerings given at (1) the Boulder campus and (2) the Denver campus.

4. Write SQL SELECT statements to define two derived horizontal fragments as enrollments associated with offerings given at (1) the Boulder campus and (2) the Denver campus.

5. Write a SELECT statement to list the information systems courses offered in spring quarter 2001. Information systems courses contain the string "IS" in the course description. Include the course number, the description, the offer number, and the time in the result. Assume fragmentation transparency in your formulation.

6. Write a SELECT statement to list the information systems courses offered in spring quarter 2001. Information systems courses contain the string "IS" in the course description. Include the course number, the description, the offer number, and the time in the result. Assume location transparency in your formulation.

7. Write a SELECT statement to list the information systems courses offered in spring quarter 2001. Information systems courses contain the string "IS" in the course description. Include the course number, the description, the offer number, and the time in the result. Assume local mapping transparency in your formulation. The *Offering* fragments are allocated to the Boulder and the Denver sites. The *Course* table is replicated at both sites.

8. Move offering number O1 from the Boulder to the Denver campus. In addition to moving the offering between campuses, change its location to Plaza 112. Assume fragmentation transparency in your formulation.

9. Move offering number O1 from the Boulder to the Denver campus. In addition to moving the offering between campuses, change its location to Plaza 112. Assume location transparency in your formulation.

10. Move offering number O1 from the Boulder to the Denver campus. In addition to moving the offering between campuses, change its location to Plaza 112. Assume local mapping transparency in your formulation.

11. For the following query, compute communication time (*CT*) for the distributed access plans listed below. Use the formulas in Section 15.6.1 and the query and network statistics (Table 15–10) in your calculations.

```
SELECT Course.CourseNo, CrsDesc, OfferNo, OffTime, FacName
  FROM BoulderOfferings BOF, Course, DenverFaculty DF
  WHERE Course.CourseNo = BOF.Course AND OffTerm = 'Spring'
    AND OffYear = 2001 AND DF.FacNo = BF.FacNo
    AND FacDept = 'Information Systems'
```

11.1 Move the entire *DenverFaculty* fragment to the Boulder site and perform the query.

11.2 Move the entire *BoulderOfferings* fragment to the Denver site and perform the query.

11.3 Move the restricted *BoulderOfferings* fragment to the Denver site and perform the query.

11.4 Move the restricted *DenverFaculty* fragment to the Boulder site and perform the query.

11.5 Restrict the *DenverFaculty* fragment and move the join values (*FacNo*) to the Boulder site. Join the *FacNo* values with the *Course* table and the

TABLE 15–10   **Statistics for Problem 11**

Record length is 1,000 bits for each table.

32 bits for *FacNo*.

20 information systems faculty.

5,000 spring 2001 offerings.

10 spring 2001 Boulder offerings taught by Denver faculty.

4,000 courses, 20,000 offerings, and 2,000 faculty in the fragments.

Course table is replicated at both the Denver and the Boulder sites.

BoulderOfferings fragment is located at the Boulder site.

DenverFaculty fragment is located at the Denver site.

Delay per message is 0.1 second.

Data rate is 100,000 bits per second.

BoulderOfferings fragment at the Boulder site. Move the result back to the Denver site to join with the *DenverFaculty* fragment.

12. Investigate the client–server computing options of a major DBMS. Identify the tools provided by the database vendor to develop two-tier, three-tier, and multiple-tier architectures with and without the Internet.

REFERENCES FOR FURTHER STUDY

This chapter, although providing a broad coverage of distributed processing and data, has only covered the basics. Specialized books on distributed database management include the classic by Ceri and Pelagatti (1984) and the more recent book by Ozsu and Valduriez (1991). The book by Ceri and Pelagatti has a well-written chapter on distributed database design. C. J. Date (1990) presents 12 objectives for distributed systems with the most emphasis on distributed DBMSs. Bernstein (1996) provides a detailed presentation of the role of middleware in client–server architectures. There are many trade books and magazines that cover client–server databases and Web database connectivity. Orfali, Harkey, and Edwards (1996) provide a detailed, practical guide to client–server computing including a lot of material on client–server databases. Many practical articles about client–server and distributed databases can be found in the database information center of the *Intelligent Enterprise* magazine (http://www.iemagazine.com/). Some good websites on client–server computing are the CGI Resource Index (http://www.cgi-resources.com/), the Object Management Group (http://www.omg.org), and the Software Engineering Institute's description of client–server computing (http://www.sei.cmu.edu/str/descriptions/clientserver.html).

Chapter 16

Object Database Management Systems

This chapter describes extensions to DBMSs to support complex data and operations. After this chapter, the student should have acquired the following knowledge and skills:

- List business reasons for using object database technology.

- Define the principles of object-oriented computing.

- Compare and contrast architectures for object database management.

- Understand features in SQL3 to define user-defined types and subtable families.

- Understand features in SQL3 to manipulate complex objects and navigate subtable families.

OVERVIEW

Chapter 15 described client–server processing to utilize remote processing capabilities and computer networks. An increasing amount of client–server processing involves complex data and operations that DBMSs do not support. In many cases, client–server processing can be improved if new kinds of data and operations are more closely integrated with traditional data. In this chapter, you will learn about extensions to DBMSs for objects, combinations of complex data and operations.

This chapter provides a broad introduction to object DBMSs. You will learn first about the business reasons to extend database technology. This chapter discusses the increasing use of complex data and the mismatch between DBMSs and programming languages as the driving forces behind object database technology. After grasping the motivation, you are ready to learn about object technology and its impact on DBMSs. You will first learn about the principles of object-oriented computing and DBMS architectures to support these principles. This chapter presents inheritance, encapsulation, and polymorphism as the underlying principles of object technology. To support these principles, this chapter presents five architectures for object DBMSs. The last part of this chapter presents SQL3, the emerging standard for object relational DBMSs. You will learn about data definition and data manipulation features in SQL3 for object databases.

16.1 MOTIVATION FOR OBJECT DATABASE MANAGEMENT

This section discusses two forces driving the demand for object database management. After a discussion of these forces, example applications are presented to depict the need for object database management.

16.1.1 Complex Data

Most relational DBMSs support only a few data types. Common data types supported in SQL2 include whole numbers, real numbers, fixed-precision numbers (currency), dates, times, and text. These data types are sufficient for many business applications, or at least significant parts of many applications. Many business databases contain fields for names, prices, addresses, and transaction dates that readily conform to the standard data types.

Advances in hardware and software capability have enabled complex data to be captured and manipulated in a digital format. Almost any kind of complex data such as images, audio, video, maps, and three-dimensional graphics can be digitally stored. For example, an image can be represented as a two-dimensional array of pixels (picture elements) where each pixel contains a numeric property representing its color or shade of gray. Digital storage is usually cheaper and more reliable than traditional means such as paper, film, or slides. In addition, digital storage allows easier retrieval and manipulation. For example, you can retrieve digital images by content and similarity to other images. Digital images can be manipulated in an image editor with operations such as cropping, texturing, and color tuning.

The ability to store and manipulate complex data does not by itself drive the demand for object database technology. Rather, the need to store large amounts of complex data and integrate complex data with simple data drives the demand for object database technology. Many business applications require large amounts of complex data. For example, insurance claims processing and medical records can involve large amounts of image data. Storing images in separate files becomes tedious for a large collection of images.

The ability to simultaneously retrieve complex and simple data is becoming important in many business applications. For example, to review a patient's condition, a physician may request X-rays along with vital statistics. Without integration, two separate programs are required to display the data: an image editor to display the X-rays and a

DBMS to retrieve the vital statistics. The ability to retrieve both image and vital statistics in a single query is a large improvement. Besides retrieving complex data, new operations also may be necessary. For example, a physician may want to compare the similarity of a patient's X-rays with X-rays that show abnormalities.

16.1.2 Type System Mismatch

Increasingly, software written in a procedural language needs to access a database. Procedural languages support customized interfaces for data entry forms and reports, operations beyond the capability of SQL, and batch processing. For example, writing a computer program is often necessary to operate on self-referencing data such as a parts hierarchy. Embedded SQL is often used to access a database from within a computer program. After executing an embedded SQL statement, database fields are stored in program variables that can be manipulated further.

A mismatch between the data types in a relational DBMS and the data types of a programming language makes software more complex and difficult to develop. For example, payroll processing can involve many kinds of benefits, deductions, and compensation. A relational database may have one representation for benefits, deductions, and compensation while a programming language may have a rather different representation. Before coding the complex calculations, the data must by transformed from the relational database representation (tables) into the programming language representation (records or objects). After the calculations, the data must be transformed back into the relational database representation.

This data type mismatch is even more pronounced for complex data. Programming languages usually have richer type systems than DBMSs. For example, relational databases provide a tedious representation of geometric shapes in a building's floor plan. Objects such as points, lines, and polygons may be represented as one text field or as several numeric fields such as X and Y coordinates for points. In contrast, a programming language may have custom data types for points, lines, and polygons. There may be considerable coding to transform between the relational database representation and the programming language representation.

In addition, a relational DBMS cannot perform elementary operations on complex data. Thus, a computer program must be written instead of using a query language. For example, a complex program must be written to compute the similarity between two images. The program will probably contain 10 to 100 times the amount of code found in a query. In addition, the program must transform between the database and the programming language representations.

16.1.3 Application Examples

This section depicts several applications that involve a mix of simple and complex data as well as ad hoc queries. These applications have features increasingly found in many business applications. As you will see, object DBMSs support the requirements of these kinds of applications.

Dental Office Support

Dental offices use a mix of simple and complex data to make appointments, generate bills, and conduct examinations. Setting appointments requires a calendar with time blocks for service providers (dentists and hygienists). In conducting examinations, service providers use dental charts (graphic of mouth with each tooth identified), X-rays, patient facts, and dental histories. After an examination, bill preparation uses the list of services in the examination and patient insurance data. Queries that involve both complex and simple data include showing a dental chart with recent dental problems highlighted and comparing X-rays for increasing gum loss.

Real Estate Listing Service

Real estate listing services increasingly use complex data to facilitate customer searches. A real estate listing includes a mix of simple and complex data. The simple data include numerous facts about homes such as the number of bedrooms, the square feet, and the listing price. Complex data include photographs of homes, floor plans, video tours, and area maps. Queries can involve a mix of simple and complex data. Customers want to see homes in a specified neighborhood with selected features. Some customers may want to see homes with the closest match to a set of ideal features where the customer assigns a weight to each feature. After selecting a set of homes, a customer wants to explore the appearance, the floor plan, and the facts about the homes.

Auto Insurance Claims

Auto insurance companies use complex data to settle claims. Analyzing claims involves complex data such as photographs, accident reports, and witness statements as well as simple data such as driver and vehicle descriptions. Settling claims involves a map showing service providers as well as service provider rates and service history. Queries for accident data and a list of service providers in close proximity to a customer involve both simple and complex data.

16.2 OBJECT-ORIENTED PRINCIPLES

To provide a foundation to understand the architectures and features of object DBMSs, this section presents three fundamental principles of object-oriented computing. After presenting the principles, this section discusses their impact on object DBMSs and object-oriented programming languages.

16.2.1 Encapsulation

An object is a combination of data and procedures. The data are sometimes referred to as variables and the procedures as methods. Each object has a unique identifier that never changes unless the object is destroyed. Object identifiers are not visible to users. In contrast, primary keys in relational databases are visible.

Classes contain collections of objects. A class definition consists of a collection of variables and methods. The variables are sometimes called instance variables to distinguish them from variables that apply to the entire class (called class variables). Example 16.1[1] shows the class *Point* with two variables (*x* and *y* denoting the Cartesian coordinates) and two methods (*Distance* and *Equals*). Each variable has an associated data type. Each method has an interface and an implementation. The interface shows the in-

---

[1]The examples in this section conform to the Object Specification Language standard defined by the Object Database Management Group. The notation resembles the C and C++ languages.

puts and the outputs of the method. The implementation shows the detailed coding. For brevity, implementations are not shown in the examples. Example 16.2 depicts a more business-oriented example.

EXAMPLE 16.1   Partial *Point* Class

```
CLASS Point {
// VARIABLES:
  Real x;    // X coordinate
  Real y;    // Y coordinate
// METHODS:
  Real Distance(Point aPoint);
    // Computes the Distance between 2 points
  Boolean Equals (Point aPoint);
    // Determines if two Points have the same coordinates };
```

EXAMPLE 16.2   Partial *Bond* Class

```
CLASS Bond {
// VARIABLES:
  Real IntRate; // Interest Rate
  Date Maturity; // Maturity Date
// METHODS:
  Real Yield();
    // Computes the Bond's Yield };
```

Encapsulation objects can be accessed only through their interfaces.

Encapsulation means that objects can be accessed only through their interfaces. The internal details (variables and method implementations) are not accessible. For example, you can use the *Distance* and *Equals* methods only to manipulate *Point* objects. To use the *Distance* method, you supply two *Point* objects. The first *Point* object is implicit in the interface because *Distance* is a method of *Point*. To make *Point* objects more usable, there should be additional methods for creating points, destroying points, and moving points.

Encapsulation provides two benefits for managing software complexity. First, a class is a larger unit of reusability than a procedure. In many cases, classes can be reused rather than just individual procedures. More complex classes can be defined using simpler classes. Examples 16.3 and 16.4 depict classes that use the *Point* and the *Bond* classes defined in Examples 16.1 and 16.2. The new classes (*Rectangle* and *Portfolio*) do not need to recode the variables and methods of the *Point* and the *Bond* classes, respectively.

EXAMPLE 16.3   *Rectangle* Class Using the *Point* Class

```
CLASS Rectangle {
// VARIABLES:
  Point UpperLeftCorner;  // Upper Left Point
  Point LowerRightCorner;  // Lower Right Point
```

```
// METHODS:
  Real Area();
    // Computes the Area of the Rectangle
  Real Length ();
    // Computes the Length
  Real Height ();
    // Computes the Height };
```

EXAMPLE 16.4

Portfolio Class Using the *Bond* Class

```
CLASS Portfolio {
// VARIABLES:
  Set<Bond> BondHoldings; // set of Bonds
  Set<Stock> StockHoldings; // Set of Stocks
// METHODS:
  Real PortfolioReturn();
    // Computes the Portfolio's Return };
```

As a second benefit, encapsulation provides a form of data independence. Because internal details of objects are hidden, changes to the internal details can be made without changing the code that uses the objects. Recall from Chapter 1 that data independence promotes reduced software maintenance costs.

16.2.2 Inheritance

Inheritance   sharing of data and code among similar classes (classes and subclasses).

Chapter 7 presented classification and inheritance for the Entity Relationship Model. These concepts are similar in object-oriented models except that inheritance applies to both data and procedures. Chapter 7 described inheritance only for attributes of an entity type. Examples 16.5 and 16.6 present classes that inherit from the *Point* and the *Bond* classes. Figure 16.1 depicts a graphical representation of the inheritance relationships. A color point is a point with color. Likewise a corporate bond is a bond with an issuing company and an investment rating. In the subclasses (a child class that inherits from a parent class), the variables and the methods of the parent classes are not repeated. When using the subclasses, the methods in the parent classes can be used.

EXAMPLE 16.5

ColorPoint Example (Subclass of *Point*)

```
CLASS ColorPoint: Point {
// VARIABLES:
  Integer Color;  // Integer value denoting a color
// METHODS:
  Integer Brighten(Real Intensity);
    // Computes a new color that is brighter };
```

EXAMPLE 16.6

Corporate Bond Example (Subclass of *Bond*)

```
CLASS Corporate: Bond {
// VARIABLES:
```

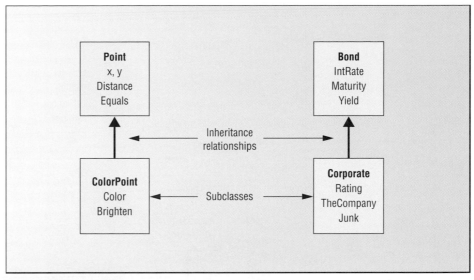

| Figure 16.1 | Class hierarchies with the *ColorPoint* and the *Corporate* subclasses. |

```
Ref<Company> TheCompany ; // Company issuing the Bond
String Rating; // Moody's Rating
// METHODS:
Boolean Junk();
    // TRUE if the bond's rating means low quality };
```

As discussed in Chapter 7, inheritance can extend to multiple levels. For example, if *Investment* is the parent class of *Bond,* the *Corporate* class inherits from both *Investment* and *Bond.* Inheritance also can extend to multiple parents. Figure 16.2 depicts an investment class hierarchy with multiple inheritance. A convertible security is a bond that becomes a stock if the bondholder chooses. The conversion price and the conversion ratio determine whether a bondholder should convert. The *Convertible* class inherits directly from the *Stock* and the *Bond* classes. Multiple inheritance can be problematic because of conflicts. In Figure 16.2, the *Yield* method can be inherited from either *Stock* or *Bond.* There are various schemes for resolving inheritance conflicts. Ultimately, the database designer must decide on the class from which to inherit.

Inheritance provides an improved organization of software and incremental reusability. The graphical class organization depicts similarity among classes. Programmers can reduce their time to search for similar code by using the graphical class organization. After finding a similar class, database designers and programmers can incrementally add more features (variables and methods). The only new coding is for the new features, not the existing features.

16.2.3 Polymorphism

Polymorphism ability of a computing system to choose among multiple implementations of a method.

Polymorphism literally means "of many forms." In object-oriented computing, polymorphism permits a method to have multiple implementations. A method implementation in a subclass can override the method implementation in a parent class. Some methods must be overridden because the meaning of the method changes for a subclass. For example, the *Equals* method in class *ColorPoint* compares the coordinates and the color

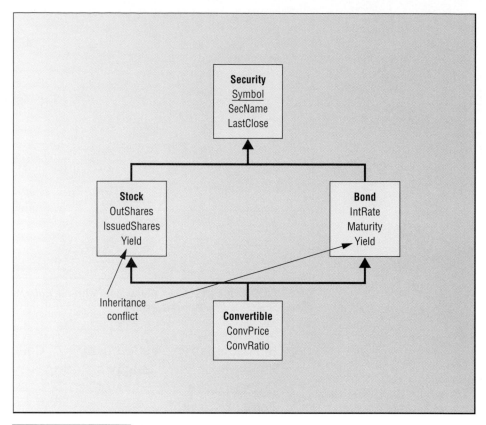

Figure 16.2   **Investment class hierarchy.**

whereas the method implementation in the *Point* class only compares the coordinates. In contrast, the *Area* method has a more efficient implementation for the *Rectangle* class than for the parent *Polygon* class. As another example, the *Yield* method (Figure 16.2) must be overridden in the *Convertible* subclass to combine the calculations in the parent *Stock* and *Bond* classes.

Requesting a method execution involves sending a message to an object. A message contains a method name and parameters, similar to a procedure call. One of the parameters is the object that receives the message. The receiver object decides what action to take. If the object's class contains the method, it is executed. Otherwise, the object forwards the message to its parent class for execution. In Figure 16.3, a *ColorPoint* object receives a message requesting a distance calculation. Since the *ColorPoint* class does not contain an implementation of the *Distance* method, the message is sent to the parent class, *Point*. The *Point* class executes the method because it contains an implementation of the *Distance* method.

Because object-oriented computing involves messages, client–server processing and object-oriented computing are closely related. Clients and servers are often objects communicating through messages. Client–server processing allows objects to be located on different computers.

In processing a message, the object DBMS assumes responsibility for choosing the appropriate implementation of a method. Associating or binding a message to a method implementation can be done statically when code is compiled or dynamically when code

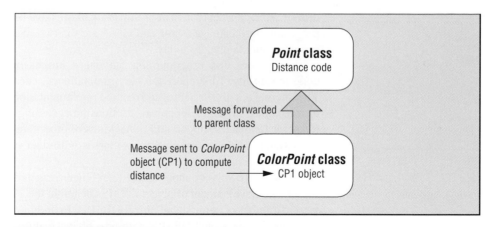

Figure 16.3   Processing a message.

is executed. Static binding is more efficient but dynamic binding can be more flexible. Dynamic binding is sometimes called "late" binding because it happens just before code execution.

Along with binding, the DBMS ensures that objects and methods are compatible. This function is known as type checking. Strong type checking ensures that there are no incompatibility errors in code. For example, strong type checking prevents computing an area for a point object because the *Area* method applies to polygons not points. Because complex expressions can involve many methods and objects, strong type checking is an important kind of consistency check in object-oriented computing.

Polymorphism supports fewer, more reusable methods. Because a method can have multiple implementations, the number of method names is reduced. A user needs to know only the method name and interface, not the appropriate implementation to use. For example, a user needs to know only that the *Area* method applies to polygons, not the appropriate implementation for a rectangle. The DBMS assumes responsibility for finding the appropriate implementation.

Polymorphism also supports incremental modification of code. In coding another implementation of a method for a subclass, much of the code for the method's implementation in the parent class often can be used. For example, to code the redefinition of the *Equals* method in the *ColorPoint* class, another equality condition (for the color of a point) should be added to the conditions to test the *x* and *y* coordinates.

16.2.4 Programming Languages versus DBMSs

These principles apply to both object-oriented programming languages and object DBMSs. However, the application of the principles varies somewhat between programming languages and DBMSs.

Programming languages have used object-oriented principles for many years. Simula, a language developed in the 1960s, is the first reported object-oriented programming language. As its name implies, Simula was originally developed as a simulation language. Objects and messages are natural in modeling simulations. Smalltalk, a language developed during the 1970s at the Xerox Palo Alto Research Center, was the first popular object-oriented programming language. Smalltalk originally emphasized objects for graphical user interfaces. Inheritance among classes for windows and controls is a nat-

---

Strong Type Checking
the ability to ensure that programming code contains no incompatibility errors. Strong type checking is an important kind of error checking for object-oriented coding.

ural fit. Since the development of Smalltalk, there have been many other object-oriented programming languages. Java and C++ are the two most widely used object-oriented programming languages today.

Object-oriented programming languages emphasize software maintenance and code reusability. To support software maintenance, encapsulation is strictly enforced. The internal details (variables and method implementations) cannot be referenced. In addition, some languages support restrictions on accessing methods. To support reusability, some languages support additional kinds of inheritance to share code. Reuse of code can extend to collections of classes, classes with data type parameters, and redefined code in a subclass.

Object DBMSs are more recent than object-oriented programming languages. Research and development of object DBMSs began in the 1980s. By the early 1990s, there were a number of commercial object DBMSs. In addition, there was considerable work on extending relational DBMSs with new object features. The next section describes a number of architectures for object DBMSs.

Because early object DBMSs began as outgrowths of object-oriented programming languages, query language support did not exist. Instead, early object DBMSs provided support for persistent data that last longer than the execution of the program. Large amounts of persistent data could be accessed although in a procedural manner. The early object DBMSs were designed to support applications with large amounts of complex data such as computer-aided design.

Most object DBMSs now support nonprocedural data access. Some of the object-oriented principles are relaxed to accommodate this emphasis. Encapsulation usually is relaxed so that an object's data can be referenced in a query. Inheritance mechanisms usually are simpler because it is assumed that most coding is through a query language, not a procedural language. In addition, most object DBMSs now provide query optimization and transaction processing capabilities.

16.3 ARCHITECTURES FOR OBJECT DATABASE MANAGEMENT

Although adding object-oriented features to a DBMS is a good idea, there is no widespread agreement about what features to add and how features should be added. Some approaches provide small extensions that leave most of the object-oriented processing outside of the DBMS. Other approaches involve a complete rewrite of the DBMS to accommodate objects. The marketplace probably will support a variety of approaches because of the different requirements among customers. This section describes several object database management architectures along with their strengths and weaknesses.

16.3.1 Large Objects and External Software

Large Object Architecture storage of large objects (binary or text) in a database along with external software to manipulate large objects. The BLOB (binary large object) and large text data types are used to store fields with large objects.

The earliest approach to add objects to relational databases was to use large objects with external software. Complex data are stored in a field as a binary or text large object. For example, an image is stored in a field using the <u>BLOB (binary large object)</u> data type. As depicted in Figure 16.4, large objects usually are stored separately from other data in a table. A query can retrieve but not display large objects. Software external to the DBMS displays and manipulates large objects. External software includes ActiveX controls, Java applets, and Web browser plug-ins.

The large object approach is simple to implement and universal. Only small changes to a DBMS are required. All kinds of complex data can be stored. In addition, a large market for third-party software may be available for prominent kinds of complex data. For example, many third-party tools have been implemented for popular image formats.

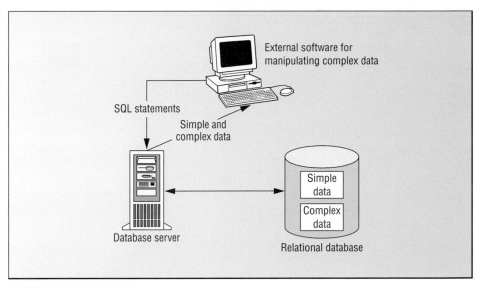

External software for manipulating complex data

SQL statements

Simple and complex data

Database server

Simple data

Complex data

Relational database

Figure 16.4   **Large object architecture.**

Despite some advantages, the large object approach suffers from serious performance drawbacks. Because the DBMS does not understand the structure and the operations of complex data, no optimization is possible. Data cannot be filtered using characteristics of large objects. No indexes can be used to select records using characteristics of large objects. Because large objects are stored separately from other data, additional disk accesses may be necessary. The order of the large objects may not coincide with the order of other table data.

16.3.2 Specialized Media Servers

Specialized Media Server Architecture the use of a dedicated server to manage complex data outside of a database. Programmers use an application programming interface to access complex data.

In the specialized media server approach, complex data reside outside of the DBMS, as depicted in Figure 16.5. A separate server may be dedicated to manipulating a single kind of complex data such as video or images. Programmers use an application programming interface (API) to access complex data through a media server. The API provides a set of procedures to retrieve, update, and transform a specific kind of complex data. To simultaneously manipulate simple data and complex data, program code contains a mix of embedded SQL and API calls to the media server.

Specialized media servers provide better performance than the large object approach but sacrifice some flexibility. Dedicated servers and highly specialized APIs provide good performance for specific kinds of complex data. Because an API is provided rather than a query language, the range of operations may be limited though. For example, a video server may support fast streaming of video but not searching by content.

When combining simple and complex data, the specialized server approach may perform poorly. A query optimizer cannot jointly optimize retrieval of simple and complex data because the DBMS is not aware of complex data. In addition, a media server may not provide indexing techniques for search conditions. Transaction processing is limited to simple data because specialized media servers do not typically support transaction processing.

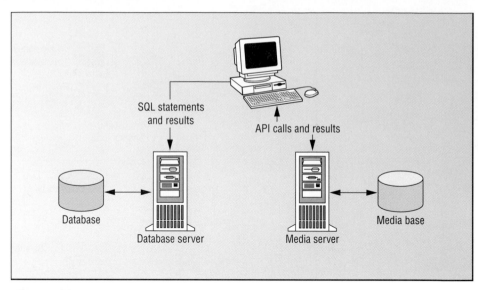

| Figure 16.5 | **Specialized media server architecture.** |

16.3.3 Object Database Middleware

Object Database Middleware   the use of middleware to manage complex data possibly stored outside of a database along with traditional data stored in a database.

Object database middleware circumvents problems with media servers by simulating object features. Clients no longer directly access media servers, as shown in Figure 16.6. Instead, clients send SQL statements to middleware, which makes API calls to media servers and sends SQL statements to database servers. The SQL statements can combine traditional operations on simple data with specialized operations on complex data. Object database middleware relieves the user of knowing a separate API for each media server. In addition, object database middleware provides location independence because users do not need to know where complex data reside.

Object middleware provides a way to integrate complex data stored on PCs and remote servers with relational databases. Without object middleware, some of the complex data could not be combined easily with simple data. Even if an architecture that integrates more tightly with the DBMS is desired, the object middleware approach can be used for complex data that users do not want to store in a database.

Object middleware can suffer performance problems because of a lack of integration with a DBMS. Combining complex and simple data suffers the same performance problems as with specialized media servers. The DBMS cannot optimize requests that simultaneously combine simple and complex data. Middleware can provide transaction processing that combines simple and complex data. However, transaction performance can be slow because two phase commit and distributed concurrency control techniques must be used.

16.3.4 Object Relational Database Management Systems for User-Defined Types

The first three approaches involve little or no change to the DBMS but provide only limited query and optimization capabilities. With larger changes to the DBMS, more query and optimization capabilities are possible.

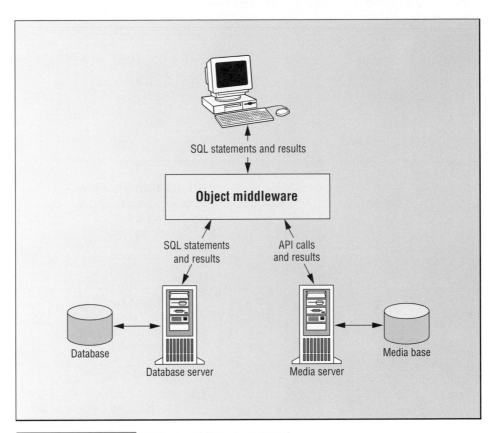

Figure 16.6	Object middleware approach.

To provide additional query capabilities, object relational DBMSs support user-defined types and functions. Almost any kind of complex data can be added as a user-defined type. Image data, spatial data, time series, and video are just a few of the possible data types. For each user-defined type, a collection of functions can be defined. These functions can be used in SQL statements, not just in programming language code. Inheritance and polymorphism apply to the user-defined data types. To improve performance, specialized storage structures can be used when accessing complex data. For example, multidimensional Btrees can be provided for accessing spatial data. Section 16.4 describes examples of user-defined types and functions in SQL3, the emerging standard for object relational DBMSs.

User-defined types involve a table-driven architecture, as depicted in Figure 16.7. The object query processor uses table-driven code for user-defined types. The parser decomposes references to expressions involving user-defined types and functions. The display manager controls the presentation of simple and complex data. The optimizer searches for storage structures for expressions involving user-defined types and functions. The relational kernel comprises transaction processing, storage management, and buffer management. It provides the engine used by the object query processor. Little or no changes are necessary to the relational kernel.

Object relational DBMSs provide good integration of complex data but reliability may be a concern. The integration of simple and complex data involves considerable changes to the parser, display manager, and optimizer. However, the base of code in the

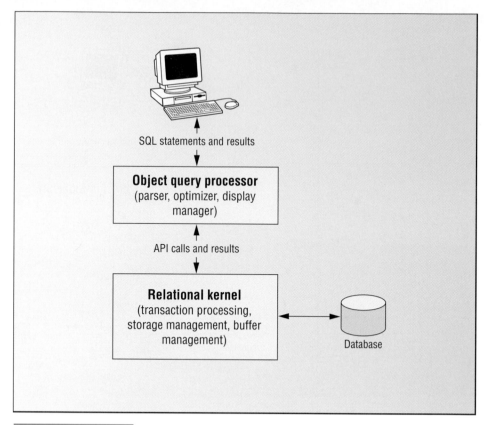

SQL statements and results

Object query processor
(parser, optimizer, display
manager)

API calls and results

Relational kernel
(transaction processing,
storage management, buffer
management)

Database

Figure 16.7   **Component architecture for object relational DBMSs.**

kernel remains unchanged. Reliability can be compromised in the implementations of user-defined functions and storage structures. DBMS vendors, third-party vendors, and in-house developers can provide user-defined types, which can be complex and difficult to implement. Implementation errors can affect the integrity of both simple and complex data. In addition, third-party data types can be subject to viruses.

16.3.5 Object-Oriented Database Management Systems

Object-Oriented DBMS
a new kind of DBMS designed especially for objects. Object-oriented DBMSs have an object query processor and an object kernel. The Object Data Management Group provides the standard for object-oriented DBMSs.

Some experts have argued that more fundamental changes to a DBMS are needed to support objects. Both the data model and the kernel must be changed to accommodate objects. This conviction has driven a number of start-up software companies to implement a new class of object DBMSs, as depicted in Figure 16.8. The software companies have banded together to form the Object Database Management Group (ODMG). The ODMG has proposed an object definition language and an object query language (OQL). These languages are the counterpart of SQL for object-oriented DBMSs.

Despite some important advantages of object-oriented DBMSs, they continue to occupy a market niche. Most of the products are used in applications where ad hoc query and transaction processing are not important. Instead, the products emphasize support for complex data in large software systems. Most of the object-oriented DBMSs began as extended programming languages with support for persistent objects (i.e., objects that exist after a program terminates). Gradually, the object-oriented DBMSs have provided

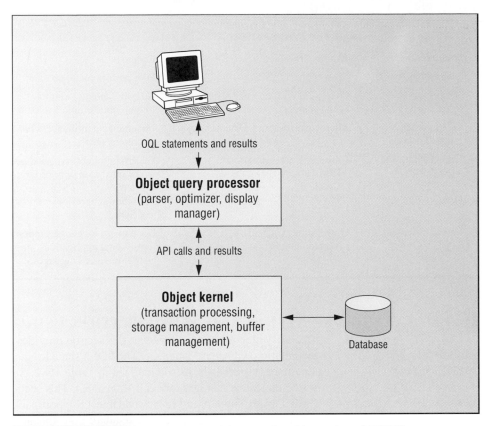

OQL statements and results

Object query processor
(parser, optimizer, display manager)

API calls and results

Object kernel
(transaction processing, storage management, buffer management)

Database

| Figure 16.8 | Component architecture for object-oriented DBMSs. |

ad hoc query and efficient transaction support. Still, questions remain about the ability of object-oriented DBMSs to provide high performance for traditional business applications. As object kernel technology matures, these concerns should cease. However, gaining significant market share against the established market-leading relational products will be difficult.

The ODMG and SQL standards groups have recognized the need for a unified standard. In a few years, a unified standard may emerge that allows portability between SQL3 and ODMG-compliant DBMSs. Even when this unification occurs, considerable time may elapse before most products support the unified standard. Both ODMG and SQL3 are very large standards. Most DBMS vendors will support only a subset of the standards.

16.3.6 Summary of Object Database Architectures

To help you remember the architectures for object DBMSs, Table 16–1 provides a convenient summary. All of the architectures fulfill a certain market niche. The simpler architectures (large objects and media servers) should become less popular over time. The struggle for dominance among the other three architectures may not be decided for some time. The object database middleware architecture will likely co-exist with the other architectures to handle complex data stored outside of a database.

TABLE 16–1	Summary of Architectures

Architecture	Example Products	Comments
Large objects	Most SQL2 DBMSs	Poor performance; no query language support
Media servers	Oracle 7.3 with text and spatial data servers	No query language support; poor performance when combining simple and complex data
Object database middleware	Microsoft Universal Data Access	Uncertain performance when combining simple and complex data
Object relational (SQL3)	Informix Universal Server, IBM Universal Database, Oracle 8	Uncertain reliability; good query language support; some type mismatch with programming languages. These products are not SQL3 compliant as of February 2000, but they support object relational extensions in the spirit of SQL3.
Object-oriented (ODMG)	ObjectStore, UniSQL, O2, Versant, Gemstone	Good query language support; uncertain performance for traditional applications; good type match with programming languages

16.4 DATABASE DEFINITION AND MANIPULATION USING SQL3

To clarify object database concepts, this section provides examples using SQL3, the object relational database language. The SQL3 standard includes a core language part and a number of packages, as summarized in Table 16–2. Several books are needed to describe the entire standard (about 2,100 pages). This section presents examples from the Basic Object Support and Enhanced Object Support packages.

Because SQL2 is a dominant standard now, this author anticipates that SQL3 will become the dominant standard for object database management. Because of the size and scope of the standard, vendors may take several years to adopt its most popular parts. Over time, major vendors will be forced to adhere to most of the SQL3 standard due to market pressures.

The examples in this section use the real estate database discussed in Section 16.1. This section extends the real estate database with residential properties, owners, and agents.

16.4.1 User-Defined Types

One of the most fundamental extensions in SQL3 is the user-defined type for bundling data and procedures together. User-defined types support definition of new structured data types rather than refinement of the standard data types. A structured data type has a collection of properties and methods. The CREATE DOMAIN statement supports refinements to standard data types.

Example 16.7 shows the *Point* type to contrast with the ODMG notation shown in Example 16.1. Some differences are apparent, such as keywords (TYPE versus CLASS) and the order of specification (the field name before the data type). The first part of a user-defined type contains the attribute definitions. The double hyphen denotes a comment. The keywords NOT FINAL mean that subtypes can be defined. For methods, the first parameter is implicit like the ODMG notation. For example, the *Distance* method lists only one *Point* parameter because the other *Point* parameter is implicit. The body of methods is not shown in the CREATE TYPE statement but rather in the CREATE METHOD statement.

TABLE 16–2	Overview of the SQL3 Standard

SQL3 Package	*Scope*
Core	SQL environment, SQL implementation, tables, views, predefined data types, SQL statements, conformance specifications
Persistent Stored Modules	Computational completeness, stored modules, function overloading
Call Level Interface	Call interface for SQL
Enhanced Datetime Facilities	Time zone specification, interval data type
Enhanced Integrity Management	Assertions, triggers, constraint management
OLAP Facilities	Cube and roll-up operators, row and table constructors, FULL JOIN and INTERSECT operators
Basic Object Support	User-defined data types, single inheritance, reference types, arrays
Enhanced Object Support	Path expressions, subtable definition, subtable search, subtypes

EXAMPLE 16.7	*Point* Type

```
CREATE TYPE Point AS
     x FLOAT(15),    -- X coordinate
     y FLOAT(15)     -- Y coordinate
     NOT FINAL
     METHOD Distance(P2 Point) RETURNS FLOAT(15),
     -- Computes the distance between 2 points
     METHOD Equals (P2 Point) RETURNS BOOLEAN
     -- Determines if 2 points are equivalent;
```

Example 16.8 shows the *ColorPoint* type, a subtype of *Point*. The UNDER keyword indicates the parent type. Because SQL3 does not support multiple inheritance, only a single type name can follow the UNDER keyword. In the method definitions, the OVERRIDING keyword indicates that the method overrides the definition in a parent type.

EXAMPLE 16.8	*ColorPoint* Type

```
CREATE TYPE ColorPoint UNDER Point AS
     Color INTEGER
     FINAL
     METHOD Brighten (Intensity INTEGER) RETURNS
INTEGER,
     -- Increases color intensity
     OVERRIDING METHOD Equals (CP2 ColorPoint)
          RETURNS BOOLEAN;
     -- Determines if 2 ColorPoints are equivalent
```

Besides the explicit methods listed in the CREATE TYPE statement, user-defined types have implicit methods that can be used in stored procedures, as shown below:

- **Constructor method:** creates an empty instance of the type. The constructor method has the same name as the data type. For example, Point() is the constructor method for the *Point* type.
- **Observer methods:** retrieve values from attributes. Each observer method uses the same name as its associated attribute. For example, x() is the observer method for the *x* attribute of the *Point* type.
- **Mutator methods:** change values stored in attributes. Each mutator method uses the same name as its associated attribute with one parameter for the value. For example, x(45.0) changes the value of the *x* attribute.

SQL3 features the ARRAY collection type to support types with more than one value such as time series and geometric shapes. Example 16.9 uses an ARRAY to define a polygon type with a maximum of 10 corners. The number following the ARRAY keyword indicates the maximum size of the array. Arrays can store any data type except other arrays and reference types presented in Section 16.4.2.

EXAMPLE 16.9   *Polygon* Type Using an ARRAY

```
CREATE TYPE Polygon AS
    Corners Point ARRAY[10], -- Array of Corner Points
    Color INTEGER
    NOT FINAL
    METHOD Area() RETURNS FLOAT(15),
      -- Computes the area
    METHOD Scale (Factor FLOAT(15)) RETURNS Polygon;
      -- Computes a new polygon scaled by factor
```

User-defined types can be used as data types for columns in tables, passed as parameters, and returned as values. User-defined functions can be used in expressions in the SELECT, the WHERE, and the HAVING clauses. The next sections provide examples of user-defined types in table definitions and queries. As you will see, user-defined types are integrated into the heart of SQL3.

16.4.2 Table Definitions and Subtable Families

SQL3 supports two styles of table definitions. The traditional SQL2 style uses foreign keys to link two tables. Example 16.10 depicts the *Property* table using a foreign key to reference the agent representing the property. The view column uses the user-defined type JPEG, a popular image format. The columns in a table are not encapsulated. Thus, an SQL3 query can reference the columns just like an SQL2 query.

EXAMPLE 16.10   *Property* and *Agent* Tables

```
CREATE TABLE Property
(PropNo    INTEGER,
  Street    VARCHAR(100),
  City      VARCHAR(100),
```

```
State      CHAR(2),
Zip        CHAR(9),
SqFt       INTEGER,
View       JPEG,
AgentNo    INTEGER,
Location   Point,
CONSTRAINT PropertyPK PRIMARY KEY(PropNo),
CONSTRAINT AgentFK FOREIGN KEY(AgentNo)
     REFERENCES Agent )


CREATE TABLE Agent
(AgentNo    INTEGER,
 Name       VARCHAR(50),
 Street     VARCHAR(100),
 City       VARCHAR(100),
 State      CHAR(2),
 Zip        CHAR(9),
 Phone      CHAR(10),
 Email      VARCHAR(50),
 CONSTRAINT AgentPK PRIMARY KEY(AgentNo) )
```

SQL3 supports the row type constructor to allow rows of a table to be stored as variables, used as parameters, and returned by functions. A row type is a sequence of name/value pairs. One use of a row type is to collect related columns together so that they can be stored as a variable or passed as a parameter. Example 16.11 depicts the *Property* table using a row type for the address columns (*Street, City, State,* and *Zip*).

EXAMPLE 16.11   Revised *Property* Table Definition with a Row Type

```
CREATE TABLE Property
(PropNo INTEGER,
  Address ROW (Street      VARCHAR,
               City        VARCHAR,
               State       CHAR(2),
               Zip         CHAR(9) ),
  SqFt       INTEGER,
  View       JPEG,
  AgentNo    INTEGER,
  Location   Point,
  CONSTRAINT PropertyPK PRIMARY KEY(PropNo),
  CONSTRAINT AgentFK FOREIGN KEY(AgentNo)
       REFERENCES Agent )
```

SQL3 provides an alternative style of table definition to support object identifiers and object references. In this style, a table definition refers to a user-defined type rather than a list of columns. Example 16.12 depicts the *AgentType* user-defined type and the *Agent* table referring to *AgentType*. The REF clause defines an object identifier for the table. The SCOPE clause in a table definition limits a reference to the rows of a table rather than objects of the type.

EXAMPLE *16.12*   Definition of *AgentType,* Followed by the *Agent* Table Based on *AgentType*

```
CREATE TYPE AgentType AS
   AgentNo  INTEGER,
   Name     VARCHAR,
   Address  ROW (Street  VARCHAR(100),
                 City     VARCHAR(100),
                 State    CHAR(2),
                 Zip      CHAR(9) ),
   Phone    CHAR(10),
   Email    VARCHAR(50)
   NOT FINAL )


CREATE TABLE Agent OF AgentType
   REF IS AgentId  -- defines an object identifier
   CONSTRAINT AgentPK PRIMARY KEY(AgentNo) )
```

Other tables can reference tables based on user-defined types. Object references provide an alternative to value references of foreign keys. Example 16.13 depicts a revised definition of the *Property* table with a reference to the *AgentType*. The SCOPE clause limits a reference to the rows of a table rather than objects of the type.

EXAMPLE *16.13*   Definition of the *Property* Table with a Reference to the *Agent* Table

```
CREATE TABLE Property
   (PropNo    INTEGER,
    Address   ROW (Street   VARCHAR(100),
                   City     VARCHAR(100),
                   State    CHAR(2),
                   Zip      CHAR(9) ),
    SqFt      INTEGER,
    View      JPEG,
    Location  Point,
    AgentRef  REF(AgentType) SCOPE Agent,
    CONSTRAINT PropertyPK PRIMARY KEY(PropNo) )
```

Inheritance applies to tables in a similar way as it applies to user-defined types. A table can be declared as a subtable of another table. A subtable inherits the columns of its parent tables. SQL3 limits inheritance for tables to single inheritance. The *Residential* table in Example 16.14 inherits the columns of the *Property* table.

<table>
<tr><td>**EXAMPLE 16.14**</td><td>Subtable of *Property* Table</td></tr>
</table>

```
CREATE TABLE Residential UNDER Property
 (BedRooms INTEGER,
  BathRoomsINTEGER,
  FloorPlan  AutoCAD,
  InteriorViews JPEG ARRAY[10] )
```

Set inclusion determines the relationship of a table to its subtables. Every row in a subtable is also a row in each of its parent tables. Each row of a parent table corresponds to at most one row in direct subtables. This set inclusion relationship extends to an entire subtable family, including the root table and all subtables directly or indirectly under the root table. For example, a subtable family includes security as the root; bond and stock under investment; and corporate, municipal, and federal under bond. The root of a subtable family is known as the maximal table. Security is the maximal table in this example.

Data manipulation operations on a row in a subtable family affect related rows in parent tables and subtables. The following is a brief description of side effects when manipulating rows in subtable families.

- If a row is inserted into a subtable, then a corresponding row (with the same values for inherited columns) is inserted into each parent table. The insert cascades upward in the subtable family until it reaches the maximal table.
- If a column is updated in a parent table, then the column is also updated in all direct and indirect subtables that inherit the column.
- If an inherited column is updated in a subtable, then the column is changed in the corresponding rows of direct and indirect parent tables. The update cascade stops in the parent table in which the column is defined, not inherited.
- If a row in a subtable family is deleted, then every corresponding row in both parent and subtables is also deleted.

16.4.3 Manipulating Complex Objects and Subtable Families

The richer data definition capabilities of SQL3 lead to new features for data retrieval. SQL3 features path expressions to manipulate columns with row references. Example 16.15 depicts the use of path expressions in the SELECT and WHERE clauses. The expression `Address.City` references the city component of the *Address* row column. The expression `AgentRef->name` references the *Name* column of the related *Agent* row. The dereference operator (->) traverses the row of type `REF(AgentType)`. Path expressions provide an alternative to value-based joins in SQL2. Example 16.16 shows the corresponding query using the SQL2 join notation.

<table>
<tr><td>**EXAMPLE 16.15**</td><td>SELECT Statement with Path Expressions Using Tables from Examples 16.12 and 16.13</td></tr>
</table>

```
SELECT PropNo, Address.City, AgentRef->Address
  FROM Property
  WHERE AgentRef->Name = 'Sue Smith'
```

EXAMPLE 16.16   SQL2 SELECT Statement Using Tables in Example 16.10

```
SELECT PropNo, City, A.Street, A.City, A.State, A.Zip
   FROM Property P, Agent A
   WHERE A.Name = 'Sue Smith' AND P.AgentNo = A.AgentNo
```

As a second new feature, SQL3 supports references to methods in expressions. To reference a method of a user-defined type, you can use the dot notation. Example 16.17 uses the *Similarity* method (a method of the *JPEG* type) to compare an image of a residential property with the image of property number 123467. The *Similarity* method returns a real number between 0 and 1. The method *DistMiles* of the *Point* type returns the miles between two points on a map. The *Similarity* and *DistMiles* methods are complex methods that would typically be provided by the DBMS vendor or a third party.

EXAMPLE 16.17   Retrieval with Methods of User-Defined Types

```
SELECT PropNo, Address, R.View. Similarity(R1.View)
   FROM Residential R, Residential R1
   WHERE R1.PropNo = 123467 AND R.PropNo <> 123467
   AND      R.View.Similarity(R1.View) > 0.8
   AND      R.Location.DistMiles(R1.Location) < 10
```

Example 16.17 also demonstrates the use of inherited columns. The fields *View* and *Location* were defined in the parent table, *Property*. Since all residential properties are properties, the inherited columns can be used. No reference to the parent table is necessary.

Sometimes you need to test membership in a specific table without being a member of any subtables. Example 16.18 retrieves bonds satisfying conditions on interest rate and maturity date. The FROM clause restricts the scope to bonds that are not members of any subtables. Thus, Example 16.18 does not retrieve any rows of the *Convertible* table, a subtable of the *Bond* table.

EXAMPLE 16.18   Using ONLY to Restrict the Range of a Table in a Subtable Family

```
SELECT Symbol, Maturity, IntRate
   FROM ONLY Bond
   WHERE IntRate > 0.8 AND Maturity < '1/1/2003'
```

CLOSING THOUGHTS

This chapter has described the motivation, principles, and architectures of object DBMSs. Object database technology is driven by demands to integrate complex and simple data and software productivity problems due to type mismatches between DBMSs and programming languages. Three principles of object-oriented computing—encapsulation, inheritance, and polymorphism—guide the development of object DBMSs. Encapsulation, the hiding of implementation details, supports data independence. Encapsulation is often relaxed for DBMSs to allow ad hoc queries. Inheritance, the sharing of code and data, supports software reusability. Polymorphism, the allowance of multiple implementations for procedures, permits incremental modification and a smaller vocabulary of procedures.

Because of the variety of ways to implement the object-oriented principles and the difficulty of implementation, a number of object DBMS architectures are commercially available. This chapter described five architectures and discussed their advantages and disadvantages. The first two architectures do not fully support the object-oriented principles as they involve simple schemes to store large objects and invoke specialized servers outside of a DBMS. The last three architectures provide different paths to implement the object-oriented principles. The architectures differ primarily on the level of integration with a DBMS. Object database middleware involves the least integration with a DBMS but provides the widest scope of complex data. Object relational DBMSs contain an object query processor on top of a relational kernel. Object-oriented DBMSs contain both an object query processor and an object kernel. The marketplace has not yet decided on the superiority of the latter three architectures.

To provide a more concrete view of object databases, this chapter presented object database definition and manipulation using SQL3, the emerging revision of SQL2. SQL3 supports user-defined types to accommodate new kinds of complex data. Expressions in queries can reference columns based on user-defined types as well as the methods of the user-defined types. SQL3 supports inheritance and polymorphism for user-defined types. A separate inheritance capability for subtable families is also provided. Inheritance for subtable families involves set inclusion relationships. Because SQL3 is a complex extension of SQL2, it may not be fully implemented for a number of years.

REVIEW CONCEPTS

- Examples of complex data that can be stored in digital format.
- Use of complex data as a motivation for object database technology.
- Type mismatches as a motivation for object database technology.
- Encapsulation as a kind of data independence.
- Relaxing encapsulation to support ad hoc queries.
- Inheritance as a way to share code and data.
- Polymorphism to reduce the vocabulary of procedures and allow incremental sharing of code.
- Difference between static and dynamic binding.
- Strong type checking to eliminate incompatibility errors in expressions.
- Reasons for marketplace support for a variety of object database management architectures.
- Level of integration with a DBMS for each object database management architecture.
- Characteristics of each object database management architecture.
- Reasons for the existence of two standards for object query languages.
- User-defined types and functions in SQL3: encapsulation, inheritance, and polymorphism.
- Subtable families in SQL3: inheritance and set inclusion.
- Relationship of subtable families and user-defined types.
- Use of the SQL3 row type to define tables with references.
- Use of path expressions and the dereference operator ($\rightarrow$) in SQL3 SELECT statements.
- Referencing subtables in SELECT statements.

QUESTIONS

1. How does the use of complex data drive the need for object database technology?

2. What problems are caused by mismatches between the types provided by a DBMS and a programming language?

3. Present an example application that uses both simple and complex data. Use a different application than discussed in Section 16.1.3.

4. Define encapsulation. How does encapsulation support the goal of data independence?

5. How do object DBMSs relax encapsulation? Why is encapsulation relaxed?

6. Define inheritance. What are the benefits of inheritance?

7. Define polymorphism. What are the benefits of polymorphism?

8. What is strong type checking? Why is strong type checking important?

9. What is the difference between static and dynamic binding?

10. Which implementation of object-oriented principles occurred first: object-oriented programming languages or object DBMSs?

11. Compare the emphasis in object-oriented programming languages to object DBMSs.

12. Discuss the reasons that multiple object DBMS architectures have been developed.

13. Discuss the benefits and limitations of storing large objects in the database. Why is external software needed when large objects are stored in a database?

14. Discuss the benefits and the limitations of using specialized media servers.

15. Discuss the benefits and the limitations of using object database middleware. Why does object database middleware support the broadest range of complex data?

16. Discuss the benefits and the limitations of using an object relational DBMS. What changes are made to the query processor of a relational DBMS to convert it into an object relational DBMS?

17. Discuss the benefits and the limitations of using an object-oriented DBMS. How does an object-oriented DBMS differ from an object-relational DBMS?

18. Why have object-oriented DBMSs occupied a market niche compared to relational DBMSs?

19. Which object DBMS architecture do you think will dominate in five years?

20. What is a persistent object? What is the difference between a persistent object and a temporary object?

21. Why are there two standard languages for object DBMSs?

22. What are the components of a user-defined type in SQL3?

23. How are SQL3 user-defined types used in table definitions and expressions?

24. What is a row type? How are row types used in SQL3 table definitions?

25. Explain the encapsulation differences for user-defined types versus tables in SQL3.

26. Discuss the relationship of subtable families and set inclusion.

27. What side effects occur when a row is inserted in a subtable?

28. What side effects occur when a subtable row is updated?

29. What side effects occur when a subtable row is deleted?

30. What is the difference between a foreign key and a reference?

31. What is the difference in notation between combining tables that are linked by a foreign key versus a column with a reference type?

32. What is a path expression? When do you use a path expression?

33. When do you need to use the dereference operator ($\rightarrow$) in an expression?

PROBLEMS

ORDER

The problems provide practice with using SQL3 to define user-defined types and tables as well as to query tables.

1. Use SQL3 to define a user-defined type for a time series. The variables of a time series include an array of floating-point values (maximum of 365), the begin date, a calendar (business or U.S.), and a period (day, week, month, year). Define methods as listed in Table 16P–1. You need to define the parameters for the methods, not the code to implement the methods. The TimeSeries parameter refers to the implicit TimeSeries object.

2. Define a table for securities. A security has fields for the unique symbol, the security name, and a time series of closing prices. The *Security* table has no parent table.

3. Define a table for stocks. A stock has fields for the number of issued shares, the number of outstanding shares, and the time series of closing prices. The *Stock* table inherits from the *Security* table.

4. Define a table for bonds. A bond has fields for the interest rate and the maturity date. The *Bond* table inherits from the *Security* table.

TABLE 16P–1	List of Methods for the TimeSeries Type	
Name	*Parameters*	*Result*
WeeklyAvg	TimeSeries	TimeSeries
MonthlyAvg	TimeSeries	TimeSeries
YearlyAvg	TimeSeries	TimeSeries
MovingAvg	TimeSeries, Start Date, Number of Values	Float
RetrieveRange	TimeSeries, Start Date, Number of Values	TimeSeries

5. Define a table for customers. A customer has fields for the unique customer number, the name, the address, the phone, and the e-mail address. The address field is a row type with fields for street, city, state, and zip. The phone field is a row type with fields for country code, area code, and local number. The *Customer* table has no parent table.

6. Define a table for a portfolio holding. A holding has fields for the customer, the security, and the shares held. The primary key of the *Holding* table is a combination of the *CustNo* field of the related customer and the *Symbol* field of the related security. The *Holding* table has no parent table.

7. Write a SELECT statement to list the securities held by Denver customers. Only list the securities with more than 100 shares held. Include the customer name, the symbol, and the shares held in the result.

8. Write a similar SELECT statement as in problem 7 except that the result only includes stocks, not bonds.

9. List the stocks with more than 1,000,000 shares outstanding. Include the symbol, the shares outstanding, and the closing price moving average of the 200 days beyond January 1, 2000. Hint: use a method that is part of a user-defined type that you defined in a previous problem.

10. List the holdings of Denver customers along with the weekly averages of the closing prices of each holding. Include the customer name, the symbol, and the weekly average of the closing prices in the result.

11. Define a customer type and a customer table based on the type. The customer type has the same attributes as the customer table in problem 5.

12. Redefine the portfolio holding table from problem 6. Modify the foreign key to the customer table with a reference to the *Customer* table.

13. Rewrite problem 7 with the revised *Customer* and *Holding* tables.

REFERENCES FOR FURTHER STUDY

This chapter has only introduced a very broad and deep subject. For more details, you are encouraged to consult specialized books, articles, and websites. Specialized books on object database management include Stonebraker and Moore (1996) on object relational DBMSs and Cattell and Barry (1997) on the object data management standard. Articles comparing the SQL3 and the object data management standard can be found in the December 1994 issue of the *IEEE Data Engineering Bulletin* (Bancilhon and Ferran, Manola and Mitchell, and Melton). An Informix White Paper by Stonebraker (available at http://www.informix.com/informix/whitepapers/index.html) provided background for Section 16.3. The ISO committee drafts (1996, 1998) and the book by Gulutzan and Pelzer (1999) provided background for the SQL3 examples in Section 16.4.

More recent trade articles on object DBMSs can be found at the *Intelligent Enterprise Magazine* (http://www.iemagazine.com/) and Advisor.com (http://www.advisor.com/) sites. Some good websites on object databases include the Object Data Management Group (http://www.odmg.org/) and the Object Information Management Technical Committee (http://www.objs.com/x3h7/h7home.htm). The major DBMS vendors also provide a wealth of information about their respective object DBMSs.

GLOSSARY

A

Access Plan   a tree that encodes decisions about file structures to access individual tables, the order of joining tables, and the algorithm to join tables. Access plans are generated by the optimization component to implement queries submitted by users.

ACID Properties   transaction properties supported by DBMSs. ACID is an acronym for atomic, consistent, isolated, and durable. Atomic means all or nothing. Consistent means that a database does not violate integrity constraints before or after a transaction commits. Isolated means that other transactions cannot see the updates made by a transaction until after the transaction terminates. Durable means that the effects of a transaction are permanent after committing even if a failure occurs.

Aggregate Function   a summary or statistical function. The standard aggregate functions in SQL are MIN, MAX, COUNT, SUM, and AVG.

Analyst/Programmer   an information system professional who is responsible for collecting requirements, designing applications, and implementing information systems. An analyst/programmer may create and use external views to develop forms, reports, and other parts of an information system.

Analytic Hierarchy Process   a decision theory technique to evaluate problems with multiple objectives. The Analytic Hierarchy Process can be used to select and evaluate DBMSs by allowing a systematic assignment of weights to requirements and scores to features of candidate DBMSs.

ANSI   American National Standards Institute, one of the groups responsible for SQL standards.

Application Profile   a statistical summary of the forms, reports, and queries that access a database. Application profiles are an important input of the physical database design phase because they are used to predict demand for the database.

Assertion   the most general kind of integrity constraint supported in SQL2. An assertion can involve a SELECT statement of arbitrary complexity. The CREATE ASSERTION statement defines assertions in SQL2.

Associative Entity Type   a weak entity type that depends on two or more entity types for its primary key. In the Crow's Foot ERD notation, associative entity types represent M-way relationships.

Attribute   a property of an entity type or relationship. Each attribute has a data type defining allowable values and operations. Attribute is synonymous with field and column.

Authorization Rules   define authorized users, allowable operations, and accessible parts of a database. The database security system stores authorization rules and enforces them for each database access. Also known as security constraints.

B

Binary Large Object (BLOB)   a data type for fields containing large binary data such as images. BLOB data can be retrieved but not displayed. The BLOB data type provides a simple way to extend a DBMS with object features. See also the Large Object Architecture.

Binding   in object-oriented computing, associating a method name with its implementation. Binding can be static (decided at compile-time) or dynamic (decided at run-time). Static binding is more efficient but sometimes less flexible than dynamic binding. See also message.

Bottom-Up Data Warehouse Architecture   an architecture for a data warehouse in which data marts are built for user departments. If a need for an enterprise data model emerges, the data marts will evolve to a data warehouse. See also two-tier data warehouse architecture and three-tier data warehouse architecture.

Boyce-Codd Normal Form (BCNF)   a table is in BCNF if every determinant is a candidate key. BCNF is a revised definition for 3NF.

Btree File   a popular file structure supported by most DBMSs because it provides good performance both on key search as well as sequential search. A Btree file is a balanced, multiway tree. The most popular variation of the Btree is the B+tree in which all keys are redundantly stored in the leaf nodes. The B+tree provides improved performance on sequential and range searches.

Buffer   an area in main memory containing physical database records transferred from disk.

C

Candidate Key   a minimal superkey. A superkey is minimal if removing any columns makes it no longer unique.

Cardinality   a constraint on the number of entities participating in a relationship. In an entity relationship diagram, the minimum and maximum number of entities are specified for both directions of a relationship.

CASE Tool   a tool to facilitate database and information systems development. CASE tools support features for drawing, analysis, prototyping, and data dictionary. CASE is an acronym for computer-aided software engineering.

Checkpoint   the act of writing a record to the checkpoint table, writing a checkpoint record to the log, and force writing buffers to disk. A checkpoint record contains the current position of the log. The checkpoint record in the log contains the list of active transactions. The purpose of a checkpoint is to reduce the time to recover from failures.

Class   a collection of objects. A class definition includes variables for object data and methods for object procedures.

Client   a program that submits requests to a server such as accessing or updating a database.

Client–Server Architecture   an arrangement of components (clients and servers) among computers connected by a network. The client–server architecture supports efficient processing of messages (requests for service) between clients and servers.

Client-Side Connectivity   a style of computing on the World Wide Web in which client computing capacity can be more fully utilized without storing code on the client. Client-side connectivity can enhance database connectivity by providing a more customized interface

than permitted by HTML and by allowing data buffering by the client.

Column   a field or attribute in a table. Each column has a data type defining allowable values and operations. Column is synonymous with field and attribute.

Combined Primary Key   a combination of columns (more than one) designated as the primary key. Also known as a composite primary key.

Common Gateway Interface (CGI)   an interface that allows a Web server to invoke an external program on the same computer. CGI was the earliest and still is the most universal way to achieve Web database connectivity.

Conceptual Evaluation Process   the sequence of operations and intermediate tables used to derive the result of a SELECT statement. The evaluation process is conceptual because most SQL compilers will take many shortcuts to produce the result. The conceptual evaluation process may help you gain an initial understanding of the SELECT statement as well as help you to understand more difficult problems.

Conceptual Schema   a data description that covers all entities and relationships in a database. The conceptual schema is concerned with the meaning of the database, not its physical implementation. See also schema, internal schema, external view, and Three Schema Architecture.

Concurrency Transparency   a service provided by a DBMS so that users perceive a database as a single-user system even though there may be many simultaneous users. The concurrency control manager is the component of a DBMS responsible for concurrency transparency.

Cross Product Style   a way to formulate joins in a SELECT statement. The cross product style lists the tables in the FROM clause and the join conditions in the WHERE clause.

D

Data Administrator   a management position that performs planning and policy setting for the information resources of an entire organization.

Data Cube   a multidimensional format in which cells contain numeric data called measures organized by subjects called dimensions. A data cube is sometimes known as a hypercube because conceptually it can have an unlimited number of dimensions.

Data Independence   a database should have an identity separate from the applications (computer programs, forms, and reports) that use it. The separate identity allows the database definition to be changed without affecting related applications.

Data Mart   a subset or view of a data warehouse, typically at a department or functional level, that contains all the data required for decision support tasks of that department. In addition, a data mart insulates departmental users from data used by other departments. In some organizations, a data mart is a small data warehouse rather than a view of a larger data warehouse.

Data Mining   the process of discovering implicit patterns in data stored in a data warehouse and using those patterns for business advantage such as predicting future trends.

Data Type   defines a set of values and permissible operations on the values. Each column of a table is associated with a data type.

Data Warehouse   a central repository for summarized and integrated data from operational databases and external data sources.

Database   a collection of persistent data that can be shared and interrelated.

Database Administrator   a support position that specializes in managing individual databases and DBMSs.

Database Management System (DBMS)   a collection of components that support data acquisition, dissemination, maintenance, retrieval, and formatting. An enterprise DBMS supports databases that are critical to an organization. A desktop DBMS supports databases for small workgroups and small businesses.

Database Security   protecting databases from unauthorized access and malicious destruction.

Datasheet   a way to display a table in which the column names appear in the first row and the body in the other rows. Datasheet is a Microsoft Access term.

Deadlock   a problem of mutual waiting that can occur when using locks. If a deadlock is not resolved, the involved transactions will wait forever.

Deferred Constraint Checking   enforcing integrity constraints at end of transaction rather than immediately after each manipulation statement. Complex constraints may benefit from deferred checking.

Deferred Update Approach   an approach used by a recovery manager to record database changes on disk. In this approach, database updates are written only after a transaction commits. To restore a database, only redo operations are used.

Denormalization   combining tables so that they are easier to query. Denormalization is the opposite of normalization. Denormalization can be useful to improve query performance or to ignore a dependency that does not cause significant storage anomalies.

Detail Line   the innermost (most nested) line on a hierarchical report

Determinant   the column(s) appearing on the left-hand side (LHS) of a functional dependency. Alternatively known as a LHS for left-hand side.

Dice   a data cube operator in which a dimension is replaced by a subset of its values. See also slice.

Difference   an operator of relational algebra that combines rows from two tables. The difference operator extracts rows that belong to the first table only. Both tables must be union compatible to use the difference operator.

Dimension Table   a table in a star schema or snowflake schema that stores dimensions or themes used to aggregate facts.

Discretionary Access Control   users are assigned access rights or privileges to specified parts of a database. Discretionary access control is the most common kind of security control supported by commercial DBMSs.

Distributed DBMS   a collection of components that supports requests for data residing on multiple sites. A distributed DBMS finds remote data, optimizes global requests, and coordinates transactions at multiple sites. Also known as a distributed database management system (DDBMS).

Distributed Processing   allows geographically dispersed computers to cooperate when providing data access and other services. See also client–server architecture.

Divide   an operator of relational algebra that combines rows from two tables. The divide operator produces a table in which the values of a column from one input table are associated with all the values from a column of the second table.

DOLAP   an acronym for Desktop On-Line Analytical Processing. DOLAP systems can be used for small data marts or to manipulate views of a large data warehouse.

Drill-Down   a data cube operator that supports navigation from a more general level of a dimension to a more specific level of a dimension. See also roll-up.

E

Embedded SQL   using SQL inside a host programming language such as COBOL or Visual Basic. Additional SQL statements that can be used only in a programming language cause other SQL statements to be executed and use database results inside the program. See also Standalone SQL.

Encapsulation   a principle of object-oriented computing in which an object can be accessed only through its interface. The internal details (variables and method implementations) cannot be accessed. Encapsulation supports lower software maintenance costs.

Encryption   involves the encoding of data to obscure their meaning. An encryption algorithm changes the original data (known as the plaintext). To decipher the data, the user supplies an encryption key to restore the encrypted data (known as the ciphertext) to its original (plaintext) format.

Enterprise Data Model   a conceptual data model of an organization. An enterprise data model can be used for data planning (what databases to develop) and decision support (how to integrate and summarize existing databases).

Entity   a cluster of data usually about a single topic that can be accessed together. An entity can denote a person, place, event, or thing.

Entity Integrity   a constraint involving primary keys. No two rows of a table can contain the same value for the primary key. In addition, no row can contain a null value for any columns of a primary key.

Entity Type   a collection of entities (persons, places, events, or things) of interest in an application, represented by a rectangle in an entity relationship diagram.

Environment Interaction Model   a graphical model showing the relationships between events and processes. An event such as the passage of time or an action from the environment can trigger a process to start or stop.

Equi-join   a join operator where the join condition involves equality. See also join and natural join.

Exact String Matching   searching for one string value using the equality comparison operator. See also inexact string matching.

Exclusive Lock   a lock that prevents other users from accessing a database item. Exclusive locks conflict with all other kinds of locks (shared, other exclusive locks, and intent). An exclusive lock indicates that a user will change the value of a database item. Also known as an X lock.

Existence Dependency   an entity that cannot exist unless another related entity exists. A mandatory relationship produces an existence dependency. See also mandatory relationship.

Expression   a combination of constants, column names, functions and operators that produces a value. In conditions and results columns, expressions can be used in any place that column names can appear.

Extended Cross Product   an operator of relational algebra that combines two tables. The extended cross product (product for short) operator builds a table from two tables consisting of all possible combinations of rows, one from each of the two input tables.

External View   a description of derived data appropriate for a given user group. Also known as external schema and view. See also schema and three schema architecture.

F

Fact Table   a table in a star schema or snowflake schema that stores numeric values of relevance to a decision maker. See also star schema and snowflake schema.

File   a collection of data on a permanent storage device such as a hard disk. The data or physical records on the file are organized to support efficient processing. Files are part of the internal schema of a database.

File Sharing   a method to share data over a computer network in which a personal computer requests a file from another computer on the network.

First Generation Database Technology   proprietary file structures and program interfaces that supported sequential and random searching. However, the user was required to write a computer program to access data. First generation database technology was largely developed during the 1960s.

Force Writing   the ability to control when data are transferred to nonvolatile storage. This ability is fundamental to recovery management. Force writing typically occurs at end of transaction and checkpoint time.

Foreign Key   a column or combination of columns in which the values must match those of a candidate key. A foreign key must have the same data type as its associated candidate key. In the CREATE TABLE statement of SQL2, a foreign key must be associated with a primary key rather than merely a candidate key.

Form   a document used in a business process, formatted to provide a convenient way to enter and edit data. A form is designed to support a business task such as processing an order, registering for classes, or making an airline reservation.

Form Entity Type   in the form analysis process, the form entity type is derived from the primary key of the form. The form entity type should be placed in the center of the ERD.

Form Structure   a hierarchy depicting the relationship among form fields. A group of form fields is known as a node. Most forms have a simple structure with a parent node (main form) and a child node (subform).

Forward Engineering   the ability to generate definitions for a target database management system from an ERD and data dictionary properties. See also CASE tool and reverse engineering.

Fourth Generation Database Technology   extend the boundaries of database technology to unconventional data and the Internet. Fourth generation systems can store and manipulate unconventional data types such as images, videos, maps, sounds, and animations as well as provide Web access to databases. Fourth generation database technology was largely commercialized during the 1990s.

Fourth Normal Form (4NF)   a table is in 4NF if it does not contain any nontrivial MVDs. A nontrivial MVD is an MVD that is not also an FD.

Fragment   a subset of a table that is allocated to sites. Fragments can be horizontal subsets (restrict operator), vertical subsets (project operator), derived horizontal subsets (semi-join operator), and combinations of these kinds of fragments. See also semi-join operator, fragmentation transparency, location transparency, and local mapping transparency.

Fragmentation Transparency a level of independence in distributed DBMSs in which queries can be formulated without knowledge of fragments. See location transparency and local mapping transparency.

Full Outer Join an outer join that produces the matching rows (the join part) as well as the nonmatching rows from both tables.

Functional Dependency (FD) a constraint about two or more columns of a table. X determines Y $(X \rightarrow Y)$ if there exists at most one value of Y for every value of X. A functional dependency is like a primary key because if X and Y are placed in a separate table, X is the primary key.

G

Generalization Hierarchy a collection of entity types arranged in a hierarchical structure to show similarity in attributes. Each subtype or child entity represents a subset of its supertype or parent entity. See also supertype and subtype.

Group Condition a comparison involving an aggregate function such as SUM or COUNT. Group conditions cannot be evaluated until after the GROUP BY clause is evaluated.

H

Hash File a specialized file structure that supports search by key. Hash files transform a key value into an address to provide fast access. Hash files may have poor performance for sequential access. A hash file may be static (requires periodic reorganization) or dynamic (does not require periodic reorganization).

Hierarchical Form a formatted window for data entry and display using a fixed (main form) and variable (subform) part. One record is shown in the main form and multiple, related records are shown in the subform.

Hierarchical Report a formatted display of a query using indentation to show grouping and sorting. Also known as a control break report.

Histogram a two-dimensional graph where the x-axis represents column ranges and the y-axis represents the number of rows containing the range of values. Histograms support more detailed distribution data than the uniform value assumption. Histograms are part of a table profile.

HOLAP an acronym for Hybrid On-Line Analytical Processing. HOLAP is an implementation approach that combines the MOLAP and the ROLAP approaches. HOLAP systems can choose and combine dynamically generated data cubes managed by ROLAP systems with precomputed data cubes managed by MOLAP systems. See also MOLAP and ROLAP.

Hot Spot common data that multiple users try to change simultaneously. Without adequate concurrency control, users may interfere with each other on hot spots. A system-independent hot spot does not depend on the details of a particular concurrency control manager. Typically, system-independent hot spots involve fields or rows in a database. A system-dependent hot spot depends on the details of the concurrency control manager, especially the locking granularity.

HTML (HyperText Markup Language) the language in which most Web documents are written. HTML combines the structure, the content, and the layout of a document. See also XML and XSL.

I

Identification Dependency involves a weak entity and one or more identifying relationships. See also weak entity and identifying relationship.

Identifying Relationship a relationship that provides a component of the primary key to a weak entity. See also weak entity and identification dependency.

Immediate Update Approach an approach used by a recovery manager to record database changes on disk. In this approach, database updates are written to the disk when they occur but after the corresponding log updates. To restore a database, both undo and redo operations may be needed. See also deferred update approach and write ahead log protocol.

Incorrect Summary a concurrency control problem in which a transaction reads several values, but another transaction updates some of the values while the first transaction is still executing. Also known as an inconsistent analysis and a nonrepeatable read.

Incremental Integration an approach to view integration where a partially integrated ERD is merged with the next view. To integrate n views, there are $n - 1$ integration steps.

Index a secondary file structure that provides an alternative path to the data. Indexes typically contain only key values, not the other fields in a logical record. Indexes may be organized as Btrees or hash files.

Index Selection for each table, select at most one clustering index and zero or more nonclustering indexes. In a clustering index, the order of the data records is close to the index order. In a nonclustering index, the order of the data records is unrelated to the index order. Index selection is an important subproblem of physical database design.

Indirect User   user who accesses a database through reports or data extracts rather than through their own initiative. See also parametric user and power user.

Inexact String Matching   searching for a pattern of strings rather than just one string. In SQL, inexact matching uses the LIKE operator and pattern-matching characters.

Information Life Cycle   the stages of information transformation in an organization. Typical stages of an information life cycle include acquisition, storage, protection, processing, formatting, dissemination, and usage.

Information Resource Dictionary (IRD)   a database of metadata that describes the entire information systems life cycle. The information resource dictionary system manages access to an IRD. Also known as the repository.

Information Resource Management   a broad management philosophy that seeks to use information technology as a tool for processing, distributing, and integrating information throughout an organization.

Information System   a system that accepts data from its environment, processes the data, and produces output data for decision making. An information system consists of people, procedures, input data, output data, databases, software, and hardware.

Information Systems Planning   the process of developing enterprise models of data, processes, and organizational roles. Information systems planning evaluates existing systems, identifies opportunities to apply information technology for competitive advantage, and plans new systems. Also known as business systems planning, information systems engineering, and information systems architecture.

Inheritance   a data modeling feature that supports sharing of attributes between a supertype and a subtype. Subtypes inherit attributes from their supertypes. In SQL3, inheritance applies to both user-defined types and subtable families. Inheritance supports sharing of data and code among similar objects.

Integration Strategy   a mix of incremental and parallel approaches to integrate a set of views. The views are divided into subsets. For each subset of views, incremental integration is used. Parallel integration is usually applied to the ERDs resulting from integrating the view subsets.

Intent Lock   a lock on a large database item (such as a table) that indicates that the user intends to lock smaller items contained in the larger item. Intent locks conflict with shared or exclusive locks on the large database item but do not conflict with locks on smaller contained items.

Internal Schema   a description of the physical implementation of a database. See also schema, conceptual schema, external view, and Three Schema Architecture.

Internet   a global "network of networks" that is built from standard protocols.

Interrelated   a fundamental characteristic of databases. Interrelated means that data stored as separate units can be connected to provide a whole picture. To support the interrelated characteristic, databases contain clusters of data known as entities and relationships connecting entities.

Intersection   an operator of relational algebra that combines rows from two tables. The intersection operator finds rows that are common to both tables. Both tables must be union compatible to use the intersection operator.

ISO   International Standards Organization, one of the groups responsible for SQL standards.

Isolation Level   defines the degree to which a transaction is separated from actions of other transactions. A transaction designer can balance concurrency control overhead with interference problems prevented by specifying the appropriate isolation level.

J

Join   an operator of relational algebra used to combine rows from two tables. The join operator produces a table containing rows that match on a condition involving a column from each input table. See also equi-join and natural join.

Join Operator Style   a way to formulate joins in a SELECT statement. The join operator style lists join operations in the FROM clause using the INNER JOIN and ON keywords.

K

Key Preserving Table   an Oracle term for the updatable table in a multiple-table view. The multiple-table view contains the primary key of the key preserving table.

Knowledge Management   applying information technology with human information processing capabilities and organization processes to support rapid adaptation to change.

L

Large Object Architecture   an architecture for object databases in which large objects (binary or text) are stored in a database along with external software to manipulate large objects.

Law of Transitivity a rule that states if an object A is related to an object B and B is related to C, then conclude that A is related to C. Functional dependencies obey the law of transitivity. See also functional dependency and transitive dependency.

Local Mapping Transparency a level of independence in distributed DBMSs in which queries can be formulated without knowledge of local formats. However, knowledge of fragments and fragment allocations is necessary. See also fragment, fragmentation transparency, and location transparency.

Location Transparency a level of independence in distributed DBMSs in which queries can be formulated without knowledge of locations. However, knowledge of fragments is necessary. See also fragment, fragmentation transparency, and local mapping transparency.

Lock a fundamental tool of concurrency control. A lock on a database item prevents other transactions from performing conflicting actions on the same item. See also exclusive lock, intent lock, and shared lock.

Locking Granularity the size of the database item locked. Locking granularity is a trade-off between waiting time (amount of concurrency permitted) and overhead (number of locks held).

Logical Expression an expression resulting in a true or false (Boolean) value. Logical expressions can involve comparisons and the logical operators (AND, OR, NOT, etc.).

Lost Update a concurrency control problem in which one user's update overwrites another user's update.

M

Main Form the fixed part of a hierarchical form. The main form shows one record at a time.

Mandatory Access Control a database security approach for highly sensitive and static databases. In mandatory control approaches, each object is assigned a classification level and each user is given a clearance level. A user can access a database element if the user's clearance level provides access to the classification level of the element.

Mandatory Relationship a relationship with a minimum cardinality of one or more. A mandatory relationship produces an existence dependency on the entity type associated with the minimum cardinality of one. See also optional relationship and existence dependency.

Many-to-Many (M-N) Relationship in the Entity Relationship Model, a relationship in which objects of

each entity type can be related to many objects of the other entity type. M-N relationships have maximum cardinalities of more than one in each direction. In the Relational Model, two 1-M relationships and a linking or associative table represent an M-N relationship. See also one-to-many relationship and relationship.

Message a request to invoke a method on an object. When an object receives a message, it looks for an implementation in its own class. If an implementation cannot be found, the message is sent to the object's parent class. See also binding.

Message-Oriented Middleware maintain a queue of messages. A client process can place a message on a queue and a server can remove a message from a queue. Message-oriented middleware supports complex messages among clients and servers.

Metadata data that describe other data including the source, use, value, and meaning of the data.

Middleware a software component in a client–server architecture that performs process management. Middleware allows servers to efficiently process messages from a large number of clients. In addition, middleware can allow clients and servers to communicate across heterogeneous platforms. Prominent kinds of database middleware include transaction-processing monitors, message-oriented middleware, and object-request brokers.

Modification Anomaly an unexpected side effect that occurs when changing the data in a table with excessive redundancies.

MOLAP an acronym for Multidimensional On-Line Analytical Processing. MOLAP is an implementation approach for a multidimensional database in which data cubes are precalculated and managed by a specially designed DBMS for data cubes.

Multiple-Tier Architecture a client–server architecture with more than three layers: a PC client, a backend database server, an intervening middleware server, and application-servers. The application-servers perform business logic and manage specialized kinds of data such as images. See also two-tier architecture and three-tier architecture.

Multivalued Dependency a constraint involving three columns. The MVD $A \rightarrow\rightarrow B|C$ (read A multidetermines B or C) means that (1) a given A value is associated with a collection of B and C values and (2) B and C are independent, given the relationships between A and B and A and C. All FDs are also MVDs but not all MVDs are FDs. An MVD is nontrivial if it is also not an FD. See also relationship independence and functional dependency.

M-Way (Multiway) Relationship   a relationship involving more than two entity types. In some ERD notations such as the Crow's Foot, an M-way relationship is represented as an associative entity type.

N

Name Qualification   preceding a column name with its table name. The column name alone is an abbreviation. If the same column name occurs in two tables in an SQL statement, the column name must be qualified with its table name. The combination of the table name and column name must be unique across all tables in a database.

Natural Join   a variation of the join operator of relational algebra. In a natural join, the matching condition is equality (equi-join), one of the matching columns is discarded in the result table, and the join columns have the same unqualified names. See also equi-join and join.

Nested Query   a query inside a query. In an SQL SELECT statement, a SELECT statement can be part of conditions in the HAVING and WHERE clauses. See Type I and Type II nested queries for two variations. Also known as a subquery and an inner query.

Node Key   a field(s) in a node of a form structure with unique values. The key of the root node is unique among all form instances. The key of a child node is unique within its parent node.

Nonprocedural Database Language   a language such as SQL that allows you to specify what part of a database to access rather than to code a complex procedure. Nonprocedural languages do not include looping statements.

Normal Form   a rule about allowable dependencies.

Normalization   the process of removing redundancies from tables so that the tables are easier to change. To normalize a table, list the functional dependencies and make tables that satisfy a normal form, usually third normal form (3NF) or Boyce-Codd normal form (BCNF).

Null Value   a special value that represents the absence of an actual value. A null value can mean that the actual value is unknown or does not apply to the given row.

O

Object   an instance of a class in object-oriented computing. An object has a unique identifier that is invisible and nonchangeable.

Object Database Middleware   an architecture for object databases in which middleware manages complex data possibly stored outside of a database along with traditional data stored in a database.

Object-Oriented DBMS   a new kind of DBMS designed especially for objects. Object-oriented DBMSs have an object query processor and an object kernel. The Object Data Management Group provides the standard for object-oriented DBMSs.

Object Relational DBMS   a relational DBMS extended with an object query processor for user-defined data types. SQL3 provides the standard for object relational DBMSs.

Object-Request Broker   a kind of middleware that provides a high level of interoperability and message intelligence. To use an object-request broker, messages must be encoded in a standard interface description language. An object-request broker resolves platform differences between a client and a server and allows communication without knowing the location of the server.

OLAP (On-line Analytical Processing)   general name of technology to support multidimensional databases. OLAP technology encompasses the multidimensional data model and implementation approaches.

One-Sided Outer Join   an outer join that produces the matching rows (the join part) as well as the nonmatching rows from only one of the tables, the designated input table.

One-to-Many (1-M) Relationship   in the Entity Relationship Model, a relationship in which the maximum cardinality is 1 in one direction and M in the other direction. In the Relational Data Model, a referential integrity constraint usually indicates a 1-M relationship. See also relationship and many-to-many relationship.

One-to-Many (1-M) Updatable Query   a type of updatable view in Microsoft Access involving one or more 1-M relationships.

Operational Database   a database to support the daily operations of an organization. Operational databases directly support major functions such as order processing, manufacturing, accounts payable, and product distribution.

Optional Relationship   a relationship with a minimum cardinality of zero. An optional relationship means that entities can be stored without participation in the relationship. See also mandatory relationship.

Outer Join   an operator of relational algebra that combines two tables. In an outer join, the matching and nonmatching rows are retained in the result. See one-sided and full outer join for two variations of this operator.

P

Parallel Integration   an approach to view integration where all views are integrated in one step. To integrate *n* views, there are *n* view design steps and one integration step. The view design steps may be performed in parallel by separate design teams.

Parametric User   someone who uses a database by requesting existing forms or reports using parameters, input values that change from usage to usage. See also indirect user and power user.

Persistent   a fundamental characteristic of databases. Persistent means that data has a lifetime longer than the execution of a computer program. To be persistent, data must reside on stable storage such as magnetic disk.

Phantom Read   a variation of the incorrect summary problem in which a transaction executes a query with record conditions but another transaction inserts new rows or modifies existing rows while the first transaction is still executing. The first transaction then executes the original query again but the results are different than for the first execution. The new rows are phantom because they did not exist for the first execution of the query.

Physical Record   collection of bytes that are transferred between volatile storage in main memory and stable storage on a disk. The number of physical record accesses is an important measure of database performance.

Pivot   a data cube operator in which the dimensions in a data cube are rearranged. See also data cube.

Polymorphism   a principle of object-oriented computing in which a computing system has the ability to choose among multiple implementations of a method. The appropriate implementation is chosen by the system (object DBMS or object-oriented programming language). Polymorphism permits a smaller vocabulary of procedures and incremental sharing of code.

Power User   someone who uses a database by submitting unplanned or ad hoc requests for data. Power users should have a good understanding of nonprocedural access. See also indirect user and parametric user.

Primary Copy Protocol   a protocol for concurrency control of distributed transactions. Each replicated fragment is designated as either the primary copy or a secondary copy. During distributed transaction processing, only the primary copy is guaranteed to be current at end of transaction. Updates may be propagated to secondary copies after end of transaction.

Primary Key   a specially designated candidate key. The primary key for a table cannot contain null values.

Procedural Language Interface   a method to combine a nonprocedural language such as SQL with a programming language such as COBOL or Visual Basic. Embedded SQL is an example of a procedural language interface.

Process Model   a graphical model showing the relationships between processes. A process can provide input data used by other processes or use output data of other processes. The well-known data flow diagram is an example of a process model.

Project   an operator of relational algebra. A project operation retrieves a subset of specified columns of the input table. Duplicate rows are eliminated in the result if present.

Prototype   a fast implementation of an application in an information system. Prototypes can demonstrate forms, reports, and menus to enable feedback from users.

Q

Query   request to extract useful data. Query formulation involves translating a problem into a language (such as an SQL SELECT statement) understood by a DBMS.

Query Binding   the process of associating a query with an access plan. Some DBMSs rebind automatically if a query changes or the database changes (file structures, table profiles, data types, etc.).

R

RAID (Redundant Arrays of Independent Disks)   a collection of disks (a disk array) that operates as a single disk. RAID storage supports parallel read and write operations with high reliability.

RAID-1   an architecture for RAID storage in which redundant arrays of disks provide high reliability and performance but with large storage overhead. RAID-1 uses disk mirroring to achieve high performance and reliability.

RAID-5   an architecture for RAID storage in which randomly located error-correcting pages provide high reliability without excessive storage overhead. RAID-5 uses striping to achieve good performance and reliability without excessive storage overhead.

Read-Only View   a view that can be used in SELECT statements but not in UPDATE, INSERT, and DELETE statements. All views are at least read-only.

Recovery Transparency   a service provided by a DBMS to automatically restore a database to a consistent state after a failure. The recovery manager is the component of a DBMS responsible for recovery transparency.

Referential Integrity   an integrity constraint involving a candidate key in one table with the related foreign key of another table. Only two kinds of values can be stored in a foreign key: (1) a value matching a candidate key value in some row of the table containing the associated candidate key or (2) a null value. See also primary key, candidate key, and foreign key.

Relation   synonymous with table. A term typically used in academic research about databases.

Relational Algebra   a set of operators to manipulate relational databases. Each operator uses one or two tables as input and produces a new table as output.

Relational Data Model   using tables, matching values for connections among tables, and table operators to represent a collection of data.

Relational DBMS   a system that uses the Relational Data Model to manage collections of data.

Relationship   in the Entity Relationship Model, a relationship is a named association among entity types. In the Relational model, a relationship is a connection among tables shown by column values in one table that matches column values in another table. Referential integrity constraints and foreign keys indicate relationships in the Relational Model. See also one-to-many relationship, many-to-many relationship, and referential integrity.

Relationship Equivalence   a rule about the equivalence between 1-M and M-N relationships. An M-N relationship can be replaced by an associative entity type and two identifying 1-M relationships. See also associative entity type and identifying relationship.

Relationship Independence   a relationship that can be derived from two independent relationships.

Remote Procedure Call   a method to share processing resources over a computer network in which a personal computer invokes a stored procedure on another computer in the network.

Report   a stylized presentation of data appropriate to a selected audience. Reports enhance the appearance of data that are displayed or printed. See also hierarchical report.

Restrict   an operator of relational algebra. A restrict operation retrieves a subset of rows of the input table that satisfy a given condition.

Reverse Engineering   the ability to extract definitions from a target database management system and use the definitions to create an ERD and data dictionary properties. See also CASE tool and forward engineering.

ROLAP   an acronym for Relational On-Line Analytical Processing. ROLAP is a relational database implementation of a multidimensional database in which data cubes (or parts of data cubes) are dynamically constructed from relational tables when requested in queries.

Roll-Up   a data cube operator that supports navigation from a more specific level of a dimension to a more general level of a dimension. The roll-up operator requires a hierarchical dimension. See also drill-down.

Row Condition   a comparison not involving an aggregate function. Row conditions are evaluated in the WHERE clause.

Rules about Referenced Rows   rules that describe actions on related rows when a row in a primary key table (the referenced row) is deleted or its primary key is updated.

S

Save Point   an intermediate point in a transaction in which a rollback may occur. Save points are supported by proprietary SQL extensions and by the new SQL3 standard.

Schema   a definition of the conceptual, external, or internal parts of a database. At the conceptual level, a schema is a diagram depicting the entities and relationships in a database. See also the Three Schema Architecture, external view, conceptual schema, and internal schema.

Schema Mapping   describes how a schema at a higher level is derived from a schema at a lower level. A mapping provides the knowledge to convert a request from a higher schema representation to a lower schema representation. See also Three Schema Architecture and schema.

Second Generation Database Technology   the first true DBMSs that managed multiple entity types and relationships. However, to obtain access to data, a computer program still had to be written. Second generation database technology was largely developed during the 1970s.

Second Normal Form (2NF)   a table is in 2NF if every nonkey column is dependent on the whole key, not part of the key.

Self-Join   a join between a table and itself (two copies of the same table). Typically, a self-join is used to query self-referencing relationships.

Self-Referencing Relationship   a relationship involving the same table or entity type. Self-referencing relationships represent associations among members of the same set. Also known as a unary, reflexive, or recursive relationship.

Semi-Join Operator   an operator of relational algebra that is especially useful for distributed database processing. A semi-join is half of a join: the rows of one table that match with at least one row of another table.

Sequential File   a simple file organization in which records are stored in insertion order or by key value. Sequential files are simple to maintain and provide good performance for processing large numbers of records.

Server   a program that processes requests on behalf of a client. A database server may interpret SQL statements, locate data, update tables, check integrity rules, and return data back to clients.

Server-Side Connectivity   an approach to Web database connectivity in which a browser communicates with a database server without invoking an external program. Although server-side connectivity is more scalable than the Common Gateway Interface, it requires a specialized Web server or a separate middleware server.

Shared   a fundamental characteristic of databases. Shared means that a database can have multiple uses and users. A large database may have hundreds of functions that use it as well as thousands of users simultaneously accessing it.

Shared Lock   a lock that allows other users to read a database item but prevents other users from changing the value of a database item. Shared locks conflict with exclusive locks but not other shared locks. A shared lock indicates that a user will read but not change the value of a database item. Also known as an S lock.

Simple Synthesis Procedure   a set of steps to produce tables in BCNF using a collection of functional dependencies. The simple synthesis procedure is limited to simple dependency structures.

Slice   a data cube operator in which a dimension is replaced by a single member value or with a summary of its member values. See also dice.

Snowflake Schema   a relational database representation for multidimensional databases. A snowflake schema has multiple fact tables related to dimension tables. Use the snowflake schema instead of the star schema for large dimension tables with hierarchical dimensions. See also star schema, fact table, and dimension table.

Sparsity   the extent of empty cells in a data cube. If a large number of cells are empty, the data cube can waste space and be slow to process. Special compression techniques can be used to reduce the size of sparse data cubes. Sparsity can be a problem if two or more dimensions are related such as products and regions where products are sold. See also data cube.

Specialized Media Server Architecture   an architecture for object databases in which a dedicated server manages complex data outside of a database. Programmers use an application programming interface to access complex data.

SQL   an acronym for the Structured Query Language. SQL is an industry standard database language that includes statements for database definition (such as the CREATE TABLE statement), database manipulation (such as the SELECT statement), and database control (such as the GRANT statement). SQL began as a proprietary language developed by IBM. SQL is now a widely supported international standard for databases. The current standard, SQL2, was adopted in 1992. The new standard, SQL3, was approved in late 1999.

SQL3   the new standard of the Structured Query Language. SQL3 supports numerous extensions beyond SQL2. An important extension is support for object relational databases. The SQL3 standard is so large that it may not be implemented for a number of years after its 1999 release.

Standalone SQL   using a specialized editor that submits SQL statements directly to the DBMS and displays the results returned from the DBMS. See also embedded SQL.

Star Schema   a relational database representation for multidimensional databases. A star schema has a fact table in the center related to multiple dimension tables. See also snowflake schema, fact table, and dimension table.

Stored Procedure   a collection of statements that are managed by a DBMS. Stored procedures extend the capabilities of SQL. Most DBMSs provide a proprietary language in which to write stored procedures.

Stripe   the set of physical records that can be read or written in parallel in RAID storage. Normally, a stripe contains a set of adjacent physical records.

Striping   a technique for allocating physical records in RAID storage so that parallel read and write operations are possible.

Strong Type Checking   the ability to ensure that expressions contain no incompatibility errors. Strong type checking is an important kind of error checking for object-oriented coding.

Subform   the variable or repeating part of a hierarchical form. The subform can show multiple records at a time.

Subquery   see nested query.

Subtype   a child entity type in a generalization hierarchy. A subtype represents a more specialized entity type than its supertype.

Summarize   an operator of relational algebra that compresses the rows of a table. A summarize operation produces a table with rows that summarize the rows of the input table. Aggregate functions are used to summarize the rows of the input table.

Superkey   a column or combination of columns containing unique values for each row. The combination of every column in a table is always a superkey because rows in a table must be unique.

Supertype   a parent entity type in a generalization hierarchy. A supertype represents a more general entity type than its subtypes.

System   a set of related components that work together to accomplish some objectives.

T

Table   a named, two-dimensional arrangement of data. A table consists of a heading part and a body part.

Table Body   synonymous with the rows of a table.

Table Heading   consists of the table name, the column names, and a data type for each column.

Table Profile   a statistical summary of the rows, columns, and participating relationships of a table. Table profiles are an important input of the physical database design phase because they are used to predict the fraction of a table accessed in a query.

Ternary Relationship   a relationship involving three entity types. In some ERD notations such as the Crow's Foot notation, a ternary relationship is represented as an associative entity type with three 1-M relationships.

Third Generation Database Technology   relational DBMSs incorporating nonprocedural access, optimization technology, and transaction processing capabilities. Third generation database technology was largely commercialized during the 1980s.

Third Normal Form (3NF)   a table is in 3NF if it is in 2NF and every nonkey column is dependent only on the key.

Three Schema Architecture   an architecture for compartmentalizing database descriptions. The Three Schema Architecture contains the external or user level, the conceptual level, and the internal or physical level. The Three Schema Architecture was proposed as a way to achieve data independence.

Three-Tier Architecture   a client–server architecture with three layers: a PC client, a backend database server, and either a middleware or an application server. See also two-tier architecture and multiple-tier architecture.

Three-Tier Data Warehouse Architecture   an architecture for a data warehouse in which user departments access data marts rather than the data warehouse. An extraction process involving the data warehouses periodically refreshes the data marts. See also two-tier data warehouse architecture and bottom-up data warehouse architecture.

Timesharing   a computer network in which computer terminals are connected to a mainframe computer. Timesharing supports only small amounts of data transmitted between a mainframe computer and terminals.

Traditional Set Operators   the union, intersection, and difference operators of relational algebra are known as the traditional set operators.

Transaction   a unit of work that should be processed reliably. DBMSs provide recovery and concurrency control services to process transactions efficiently and reliably.

Transaction Boundary   an important decision of transaction design in which an application consisting of a collection of SQL statements is divided into one or more transactions. Transaction boundary decisions can affect (positively or negatively) transaction throughput.

Transaction Log   a table that contains a history of all database changes. The recovery manager uses the log to recover from failures.

Transaction Processing   reliable and efficient processing of large volumes of repetitive work. DBMSs ensure that simultaneous users do not interfere with each other and that failures do not cause lost work. See also transaction.

Transaction-Processing Monitor   an early and still important kind of database middleware. A transaction-processing monitor receives transactions, schedules them, and manages them to completion. Transaction-processing monitors also may support updating multiple databases in a single transaction.

Transaction Throughput   the number of transactions processed per time interval. It is an important measure of transaction processing performance. Typically, transaction throughput is reported in transactions per minute.

Transitive Dependency   a functional dependency derived by the law of transitivity. Transitive FDs should not be recorded as input to the normalization process. See also functional dependency and law of transitivity.

Trigger   a rule that is stored and executed by the database rule system. Because triggers typically involve an event, a condition, and an action, they are sometimes known as event–condition–action rules. Triggers are not part of SQL2 but many vendors provide extensions for them. Triggers are part of SQL3.

Two Phase Commit Protocol (2PC)   a rule to ensure that distributed transactions are atomic. 2PC uses a voting and a decision phase to coordinate commits of local transactions.

Two Phase Locking Protocol (2PL)   a rule to ensure that concurrent transactions do not interfere with each other. 2PL requires that locks are used before reading or writing a database item and locks are not released until end of transaction.

Two-Tier Architecture   a client–server architecture in which a PC client and a database server interact directly to request and transfer data. The PC client contains the user interface code, the server contains the data access logic, and the PC client and the server share the validation and business logic. See also three-tier architecture and multiple-tier architecture.

Two-Tier Data Warehouse Architecture   an architecture for a data warehouse in an organization in which user departments directly use the data warehouse rather than smaller data marts. See also three-tier data warehouse architecture and bottom-up data warehouse architecture.

Type I Nested Query   a nested query in which the inner query does not reference any tables used in the outer query. Type I nested queries can be used for some join problems and some difference problems.

Type II Nested Query   a nested query in which the inner query references a table used in the outer query. Type II nested queries can be used for difference problems but should be avoided for join problems.

U

Uncommitted Dependency   a concurrency control problem in which one transaction reads data written by another transaction before the other transaction commits. If the second transaction aborts, the first transaction has read phantom data that will no longer exist. Also known as a dirty read.

Uniform Value Assumption   assuming that each column value is equally likely (has the same number of rows). The uniform value assumption allows compact representation of a distribution, but it can lead to large estimation errors that lead to poor choices in query optimization and index selection.

Union   an operator of relational algebra that combines rows from two tables. The result of a union operation has all the rows from either table. Both tables must be union compatible to use the union operator.

Union Compatibility   a requirement for the union, intersection, and difference operators of relational algebra. Union compatibility requires that both tables must have the same number of columns and each corresponding column must have the same data type.

Updatable View   a view that can be used in SELECT statements as well as UPDATE, INSERT, and DELETE statements. When modifying the rows of an updatable view, the DBMS translates the view modifications into modifications to rows of the base tables.

V

View   virtual or derived table. A view is derived from base or physical tables using a query.

View Materialization   a method to process a query on a view by executing the query defining the view followed by the query using the view.

View Modification   a method to process a query on a view involving the execution of only one query. A query using a view is translated into a query using base tables by replacing references to the view with its definition.

Volatile Storage   storage that loses its state when the power is disconnected. Main memory is typically volatile. Nonvolatile storage does not lose its state when power is disconnected. A hard disk is an example of nonvolatile storage.

W

Waterfall Model   a reference framework for information systems development. The waterfall model consists of iteration among analysis, design, and implementation.

Weak Entity   an entity type that borrows all or part of its primary key from another entity type. A weak entity is also existent dependent. See also identification dependency and identifying relationship.

Web Database Connectivity   client–server architectures that allow a Web page to query and update remote databases managed by servers on the Internet.

WITH CHECK OPTION   a clause in the CREATE VIEW statement that can be used to prevent updates with side effects. If the WITH CHECK OPTION is specified, INSERT or UPDATE statements that violate a view's WHERE clause are rejected.

Workflow   a collection of related tasks structured to accomplish a business process.

World Wide Web (WWW)   a collection of pages that can be viewed over the Internet. In the WWW, a browser displays pages sent by a Web server. The WWW is the most popular application on the Internet.

Write Ahead Log Protocol   in the immediate update recovery process, log records must be written to stable storage before database records.

X

XML (eXtensible Markup Language)   a language for defining the structure and the content of documents on the World Wide Web. XML supports the development of industry-specific standards for document content and structure.

XSL (eXtensible Style Language)   a language for defining the format of documents on the World Wide Web. XSL supports the transformation of XML documents into HTML and other layout languages. XSL allows device-dependent layout of Web documents.

Elmasri, R., and S. Navathe. *Fundamentals of Database Systems.* 3rd ed. Redwood City, CA: Benjamin Cummins, 1999.

Ensor, D., and D. Stevenson. *Oracle Design.* Sebastopol, CA: O'Reilly and Associates, 1997.

Fagin, R. "A Normal Form for Relational Databases That Is Based on Domains and Keys." *ACM Transactions on Database Systems* 6, no. 3 (September 1981).

Fernandez, E.; R. Summers; and C. Wood. *Database Security and Integrity.* Reading, MA: Addison-Wesley, 1981.

Finkelstein, S.; M. Schkolnick; and T. Tiberio. "Physical Database Design for Relational Databases." *ACM Transactions on Database Systems* 13, no. 1 (March 1988), pp. 91–128.

Fowler, M., and K. Scott. *UML Distilled.* Reading, MA: Addison-Wesley, 1997.

Gardner, S. "Building the Data Warehouse." *Communications of the ACM* 41, no. 9 (September 1998), pp. 52–57.

Gibson, M.; C. Hughes; W. Remington. "Tracking the Trade-Offs with Inverted Lists." *Database Programming and Design* 2, no. 1 (January 1989), pp. 28–34.

Gillette, R.; D. Muench; and J. Tabaka. *Physical Database Design for Sybase SQL Server.* Upper Saddle River, NJ: Prentice Hall, 1996.

Graefe, G. "Options for Physical Database Design." *ACM SIGMOD Record* 22, no. 3 (September 1993), pp. 76–83.

Gray, J., and A. Reuter. *Transaction Processing: Concepts and Techniques.* San Francisco, CA: Morgan Kaufmann, 1993.

Groff, J., and P. Weinberg. *SQL: The Complete Reference.* New York: Osborne McGraw Hill, 1999.

Guimaraes, T. "Information Resources Management: Improving the Focus." *Information Resources Management Journal* 1 (Fall 1988), pp. 10–21.

Gulutzan, P., and T. Pelzer. *SQL-99 Complete, Really.* Lawrence, KS: R & D Books, 1999.

Hackathorn, R., and J. Karimi. "A Framework for Comparing Information Engineering Methods." *MIS Quarterly* 12, no. 2 (June 1988), pp. 203–219.

Hawryszkiewycz, I. *Database Analysis and Design.* New York: SRA, 1984.

Inmon, W. *Information Systems Architecture.* New York: John Wiley & Sons, 1986.

Inmon, W. *Building the Data Warehouse.* 2nd ed. New York: John Wiley & Sons, 1996.

International Standards Organization. ISO/IEC JTC1/SC21 N10489, ISO//IEC 9075, Part 8. Committee Draft (CD). Database Language SQL—Part 8: SQL/Object, July 1996.

International Standards Organization. *Database Language SQL—Part 1: Framework.* ISO Working Draft. May 1998. Available for download from ftp://jerry.ece.umassd.edu/isowg3/dbl/BASEdocs/public/.

International Standards Organization. *Database Language SQL—Part 2: Foundation.* ISO Working Draft. September 1998. Available for download from ftp://jerry.ece.umassd.edu/isowg3/dbl/BASEdocs/public/.

Jarke, M., and J. Koch. "Query Optimization in Database Systems." *ACM Computing Surveys* 16, no. 2 (June 1984), pp. 111–152.

Kent, W. "A Simple Guide to the Five Normal Forms in Relational Database Theory." *Communications of the ACM* 26, no. 2 (February 1983), pp. 120–125.

Kimball, R. "Dealing with Dirty Data." *DBMS* 9, no. 10 (September 1996), pp. 55–62.

Kimball, Ralph. *The Data Warehouse Lifecycle Toolkit.* New York: John Wiley & Sons, 1998.

Mannino, M.; P., Chu; and T. Sager. "Statistical Profile Estimation in Database Systems." *ACM Computing Surveys* 20, no. 3 (September 1988), pp. 191–221.

Manola, F., and G. Mitchell. "A Comparison of Object Models in ODBMS-Related Standards." *IEEE Data Engineering Bulletin* 17, no. 4 (December 1994), pp. 27–35.

Martin, J. *Strategic Data-Planning Methodologies.* Englewood Cliffs, NJ: Prentice Hall, 1982.

Melton, J., "Object Technology and SQL: Adding Objects to a Relational Language." *IEEE Data Engineering Bulletin* 17, no. 4 (December 1994), pp. 15–26.

Melton, J., and A. Simon. *Understanding the New SQL: A Complete Guide.* San Mateo, CA: Morgan-Kauffman, 1992.

Muller, R. *Database Design for Smarties—Using UML for Data Modeling.* San Francisco, CA: Morgan Kaufmann, 1999.

Nelson, M., and L. DeMichiel. "Recent Trade-Offs in SQL3." *ACM SIGMOD Record* 23, no. 4 (December 1994), pp. 84–89.

Nijssen, G., and T. Halpin. *Conceptual Schema and Relational Database Design.* Prentice Hall of Australia, 1989.

Orfali, R.; D. Harkey; and J. Edwards. *The Essential Client/Server Survival Guide.* 2nd ed. New York: John Wiley and Sons, 1996.

Ozsu, T., and P. Valduriez. *Principles of Distributed Database Systems.* Englewood Cliffs, NJ: Prentice Hall, 1991.

Peinl, P.; A. Reuter; and H. Sammer. "High Contention in a Stock Trading Database: A Case Study." In *Proceedings of the ACM SIGMOD Conference,* Chicago, IL: May 1988, pp. 260–268.

Prusak, L., ed. *Knowledge in Organizations.* Boston, MA: Butterworth-Heinemann, 1997.

Redman, T. *Data Quality: Management and Technology.* New York: Bantam Books, 1992.

Rodgers, U. "Denormalization: Why, What, and How?" *Database Programming and Design* 2, no. 12 (December 1989), pp. 46–53.

Saaty, T. *The Analytic Hierarchy Process.* New York: McGraw-Hill, 1988.

Schumacher, R. "Oracle Performance Strategies." *DBMS* 10 (1994), pp. 89–93.

Scott, J. "Warehousing over the Web." *Communications of the ACM* 41, no. 9 (September 1998), pp. 64–65.

Sheth, A.; D. Georgakopoulos; and M. Hornrick. "An Overview of Workflow Management: From Process Modeling to

Workflow Automation Infrastructure." *Distributed and Parallel Databases* 3 (1995), pp. 119–153.

Sigal, M. "A Common Sense Development Strategy." *Communications of the ACM* 41, no. 9 (September 1998), pp. 42–48.

Stonebraker, M., with D. Moore. *Object Relational DBMSs: The Next Great Wave.* San Francisco, CA: Morgan Kauffman, 1996.

Strong, D.; Y. Lee; and R. Wang. "10 Potholes in the Road to Information Quality." *IEEE Computer* 30, no. 8 (August 1997), pp. 38–46.

Su, S.; J. Dujmovic; D. Batory; S. Navathe; and R. Elnicki. "A Cost-Benefit Decision Model: Analysis, Comparison, and Selection of Data Management Systems." *ACM Transactions on Database Systems* 12, no. 3 (September 1987), pp. 472–520.

Sutter, J. "Project-Based Warehouses." *Communications of the ACM* 41, no. 9 (September 1998), pp. 49–51.

Teorey, T. *Database Modeling and Design.* 3rd ed. San Francisco, CA: Morgan Kauffman, 1999.

Teorey, T., and J. Fry. *Design of Database Structures.* Englewood Cliffs, NJ: Prentice Hall, 1982.

Ullman, J. *Principles of Database and Knowledge Base Systems.* Vol. I. Rockville, MD: Computer Science Press, 1988.

Viehman, P. "24 Ways to Improve Database Performance." *Database Programming and Design* 7, no. 2 (February 1994), pp. 32–41.

Watson, H., and B. Haley. "Managerial Considerations." *Communications of the ACM* 41, no. 9 (September 1998), pp. 32–37.

Watson, R. *Data Management: An Organizational Perspective.* New York: John Wiley & Sons, 1996.

Weldon, J. *Data Base Administration.* New York: Plenum Press, 1981.

Whitten, J., and L. Bentley. *Systems Analysis and Design Methods.* New York: Irwin/McGraw-Hill, 2001.

Zahedi, F. "The Analytic Hierarchy Process: A Survey of the Method and Its Applications." *Interfaces* 16, no. 4 (1986), pp. 96–108.

WEB RESOURCES

CASE Tools for Database Development

PowerDesigner: http://www.sybase.com/products/powerdesigner/

Oracle Designer: http://www.oracle.com/tools/designer/index.html

Visio 2000 Enterprise: http://www.visio.com/visio2000/enterprise/

ER *win:* http://www.cai.com/products/platinum/appdev/erwin_ps.htm

ER/Studio: http://www.embarcadero.com/products/Design/design.htm

Visible Analyst: http://www.visible.com/dataapp/dappprods/vaw.htm

Client–Server Architectures

George Schusel article: http://www.dciexpo.com/geos/dbsejava.htm

Overview of Client/Server Software Architectures by Software Engineering Institute:
http://www.sei.cmu.edu/str/descriptions/clientserver.html

Middleware Overview by Software Engineering Institute:
http://www.sei.cmu.edu/str/descriptions/middleware_body.html

Datamation middleware articles (search on middleware):

http://datametron.earthweb.com

Data Mining

Data Mining and Knowledge Discovery Journal:
http://www.research.microsoft.com/datamine/

Data Mining for Competitive Advantage:
http://www.Datamindcorp.com/paper_advantage.html

Swami, A. "Data Mining with Silicon Graphics Technology." Silicon Graphics White
Paper: http://www.sgi.com/Technology/data-mining.html

Data Mining, Web Mining, and Knowledge Discovery Resources:
http://www.kdnuggets.com/

Glossary of Data Mining Terms by Pilot Software:
http://www.pilotsw.com/r_and_t/whtpaper/datamine/dmglos.htm

INDEX

A

Access; *see* Microsoft Access
Access control
   discretionary, 393–394, 395
   mandatory, 394
Access plans, 334–335
ACID properties, 420–421, 441–442
Aggregate functions, 48, 74–75, 141–142
Analysis tools, 204–205
Analyst/programmers, 19
Analytic hierarchy process, 404–406
AND operator, 71–72
Anomalies
   deletion, 265
   insertion, 264–265
   modification, 264–265
   update, 265
Application development, 7, 10–11
Application profiles, 321–322
Associative entity types, 221–223
Atomic property, 420
Attributes, 213
AVG function, 74

B

Backups of databases, 431
BCNF (Boyce-Codd normal form),
   271–273
BEGIN TRANSACTION statement,
   419–420
BETWEEN-AND operator, 70
Binary large objects (BLOBs), 534
Binding, 532–533
BLOBs (binary large objects), 534
Body of tables, 26
BOOLEAN data type, 27
Bottom-up data warehouse architecture,
   456–457, 459

Boyce-Codd normal form (BCNF),
   271–273
Btree (multiway tree) files, 326–331
B+tree files, 328, 331

C

Candidate keys, 30, 269
Cardinality of relationships, 213–216
CASE tools; *see* Computer-aided software
   engineering (CASE) tools
Catalog tables, 400–401
CGI (Common Gateway Interface),
   499–500
CHAR data type, 27
CHECK constraint clause, 397–398,
   415–416
Checkpoint tables, 430–431
Chen notation, 228, 229
Ciphertext, 394
Class diagrams, 260–262
Classes
   as collections of objects, 528–531
   of data cubes, 463
Client-server database architectures; *see*
   also Distributed databases
   definition of, 17, 490
   design issues, 490–492
   distributed processing and, 17–18
   introduction to, 490
   multiple-tier, 494–496
   three-tier, 493–494
   two-tier, 492–493
Client-side connectivity, 501–502
Clients, 17, 487
Clustering indexes, 336–337
Codd, Dr. Ted, 62–63
Columns, matching, 85
Combined measure of database
   performance, 318

Combined primary keys, 32
COMMIT statement, 419–420
Common Gateway Interface (CGI), 499–500
Comparison operators, 68
Completeness constraints, 226
Composite primary keys, 32
Computer-aided software engineering
   (CASE) tools
   analysis tools, 204–205
   commercial, 205–208
   diagramming tools, 204
   documentation tools, 204
   introduction to, 203–204
   prototyping tools, 205
Computer-oriented workflows, 440
Conceptual data modeling, 197–198,
   200–201
Conceptual schemas, 16
Concurrency control
   distributed, 515–516
   interference problems, 422–424, 425
   introduction to, 422
   objective of, 422
   optimistic, 428
   tools, 424–428
Concurrency transparency, 421
Connectivity
   client-side, 501–502
   server-side, 500–501
Consistent property, 421
CONSTRAINT clause, 31–34, 36–37
Constraint timing clause, 451
Constraints
   completeness, 226
   deferred constraint checking, 438–439
   disjointness, 225–226
   foreign key (FK), 265
   integrity, 395–398
   primary key (PK), 265
   value-based, 265
   value-neutral, 265

COUNT function, 74–75, 134–138
CREATE ASSERTION statement,
    396–397, 415
CREATE DOMAIN statement, 395–396,
    415
CREATE FRAGMENT statement,
    508–509
CREATE INDEX statement, 342, 354
CREATE TABLE statement
    CHECK constraints, 397–398
    CONSTRAINT clause, 31–34, 36–37
    introduction to, 27, 28
    SQL2 syntax, 59–60
    SQL3 use, 542–545
    Student Loan Limited database, 380–383
    university database, 57–58
CREATE TRIGGER statement, 398–399
CREATE TYPE statement, 540–542, 544
CREATE VIEW statement, 155–156,
    161–162, 163, 186
Cross product style, 85–89
Crow's Foot notation, 212–213, 214, 228
CUBE operator, 468

D

DAs; see Data administrators (DAs)
Data
    complex, 526–527
    multidimensional representation of
        data cube operators, 465–468
        data cubes, 460–464
        introduction to, 460
        key terminology, 462–463
        multidimensional database
            technologies, 469–472
        relational data modeling for
            multidimensional data, 468–469,
            470
        time-series data, 464
    time-series, 464
Data administrators (DAs)
    definition of, 390
    environment management
        data warehouse processing, 407–408
        distributed environments, 408, 409
        object database management, 408–409
        transaction processing, 407
    introduction to, 20–21
    processes for
        data planning, 402–403
        introduction to, 401
        selection and evaluation of DBMSs,
            403–406
Data cubes, 460–464
    operators for, 465–468
Data dictionary manipulation, 400–401,
    402
Data Encryption Standard, 394

Data extraction, 475–477
Data independence
    definition of, 15
    Three Schema Architecture and, 15–17
Data marts, 456
Data mining, 457–459
Data modeling, 197–198, 200–201; see
    also Entity relationship diagrams
    (ERDs); Relationships; Unified
    Modeling Language (UML) class
    diagrams
Data models
    enterprise (EDW), 391–392, 456
    introduction to, 195
Data planning, 402–403
Data types, 27
Data warehouses
    basic concepts
        applications, 459–460
        architectures, 456–457, 458, 459
        characteristics, 455–456
        data mining, 457–459
        introduction to, 454
        transaction processing versus decision
            support, 454
    building
        data extraction, 475–477
        introduction to, 472
        logical and physical design, 473–474
        practical considerations, 477–478
        requirements specification, 472–473
    data specialist responsibilities, 408
    definition of, 455
    introduction to, 407
    maintaining
        introduction to, 478
        query phase, 478–479
        refresh phase, 479
    multidimensional representation of data
        data cube operators, 465–468
        data cubes, 460–464
        introduction to, 460
        key terminology, 462–463
        multidimensional database
            technologies, 469–472
        relational data modeling for
            multidimensional data, 468–469,
            470
        time-series data, 464
    operational databases versus, 455–456
Database administration tools
    data dictionary manipulation, 400–401,
        402
    integrity constraints, 395–398
    introduction to, 392
    security, 392–395
    triggers and stored procedures, 398–400
Database administrators (DBAs)
    definition of, 390–391
    environment management

data warehouse processing, 407–408
    distributed environments, 408, 409
    object database management, 408–409
    transaction processing, 407
introduction to, 19, 20
joint application requirement (JAR)
    sessions with, 472–473
processes for
    data planning, 402–403
    introduction to, 401
    selection and evaluation of DBMSs,
        403–406
Database definition, 7–8
Database design; see Logical database
    design; Physical database design;
    Student Loan Limited database design
Database development; see also
    Information systems
    goals of
        business rule definition, 195–196
        common vocabulary, 195
        data quality, 196–197
        efficient implementation, 197
        introduction to, 195
    phases of
        conceptual data modeling, 197–198,
            200–201
        cross checking with application
            development, 201, 202
        distributed database design, 199–200
        introduction to, 197, 198
        logical database design, 198–199
        physical database design, 200
        splitting conceptual design for large
            projects, 200–201
    skills in, 201–203
    tools of; see Computer-aided software
        engineering (CASE) tools
Database management
    environments
        data warehouse processing, 407–408
        distributed environments, 408, 409
        introduction to, 407
        object database management, 408–409
        transaction processing, 407
    organizational context for
        database support for management
            decision-making, 388–389
        information management to
            knowledge management,
            389–390
        introduction to, 388
        responsibilities of data administrators
            and database administrators,
            390–392
    processes for data specialists, 401
    processes for database specialists
        data planning, 402–403
        selection and evaluation of DBMSs,
            403–406

tools of database administration
  data dictionary manipulation,
    400–401, 402
  integrity constraints, 395–398
  introduction to, 392
  security, 392–395
  triggers and stored procedures,
    398–400
Database management systems (DBMSs)
  architectures
    data independence and the Three
      Schema Architecture, 15–17
    distributed processing and the client-
      server architecture, 17–18
    introduction to, 15
  definition of, 7
  desktop, 12
  enterprise, 12
  features
    application development, 7, 10–11
    database definition, 7–8
    database tuning, 7, 12
    introduction to, 7
    nonprocedural access, 7, 8–10
    procedural language interface, 7, 11
    transaction processing, 7, 11
  object-oriented, 538–539
  programming languages versus, 533–534
  selection and evaluation of, 403–406
  third-party software for, 12
Database performance, 318
Database security, 392–395
Database software market, 14–15
Database technology
  development of, 12–14
  organizational impacts of, 18–21
Database tuning, 7, 12
Databases; *see also* Distributed databases;
    Hospital database; Object databases;
    Relational databases; University
    database; Water utility database
  backups of, 431
  characteristics, 4–6
  definition of, 4
  interacting with, 18–19
  interrelated characteristic, 5
  operational, 388
    data warehouses versus, 455–456
  persistent characteristic, 4
  shared characteristic, 4
  storage level of, 316–317
DATE/TIME data type, 27
DB2 syntax differences with other
  products, 114
DBAs; *see* Database administrators
  (DBAs)
DBMSs; *see* Database management
  systems (DBMSs)
Deadlocks, 426–427
DECIMAL data type, 27

Decision support versus transaction
  processing, 454
Deferred constraint checking, 438–439
Deferred update approach, 433–434
DELETE statement, 96, 97, 113
Deletion anomalies, 265
Denormalization, 282, 342–344, 373–374
Dependencies
  existence, 214
  functional dependencies (FDs), 265–267
  identification, 217–218
  multivalued dependencies (MVDs),
    279–280
  relationship independence, 276–279
  transitive, 270
  uncommitted, 423–424
Desktop database management systems
  (DBMSs), 12
Desktop OLAP (DOLAP), 471
Determinant (left-hand side (LHS)), 266
Diagramming tools, 204
Dice data cube operator, 465–466, 467
Difference operator, 45–48, 51, 52
Dimension tables, 468–469
Dimensions of data cubes, 462
Dirty reads, 423–424
Discretionary access control, 393–394, 395
Disjointness constraints, 225–226
DISTINCT keyword, 74–75, 78, 79, 137
Distributed databases; *see also* Client-
    server database architectures
  architectures for distributed DBMSs
    component architecture, 502–505
    introduction to, 502
    schema architectures, 505–507
  data specialist responsibilities, 408, 409
  design, 199–200
  distributed database processing
    client-server architecture and, 17–18
    distributed query processing, 513–515
    distributed transaction processing,
      515–517
    introduction to, 513
  introduction to, 408
  overview of distributed processing and
      distributed data
    evolution, 486–488
    introduction to, 486
    motivation for distributed data,
      489–490
    motivation for distributed processing,
      488–489
    summary of advantages and
      disadvantages, 490
  transparency for distributed database
      processing
    fragmentation transparency, 509–510
    introduction to, 507
    local mapping transparency, 511–513
    location transparency, 510–511

  motivating example, 507–509
  Web database connectivity
    client-side connectivity, 501–502
    definition of, 496
    Internet basics, 496–499
    introduction to, 496
    server-side connectivity, 500–501
    summary of, 502, 503
Distributed object management, 440–441
Divide operator, 49–50, 51, 52, 133; *see
    also* Division problems
Division problems
  Access formulation of, 150
  advanced, 136–138
  introduction to, 133
  review of the divide operator, 133–134
  simple, 134–136
DKNF (domain key normal form), 281
Documentation tools, 204
DOLAP (Desktop OLAP), 471
Domain key normal form (DKNF), 281
Drill-down data cube operator, 466, 467
Drill-up (roll-up) data cube operator, 465,
    466, 467
DROP ASSERTION statement, 415
DROP DOMAIN statement, 415
DROP INDEX statement, 354
DROP VIEW statement, 186
Durable property, 421

E

EDW (enterprise data model), 391–392,
    456
Embedded context, 64
Encapsulation, 528–530
Encryption, 394
Enterprise data model (EDW), 391–392,
    456
Enterprise database management systems
  (DBMSs), 12
Enterprise models, 402–403
Entities
  definition of, 5
  integrity of, 30, 31
  weak, 217–218
Entity relationship diagrams (ERDs); *see
    also* View design and integration
  basic symbols, 212–213
  Chen notation, 228, 229
  classification and
    disjointness and completeness
      constraints, 225–226
    generalization hierarchies, 225
    introduction to, 224–225
    multiple levels of generalization,
      226–227
  comparison to relational database
    diagrams, 216–217, 230

converting to relational tables
   basic conversion rules, 236–240, 241
   comprehensive conversion example, 245–248
   converting 1-1 relationships, 245, 246
   converting generalization hierarchies, 242–245
   converting optional 1-M relationships, 240–242
   introduction to, 235–236
  created with Visio Professional, 12
  Crow's Foot notation, 212–213, 214, 228
  diagram variations, 227–230
  introduction to, 197–198, 199, 212
  loan origination form, 361–362
  notation review, 227–230
  relationship cardinality, 213–216
  water utility database
   conversion to relational tables, 245–248
   database description, 230–231
   finalizing the ERD, 235
   initial ERD, 231–232
   introduction to, 230
   refinements to the initial ERD, 232–234
Entity types
  associative, 221–223
  definition of, 212
  subtypes, 225
  supertypes, 225
Environment interaction models, 195
Equi-join operator, 41
ERDs; *see* Entity relationship diagrams (ERDs)
Exact matching, 70
EXCEPT keyword, 94, 95, 129
Exclusive (X) locks, 424, 425
Existence dependencies, 214
EXISTS operator, 126–129
Expressions, 64
Extended cross product (product) operator, 39–40, 51, 52
  eXtensible Markup Language (XML), 498–499
  eXtensible Style Language (XSL), 498–499
External schemas, 16

F

Fact tables, 468–469
FDs (functional dependencies), 265–267
Fifth normal form (5NF), 280–281
File sharing, 486, 487
File structures
  hash files, 323–326
  introduction to, 322
  multiway tree (Btree) files, 326–331
  sequential files, 322–323
  summary of, 331–332

First-generation database technology, 13
First normal form (1NF), 268–269
FK (foreign key) constraints, 265
Flexibility, 488
FLOAT data type, 27
Force writing, 431
Foreign key (FK) constraints, 265
Foreign keys, 31, 33
Forms
  hierarchical
   definition of, 167
   introduction to, 167–168
   query formulation skills for, 169–173
   relationship between hierarchical forms and tables, 168–169
  introduction to, 10
  precedence relationships among, 306
  view design with
   analysis of M-way relationships using forms, 299–300, 302–303, 304
   form analysis, 293–299, 300, 301
   introduction to, 293
Forward engineering, 204
Fourth-generation database technology, 13, 14
Fourth normal form (4NF), 280
Fragmentation of schema architectures, 506–513
Fragmentation transparency, 509–510
FROM clause, 73
Full outer joins, 43, 44, 119–121
Functional dependencies (FDs), 265–267

G

Generalization hierarchies, 225
Grain of tables, 469
GRANT statement, 393–394, 415
GROUP BY clause, 74–77, 78, 468
Group conditions, expanded syntax for, 151
Grouping, combining joins and, 93–94
GROUPING SETS operator, 468

H

Hash files, 323–326
HAVING clause, 75; *see also* Nested queries
Headings for tables, 26
Hierarchical forms
  definition of, 167
  introduction to, 167–168
  query formulation skills for, 169–173
  relationship between hierarchical forms and tables, 168–169
Hierarchical reports
  definition of, 173

  introduction to, 173–175
  query formulation skills for, 175–176
Hierarchies of data cubes, 463
Histograms, 321
HOLAP (Hybrid OLAP), 471
Homonyms, 307
Hospital database, 6
Hot spots, 422, 435
HTML (Hypertext Markup Language), 497, 498–499
HTTP (Hypertext Transfer Protocol), 496–497
Human-oriented workflows, 440
Hybrid OLAP (HOLAP), 471
Hypertext Markup Language (HTML), 497, 498–499
Hypertext Transfer Protocol (HTTP), 496–497

I

IBM DB2 syntax differences with other products, 114
Identification dependencies, 217–218
Immediate update approach, 432–433
Incorrect summaries, 424, 425
Incremental approach to view integration, 304, 305, 307–309
Incremental integration in the Sudent Loan Limited database
  after adding the disclosure letter, 363–364
  after adding the loan activity report, 366–367
  after adding the statement of account, 364–365
Index selection
  introduction to, 336
  problem definition, 336–337, 338
  selection rules, 340–342
  Student Loan Limited database, 372–373
  trade-offs and difficulties, 337, 339–340
Indexes
  clustering, 336–337
  definition of, 336
  nonclustering, 337, 338
Indirect users, 19
Inexact matching, 69–70
Information life cycles, 389–390
Information resource dictionary (IRD), 401
Information resource dictionary system (IRDS), 401, 402
Information resource management, 19–21
Information systems; *see also* Database development
  components of, 192–193
  definition of, 192
  development process, 193–195
  planning, 402–403

Inheritance, 225, 530–531
Initial design approach to normalization,
    282
Inner joins, mixing with outer joins,
    121–123
INSERT statement, 96, 112
Insertion anomalies, 264–265
INTEGER data type, 27
Integration strategies for view integration,
    304–306
Integrity
    entity, 30, 31
    referential, 30, 31, 34–35
Integrity constraints, 395–398
Integrity rules
    applying, 31–34
    definition of, 30–31
    graphical representation of referential
        integrity, 34–35
    introduction to, 30
Intent locks, 426
Interacting with databases, 18–19
Internal schemas, 16
Internet, 496, 497; *see also* Web database
    connectivity
Internet Protocol (IP), 496
Interoperability, 489
Interrelated characteristic of databases, 5
INTERSECT keyword, 94, 95
Intersection operator, 45–48, 51, 52
Intranets, 496, 497
IP (Internet Protocol), 496
IRD (information resource dictionary), 401
IRDS (information resource dictionary
    system), 401, 402
Isolated property, 421
Isolation levels, 436–437

J

JAR (joint application requirement)
    sessions, 472–473
Join operator style, 89–91
Join views, updatable, Oracle rules for, 187
Joining tables
    with the cross product style, 85–89
    introduction to, 72–73
    multiple tables with the join operator
        style, 89–91
Joins
    combining joins and grouping, 93–94
    equi-join, 41
    full outer, 43, 44, 119–121
    inner, mixing with outer joins, 121–123
    introduction to, 41–43, 51, 52
    multiple, 91–92
    natural, 41–42
    one-sided outer, 44, 116–119, 121–123
    outer

expanded syntax for, 151
introduction to, 43–45, 46, 51, 52
mixing with inner joins, 121–123
SQL support for outer join problems,
    116–121
self-joins, 91–92
semi-join, 507
Joint application requirement (JAR)
    sessions, 472–473

K

Keys
    candidate, 30, 269
    combined primary, 32
    composite primary, 32
    in domain key normal form (DKNF),
        281
    foreign, 31, 33
    null values in, 30, 33
    potential primary, 266
    primary, 31, 32
    superkeys, 30
Knowledge management, 390

L

Large object architecture, 534–535
LEFT (OUTER) JOIN keyword, 116, 117,
    118
Left-hand side (determinant, LHS), 266
Life cycle for systems development,
    193–194
LIKE operator, 69–70
Local mapping transparency, 511–513
Location transparency, 510–511
Locking granularity, 425, 426
Locks
    deadlocks, 426–427
    exclusive (X), 424, 425
    intent, 426
    introduction to, 424–426
    shared (S), 424, 425
    Two Phase Locking (2PL) protocol,
        427–428
Logical database design, 198–199
Logical records, 316–317
Loosely integrated distributed DBMSs, 505
Lost updates, 422–423
Lower function (Oracle), 70

M

M-N relationships; *see* Many-to-many (M-
    N) relationships
M-way relationships; *see* Multiway (M-
    way) relationships

Maintenance phase, 193, 194
Managing databases; *see* Database
    management
Mandatory access control, 394
Mandatory relationships, 214
Many-to-many (M-N) relationships
    with attributes, 219–220
    equivalence between 1-M and M-N
        relationships, 223–224
    introduction to, 35
Market for database software, 14–15
Matching
    exact, 70
    inexact, 69–70
Matching columns, 85
MAX function, 74
Measures of data cubes, 462, 463
Members of data cubes, 462
Message-oriented middleware, 492
Microsoft Access
    combining cross product and join
        operator styles, 91
    combining grouping and joins, 77
    combining nested query and join
        operator style
        Type I nested query, 124
        Type II nested query, 127
    conditions on date columns, 71
    DELETE statement
        using join operator style, 97
        using INNER JOIN operation, 125
    division problem
        formulation, 150
        with a join, 136
    ERDs compared to relational database
        diagrams, 216–217, 230
    expressions in SELECT and WHERE
        clauses, 69
    form for assigning courses to faculty, 10
    full outer joins using a union of two one-
        sided outer joins, 120
    inexact matching with LIKE, 70
    join tables
        and show columns from both tables,
            73
        using a join operator in the FROM
            clause, 73
    joining tables using the join operator
        style
        two tables, 89
        three tables, 90
        four tables, 90
    mixing a one-sided outer join and inner
        joins
        one inner join, 121
        two inner joins, 122
    more difficult difference problem using a
        Type II nested query, 131–132
    multiple-table read-only query, 164–165
    multiple-table updatable query, 164

one-sided outer join
with only nonmatching rows, 119
using LEFT JOIN, 117
using RIGHT JOIN, 118
one-to-many (1-M) updatable query
with three tables, 166
with four tables, 166–167
Query Design window, 9
Relationship Definition window, 9
report of faculty workload, 11
syntax differences with other products, 114
Table Definition window, 8
Microsoft SQL Server syntax differences with other products, 114
Middleware, 491–492, 536, 537
MIN function, 74
MINUS keyword, 95, 129–130
Modification anomalies, 264–265
Modification statements in SQL, 96–97
Multidimensional OLAP (MOLAP), 470–471
Multiple joins, 91–92
Multiple-table updatable views, 164–167
Multiple-tier client-server architecture, 494–496
Multivalued dependencies (MVDs), 279–280
Multiway (M-way) relationships
analysis of, using forms, 299–300, 302–303, 304
associative entity types representing, 221–223
introduction to, 276
multivalued dependencies (MVDs) and fourth normal form (4NF), 279–280
relationship independence, 276–279
Multiway tree (Btree) files, 326–331
MVDs (multivalued dependencies), 279–280

N

Natural join operator, 41–42
Nested queries
definition of, 123
introduction to, 123
Type I, 123–125
Type II
definition of, 125
introduction to, 125–127
solving difference problems with, 127–133
Nonclustering indexes, 337, 338
Nonprocedural access, 7, 8–10
Nonvolatile memory, 429
Normalization of relational tables
definition of, 267
denormalization, 282, 342–344, 373–374

normal forms
Boyce-Codd normal form (BCNF), 271–273
definition of, 267
domain key normal form (DKNF), 281
fifth normal form (5NF), 280–281
first normal form (1NF), 268–269
fourth normal form (4NF), 280
introduction to, 267–268, 280
second normal form (2NF), 269–271
simple synthesis procedure, 273–276
third normal form (3NF), 269, 270–271, 272–273
practical concerns about
analyzing the normalization objective, 282–283
introduction to, 281–282
role of normalization in the database development process, 282
refining M-way relationships
introduction to, 276
multivalued dependencies (MVDs) and fourth normal form (4NF), 279–280
relationship independence, 276–279
refining the conceptual schema and, 369–370
relational database design overview
avoidance of modification anomalies, 264–265
functional dependencies (FDs), 265–267
introduction to, 264
NOT DEFERRABLE keyword, 438–439
NOT FINAL keyword, 540
Null values
effect on aggregate calculations and grouping, 141–142
effect on compound conditions, 139–141
effect on simple conditions, 138–139
introduction to, 138
in keys, 30, 33

O

Object Database Management Group (ODMG), 538, 539
Object database middleware, 536, 537
Object databases
architectures for object database management
introduction to, 534
large objects and external software, 534–535
object database middleware, 536, 537
object-oriented DBMSs, 538–539
object relational DBMSs for user-defined types, 536–538

specialized media servers, 535–536
summary of, 539–540
data specialist responsibilities, 409
introduction to, 408–409
motivation for object database management
application examples, 527–528
complex data, 526–527
introduction to, 526
type system mismatch, 527
object-oriented principles
encapsulation, 528–530
inheritance, 530–531
introduction to, 528
polymorphism, 531–533
programming languages versus DBMSs, 533–534
SQL3 database definition and manipulation
introduction to, 540, 541
manipulating complex objects and subtable families, 545–546
table definitions and subtable families, 542–545
user-defined types, 540–542
Object-oriented DBMSs, 538–539
Object-oriented principles
encapsulation, 528–530
inheritance, 225, 530–531
introduction to, 528
polymorphism, 531–533
programming languages versus DBMSs, 533–534
Object query language (OQL), 538
Object relational DBMSs, 536–538
Object-request brokers, 492
Objects, 528
ODMG (Object Database Management Group), 538, 539
OLAP (On-line Analytical Processing), 469–472
ON DELETE clause, 36–37
On-line Analytical Processing (OLAP), 469–472
ON UPDATE clause, 36–37
One-sided outer joins, 44, 116–119, 121–123
One-to-many (1-M) relationships
equivalence between 1-M and M-N relationships, 223–224
introduction to, 34–35
Operational databases, 388
data warehouses versus, 455–456
Operators; see also Joins
AND, 71–72
BETWEEN-AND, 70
comparison, 68
CUBE, 468
data cube, 465–468
difference, 45–48, 51, 52

divide, 49–50, 51, 52, 133; *see also*
  Division problems
EXISTS, 126–129
extended cross product (product), 39–40,
  51, 52
GROUPING SETS, 468
intersection, 45–48, 51, 52
LIKE, 69–70
OR, 71–72
project, 38–39, 51, 52
restrict (select), 38–39, 51, 52
ROLLUP, 468
set, 45–48, 51, 52, 94–95
summarize, 48–49, 51, 52
summary of, 50–52
union, 45–48, 51, 52
union compatibility, 47–48
Optimistic concurrency control, 428
OQL (object query language), 538
OR operator, 71–72
Oracle
  catalog tables, 401
  combining a nested query and the cross
    product style
    Type I nested query, 124
    Type II nested query, 127
  combining grouping and joins, 77
  conditions on date columns, 71
  counting rows and unique column
    values, 75
  difference query, 95, 129–130
  division problems
    with DISTINCT inside COUNT,
      137–138
    with a join, 136–137
  expressions in SELECT and WHERE
    clauses, 69
  full outer joins using a union of two one-
    sided outer joins, 121
  inexact matching with LIKE, 70
  INTERSECT query, 95
  join of the faculty and offering tables,
    339
  join tables and show columns from both
    tables, 73
  mixing a one-sided outer join and inner
    joins
    one inner join, 122
    two inner joins, 122–123
  more difficult difference problem using a
    Type II nested query, 132
  one-sided outer join
    with only nonmatching rows, 119
    using LEFT JOIN, 118
    using RIGHT JOIN, 118
  stored procedure, 399–400
  syntax differences with other products,
    114
  updatable join view rules, 187
ORDER BY clause, 77–78

Organizational impacts of database
  technology, 18–21
Outer joins
  expanded syntax for, 151
  introduction to, 43–45, 46, 51, 52
  mixing with inner joins, 121–123
  SQL support for outer join problems,
    116–121
OVERRIDING keyword, 541

P

Parallel approach to view integration, 304,
  305, 309
Parallel processing, 345–347
Parametric users, 19
Persistent characteristic of databases, 4
Phantom read problems, 424
Physical database design
  denormalization, 282, 342–344, 373–374
  file structures
    hash files, 323–326
    introduction to, 322
    multiway tree (Btree) files, 326–331
    sequential files, 322–323
    summary of, 331–332
  index selection
    introduction to, 336
    problem definition, 336–337, 338
    selection rules, 340–342
    Student Loan Limited database,
      372–373
    trade-offs and difficulties, 337,
      339–340
  inputs of
    application profiles, 321–322
    introduction to, 320
    table profiles, 320–321
  introduction to, 200
  other ways to improve performance, 347
  overview of
    difficulties, 320
    inputs, outputs, and environment,
      318–319
    objectives and constraints, 318
    storage level of databases, 316–317
  parallel processing, 345–347
  query optimization
    introduction to, 332
    optimization tips, 335–336
    translation tasks, 332–335
  record formatting, 344–345
  Redundant Arrays of Independent Disks
    (RAID), 345–347
  Student Loan Limited
    application and table profiles,
      370–372
    derived data and denormalization
      decisions, 373–374

    index selection, 372–373
    introduction to, 370
    other implementation decisions, 374
Physical records, 316–317
Pivot data cube operator, 467
PK (primary key) constraints, 265
Plaintext, 394
Polymorphism, 531–533
Potential primary keys, 266
Power users, 19
Precedence relationships among forms, 306
Preliminary investigation phase, 193, 194
Primary copy protocol, 516
Primary key (PK) constraints, 265
Primary keys, 31, 32
Procedural language interface, 7, 11
Process models, 195
Product (extended cross product) operator,
  39–40, 51, 52
Production data extract systems, 475
Programming languages versus DBMSs,
  533–534
Project operator, 38–39, 51, 52
Prototypes, 194
Prototyping tools, 205
Public-Key Encryption algorithm, 394

Q

Qualified names, 72
Query binding, 335
Query formulation; *see also* Nested
    queries; SELECT statement; Views
  critical questions for, 84–85
  division problems
    Access formulation of, 150
    advanced, 136–138
    introduction to, 133
    review of the divide operator,
      133–134
    simple, 134–136
  examples
    combining joins and grouping, 93–94
    joining multiple tables with the cross
      product style, 85–89
    joining multiple tables with the join
      operator style, 89–91
    self-joins and multiple joins between
      two tables, 91–92
    traditional set operators, 94–95
  hierarchical form skills, 169–173
  hierarchical report skills, 175–176
  null value considerations
    effect on aggregate calculations and
      grouping, 141–142
    effect on compound conditions,
      139–141
    effect on simple conditions, 138–139
    introduction to, 138

outer join problems
  introduction to, 116
  mixing inner and outer joins, 121–123
  SQL support for, 116–121
SQL modification statements, 96–97
subqueries, 151
Query optimization
  introduction to, 332
  optimization tips, 335–336
  translation tasks, 332–335
Query processing, distributed, 513–515

R

RAID (Redundant Arrays of Independent
    Disks), 345–347
READ COMMITTED keyword, 437
READ UNCOMMITTED keyword, 437
Record formatting, 344–345
Record-oriented terminology, 29–30
Records, 316–317
Recovery management
  data storage devices and failure types,
    429
  distributed, 516–517
  introduction to, 429
  processes, 431–434
  tools, 430–431
Recovery transparency, 421
Redo operations, 430
Redundant Arrays of Independent Disks
    (RAID), 345–347
Referenced rows, 35–37
Referential integrity, 30, 31, 34–35
Refinement approach to normalization, 282
Relational algebra, 37; see also Operators
Relational databases
  alternative terminology for, 29–30
  basic elements, 20; see also Integrity
    rules; Operators; Tables
  design overview
    avoidance of modification anomalies,
      264–265
    functional dependencies (FDs),
      265–267
    introduction to, 264
  ERD comparison to relational database
    diagrams, 216–217, 230
  object relational DBMSs, 536–538
Relational OLAP (ROLAP), 470
Relationship independence, 276–279
Relationships; see also Many-to-many (M-
    N) relationships; Multiway (M-way)
    relationships; One-to-many (1-M)
    relationships
  cardinality of, 213–216
  definition of, 28, 213
  identification dependency (weak entities
    and identifying relationships),
    217–218

introduction to, 5, 28–29
mandatory, 214
precedence, among forms, 306
self-referencing (unary), 34, 35,
    220–221
ternary, 222
Remote procedure calls, 486, 487
REPEATABLE READ keyword, 437
Reports
  hierarchical
    definition of, 173
    introduction to, 173–175
    query formulation skills for, 175–176
  introduction to, 10
Restrict (select) operator, 38–39, 51, 52
Reverse engineering, 204
REVOKE statement, 393, 394, 415
RIGHT (OUTER) JOIN keyword, 116, 118
ROLAP (Relational OLAP), 470
Roll-up (drill-up) data cube operator, 465,
    466, 467
ROLLBACK statement, 20, 429, 442
ROLLUP operator, 468
Rows
  expanded syntax for row conditions, 151
  referenced, 35–37

S

S (shared) locks, 424, 425
SAVEPOINT statement, 442
Scalability, 489
Schema architectures, 505–507
Schemas
  conceptual, 16
  definition of, 15–16
  external, 16
  internal, 16
  refining the conceptual schema
    introduction to, 367
    normalization, 369–370
    schema conversion, 367–368
  snowflake, 469, 470
Second-generation database technology, 13
Second normal form (2NF), 269–271
Security of databases, 392–395
Select (restrict) operator, 38–39, 51, 52
SELECT statement
  conceptual evaluation process for, 79–84
  improving the appearance of results,
    77–79
  introduction to, 64–66
  joining tables, 72–73
  single table problems, 66–72
  SQL2 syntax, 111–112, 151
  SQL3 use, 545–546
  summarizing tables with GROUP BY
    and HAVING, 74–77
  syntax differences among products, 114
  using views in, 156–158

Self-joins, 91–92
Self-referencing (unary) relationships, 34,
    35, 220–221
Semi-join operator, 507
SEQUEL language, 63
Sequential files, 322–323
SERIALIZABLE keyword, 437
Server-side connectivity, 500–501
Servers, 17, 487
SET CONSTRAINTS statement, 439, 451
Set operators, 45–48, 51, 52, 94–95
Set-oriented terminology, 29–30
SET TRANSACTION statement, 437, 452
Shared (S) locks, 424, 425
Shared characteristic of databases, 4
Single-table updatable views, 160–163
Slice data cube operator, 465, 466, 467
Snowflake schema, 469, 470
Specialized media server architecture,
    535–536
SQL; see Structured Query Language
    (SQL)
SQL Server syntax differences with other
    products, 114
SQUARE language, 62–63
Stand-alone context, 64
Standards for SQL, 63
Stored procedures, 399–400
Striping, 346, 347
Strong type checking, 533
Structured Query Language (SQL); see
    also Operators; Query formulation
  BEGIN TRANSACTION statement,
    419–420
  CHECK constraint clause, 397–398,
    415–416
  COMMIT statement, 419–420
  CONSTRAINT clause, 31–34, 36–37
  constraint timing clause, 451
  COUNT function, 74–75, 134–138
  CREATE ASSERTION statement,
    396–397, 415
  CREATE DOMAIN statement, 395–396,
    415
  CREATE INDEX statement, 342, 354
  CREATE TABLE statement
    CHECK constraint clause, 397–398,
      415–416
    CONSTRAINT clause, 31–34, 36–37
    introduction to, 27, 28
    SQL2 syntax, 59–60
    SQL3 use, 542–545
    Student Loan Limited database,
      380–383
    university database, 57–58
  CREATE TRIGGER statement, 398–399
  CREATE TYPE statement, 540–542,
    544
  CREATE VIEW statement, 155–156,
    161–162, 163, 186
  data types, 27

definition of, 8
DELETE statement, 96, 97, 113
DISTINCT keyword, 74–75, 78, 79, 137
DROP ASSERTION statement, 415
DROP DOMAIN statement, 415
DROP INDEX statement, 354
DROP VIEW statement, 186
EXCEPT keyword, 94, 95, 129
FROM clause, 73
GRANT statement, 393–394, 415
GROUP BY clause, 74–77, 78, 468
HAVING clause, 75; *see also* Nested
    queries
history of, 62–63
INSERT statement, 96, 112
INTERSECT keyword, 94, 95
introduction to, 8
MINUS keyword, 95, 129–130
modification statements, 96–97
NOT DEFERRABLE keyword, 438–439
NOT FINAL keyword, 540
ON DELETE clause, 36–37
ON UPDATE clause, 36–37
ORDER BY clause, 77–78
outer join problem support, 116–121
OVERRIDING keyword, 541
READ COMMITTED keyword, 437
READ UNCOMMITTED keyword, 437
refining the conceptual schema
    introduction to, 367
    schema conversion, 367–368
REPEATABLE READ keyword, 437
REVOKE statement, 393, 394, 415
ROLLBACK statement, 20, 429, 442
SAVEPOINT statement, 442
scope of, 63–64
SELECT statement
    conceptual evaluation process for,
        79–84
    improving the appearance of results,
        77–79
    introduction to, 64–66
    joining tables, 72–73
    single table problems, 66–72
    SQL2 syntax, 111–112, 151
    SQL3 use, 545–546
    summarizing tables with GROUP BY
        and HAVING, 74–77
    syntax differences among products,
        114
    using views in, 156–158
SERIALIZABLE keyword, 437
SET CONSTRAINTS statement, 439,
    451
SET TRANSACTION statement, 437,
    452
SQL3 database definition and
    manipulation
    introduction to, 540, 541
    manipulating complex objects and
        subtable families, 545–546

table definitions and subtable families,
    542–545
user-defined types, 540–542
standards, 63
UNDER keyword, 541
UNION keyword, 94, 95
UNIQUE keyword, 31, 32
UPDATE statement, 96–97, 113
usage contexts, 64
WHERE clause, 66–73, 75, 545–546;
    see also Nested queries
WITH CHECK OPTION clause, 163
Student Loan Limited database design
case description
    flow of work, 356–361
    introduction to, 356
    overview, 356
conceptual data modeling
    ERD for the loan origination form,
        361–362
    incremental integration after adding
        the disclosure letter, 363–364
    incremental integration after adding
        the loan activity report, 366–367
    incremental integration after adding
        the statement of account,
        364–365
    introduction to, 361
CREATE TABLE statements, 380–383
form and report fields, 377–379
physical database design
    application and table profiles,
        370–372
    derived data and denormalization
        decisions, 373–374
    index selection, 372–373
    introduction to, 370
    other implementation decisions, 374
    refining the conceptual schema, 369–370
Subqueries, 151
Subtypes, 225
SUM function, 74
Summarize operator, 48–49, 51, 52
Superkeys, 30
Supertypes, 225
Synonyms, 306–307
System-dependent hot spots, 435
System-independent hot spots, 435
Systems, 192
Systems analysis phase, 193, 194
Systems design phase, 193, 194
Systems implementation phase, 193, 194

T

Table-oriented terminology, 29–30
Table profiles, 320–321
Tables; *see also* Normalization of relational
    tables; Relationships; Views
    alternative terminology, 29–30

body of, 26
catalog, 400–401
checkpoint, 430–431
converting ERDs to
    basic conversion rules, 236–240, 241
    comprehensive conversion example,
        245–248
    converting 1-1 relationships, 245, 246
    converting generalization hierarchies,
        242–245
    converting optional 1-M relationships,
        240–242
    introduction to, 235–236
definition of, 7, 26
delete and update actions for referenced
    rows, 35–37
dimension, 468–469
fact, 468–469
grain of, 469
headings for, 26
introduction to, 26–29
joining
    introduction to, 72–73
    multiple tables with the cross product
        style, 85–89
    multiple tables with the join operator
        style, 89–91
    multiple joins between, 91–92
    referenced rows, 35–37
    relationship between hierarchical forms
        and, 168–169
    relationships among, 28–29
    self-joins between, 91–92
Task complexity, 440
Task structure, 440
TCP (Transmission Control Protocol),
    496
Ternary relationships, 222
Third-generation database technology,
    13–14
Third normal form (3NF), 269, 270–271,
    272–273
Third-party software for database
    management systems (DBMSs), 12
Three Schema Architecture, 15–17
Three-tier client-server architecture,
    493–494
Three-tier data warehouse architecture,
    456, 458
Tightly integrated distributed DBMSs, 503,
    505
Time-series data, 464
Timesharing, 486, 487
Transaction boundaries, 434–435
Transaction logs, 430
Transaction processing
    versus decision support, 454
    definition of, 11
    distributed, 515–517
    introduction to, 7, 11
    monitors, 491–492